READING

THE

WORLD

READING THE WORLD

Ideas That Matter

THIRD EDITION

MICHAEL AUSTIN

UNIVERSITY OF EVANSVILLE

W. W. NORTON & COMPANY

NEW YORK LONDON

W. W. Norton & Company has been independent since its founding in 1923, when William Warder Norton and Mary D. Herter Norton first published lectures delivered at the People's Institute, the adult education division of New York City's Cooper Union. The firm soon expanded its program beyond the Institute, publishing books by celebrated academics from America and abroad. By mid-century, the two major pillars of Norton's publishing program—trade books and college texts—were firmly established. In the 1950s, the Norton family transferred control of the company to its employees, and today—with a staff of four hundred and a comparable number of trade, college, and professional titles published each year—W. W. Norton & Company stands as the largest and oldest publishing house owned wholly by its employees.

Editor: Marilyn Moller
Associate Editor: Ariella Foss
Assistant Editor: Claire Wallace
Project Editor: Caitlin Moran
Marketing Manager: Megan Zwilling
Emedia Editor: Erica Wnek
Production Manager: Andy Ensor
Permissions Manager: Megan Jackson
Text Designer: Jo Anne Metsch
Art Researcher: Trish Marx
Composition: Cenveo® Publisher Services
Manufacturing: Quad / Graphics—Fairfield, PA

The Library of Congress has cataloged an earlier edition as follow:

Library of Congress Cataloging-in-Publication Data

Reading the world: ideas that matter / edited by Michael Austin.—Third edition
    pages cm—(Third edition).
  Includes bibliographical references and index.
  ISBN 978-0-393-93630-8 (pbk.)
1. College readers.   2. English language—Rhetoric—Problems, exercises, etc.
3. Critical thinking—Problems, exercises, etc.   I. Austin, Michael, 1966   II. Title
   PE1417.R396   2015
   808'.0427—dc23   20140338120

This edition: ISBN 978-0-393-61742-9

Instructor's Edition ISBN: 978-0-393-93845-6

W. W. Norton & Company, Inc., 500 Fifth Avenue, New York, NY 10110
wwnorton.com

W. W. Norton & Company Ltd., 15 Carlisle Street, London W1D 3BS

3 4 5 6 7 8 9 0

Contents

◻

◻ *Image*

PART 2 A GUIDE TO READING AND WRITING

Preface

FROM THE START *Reading the World: Ideas That Matter* has been based on a simple premise: that the great-ideas tradition is fully compatible with the objectives of multiculturalism. To me, this has always seemed obvious. Great ideas are not the exclusive province of any culture, or of any historical epoch. Understanding diversity—really understanding it—requires us to understand the great ideas that have formed diverse societies. And overcoming prejudice requires us to see the essential sameness between our own experiences and those that seem alien to us. By exploring the most important and influential ideas of a variety of human cultures, we can accomplish both objectives.

In the world of contemporary writing instruction, however, these two approaches have come to be seen as, if not quite antithetical, at least incompatible. Multicultural readers largely confine themselves to twentieth- and twenty-first-century issues and readings, while great-ideas readers focus almost exclusively on Western traditions. Those who argue in favor of a multicultural approach to teaching reading and writing often find themselves—in the textbook debates for which English departments are justly famous—on the other side of the table from those who value a rigorous introduction to the great-ideas tradition. *Reading the World places* itself, squarely and unapologetically, on both sides of the table.

I have been extremely gratified by the responses to *Reading the World: Ideas That Matter*. Since it first appeared, I have heard from many instructors who have used the book and a number of students who have benefitted from its unique approach. What has gratified me the most is the number of readers who have "gotten it," who have understood the power of the two approaches that I have tried to combine in this textbook. I believe now more than ever in both the importance and the viability of a meaningfully multicultural, intellectually rigorous introduction to the intellectual traditions of the world's cultures.

Like earlier editions, the new edition groups its reading into chapters devoted to universal themes. Several possible chapter groupings are purposely absent. The book does not have, for example, a chapter called "Religion," but not because religion is unimportant in the world's intellectual traditions—quite the opposite. Religion has been so important to the development of ideas that its influence can be seen across the spectrum of human thought. *Reading the World* attempts to show this influence by presenting the ideas of the world's great religions and religious leaders in every chapter of the book. Likewise, *Reading the World* includes no chapter titled "Women" or "Feminism." To include such a chapter would, in my view, suggest that women writers have limited themselves to a narrow set of issues. Women have written about all the issues covered by this book; therefore, women writers appear in all of its sections. Every chapter in *Reading the World* has been carefully constructed to incorporate multiple perspectives on a particular theme.

English translations of many texts in this volume vary greatly. I have tried to maintain consistency among the different translations while, at the same time, remaining faithful to the original sources. In some cases, however, fidelity seemed more important to the goals of this book than consistency. Thus, the translated texts include some minor variations in spelling, accenting, diacritic marks, and other types of punctuation. Similarly, all British spellings and punctuation have been retained in translated and nontranslated texts.

HIGHLIGHTS

The third edition of *Reading the World* includes a number of new and updated texts. In deciding which texts to add and which to retire, I have been guided by the feedback that I have received from both instructors and students who have used the first two editions. Some of this feedback has been very specific—comments about the ways that specific texts have worked in a classroom setting. Much of it, though, fits into several large patterns that I have tried to address in the third edition. Among the changes that readers will find are the following:

A new chapter, "The Arts," explores our appreciation of art—and seeks to understand our fascination with it. With selections from Boethius, Murasaki Shikibu, Leo Tolstoy, Alice Walker, and more, this chapter explores music, painting, poetry, novels, aesthetics, and other ways that human beings have exercised their desire to create.

An expanded chapter, "Human Nature and the Mind," highlights the role of the mind in fashioning human nature. A drawing from Carl Jung's *The Red Book* and an excerpt from Daniel Kahneman's bestselling book *Thinking, Fast and Slow* are two examples of this chapter's exploration of our attempts to understand the mind in all its complexity.

More selections by women: Selections by women have always been important to *Reading the World*. In the third edition, they have become more important than ever.

New readings from important women across time and culture include selections from Sor Juana Inés de la Cruz, Virginia Woolf, Zeynep Tufekci, and Nobel Prize winners Wangari Maathai and Tawakkol Karman.

More readings from contemporary authors: Along with the classical texts and influential ideas from across the spectrum of human cultures, the new edition includes more recent texts from such influential thinkers as Martha Nussbaum, Joseph Stiglitz, Vandana Shiva, and Elaine Scarry.

I believe that these changes will help students get more out of their experience with the new ideas that they will encounter in *Reading the World*. The essential features of the book remain unchanged and include

Challenging texts made accessible: The detailed editorial apparatus in *Reading the World* will guide students through the process of reading and writing about sophisticated texts and ideas. Chapter introductions begin with a single question that all of the selections in a chapter are responding to in some way. These introductions set out the major issues and concerns that each chapter deals with and situate each reading in a bigger overall scheme. Text headnotes offer necessary historical contextual information about the authors and texts. Explanatory footnotes describe unfamiliar terms, concepts, and references in the selections. Study questions prompt students to think about the major ideas in each selection, consider the elements of writing, and think about how texts interact. And writing suggestions prompt creative, analytical, and comparative responses.

A balance of Western and non-Western texts: Nearly half of the selections come from Eastern, Islamic, African, and South American sources. These texts highlight both the differences between Western and non-Western thinking and the similarities in the ways that all human cultures have formulated and approached essential problems.

A substantial yet flexible guide to reading and writing: At the end of *Reading the World* you can find Part 2, The Guide to Reading and Writing, which explores the writing process from reading critically to generating topic ideas to organization and support to evaluating and documenting sources. This substantial segment draws examples largely from the selections in the book.

Readings on language and rhetoric: One full chapter of the reader is devoted to primary sources on language and rhetoric. Here, students involved in the writing process can read accessible selections from writers such as Plato, Aristotle, Gloria Anzaldúa, and Toni Morrison.

Images as texts: Great ideas are not always expressed in words; sometimes, they are conveyed through visual texts. Included throughout *Reading the World*, therefore, are the kinds of visual texts that contemporary students need to decode on a daily basis: drawings, paintings, photographs, monuments, and so on. Not merely illustrations or visual aids, these complex texts make substantial arguments in their own right, and they are presented here *as texts*, with headnotes, study questions, and writing suggestions.

Mix of longer and shorter readings: To meet a variety of teaching and assignment styles, the selections in *Reading the World* vary widely in length. Each chapter includes some pieces of only a page or two, which can be read quickly and incorporated into group discussions and in-class writing assignments. Each chapter also includes several medium-length selections, and one or two lengthy selections, which require in-depth reading and extensive discussion.

Cross-textual connections: The readings work together both within and across chapters. Following each reading, a set of questions titled "Making Connections" prompts students to explore these threads.

ACKNOWLEDGMENTS

Reading the World: Ideas That Matter truly has many authors. It owes its existence to the great writers, artists, philosophers, and critics whose works fill its pages. Those pages, in turn, are the product of the attention, support, and creative energy of many people.

After the publication of the first edition, the writing programs at both Shepherd University and the Catholic University of America invited me to speak with instructors using the book. I thank these instructors and their students for the crucial feedback that they provided. My colleagues at Newman University were also extremely supportive as I prepared this new edition. I am especially grateful to President Noreen M. Carrocci for enduring a provost who was occasionally missing in action as deadlines for the new edition approached.

The staff at W. W. Norton provided more support than I ever imagined possible. This support began very early in the process, when John Kelly "discovered" the book during a meeting in my office on other textbook concerns. Marilyn Moller, who believed in the project from the beginning, was enormously helpful in giving the book its current shape and configuration—which is far superior to the shape and configuration that I originally had in mind. Ariella Foss, who edited the third edition, and Erin Granville, who edited the first two editions, were both outstanding in every regard. They held me to the same standards of clarity, concision, and logical consistency that I ask of all students who use *Reading the World*. Megan Jackson performed the task of clearing permissions for all the readings. Caitlin Moran did a superb job project editing the text; and Jillian Burr, Andy Ensor, Sophie Hagen, Rebecca Homiski, Ben Reynolds, and Claire Wallace were instrumental in managing the production and editing of this edition. I am also grateful to Carin Berger and Debra Morton Hoyt for the wonderful cover design.

Reading the World has also benefited tremendously from the teachers and scholars who took valuable time to review the second edition: Alex Blazer (Georgia College of State University), Robert Epstein (Fairfield University), Mark A. Graves (Morehead State University), David Holler (University of San Francisco), Mai Nguyen (Univerity of Tampa), Jonathan Rovner (American University of Iraq, Sulaimani), and Kelly A. Shea (Seton Hall University). And I also want to thank the teachers and scholars who reviewed the second edition, and read new selections for the third: Jenny Bangsund (University of Sioux Falls), Nancy Enright (Seton Hall University), Keely McCarthy (Chestnut Hill College), Anthony J. Sams (Ivy Tech Community College), and Thomas Wilmeth (Concordia University).

Finally, *Reading the World* is the result of personal debts that can never be adequately repaid. These include debts to my parents, Roger and Linda Austin, who taught me how to read and who always made sure that I lived in a house full of books and ideas; to my wife, Karen Austin, for her emotional and intellectual nurturing during the entire process of conceiving and executing this book—and for taking a lead role in writing the instructor's manual that accompanies it; and to my children, Porter and Clarissa Austin, who patiently endured more than a year of seeing their daddy always at the computer. My greatest hope is that they will someday understand why.

Timeline

ca. 3000–1500 BCE	Indus Valley civilization flourishes in present-day northeast India. Writing present
ca. 3000 BCE	Mesopotamia. Cuneiform writing on clay tablets
ca. 2575–2130 BCE	Old Kingdom in Egypt (Great Pyramids, Sphinx)
ca. 2130–1540 BCE	Middle Kingdom in Egypt
ca. 2070–1600 BCE	Xia Dynasty flourishes in present-day China
1600–1046 BCE	Shang Dynasty in China. Ideograph writing on oracle bones
ca. 1539–1200 BCE	New Kingdom in Egypt
ca. 1200 BCE	Moses leads Hebrews out of Egypt to Palestine
1030 BCE	Kingdom of Israel founded
776 BCE	First recorded Olympics held in Greece
753–510 BCE	Roman Kingdom founded
700 BCE	Emergence of kingdoms and republics in northern India
648 BCE	Rise of first Persian state
600–400 BCE	Lao Tzu, *Tao Te Ching*
510 BCE	Roman Republic founded with the overthrow of the Roman Kingdom
475–221 BCE	Period of Warring States in China. "Hundred Schools of Thought" flourish
431 BCE	Pericles, *The Funeral Oration*
425 BCE	Mo Tzu, *Against Music* • Mo Tzu, *Against Offensive Warfare*
400–320 BCE	Sun Tzu, *The Art of War*
399 BCE	Socrates, tried for impiety and corrupting the youth of Athens, sentenced to death by hemlock
380 BCE	Plato, *Gorgias*

Many dates, especially ancient ones, are approximate.
Boldface *titles indicate works in the anthology.*

350 BCE	Aristotle, *Rhetoric*
331–330 BCE	Alexander the Great conquers Syria, Mesopotamia, and Iran
330–323 BCE	Alexander the Great conquers Central Asia and Indus Valley, but dies in Babylon. His generals divide his empire and found the Ptolemaic Dynasty in Egypt and Seleucid Empire in Syria, Mesopotamia, and Iran
300 BCE	Mencius, *Man's Nature Is Good* • Hsün Tzu, *Man's Nature Is Evil*
250 BCE	Hsün Tzu, *Encouraging Learning*
221–207 BCE	Qin Dynasty established in China. Rule guided primarily by Legalist philosophy
206 BCE–220 CE	Han Dynasty founded. Rule guided by a mixture of Legalist and Confucian philosophies
2nd–1st centuries BCE	Buddhism spreads to China
49 BCE	Beginning of civil war that ends the Roman Republic and leads to the Roman Empire
30 BCE	Rome conquers Egypt
ca. 6	Birth of Jesus
90	*New Testament*
ca. 100	Lucretius, *De Rerum Natura* • Epictetus, *To Those Who Fear Want*
131–134	Jewish revolt against Roman rule; Jews expelled from Palestine
200–350	Introduction and spread of Christianity in North Africa
4th–6th centuries	Clans ally to form Yamato, precursor of Japanese state
330	Constantine moves capital of the Roman Empire to Byzantium and renames it Constantinople
367	Final canon of the New Testament of the Bible established
395	Roman Empire divided into the Eastern and Western Empires
426	Augustine, *On Christian Doctrine*
476	Last emperor of the Western Empire deposed
ca. 500	Boethius, *Of Music*
500–1495	Rise of the West African savanna empires
550–700	Asuka period in Japan develops around the rule of the Yamato clan. Buddhism introduced to the Japanese archipelago by way of Korea
570 CE	Birth of Mohammed
610–1000	Introduction and spread of Islam in East and West Africa
610–632	Period of Mohammed's prophesy, the growth of his following, his flight to Medina, and his return to Mecca
800	Po-Chü-I, *The Flower Market*

819–1005	The Samanids, the first Persian Muslim dynasty, become hereditary governors of eastern Iran and central Asia
1000	Lady Murasaki Shikibu, *On the Art of the Novel*
1096–1290	European Crusades to regain Christian control of the Holy Lands
1265–1274	St. Thomas Aquinas, *Summa Theologica*
1281–1924	Ottoman rulers gradually establish the last great Islamic dynasty to rule in the Middle East. They dominate the region until World War II
1300–1500	Rise of the Kongo kingdom on the lower Zaire
1338–1453	Hundred Years' War between France and England
1350	Laurentius de Voltolina, *Liber Ethicorum des Henricus de Alemania*
1405	Christine de Pizan, *The Treasure of the City of Ladies*
1453	Constantinople falls to the Turks, increasing dissemination of Greek culture in western Europe
1492	Columbus lands in America
1513	Niccolò Machiavelli, *The Prince*
1515	Erasmus, *Against War*
1517	Luther's Ninety-five Theses denounce abuses of the Roman Church
1534	Henry VIII breaks with Rome and becomes head of the Church of England
late 16th–mid 19th centuries	Atlantic slave trade
1620	Colony founded by Pilgrims at Plymouth, Massachusetts
1651	Thomas Hobbes, *Leviathan* • Abraham Bosse, *Frontispiece of Thomas Hobbes's* Leviathan
ca. 1666	Johannes Vermeer, *Study of a Young Woman*
1689	Matsuo Bashō, *The Narrow Road to the Interior*
1690	John Locke, *Of Ideas*
1691	Sor Juana Inés de la Cruz, *La Respuesta*
1751	William Hogarth, *Gin Lane*
1756–1763	Seven Years' War, involving nine European powers
1757	Edmund Burke, *The Sublime and Beautiful*
1768	Joseph Wright of Derby, *An Experiment on a Bird in the Air Pump*
1775–1783	American War of Independence; Declaration of Independence
1785	James Madison, *Memorial and Remonstrance Against Religious Assessments*

1789	French Revolution begins. French National Assembly adopts the Declaration of the Rights of Man
1794	William Blake, *The Tyger*
1798	Thomas Malthus, *An Essay on the Principle of Population*
1802	William Paley, *Natural Theology*
1830	Eugène Delacroix, *Liberty Leading the People*
1845	Frederick Douglass, *Learning to Read*
1852	John Henry Newman, *Knowledge Its Own End*
1859	Charles Darwin, *Natural Selection; or the Survival of the Fittest*
1861–1865	American Civil War. Lincoln signs the Emancipation Proclamation, freeing the slaves in the Confederate States of America
1868	Meiji restoration in Japan overthrows the Tokugawa Shogunate and results in rapid modernization
1891	*Phrenology Chart*
1896	Leo Tolstoy, *What is Art?*
1899–1902	Boxer Rebellion in China in response to the European presence. The combined response of the European powers and Japan is something of the world's first international peacekeeping mission
1904–1905	Japan becomes the first Asian power to defeat a Western nation, when it wins the Russo-Japanese War
1911	China is thrown into decades of chaos when the Qing Dynasty is overthrown and the last emperor is deposed
1914–1918	World War I in Europe and the colonies. The United States enters in 1917
1916	Mohandas Gandhi, *Economics and Moral Progress*
1917	Russian Revolution overthrows the Romanov Dynasty
1923	Rabindranath Tagore, *To Teachers*
1929	American stock market crash heralds beginning of world economic crisis; Great Depression lasts until 1939 • Virginia Woolf, *Shakespeare's Sister*
ca. 1930	Carl Jung, *The Red Book*
1933	Adolf Hitler given dictatorial powers in Germany
1934	Ruth Benedict, *The Individual and the Pattern of Culture*
1936–1938	Spanish Civil War. After the Nationalist side prevails against the Republican side, Francisco Franco is installed as dictator
1936	Dorothea Lange, *Migrant Mother*
1937	Pablo Picasso, *Guernica* • Japan invades China
1939	Germany invades Poland, pulling all of Europe into war
ca. 1940	Simone Weil, *Equality*

1940	Margaret Mead, *Warfare: An Invention—Not a Biological Necessity*
1941	Japan attacks Pearl Harbor. The United States enters World War II
1942	George Orwell, *Pacifism and the War*
1945	World War II ends with the United States dropping atomic bombs on Hiroshima and Nagasaki. United Nations founded
1946	Cold War begins with Winston Churchill's "Iron Curtain" speech
1948	State of Israel founded
1949	Mao Zedong's Communists push the Nationalist forces off mainland China and establish the People's Republic of China • Apartheid instituted in South Africa
1950	Octavio Paz, *The Day of the Dead*
1950–1953	Korean War involves North and South Korea, the United Nations, and China
1952	Revolution in Egypt, which becomes a republic in 1953
1960–1962	Independence for Belgian Congo, Uganda, Tanganyika, Nigeria
1961	Yuri Gagarin becomes first human in space
1962–1973	United States engaged in Vietnam War
1962	Rachel Carson, *The Obligation to Endure*
1963	Martin Luther King Jr., *Letter from Birmingham Jail*
	Wayne Booth, *The Rhetorical Stance*
	Karl Popper, *Science as Falsification*
1966–1969	Mao Zedong's Cultural Revolution attacks Confucian tradition and intellectuals in China
1969	Neil Armstrong becomes first human on the moon
1971	Barry Commoner, *The Four Laws of Ecology*
1973	Arab oil producers cut off shipments to nations supporting Israel. Ensuing energy crisis reshapes global economy
1974	Garrett Hardin, *Lifeboat Ethics: The Case against Helping the Poor*
1983	Alice Walker, *Beauty: When the Other Dancer Is the Self*
1985	Richard Feynman, *O Americano Outra Vez*
1987	Gloria Anzaldúa, *How to Tame a Wild Tongue*
1990	Aung San Suu Kyi, *In Quest of Democracy* • East and West Germany united
1991	Soviet Union dissolved
1993	Toni Morrison, *Nobel Lecture* • World Wide Web established
1994	Nelson Mandela becomes president of South Africa after first multiracial elections there

1997	Desmond Tutu, *Nuremberg or National Amnesia: A Third Way*
1998	Edward O. Wilson, *The Fitness of Human Nature*
	Marevasei Kachere, *War Memoir*
1999	Elaine Scarry, *On Beauty and Being Just*
2001	Islamists fly jets into the United States Pentagon and the World Trade Center
2003	United States invades Iraq
	Lisa Yuskavage, *Babie I*
2005	*Women of World War II Monument*
2006	Wangari Maathai, *Foresters without Diplomas*
2007	*Brain Scan*
2009	Vandana Shiva, *Soil, Not Oil*
2008	Barack Obama, *A More Perfect Union*
2010	Martha Nussbaum, *Education for Profit, Education for Democracy*
	Nicholas Carr, *A Thing Like Me*
2011	Daniel Kahneman, *Thinking, Fast and Slow*
	Tawakkol Karman, *Nobel Lecture*
2012	Joseph Stiglitz, *Rent Seeking and the Making of an Unequal Society*
2013	Zeynep Tufekci, *Networked Politics from Tahrir to Taksim*

Pronunciation Guide

PHONETIC KEY

a as in c**a**t	**ee** as in str**ee**t	**j** as in **j**oke	**or** as in b**or**e
ah as in f**a**ther	**ehr** as in **air**	**nh** a nasal sound	**ow** as in n**ow**
ai as in l**i**ght	**er** as in b**ir**d	**o** as in p**o**t	**s** as in me**ss**
ay as in d**ay**	**eu** as in l**u**rk	**oh** as in n**o**	**u** as in p**u**t
aw as in r**aw**	**g** as in **g**ood	**oo** as in b**oo**t	**uh** as in **u**s
e as in p**e**t	**i** as in s**i**t	**oy** as in t**oy**	**zh** as in vi**s**ion

NAMES, TERMS, AND TITLES

Abraham Bosse   *ah-brahm' bahs'-uh*

Aeschylus   *esh'-kuh-luhs*

Anzaldúa   *ahn-zuhl-doo'-uh*

Aung San Suu Kyi   *owng sahn soo chee*

Boethius   *boh-ee'-thee-uhs*

Carl Jung   *kahrl yung*

Christine de Pizan   *kris-teen' day pee-zanh'*

Daniel Kahneman   *dan'-yel khan'-i-min*

Epictetus   *eh-pic-tay'-tus*

Erasmus   *eh-raz'-muz*

Eugène Delacroix   *eu-zhen' duh-lah-krwah'*

Feynman   *fain'-mun*

Hsün Tzu *shinh tsuh*

Johannes Vermeer *yoh-hahn'-uhs ver-meer'*

Lao Tzu *low tsuh*

Laurentius de Voltolina *lahr-en'-ti-uhs day vohl-tow-leen'-uh*

Marevasei Kachere *mahr-e-vah-sai' kuh-cher'-ai*

Matsuo Bashō *maht-soo-oh bah-shoh*

Mencius *men'-chee-oos*

Mo Tzu *mor tsuh*

Murasaki Shikibu *mu-ruh-saw'-kee shi-kee'-boo*

Octavio Paz *ohk-tahv-'ee-oh pahz*

Pericles *pehr'-uh-klees*

Po-Chü-I *bo-choo-ee'*

Rabindranath Tagore *ra-bin'-dra-nahth tah-gor'*

Seneca *sen'-ah-kah*

Simone Weil *see-mohn' vyle*

Sor Juana Inés de la Cruz *sor wahnah een-nez day lah krooz*

Sun Tzu *shunh tsuh*

Tawakkol Karman *ta-wah-kohl kahr-mahn'*

Vandana Shiva *van'-dah-nah shee'-vuh*

Wangari Maathai *wawn-gah-ree mah-tai*

Yuskavage *you-skah/-vidge*

Zeynep Tufekci *zay'-nef too-fetch'-ee*

READING
THE
WORLD

PART 1

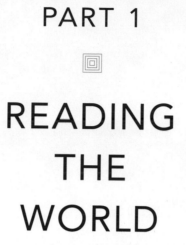

READING
THE
WORLD

1

EDUCATION

What Does It Mean to Be
an Educated Person?

Such is the constitution of the human mind, that any kind of knowledge,
if it be really such, is its own reward.
—John Henry Newman

IN 1854, the great English scholar and Catholic convert, John Henry Newman, was appointed the rector of the newly created Catholic University of Ireland. In this capacity, Newman delivered a series of lectures about the nature and purpose of higher education. In 1858, these lectures were published together as *The Idea of a University*—which became one of the nineteenth century's most influential books on the purpose of education. Newman argued that education had to do more than just prepare people for different careers—it had to teach a body of knowledge and set of skills that, while not immediately applicable to any kind of work, were vital to the growth and development of a human being. Knowledge, he believed, was capable of being its own reward.

Since the middle of the twentieth century, educators at all levels have struggled with this concept of education. Parents, communities, government agencies, and business leaders now demand that schools teach practical skills that will lead to good jobs for graduates and a strong economy for everybody. As schools have become more and more driven by standardized tests and accountability scorecards, it has become more and more difficult for them to justify the kind of abstract knowledge that Newman saw as the cornerstone of a good education. This, in turn, has lead to a definition of "educated" that is roughly the same as the definition of "employable." But this has not always been the case. This chapter examines the various ways that people in different eras and cultures have defined what it means to be educated.

The discussion begins with two ancient treatises on learning. From China, Hsün Tzu's "Encouraging Learning," working in the Confucian tradition, argues that education is necessary to shape an inherently evil human nature. From ancient Rome, Seneca's "On Liberal and Vocational Studies" highlights connections between education and the moral development necessary for a citizen. These readings are followed by one of the most striking classroom scenes ever painted: Laurentius de Voltolina's fourteenth-century illustration *Lecture of Henricus de Alemania*, which depicts a classroom lecture at a medieval university that in many ways looks like a lecture you might attend today.

The chapter also presents a series of modern and contemporary texts that give divergent perspectives on the function of education. Two of these readings come from theorists and philosophers. Newman's "Knowledge Its Own End" argues that the attainment of knowledge is an independent good needing no further utilitarian justification. Richard Feynman's "O Americano Outra Vez" relates a famous scientist's experience with the Brazilian educational system.

A second group of readings come from the margins of society. Virginia Woolf's "Shakespeare's Sister" takes the form of an elaborate thought experiment, imagining the life of a woman during Shakespeare's time if she were equipped with the playwright's intelligence and creativity. A selection from Frederick Douglass's autobiography describes how he, while enslaved, learned to read and write in violation of the law and, in the process, discovered the value of freedom. A speech by the Indian writer Rabindranath Tagore compares early twentieth-century schools to factories and advocates for an approach to education that honors children's natural curiosity.

The final reading in the chapter, "Education for Profit, Education for Democracy" by Martha Nussbaum, builds on Tagore's ideas. Nussbaum argues that democratic nations have a responsibility to train their citizens to become critical thinkers so that they can take part in the task of self-government that democracy requires.

HSÜN TZU
Encouraging Learning
[CIRCA 250 BCE]

THE GREAT CHINESE PHILOSOPHER Confucius (551–479 BCE) taught his disciples that human beings must always strive for perfection through strict attention to duty, order, and ritual. He did not, however, clearly state his opinions on human nature. Some time after Confucius's death, his disciples split into two camps. The majority of Confucians followed the teachings of Mencius, who believed that the rites that Confucius advocated could produce virtue and rectitude only because humans inherently possessed these qualities. A second group of Confucians believed exactly the reverse: that the Confucian program of rites and observances was necessary because humans were inherently evil. The most famous advocate of this position was the scholar Hsün Tzu.

Hsün Tzu (circa 300–230 BCE) believed that becoming virtuous meant altering human nature, and was therefore one of the ancient world's strongest advocates of education. He believed that only rigorous training and devoted study could produce virtue. He compared the process of educating a child to the process of straightening a piece of wood against a board or sharpening a piece of metal with a stone. If done correctly, each process permanently transforms the nature of the thing: the wood becomes straight, the metal becomes sharp, and the child becomes a "gentleman," as Confucius termed a person of moral character.

Confucius's ideas have come down to us only as epigrams recorded by his disciples; Lao Tzu wrote poems and prose pieces marked by paradox; Mencius wrote dialogues, parables, and indirect narratives. Hsün Tzu, the most systematic of the classical Chinese philosophers, developed brief essays that introduce and support clearly labeled, easy-to-follow arguments. In "Encouraging Learning," he employs his straightforward style on a series of metaphors and object lessons, drawn from the natural world, to illustrate his principal point: that education can compensate for natural human defects and make people good.

Long after Hsün Tzu's death, Confucianism became the official state philosophy of China. However, the later, official versions of Confucian doctrine rejected Hsün Tzu's arguments about human nature and instead accepted Mencius's more optimistic theories. Nonetheless, Hsün Tzu, as the first philosopher to turn Confucius's aphorisms into a complete system of thought, remains an important figure in the development of Chinese philosophy. Unlike his views on human nature, his views on the importance of education became part of the Confucian mainstream and have influenced many people throughout Chinese history to devote their lives to scholarly pursuits.

Hsün Tzu's primary method of supporting his arguments in this selection is to give examples, either from the natural world or from figures in Chinese history. Pay close attention to these examples and to the claims that they support.

The gentleman[1] says: Learning should never cease. Blue comes from the indigo plant but is bluer than the plant itself. Ice is made of water but is colder than water ever is. A piece of wood as straight as a plumb line may be bent into a circle as true as any drawn with a compass and, even after the wood has dried, it will not straighten out again. The bending process has made it that way. Thus, if wood is pressed against a straightening board, it can be made straight; if metal is put to the grindstone, it can be sharpened; and if the gentleman studies widely and each day examines himself, his wisdom will become clear and his conduct be without fault. If you do not climb a high mountain, you will not comprehend the highness of the heavens; if you do not look down into a deep valley, you will not know the depth of the earth; and if you do not hear the words handed down from the ancient kings, you will not understand the greatness of learning. Children born among the Han or Yüeh people of the south and among the Mo barbarians of the north cry with the same voice at birth, but as they grow older they follow different customs. Education causes them to differ. The Odes[2] says:

> Oh, you gentlemen,
> Do not be constantly at ease and rest!
> Quietly respectful in your posts,
> Love those who are correct and upright
> And the gods will hearken to you
> And aid you with great blessing.

There is no greater godliness than to transform yourself with the Way,[3] no greater blessing than to escape misfortune.

I once tried spending the whole day in thought, but I found it of less value than a moment of study. I once tried standing on tiptoe and gazing into the distance, but I found I could see much farther by climbing to a high place. If you climb to a high place and wave to someone, it is not as though your arm were any longer than usual, and yet people can see you from much farther away. If you shout down the

---

Some of the translator's footnotes have been omitted.

1. **Gentleman:** the Confucian term for a person of virtue and breeding—one who always fulfills the appropriate roles for a person of his or her rank.

2. **The Odes:** Chinese poetic writings much older than Confucianism that Confucius and his followers considered sources of ancient wisdom. Confucius is traditionally considered the editor

and compiler of the Shih Ching, or Book of Odes, in which these odes are collected.

3. **The Way:** Tao, which can be translated as "the Way" or "the Path," is a vital concept in almost all classical Chinese philosophy; however, its meaning is not the same for Confucians as it is for Taoists. For Lao Tzu (p. 384), the Way means something like "the way of nature" or "the natural order of things." For Confucius, it means something more like "the path to perfection."

wind, it is not as though your voice were any stronger than usual, and yet people can hear you much more clearly. Those who make use of carriages or horses may not be any faster walkers than anyone else, and yet they are able to travel a thousand *li*.[4] Those who make use of boats may not know how to swim, and yet they manage to get across rivers. The gentleman is by birth no different from any other man; it is just that he is good at making use of things.

In the south there is a bird called the *meng* dove. It makes a nest out of feathers woven together with hair and suspends it from the tips of the reeds. But when the wind comes, the reeds break, the eggs are smashed, and the baby birds killed. It is not that the nest itself is faulty; the fault is in the thing it is attached to. In the west there is a tree called the *yeh-kan*. Its trunk is no more than four inches tall and it grows on top of the high mountains, from whence it looks down into valleys a hundred fathoms deep. It is not a long trunk which affords the tree such a view, but simply the place where it stands. If pigweed grows up in the midst of hemp, it will stand up straight without propping. If white sand is mixed with mud, it too will turn black. The root of a certain orchid is the source of the perfume called *chih*; but if the root were to be soaked in urine, then no gentleman would go near it and no commoner would consent to wear it. It is not that the root itself is of an unpleasant quality; it is the fault of the thing it has been soaked in. Therefore a gentleman will take care in selecting the community he intends to live in, and will choose men of breeding for his companions. In this way he wards off evil and meanness, and draws close to fairness and right.

Every phenomenon that appears must have a cause. The glory or shame that come to a man are no more than the image of his virtue. Meat when it rots breeds worms; fish that is old and dry brings forth maggots. When a man is careless and lazy and forgets himself, that is when disaster occurs. The strong naturally bear up under weight; the weak naturally end up bound. Evil and corruption in oneself invite the anger of others. If you lay sticks of identical shape on a fire, the flames will seek out the driest ones; if you level the ground to an equal smoothness, water will still seek out the dampest spot. Trees of the same species grow together; birds and beasts gather in herds; for all things follow after their own kind. Where a target is hung up, arrows will find their way to it; where the forest trees grow thickest, the axes will enter. When a tree is tall and shady, birds will flock to roost in it; when vinegar turns sour, gnats will collect around it. So there are words that invite disaster and actions that call down shame. A gentleman must be careful where he takes his stand.

Pile up earth to make a mountain and wind and rain will rise up from it. Pile up water to make a deep pool and dragons will appear. Pile up good deeds to create virtue and godlike understanding will come of itself; there the mind of the sage will find completion. But unless you pile up little steps, you can never journey a thousand *li*; unless you pile up tiny streams, you can never make a river or a sea. The finest

5

---

4. **Li**: a traditional Chinese unit of distance; about one-third of a mile.

thoroughbred cannot travel ten paces in one leap, but the sorriest nag can go a ten days' journey. Achievement consists of never giving up. If you start carving and then give up, you cannot even cut through a piece of rotten wood; but if you persist without stopping, you can carve and inlay metal or stone. Earthworms have no sharp claws or teeth, no strong muscles or bones, and yet above ground they feast on the mud, and below they drink at the yellow springs. This is because they keep their minds on one thing. Crabs have six legs and two pincers, but unless they can find an empty hole dug by a snake or a water serpent, they have no place to lodge. This is because they allow their minds to go off in all directions. Thus if there is no dark and dogged will, there will be no shining accomplishment; if there is no dull and determined effort, there will be no brilliant achievement. He who tries to travel two roads at once will arrive nowhere; he who serves two masters will please neither. The wingless dragon has no limbs and yet it can soar; the flying squirrel has many talents but finds itself hard pressed. The *Odes* says:

> Ringdove in the mulberry,
> Its children are seven.
> The good man, the gentleman,
> His forms are one.
> His forms are one,
> His heart is as though bound.

Thus does the gentleman bind himself to oneness.

In ancient times, when Hu Pa played the zither, the fish in the streams came forth to listen; when Po Ya played the lute, the six horses of the emperor's carriage looked up from their feed trough. No sound is too faint to be heard, no action too well concealed to be known. When there are precious stones under the mountain, the grass and trees have a special sheen; where pearls grow in a pool, the banks are never parched. Do good and see if it does not pile up. If it does, how can it fail to be heard of?

Where does learning begin and where does it end? I say that as to program, learning begins with the recitation of the Classics and ends with the reading of the ritual texts; and as to objective, it begins with learning to be a man of breeding, and ends with learning to be a sage. If you truly pile up effort over a long period of time, you will enter into the highest realm. Learning continues until death and only then does it cease. Therefore we may speak of an end to the program of learning, but the objective of learning must never for an instant be given up. To pursue it is to be a man, to give it up is to become a beast. The *Book of Documents*[5] is the record of government affairs, the *Odes* the repository of correct sounds, and the rituals are

---

5. **Book of Documents:** the *Shu Ching*, a collection of speeches, legal codes, government actions, and other reputedly primary texts from pre-Confucian Chinese dynasties.

the great basis of law and the foundation of precedents. Therefore learning reaches its completion with the rituals, for they may be said to represent the highest point of the Way and its power. The reverence and order of the rituals, the fitness and harmony of music, the breadth of the *Odes* and *Documents*, the subtlety of the *Spring and Autumn Annals*[6]—these encompass all that is between heaven and earth.

The learning of the gentleman enters his ear, clings to his mind, spreads through his four limbs, and manifests itself in his actions. His smallest word, his slightest movement can serve as a model. The learning of the petty man enters his ear and comes out his mouth. With only four inches between ear and mouth, how can he have possession of it long enough to ennoble a seven-foot body? In old times men studied for their own sake; nowadays men study with an eye to others.[7] The gentleman uses learning to ennoble himself; the petty man uses learning as a bribe to win attention from others. To volunteer information when you have not been asked is called officiousness; to answer two questions when you have been asked only one is garrulity.[8] Both officiousness and garrulity are to be condemned. The gentleman should be like an echo.

In learning, nothing is more profitable than to associate with those who are learned. Ritual and music present us with models but no explanations; the *Odes* and *Documents* deal with ancient matters and are not always pertinent; the *Spring and Autumn Annals* is terse and cannot be quickly understood. But if you make use of the erudition of others and the explanations of gentlemen, then you will become honored and may make your way anywhere in the world. Therefore I say that in learning nothing is more profitable than to associate with those who are learned, and of the roads to learning, none is quicker than to love such men. Second only to this is to honor ritual. If you are first of all unable to love such men and secondly are incapable of honoring ritual, then you will only be learning a mass of jumbled facts, blindly following the *Odes* and *Documents*, and nothing more. In such a case you may study to the end of your days and you will never be anything but a vulgar pedant.[9] If you want to become like the former kings and seek out benevolence and righteousness, then ritual is the very road by which you must travel. It is like picking up a fur coat by the collar: grasp it with all five fingers and the whole coat can easily be lifted. To lay aside the rules of ritual and try to attain your objective with the *Odes* and *Documents* alone is like trying to measure the depth of a river with your finger, to pound millet with a spear point, or to eat a pot of stew with an awl. You will get nowhere. Therefore one who honors ritual, though he may not yet have full understanding, can be called a model man of breeding; while one who does not honor ritual, though he may have keen perception, is no more than a desultory pedant.

6. *Spring and Autumn Annals*: the Ch'un Ch'iu, a work of ancient history, traditionally thought to have been compiled by Confucius.
7. This sentence is quoted from *Analects* XIV, 25, where it is attributed to Confucius. [Translator's note]

8. **Garrulity**: talkativeness.
9. **Vulgar pedant**: literally, "vulgar Confucian," but here and below Hsün Tzu uses the word *ju* in the older and broader sense of a scholar. [Translator's note]

Do not answer a man whose questions are gross. Do not question a man whose answers are gross. Do not listen to a man whose theories are gross. Do not argue with a contentious man. Only if a man has arrived where he is by the proper way should you have dealings with him; if not, avoid him. If he is respectful in his person, then you may discuss with him the approach to the Way. If his words are reasonable, you may discuss with him the principles of the Way. If his looks are gentle, you may discuss with him the highest aspects of the Way. To speak to someone you ought not to is called officiousness; to fail to speak to someone you ought to is called secretiveness; to speak to someone without first observing his temper and looks is called blindness. The gentleman is neither officious, secretive, nor blind, but cautious and circumspect in his manner. This is what the *Odes* means when it says:

> Neither overbearing nor lax,
> They are rewarded by the Son of Heaven.

He who misses one shot in a hundred cannot be called a really good archer; he who sets out on a thousand-mile journey and breaks down half a pace from his destination cannot be called a really good carriage driver; he who does not comprehend moral relationships and categories and who does not make himself one with benevolence and righteousness cannot be called a good scholar. Learning basically means learning to achieve this oneness. He who starts off in this direction one time and that direction another is only a commoner of the roads and alleys, while he who does a little that is good and much that is not good is no better than the tyrants Chieh and Chou or Robber Chih.[10]

The gentleman knows that what lacks completeness and purity does not deserve to be called beautiful. Therefore he reads and listens to explanations in order to penetrate the Way, ponders in order to understand it, associates with men who embody it in order to make it part of himself, and shuns those who impede it in order to sustain and nourish it. He trains his eye so that they desire only to see what is right, his ears so that they desire to hear only what is right, his mind so that it desires to think only what is right. When he has truly learned to love what is right, his eyes will take greater pleasure in it than in the five colors; his ears will take greater pleasure than in the five sounds; his mouth will take greater pleasure than in the five flavors; and his mind will feel keener delight than in the possession of the world. When he has reached this stage, he cannot be subverted by power or the love of profit; he cannot be swayed by the masses; he cannot be moved by the world. He follows this one thing in life; he follows it in death. This is what is called

---

10. **Chieh and Chou or Robber Chih:** traditional figures in Chinese history. Cheih and Chou were tyrannical kings; Robber Chih led a band of nine thousand criminals who terrorized all of China.

constancy of virtue. He who has such constancy of virtue can order himself, and, having ordered himself, he can then respond to others. He who can order himself and respond to others—this is what is called the complete man. It is the characteristic of heaven to manifest brightness, of earth to manifest breadth, and of the gentleman to value completeness.

UNDERSTANDING THE TEXT

1. What distinction does Hsün Tzu draw between "thought" and "study"? Why does he privilege study over thought in education? How have your teachers emphasized "study" and "thought" differently as you have progressed through school?

2. How would you classify Hsün Tzu's methods of supporting his argument? What kinds of support does he include? What kinds does he omit? How persuasive are his methods?

3. Several of Hsün Tzu's metaphors suggest that hard work and study, rather than natural ability, determine success. How is this assertion important to his overall argument? Do you agree with his assessment? Why or why not?

4. According to Hsün Tzu, what should be part of the education of a gentleman? What, by implication, should not be part of such an education?

5. What role do associations with other people play in a good education? Would it be possible to follow Hsün Tzu's educational program by reading in isolation?

6. According to Hsün Tzu, what is the ultimate objective of education? What reward can an educated person expect? In your opinion, is this reward a sufficient motivation to pursue learning? Why or why not?

MAKING CONNECTIONS

1. Consider "Encouraging Learning" in the context of the debate between Hsün Tzu and Mencius about human nature. How do Hsün Tzu's ideas about education flow from the position that he articulates in "Man's Nature Is Evil" (p. 84)?

2. Compare Hsün Tzu's implied definition of "education" with those of Seneca (p. 13). For each thinker, what does the best kind of education focus on?

3. How might Hsün Tzu respond to one of Plato's major arguments in *Gorgias* (p. 166), that educating people often increases their ability to act unvirtuously? Would the kind of education that Hsün Tzu advocates be susceptible to abuse by the unscrupulous?

4. Compare Hsün Tzu's views on the need to alter human nature with those of Lao Tzu (p. 384). What specific statements in the *Tao Te Ching* might apply to education or learning in general?

WRITING ABOUT THE TEXT

1. Write an essay supporting or opposing Hsün Tzu's assumption that education should promote virtue. Do schools have the responsibility to teach people to act ethically? What problems might arise (or have arisen) when schools teach ethics?

2. Respond to Hsün Tzu from the perspective of someone who believes that human beings are inherently good. What kind of education would result from this assumption?

3. Compare the purpose of education that Hsün Tzu describes with the one described by either Frederick Douglass (p. 24) or Rabindranath Tagore (p. 40). What philosophical assumptions shape one's view of education? How so?

SENECA
On Liberal and Vocational Studies
[CIRCA 55 CE]

LUCIUS ANNAEUS SENECA (4 BCE–65 CE), sometimes called "Seneca the Younger," was a member of the early Roman Empire's most celebrated literary family. His father, Marcus Annaeus Seneca, or Seneca the Elder (circa 54 BCE–circa 39 CE), was a noted orator and writer. His nephew, Lucian (39–65 CE), was a celebrated poet who made important contributions to the development of satire. Seneca the Younger distinguished himself as a scientist, scholar, playwright, and philosopher—as well as a politician whose career rose and fell on the whims of three powerful emperors.

Seneca received a first-rate education and as a young man became a successful politician. But in 37 CE, he came into conflict with the emperor Caligula and barely escaped a death sentence. Four years later, in 41 CE, Seneca was accused of having an improper relationship with the niece of the emperor Claudius, who consequently banished him to the island of Corsica. Seneca remained there until 49 CE, when he was summoned back to Rome to tutor the twelve-year-old Nero, who would become emperor in 54 CE after Claudius's death. Seneca became one of the young Nero's most trusted and powerful advisors, but as the emperor became more corrupt, Seneca became less powerful. He received permission to retire in 62 CE, but three years later, Nero accused Seneca of conspiring against him and ordered Seneca to commit suicide by slitting his own wrists.

Seneca was a well-known member of the Stoic school of philosophy. Stoics held that people achieved the greatest good by living a life founded on reason and in harmony with nature. Stoics also believed that wealth and social position were ultimately unimportant because reason and virtue were available to everybody. In fact, two of the most famous Roman Stoics were the slave Epictetus (55–153) and the emperor Marcus Aurelius (121–180). As a Stoic, Seneca believed that excessive passions diluted the influence of reason, that the point of living is to live virtuously, and that one could be happy and virtuous in any physical or economic condition.

"On Liberal and Vocational Studies" is the eighty-eighth of 124 letters from Seneca that are collectively known as the "Moral Epistles." In this letter, Seneca attempts to define liberal studies and separate them clearly from vocational training. During Seneca's time, a "liberal" education was the kind of education appropriate for a *liber*, or a free person. Unlike many of his contemporaries, Seneca was unwilling to defend pursuits such as literature, music, geometry, and astronomy by arguing that they made people virtuous. This argument, Seneca believed, reduced the liberal arts to a sort of moral propaganda. They do not convert people to virtue, he insists; rather, they are the raw materials out of which a virtuous life can be built—and as such they are indispensible to the functioning of a free society.

Much of Seneca's philosophical work comes to us in the form of letters to other people. As you read Seneca's argument, consider how his use of the second-person address ("You want to know . . . ", "You teach me") creates a connection with the reader and constructs his own ethos as a writer.

Letter LXXXVIII

You want to know my attitude towards liberal studies. Well, I have no respect for any study whatsoever if its end is the making of money. Such studies are to me unworthy ones. They involve the putting out of skills to hire, and are only of value in so far as they may develop the mind without occupying it for long. Time should be spent on them only so long as one's mental abilities are not up to dealing with higher things. They are our apprenticeship, not our real work. Why "liberal studies" are so called is obvious: it is because they are the ones considered worthy of a free man.[1] But there is really only one liberal study that deserves the name—because it makes a person free—and that is the pursuit of wisdom. Its high ideals, its steadfastness and spirit make all other studies puerile and puny in comparison. Do you really think there is anything to be said for the others when you find among the people who profess to teach them quite the most reprehensible and worthless characters you could have as teachers? All right to have studied that sort of thing once, but not to be studying them now.

The question has sometimes been posed whether these liberal studies make a man a better person. But in fact they do not aspire to any knowledge of how to do this, let alone claim to do it. Literary scholarship concerns itself with research into language, or history if a rather broader field is preferred, or, extending its range to the very limit, poetry. Which of these paves the way to virtue? Attentiveness of words, analysis of syllables, accounts of myths, laying down the principles of prosody? What is there in all this that dispels fear, roots out desire, or reins in passion? Or let us take a look at music, at geometry; you will not find anything in them which tells us not to be afraid of this or desire that—and if anyone lacks this kind of knowledge all his other knowledge is valueless to him. The question is whether or not that sort of scholar is teaching virtue. For if he is not, he will not even be imparting it incidentally. If he is teaching it he is a philosopher. If you really want to know how far these persons are from the position of being moral teachers, observe the absence of connexion between all the things they study; if they were teaching one and the same thing a connexion would be evident. . . .

Turning to the musical scholar I say this. You teach me how bass and treble harmonize, or how strings producing different notes can give rise to concord. I would

1. . . . **Free man:** The word for "free man" in Latin is *liber*, the root word of *liberal*.

rather you brought about some harmony in my mind and got my thoughts into tune. You show me which are the plaintive keys. I would rather you showed me how to avoid uttering plaintive notes when things go against me in life.

The geometrician teaches me how to work out the size of my estates—rather than how to work out how much a man needs in order to have enough. He teaches me to calculate, putting my fingers into the service of avarice, instead of teaching me that there is no point whatsoever in that sort of computation and that a person is none the happier for having properties which tire accountants out, or to put it another way, how superfluous a man's possessions are when he would be a picture of misery if you forced him to start counting up single-handed how much he possessed. What use is it to me to be able to divide a piece of land into equal areas if I'm unable to divide it with a brother? What use is the ability to measure out a portion of an acre with an accuracy extending even to the bits which elude the measuring rod if I'm upset when some high-handed neighbour encroaches slightly on my property? The geometrician teaches me how I may avoid losing any fraction of my estates, but what I really want to learn is how to lose the lot and still keep smiling. . . . Oh, the marvels of geometry! You geometers can calculate the areas of circles, can reduce any given shape to a square, can state the distances separating stars. Nothing's outside your scope when it comes to measurement. Well, if you're such an expert, measure a man's soul; tell me how large or how small that is. You can define a straight line; what use is that to you if you've no idea what straightness means in life?

I come now to the person who prides himself on his familiarity with the heavenly   5
bodies:

> Towards which quarter chilly Saturn draws,
> The orbits in which burning Mercury roams.[2]

What is to be gained from this sort of knowledge? Am I supposed to feel anxious when Saturn and Mars are in opposition or Mercury sets in the evening in full view of Saturn, instead of coming to learn that bodies like these are equally propitious wherever they are, and incapable of change in any case. They are swept on in a path from which they cannot escape, their motion governed by an uninterrupted sequence of destined events, making their reappearances in cycles that are fixed. They either actuate or signalize all that comes about in the universe. If every event is brought about by them, how is mere familiarity with a process which is unchangeable going to be of any help? If they are pointers to events, what difference does it make to be aware in advance of things you cannot escape? They are going to happen whether you know about them or not. . . .

"So we don't," you may ask, "in fact gain anything from the liberal studies?" As far as character is concerned, no, but we gain a good deal from them in other directions—just

2. **Mercury roams:** Virgil, *Georgics*, I: 336–7. The person meant is of course the astrologer, not the astronomer. [Translator's note]

as even these admittedly inferior arts which we've been talking about, the ones that are based on use of the hands, make important contributions to the amenities of life although they have nothing to do with character. Why then do we give our sons a liberal education? Not because it can make them morally good but because it prepares the mind for the acquisition of moral values. Just as that grounding in grammar, as they called it in the old days, in which boys are given their elementary schooling, does not teach them the liberal arts but prepares the ground for knowledge of them in due course, so when it comes to character the liberal arts open the way to it rather than carry the personality all the way there. . . .

In this connexion I feel prompted to take a look at individual qualities of character. Bravery is the one which treats with contempt things ordinarily inspiring fear, despising and defying and demolishing all the things that terrify us and set chains on human freedom. Is she in any way fortified by liberal studies? Take loyalty, the most sacred quality that can be found in a human breast, never corrupted by a bribe, never driven to betray by any form of compulsion, crying: "Beat me, burn me, put me to death, I shall not talk—the more the torture probes my secrets the deeper I'll hide them!" Can liberal studies create that kind of spirit? Take self-control, the quality which takes command of the pleasures; some she dismisses out of hand, unable to tolerate them; others she merely regulates, ensuring that they are brought within healthy limits; never approaching pleasures for their own sake, she realizes that the ideal limit with things you desire is not the amount you would like to but the amount you ought to take. Humanity is the quality which stops one being arrogant towards one's fellows, or being acrimonious. In words, in actions, in emotions she reveals herself as kind and good-natured towards all. To her the troubles of anyone else are her own, and anything that benefits herself she welcomes primarily because it will be of benefit to someone else. Do the liberal studies inculcate these attitudes? No, no more than they do simplicity, or modesty and restraint, or frugality and thrift, or mercy, the mercy that is as sparing with another's blood as though it were its own, knowing that it is not for man to make wasteful use of man.

Someone will ask me how I can say that liberal studies are of no help towards morality when I've just been saying that there's no attaining morality without them. My answer would be this: there's no attaining morality without food either, but there's no connexion between morality and food. The fact that a ship can't begin to exist without the timbers of which it's built doesn't mean that the timbers are of "help" to it. There's no reason for you to assume that, X being something without which "Y" could never have come about, Y came about as a result of the assistance of X. And indeed it can actually be argued that the attainment of wisdom is perfectly possible without the liberal studies; although moral values are things which have to be learnt, they are not learnt through these studies. Besides, what grounds could I possible have for supposing that a person who has no acquaintance with books will never be a wise man? For wisdom does not lie in books. Wisdom publishes not words but truths—and I'm not sure that the memory isn't more reliable when it has no external aids to fall back on.

There is nothing small or cramped about wisdom. It is something calling for a lot of room to move. There are questions to be answered concerning physical as well as human matters, questions about the past and about the future, questions about things eternal and things ephemeral, questions about time itself. On this one subject of time just look how many questions there are. To start with, does it have an existence of its own? Next, does anything exist prior to time, independently of it? Did it begin with the universe, or did it exist even before then on the grounds that there was something in existence before the universe? There are countless questions about the soul alone—where it comes from, what its nature is, when it begins to exist, and how long it is in existence; whether it passes from one place to another, moving house, so to speak, on transfer to successive living creatures, taking on a different form with each, or is no more than once in service and is then released to roam the universe; whether it is a corporeal substance or not; what it will do when it ceases to act through us, how it will employ its freedom once it has escaped its cage here; whether it will forget its past and become conscious of its real nature from the actual moment of its parting from the body and departure for its new home on high. Whatever the field of physical or moral sciences you deal with, you will be given no rest by the mass of things to be learnt or investigated. And to enable matters of this range and scale to find unrestricted hospitality in our minds, everything superfluous must be turned out. Virtue will not bring herself to enter the limited space we offer her; something of great size requires plenty of room. Let everything else be evicted, and your heart completely opened to her.

"But it's a nice thing, surely, to be familiar with a lot of subjects." Well, in that case let us retain just as much of them as we need. Would you consider a person open to criticism for putting superfluous objects on the same level as really useful ones by arranging on display in his house a whole array of costly articles, but not for cluttering himself up with a lot of superfluous furniture in the way of learning? To want to know more than is sufficient is a form of intemperance. Apart from which this kind of obsession with the liberal arts turns people into pedantic, irritating, tactless, self-satisfied bores, not learning what they need simply because they spend their time learning things they will never need. The scholar Didymus wrote four thousand works: I should feel sorry for him if he had merely read so many useless works. In these works he discusses such questions as Homer's origin, who was Aeneas' real mother, whether Anacreon's manner of life was more that of a lecher or that of a drunkard, whether Sappho[3] slept with anyone who asked her, and other things that would be better unlearned if one actually knew them! Don't you go and tell

10

3. **Sappho (circa 630–circa 570 BCE)**: a Greek poet from the isle of Lesbos who was reputed to have loved both men and women. **Homer's origin:** Very little was known about Homer, the author of the *Iliad* and the *Odyssey*. **Aeneas's real mother:** Aeneas, the hero of Virgil's epic *The Aeneid*, was the son of the goddess Venus, who tried to keep the fact that she had a mortal child a secret. **Anacreon (570–480 BCE)**: a lyric poet known for his drinking songs.

me now that life is long enough for this sort of thing! When you come to writers in our own school, for that matter, I'll show you plenty of works which could do with some ruthless pruning. It costs a person an enormous amount of time (and other people's ears an enormous amount of boredom) before he earns such compliments as "What a learned person!" Let's be content with the much less fashionable label, "What a good man!" . . .

I have been speaking about liberal studies. Yet look at the amount of useless and superfluous matter to be found in the philosophers. Even they have descended to the level of drawing distinctions between the uses of different syllables and discussing the proper meanings of prepositions and conjunctions. They have come to envy the philologist and the mathematician, and they have taken over all the inessential elements in those studies—with the result that they know more about devoting care and attention to their speech than about devoting such attention to their lives. Listen and let me show you the sorry consequences to which subtlety carried too far can lead, and what an enemy it is to truth. Protagoras[4] declares that it is possible to argue either side of any question with equal force, even the question whether or not one can equally argue either side of any question! Nausiphanes[5] declares that of the things which appear to us to exist, none exists any more than it does not exist. Parmenides[6] declares that of all these phenomena none exists except the whole. Zeno of Elea[7] has dismissed all such difficulties by introducing another; he declares that nothing exists. The Pyrrhonean, Megarian, Eretrian, and Academic schools[8] pursue more or less similar lines; the last named have introduced a new branch of knowledge, non-knowledge.

Well, all these theories you should just toss on top of that heap of superfluous liberal studies. The people I first mentioned provide me with knowledge which is not going to be of any use to me, while the others snatch away from me any hopes of ever acquiring any knowledge at all. Superfluous knowledge would be preferable to no knowledge. One side offers me no guiding light to direct my vision towards the truth, while the other just gouges my eyes out. If I believe Protagoras there is nothing certain in the universe; if I believe Nausiphanes there is just the one certainty, that nothing is certain; if Parmenides, only one thing exists; if Zeno, not even one. Then what are we? The things that surround us, the things on which we live, what are they? Our whole universe is no more than a semblance of reality,

---

4. **Protagoras (490–420 BCE):** an early Sophist philosopher.

5. **Nausiphanes (circa 325 BCE):** a Greek philosopher and scientist.

6. **Parmenides (fifth century BCE):** an early Greek philosopher whose belief that truth can be derived only from reason, and not through the senses, was a significant influence on Plato.

7. **Zeno of Elea (circa 490–circa 430 BCE):** a Greek philosopher noted for his paradoxes.

8. **Pyrrhonean, Megarian, Eretrian, and Academic schools:** philosophical schools in ancient Greece that practiced some form of skepticism, or mistrust of claims to philosophical and scientific truth.

perhaps a deceptive semblance, perhaps one without substance altogether. I should find it difficult to say which of these people annoy me most, those who would have us know nothing or the ones who refuse even to leave us the small satisfaction of knowing that we know nothing.

UNDERSTANDING THE TEXT

1. What does Seneca see as the connection between a liberal studies education and the status of a free person? Think of other words based on the Latin word *liber* (liberty, liberate, library) and explain how these concepts might all be connected through Seneca's concept of liberal studies.

2. What does Seneca consider the only subject that deserves to be called "liberal"? Are the other disciplines that he mentions (music, mathematics, etc.) subsets of a larger discipline? If so, how? If not, why not?

3. What does Seneca see as the distinguishing feature between liberal and vocational studies? Is this distinction still valid in education today? Explain.

4. Why does Seneca reject the ideal that liberal studies make people virtuous? Given that he is writing in support of liberal studies, why does he spend more than half of the essay demonstrating the inability of liberal studies to produce moral behavior?

5. What, for Seneca, is the difference between studies that make people morally good and studies that lay a foundation that people can use in acquiring moral values?

MAKING CONNECTIONS

1. How does Seneca's view of liberal education compare with John Henry Newman's (p. 31)? How would they compare practical and vocational studies? Do the two philosophers have similar definitions of "liberal education"?

2. Compare Seneca's view of useless knowledge with the view implied in Richard Feynman's "O Americano Outra Vez" (p. 53). Does Seneca agree with Feynman's point that even very important subjects can be taught in such a way that they lose their value?

3. Seneca and Mo Tzu (p. 236) both see music as a thing with no practical value. Why, then, does Seneca value music while Mo Tzu opposes it?

4. Compare Seneca's view of the political importance of knowledge with the view that Frederick Douglass advances in "Learning to Read" (p. 24). Would Seneca view Douglass's arguments for literacy education as "liberal" in the sense of befitting a free person? Why or why not?

WRITING ABOUT THE TEXT

1. Write an essay that explores the connection between education and freedom. Explain how you think education should function in a free society and how educational institutions should prepare people to be citizens.

2. Provide a rebuttal to Seneca's view of vocational training as inconsistent with liberal education as he defines it. Consider how training people for careers might be important for "free people."

3. Choose one of the disciplines that Seneca lists—literature, music, geometry, or astronomy—and either agree or disagree with his reasoning that these studies do not directly produce virtue in those who study them.

4. Examine a current catalog from your college and write an essay describing one subject that Seneca would consider a liberal art and one that he would not. Support your position with quotations from Seneca's letter.

LAURENTIUS DE VOLTOLINA

Liber Ethicorum des Henricus de Alemania

[CIRCA 1350]

WE KNOW ALMOST NOTHING about the fourteenth-century Italian painter Laurentius de Voltolina, except that his signature appears on one of the most remarkable images of the late Middle Ages. The drawing appears in a preserved copy of a parchment manuscript called *Liber Ethicorum or Book of Moral Philosophy* by a medieval scholar named Henricus de Alemania (Henry the German). We know scarcely more about Henricus than we do about Laurentius. All we can say for sure is that he is the figure at the front of the class in the famous illustration that decorates his book.

This drawing by an obscure painter in a virtually unknown manuscript has become famous in our day as one of the earliest concrete pictures of a medieval university classroom. The image shows Henricus sitting at a *cathedra*, or lectern, reading passages to his students at the University of Bologna, one of the great medieval centers of learning whose faculty included the great poets Dante and Petrarch and the famous astronomer Nicholas Copernicus.

The reactions of the students give us a window into education in the fourteenth century. As Henricus reads his lecture, some of the students, primarily in the front row, listen to his words with rapt attention. Others follow along studiously in the text. Towards the back of the room, students seem more distracted; some look bored, others are socializing with each other, and at least two appear to have fallen asleep. It is, in other words, like many college classrooms today.

Some educators use this image and others like it to argue that not much about higher education has changed in the past 700 years: professors still lecture from a privileged position, some people will always pay attention, and other people will always find distractions. However one interprets the painting, it is clear that viewers today recognize more than a few similarities between the education they have experienced and the world of Laurentius de Voltolina and Henricus de Alemania.

LAURENTIUS DE VOLTOLINA
Liber Ethicorum des Henricus de Alemania, circa 1350 (book illustration on parchment)
Wikimedia Commons
See p. C-1 in the color insert for a full-color reproduction of this image.

UNDERSTANDING THE TEXT

1. Examine the teacher's position behind the podium. How does his position contribute to his authority? What does it say about the relationship he has with his students?

2. How many of the students would you say are engaged in the lecture? How many are disengaged? How many kinds of disengaged behaviors can you identify?

3. How does Henricus appear to be responding to his class? Does he seem concerned about the students who are disruptive?

4. Do you think it is fair to say that teachers and students today behave in many of the same ways depicted in this illustration? What do you think accounts for the similarities?

MAKING CONNECTIONS

1. How might Rabindranath Tagore (p. 40) interpret Voltolina's illustration? How might the teacher and students of Tagore's classroom be arranged in such an illustration?

2. Compare the authority of the teacher in this drawing to the authority of Liberty in *Liberty Leading the People* (p. 494). From what source do the main figures seem to derive their authority?

WRITING ABOUT THE TEXT

1. Write an essay describing your own educational experiences as they relate to the drawing by Laurentius de Voltolina. Have you ever taken classes like the one depicted in the painting? What, in your experience, makes for an engaging class-room? a disengaging one?

2. Analyze the painting closely and explain why some students seem engaged while others do not. Is this the result of the way the information is being presented? If so, what about the presentation seems to work so well for the students in the front row?

3. Locate a photograph of a college or university lecture online and compare the students, teacher, and pedagogical strategies in that photo with those in the drawing.

FREDERICK DOUGLASS
Learning to Read
[1845]

FREDERICK DOUGLASS (1817–1895) was the most famous and respected African American in the United States for much of the nineteenth century. In 1845, he published his autobiography, *Narrative of the Life of Frederick Douglass, an American Slave*, which tells of his birth as the son of an enslaved woman and an unknown white man, his early life as a slave in Maryland, and his escape to freedom in 1837. The book became an international bestseller and catapulted him into a prominent position that he maintained for the rest of his life. He became a leader of the abolitionist movement and tirelessly spoke and wrote about the evils of slavery.

The turning point in Douglass's early life, as he presents it in his autobiography, was when he learned to read and write. His master's wife, Mrs. Auld, first taught him the alphabet—illegally, since slaves were forbidden to read or write. However, under pressure from her husband, she soon abandoned the effort, and he was left to learn on his own. His one guide in this effort was the children's schoolbook *The Columbian Orator*, a collection of great speeches, poems, soliloquies, and occasional pieces used to teach rhetoric and public speaking. In *The Columbian Orator*, Douglass learned a perplexing truth: the same country that had enslaved him had fought a revolution in the name of freedom. For the rest of his life, he drew on this tradition to call attention to the hypocrisy of slavery in a nation founded on principles of, in his words, "justice, liberty, prosperity, and independence."

In the example that follows, Douglass describes the strategies that he used to learn to read and write. The passage is important not only because it records Douglass's determination and perseverance but also because it reveals his keen understanding of the link between education and a desire for justice. For a time, Douglass relates, he felt oppressed by the fact that he had become more educated than most other slaves and wished that he could be as ignorant as they. In time, however, his education helped him to escape slavery and to make substantial contributions to its abolition.

Douglass is keenly aware of his story's great irony: that the white masters who tried to prevent slaves from being educated on the grounds that it would make them unfit for slavery were absolutely correct. Education, Douglass insists, goes hand in hand with freedom, and the only way to keep people enslaved is to prevent them from learning and acquiring knowledge. The *Narrative of the Life of Frederick Douglass* is both an account of and a testimony to the emancipatory power of education.

Douglass relies heavily on emotional appeals as he narrates his early experiences with reading and literacy. These experiences were both positive and negative, and his emotional reflections are both joyful and disconcerting. They all, though, have the effect of pulling the reader in and creating sympathy for Douglass.

I lived in Master Hugh's family about seven years. During this time, I succeeded in learning to read and write. In accomplishing this, I was compelled to resort to various stratagems. I had no regular teacher. My mistress, who had kindly commenced to instruct me, had, in compliance with the advice and direction of her husband, not only ceased to instruct, but had set her face against my being instructed by anyone else. It is due, however, to my mistress to say of her, that she did not adopt this course of treatment immediately. She at first lacked the depravity indispensable to shutting me up in mental darkness. It was at least necessary for her to have some training in the exercise of irresponsible power, to make her equal to the task of treating me as though I were a brute.

My mistress was, as I have said, a kind and tender-hearted woman; and in the simplicity of her soul she commenced, when I first went to live with her, to treat me as she supposed one human being ought to treat another. In entering upon the duties of a slaveholder, she did not seem to perceive that I sustained to her the relation of a mere chattel, and that for her to treat me as a human being was not only wrong, but dangerously so. Slavery proved as injurious to her as it did to me. When I went there, she was a pious, warm, and tender-hearted woman. There was no sorrow or suffering for which she had not a tear. She had bread for the hungry, clothes for the naked, and comfort for every mourner that came within her reach. Slavery soon proved its ability to divest her of these heavenly qualities. Under its influence, the tender heart became stone, and the lamblike disposition gave way to one of tiger-like fierceness. The first step in her downward course was in her ceasing to instruct me. She now commenced to practise her husband's precepts. She finally became even more violent in her opposition than her husband himself. She was not satisfied with simply doing as well as he had commanded; she seemed anxious to do better. Nothing seemed to make her more angry than to see me with a newspaper. She seemed to think that here lay the danger. I have had her rush at me with a face made all up of fury, and snatch from me a newspaper, in a manner that fully revealed her apprehension. She was an apt woman; and a little experience soon demonstrated, to her satisfaction, that education and slavery were incompatible with each other.

From this time I was most narrowly watched. If I was in a separate room any considerable length of time, I was sure to be suspected of having a book, and was at once called to give an account of myself. All this, however, was too late. The first step had been taken. Mistress, in teaching me the alphabet, had given me the *inch*, and no precaution could prevent me from taking the *ell*.[1]

---

1. ***Ell:*** an archaic unit of measurement equal to forty-five inches. The saying "give him an inch and he will take an ell" is the forerunner of the current proverb "give him an inch and he will take a mile."

The plan which I adopted, and the one by which I was most successful, was that of making friends of all the little white boys whom I met in the street. As many of these as I could, I converted into teachers. With their kindly aid, obtained at different times and in different places, I finally succeeded in learning to read. When I was sent of errands, I always took my book with me, and by doing one part of my errand quickly, I found time to get a lesson before my return. I used also to carry bread with me, enough of which was always in the house, and to which I was always welcome; for I was much better off in this regard than many of the poor white children in our neighborhood. This bread I used to bestow upon the hungry little urchins, who, in return, would give me that more valuable bread of knowledge. I am strongly tempted to give the names of two or three of those little boys, as a testimonial of the gratitude and affection I bear them; but prudence forbids;—not that it would injure me, but it might embarrass them; for it is almost an unpardonable offence to teach slaves to read in this Christian country. It is enough to say of the dear little fellows, that they lived on Philpot Street, very near Durgin and Bailey's ship-yard. I used to talk this matter of slavery over with them. I would sometimes say to them, I wished I could be as free as they would be when they got to be men. "You will be free as soon as you are twenty-one, *but I am a slave for life!* Have not I as good a right to be free as you have?" These words used to trouble them; they would express for me the liveliest sympathy, and console me with the hope that something would occur by which I might be free.

I was now about twelve years old, and the thought of being *a slave for life* began   5
to bear heavily upon my heart. Just about this time, I got hold of a book entitled "The Columbian Orator." Every opportunity I got, I used to read this book. Among much of other interesting matter, I found in it a dialogue between a master and his slave. The slave was represented as having run away from his master three times. The dialogue represented the conversation which took place between them, when the slave was retaken the third time. In this dialogue, the whole argument in behalf of slavery was brought forward by the master, all of which was disposed of by the slave. The slave was made to say some very smart as well as impressive things in reply to his master—things which had the desired though unexpected effect; for the conversation resulted in the voluntary emancipation of the slave on the part of the master.

In the same book, I met with one of Sheridan's[2] mighty speeches on and in behalf of Catholic emancipation. These were choice documents to me. I read them over and over again with unabated interest. They gave tongue to interesting thoughts of my own soul, which had frequently flashed through my mind, and died away for want of utterance. The moral which I gained from the dialogue was the power of truth over the conscience of even a slaveholder. What I got from Sheridan was

---

2. **Sheridan's:** Richard Brinsley Sheridan (1751–1816) was a well-known Irish playwright and advocate for Catholic civil rights.

a bold denunciation of slavery, and a powerful vindication of human rights. The reading of these documents enabled me to utter my thoughts, and to meet the arguments brought forward to sustain slavery; but while they relieved me of one difficulty, they brought on another even more painful than the one of which I was relieved. The more I read, the more I was led to abhor and detest my enslavers. I could regard them in no other light than a band of successful robbers, who had left their homes, and gone to Africa, and stolen us from our homes, and in a strange land reduced us to slavery. I loathed them as being the meanest as well as the most wicked of men. As I read and contemplated the subject, behold! that very discontentment which Master Hugh had predicted would follow my learning to read had already come, to torment and sting my soul to unutterable anguish. As I writhed under it, I would at times feel that learning to read had been a curse rather than a blessing. It had given me a view of my wretched condition, without the remedy. It opened my eyes to the horrible pit, but to no ladder upon which to get out. In moments of agony, I envied my fellow-slaves for their stupidity. I have often wished myself a beast. I preferred the condition of the meanest reptile to my own. Any thing, no matter what, to get rid of thinking! It was this everlasting thinking of my condition that tormented me. There was no getting rid of it. It was pressed upon me by every object within sight or hearing, animate or inanimate. The silver trump of freedom had roused my soul to eternal wakefulness. Freedom now appeared, to disappear no more forever. It was heard in every sound, and seen in every thing. It was ever present to torment me with a sense of my wretched condition. I saw nothing without seeing it, I heard nothing without hearing it, and felt nothing without feeling it. It looked from every star, it smiled in every calm, breathed in every wind, and moved in every storm.

I often found myself regretting my own existence, and wishing myself dead; and but for the hope of being free, I have no doubt but that I should have killed myself, or done something for which I should have been killed. While in this state of mind, I was eager to hear any one speak of slavery. I was a ready listener. Every little while, I could hear something about the abolitionists. It was some time before I found what the word meant. It was always used in such connections as to make it an interesting word to me. If a slave ran away and succeeded in getting clear, or if a slave killed his master, set fire to a barn, or did any thing very wrong in the mind of a slaveholder, it was spoken of as the fruit of *abolition*. Hearing the word in this connection very often, I set about learning what it meant. The dictionary afforded me little or no help. I found it was "the act of abolishing"; but then I did not know what was to be abolished. Here I was perplexed. I did not dare to ask any one about its meaning, for I was satisfied that it was something they wanted me to know very little about. After a patient waiting, I got one of our city papers, containing an account of the number of petitions from the north, praying for the abolition of slavery in the District of Columbia, and of the slave trade between the States. From this time I understood the words *abolition* and *abolitionist*, and always drew near when that word was spoken, expecting to hear something of importance to myself and fellow-slaves. The light broke in upon me by degrees. I went one day down on the wharf of Mr. Waters; and seeing two Irishmen unloading a scow of stone, I went, unasked, and helped them. When we had finished, one of them came to me and asked me if I were a slave. I told him I was. He asked, "Are ye a slave for life?" I told him that I was. The good Irishman seemed to be deeply affected by the statement. He said to the other that it was a pity so fine a little fellow as myself should be a slave for life. He said it was a shame to hold me. They both advised me to run away to the north; that I should find friends there, and that I should be free. I pretended not to be interested in what they said, and treated them as if I did not understand them; for I feared they might be treacherous. White men have been known to encourage slaves to escape, and then, to get the reward, catch them and return them to their masters. I was afraid that these seemingly good men might use me so; but I nevertheless remembered their advice, and from that time I resolved to run away. I looked forward to a time at which it would be safe for me to escape. I was too young to think of doing so immediately; besides, I wished to learn how to write, as I might have occasion to write my own pass. I consoled myself with the hope that I should one day find a good chance. Meanwhile, I would learn to write.

The idea as to how I might learn to write was suggested to me by being in Durgin and Bailey's ship-yard, and frequently seeing the ship carpenters, after hewing, and getting a piece of timber ready for use, write on the timber the name of that part of the ship for which it was intended. When a piece of timber was intended for the larboard side, it would be marked thus—"L." When a piece was for the starboard side, it would be marked thus—"S." A piece for the larboard side forward, would be marked thus—"L. F." When a piece was for starboard side forward it would be marked thus—"S. F." For larboard aft, it would be marked thus— "L. A." For starboard aft, it would be marked thus— "S. A." I soon learned the names of these letters, and for what they were intended when placed upon a piece of timber in the shipyard. I immediately commenced copying them, and in a short time was able to make the four letters named. After that, when I met with any boy who I knew could write, I would tell him I could write as well as he. The next word would be, "I don't believe you. Let me see you try it." I would then make the letters which I had been so fortunate as to learn, and ask him to beat that. In this way I got a good many lessons in writing, which it is quite possible I should never have gotten in any other way. During this time, my copy-book was the board fence, brick wall, and pavement; my pen and ink was a lump of chalk. With these, I learned mainly how to write. I then commenced and continued copying the Italics in Webster's Spelling Book, until I could make them all without looking on the book. By this time, my little Master Thomas had gone to school, and learned how to write, and had written over a number of copy-books. These had been brought home, and shown to some of our near neighbors, and then laid aside. My mistress used to go to class meeting at the Wilk Street meetinghouse every Monday afternoon, and leave me to take care of the house. When left thus, I used to spend the time in writing in the spaces left in Master Thomas's copy-book, copying what he had written. I continued to do this until I could write a hand very similar to that of Master Thomas. Thus, after a long, tedious effort for years, I finally succeeded in learning how to write.

UNDERSTANDING THE TEXT

1. What effect does Douglass believe slavery has on slaveholders? How do the actions of his former mistress support his assertion?

2. Why does Douglass not name the white boys who helped him learn to read? What does this decision say about the society he was living in when he wrote his autobiography?

3. What kinds of ideas did Douglass encounter when he read *The Columbian Orator*? How did these ideas influence him?

4. Why did Douglass become depressed after reading *The Columbian Orator*? Why did he feel that he would have been better off not knowing how to read?

5. What role does Douglass suggest education has in ending oppression? Why do oppressors keep their victims in ignorance?

6. How well does Douglass's narrative support his argument? How would you phrase that argument as a single thesis (p. 634)?

MAKING CONNECTIONS

1. Compare "Learning to Read" with Martin Luther King Jr.'s "Letter from Birmingham Jail" (p. 425). How does each writer draw on noncontroversial sources and ideas to support his then-controversial assertions?

2. Compare Douglass's experience of educating himself with John Henry Newman's understanding of "liberal education" (p. 31). How well does Douglass's learning correspond to the kind of education that Newman advocates? How "useful" to Douglass are the things he learns?

3. What role does rhetoric, as exemplified by the dialogue and speech in *The Columbian Orator*, play in Douglass's education? Consider the impact of this material on Douglass from the standpoint of Plato's (p. 166) and Aristotle's (p. 177) conflicting views on the usefulness of rhetoric.

4. Contrast Douglass's view of the importance of learning to read and write in Standard English with the views of Gloria Anzaldúa (p. 205) on the importance of cultural minorities' retaining their linguistic distinctiveness. Might the two positions be reconciled? Why or why not?

WRITING ABOUT THE TEXT

1. Write a personal essay about an early experience that significantly influenced your education. If appropriate, describe how something that you read had an impact on you and your course(s) of study.

2. Imagine that a person from another country arrived in your community able to speak English but not able to read and write. You are that person's tutor. How would you begin to teach? What reading materials would you use?

3. Other abolitionists criticized Douglass for accepting the tenets of the U.S. Constitution, because it did not repudiate slavery. Write an essay examining the Constitution as it stood in Douglass's day and arguing for or against Douglass's proposition that it is inherently antislavery. Perhaps also examine other founding American documents and judge how Douglass might have viewed them.

4. Explain the connections between education and liberty by using Seneca (p. 13) as a theoretical background and Douglass as a primary example.

JOHN HENRY NEWMAN
from *Knowledge Its Own End*
[1852]

JOHN HENRY NEWMAN (1801–1890) shocked his students, his colleagues, and much of England when, in 1845, he resigned his positions as Anglican minister and Oxford professor and converted to Roman Catholicism. At the time, Catholics held an extremely tenuous position in English society; they had received the right to vote only sixteen years earlier, in 1829, and the Catholic Church had no formal organization in England. Newman's conversion was a matter of deep, personal conviction, which he discussed in his famous 1864 autobiography, *Apologia Pro Vita Sua*. In 1879, Pope Leo XIII named Newman a cardinal, and in 1991, Pope John Paul II set in motion the process to proclaim him a saint. Newman was as committed to education as he was to Catholicism, and, from his conversion to his death, he was a prominent spokesperson for both.

Newman's conversion meant that he was forbidden to teach at Oxford or any other English university. However, the Catholic population of Ireland was large enough to support a major university. In 1852, Newman traveled to Dublin to deliver a series of lectures on the importance of Catholic education. Two years later, in 1854, he helped found the Catholic University of Ireland and was named its first rector. In this capacity, he revised his early lectures on education, which were published in 1873 as *The Idea of a University*.

The Idea of a University reflects on much more than the role of education in a religious life. Newman understood "Catholic" in its broadest sense, including the meaning "universal," and he believed that a "Catholic education" involved all branches of knowledge. *The Idea of a University* argues for a "liberal" education, meaning an education that crosses disciplinary boundaries and gives students a solid background in the arts, sciences, and humanities. Newman's concept of a liberal education had a tremendous impact on the subsequent development of universities in England and the United States. Even today, most colleges and universities have a general education component whose core values can be traced back to the ideas that Newman articulates in this book.

"Knowledge Its Own End" was the fifth of Newman's original lectures on education to Irish Catholics. In it, Newman argues that a true education need not, and in many cases cannot, be attached to practical purposes. Relying on quotations from Cicero, Aristotle, Xenophon, and Francis Bacon, Newman draws a sharp distinction between "useful knowledge" (knowledge that has a practical application) and "liberal knowledge" (knowledge that is pursued for its own sake). Newman acknowledges that useful knowledge is important—people need to be trained for careers, taught to accomplish tasks, and provided with ways to make their lives more fulfilling. However, Newman also sees tremendous value in education that exists solely for the sake of imparting knowledge and fostering inquiry. This kind of knowledge, for Newman, lies at the heart of a university. His own essay on liberal education draws much of its authority from the words of thinkers that most educated people in Newman's day were familiar with.

2.

I am asked what is the end of University Education, and of the Liberal or Philosophical Knowledge which I conceive it to impart: I answer, that what I have already said has been sufficient to show that it has a very tangible, real, and sufficient end, though the end cannot be divided from that knowledge itself. Knowledge is capable of being its own end. Such is the constitution of the human mind, that any kind of knowledge, if it be really such, is its own reward. And if this is true of all knowledge, it is true also of that special Philosophy, which I have made to consist in a comprehensive view of truth in all its branches, of the relations of science to science, of their mutual bearings, and their respective values. What the worth of such an acquirement is, compared with other objects which we seek, wealth or power or honour or the conveniences and comforts of life, I do not profess here to discuss; but I would maintain, and mean to show, that it is an object, in its own nature so really and undeniably good, as to be the compensation of a great deal of thought in the compassing, and a great deal of trouble in the attaining.

Now, when I say that Knowledge is, not merely a means to something beyond it, or the preliminary of certain arts into which it naturally resolves, but an end sufficient to rest in and to pursue for its own sake, surely I am uttering no paradox, for I am stating what is both intelligible in itself, and has ever been the common judgment of philosophers and the ordinary feeling of mankind. I am saying what at least the public opinion of this day ought to be slow to deny, considering how much we have heard of late years, in opposition to Religion, of entertaining, curious, and various knowledge. I am but saying what whole volumes have been written to illustrate, viz.,[1] by a "selection from the records of Philosophy, Literature, and Art, in all ages and countries, of a body of examples, to show how the most unpropitious circumstances have been unable to conquer an ardent desire for the acquisition of knowledge."[2] That further advantages accrue to us and redound to others by its possession, over and above what it is in itself, I am very far indeed from denying; but, independent of these, we are satisfying a direct need of our nature in its very aquisition; and

1. **Viz.:** namely.
2. The quotation is from *The Pursuit of Knowledge* *under Difficulties* (1866), by the American essayist Mary Abigail Dodge (1833–1896).

whereas our nature, unlike that of the inferior creation, does not at once reach its perfection, but depends, in order to it, on a number of external aids and appliances, Knowledge, as one of the principal of these, is valuable for what its very presence in us does for us after the manner of a habit, even though it be turned to no further account, nor subserve any direct end.

3.

Hence it is that Cicero,[3] in enumerating the various heads of mental excellence, lays down the pursuit of Knowledge for its own sake, as the first of them. "This pertains most of all to human nature," he says, "for we are all of us drawn to the pursuit of Knowledge; in which to excel we consider excellent, whereas to mistake, to err, to be ignorant, to be deceived, is both an evil and a disgrace." And he considers Knowledge the very first object to which we are attracted, after the supply of our physical wants. After the calls and duties of our animal existence, as they may be termed, as regards ourselves, our family, and our neighbours, follows, he tells us, "the search after truth. Accordingly, as soon as we escape from the pressure of necessary cares, forthwith we desire to see, to hear, and to learn; and consider the knowledge of what is hidden or is wonderful a condition of our happiness."

This passage, though it is but one of many similar passages in a multitude of authors, I take for the very reason that it is so familiarly known to us; and I wish you to observe, Gentlemen, how distinctly it separates the pursuit of Knowledge from those ulterior objects to which certainly it can be made to conduce, and which are, I suppose, solely contemplated by the persons who would ask of me the use of a University or Liberal Education. So far from dreaming of the cultivation of Knowledge directly and mainly in order to our physical comfort and enjoyment, for the sake of life and person, of health, of the conjugal and family union, of the social tie and civil security, the great Orator implies, that it is only after our physical and political needs are supplied, and when we are "free from necessary duties and cares," that we are in a condition for "desiring to see, to hear, and to learn." Nor does he contemplate in the least degree the reflex or subsequent action of Knowledge, when acquired, upon those material goods which we set out by securing before we seek it; on the contrary, he expressly denies its bearing upon social life altogether, strange as such a procedure is to those who live after the rise of the Baconian philosophy,[4] and he cautions us against such a cultivation of it as will interfere with our duties to our fellow-creatures. "All these methods," he says, "are engaged in the investigation of truth; by the pursuit of which to be carried off from public occupations is a

---

3. **Cicero:** Marcus Tullius Cicero (106–43 BCE), Roman orator and statesman. The quotation below comes from his work *De Officiis*, or "On Duties" (44 BCE).

4. **Baconian philosophy:** the theory of knowledge derived from the writings of Francis Bacon (1561–1626), who emphasized the way that scientific inquiry could improve the human condition.

transgression of duty. For the praise of virtue lies altogether in action; yet intermissions often occur, and then we recur to such pursuits; not to say that the incessant activity of the mind is vigorous enough to carry us on in the pursuit of knowledge, even without any exertion of our own." The idea of benefiting society by means of "the pursuit of science and knowledge" did not enter at all into the motives which he would assign for their cultivation. . . .

4.

Things, which can bear to be cut off from every thing else and yet persist in living, 5
must have life in themselves; pursuits, which issue in nothing, and still maintain their ground for ages, which are regarded as admirable, though they have not as yet proved themselves to be useful, must have their sufficient end in themselves, whatever it turn out to be. And we are brought to the same conclusion by considering the force of the epithet, by which the knowledge under consideration is popularly designated. It is common to speak of "*liberal* knowledge," of the "*liberal* arts and studies," and of a "*liberal* education," as the especial characteristic or property of a University and of a gentleman; what is really meant by the word? Now, first, in its grammatical sense it is opposed to *servile*; and by "servile work" is understood, as our catechisms inform us, bodily labour, mechanical employment, and the like, in which the mind has little or no part. . . . As far as this contrast may be considered as a guide into the meaning of the word, liberal education and liberal pursuits are exercises of mind, of reason, of reflection.

But we want something more for its explanation, for there are bodily exercises which are liberal, and mental exercises which are not so. For instance, in ancient times the practitioners in medicine were commonly slaves; yet it was an art as intellectual in its nature, in spite of the pretence, fraud, and quackery with which it might then, as now, be debased, as it was heavenly in its aim. And so in like manner, we contrast a liberal education with a commercial education or a professional; yet no one can deny that commerce and the professions afford scope for the highest and most diversified powers of mind. There is then a great variety of intellectual exercises, which are not technically called "liberal;" on the other hand, I say, there are exercises of the body which do receive that appellation. Such, for instance, was the palæstra,[5] in ancient times; such the Olympic games, in which strength and dexterity of body as well as of mind gained the prize. In Xenophon[6] we read of the young Persian nobility being taught to ride on horseback and to speak the truth; both being among the accomplishments of a gentleman. War, too, however rough a profession, has ever been accounted liberal, unless in cases when it becomes heroic, which would introduce us to another subject.

5. **The palæstra:** in ancient Greece, the site of boxing, wrestling, and other physical competitions.

6. **Xenophon:** a student (circa 431–circa 352 BCE) of Socrates and contemporary of Plato who wrote a series of works on the history of Athens during his own times. His best-known work, the *Anabasis*, tells of his travels through the Persian Empire.

Now comparing these instances together, we shall have no difficulty in determining the principle of this apparent variation in the application of the term which I am examining. Manly games, or games of skill, or military prowess, though bodily, are, it seems, accounted liberal; on the other hand, what is merely professional, though highly intellectual, nay, though liberal in comparison of trade and manual labour, is not simply called liberal, and mercantile occupations are not liberal at all. Why this distinction? because that alone is liberal knowledge, which stands on its own pretensions, which is independent of sequel, expects no complement, refuses to be *informed* (as it is called) by any end, or absorbed into any art, in order duly to present itself to our contemplation. The most ordinary pursuits have this specific character, if they are self-sufficient and complete; the highest lose it, when they minister to something beyond them. It is absurd to balance, in point of worth and importance, a treatise on reducing fractures with a game of cricket or a fox-chase; yet of the two the bodily exercise has that quality which we call "liberal," and the intellectual has it not. And so of the learned professions altogether, considered merely as professions; although one of them be the most popularly beneficial, and another the most politically important, and the third the most intimately divine of all human pursuits, yet the very greatness of their end, the health of the body, or of the commonwealth, or of the soul, diminishes, not increases, their claim to the appellation "liberal," and that still more, if they are cut down to the strict exigencies of that end. If, for instance, Theology, instead of being cultivated as a contemplation, be limited to the purposes of the pulpit or be represented by the catechism, it loses,—not its usefulness, not its divine character, not its meritoriousness (rather it gains a claim upon these titles by such charitable condescension),—but it does lose the particular attribute which I am illustrating; just as a face worn by tears and fasting loses its beauty, or a labourer's hand loses its delicateness;—for Theology thus exercised is not simple knowledge, but rather is an art or a business making use of Theology. And thus it appears that even what is supernatural need not be liberal, nor need a hero be a gentleman, for the plain reason that one idea is not another idea. And in like manner the Baconian Philosophy, by using its physical sciences in the service of man, does thereby transfer them from the order of Liberal Pursuits to, I do not say the inferior, but the distinct class of the Useful. And, to take a different instance, hence again, as is evident, whenever personal gain is the motive, still more distinctive an effect has it upon the character of a given pursuit; thus racing, which was a liberal exercise in Greece, forfeits its rank in times like these, so far as it is made the occasion of gambling.

All that I have been now saying is summed up in a few characteristic words of the great Philosopher. "Of possessions," he says, "those rather are useful, which bear fruit; those *liberal, which tend to enjoyment.* By fruitful, I mean, which yield revenue; by enjoyable, where *nothing accrues of consequence beyond the using.*"[7] . . .

---

7. This quotation comes from the fifth chapter of the first book of Aristotle's *Rhetoric.*

9.

Useful Knowledge then, I grant, has done its work; and Liberal Knowledge as certainly has not done its work,—that is, supposing, as the objectors assume, its direct end, like Religious Knowledge, is to make men better; but this I will not for an instant allow, and, unless I allow it, those objectors have said nothing to the purpose. I admit, rather I maintain, what they have been urging, for I consider Knowledge to have its end in itself. For all its friends, or its enemies, may say, I insist upon it, that it is as real a mistake to burden it with virtue or religion as with the mechanical arts. Its direct business is not to steel the soul against temptation or to console it in affliction, any more than to set the loom in motion, or to direct the steam carriage; be it ever so much the means or the condition of both material and moral advancement, still, taken by and in itself, it as little mends our hearts as it improves our temporal circumstances. And if its eulogists claim for it such a power, they commit the very same kind of encroachment on a province not their own as the political economist who should maintain that his science educated him for casuistry or diplomacy. Knowledge is one thing, virtue is another; good sense is not conscience, refinement is not humility, nor is largeness and justness of view faith. Philosophy, however enlightened, however profound, gives no command over the passions, no influential motives, no vivifying principles. Liberal Education makes not the Christian, not the Catholic, but the gentleman. It is well to be a gentleman, it is well to have a cultivated intellect, a delicate taste, a candid, equitable, dispassionate mind, a noble and courteous bearing in the conduct of life;—these are the natural qualities of a large knowledge; they are the objects of a University; I am advocating, I shall illustrate and insist upon them; but still, I repeat, they are no guarantee for sanctity or even for conscientiousness, they may attach to the man of the world, to the profligate, to the heartless,—pleasant, alas, and attractive as he shows when decked out in them. Taken by themselves, they do but seem to be what they are not; they look like virtue at a distance, but they are detected by close observers, and on the long run; and hence it is that they are popularly accused of pretence and hypocrisy, not, I repeat, from their own fault, but because their professors and their admirers persist in taking them for what they are not, and are officious in arrogating for them a praise to which they have no claim. Quarry the granite rock with razors, or moor the vessel with a thread of silk; then may you hope with such keen and delicate instruments as human knowledge and human reason to control against those giants, the passion and the pride of man.

Surely we are not driven to theories of this kind, in order to vindicate the value and dignity of Liberal Knowledge. Surely the real grounds on which its pretensions rest are not so very subtle or abstruse, so very strange or improbable. Surely it is very intelligible to say, and that is what I say here, that Liberal Education, viewed in itself, is simply the cultivation of the intellect, as such, and its object is nothing more or less than intellectual excellence. Every thing has its own perfection, be it

10

higher or lower in the scale of things; and the perfection of one is not the perfection of another. Things animate, inanimate, visible, invisible, all are good in their kind, and have a *best* of themselves, which is an object of pursuit. Why do you take such pains with your garden or your park? You see to your walks and turf and shrubberies; to your trees and drives; not as if you meant to make an orchard of the one, or corn or pasture land of the other, but because there is a special beauty in all that is goodly in wood, water, plain, and slope, brought all together by art into one shape, and grouped into the whole. Your cities are beautiful, your palaces, your public buildings, your territorial mansions, your churches; and their beauty leads to nothing beyond itself. There is a physical beauty and a moral: there is a beauty of person, there is a beauty of our moral being, which is natural virtue; and in like manner there is a beauty, there is a perfection, of the intellect. There is an ideal perfection in these various subject-matters, towards which individual instances are seen to rise, and which are the standards for all instances whatever. The Greek divinities and demigods, as the statuary has moulded them, with their symmetry of figure, and their high forehead and their regular features, are the perfection of physical beauty. The heroes, of whom history tells, Alexander, or Cæsar, or Scipio, or Saladin, are the representatives of that magnanimity or self-mastery which is the greatness of human nature. Christianity too has its heroes, and in the supernatural order, and we call them Saints. The artist puts before him beauty of feature and form; the poet, beauty of mind; the preacher, the beauty of grace: then intellect too, I repeat, has its beauty, and it has those who aim at it. To open the mind, to correct it, to refine it, to enable it to know, and to digest, master, rule, and use its knowledge, to give it power over its own faculties, application, flexibility, method, critical exactness, sagacity, resource, address, eloquent expression, is an object as intelligible. . . . as the cultivation of virtue, while, at the same time, it is absolutely distinct from it.

10.

This indeed is but a temporal object, and a transitory possession: but so are other things in themselves which we make much of and pursue. The moralist will tell us that man, in all his functions, is but a flower which blossoms and fades, except so far as a higher principle breathes upon him, and makes him and what he is immortal. Body and mind are carried on into an eternal state of being by the gifts of Divine Munificence; but at first they do but fail in a failing world; and if the powers of intellect decay, the powers of the body have decayed before them, and, as an Hospital or an Almshouse, though its end be ephemeral, may be sanctified to the service of religion, so surely may a University, even were it nothing more than I have as yet described it. We attain to heaven by using this world well, though it is to pass away; we perfect our nature, not by undoing it, but by adding to it what is more than nature, and directing it towards aims higher than its own.

UNDERSTANDING THE TEXT

1. What are some of the practical applications of different kinds of knowledge? Is Newman correct in saying that knowledge need not serve any "useful" social purpose to be worth acquiring? Why or why not?

2. How does Newman define "liberal" as it applies to knowledge? Which subjects in a contemporary college or university would Newman consider "liberal knowledge"? Which would he consider "useful knowledge"? Is this distinction valuable? Why or why not?

3. What kinds of physical exercises does Newman consider "liberal"? What is the difference between useful physical exercise and "liberal exercise"? Is the distinction the same as it is for intellectual pursuits?

4. According to Newman, what is the consequence of requiring that education correspond to certain notions of "virtue"?

5. In Newman's opinion, what role does enjoyment play in the motivation to acquire knowledge? In your opinion, is learning most enjoyable for its own sake or for its practical use?

6. Examine the ways that Newman incorporates quotations and references from ancient Greek and Roman authors. How well do these citations prove his points? How well do they illustrate his arguments?

7. Does Newman believe that liberal education is more valuable than career-oriented education? Which kinds of education would his ideal university accomplish?

MAKING CONNECTIONS

1. How does Newman's view of the value of education compare with that of Frederick Douglass (p. 24)? Do you think that Douglass would agree that acquiring knowledge is an end of its own? Why or why not?

2. Does Newman's religious approach to education resemble that of Hsün Tzu (p. 5), Seneca (p. 13), or Nussbaum (p. 61)? In what way can an education that does not specifically promote virtue be "religious"?

3. Compare Newman's understanding of the role of "useful education" with Richard Feynman's view that education must be practical and hands-on to be understood (p. 53). Do the two views contradict each other? Why or why not?

4. How might Newman respond to Gorgias (p. 166) or someone else who argues that rhetoric always has as its purpose the persuasion of others? Is it possible for rhetoric to be "liberal" in Newman's sense of the word?

WRITING ABOUT THE TEXT

1. Obtain a catalog from your own college or university and examine the general education curriculum. Write an essay discussing this curriculum in relation to

Newman's "Knowledge Its Own End." Support or oppose these requirements for all students, regardless of their majors.

2. Compare Newman's view of liberal education with Seneca's (p. 13). In what ways does Seneca mirror Newman's contention that education does not need to be useful?

3. How "useful" or helpful do you find Newman's distinction between "useful" and "liberal" knowledge? Consider your education thus far. How much of your knowledge meets all the qualifications of "liberal knowledge"? How much is "useful" and practical? Where do the two kinds overlap?

4. Write an essay titled "The Idea of a University," explaining your view of what college should be and how it should function. Do not feel bound to Newman's ideas, but refer to them when appropriate.

RABINDRANATH TAGORE
To Teachers

[1923]

RABINDRANATH TAGORE (1861–1941) is considered by many to be one of India's most important literary figures. Born and raised in Calcutta, Tagore primarily spoke and wrote in Bengali—the second most spoken language in India and the seventh most spoken language in the world. He was a scholar, educator, novelist, musician, painter, and poet. It would be difficult to overstate Tagore's influence on the culture of his region, where he is held in the same regard as William Shakespeare in England or Benjamin Franklin in the United States. Two modern nations—India and Bangladesh—use songs written by Tagore as their national anthems.

Outside of India, Tagore is best known for his book of poetry *Gitanjali or Song Offerings* (1910), the first Indian work to be widely read and praised in the West. In 1912, Tagore translated the poems into English himself and published them in London, where they quickly became a sensation. The next year, Tagore became the first non-European writer to win the Nobel Prize for Literature. He used his prize money from the Nobel committee to start Visva-Bharati, now called Visva-Bharati University, one of the premier institutions of higher education in India.

Visva-Bharati grew out of a coeducational school for children that Tagore established on his family property in 1901. Its name means "the communion of the world with India," and Tagore frequently invited notable people from India or Europe to spend time at the school. Classes were often held outdoors, as Tagore believed that students learned best when they were close to nature. And courses did not begin and end on specific dates on the calendar. Students continued taking the course until both they and the instructor were satisfied that they had learned the material.

In 1924, Tagore was invited to China to give a series of lectures on education and the philosophy behind Visva-Bharati. He spent nearly two months touring the country and speaking at universities. His generally conservative approach to education was not well received by students, who were in the midst of a revolutionary fervor that would soon overthrow the Confucian and Buddhist traditions that he supported. But these lectures did give him the opportunity to distill his educational philosophies into concrete statements of value and purpose.

The essay that follows, "To Teachers," comes from Tagore's own published account of his trip to China. It consists of a lecture that he gave, probably multiple times, to the faculty of the schools he visited. Tagore builds this lecture around a set of contrasts: natural versus artificial, childhood versus adulthood, freedom versus constraint, and others. Each of these contrasts contributes to the overall picture of education that Tagore draws: a school should work with the natural curiosity of a child's mind to stimulate creativity and understanding, and should introduce children to people from as many different backgrounds and worldviews as possible so that they do not grow up with the prejudices and blind spots of their elders. It should not be an "education factory" that warehouses students and teaches them in ways most convenient for adults. Such is the vision that Tagore had for his beloved Visva-Bharati.

I have been told that you would like to hear about the educational crusade I have undertaken, but it will be difficult for me to give you a distinct idea of my institution of learning, which has grown gradually during the last twenty-four years. My own mind has grown with it, and my own ideal of education has reached its fullness so slowly and so naturally, that I find it difficult to analyze and place it before you.

The first question you may all ask is: what urged me to take up education. Until I was forty or more, I had spent most of my time in literary pursuits. I had never any desire to participate in practical work because I had a conviction that I did not have the gift. Perhaps you know the truth, or shall I make a confession? When I was thirteen I finished going to school. I do not want to boast about it, I merely give it to you as a historical fact.

So long as I was forced to attend school, I felt an unbearable torture. I often counted the years before I would have my freedom. My elder brothers had finished their academic career and were engaged in life, each in his own way. How I envied them when, after a hurried meal in the morning, I found the inevitable carriage that took us to school, ready at the gate. How I wished that, by some magic spell, I could cross the intervening fifteen or twenty years and suddenly become a grown-up man. I afterwards realized that what then weighed on my mind was the unnatural pressure of a system of education which prevailed everywhere.

Children's minds are sensitive to the influences of the world. Their subconscious minds are active, always imbibing some lesson, and realizing the joy of knowing. This sensitive receptivity helps them, without any strain, to master language, which is the most complex and difficult instrument of expression, full of indefinable ideas and abstract symbols. Through their natural ability to guess they learn the meaning of words which we cannot explain. It may be easy for a child to know what the word "water" means, but how difficult it must be for him to know what idea is associated with the simple word "yesterday." Yet how easily they overcome such innumerable difficulties because of the extraordinary sensitiveness of their subconscious mind. Because of this their introduction to the world of reality is easy and joyful.

In this critical period, the child's life is subjected to the education factory, lifeless, colorless, dissociated from the context of the universe, within bare white walls staring like eyeballs of the dead. We are born with that God-given gift of taking delight in the world, but such delightful activity is fettered and imprisoned, muted by a force called discipline which kills the sensitiveness of the child mind which is always on the alert, restless and eager to receive first-hand knowledge from mother nature. We sit inert, like dead specimens of some museum, while lessons are pelted at us from on high, like hail stones on flowers.

In childhood we learn our lessons with the aid of both body and mind, with all the senses active and eager. When we are sent to school, the doors of natural information are closed to us; our eyes see the letters, our ears hear the abstract lessons, but our mind misses the perpetual stream of ideas from nature, because the teachers, in their wisdom, think these bring distraction, and have no purpose behind them.

When we accept any discipline for ourselves, we try to avoid everything except that which is necessary for our purpose; it is this purposefulness, which belongs to the adult mind, that we force upon school children. We say, "Never keep your mind alert, attend to what is before you, what has been given you." This tortures the child because it contradicts nature's purpose, and nature, the greatest of all teachers, is thwarted at every step by the human teacher who believes in machine-made lessons rather than life lessons, so that the growth of the child's mind is not only injured, but forcibly spoiled.

Children should be surrounded with the things of nature which have their own educational value. Their minds should be allowed to stumble upon and be surprised at everything that happens in today's life; the new tomorrow will stimulate their attention with new facts of life. What happens in a school is that every day, at the same hour, the same book is brought and poured out for him. His attention is never alerted by random surprises from nature.

Our adult mind is always full of things we have to arrange and deal with, and therefore the things that happen around us, such as the coming of morning, leave no mark upon us. We do not allow them to because our minds are already crowded; the stream of lessons perpetually flowing from the heart of nature does not touch us, we merely choose those which are useful, rejecting the rest as undesirable because we want the shortest path to success.

Children have no such distractions. With them every new fact or event comes to   10
a mind that is always open with an abundant hospitality, and through this exuberant, indiscriminate acceptance, they learn innumerable facts within an amazingly short time, compared with our own slowness. These are the most important lessons in life, and what is still more wonderful is that the greater part of them are abstract truths.

The child learns so easily because he has a natural gift, but adults, because they are tyrants, ignore natural gifts and say that children must learn through the same process that they learned by. We insist upon forced mental feeding and our lessons become a form of torture. This is one of man's most cruel and wasteful mistakes.

Because I underwent this process when I was young, and remembered the torture of it, I tried to establish a school where boys might be free in spite of the school. Knowing something of the natural school which Nature supplies to all her creatures, I established my institution in a beautiful spot, far away from town, where the children had the greatest freedom possible, especially in my not forcing upon them lessons for which their mind was unfitted. I do not wish to exaggerate, however, and I must admit that I have not been able to follow my own plan in every way. Forced as we are to live in a society which is itself tyrannical, and which cannot always be gainsaid, I was often obliged to concede to what I did not believe in, but what the others around me insisted on. Yet I always had it in my mind to create an atmosphere; I felt this was more important than classroom teaching.

The atmosphere was there; how could I create it? The birds sang to the awakening light of the morning, the evening came with its own silence, and the stars brought the peace of night.

We had the open beauty of the sky, and the seasons in all their magnificent color. Through this intimacy with nature we took the opportunity of instituting festivals. I wrote songs to celebrate the coming of spring and the rainy season which follows the long months of drought; we had dramatic performances with decorations appropriate to the seasons.

I invited artists from the city to live at the school, and left them free to produce   15
their own work. If the boys and girls felt inclined to watch, I allowed them to do so. The same was true with my own work; I was composing songs and poems, and would often invite the teachers to sing or read with them. This helped to create an atmosphere in which they could imbibe something intangible, but lifegiving. . . .

When races come together, as in the present age, it should not be merely the gathering of a crowd; there must be a bond of relation, or they will collide with each other.

Education must enable every child to understand and fulfill this purpose of the age, not defeat it by acquiring the habit of creating divisions and cherishing national prejudices. There are of course natural differences in human races which should be preserved and respected, and the task of our education should be to realize unity in spite of them, to discover truth through the wilderness of their contradictions.

We have tried to do this in Visva-Bharati. Our endeavor has been to include this ideal of unity in all the activities in our institution, some educational, some that comprise different kinds of artistic expression, some in the shape of service to our neighbors by helping the reconstruction of village life.

The children began to serve our neighbors, to help them in various ways and to be in constant touch with the life around them. They also had the freedom to grow, which is the greatest possible gift to a child. We aimed at another kind of freedom; a sympathy with all humanity, free from all racial and national prejudices.

The minds of children are usually shut inside prison houses, so that they become   20
incapable of understanding people who have different languages and customs. This causes us to grope after each other in darkness, to hurt each other in ignorance, to suffer from the worst form of blindness. Religious missionaries themselves have contributed to this evil; in the name of brotherhood and in the arrogance of sectarian pride they have created misunderstanding. They make this permanent in their textbooks, and poison the minds of children.

I have tried to save children from the vicious methods which alienate their minds, and from other prejudices which are fostered through histories, geographies and lessons full of national prejudices. In the East there is a great deal of bitterness against other races, and in our own homes we are often brought up with feelings of hatred. I have tried to save the children from such feelings, with the help of friends from the West, who, with their understanding and their human sympathy and love, have done us a great service.

We are building our institution upon the ideal of the spiritual unity of all races. I want to use the help of all other races, and when I was in Europe I appealed to the great scholars of the West, and was fortunate enough to receive their help. They left their own schools to come to our institution, which is poor in material things, and they helped us develop it.

I have in my mind not merely a University, for that is only one aspect of our Visva-Bharati, but the idea of a great meeting place for individuals from all countries where men who believe in spiritual unity can come in touch with their neighbors. There are such idealists, and when I traveled in the West, even in remote places, many persons without any special reputation wanted to join this work.

It will be a great future, when base passions are no longer stimulated within us, when human races come closer to one another, and when through their meeting new truths are revealed.

There will be a sunrise of truth and love through insignificant people who have suffered martyrdom for humanity, like the great personality who had only a handful of disciples from among the fisherfolk and who at the end of his career seemingly presented a picture of failure at a time when Rome was at the zenith of her glory. He was reviled by those in power, ignored by the crowd, and he was crucified; yet through that symbol he lives forever.

There are martyrs of today who are sent to prison and persecuted, who are not men of power, but who belong to a deathless future.

UNDERSTANDING THE TEXT

1. What purpose do Tagore's reflections on his own educational experiences serve in the lecture? Why does he talk about how much he hated school? What about the school's educational system made him feel that way?

2. What kind of school does Tagore call "the education factory"? What impact does this kind of education have on students?

3. According to Tagore, what "natural gift" do children have? How can teachers use this gift to create stimulating educational experiences? Why do so many teachers fail to do this?

4. Why does Tagore believe that it is more important to create an atmosphere for learning than to actually teach important material?

5. How does Tagore believe that students of different races should be taught to interact with each other? What can schools do to encourage this?

MAKING CONNECTIONS

1. Martha Nussbaum (p. 61) cites Tagore as one of the major theorists of what she calls "education for democracy." In what ways do Tagore's views on education seem especially useful for democratic government?

2. Tagore and Mohandas Gandhi (p. 560) knew and admired each other, but often disagreed about the role of education in society—Tagore believed that only education could ultimately free India from British rule while Gandhi saw formal education as a tool of imperialism. How would you compare the underlying assumptions of these divergent beliefs?

WRITING ABOUT THE TEXT

1. Compare Rabindranath Tagore's view of education to that of Hsün Tzu in "Encouraging Learning" (p. 5). What assumptions about human nature lie beneath these views of education?

2. Using Tagore's essay and other sources in this chapter, compose an argument in which you try to persuade your teacher to hold class outside for the rest of the semester.

3. Describe your own experience with what Tagore calls "the education factory." What elements of your elementary or secondary education were factory-like? Which elements were not? Are there classrooms today that incorporate some of Tagore's principles?

VIRGINIA WOOLF
Shakespeare's Sister
[1929]

VIRGINIA WOOLF (1882–1941) was one of the most important English writers of the twentieth century. Her father, the eminent scholar and religious freethinker Sir Leslie Stephen, raised her in an intellectually stimulating environment and encouraged her academic pursuits. After her father's death in 1904, she began to associate with a group of London artists and intellectuals known as the Bloomsbury Group, whose members included the novelist E. M. Forster, the painter Roger Fry, the economist John Maynard Keynes, and the political theorist Leonard Woolf, who became her husband in 1912.

Woolf published her first novel, *The Voyage Out,* in 1915. She would go on to publish several other novels of lasting influence, including *Mrs. Dalloway* (1925), *To the Lighthouse* (1927), *Orlando* (1928), and *The Waves* (1931). In her fiction, Woolf often experimented with many features of Modernist literature: non-sequential plot, stream-of-consciousness narrative, and interior monologue that explored the inner landscapes of her characters.

During her lifetime, Woolf gained fame as one of the best nonfiction writers of the Modernist period. In the second half of the twentieth century, she would be considered by modern feminists as one of the founders of their movement. One of her most famous works is the book-length essay *A Room of One's Own,* which grew out of lectures she delivered at the women's colleges of Cambridge University. In this essay, she explores the long and impressive history of women as the subjects of literature and contrasts it to the small number of women who actually wrote literature. In Woolf's day, only a handful of women rose to the status of major writers, and most of these women had either published their works anonymously (such as Jane Austen) or used a male pseudonym (such as George Eliot). Woolf wanted to understand these phenomena.

Her conclusion, which provides the title of the essay, is that a woman can only become a writer if she has "money and a room of her own"—two things that most women throughout history have not had. No matter how much innate talent women of the past possessed, Woolf argues, they did not have the economic or cultural freedom to put that talent to good use. In the passage reprinted here, Woolf imagines what would have happened if a woman in Shakespeare's day had been born with all of the innate talent of Shakespeare. No such woman could ever have become Shakespeare's equal, she insists, because she would never have had access to all of the things that make great writing possible.

Woolf tells the story of Judith Shakespeare, a fictional female writer with all of William Shakespeare's talent but none of his opportunities. Among other things, "Shakespeare's Sister" demonstrates the rhetorical power of narrative. Though Woolf invents many of the details of Judith Shakespeare's life, her creation dramatizes the very real limitations that women have faced in nearly every period and culture of the world's history.

It was disappointing not to have brought back in the evening some important statement, some authentic fact. Women are poorer than men because—this or that. Perhaps now it would be better to give up seeking for the truth, and receiving on one's head an avalanche of opinion hot as lava, discoloured as dish-water. It would be better to draw the curtains; to shut out distractions; to light the lamp; to narrow the enquiry and to ask the historian, who records not opinions but facts, to describe under what conditions women lived, not throughout the ages, but in England, say in the time of Elizabeth.

For it is a perennial puzzle why no woman wrote a word of that extraordinary literature when every other man, it seemed, was capable of song or sonnet. What were the conditions in which women lived, I asked myself; for fiction, imaginative work that is, is not dropped like a pebble upon the ground, as science may be; fiction is like a spider's web, attached ever so lightly perhaps, but still attached to life at all four corners. Often the attachment is scarcely perceptible; Shakespeare's plays, for instance, seem to hang there complete by themselves. But when the web is pulled askew, hooked up at the edge, torn in the middle, one remembers that these webs are not spun in midair by incorporeal creatures, but are the work of suffering human beings, and are attached to grossly material things, like health and money and the houses we live in.

I went, therefore, to the shelf where the histories stand and took down one of the latest, Professor Trevelyan's *History of England*.[1] Once more I looked up Women, found "position of" and turned to the pages indicated. "Wife-beating", I read, "was a recognised right of man, and was practised without shame by high as well as low. . . . Similarly," the historian goes on, "the daughter who refused to marry the gentleman of her parents' choice was liable to be locked up, beaten and flung about the room, without any shock being inflicted on public opinion. Marriage was not an affair of personal affection, but of family avarice, particularly in the 'chivalrous' upper classes. . . . Betrothal often took place while one or both of the parties was in the cradle, and marriage when they were scarcely out of the nurses' charge." That was about 1470, soon after Chaucer's time. The next reference to the position of women is some two hundred years later, in the time of the Stuarts.[2] "It was still the exception for

1. **Professor Trevelyon:** George Macaulay Trevelyan (1876–1962) was a British historian. His *History of England* was published in 1926, three years before *A Room of One's Own*.

2. **Stuarts:** The kings and queens who ruled England for most of the seventeenth century.

women of the upper and middle class to choose their own husbands, and when the husband had been assigned, he was lord and master, so far at least as law and custom could make him. Yet even so," Professor Trevelyan concludes, "neither Shakespeare's women nor those of authentic seventeenth-century memoirs, like the Verneys and the Hutchinsons[3], seem wanting in personality and character." Certainly, if we consider it, Cleopatra must have had a way with her; Lady Macbeth, one would suppose, had a will of her own; Rosalind, one might conclude, was an attractive girl. Professor Trevelyan is speaking no more than the truth when he remarks that Shakespeare's women do not seem wanting in personality and character. Not being a historian, one might go even further and say that women have burnt like beacons in all the works of all the poets from the beginning of time—Clytemnestra, Antigone, Cleopatra, Lady Macbeth, Phèdre, Cressida, Rosalind, Desdemona, the Duchess of Malfi, among the dramatists; then among the prose writers: Millamant, Clarissa, Becky Sharp, Anna Karenina, Emma Bovary, Madame de Guermantes—the names flock to mind, nor do they recall women "lacking in personality and character." Indeed, if woman had no existence save in the fiction written by men, one would imagine her a person of the utmost importance; very various; heroic and mean; splendid and sordid; infinitely beautiful and hideous in the extreme; as great as a man, some think even greater.[*] But this is woman in fiction. In fact, as Professor Trevelyan points out, she was locked up, beaten and flung about the room.

A very queer, composite being thus emerges. Imaginatively she is of the highest importance; practically she is completely insignificant. She pervades poetry from cover to cover; she is all but absent from history. She dominates the lives of kings and conquerors in fiction; in fact she was the slave of any boy whose parents forced a ring upon her finger. Some of the most inspired words, some of the most profound

3. The **Verneys** and the **Hutchinsons** were both prominent families during the English Civil Wars of the seventeenth century. Frances Parthenope Verney (1819–1890) wrote *Memoirs of the Verney Family during the 17th Century;* which was published posthumously in 1904 (and which gained some fame in connection with Frances's younger sister, Florence Nightingale). Lucy Hutchinson (1620–1681) wrote the biography of her husband, John Hutchinson, in *Memoirs of the Life of Colonel Hutchinson,* which was not published until 1806. Lucy Hutchinson also produced the first known English translation of Lucretius's *De Rerum Natura.*

* "It remains a strange and almost inexplicable fact that in Athena's city, where women were kept in almost Oriental suppression as odalisques or drudges, the stage should yet have produced figures like Clytemnestra and Cassandra, Atossa and Antigone, Phèdre and Medea, and all the other heroines who dominate play after play of the "misogynist" Euripides. But the paradox of this world where in real life a respectable woman could hardly show her face alone in the street, and yet on the stage woman equals or surpasses man, has never been satisfactorily explained. In modern tragedy the same predominance exists. At all events, a very cursory survey of Shakespeare's work (similarly with Webster, though not with Marlowe or Jonson) suffices to reveal how this dominance, this initiative of women, persists from Rosalind to Lady Macbeth. So too in Racine; six of his tragedies bear their heroines' names; and what male characters of his shall we set against Hermione and Andromaque, Bérénice and Roxane, Phèdre and Athalie? So again with Ibsen; what men shall we match with Solveig and Nora, Hedda and Hilda Wangel and Rebecca West?"—F. L. Lucas, Tragedy, pp. 114–15. [Author's note]

thoughts in literature fall from her lips; in real life she could hardly read, could scarcely spell, and was the property of her husband.

It was certainly an odd monster that one made up by reading the historians first   5
and the poets afterwards—a worm winged like an eagle; the spirit of life and beauty in a kitchen chopping up suet. But these monsters, however amusing to the imagination, have no existence in fact. What one must do to bring her to life was to think poetically and prosaically at one and the same moment, thus keeping in touch with fact—that she is Mrs. Martin, aged thirty-six, dressed in blue, wearing a black hat and brown shoes; but not losing sight of fiction either—that she is a vessel in which all sorts of spirits and forces are coursing and flashing perpetually. The moment, however, that one tries this method with the Elizabethan woman, one branch of illumination fails; one is held up by the scarcity of facts. . . .

. . . All these facts lie somewhere, presumably, in parish registers and account books; the life of the average Elizabethan woman must be scattered about somewhere, could one collect it and make a book of it. It would be ambitious beyond my daring, I thought, looking about the shelves for books that were not there, to suggest to the students of those famous colleges that they should re-write history, though I own that it often seems a little queer as it is, unreal, lop-sided; but why should they not add a supplement to history? calling it, of course, by some inconspicuous name so that women might figure there without impropriety? For one often catches a glimpse of them in the lives of the great, whisking away into the background, concealing, I sometimes think, a wink, a laugh, perhaps a tear. And, after all, we have lives enough of Jane Austen; it scarcely seems necessary to consider again the influence of the tragedies of Joanna Baillie[4] upon the poetry of Edgar Allan Poe; as for myself, I should not mind if the homes and haunts of Mary Russell Mitford were closed to the public for a century at least. But what I find deplorable, I continued, looking about the bookshelves again, is that nothing is known about women before the eighteenth century. I have no model in my mind to turn about this way and that. Here am I asking why women did not write poetry in the Elizabethan age, and I am not sure how they were educated; whether they were taught to write; whether they had sitting-rooms to themselves; how many women had children before they were twenty-one; what, in short, they did from eight in the morning till eight at night. They had no money evidently; according to Professor Trevelyan they were married whether they liked it or not before they were out of the nursery, at fifteen or sixteen very likely. It would have been extremely odd, even upon this showing, had one of them suddenly written the plays of Shakespeare, I concluded, and I thought of that old gentleman, who is dead now, but was a bishop, I think, who declared that it was impossible for any woman, past, present, or to come, to have the genius

4. **Joanna Baillie:** Scottish poet and playwright (1762–1851); **Mary Russell Mitford:** English poet (1787–1855). Both women were celebrated in their lifetimes for their literary achievements, rare examples, for Woolf, of women writers whose lives and writings are well known to the public.

of Shakespeare. He wrote to the papers about it. He also told a lady who applied to him for information that cats do not as a matter of fact go to heaven, though they have, he added, souls of a sort. How much thinking those old gentlemen used to save one! How the borders of ignorance shrank back at their approach! Cats do not go to heaven. Women cannot write the plays of Shakespeare.

Be that as it may, I could not help thinking, as I looked at the works of Shakespeare on the shelf, that the bishop was right at least in this; it would have been impossible, completely and entirely, for any woman to have written the plays of Shakespeare in the age of Shakespeare. Let me imagine, since facts are so hard to come by, what would have happened had Shakespeare had a wonderfully gifted sister, called Judith, let us say. Shakespeare himself went, very probably—his mother was an heiress—to the grammar school, where he may have learnt Latin—Ovid, Virgil and Horace— and the elements of grammar and logic. He was, it is well known, a wild boy who poached rabbits, perhaps shot a deer, and had, rather sooner than he should have done, to marry a woman in the neighbourhood, who bore him a child rather quicker than was right. That escapade sent him to seek his fortune in London. He had, it seemed, a taste for the theatre; he began by holding horses at the stage door. Very soon he got work in the theatre, became a successful actor, and lived at the hub of the universe, meeting everybody, knowing everybody, practising his art on the boards, exercising his wits in the streets, and even getting access to the palace of the queen. Meanwhile his extraordinarily gifted sister, let us suppose, remained at home. She was as adventurous, as imaginative, as agog to see the world as he was. But she was not sent to school. She had no chance of learning grammar and logic, let alone of reading Horace and Virgil. She picked up a book now and then, one of her brother's perhaps, and read a few pages. But then her parents came in and told her to mend the stockings or mind the stew and not moon about with books and papers. They would have spoken sharply but kindly, for they were substantial people who knew the conditions of life for a woman and loved their daughter—indeed, more likely than not she was the apple of her father's eye. Perhaps she scribbled some pages up in an apple loft on the sly, but was careful to hide them or set fire to them. Soon, however, before she was out of her teens, she was to be betrothed to the son of a neighbouring wool-stapler. She cried out that marriage was hateful to her, and for that she was severely beaten by her father. Then he ceased to scold her. He begged her instead not to hurt him, not to shame him in this matter of her marriage. He would give her a chain of beads or a fine petticoat, he said; and there were tears in his eyes. How could she disobey him? How could she break his heart? The force of her own gift alone drove her to it. She made up a small parcel of her belongings, let herself down by a rope one summer's night and took the road to London. She was not seventeen. The birds that sang in the hedge were not more musical than she was. She had the quickest fancy, a gift like her brother's, for the tune of words. Like him, she had a taste for the theatre. She stood at the stage door; she wanted to act, she said. Men laughed in her face. The manager—a fat, loose-lipped man—guffawed.

He bellowed something about poodles dancing and women acting—no woman, he said, could possibly be an actress. He hinted—you can imagine what. She could get no training in her craft. Could she even seek her dinner in a tavern or roam the streets at midnight? Yet her genius was for fiction and lusted to feed abundantly upon the lives of men and women and the study of their ways. At last—for she was very young, oddly like Shakespeare the poet in her face, with the same grey eyes and rounded brows—at last Nick Greene the actor-manager took pity on her; she found herself with child by that gentleman and so—who shall measure the heat and violence of the poet's heart when caught and tangled in a woman's body?—killed herself one winter's night and lies buried at some cross-roads where the omnibuses now stop outside the Elephant and Castle.[5]

That, more or less, is how the story would run, I think, if a woman in Shakespeare's day had had Shakespeare's genius.

UNDERSTANDING THE TEXT

1. What is the significance of Woolf's spiderweb image? What does it mean that a work of fiction, like the web of a spider, must be "attached to life at all four corners"?

2. Why does Woolf quote extensively from Trevelyan's *History of England*? For what material facts about women's lives does she want historical evidence? How are these facts connected to her overall point that a woman needs "a room of her own" to become a writer?

3. What female literary characters does Woolf cite as proof that women have been extremely important to the Western literary imagination? How does the importance of women *in* literature compare with the importance of women writers *to* literature?

4. To what facts about the lives of women during the Elizabethan period does Virginia Woolf not have access? How does her limited knowledge affect the narrative she is constructing?

5. What is the major point of the story Woolf invents about Judith Shakespeare? How does the character of Judith Shakespeare function rhetorically in her larger argument?

MAKING CONNECTIONS

1. Compare Woolf's fictional account of Judith Shakespeare to Fredrick Douglass's account of his own life in "Learning to Read" (p. 24). How is Douglass able to overcome some of the obstacles that Woolf describes? Do you think that Frederick Douglass could have become a writer and activist if he had been a woman?

2. How does Woolf's portrayal of the woman writer compare with Christine de Pisan's view of women who exercise influence in political matters? Does somebody like Christine de Pisan refute any part of Woolf's argument?

5. **Elephant and Castle:** A well-known London pub tracing back to the eighteenth century that became a bus stop.

3. Compare the character of Judith Shakespeare in Woolf's essay and the symbol of the bird in Toni Morrison's Nobel Lecture (p. 217). In what way might her use of Judith Shakespeare be similar to Morrison's use of the bird?

WRITING ABOUT THE TEXT

1. Analyze Woolf's use of fictional narrative as a rhetorical device in "Shakespeare's Sister." Use your analysis as a springboard to discuss the rhetorical value of stories generally.

2. Compare Woolf's use of fictional narrative with Jesus's use of parables in the Book of Luke (p. 541), or Plato's use of a fictionalized myth in "The Speech of Aristophanes" (p. 74).

3. Write an essay in which you support or refute the claim that women writers are still disadvantaged by some of the challenges that Woolf articulates in "Shakespeare's Sister."

RICHARD FEYNMAN
O Americano Outra Vez
[1985]

RICHARD P. FEYNMAN (1918–1988) was one of the most respected theoretical physicists of the twentieth century. As a young man, he worked on the Manhattan Project to develop a nuclear bomb during World War II. In the years that followed, he taught physics at both Cornell University and the California Institute of Technology and conducted research in quantum mechanics and particle physics. He received the Nobel Prize in Physics in 1965 for his contributions to the theory of quantum electrodynamics.

Unlike many of his colleagues in the highest levels of theoretical physics, Feynman had a reputation as a patient and talented classroom teacher. He frequently remarked that if a teacher could not explain a scientific concept clearly to a college freshman, the teacher didn't really understand it. His classroom lectures to undergraduate students at Caltech were compiled in the three-volume *Feynman Lectures on Physics* (1970), which has become a widely read introductory text to some of science's most difficult concepts.

In the later part of his life, Feynman became a public figure whose reputation as a quirky nonconformist was almost as well known as his reputation as a brilliant scientist. Much of this reputation derives from two bestselling books: *Surely You're Joking, Mr. Feynman* (1985) and *What Do You Care What Other People Think?* (1988). Both are composed of short, oral reminiscences collected and edited by Feynman's friend, Ralph Leighton. In these stories, Feynman presents himself as someone who has little use for rules, authorities, and structures. A recurring theme is his unwillingness to observe the rules of polite behavior and pretend to be impressed with people just because they are wealthy, famous, or in charge of resources. The Richard Feynman that emerges in these books is a man with an obsessive and insatiable curiosity—someone who grew up fixing radios and picking locks and never stopped trying to figure out how things worked.

"O Americano Outra Vez" ("The American Again") is taken from *Surely You're Joking, Mr. Feynman*. It tells the story of Feynman's trip to Brazil in the summer of 1950 to spend time at the Brazilian Center for Physical Research. While there, Feynman interacted with a number of Brazilian students who were preparing for teaching careers. He discovered that their educations had equipped them with surface facts about physics rather than a genuine understanding of physical processes. This experience became a platform for Feynman to discuss the difference between learning something and learning *about* something—one of the most important themes in all of his lectures and published works. "You can know the name of a bird in all the languages of world, but when you're finished, you'll know absolutely nothing whatever about the bird," Feynman once wrote. "So let's look at the bird and see what it's doing—that's what counts."

Feynman organizes this selection as a single narrative from which he draws a simple conclusion. He goes on, though, to use inductive reasoning to generalize this conclusion to the whole country of Brazil and its educational system.

In regard to education in Brazil, I had a very interesting experience. I was teaching a group of students who would ultimately become teachers, since at that time there were not many opportunities in Brazil for a highly trained person in science. These students had already had many courses, and this was to be their most advanced course in electricity and magnetism—Maxwell's equations,[1] and so on.

The university was located in various office buildings throughout the city, and the course I taught met in a building which overlooked the bay.

I discovered a very strange phenomenon: I could ask a question, which the students would answer immediately. But the next time I would ask the question—the same subject, and the same question, as far as I could tell—they couldn't answer it at all! For instance, one time I was talking about polarized light, and I gave them all some strips of polaroid.

Polaroid passes only light whose electric vector is in a certain direction, so I explained how you could tell which way the light is polarized from whether the polaroid is dark or light.

We first took two strips of polaroid and rotated them until they let the most light through. From doing that we could tell that the two strips were now admitting light polarized in the same direction—what passed through one piece of polaroid could also pass through the other. But then I asked them how one could tell the *absolute* direction of polarization, from a *single* piece of polaroid.

They hadn't any idea.

I knew this took a certain amount of ingenuity, so I gave them a hint: "Look at the light reflected from the bay outside."

Nobody said anything.

Then I said, "Have you ever heard of Brewster's Angle?"

"Yes, sir! Brewster's Angle is the angle at which light reflected from a medium with an index of refraction is completely polarized."

"And which way is the light polarized when it's reflected?"

"The light is polarized perpendicular to the plane of reflection, sir." Even now, I have to think about it; they knew it cold! They even knew the tangent of the angle equals the index!

I said, "Well?"

1. **Maxwell's equations:** equations that describe the properties of electric and magnetic fields.

Still nothing. They had just told me that light reflected from a medium with an index, such as the bay outside, was polarized; they had even told me which *way* it was polarized.

I said, "Look at the bay outside, through the polaroid. Now turn the polaroid."   15
"Ooh, it's polarized!" they said.

After a lot of investigation, I finally figured out that the students had memorized everything, but they didn't know what anything meant. When they heard "light that is reflected from a medium with an index," they didn't know that it meant a material *such as water*. They didn't know that the "direction of the light" is the direction in which you *see* something when you're looking at it, and so on. Everything was entirely memorized, yet nothing had been translated into meaningful words. So if I asked, "What is Brewster's Angle?" I'm going into the computer with the right keywords. But if I say, "Look at the water," nothing happens—they don't have anything under "Look at the water"!

Later I attended a lecture at the engineering school. The lecture went like this, translated into English: "Two bodies . . . are considered equivalent . . . if equal torques . . . will produce . . . equal acceleration. Two bodies, are considered equivalent, if equal torques, will produce equal acceleration." The students were all sitting there taking dictation, and when the professor repeated the sentence, they checked it to make sure they wrote it down all right. Then they wrote down the next sentence, and on and on. I was the only one who knew the professor was talking about objects with the same moment of inertia, and it was hard to figure out.

I didn't see how they were going to learn anything from that. Here he was talking about moments of inertia, but there was no discussion about how hard it is to push a door open when you put heavy weights on the outside, compared to when you put them near the hinge—*nothing!*

After the lecture, I talked to a student: "You take all those notes—what do you   20
do with them?"
"Oh, we study them," he says. "We'll have an exam."
"What will the exam be like?"
"Very easy. I can tell you now one of the questions." He looks at his notebook and says, "'When are two bodies equivalent?' And the answer is, 'Two bodies are considered equivalent if equal torques will produce equal acceleration.'" So, you see, they could pass the examinations, and "learn" all this stuff, and not *know* anything at all, except what they had memorized.

Then I went to an entrance exam for students coming into the engineering school. It was an oral exam, and I was allowed to listen to it. One of the students was absolutely super: He answered everything nifty! The examiners asked him what diamagnetism was, and he answered it perfectly. Then they asked, "When light comes at an angle through a sheet of material with a certain thickness, and a certain index N, what happens to the light?"

"It comes out parallel to itself, sir—displaced."

"And how much is it displaced?"

"I don't know, sir, but I can figure it out." So he figured it out. He was very good. But I had, by this time, my suspicions.

After the exam I went up to this bright young man, and explained to him that I was from the United States, and that I wanted to ask him some questions that would not affect the result of his examination in any way. The first question I ask is, "Can you give me some example of a diamagnetic substance?"[2]

"No."

Then I asked, "If this book was made of glass, and I was looking at something on the table through it, what would happen to the image if I tilted the glass?"

"It would be deflected, sir, by twice the angle that you've turned the book."

I said, "You haven't got it mixed up with a mirror, have you?"

"No, sir!"

He had just told me in the examination that the light would be displaced, parallel to itself, and therefore the image would move over to one side, but would not be turned by any angle. He had even figured out how *much* it would be displaced, but he didn't realize that a piece of glass is a material with an index, and that his calculation had applied to my question.

I taught a course at the engineering school on mathematical methods in physics, in which I tried to show how to solve problems by trial and error. It's something that people don't usually learn, so I began with some simple examples of arithmetic to illustrate the method. I was surprised that only about eight out of the eighty or so students turned in the first assignment. So I gave a strong lecture about having to actually *try* it, not just sit back and watch *me* do it.

After the lecture some students came up to me in a little delegation, and told me that I didn't understand the backgrounds that they have, that they can study without doing the problems, that they have already learned arithmetic, and that this stuff was beneath them.

So I kept going with the class, and no matter how complicated or obviously advanced the work was becoming, they were never handing a damn thing in. Of course I realized what it was: They couldn't *do* it!

One other thing I could never get them to do was to ask questions. Finally, a student explained it to me: "If I ask you a question during the lecture, afterwards everybody will be telling me, 'what are you wasting our time for in the class? We're trying to *learn* something. And you're stopping him by asking a question.'"

It was a kind of one-upmanship, where nobody knows what's going on, and they'd put the other one down as if they *did* know. They all fake that they know, and if one student admits for a moment that something is confusing by asking a question,

---

2. **Diamagnetic substance:** a substance that creates a magnetic field when another magnetic field is applied externally.

the others take a high-handed attitude, acting as if it's not confusing at all, telling him that he's wasting their time.

I explained how useful it was to work together, to discuss the questions, to talk   40
it over, but they wouldn't do that either, because they would be losing face if they had to ask someone else. It was pitiful! All the work they did, intelligent people, but they got themselves into this funny state of mind, this strange kind of self-propagating "education" which is meaningless, utterly meaningless!

At the end of the academic year, the students asked me to give a talk about my experiences of teaching in Brazil. At the talk there would be not only students, but professors and government officials, so I made them promise that I could say whatever I wanted. They said, "Sure. Of course. It's a free country."

So I came in, carrying the elementary physics textbook that they used in the first year of college. They thought this book was especially good because it had different kinds of typeface—bold black for the most important things to remember, lighter for less important things, and so on.

Right away somebody said, "You're not going to say anything bad about the textbook, are you? The man who wrote it is here, and everybody thinks it's a good textbook."

"You promised I could say whatever I wanted."

The lecture hall was full. I started out by defining science as an understanding of   45
the behavior of nature. Then I asked, "What is a good reason for teaching science? Of course, no country can consider itself civilized unless . . . yak, yak, yak." They were all sitting there nodding, because I know that's the way they think.

Then I say, "That, of course, is absurd, because why should we feel we have to keep up with another country? We have to do it for a *good* reason, a *sensible* reason; not just because other countries do." Then I talked about the utility of science, and its contribution to the improvement of the human condition, and all that—I really teased them a little bit.

Then I say, "The main purpose of my talk is to demonstrate to you that *no* science is being taught in Brazil!"

I can see them stir, thinking, "What? No science? This is absolutely crazy! We have all these classes."

So I tell them that one of the first things to strike me when I came to Brazil was to see elementary school kids in bookstores, buying physics books. There are so many kids learning physics in Brazil, beginning much earlier than kids do in the United States, that it's amazing you don't find many physicists in Brazil—why is that? So many kids are working so hard, and nothing comes of it.

Then I gave the analogy of a Greek scholar who loves the Greek language,   50
who knows that in his own country there aren't many children studying Greek. But he comes to another country, where he is delighted to find everybody studying Greek—even the smaller kids in the elementary schools. He goes to the examination of a student who is coming to get his degree in Greek, and asks him, "What were

Socrates' ideas on the relationship between Truth and Beauty?"—and the student can't answer. Then he asks the student, "What did Socrates say to Plato in the Third Symposium?" the student lights up and goes, "*Brrrrrrrr-up*"—he tells you everything, word for word, that Socrates said, in beautiful Greek.

But what Socrates was talking about in the Third Symposium was the relationship between Truth and Beauty!

What this Greek scholar discovers is, the students in another country learn Greek by first learning to pronounce the letters, then the words, and then sentences and paragraphs. They can recite, word for word, what Socrates said, without realizing that those Greek words actually *mean* something. To the student they are all artificial sounds. Nobody has ever translated them into words the students can understand.

I said, "That's how it looks to me, when I see you teaching the kids 'science' here in Brazil." (Big blast, right?)

Then I held up the elementary physics textbook they were using. "There are no experimental results mentioned anywhere in this book, except in one place where there is a ball, rolling down an inclined plane, in which it says how far the ball got after one second, two seconds, three seconds, and so on. The numbers have 'errors' in them—that is, if you look at them, you think you're looking at experimental results, because the numbers are a little above, or a little below, the theoretical values. The book even talks about having to correct the experimental errors—very fine. The trouble is, when you calculate the value of the acceleration constant from these values, you get the right answer. But a ball rolling down an inclined plane, *if it is actually done*, has an inertia to get it to turn, and will, *if you do the experiment*, produce five-sevenths of the right answer, because of the extra energy needed to go into the rotation of the ball. Therefore this single example of experimental 'results' is obtained from a *fake* experiment. Nobody had rolled such a ball, or they would never have gotten those results!

"I have discovered something else," I continued. "By flipping the pages at random, and putting my finger in and reading the sentences on that page, I can show you what's the matter—how it's not science, but memorizing, in *every* circumstance. Therefore I am brave enough to flip through the pages now, in front of this audience, to put my finger in, to read, and to show you."

So I did it. *Brrrrrrrup*—I stuck my finger in, and I started to read: "Triboluminescence. Triboluminescence is the light emitted when crystals are crushed . . . "

I said, "And there, have you got science? No! You have only told what a word means in terms of other words. You haven't told anything about nature—*what* crystals produce light when you crush them, *why* they produce light. Did you see any student go home and *try* it? He can't.

"But if, instead, you were to write, 'When you take a lump of sugar and crush it with a pair of pliers in the dark, you can see a bluish flash. Some other crystals do that too. Nobody knows why. The phenomenon is called "triboluminescence."'

55

Then someone will go home and try it. Then there's an experience of nature." I used that example to show them, but it didn't make any difference where I would have put my finger in the book; it was like that everywhere.

Finally, I said that I couldn't see how anyone could be educated by this self-propagating system in which people pass exams, and teach others to pass exams, but nobody knows anything. "However," I said, "I must be wrong. There were two students in my class who did very well, and one of the physicists I know was educated entirely in Brazil. Thus, it must be possible for some people to work their way through the system, bad as it is."

Well, after I gave the talk, the head of the science education department got up and said, "Mr. Feynman has told us some things that are very hard for us to hear, but it appears to be that he really loves science, and is sincere in his criticism. Therefore, I think we should listen to him. I came here knowing we have some sickness in our system of education; what I have learned is that we have a *cancer!*"—and he sat down.

That gave other people the freedom to speak out, and there was a big excitement. Everybody was getting up and making suggestions. The students got some committee together to mimeograph the lectures in advance, and they got other committees organized to do this and that.

Then something happened which was totally unexpected for me. One of the students got up and said, "I'm one of the two students whom Mr. Feynman referred to at the end of his talk. I was not educated in Brazil; I was educated in Germany, and I've just come to Brazil this year."

The other student who had done well in class had a similar thing to say. And the professor I had mentioned got up and said, "I was educated here in Brazil during the war, when, fortunately, all of the professors had left the university, so I learned everything by reading alone. Therefore I was not really educated under the Brazilian system."

I didn't expect that. I knew the system was bad, but 100 percent—it was terrible!

Since I had gone to Brazil under a program sponsored by the United States Government, I was asked by the State Department to write a report about my experiences in Brazil, so I wrote out the essentials of the speech I had just given. I found out later through the grapevine that the reaction of somebody in the State Department was, "That shows you how dangerous it is to send somebody to Brazil who is so naive. Foolish fellow; he can only cause trouble. He didn't understand the problems." Quite the contrary! I think this person in the State Department was naive to think that because he saw a university with a list of courses and descriptions, that's what it was.

65

UNDERSTANDING THE TEXT

1. How would you characterize the difference between the knowledge possessed by the students that Feynman encounters and the knowledge that Feynman believes that they should have?

2. What is the purpose of examinations in the educational system that Feynman describes?

3. How does Feynman characterize the role of social pressures in perpetuating Brazil's flawed educational system? What kinds of peer pressures do the students he meets describe?

4. How would Feynman recommend that science be taught in elementary schools? How does this compare with the way that science usually is taught? Compare your own educational experiences to those described in the text.

5. How does Feynman characterize his experience with the U.S. government when he wrote a report about his experience in Brazil? Why do you think he includes this final reflection? What parallels can we draw between Brazilian science students and American government workers?

MAKING CONNECTIONS

1. Are the methods of teaching physics that Feynman describes culturally specific phenomena, such as those described by Ruth Benedict (p. 112)? Is it unreasonable for Feynman to expect students from a different culture to understand and teach science the way that he does? Why or why not?

2. Compare Feynman's approach to teaching physics with Edmund Burke's understanding of aesthetics in "The Sublime and Beautiful" (p. 256). How might Feynman characterize the "sublime" that is central to Burke's work?

WRITING ABOUT THE TEXT

1. Describe your own experience learning science in school. Was your education one that Feynman would have approved of, or would he have made the same accusations of your instructors as he did of the Brazilian educational system?

2. Many educators would challenge Feynman's belief that knowing the names of things and being able to define them is "meaningless." Being able to define concepts, they argue, is an essential part of being able to understand them at any level. Write an essay in which you agree or disagree with this position.

3. Describe how Feynman's distinction between knowing the name of a thing and truly understanding how to do it applies to the writing process. Which do you believe is the more effective way to teach writing? Why?

MARTHA NUSSBAUM
Education for Profit, Education for Democracy
[2010]

MARTHA NUSSBAUM (b. 1947) is an American philosopher, classicist, and legal theorist. She received her Ph.D. from Harvard University in 1975 and taught at Harvard, Brown, and Oxford Universities before moving to the University of Chicago, where she is the Ernst Freund Distinguished Service Professor of Law. She is the author or editor of more than twenty books on topics in ethics, aesthetics, social policy, and education reform.

In her book *Cultivating Humanity* (1997), Nussbaum argued that institutions of higher education should look to Greek and Roman models of learning for inspiration as they reform their curricula and approaches to education. Nussbaum cites the arguments of Plato and Seneca to argue that education should encourage critical self-examination and prepare students to be "citizens of the world," which requires them to understand and appreciate culture, gender, religion, and other forms of diversity. *Cultivating Humanity* was written partially in response to conservative thinkers who had strongly criticized modern colleges and universities for their focus on "multiculturalism" at the expense of the Western tradition.

The selection in this chapter is taken from Nussbaum's second major book on higher education: *Not for Profit: Why Democracy Needs the Humanities* (2010). In this book, Nussbaum argues that the current focus on education as a form of career training fails to teach students the skills necessary to participate in the political process. If this trend is not reversed, "nations all over the world will soon be producing generations of useful machines, rather than complete citizens who can think for themselves, criticize tradition, and understand the significance of another person's sufferings and achievements. The future of the world's democracies hangs in the balance." In other words, government by the people requires that the citizens it governs be capable of thinking critically about political issues and participating fully in the political process. And it is education in the humanities, not training in the professions, that makes this possible.

In this chapter, "Education for Profit, Education for Democracy," Nussbaum compares two possible paradigms for education: education for economic growth and education for human development. Using the United States and India as her primary examples, Nussbaum argues that democratic nations tend to approve abstractly of human development goals, or goals to improve the overall quality of the life of their citizens, but under economic pressure to grow, often ignore their own values and force education into the narrow role of facilitating economic growth.

In this selection, Nussbaum illustrates the discrepancies between what democratic societies value and what they actually do. By beginning with quotations from the American and Indian constitutions, she demonstrates that both nations have a deep commitment to democracy, dignity, and quality of life for all of their citizens. This provides a springboard for her analysis of the distance between these goals and current educational policies, which focus on economic growth at any cost.

> We, the People of the United States, in Order to form a more perfect Union, establish Justice, insure domestic Tranquility, provide for the common defence, promote the general Welfare, and secure the Blessings of Liberty to ourselves and our Posterity, do ordain and establish this Constitution for the United States of America.
> —Preamble, *Constitution of the United States, 1787*

> We, the people of India, having solemnly resolved to . . .
> secure to all its citizens:
> Justice, economic and political;
> Liberty of thought, expression, belief, faith and worship;
> Equality of status and of opportunity
> and to promote among them all
> Fraternity assuring the dignity of the individual and the
> unity and integrity of the Nation;
> In our constituent assembly this twenty-sixth day of November, 1949,
> do hereby adopt, enact and give to
> ourselves this constitution.
> —Preamble, *Constitution of India, 1949*

> Education shall be directed to the full development of the human personality and to the strengthening of respect for human rights and fundamental freedoms. It shall promote understanding, tolerance and friendship among all nations, racial or religious groups.
> —*Universal Declaration of Human Rights, 1948*

To think about education for democratic citizenship, we have to think about what democratic nations are, and what they strive for. What does it mean, then, for a nation to advance? In one view it means to increase its gross national product per capita. This measure of national achievement has for decades been the standard one used by development economists around the world, as if it were a good proxy for a nation's overall quality of life.

The goal of a nation, says this model of development, should be economic growth. Never mind about distribution and social equality, never mind about the preconditions of stable democracy, never mind about the quality of race and gender relations, never mind about the improvement of other aspects of a human being's quality of life that are not well linked to economic growth. (Empirical studies have by now shown that political liberty, health, and education are all poorly correlated with growth.) One sign of what this model leaves out is the fact that South Africa under apartheid used to shoot to the top of development indices. There was a lot of wealth in the old South Africa, and the old model of development rewarded that achievement (or good fortune), ignoring the staggering distributional inequalities, the brutal apartheid regime, and the health and educational deficiencies that went with it.

This model of development has by now been rejected by many serious development thinkers, but it continues to dominate a lot of policy-making, especially policies influenced by the United States. The World Bank made some commendable progress, under James Wolfensohn[1] in recognizing a richer conception of development, but things then slipped badly, and the International Monetary Fund never made the sort of progress that the Bank did under Wolfensohn. Many nations, and states within nations, are pursuing this model of development. Today's India offers a revealing laboratory of such experiments, as some states (Gujarat, Andhra Pradesh) have pursued economic growth through foreign investment, doing little for health, education, and the condition of the rural poor, while other states (Kerala, Delhi, to some extent West Bengal) have pursued more egalitarian strategies, trying to ensure that health and education are available to all, that the infrastructure develops in a way that serves all, and that investment is tied to job creation for the poorest.

Proponents of the old model sometimes like to claim that the pursuit of economic growth will by itself deliver the other good things I have mentioned: health, education, a decrease in social and economic inequality. By now, however, examining the results of these divergent experiments, we have discovered that the old model really does not deliver the goods as claimed. Achievements in health and education, for example, are very poorly correlated with economic growth. Nor does political liberty track growth, as we can see from the stunning success of China. So producing economic growth does not mean producing democracy. Nor does it mean producing a healthy, engaged, educated population in which opportunities for a good life are available to all social classes. Still, everyone likes economic growth these days, and the trend is, if anything, toward increasing reliance on what I have called the "old paradigm," rather than toward a more complex account of what societies should be trying to achieve for their people.

These baneful trends have recently been challenged in both of the nations that are my focus. By choosing the Obama administration, U.S. voters opted for a group committed to greater equality in health care and a greater degree of attention to issues of equal access to opportunity generally. In India, this past May, in a surprise result, voters delivered a virtual majority to the Congress party, which has combined

5

---

1. **James Wolfensohn:** Australian banker (b. 1933) and president of the World Bank from 1995 to 2005.

moderate economic reforms with a strong commitment to the rural poor.[2] In neither nation, however, have policies been sufficiently rethought with ideas of human development clearly in view. Thus it is not clear that either nation has really embraced a human development paradigm, as opposed to a growth-oriented paradigm adjusted for distribution.

Both nations, however, have written constitutions, and in both, the constitution protects from majority whim a group of fundamental rights that cannot be abrogated even to achieve a large economic benefit. Both nations protect a range of political and civil rights, and both guarantee all citizens the equal protection of the laws regardless of racial, gender, or religious group membership. The Indian list, longer than that of the United States, also includes free compulsory primary and secondary education, and a right to freedom from desperate conditions (a life commensurate with human dignity). Even though the U.S. federal Constitution does not guarantee a right to education, numerous state constitutions do, and many add other social welfare provisions. In general, we are entitled to conclude that both the United States and India have rejected the notion that the right way for a nation to proceed is simply ro strive to maximize economic growth. It is, then, all the odder that major figures concerned with education, in both nations, continue to behave as if the goal of education were economic growth alone.

In the context of the old paradigm of what it is for a nation to develop, what is on everyone's lips is the need for an education that promotes national development seen as economic growth. Such an education has recently been outlined by the Spellings Commission Report of the U.S. Department of Education[3] focusing on higher education. It is being implemented by many European nations, as they give high marks to technical universities and university departments and impose increasingly draconian cuts on the humanities. It is central to discussions of education in India today, as in most developing nations that are trying to grab a larger share of the global market.

The United States has never had a pure growth-directed model of education. Some distinctive and by now traditional features of our system positively resist being cast in those terms. Unlike virtually every nation in the world, we have a liberal arts model of university education. Instead of entering college/university to study a single subject, students are required to take a wide range of courses in their first two years, prominently including courses in the humanities. This model of university and college education influences secondary education. Nobody is tracked too early into a nonhumanities stream, whether purely scientific or purely vocational, nor do children with a humanities focus lose all contact with the sciences at an early date. Nor is the emphasis on the liberal arts a vestige of elitism or class distinction. From early

2. **Congress Party:** One of India's two major political parties.
3. **Spellings Commission Report:** A 2006 report by the Commission on the Future of Higher Education, chaired by then Secretary of Education Margaret Spellings. The report focused on ensuring that colleges and universities were preparing students for the twenty-first-century workplace.

on, leading U.S. educators connected the liberal arts to the preparation of informed, independent, and sympathetic democratic citizens. The liberal arts model is still relatively strong, but it is under severe stress now in this time of economic hardship.

Another aspect of the U.S. educational tradition that stubbornly refuses assimilation into the growth-directed model is its characteristic emphasis on the active participation of the child in inquiry and questioning. This model of learning, associated with a long Western philosophical tradition of education theory, ranging from Jean-Jacques Rousseau in the eighteenth century to John Dewey in the twentieth, includes such eminent educators as Friedrich Froebel in Germany, Johann Pestalozzi in Switzerland, Bronson Alcott in the United States, and Maria Montessori in Italy. This tradition argues that education is not just about the passive assimilation of facts and cultural traditions, but about challenging the mind to become active, competent, and thoughtfully critical in a complex world. This model of education supplanted an older one in which children sat still at desks all day and simply absorbed, and then regurgitated, the material that was brought their way. This idea of active learning, which usually includes a large commitment to critical thinking and argument that traces its roots back to Socrates, has profoundly influenced American primary and to some extent secondary education, and this influence has not yet ceased, despite increasing pressures on schools to produce the sort of student who can do well on a standardized test.

I shall discuss these educational theories later, but I introduce them now in order   10
to point out that we are unlikely to find a pure example of education for economic growth in the United States—*so far*. India is closer; for, despite the widespread influence of the great Tagore, who tried to build his school around the idea of critical thinking and empathetic imagining, and who founded a university built around an interdisciplinary liberal arts model, India's universities today, like those of Europe, have long been structured around the single-subject rather than the liberal arts paradigm. Tagore's university, Visva-Bharati (which means "All-the-World"), was taken over by the government, and now it is just like any other single-subject-model university, largely aiming at market impact. Similarly, Tagore's school has long ceased to define the goals of primary and secondary education. Socratic active learning and exploration through the arts have been rejected in favor of a pedagogy of force-feeding for standardized national examinations. The very model of learning that Tagore (along with the Europeans and Americans I have named) passionately repudiated—in which the student sits passively at a desk while teachers and textbooks present material to be uncritically assimilated—is a ubiquitous reality in India's government schools. When we imagine what education for economic growth would be like, pursued without attention to other goals, we are likely, then, to come up with something that lies relatively close to what India's government-sector schools usually offer.

Nonetheless, our aim is to understand a model that has influence around the world, not to describe a particular school system in a particular nation, so let us simply pose our questions abstractly.

What sort of education does the old model of development suggest? Education for economic growth needs basic skills, literacy, and numeracy. It also needs some people to have more advanced skills in computer science and technology. Equal access, however, is not terribly important; a nation can grow very nicely while the rural poor remain illiterate and without basic computer resources, as recent events in many Indian states show. In states such as Gujarat and Andhra Pradesh, we have seen the creation of increased GNP per capita through the education of a technical elite who make the state attractive to foreign investors. The results of this growth have not trickled down to improve the health and well-being of the rural poor, and there is no reason to think that economic growth requires educating them adequately. This was always the first and most basic problem with the GNP per capita paradigm of development. It neglects distribution, and can give high marks to nations or states that contain alarming inequalities. This is very true of education: Given the nature of the information economy, nations can increase their GNP without worrying too much about the distribution of education, so long as they create a competent technology and business elite.

Here we see yet another way in which the United States has traditionally diverged, at least in theory, from the economic growth paradigm. In the U.S. tradition of public education, ideas of equal opportunity and equal access, though never robust in reality, have always been notional goals, defended even by the most growth-focused politicians, such as the authors of the Spellings Report.

After basic skills for many, and more advanced skills for some, education for economic growth needs a very rudimentary familiarity with history and with economic fact—on the part of the people who are going to get past elementary education in the first place, and who may turn out to be a relatively small elite. But care must be taken lest the historical and economic narrative lead to any serious critical thinking about class, about race and gender, about whether foreign investment is really good for the rural poor, about whether democracy can survive when huge inequalities in basic life-chances obtain. So critical thinking would not be a very important part of education for economic growth, and it has not been in states that have pursued this goal relentlessly, such as the Western Indian state of Gujarat, well known for its combination of technological sophistication with docility and group-think. The student's freedom of mind is dangerous if what is wanted is a group of technically trained obedient workers to carry out the plans of elites who are aiming at foreign investment and technological development. Critical thinking will, then, be discouraged—as it has so long been in the government schools of Gujarat.

History, I said, might be essential. But educators for economic growth will not want a study of history that focuses on injustices of class, caste, gender, and ethnoreligious membership, because this will prompt critical thinking about the present. Nor will such educators want any serious consideration of the rise of nationalism, of the damages done by nationalist ideals, and of the way in which the moral imagination too often becomes numbed under the sway of technical mastery—all themes developed with scathing pessimism by Rabindranath Tagore in *Nationalism*, lectures

15

delivered during the First World War, which are ignored in today's India, despite the universal fame of Tagore as Nobel Prize–winning author. So the version of history that will be presented will present national ambition, especially ambition for wealth, as a great good, and will downplay issues of poverty and of global accountability. Once again, real-life examples of this sort of education are easy to find.

A silent example of this approach to history can be found in the textbooks created by the BJP, India's Hindu-nationalist political party, which also pursues aggressively an economic-growth-based development agenda. These books (now, fortunately, withdrawn, since the BJP lost power in 2004) utterly discouraged critical thinking and didn't even give it material to work with. They presented India's history as an uncritical story of material and cultural triumph in which all trouble was caused by outsiders and internal "foreign elements." Criticism of injustices in India's past was made virtually impossible by the content of the material and by its suggested pedagogy (for example, the questions at the end of each chapter), which discouraged thoughtful questioning and urged assimilation and regurgitation. Students were asked simply to absorb a story of unblemished goodness, bypassing all inequalities of caste, gender, and religion.

Contemporary development issues, too, were presented with an emphasis on the paramount importance of economic growth and the relative insignificance of distributional equality. Students were told that what matters is the situation of the *average* person (not, for example, how the least well-off are doing). And they were even encouraged to think of themselves as parts of a large collectivity that is making progress, rather than as separate people with separate entitlements: "In social development, whatever benefit an individual derives is only as a collective being." This controversial norm (which suggests that if the nation is doing well, you must be doing well, even if you are extremely poor and suffering from many deprivations) is presented as a fact that students must memorize and regurgitate on mandatory national examinations.

Education for economic growth is likely to have such features everywhere, since the unfettered pursuit of growth is not conducive to sensitive thinking about distribution or social inequality. (Inequality can reach astonishing proportions, as it did in yesterday's South Africa, while a nation grows very nicely.) Indeed, putting a human face on poverty is likely to produce hesitation about the pursuit of growth; for foreign investment often needs to be courted by policies that strongly disadvantage the rural poor. (In many parts of India, for example, poor agricultural laborers hold down land that is needed to build factories, and they are not likely to be the gainers when their land is acquired by the government—even if they are compensated, they do not typically have the skills to be employed in the new industries that displace them.)

What about the arts and literature, so often valued by democratic educators? An education for economic growth will, first of all, have contempt for these parts of a child's training, because they don't look like they lead to personal or national economic advancement. For this reason, all over the world, programs in arts and the humanities, at all levels, are being cut away, in favor of the cultivation of the technical. Indian parents take pride in a child who gains admission to the Institutes of Technology and Management; they are ashamed of a child who studies literature, or philosophy, or who wants to paint or dance or sing. American parents, too, are moving rapidly in this direction, despite a long liberal arts tradition.

But educators for economic growth will do more than ignore the arts. They will fear them. For a cultivated and developed sympathy is a particularly dangerous enemy of obtuseness, and moral obtuseness is necessary to carry out programs of economic developmenr that ignore inequality. It is easier to treat people as objects to be manipulated if you have never learned any other way to see them. As Tagore said, aggressive nationalism needs to blunt the moral conscience, so it needs people who do not recognize the individual, who speak group-speak, who behave, and see the world, like docile bureaucrats. Art is a great enemy of that obtuseness, and artists (unless thoroughly browbeaten and corrupted) are not the reliable servants of any ideology, even a basically good one—they always ask the imagination to move beyond its usual confines, to see the world in new ways. So, educators for economic growth will campaign against the humanities and arts as ingredients of basic education. This assault is currently taking place all over the world.

Pure models of education for economic growth are difficult to find in flourishing democracies since democracy is built on respect for each person, and the growth model respects only an aggregate. However, education systems all over the world are moving closer and closer to the growth model without much thought about how ill-suited it is to the goals of democracy.

How else might we think of the sort of nation and the sort of citizen we are trying to build? The primary alternative to the growth-based model in international development circles, and one with which I have been associated, is known as the Human Development paradigm. According to this model, what is important is the opportunities, or "capabilities," each person has in key areas ranging from life, health, and bodily integrity to political liberty, political participation, and education. This model of development recognizes that all individuals possess an inalienable human dignity that must be respected by laws and institutions. A decent nation, at a bare minimum, acknowledges that its citizens have entitlements in these and other areas and devises strategies to get people above a threshold level of opportunity in each.

The Human Development model is committed to democracy, since having a voice in the choice of the policies that govern one's life is a key ingredient of a life worthy of human dignity. The sort of democracy it favors will, however, be one with a strong role for fundamental rights that cannot be taken away from people by majority whim—it will thus favor strong protections for political liberty; the freedoms of speech, association, and religious exercise; and fundamental entitlements in yet other areas such as education and health. This model dovetails well with the aspirations pursued in India's constitution (and that of South Africa). The United States has never given constitutional protection, at least at the federal level, to

20

entitlements in "social and economic" areas such as health and education; and yet Americans, too, have a strong sense that the ability of all citizens to attain these entitlements is an important mark of national success. So the Human Development model is not pie-in-the-sky idealism; it is closely related to the constitutional commitments, not always completely fulfilled, of many if not most of the world's democratic nations.

If a nation wants to promote this type of humane, people-sensitive democracy dedicated to promoting opportunities for "life, liberty and the pursuit of happiness" to each and every person, what abilities will it need to produce in its citizens? At least the following seem crucial:

- The ability to think well about political issues affecting the nation, to examine, reflect, argue, and debate, deferring to neither tradition nor authority
- The ability to recognize fellow citizens as people with equal rights, even though they may be different in race, religion, gender, and sexuality: to look at them with respect, as ends, not just as tools to be manipulated for one's own profit
- The ability to have concern for the lives of others, to grasp what policies of many types mean for the opportunities and experiences of one's fellow citizens, of many types, and for people outside one's own nation
- The ability to imagine well a variety of complex issues affecting the story of a human life as it unfolds: to think about childhood, adolescence, family relationships, illness, death, and much more in a way informed by an understanding of a wide range of human stories, not just by aggregate data
- The ability to judge political leaders critically, but with an informed and realistic sense of the possibilities available to them
- The ability to think about the good of the nation as a whole, not just that of one's own local group
- The ability to see one's own nation, in turn, as a part of a complicated world order in which issues of many kinds require intelligent transnational deliberation for their resolution

This is only a sketch, but it is at least a beginning in articulating what we need.   25

UNDERSTANDING THE TEXT

1. Why does Nussbaum begin with selections from the constitutions of both the United States and India? What is she trying to suggest about the ultimate values of both countries as expressed in their most fundamental documents?

2. What disadvantages does Nussbaum see to using economic development as the primary metric for measuring progress in a country?

3. Why does Nussbaum believe that economic growth will not automatically produce democracy? What examples does she cite to prove this thesis?

4. Why is it important to Nussbaum's argument that both the United States and India have enshrined in their constitutions "a group of fundamental rights that cannot be abrogated even to achieve a large economic benefit"? What role does education have in protecting these rights?

5. For education that is aimed at producing economic growth, what subjects are important to learn? What subjects are unimportant to this goal?

6. Why does Nussbaum believe that education for economic growth discourages critical thinking? What about critical thinking is dangerous to this educational paradigm?

7. Summarize in your own words Nussbaum's proposals for a human development paradigm in education. What are the most important goals that such a paradigm should have?

MAKING CONNECTIONS

1. Nussbaum makes the point that Rabindranath Tagore set up a school to facilitate critical thinking and cultural understanding, but that it was eventually turned into a standard state school by India's government. Do the goals for education that she articulates seem the same as Tagore's goals for education in "To Teachers" (p. 40)? How are they similar and different?

2. Compare Nussbaum's views of education with Gandhi's views of progress in "Economic and Moral Progress" (p. 560). Does her division between education for economic growth and education for human development seem the same as Gandhi's division between economic progress and moral progress?

3. Compare Nussbaum's views of economic inequality with those of Joseph Stiglitz in "Rent Seeking and the Making of an Unequal Society" (p. 594). How do Nussbaum and Stiglitz see great disparities in wealth affecting the democratic process?

WRITING ABOUT THE TEXT

1. Compare Nussbaum's view of the role of education with that of Seneca and John Henry Newman. How might the two earlier philosophers have characterized what she calls "education for economic growth"? Explain where they might have disagreed with her conclusions.

2. Write a paper expressing your own view of the role of education in democracy. Explain the courses and areas of study that you believe to be most important in a democratic society.

3. Write a paper either for or against the proposition that students should be required to study arts and humanities in college. Use Nussbaum and other readings in this chapter to frame your argument.

2

HUMAN NATURE
AND THE MIND

What Is the Essence of Humanity?

A man is a featherless biped with broad, flat nails.
—*philosophers at Plato's Academy*

ACCORDING TO A LEGEND of ancient Greek philosophy, the students at Plato's Academy once tried to unassailably define the phrase "human being." After months of wrangling over every fine point, the philosophical elite of Athens finally settled on a definition that would, they felt, stand throughout time: a human being is a "featherless biped." On the day that the Academy was set to announce this truth to the world, however, the famous philosopher Diogenes of Sinope—a member of the group called the Cynics (from whose name the modern word "cynic" derives)— brought a plucked chicken to the school. The philosophers, unwilling to see months of work shattered, amended their definition and announced that a human being "is a featherless biped with broad, flat nails."

For a very long time, humans have been obsessed with defining their own nature and yet have been unable to do so in any convincing fashion—even in an arena of pure speculation such as Plato's Academy. Not only has there never been a universally accepted definition of human nature, the definitions and ideas that have been proposed have historically led to very different ways of organizing and governing societies. If, for example, human beings are inherently selfish, aggressive, and antisocial, then strong laws and harsh punishments may be necessary to check their natural tendencies and ensure the cohesion of society. This was the argument of the Chinese school of thought known as Legalism, which, working from the premise that human beings were naturally evil, unified all of China under the tyrannical rule of the Ch'in Dynasty. If, on the other hand, human beings have an innate sense of morality and justice, then it follows that people should be trusted to organize their own governments and elect their own leaders. This idea led to both America's Declaration of Independence and the development of democratic governments throughout the world.

This chapter opens with three readings from the ancient world. The first comes from Plato's *Symposium*, a series of speeches paying tribute to love. The speech included here attempts to explain the nature of love allegorically, by telling of a mythical time when human beings were physically connected to each other. Through this allegory, Plato presents humans as fragmented beings in dire need of others who can complete them. The readings continue with a vigorous debate about the moral nature of humanity between two of China's most esteemed Confucian scholars: Mencius, who saw humans as essentially good, and Hsün Tzu, who believed that humans were inherently evil.

During the European Enlightenment, philosophers attempted to define human nature by imagining what people would be like in a "state of nature," in which there were no social or cultural influences to constrain their behavior. Versions of this natural state ranged from wistful descriptions of "noble savages" living idyllic, uncontaminated lives to disturbing portrayals of lawless brutes, barely better than animals, robbing each other regularly and killing at the slightest provocation. Foremost among those who held the latter view of the state of nature was the English political theorist Thomas Hobbes, whose major work Leviathan is excerpted here. The next writer, John Locke, was a contemporary of Hobbes who believed that human beings were neither essentially good nor bad but tabula rasas, "blank slates," to be formed by experience.

The next few selections in the chapter come from the nineteenth century and later, and explore the forces that interact to create a human being. The first is an illustration from the Swiss psychologist Carl. Jung, who explores notions of myth and archetype to understand the human mind. Another selection comes from Ruth Benedict, one of the foremost anthropologists of the twentieth century, who argues that much of what others have labeled "human nature" actually arises out of a complicated interplay between human beings and the cultures in which they live. Benedict asserts that such things as values, morals, and "human" traits can be studied only when they are connected to a specific culture.

A pair of images in the chapter compares two models of the brain: the first is a now outdated kind of brain-mapping called "phrenology," which appeared in the nineteenth century, while the second is a twenty-first-century brain scan made with modern imaging technology. The chapter then concludes with two readings that take advantage of the tremendous insights of cognitive psychology and neuroscience to explain the inner workings of human thought. Nicholas Carr's "A Thing Like Me," from his bestselling book *The Shallows*, argues that the internet is changing the way human beings process information. And Daniel Kahneman's *Thinking, Fast and Slow* introduces two different thought processes that determine the way we make decisions.

Diogenes and the philosophers at Plato's Academy were just one part of the world's very long tradition of debating the nature of human beings and the mind. Are human beings inherently good or inherently evil? Does civilization redeem or contaminate the natural human condition? Do we make choices freely, or do we simply follow a script that has been written by history, culture, or God? Perhaps the most convincing evidence for the existence of some kind of core human nature and mind is the fact that we persist in asking questions such as these.

PLATO
The Speech of Aristophanes
[385 BCE]

THE GREEK PHILOSOPHER PLATO (circa 428–circa 347 BCE) was one of the most influential thinkers of the ancient world. Chronologically, he was the second of three towering figures. His student, Aristotle (384–322 BCE) was the first to attempt to catalog and interpret the knowledge of his day in a structured, methodical way. Plato's mentor, Socrates (469–399 BCE), invented the term *philosophy* ("love of wisdom") and was an important public figure in Athens until his execution in 399 for the crimes of impiety and corrupting the youth. Socrates did not leave behind any written records of his own. We know him only through the descriptions of others—chiefly the descriptions of Plato, who made Socrates a character in many of his works.

Most of Plato's philosophical writings take the form of dialogues between Socrates and one or more companions. In these dialogues Socrates leads his interlocutors to the point that Plato wants to make. The *Symposium*, however, from which this selection is taken, reads more like a complete story than most of Plato's dialogues. It is the story of an evening of drinking and making speeches (*symposium* comes from a Greek word meaning "drinking party") in the home of the young poet Agathon, who has won first prize in the annual tragedy competition and is celebrating with his friends. As the party progresses, the participants each agree to make a speech in praise of love.

Among the participants are both Socrates and the comic poet Aristophanes, whose play *The Clouds* had viciously satirized Socrates as a manipulative, impractical teacher who taught students to circumvent the law. Given Plato's dislike and suspicion of Aristophanes—in *Apology* he calls *The Clouds* one of the primary reasons that the people of Athens mistrusted Socrates—we might expect the character of Aristophanes in *Symposium* to appear foolish or cruel. However, Plato assigns him the most memorable and beautiful speech in the entire volume. Aristophanes's speech takes the form of a creation myth—the story of an ancestral race of human beings who were neither male nor female but a combination of both, who grew so strong that they challenged the gods and were each split into two incomplete halves.

Plato does not cast Aristophanes's story as a serious attempt to explain human history. Rather, he is trying to create a metaphor for something that he sees as a crucial element of human nature: the deep and aching need we have to find a person who can complete what is lacking in ourselves. This need forms the basis of erotic love, which, for Plato, was not entirely sexual, as the term generally implies today. An erotic relationship in the Platonic sense is a total and all-consuming connection with another person that—whether or not it has a sexual component—is primarily a meeting of minds and a mingling of intellects.

The central rhetorical device that Plato uses in "The Speech of Aristophanes" is an extended analogy between the creatures that Aristophanes describes and real human beings, who feel the same sense of loss and emptiness because we have been designed to be fulfilled by other people.

First you must learn what Human Nature was in the beginning and what has happened to it since, because long ago our nature was not what it is now, but very different. There were three kinds of human beings, that's my first point—not two as there are now, male and female. In addition to these, there was a third, a combination of those two; its name survives, though the kind itself has vanished. At that time, you see, the word "androgynous" really meant something: a form made up of male and female elements, though now there's nothing but the word, and that's used as an insult. My second point is that the shape of each human being was completely round, with back and sides in a circle; they had four hands each, as many legs as hands, and two faces, exactly alike, on a rounded neck. Between the two faces, which were on opposite sides, was one head with four ears. There were two sets of sexual organs, and everything else was the way you'd imagine it from what I've told you. They walked upright, as we do now, whatever direction they wanted. And whenever they set out to run fast, they thrust out all their eight limbs, the ones they had then, and spun rapidly, the way gymnasts do cartwheels, by bringing their legs around straight.

Now here is why there were three kinds, and why they were as I described them: The male kind was originally an offspring of the sun, the female of the earth, and the one that combined both genders was an offspring of the moon, because the moon shares in both. They were spherical, and so was their motion, because they were like their parents in the sky.

In strength and power, therefore, they were terrible, and they had great ambitions. They made an attempt on the gods, and Homer's story about Ephialtes and Otos[1] was originally about them: how they tried to make an ascent to heaven so as to attack the gods. Then Zeus and the other gods met in council to discuss what to do, and they were sore perplexed. They couldn't wipe out the human race with thunderbolts and kill them all off, as they had the giants, because that would wipe out the worship they receive, along with the sacrifices we humans give them. On the other hand, they couldn't let them run riot. At last, after great effort, Zeus had an idea.

"I think I have a plan," he said, "that would allow human beings to exist and stop their misbehaving: they will give up being wicked when they lose their strength. So I shall now cut each of them in two. At one stroke they will lose their strength and also become more profitable to us, owing to the increase in their number. They shall walk upright on two legs. But if I find they still run riot and do not keep the peace," he said, "I will cut them in two again, and they'll have to make their way on one leg, hopping."

1. **Ephialtes and Otos:** giants and sons of Poseidon who attacked Mt. Olympus and were tricked into killing each other.

So saying, he cut those human beings in two, the way people cut sorb-apples[2]   5
before they dry them or the way they cut eggs with hairs. As he cut each one, he
commanded Apollo to turn its face and half its neck towards the wound, so that each
person would see that he'd been cut and keep better order. Then Zeus commanded
Apollo to heal the rest of the wound, and Apollo did turn the face around, and he
drew skin from all sides over what is now called the stomach, and there he made one
mouth, as in a pouch with a drawstring, and fastened it at the center of the stomach.
This is now called the navel. Then he smoothed out the other wrinkles, of which
there were many, and he shaped the breasts, using some such tool as shoemakers
have for smoothing wrinkles out of leather on the form. But he left a few wrinkles
around the stomach and the navel, to be a reminder of what happened long ago.

Now, since their natural form had been cut in two, each one longed for its own
other half, and so they would throw their arms about each other, weaving themselves
together, wanting to grow together. In that condition they would die from hunger
and general idleness, because they would not do anything apart from each other.
Whenever one of the halves died and one was left, the one that was left still sought
another and wove itself together with that. Sometimes the half he met came from
a woman, as we'd call her now, sometimes it came from a man; either way, they
kept on dying.

Then, however, Zeus took pity on them, and came up with another plan: he
moved their genitals around to the front! Before then, you see, they used to have
their genitals outside, like their faces, and they cast seed and made children, not
in one another, but in the ground, like cicadas. So Zeus brought about this reloca-
tion of genitals, and in doing so he invented interior reproduction, *by* the man *in*
the woman. The purpose of this was so that, when a man embraced a woman, he
would cast his seed and they would have children; but when male embraced male,
they would at least have the satisfaction of intercourse, after which they could stop
embracing, return to their jobs, and look after their other needs in life. This, then,
is the source of our desire to love each other. Love is born into every human being;
it calls back the halves of our original nature together; it tries to make one out of
two and heal the wound of human nature.

UNDERSTANDING THE TEXT

1. How does knowing that Aristophanes's speech was one of a series of speeches
   devoted to the same topic in a friendly competition affect your understanding of
   his words? How might he have framed the argument differently if he were writing a
   philosophical essay on the topic?

2. Why do you think that Plato chose to put this speech in the mouth of somebody
   whom, on other occasions, he strongly disagreed with? Do you think that Plato
   intended for us to read Aristophanes's speech as his own words?

2. **Sorb-apples:** small, berry-sized fruit.

3. Why does Aristophanes choose to make his point with a purely fictional story? Is the story meant to be humorous? What element of human nature does he hope to dramatize with this story?

4. How does Aristophanes understand the term *androgynous*? What does he suggest about the nature of masculinity and femininity?

5. What role does divine intervention play in Aristophanes's allegory? What might he intend to symbolize by depicting Zeus as the creator of fragmented beings?

6. What does the allegory ultimately suggest about human nature?

MAKING CONNECTIONS

1. How do Plato's arguments about erotic love compare with the sociobiological arguments advanced by Edward O. Wilson in "The Fitness of Human Nature" (p. 356)? Does modern evolutionary science support or contradict the notion that we have a deep-seated longing to form attachments with other people? How so?

2. Compare the use of a mythical "state of nature" in the "Speech of Aristophanes" with that found in Thomas Hobbes's *Leviathan* (p. 94). What do philosophers gain by presenting human beings in a mythical past and drawing conclusions from their fictional portraits?

WRITING ABOUT THE TEXT

1. Use the "Speech of Aristophanes" as the basis for an essay about the nature of masculinity and femininity. Discuss whether or not the assumptions at the basis of the allegory can be used to derive valid points about human gender.

2. Compare Aristophanes's creation myth with another creation narrative or origin myth. Analyze the power of a narrative from the past to explain things about the present.

3. Explain, in your own words, the underlying argument about human nature at the heart of the "Speech of Aristophanes."

MENCIUS
Man's Nature Is Good
[CIRCA 300 BCE]

OF THE HUNDREDS OF GREAT Chinese philosophers, poets, novelists, and statesmen whose works have been read in the West, only two have been given Latin
names: Kung Fu Tzu (551–479 BCE), who is known in the West as Confucius, and
Meng Tzu (circa 371–circa 289 BCE), who is known as Mencius. After Confucius
himself, Mencius is the most important figure in the development of Confucianism,
a system of rites, rituals, and social observances that was the official state religion
of China for nearly two thousand years.

Mencius lived and wrote during one of the most spectacular eras of social
upheaval that the world has ever known: the Period of Warring States (475–221
BCE). During this period, the area now known as China consisted of numerous
smaller states—all remnants of the great Chou Empire—that were constantly at war
against each other. Confucianism, Legalism, Moism, and Taoism all emerged during
this time as different ways to answer the most important question of the day: what
is the best way to ensure political stability? The general Confucian answer to this
question is that good government requires good leaders, and good leaders must
be good people—people who honor their ancestors, observe the ancient rites, and
act toward others with a spirit of rectitude and benevolence.

During Mencius's lifetime, Confucians were split on the question of human nature.
Confucius had been puzzlingly vague on this matter, insisting only that all people
had a duty to observe the rites and rituals handed down by their ancestors. Some,
such as Mencius, took this to mean that humans were inherently good and, with
proper training, could become perfect. Others, such as Hsün Tzu, believed that the
Confucian rites were necessary because humans were inherently evil and required
rites to keep them in check. Mencius's arguments ultimately prevailed and influenced future generations of Confucians.

The excerpt here is drawn from Chapter 21 of Mencius's major work, called the
Mencius, and consists of a series of conversations between Mencius and the philosopher Kao Tzu and his disciples. Kao Tzu believed that human nature was neither
inherently good nor inherently evil but a "blank slate" that could be conditioned in
both directions. In Kao's philosophy, the love that people feel toward their relatives
stems from internal human nature, but the respect that people show for strangers—
and for the rites and traditions that were so important to Confucianism—must be
conditioned by external forces. Mencius and his disciple Kung-tu refuse to make
this distinction and insist that both love and respect proceed from internal feelings
that form part of human beings' nature.

[handwritten margin note: so what's weird but]

78

Mencius's rhetorical style is somewhat confusing at first because, like Plato in the "Gorgias" (p. 166), he advances his own arguments in a dialogue with others. Mencius adds an additional layer of complexity to this dialogue form by filtering Kao's arguments through a student, Kung-tu, who listens to both Kao and Mencius and tries to determine which of them speaks the truth.

1

Master Kao said: "The nature of things is like willow wood, and Duty is like cups and bowls. Shaping human nature into Humanity and Duty is like shaping willow wood into cups and bowls."

"Do you follow the nature of willow wood to shape cups and bowls," replied Mencius, "or do you maul it? If you maul willow wood to make cups and bowls, then I guess you maul human nature to make Humanity and Duty. It's talk like yours that will lead people to ravage Humanity and Duty throughout all beneath Heaven."

2

this I can see

Master Kao said: "The nature of things is like swirling water: channel it east and it flows east, channel it west and it flows west. And human nature too is like water: it doesn't choose between good and evil any more than water chooses between east and west."

"It's true that water doesn't choose between east and west," replied Mencius, "but doesn't it choose between high and low? Human nature is inherently good, just like water flows inherently downhill. There's no such thing as a person who isn't good, just as there's no water that doesn't flow downhill. *good point but debatable* 5

"Think about water: if you slap it, you can make it jump over your head; and if you push and shove, you can make it stay on a mountain. But what does this have to do with the nature of water? It's only responding to the forces around it. It's like that for people too: you can make them evil, but that says nothing about human nature." . . .   *tho.*

6

Adept Kung-tu[1] said: "Master Kao said: *Human nature isn't good, and it isn't evil.* There are others who say: *Human nature can be made good, and it can be made evil. That's why the people loved goodness when Wen and Wu ruled, and they loved cruelty when Yu*

---

1. **Kung-tu:** Mencius's disciple.

and Li ruled.[2] And there are still others who say: *Human nature is inborn: some people are good and some evil. That's why a Hsiang could have Yao as his ruler, a Shun could have Blind Purblind as his father, a Lord Ch'i of Wei and Prince Pi Kan could have the tyrant Chou as their nephew and sovereign.*[3]

"But you say: *Human nature is good.* Does that mean all the others are wrong?"

"We are, by constitution, capable of being good," replied Mencius. "That's what I mean by good. If someone's evil, it can't be blamed on inborn capacities. We all have a heart of compassion and a heart of conscience, a heart of reverence and a heart of right and wrong. In a heart of compassion is Humanity, and in a heart of conscience is Duty. In a heart of reverence is Ritual, and in a heart of right and wrong is wisdom. Humanity, Duty, Ritual, wisdom—these are not external things we meld into us. They're part of us from the beginning, though we may not realize it. Hence the saying: *What you seek you will find, and what you ignore you will lose.* Some make more of themselves than others, maybe two or five or countless times more. But that's only because some people fail to realize their inborn capacities.

"The *Songs* say:

Heaven gave birth to humankind,
and whatever is has its own laws:
cleaving to what makes us human,
people delight in stately Integrity.

Of this, Confucius said: *Whoever wrote this song knew the Way well.* So whatever is must have its own laws, and whenever they cleave to what makes us human, the people must delight in stately Integrity."

10

7

Mencius said: "In good years, young men are mostly fine. In bad years, they're mostly cruel and violent. It isn't that Heaven endows them with such different capacities, only that their hearts are mired in such different situations. Think about barley: if you plant the seeds carefully at the same time and in the same place, they'll all sprout and

2. **Yu and Li:** kings singled out in the Confucian tradition for their arrogance and recklessness. **Wen and Wu:** ancient kings who were singled out by Confucius as eminent examples of virtuous rulers. In Mencius's time, philosophers commonly appealed to well-known ancient kings, good and bad, to support their arguments about statecraft.

3. **Yao:** an ancient emperor frequently cited by Confucius as the model of a righteous king. **Shun:** Yao's handpicked, equally righteous successor. **Blind Pureblind:** Shun's wicked father also called Ku-Sau. **Lord Ch'i of Wei:** a wise man who refused to serve the wicked tyrant **Chou,** who killed his own uncle **Prince Pi Kan.** The point of all these examples is to refute Mencius's major claim—that human nature is essentially good and made bad by environment—by showing that the same environments that produced some of the most righteous people in history also produced some of the worst.

grow ripe by summer solstice. If they don't grow the same—it's because of inequities in richness of soil, amounts of rainfall, or the care given them by farmers. And so, all members belonging to a given species of thing are the same. Why should humans be the lone exception? The sage and I—surely we belong to the same species of thing.

"That's why Master Lung said: *Even if a cobbler makes a pair of sandals for feet he's never seen, he certainly won't make a pair of baskets.* Sandals are all alike because feet are the same throughout all beneath Heaven. And all tongues savor the same flavors. Yi Ya[4] was just the first to discover what our tongues savor. If taste differed by nature from person to person, the way horses and dogs differ by species from me, then how is it people throughout all beneath Heaven savor the tastes Yi Ya savored? People throughout all beneath Heaven share Yi Ya's tastes, therefore people's tongues are alike throughout all beneath Heaven.

"It's true for the ear too: people throughout all beneath Heaven share Maestro K'uang's[5] sense of music, therefore people's ears are alike throughout all beneath Heaven. And it's no less true for the eye: no one throughout all beneath Heaven could fail to see the beauty of Lord Tu. If you can't see his beauty, you simply haven't eyes.

"Hence it is said: *All tongues savor the same flavors, all ears hear the same music, and all eyes see the same beauty.* Why should the heart alone not be alike in us all? But what is it about our hearts that is alike? Isn't it what we call reason and Duty? The sage is just the first to discover what is common to our hearts. Hence, reason and Duty please our hearts just like meat pleases our tongues."

8

Mencius said: "The forests were once lovely on Ox Mountain.[6] But as they were near a great city, axes cleared them little by little. Now there's nothing left of their beauty. They rest day and night, rain and dew falling in plenty, and there's no lack of fresh sprouts. But people graze oxen and sheep there, so the mountain's stripped bare. When people see how bare it is, they think that's all the potential it has. But does that mean this is the nature of Ox Mountain?

"Without the heart of Humanity and Duty alive in us, how can we be human? When we abandon this noble heart, it's like cutting those forests: a few axe blows each day, and pretty soon there's nothing left. Then you can rest day and night, take

15

4. **Yi Ya:** an ancient chef revered for his culinary talents; according to legend, he once cooked his own son for his master's table.
5. **Maestro K'uang:** the most revered musician in Chinese history. Mencius makes the point that if everyone likes the cooking of Yi Ya and everyone likes the music of K'uang, then certain preferences in human nature are not subject to individual taste.

6. **Ox Mountain:** a mountain on the Pearl River Delta, near present-day Hong Kong. Mencius argues that, though it was in the nature of the mountain to have trees and lush vegetation, the human and animal population of the large state made it appear barren. The larger point is that even people's failure to act benevolently does not mean that they lack a natural disposition toward benevolence.

in the clarity of morning's healing *ch'i*—but the values that make you human keep thinning away. All day long, you're tangled in your life. If these tangles keep up day after day, even the clarity of night's healing *ch'i* isn't enough to preserve you. And if the clarity of night's healing *ch'i* isn't enough to preserve you, you aren't much different from an animal. When people see you're like an animal, they think that's all the potential you have. But does that mean this is the human constitution?

"With proper sustenance, anything will grow; and without proper sustenance, anything will fade away. Confucius said: *Embrace it and it endures. Forsake it and it dies. It comes and goes without warning, and no one knows its route.* He was speaking of the heart."

UNDERSTANDING THE TEXT

1. What is the rhetorical purpose of the character Kao at the beginning of this selection? How does he set up Mencius's argument? What kinds of objections to his own theory does this device allow Mencius to anticipate?

2. How does Mencius present the difference between "benevolence" and "righteousness"? Why does Kao Tzu see the first as internal to human nature and the second as external to human nature?

3. What role does human nature, for Mencius, play in the love we show to our family members? What role does it play in the respect that we show to strangers?

4. A great deal of the debate between Mencius and Kao Tzu concerns the origin of propriety, or proper social behavior, which is synonymous in the text with "righteousness." For Kao Tzu, propriety is a matter of social convention that has nothing to do with human nature. For Mencius, the standards of propriety are based on qualities that are inherently part of human nature. Which of these views do you find more convincing? Why?

5. How might Mencius perceive the nature of evil? If human beings are naturally good, where might evil originate? Support your answer with evidence from the text.

6. Do you agree with Mencius's statement "Men's mouths agree in having the same relishes; their ears agree in enjoying the same sounds; their eyes agree in recognising the same beauty"? How does this idea of conformity, and with it Mencius's argument, conflict with modern ideas of the individual?

MAKING CONNECTIONS

1. Mencius and Hsün Tzu (p. 84) disagree completely about human nature, yet both are dedicated Confucians. What elements of their respective philosophies justify their inclusion as members of the same school of thought?

2. Compare the thoughts of Mencius and Kao Tzu with those of Ruth Benedict (p. 112) or Edward O. Wilson (p. 356). Does the comparison between East and West, ancient and modern, make either Chinese philosopher more relatable? Why?

3. What does Mencius imply about people who change the appearance of natural phenomena, such as trees or mountains? How is this argument similar to Rachel Carson's
   in "The Obligation to Endure" (p. 328)?

4. How would you extend Mencius's view of human nature to answer the question
   "What is good government?" If human beings are essentially good, then what kind
   of government serves them best? How does this compare to Lao Tzu's thoughts on
   government (p. 384)?

WRITING ABOUT THE TEXT

1. Take one of the metaphors that Kao Tzu and Mencius debate over—either the willow
   metaphor or the water metaphor—and use it to support your own view of human
   nature.

2. Compare Mencius's and Hsün Tzu's (p. 84) essays on human nature. How are the two
   texts similar? How are they different?

3. Examine the role of ritual in contemporary society. Where do social conventions
   such as manners, dating behavior, dressing and grooming practices, and so on come
   from? Do they have as their basis anything natural to human beings?

4. What kinds of government best suit, respectively, Mencius's and Kao Tzu's assumptions about human nature? Write an essay exploring this question, being sure to
   explain how different perceptions about the nature of human beings lead to different
   assumptions about the role of government.

HSÜN TZU

Man's Nature Is Evil

[CIRCA 300 BCE]

IN BOTH THE STYLE OF HIS WRITING and the nature of his philosophy, the Chinese scholar Hsün Tzu (circa 300–230 BCE) could not have differed more from his slightly older contemporary Mencius (circa 371–circa 289 BCE). The writings of Mencius consist largely of parables and of what appear to be transcripts of debates that he had with other philosophers. Hsün Tzu wrote sustained, well-developed philosophical arguments that, while they feel quite familiar to the modern reader, were something of an anomaly in his own time.

Both men were Confucians, but Hsün Tzu did not share Mencius's belief that human nature is inherently good, even divine. Whereas for Mencius the Confucian sense of propriety derived from inclinations that all people possessed, Hsün Tzu saw Confucian rites as valuable because they restrained and redirected humanity's inherent disposition toward evil. Hsün Tzu believed that strict discipline could make human beings good despite their natural inclinations. Most of his known writings deal with forces that, in his estimation, steered people toward righteousness: education, music, ritual, and law.

Hsün Tzu's philosophy had an enormous effect on the Chinese philosophy of Legalism. One of his pupils Han Fei Tzu, the major theorist of that school, argued that human beings must be forced into rectitude by strict laws and harsh penalties for disobedience. When the state of Ch'in unified China into a single empire (221 BCE), another of Hsün Tzu's pupils, Li Ssu, became the prime minister and put the authoritarian principles of Legalism into practice. When the Ch'in Dynasty collapsed—a mere fifteen years after it was established—the backlash against Legalist rule led subsequent regimes to ban Hsün Tzu's teachings.

The reading included here, "Man's Nature Is Evil," is section 23 of the *Hsün Tzu*, the standard collection of Hsün Tzu's writings. This essay specifically addresses the arguments about human nature Mencius advanced one generation earlier. Like Mencius, Hsün Tzu argues frequently by analogy, but unlike his predecessor, he uses sustained, developed arguments just as frequently. Like modern writers, he states his thesis early (in the very first sentence), repeats it throughout the essay, and focuses on proving this thesis.

Man's nature is evil; goodness is the result of conscious activity. The nature of man is such that he is born with a fondness for profit. If he indulges this fondness, it will lead him into wrangling and strife, and all sense of courtesy and humility will disappear. He is born with feelings of envy and hate, and if he indulges these, they

Some of the translator's footnotes have been omitted. Bracketed insertions are the translator's.

will lead him into violence and crime, and all sense of loyalty and good faith will disappear. Man is born with the desires of the eyes and ears, with a fondness for beautiful sights and sounds. If he indulges these, they will lead him into license and wantonness, and all ritual principles and correct forms will be lost. Hence, any man who follows his nature and indulges his emotions will inevitably become involved in wrangling and strife, will violate the forms and rules of society, and will end as a criminal. Therefore, man must first be transformed by the instructions of a teacher and guided by ritual principles, and only then will he be able to observe the dictates of courtesy and humility, obey the forms and rules of society, and achieve order. It is obvious from this, then, that man's nature is evil, and that his goodness is the result of conscious activity.

A warped piece of wood must wait until it has been laid against the straightening board, steamed, and forced into shape before it can become straight; a piece of blunt metal must wait until it has been whetted on a grindstone before it can become sharp. Similarly, since man's nature is evil, it must wait for the instructions of a teacher before it can become upright, and for the guidance of ritual principles before it can become orderly. If men have no teachers to instruct them, they will be inclined towards evil and not upright; and if they have no ritual principles to guide them, they will be perverse and violent and lack order. In ancient times the sage kings realized that man's nature is evil, and that therefore he inclines toward evil and violence and is not upright or orderly. Accordingly they created ritual principles and laid down certain regulations in order to reform man's emotional nature and make it upright, in order to train and transform it and guide it in the proper channels. In this way they caused all men to become orderly and to conform to the Way.[1] Hence, today any man who takes to heart the instructions of his teacher, applies himself to his studies, and abides by ritual principles may become a gentleman, but anyone who gives free rein to his emotional nature, is content to indulge his passions, and disregards ritual principles becomes a petty man. It is obvious from this, therefore, that man's nature is evil, and that his goodness is the result of conscious activity.

Mencius states that man is capable of learning because his nature is good, but I say that this is wrong. It indicates that he has not really understood man's nature nor distinguished properly between the basic nature and conscious activity. The nature is that which is given by Heaven; you cannot learn it, you cannot acquire it by effort. Ritual principles, on the other hand, are created by sages; you can learn to apply them, you can work to bring them to completion. That part of man which cannot be learned or acquired by effort is called the nature; that part of him which can be acquired by learning and brought to completion by effort is called conscious activity. This is the difference between nature and conscious activity.

1. **The Way:** Chinese philosophers from every school speak about "the Way," or the *Tao*, though each school uses the term in a different sense. For Taoists, "the Way" means "the natural order of things" and is beyond human influence. For Confucians, "the Way" means something like "the way things should be" and incorporates ideals of rectitude and propriety.

It is a part of man's nature that his eyes can see and his ears can hear. But the faculty of clear sight can never exist separately from the eye, nor can the faculty of keen hearing exist separately from the ear. It is obvious, then, that you cannot acquire clear sight and keen hearing by study. Mencius states that man's nature is good, and that all evil arises because he loses his original nature. Such a view, I believe, is erroneous. It is the way with man's nature that as soon as he is born he begins to depart from his original naïveté and simplicity, and therefore he must inevitably lose what Mencius regards as his original nature. It is obvious from this, then, that the nature of man is evil.

Those who maintain that the nature is good praise and approve whatever has   5 not departed from the original simplicity and naïveté of the child. That is, they consider that beauty belongs to the original simplicity and naïveté and goodness to the original mind in the same way that clear sight is inseparable from the eye and keen hearing from the ear. Hence, they maintain that [the nature possesses goodness] in the same way that the eye possesses clear vision or the ear keenness of hearing. Now it is the nature of man that when he is hungry he will desire satisfaction, when he is cold he will desire warmth, and when he is weary he will desire rest. This is his emotional nature. And yet a man, although he is hungry, will not dare to be the first to eat if he is in the presence of his elders, because he knows that he should yield to them, and although he is weary, he will not dare to demand rest because he knows that he should relieve others of the burden of labor. For a son to yield to his father or a younger brother to yield to his elder brother, for a son to relieve his father of work or a younger brother to relieve his elder brother—acts such as these are all contrary to man's nature and run counter to his emotions. And yet they represent the way of filial piety and the proper forms enjoined by ritual principles. Hence, if men follow their emotional nature, there will be no courtesy or humility; courtesy and humility in fact run counter to man's emotional nature. From this it is obvious, then, that man's nature is evil, and that his goodness is the result of conscious activity.

Someone may ask: if man's nature is evil, then where do ritual principles come from? I would reply: all ritual principles are produced by the conscious activity of the sages; essentially they are not products of man's nature. A potter molds clay and makes a vessel, but the vessel is the product of the conscious activity of the potter, not essentially a product of his human nature. A carpenter carves a piece of wood and makes a utensil, but the utensil is the product of the conscious activity of the carpenter, not essentially a product of his human nature. The sage gathers together his thoughts and ideas, experiments with various forms of conscious activity, and so produces ritual principles and sets forth laws and regulations. Hence, these ritual principles and laws are the products of the conscious activity of the sage, not essentially products of his human nature.

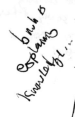

Phenomena such as the eye's fondness for beautiful forms, the ear's fondness for beautiful sounds, the mouth's fondness for delicious flavors, the mind's fondness for profit, or the body's fondness for pleasure and ease—these are all products of the emotional nature of man. They are instinctive and spontaneous; man does not have to do anything to produce them. But that which does not come into being instinctively but must wait for some activity to bring it into being is called the product of conscious activity. These are the products of the nature and of conscious activity respectively, and the proof that they are not the same. Therefore, the sage transforms his nature and initiates conscious activity; from this conscious activity he produces ritual principles, and when they have been produced he sets up rules and regulations. Hence, ritual principles and rules are produced by the sage. In respect to human nature the sage is the same as all other men and does not surpass them; it is only in his conscious activity that he differs from and surpasses other men.

It is man's emotional nature to love profit and desire gain. Suppose now that a man has some wealth to be divided. If he indulges his emotional nature, loving profit and desiring gain, then he will quarrel and wrangle even with his own brothers over the division. But if he has been transformed by the proper forms of ritual principle, then he will be capable of yielding even to a complete stranger. Hence, to indulge the emotional nature leads to the quarreling of brothers, but to be transformed by ritual principles makes a man capable of yielding to strangers.

Every man who desires to do good does so precisely because his nature is evil. A man whose accomplishments are meager longs for greatness; an ugly man longs for beauty; a man in cramped quarters longs for spaciousness; a poor man longs for wealth; a humble man longs for eminence. Whatever a man lacks in himself he will seek outside. But if a man is already rich, he will not long for wealth, and if he is already eminent, he will not long for greater power. What a man already possesses in himself he will not bother to look for outside. From this we can see that men desire to do good precisely because their nature is evil. Ritual principles are certainly not a part of man's original nature. Therefore, he forces himself to study and to seek to possess them. An understanding of ritual principles is not a part of man's original nature, and therefore he ponders and plans and thereby seeks to understand them. Hence, man in the state in which he is born neither possesses nor understands ritual principles. If he does not possess ritual principles, his behavior will be chaotic, and if he does not understand them, he will be wild and irresponsible. In fact, therefore, man in the state in which he is born possesses this tendency towards chaos and irresponsibility. From this it is obvious, then, that man's nature is evil, and that his goodness is the result of conscious activity.

Mencius states that man's nature is good, but I say that this view is wrong. All men in the world, past and present, agree in defining goodness as that which is upright, reasonable, and orderly, and evil as that which is prejudiced, irresponsible, and chaotic. This is the distinction between good and evil. Now suppose that man's nature was in fact intrinsically upright, reasonable, and orderly—then what need would there be for sage kings and ritual principles? The existence of sage kings and ritual principles could certainly add nothing to the situation. But because man's nature is in fact evil, this is not so. Therefore, in ancient times the sages, realizing that man's nature is evil, that it is prejudiced and not upright, irresponsible and lacking in order, for this reason established the authority of the ruler to control it, elucidated ritual principles to transform it, set up laws and standards to correct it, and meted out strict punishments to restrain it. As a result, all the world achieved order and conformed to goodness. Such is the orderly government of the sage kings and the transforming power of ritual principles. Now let someone try doing away with the authority of the ruler, ignoring the transforming power of ritual principles, rejecting the order that comes from laws and standards, and dispensing with the restrictive power of punishments, and then watch and see how the people of the world treat each other. He will find that the powerful impose upon the weak and rob them, the many terrorize the few and extort from them, and in no time the whole world will be given up to chaos and mutual destruction. It is obvious from this, then, that man's nature is evil, and that his goodness is the result of conscious activity.

Those who are good at discussing antiquity must demonstrate the validity of what they say in terms of modern times; those who are good at discussing Heaven must show proofs from the human world. In discussions of all kinds, men value what is in accord with the facts and what can be proved to be valid. Hence if a man sits on his mat propounding some theory, he should be able to stand right up and put it into practice, and show that it can be extended over a wide area with equal validity. Now Mencius states that man's nature is good, but this is neither in accord with the facts, nor can it be proved to be valid. One may sit down and propound such a theory, but he cannot stand up and put it into practice, nor can he extend it over a wide area with any success at all. How, then, could it be anything but erroneous?

If the nature of man were good, we could dispense with sage kings and forget about ritual principles. But if it is evil, then we must go along with the sage kings and honor ritual principles. The straightening board is made because of the warped wood; the plumb line is employed because things are crooked; rulers are set up and ritual principles elucidated because the nature of man is evil. From this it is obvious, then, that man's nature is evil, and that his goodness is the result of conscious activity. A straight piece of wood does not have to wait for the straightening board to become straight; it is straight by nature. But a warped piece of wood must wait until it has been laid against the straightening board, steamed, and forced into shape before it can become straight, because by nature it is warped. Similarly, since man's nature is evil, he must wait for the ordering power of the sage kings and the transforming power of ritual principles; only then can he achieve order and conform to goodness. From this it is obvious, then, that man's nature is evil, and that his goodness is the result of conscious activity.

Someone may ask whether ritual principles and concerted conscious activity are not themselves a part of man's nature, so that for that reason the sage is capable of producing them. But I would answer that this is not so. A potter may mold clay and produce an earthen pot, but surely molding pots out of clay is not a part of the potter's human nature. A carpenter may carve wood and produce a utensil, but surely carving utensils out of wood is not a part of the carpenter's human nature. The sage stands in the same relation to ritual principles as the potter to the things he molds and produces. How, then, could ritual principles and concerted conscious activity be a part of man's basic human nature?

As far as human nature goes, the sages Yao and Shun possessed the same nature as the tyrant Chieh or Robber Chih, and the gentleman possesses the same nature as the petty man.[2] Would you still maintain, then, that ritual principles and concerted conscious activity are a part of man's nature? If you do so, then what reason is there to pay any particular honor to Yao, Shun, or the gentleman? The reason people honor Yao, Shun, and the gentleman is that they are able to transform their nature, apply themselves to conscious activity, and produce ritual principles. The sage, then, must stand in the same relation to ritual principles as the potter to the things he molds and produces. Looking at it this way, how could ritual principles and concerted conscious activity be a part of man's nature? The reason people despise Chieh, Robber Chih, or the petty man is that they give free rein to their nature, follow their emotions, and are content to indulge their passions, so that their conduct is marked by greed and contentiousness. Therefore, it is clear that man's nature is evil, and that his goodness is the result of conscious activity.

Heaven did not bestow any particular favor upon Tseng Tzu, Min Tzu-ch'ien, or   15
Hsiao-i that it withheld from other men.[3] And yet these three men among all others proved most capable of carrying out their duties as sons and winning fame for their filial piety. Why? Because of their thorough attention to ritual principles. Heaven has not bestowed any particular favor upon the inhabitants of Ch'i and Lu which it has withheld from the people of Ch'in.[4] And yet when it comes to observing the duties of father and son and the separation of roles between husband and wife, the inhabitants of Ch'in cannot match the filial reverence and respect for proper form which marks the people of Ch'i and Lu. Why? Because the people of Ch'in give free rein to their emotional nature, are content to indulge their passions, and are careless of ritual principles. It is certainly not due to any difference in human nature between the two groups.

The man in the street can become a Yü.[5] What does this mean? What made the sage emperor Yü a Yü, I would reply, was the fact that he practiced benevolence

2. **Gentleman:** the category representing the ideal human being in the Confucian system of thought. The gentleman possesses rectitude, benevolence, integrity, honor, and a proper respect for the ancestors and the rites. The opposite of a gentleman is a "petty man." The terms do not have any class-based connotations. **Yao and Shun:** mythical ancient kings advanced by Confucians as ideals of righteous rulers. **Tyrant Chieh or Robber Chih:** according to tradition, Chieh was an evil ruler who brought down the great Hsia Dynasty. **Robber Chih** led a band of nine thousand criminals; legend has it that Confucius once tried in vain to reform him.

3. **Tseng Tzu, Min Tzu-ch'ien:** followers of Confucius who were considered especially righteous. Not much is known about **Hsiao-i.**
4. **Ch'i and Lu:** areas where Confucianism was very influential. **Ch'in's** government was officially anti-Confucian (see p. 84).
5. **Yü:** the virtuous king and founder of the ancient Hsia Dynasty. "The man in the street can become a Yü" refers to the assertion, found in section 22 of the *Mencius*, that "all men may be Yaos and Shuns" (see note 2).

and righteousness and abided by the proper rules and standards. If this is so, then benevolence, righteousness, and proper standards must be based upon principles which can be known and practiced. Any man in the street has the essential faculties needed to understand benevolence, righteousness, and proper standards, and the potential ability to put them into practice. Therefore it is clear that he can become a Yü.

Would you maintain that benevolence, righteousness, and proper standards are not based upon any principles that can be known and practiced? If so, then even a Yü could not have understood or practiced them. Or would you maintain that the man in the street does not have the essential faculties needed to understand them or the potential ability to put them into practice? If so, then you are saying that the man in the street in his family life cannot understand the duties required of a father or a son and in public life cannot comprehend the correct relationship between ruler and subject. But in fact this is not true. Any man in the street *can* understand the duties required of a father or a son and *can* comprehend the correct relationship between ruler and subject. Therefore, it is obvious that the essential faculties needed to understand such ethical principles and the potential ability to put them into practice must be a part of his make-up. Now if he takes these faculties and abilities and applies them to the principles of benevolence and righteousness, which we have already shown to be knowable and practicable, then it is obvious that he can become a Yü. If the man in the street applies himself to training and study, concentrates his mind and will, and considers and examines things carefully, continuing his efforts over a long period of time and accumulating good acts without stop, then he can achieve a godlike understanding and form a triad with Heaven and earth. The sage is a man who has arrived where he has through the accumulation of good acts.

You have said, someone may object, that the sage has arrived where he has through the accumulation of good acts. Why is it, then, that everyone is not able to accumulate good acts in the same way? I would reply: everyone is capable of doing so, but not everyone can be made to do so. The petty man is capable of becoming a gentleman, yet he is not willing to do so; the gentleman is capable of becoming a petty man but he is not willing to do so. The petty man and the gentleman are perfectly capable of changing places; the fact that they do not actually do so is what I mean when I say that they are capable of doing so but they cannot be made to do so. Hence, it is correct to say that the man in the street is *capable* of becoming a Yü but it is not necessarily correct to say that he will in fact find it possible to do so. But although he does not find it possible to do so does not prove that he is incapable of doing so.

A person with two feet is theoretically capable of walking to every corner of the earth, although in fact no one has ever found it possible to do so. Similarly, the artisan, the carpenter, the farmer, and the merchant are theoretically capable of exchanging professions, although in actual practice they find it impossible to do so. From this we can see that, although someone may be theoretically capable of becoming something, he may not in practice find it possible to do so. But although he does not find it possible to do so, this does not prove that he is not capable of doing so. To find it practically possible or impossible to do something and to be capable or incapable of doing something are two entirely different things. It is perfectly clear, then, that a man is theoretically capable of becoming something else.

Yao asked Shun, "What are man's emotions like?" Shun replied, "Man's emotions are very unlovely things indeed! What need is there to ask any further? Once a man acquires a wife and children, he no longer treats his parents as a filial son should. Once he succeeds in satisfying his cravings and desires, he neglects his duty to his friends. Once he has won a high position and a good stipend, he ceases to serve his sovereign with a loyal heart. Man's emotions, man's emotions—they are very unlovely things indeed! What need is there to ask any further? Only the worthy man is different from this."

There is the understanding of the sage, the understanding of the gentleman and man of breeding, the understanding of the petty man, and the understanding of the menial. He speaks many words but they are graceful and well ordered; all day he discourses on his reasons, employing a thousand different and varied modes of expression, and yet all that he says is united around a single principle: such is the understanding of the sage. He speaks little but what he says is brief and to the point, logical and clearly presented, as though laid out with a plumb line: such is the understanding of the gentleman and man of breeding. His words are all flattery, his actions irresponsible; whatever he does is shot through with error: such is the understanding of the petty man. His words are rapid and shrill but never to the point; his talents are varied and many but of no practical use; he is full of subtle distinctions and elegant turns of phrase that serve no practical purpose; he ignores right or wrong, disdains to discuss crooked or straight, but seeks only to overpower the arguments of his opponent: such is the understanding of the menial.

There is superior valor, there is the middle type of valor, and there is inferior valor. When proper standards prevail in the world, to dare to bring your own conduct into accord with them; when the Way of the former kings prevails, to dare to follow its dictates; to refuse to bow before the ruler of a disordered age, to refuse to follow the customs of the people of a disordered age; to accept poverty and hardship if they are in the cause of benevolent action; to reject wealth and eminence if they are not consonant with benevolent action; if the world recognizes you, to share in the world's joys; if the world does not recognize you, to stand alone and without fear: this is superior valor. To be reverent in bearing and modest in intention; to value honor and make light of material goods; to dare to promote and honor the worthy, and reject and cast off the unworthy: such is the middle type of valor. To ignore your own safety in the quest for wealth; to make light of danger and try to talk your way out of every difficulty; to rely on lucky escapes; to ignore right and wrong, just

20

and unjust, and seek only to overpower the arguments of your opponents: such is inferior valor. . . .

A man, no matter how fine his nature or how keen his mind, must seek a worthy teacher to study under and good companions to associate with. If he studies under a worthy teacher, he will be able to hear about the ways of Yao, Shun, Yü, and T'ang,[6] and if he associates with good companions, he will be able to observe conduct that is loyal and respectful. Then, although he is not aware of it, he will day by day progress in the practice of benevolence and righteousness, for the environment he is subjected to will cause him to progress. But if a man associates with men who are not good, then he will hear only deceit and lies and will see only conduct that is marked by wantonness, evil, and greed. Then, although he is not aware of it, he himself will soon be in danger of severe punishment, for the environment he is subjected to will cause him to be in danger. An old text says, "If you do not know a man, look at his friends; if you do not know a ruler, look at his attendants." Environment is the important thing! Environment is the important thing!

UNDERSTANDING THE TEXT

1. Why does Hsün Tzu repeat his thesis (p. 84) throughout this piece? Does this technique make his argument more effective? What other types of repetition does Hsün Tzu use, and how does the repetition illustrate different aspects of his argument?

2. What distinction does Hsün Tzu draw between "nature" and "conscious activity"? Are these categories mutually exclusive? What kinds of things does he place in each category?

3. What does Hsün Tzu see as the origin of ritual principles? How does this differ from Mencius's view (p. 78)?

4. Why does Hsün Tzu assert that "every man who desires to do good does so precisely because his nature is evil"? Do you agree? Are his comparisons to men who are unaccomplished, ugly, cramped, poor, and humble valid? Is it possible to desire to be something that is part of one's nature?

5. How does Hsün Tzu define "good" and "evil"? Do his definitions concur with contemporary definitions of the same words?

6. How does Hsün Tzu differentiate between capability and possibility? How are they related, and does this inclusion weaken or strengthen the validity of Hsün Tzu's argument?

7. According to Hsün Tzu, what role does environment play in how humans deal with their nature? What kind of environmental factors determine a person's inclination or rejection of human nature?

6. **T'ang:** a righteous king in mythical ancient China; should not be confused with the T'ang Dynasty, which ruled China from 618 to 907 CE, nearly a thousand years after Hsün Tzu's time.

MAKING CONNECTIONS

1. How does Hsün Tzu's writing style compare with that of Mencius (p. 78)? Are his rhetorical strategies more or less effective than those of his major philosophical opponent? Why?

2. What kind of political theory is suggested by Hsün Tzu's philosophy of human nature? How do perceptions of human nature affect political arguments? Which political theories covered in Chapter 6, "Law and Government," best reflect the kind of government that Hsün Tzu would advocate?

3. Compare this essay by Hsün Tzu with the essay by him in Chapter 1, "Encouraging Learning" (p. 5). How do his views on human nature affect his views on education?

4. Compare Hsün Tzu's use of the dialogue form with that of Plato in "Gorgias" (p. 166). Do the two philosophers use multiple voices for the same reasons? Explain.

WRITING ABOUT THE TEXT

1. Hsün Tzu states: "If a man is already rich, he will not long for wealth, and if he is already eminent, he will not long for greater power. What a man already possesses in himself he will not bother to look for outside. From this we can see that men desire to do good precisely because their nature is evil." Defend or refute this assertion, using historical examples to support your argument.

2. Compare Hsün Tzu's philosophy of human nature with that of Thomas Hobbes (p. 94). How does each philosopher feel that people should be governed?

3. Analyze the rhetoric of "Man's Nature Is Evil." What inductive and deductive arguments can you draw from the essay? (See p. 652 for explanations and examples of inductive and deductive reasoning.) How logically sound are his arguments?

4. Compare Hsün Tzu's view of human nature with the one implicit in the argument of his contemporary Mo Tzu in "Against Music" (p. 236). What elements do the texts share?

THOMAS HOBBES
from *Leviathan*
[1651]

LIKE THE PERIOD OF WARRING STATES in ancient China, the years between 1640 and 1714 in England saw great social upheaval. In 1642, a civil war broke out between King Charles I and the British Parliament under the leadership of Oliver Cromwell. The war ended in 1649 with the execution of King Charles, and for the next eleven years Cromwell ruled England as a commonwealth rather than a monarchy. Soon after Cromwell's death, Parliament invited Charles's son, Charles II, to return to the throne, but the hostilities among Anglicans, Catholics, and Dissenting Protestants continued for years and led to another revolution in 1689. Out of the chaos and uncertainty of the English revolutions emerged two of England's greatest political philosophers: Thomas Hobbes (1588–1679) and John Locke (1632–1704).

Both Locke's and Hobbes's theories of government imagine what people would be like in a "state of nature"—an environment without laws or social structures, one in which human nature existed without constraints. Locke and Hobbes posited that from a state of nature, humans established a social contract that required them to surrender some of their freedoms in exchange for the protections and opportunities of a civil society. The social contract arguments of Locke and Hobbes were extremely influential in their day. They were adopted by French philosophers such as the Baron de Montesquieu (1689–1755) and Jean-Jacques Rousseau (1712–1778) and by American revolutionaries such as Thomas Jefferson (1743–1826).

Each thinker's vision of the social contract depended on his understanding of human nature. Those who, like Locke, saw the natural state as reasonably safe and secure believed that people had the right to renegotiate, through violent revolution if necessary, their relationship with their government when that government ceased to protect them. For Hobbes, however, the state of nature was so horrible, and people in their natural state so degenerate, that any form of government was preferable to it. Hobbes therefore opposed revolution in any form, not because he thought that kings ruled by divine right but because he believed that authoritarian governments were necessary to keep human beings' worst impulses under control.

The reading that follows, "Of the Natural Condition of Mankind, As Concerning Their Felicity and Misery," is Chapter 13 of Hobbes's most important political work, *Leviathan*. Though one of the shorter chapters in the book, it has become by far the most famous chapter. In it, Hobbes lays out his theory that the natural state of humanity is war, by which he means not necessarily armed conflict but a struggle in which each person's interests are inherently opposed to everyone else's.

In such a state, human life is, in Hobbes's oft-quoted terms, "solitary, poor, nasty, brutish, and short."

This selection from *Leviathan* provides an example of reasoning by generalization. Hobbes begins by defining the nature of individual human beings and then generalizes this characterization to apply to entire societies.

Nature hath made men so equal in the faculties of body and mind as that, though there be found one man sometimes manifestly stronger in body or of quicker mind than another, yet when all is reckoned together the difference between man and man is not so considerable as that one man can thereupon claim to himself any benefit to which another may not pretend as well as he. For as to the strength of body, the weakest has strength enough to kill the strongest, either by secret machination, or by confederacy with others that are in the same danger with himself.[1]

And as to the faculties of the mind—setting aside the arts grounded upon words, and especially that skill of proceeding upon general and infallible rules called science (which very few have, and but in few things), as being not a native faculty (born with us), nor attained (as prudence) while we look after somewhat else—I find yet a greater equality amongst men than that of strength. For prudence is but experience, which equal time equally bestows on all men in those things they equally apply themselves unto. That which may perhaps make such equality incredible is but a vain conceit of one's own wisdom, which almost all men think they have in a greater degree than the vulgar, that is, than all men but themselves and a few others whom, by fame or for concurring with themselves, they approve. For such is the nature of men that howsoever they may acknowledge many others to be more witty, or more eloquent, or more learned, yet they will hardly believe there be many so wise as themselves. For they see their own wit at hand, and other men's at a distance. But this proveth rather that men are in that point equal, than unequal. For there is not ordinarily a greater sign of the equal distribution of anything than that every man is contented with his share.

From this equality of ability ariseth equality of hope in the attaining of our ends. And therefore, if any two men desire the same thing, which nevertheless they cannot both enjoy, they become enemies; and in the way to their end, which is principally their own conservation, and sometimes their delectation only, endeavour to destroy or subdue one another. And from hence it comes to pass that, where an invader hath no more to fear than another man's single power, if one plant, sow, build, or possess a convenient seat, others may probably be expected to come prepared with forces united, to dispossess and deprive him, not only of the fruit of his labour, but also of his life or liberty. And the invader again is in the like danger of another.

---

1. **By secret machination, or by confederacy:** Hobbes states that nobody is safe in a state of nature, since even the weakest people can kill the strongest, either by laying secret plans or by forming alliances with others.

And from this diffidence[2] of one another, there is no way for any man to secure himself so reasonable as anticipation, that is, by force or wiles to master the persons of all men he can, so long till he see no other power great enough to endanger him. And this is no more than his own conservation requireth, and is generally allowed. Also, because there be some that taking pleasure in contemplating their own power in the acts of conquest, which they pursue farther than their security requires, if others (that otherwise would be glad to be at ease within modest bounds) should not by invasion increase their power, they would not be able, long time, by standing only on their defence, to subsist. And by consequence, such augmentation of dominion over men being necessary to a man's conservation, it ought to be allowed him.

Again, men have no pleasure, but on the contrary a great deal of grief, in keeping company where there is no power able to over-awe them all. For every man looketh that his companion should value him at the same rate he sets upon himself, and upon all signs of contempt, or undervaluing, naturally endeavours, as far as he dares (which amongst them that have no common power to keep them in quiet, is far enough to make them destroy each other), to extort a greater value from his contemners, by damage, and from others, by the example.

So that in the nature of man we find three principal causes of quarrel: first, competition; secondly, diffidence; thirdly, glory.

The first maketh men invade for gain; the second, for safety; and the third, for reputation. The first use violence to make themselves masters of other men's persons, wives, children, and cattle; the second, to defend them; the third, for trifles, as a word, a smile, a different opinion, and any other sign of undervalue, either direct in their persons, or by reflection in their kindred, their friends, their nation, their profession, or their name.

Hereby it is manifest that during the time men live without a common power to keep them all in awe, they are in that condition which is called war, and such a war as is of every man against every man. For WAR consisteth not in battle only, or the act of fighting, but in a tract of time wherein the will to contend by battle is sufficiently known. And therefore, the notion of *time* is to be considered in the nature of war, as it is in the nature of weather. For as the nature of foul weather lieth not in a shower or two of rain, but in an inclination thereto of many days together, so the nature of war consisteth not in actual fighting, but in the known disposition thereto during all the time there is no assurance to the contrary.[3] All other time is PEACE.

Whatsoever therefore is consequent to a time of war, where every man is enemy to every man, the same is consequent to the time wherein men live without other

2. **Diffidence:** reservation. Hobbes means that people in a natural state can never trust or be genuinely close to other people because their interests might conflict and turn them into enemies.

3. Hobbes expands the common definition of "war" to include situations in which people do not have a reasonable assurance that they will not soon be at war. For Hobbes, then, "peace" means not only the absence of conflict but also the reasonable expectation that society has been structured to prevent conflict.

security than what their own strength and their own invention shall furnish them withal. In such condition there is no place for industry, because the fruit thereof is uncertain, and consequently, no culture of the earth, no navigation, nor use of the commodities that may be imported by sea, no commodious building, no instruments of moving and removing such things as require much force, no knowledge of the face of the earth, no account of time, no arts, no letters, no society, and which is worst of all, continual fear and danger of violent death, and the life of man, solitary, poor, nasty, brutish, and short.

It may seem strange, to some man that has not well weighed these things, that nature should thus dissociate, and render men apt to invade and destroy one another. And he may, therefore, not trusting to this inference made from the passions, desire perhaps to have the same confirmed by experience. Let him therefore consider with himself—when taking a journey, he arms himself, and seeks to go well accompanied; when going to sleep, he locks his doors; when even in his house, he locks his chests; and this when he knows there be laws, and public officers, armed, to revenge all injuries shall be done him—what opinion he has of his fellow subjects, when he rides armed; of his fellow citizens, when he locks his doors; and of his children and servants, when he locks his chests. Does he not there as much accuse mankind by his actions, as I do by my words? But neither of us accuse man's nature in it. The desires and other passions of man are in themselves no sin. No more are the actions that proceed from those passions, till they know a law that forbids them—which till laws be made they cannot know. Nor can any law be made, till they have agreed upon the person that shall make it.

It may peradventure[4] be thought, there was never such a time nor condition of war as this; and I believe it was never generally so, over all the world. But there are many places where they live so now. For the savage people in many places of *America* (except the government of small families, the concord whereof dependeth on natural lust)[5] have no government at all, and live at this day in that brutish manner as I said before. Howsoever, it may be perceived what manner of life there would be where there were no common power to fear, by the manner of life which men that have formerly lived under a peaceful government use to degenerate into, in a civil war.

But though there had never been any time wherein particular men were in a condition of war one against another, yet in all times kings and persons of sovereign authority, because of their independency, are in continual jealousies and in the state and posture of gladiators, having their weapons pointing and their eyes fixed on one another, that is, their forts, garrisons, and guns upon the frontiers of their kingdoms, and continual spies upon their neighbours, which is a posture of war. But because

4. **Peradventure:** perhaps.
5. **The concord whereof dependeth on natural lust:** Hobbes relies on largely inaccurate portrayals of American Indians and other tribal people to assert that they have no form of civil government beyond that of the small family, which is kept together by sexual ties between partners and by affection for children.

they uphold thereby the industry of their subjects, there does not follow from it that misery which accompanies the liberty of particular men.

To this war of every man against every man, this also is consequent: that nothing can be unjust. The notions of right and wrong, justice and injustice, have there no place. Where there is no common power, there is no law; where no law, no injustice. Force and fraud are in war the two cardinal virtues. Justice and injustice are none of the faculties neither of the body, nor mind. If they were, they might be in a man that were alone in the world, as well as his senses and passions. They are qualities that relate to men in society, not in solitude. It is consequent also to the same condition that there be no propriety, no dominion, no *mine* and *thine* distinct, but only that to be every man's that he can get, and for so long as he can keep it. And thus much for the ill condition which man by mere nature is actually placed in, though with a possibility to come out of it, consisting partly in the passions, partly in his reason.

The passions that incline men to peace are fear of death, desire of such things as are necessary to commodious living, and a hope by their industry to obtain them. And reason suggesteth convenient articles of peace, upon which men may be drawn to agreement. These articles are they which otherwise are called the Laws of Nature, whereof I shall speak more particularly in the two following chapters.

UNDERSTANDING THE TEXT

1. Why does Hobbes believe all humans are equal in the state of nature? In what ways can those who are physically weaker than others compensate for their weakness? According to Hobbes, is this equality good or bad? Why?

2. What makes people enemies in the state of nature? Is it possible to avoid this enmity? Why or why not?

3. What three principal causes of warfare and conflict does Hobbes name? Explain why Hobbes lists them in a particular order. How does one lead to the others? What do these causes imply about Hobbes's idea of human nature?

4. Under what conditions can peace occur? Considering the other tenets of human nature Hobbes puts forth, would these conditions ever be feasible?

5. According to Hobbes, how do people living in civilized states "degenerate into a civil war"? Why should people avoid doing this at all costs?

6. Why does Hobbes state that justice cannot exist in the state of nature? What conditions are necessary for it to exist?

7. What feelings propel human beings to seek "peace" and, therefore, civil government?

8. Which of Hobbes's passages appeal most to logic, or logos? Which appeal most to emotion, or pathos? Which of these two modes of persuasion (p. 649) are the most important to the presentation of his argument?

MAKING CONNECTIONS

1. Does Hobbes, like Hsün Tzu (p. 84), assert that human beings are evil? Does he advocate the same kinds of solutions to improve the natural condition of humankind? Explain.

2. According to Hobbes, any government should be tolerated because any state of peace is better than a state of war. How might Martin Luther King Jr. (p. 425) or Aung San Suu Kyi (p. 442) respond to this assertion?

3. How does Hobbes's take on the state of nature compare with Darwin's view of natural selection (p. 314)? How might Darwin evaluate the condition that Hobbes fears most: a social situation in which all humans compete with all other humans for survival?

5. How does Hobbes's idea of the state of nature compare to Plato's myth of human beings in their natural state in "The Speech of Aristophanes" (p. 74)?

WRITING ABOUT THE TEXT

1. Develop your own "state of nature" theory in which you describe how, in your opinion, human beings would behave in the absence of government or civil society.

2. Write a rebuttal to Hobbes using Martin Luther King Jr.'s distinction (p. 425) between "a negative peace which is the absence of tension" and "a positive peace which is the presence of justice" as the basis for your critique.

3. Compare Hobbes's assumptions about human nature to those of Hsün Tzu (p. 84). What kinds of assumptions might more likely lead to totalitarian governments, and what kinds might more likely lead to democratic governments?

JOHN LOCKE
Of Ideas
[1690]

LIKE HIS CONTEMPORARY Thomas Hobbes, John Locke (1632–1704) lived during one of the most turbulent times in English history. A student at Oxford University in the 1650s, Locke came of age during the brief period of republican rule that occurred in England after the execution of Charles I in 1649 and before the Restoration of Charles II in 1660. Unlike Hobbes, however, Locke did not see political unrest, or even revolution, as necessarily bad things, nor did he perceive human nature as inherently self-interested and aggressive.

In his *Second Treatise on Government* (1689), Locke argued that individuals enter into a two-way contract with the state, surrendering absolute liberty in exchange for the protection of life, liberty, and the right to own property. When the state fails to uphold its end of the bargain, he believed, the people have a right to renegotiate the terms of the contract. In his own day, Locke's ideas helped lay the groundwork for the Glorious Revolution of 1688–1689, when King James II was forced from the English throne without bloodshed. Nearly a hundred years later, Locke's ideas were incorporated almost verbatim into the American Declaration of Independence.

In addition to being one of the most important political theorists of the Enlightenment, Locke was also one of the founding figures of the school of philosophy known as "empiricism," the belief that all knowledge is gained through experience. In Locke's day, as in ours, empiricism contrasted directly with "nativism," the belief that all people share certain values and perceptions as part of their human inheritance—which can come from God, as many people in Locke's day believed, or from the mechanical operation of genes, as many scientists today affirm.

The selection below is drawn from Locke's influential *Essay Concerning Human Understanding* (1690). According to this principle, the human mind begins as a blank slate (in Latin, *tabula rasa*) and acquires knowledge through experience. For Locke, all such experience is either sensation (information acquired through the senses) or reflection (information that the mind derives through its own operations). Both sensation and reflection begin at birth, and together they entirely determine human understanding. Human nature, from this perspective, is simply the sum total of human experience.

Of Ideas in general, and their Original

1. *Idea is the object of thinking.* Every man being conscious to himself that he thinks; and that which his mind is applied about whilst thinking being the ideas

that are there, it is past doubt that men have in their minds several ideas, such as are those expressed by the words *whiteness, hardness, sweetness, thinking, motion, man, elephant, army, drunkenness*, and others: it is in the first place then to be inquired, How he come by them?

I know it is a received doctrine, that men have native ideas, and original characters, stamped upon their minds in their very first being.[1] This opinion I have at large examined already; and, I suppose what I have said in the foregoing Book[2] will be much more easily admitted, when I have shown whence the understanding may get all the ideas it has; and by what ways and degrees they may come into the mind; for which I shall appeal to every one's own observation and experience.

2. *All ideas come from sensation or reflection.* Let us then suppose the mind to be, as we say, white paper,[3] void of all characters, without any ideas: How comes it to be furnished? Whence comes it by that vast store which the busy and boundless fancy of man has painted on it with an almost endless variety? Whence has it all the materials of reason and knowledge? To this I answer, in one word, from EXPERIENCE. In that all our knowledge is founded; and from that it ultimately derives itself. Our observation employed either, about external sensible objects, or about the internal operations of our minds perceived and reflected on by ourselves, is that which supplies our understandings with all the materials of thinking. These two are the fountains of knowledge, from whence all the ideas we have, or can naturally have, do spring.

3. *The objects of sensation one source of ideas.* First, our Senses, conversant about particular sensible objects, do convey into the mind several distinct perceptions of things, according to those various ways wherein those objects do affect them. And thus we come by those ideas we have of yellow, white, heat, cold, soft, hard, bitter, sweet, and all those which we call sensible qualities; which when I say the senses convey into the mind, I mean, they from external objects convey into the mind what produces there those perceptions. This great source of most of the ideas we have, depending wholly upon our senses, and derived by them to the understanding, I call SENSATION.

4. *The operations of our minds, the other source of them.* Secondly, the other fountain from which experience furnisheth the understanding with ideas is, the perception of the operations of our own mind within us, as it is employed about the ideas it has got; which operations, when the soul comes to reflect on and consider, do furnish

5

1. The "received doctrine" of nativism, the belief that all people share certain ideas and values simply because they are all human, goes back to the philosophy of Plato; in Locke's day it was most associated with the philosophy of René Descartes (1596–1650). Some version of nativism is common in most of the world's major religious traditions.

2. **Foregoing Book:** *An Essay Concerning Human Understanding* is divided into four books.

This selection is taken from the beginning of Book Two, "Of Ideas." The "foregoing book" refers to Book One, "Of Innate Notions."

3. **White paper:** Though *An Essay Concerning Human Understanding* is generally considered the source of the term *tabula rasa*, or "blank slate," Locke himself never uses either term. "White paper" is as close as he comes.

the understanding with another set of ideas, which could not be had from things without. And such are perception, thinking, doubting, believing, reasoning, knowing, willing, and all the different actings of our own minds; which we being conscious of, and observing in ourselves, do from these receive into our understandings as distinct ideas as we do from bodies affecting our senses. This source of ideas every man has wholly in himself; and though it be not sense, as having nothing to do with external objects, yet it is very like it, and might properly enough be called internal sense. But as I call the other SENSATION, so I call this REFLECTION, the ideas it affords being such only as the mind gets by reflecting on its own operations within itself. By reflection then, in the following part of this discourse, I would be understood to mean, that notice which the mind takes of its own operations, and the manner of them, by reason whereof there come to be ideas of these operations in the understanding. These two, I say, viz. external material things, as the objects of SENSATION, and the operations of our own minds within, as the objects of REFLECTION, are to me the only originals from whence all our ideas take their beginnings. The term operations here I use in a large sense, as comprehending not barely the actions of the mind about its ideas, but some sort of passions arising sometimes from them, such as is the satisfaction or uneasiness arising from any thought.

5. *All our ideas are of the one or the other of these*. The understanding seems to me not to have the least glimmering of any ideas which it doth not receive from one of these two. External objects furnish the mind with the ideas of sensible qualities, which are all those different perceptions they produce in us; and the mind furnishes the understanding with ideas of its own operations.

These, when we have taken a full survey of them, and their several modes, combinations, and relations, we shall find to contain all our whole stock of ideas; and that we have nothing in our minds which did not come in one of these two ways. Let any one examine his own thoughts, and thoroughly search into his understanding; and then let him tell me, whether all the original ideas he has there, are any other than of the objects of his senses, or of the operations of his mind, considered as objects of his reflection. And how great a mass of knowledge soever he imagines to be lodged there, he will, upon taking a strict view, see that he has not any idea in his mind but what one of these two have imprinted; though perhaps, with infinite variety compounded and enlarged by the understanding. . . .

UNDERSTANDING THE TEXT

1. What examples of "ideas" does Locke use to begin this passage? Is his list representative of the kinds of ideas that a person might have? Can you think of kinds of ideas that might not fit easily into his theory (i.e., ideas that do not appear to be based on either sensation or reflection)?

2. What does Locke present as the two subcategories of experience? Do you agree that neither of these contain innate ideas? Explain.

3. What does Locke mean by the term "sensible qualities"? How are such qualities experienced as ideas? What examples of this kind of idea does he give?

4. What kinds of "operations of our own minds" does Locke include under the heading "reflection"? Do you agree with him that these mental operations constitute a "kind of internal sense"? Explain.

5. What appeal does Locke make to the reader at the end of this passage? How does he suggest that his ideas can be empirically tested and verified?

MAKING CONNECTIONS

1. Locke and Hobbes (p. 94) are often thought of as polar opposites of Enlightenment political theory. Do the brief selections from Locke and Hobbes in this section confirm this? Why or why not?

2. Many modern scientists, including Edward O. Wilson (p. 356), reject Locke's idea of the human mind as a blank slate. The mind, they argue, has been "written on" by genes and contains innate perceptions that are common to all cultures. How do you think Locke might have responded to Wilson and others who argue for an innate, genetically determined human nature?

WRITING ABOUT THE TEXT

1. Write an essay comparing Locke's view of human nature with that of Mencius (p. 78) and Hsün Tzu (p. 84). How would Locke respond to the argument between these two ancient Confucians?

2. Refute Locke's theory that human beings are born "blank slates" with no innate ideas. Argue against it from a religious or a scientific perspective.

3. Write an essay in which you discuss the political implications of both Locke's and Hobbes's (p. 94) views of human nature. Conduct research into each author's actual political philosophies and discuss whether or not they flow logically from the brief passages in this chapter.

Two Pictures of the Brain
[1891 AND 2007]

SINCE THE DAYS of the ancient physicians Hippocrates and Galen, people have known—or at least suspected—that the brain houses all human thoughts, perceptions, and emotions. But for nearly all of human history, the way the brain works has been a complete mystery. Until the second half of the twentieth century, scientists lacked the tools to study the brain at any level of detail and, for thousands of years, "brain science," even in top universities, was a patchwork of supposition, folklore, and dubious received wisdom.

One early form of brain science was called phrenology, invented in Germany in the late eighteenth century and popular throughout Europe and America for much of the nineteenth century. Phrenologists believed that every part of the brain had a different function and that it was possible to understand a person's temperament by measuring the shape of his or her skull. Practitioners of phrenology developed elaborate brain maps, such as the one reprinted here from the 1891 reference work *How to Read Character: A New Illustrated Hand-Book of Phrenology and Physiognomy, for Students and Examiners; with a Descriptive Chart* by Samuel Wells. These charts supposedly illustrated where different characteristics originated in the brain in order to make informed judgments about a person's character.

Phrenology's fundamental assumptions have long been debunked and reputable scientists now consider it a pseudoscience. Over the last twenty years, a new, much more sophisticated science called neuroimaging has attempted to do many of the same things that the phrenologists did—with often spectacular results. One method contemporary neuroscientists use is a procedure called functional magnetic resonance imaging (fMRI), which enables them to take pictures of the brain. With these pictures, they can see which areas of the brain receive more blood flow when people are engaged in different activities, such as sleeping, reading, arguing, praying, or solving complex problems. Another type of imaging is seen in the image of a positron emission tomography (PET) scan that follows the phrenology chart. This scan allows doctors to see how a brain is functioning and if it may be suffering from a disease, like the one produced here, which contrasts a healthy brain with one suffering from depression.

Though neurological brain scans are much more accurate than phrenology charts, they raise some of the same ethical issues that were discussed in the nineteenth century. Some people argue that any attempt to reduce a human being to chemical reactions is inherently debasing, robbing people of free will and encouraging society to limit their freedom and personal choices. Others point to brain scans like the one reproduced here—which contrasts a healthy brain and one suffering from severe depression—and argue that brain-scan science has the potential to treat people suffering from a variety of mental and personality disorders.

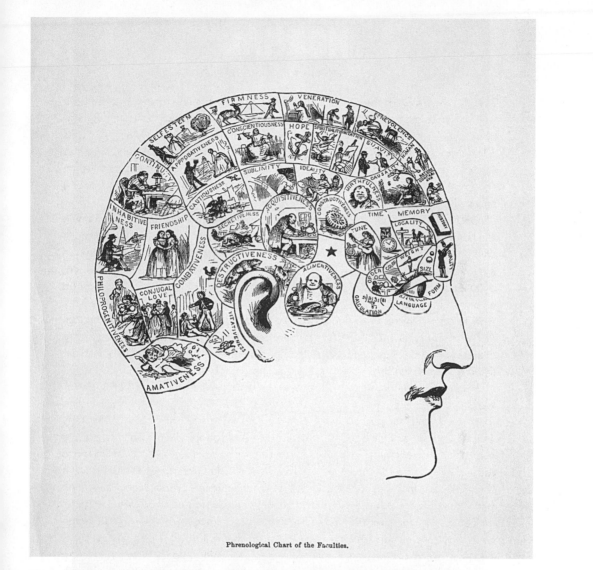

Phrenological Chart of the Faculties.

Phrenology Chart from *How to Read Character: A New Illustrated Hand-Book of Phrenology and Physiognomy for Students and Examiners, with a Descriptive Chart* by Samuel Wells, 1891. Bettman / Corbis

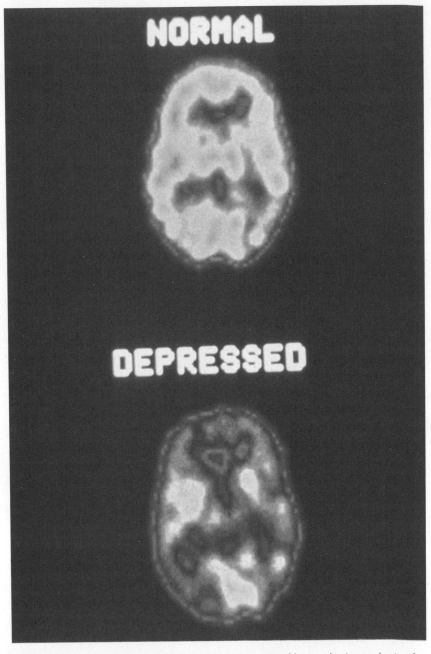

PET scan of a deoxyglucose study that compares a normal human brain to a brain of someone suffering from depression.
Science Source
See p. C-2 in the color insert for a full-color reproduction of this image.

UNDERSTANDING THE TEXT

1. How would you describe the categories of behavior in the phrenology chart? What kinds of assumptions are embedded into the categories that the chart uses for personality traits? How would changing words like "acquisitiveness" and "firmness" to "industriousness" and "stubbornness" change the meaning of the chart?

2. Why do you think that the creator of the phrenology chart drew pictures to illustrate each of the personality traits? What kinds of assumptions are contained in the pictures?

3. What assumptions are embedded in the brain-scan chart? Does the category of "depression" seem to be the same kind of character trait illustrated in the phrenology chart?

4. How might the information in either the phrenology chart or the brain scan be used to prevent certain kinds of behaviors or treat various diseases?

MAKING CONNECTIONS

1. Is there room in either the phrenology chart or the brain scan for the kind of "swerve" that Lucretius (p. 292) believes can introduce randomness in an otherwise deterministic system?

2. One of the biggest complaints about modern brain science is that it rejects free will and presents human behavior as completely mechanistic. How might a cognitive psychologist such as Daniel Kahneman (p. 134) respond to this charge?

3. Is either phrenology or brain-scan technology compatible with Locke's (p. 100) notion of the mind as a *tabula rasa*, or "blank slate"? Why or why not?

WRITING ABOUT THE TEXT

1. Write a paper examining the assumptions and value judgments behind both the phrenological chart and the brain scan. Explore the unspoken assumptions about the way that each image presents evidence and makes arguments.

2. Conduct independent research into both phrenology and brain-scan technology and write a research paper answering the question, "Is modern neuroscience a new phrenology?"

CARL JUNG
from *The Red Book*
[DATE UNKNOWN]

CARL GUSTAV JUNG (1875–1961) was a Swiss psychiatrist and early disciple of Sigmund Freud. Jung met Freud early in 1906, as he was beginning his career, and the two began a dynamic professional relationship that lasted until 1913, when Jung broke with Freud over increasingly pronounced differences in their views of the mind. Jung resigned from his position as the head of the International Psychoanalytical Association. Jung felt that Freud assigned far too much prominence to sexual conflicts in the personality development of pre-adolescent children. He also felt that Freud's view of the unconscious was too limited to explain things like dreams, visions, and religious experiences.

Jung went on to develop the psychological theory for which he is best known: the "collective unconscious." Freud saw the mind as a *tabula rasa* or "blank slate," that contained no preexisting structures, memories, or images. Jung, on the other hand, believed that the human mind retained traces of memories and images acquired by members of our species over hundreds of thousands of years and passed down through many generations. Jung first called these "primordial images," but later employed the term "archetype." Today, the term "Jungian archetype" is used to describe a pattern or image that triggers powerful associations in nearly all human minds.

For Jung archetypal images were the basis for dreams, but also for myths, religions, and literature. To understand archetypes, Jung paid special attention to the images that were common across a wide variety of cultures. Snakes, he found, represented both evil and divinity in cultures around the world. And he also found that often wise old men would help young seekers. Jung's ideas have been enormously influential in both psychology and contemporary culture. A number of the most popular books and films in history—*Star Wars, The Lord of the Rings, Harry Potter*—employ a variety of Jungian archetypes as they construct the adventures of their heroes.

The image in this chapter comes from Jung's *Liber Novus*, or "New Book," which is usually referred to as *The Red Book*. *The Red Book* consists of Jung's own elaborate calligraphy and drawings of various archetypal figures. Jung worked on *The Red Book* between 1914 and 1930, but he never submitted it for publication. After he died, his heirs kept it in a vault and allowed only a very few people to see it. It was not published until 2009, after the British scholar Sonu Shamdasani convinced the family to allow him to create a facsimile edition that would reproduce the work exactly as Jung had intended for it to be experienced.

The main figure in this image is Philemon, a character from Greek and Roman mythology (not to be confused with the recipient of Paul's *Letter to Philemon* in the New Testament), who Jung first saw in a dream in 1913 and who would become for him a symbol of wisdom and understanding as he worked out his theories of the mind. In his memoir, *Memories, Dreams, Reflections*, Jung explains his first dream of Philemon:

His figure first appeared to me in the following dream. There was a blue sky, like the sea, covered not by clouds but by flat brown clods of earth. It looked as if the clods were breaking apart and the blue water of the sea was becoming visible between them. But the water was the blue sky. Suddenly there appeared from the right a winged being sailing across the sky. . . . He held a bunch of four keys, one of which he clutched as if he were about to open a lock. He had the wings of the kingfisher with its characteristic colors. Since I did not understand this dream image, I painted it in order to impress it upon my memory.

CARL JUNG

Selection from *The Red Book*, date unknown (tempera on paper).

The Red Book by Carl G. Jung, edited by Sonu Shamdasani, translated by Mark Kyburz, John Peck, and Sonu Shamdasani. Copyright © 2009 by the Foundation of the Works of C.G. Jung. Translation © 2009 by Mark Kyburz, John Peck, and Sonu Shamdasani. Used by permission of W.W. Norton & Company, Inc. *See p. C-3 in the color insert for a full-color reproduction of this image.*

UNDERSTANDING THE TEXT

1. Why do you think that Philemon has wings? What might the "wings of the kingfisher" have represented to Jung in his dream?

2. What does the old man appear to be standing on? Why might this be significant?

3. The text in the upper left-hand corner reads, "Father of the Prophet, Beloved Philemon." What might Jung be suggesting by mixing the Judeo-Christian concept of a "prophet" with the Greek pagan character of Philemon?

4. What might the snake coiled around the tree symbolize? Why is this figure in the same image as Philemon?

5. In his initial description of his dream of Philemon, Jung describes him as holding four keys. What do you think that these keys represent? What "locks" could they be designed to open?

6. The marginal note in the upper left margin comes from the Hindu text, *The Bhagavad Gita*, and reads, "Whenever there is a decline of the law and an increase in iniquity, then I put forth myself. For the rescue of the pious and for the destruction of the evildoers, for the establishment of the law I am born in every age." How might this quotation, in which the Hindu deity Vishnu describes his decision to take on human flesh, apply to the painting?

MAKING CONNECTIONS

1. How does the view of the mind that comes through in Jung's painting compare with that found in either the phrenology or the brain-scan images (p. 104)?

2. Compare the Jungian view of archetypes in the collective unconscious with Edward O. Wilson's view of the instinctive elements of human nature (p. 356). Could the same factors be responsible for both universal behaviors and universal responses to symbols?

3. Look at the quotation from the *Bhagavad Gita* (see question #6 above) in relation to the drawing of Philemon. What might Jung be saying about law and government? How do his views compare to those incorporated into the frontispiece of Hobbes's *Leviathan* (p. 414)?

WRITING ABOUT THE TEXT

1. Write a paper comparing the two primary images in Jung's drawing: the figure of the wise old man and the figure of the snake coiled around the tree. Explain the connections or the contrasts between these two images in the same drawing.

2. Compare the image from Jung's *Red Book* with Blake's illustration of "The Tyger" from *Songs of Experience* (p. 262)? Does Blake's drawing suggest the same kind of universal archetype that Jung's painting does?

3. Conduct further research into the Jungian ideas of archetypes and the collective unconscious and use your research to explicate the images in this drawing.

RUTH BENEDICT

The Individual and the Pattern of Culture

[1934]

RUTH FULTON BENEDICT (1887–1948) was one of a key group of scholars who, in the early twentieth century, developed the discipline of cultural anthropology—a set of strategies and assumptions for studying different cultures. Benedict entered Columbia University in 1919 to study under the world-famous anthropologist Franz Boas (1858–1942). Four years later, she received a Ph.D. in anthropology and joined the faculty at Columbia, where one of her first doctoral students was Margaret Mead (1901–1978), who went on to become the best-known anthropologist of the century.

Benedict and her colleagues believed that cultures should be studied without the prejudices that most people experience when they encounter lifestyles and values different from their own. Unlike previous generations of anthropologists, who either made judgments about other cultures based on their own value systems or studied different peoples to discover "human universals" that could be applied across the spectrum of humanity, the cultural anthropologists observed other cultures impartially, evaluated them on the cultures' own terms, and described their findings without inserting their own values into the descriptions. Benedict called this approach "cultural relativism," referring to the belief that "right" and "wrong" were defined by individual cultures and could not be generalized in any fashion to all people or societies.

Benedict's first book, *Patterns of Culture*, became a national bestseller and introduced millions of Americans to anthropology. In it Benedict examines the basic assumptions of three cultures: the gentle, austere Zuñi Pueblo Indians of New Mexico; the violent, brutal Dobu tribe of New Guinea; and the highly structured, hierarchical Kwakiutl Indians of the Pacific Northwest coast, near Vancouver. After considering the practices and values of these three cultures, Benedict proposes that values are always situated within a cultural context and that a tremendous amount of what people call "human nature" must be attributed to the influence of culture.

In the selection here, the conclusion to *Patterns of Culture*, Benedict examines the relationship between the individual and his or her culture. She rejects the assumption that an inherent conflict exists between the needs of the individual and the needs of society and argues instead that individuals and society form an integrated whole, with individual personalities contributing to the fabric of a culture, and with that cultural fabric constraining the range of choices that any individual can make. Even those character traits that occur across the spectrum of human society are interpreted in very different ways by different cultures, leading to different kinds of lives for those who possess them.

Like several other writers in this chapter, Benedict builds her argument on the form of inductive reasoning known as generalization. Specifically, she examines the conventions of several historical and contemporary societies and uses her conclusions as the basis for an argument about human nature in general.

There is no proper antagonism between the role of society and that of the individual. One of the most misleading misconceptions due to this nineteenth-century dualism[1] was the idea that what was subtracted from society was added to the individual and what was subtracted from the individual was added to society. Philosophies of freedom, political creeds of *laissez faire*,[2] revolutions that have unseated dynasties, have been built on this dualism. The quarrel in anthropological theory between the importance of the culture pattern and of the individual is only a small ripple from this fundamental conception of the nature of society.

In reality, society and the individual are not antagonists. His culture provides the raw material of which the individual makes his life. If it is meagre, the individual suffers; if it is rich, the individual has the chance to rise to his opportunity. Every private interest of every man and woman is served by the enrichment of the traditional stores of his civilization. The richest musical sensitivity can operate only within the equipment and standards of its tradition. It will add, perhaps importantly, to that tradition, but its achievement remains in proportion to the instruments and musical theory which the culture has provided. In the same fashion a talent for observation expends itself in some Melanesian[3] tribe upon the negligible borders of the magico-religious field. For a realization of its potentialities it is dependent upon the development of scientific methodology, and it has no fruition unless the culture has elaborated the necessary concepts and tools.

The man in the street still thinks in terms of a necessary antagonism between society and the individual. In large measure this is because in our civilization the regulative activities of society are singled out, and we tend to identify society with the restrictions the law imposes upon us. The law lays down the number of miles per hour that I may drive an automobile. If it takes this restriction away, I am by that much the freer. This basis for a fundamental antagonism between society and the individual is naïve indeed when it is extended as a basic philosophical and political notion. Society is only incidentally and in certain situations regulative, and law is not equivalent to the social order. In the simpler homogeneous cultures collective

1. **Nineteenth-century dualism:** early anthropological theories that the rights of the individual fundamentally conflict with the needs of society.

2. ***Laissez faire:*** a French term meaning "let things alone." The economic doctrine of laissez-faire, often associated with the philosopher Adam Smith, holds that government should not interfere with the running of the economy, but

should allow economic forces to regulate themselves. In a larger political sense, a laissez-faire approach to government involves minimal laws, taxation, security procedures, and so on.

3. **Melanesian:** Melanesia refers to a group of Pacific islands north and northeast of Australia. The island of New Guinea, home to the Dobu tribe analyzed in *Patterns of Culture*, is by far the largest of these islands.

habit or custom may quite supersede the necessity for any development of formal legal authority. American Indians sometimes say: "In the old days, there were no fights about hunting grounds or fishing territories. There was no law then, so everybody did what was right." The phrasing makes it clear that in their old life they did not think of themselves as submitting to a social control imposed upon them from without. Even in our civilization the law is never more than a crude implement of society, and one it is often enough necessary to check in its arrogant career. It is never to be read off as if it were the equivalent of the social order.

Society in its full sense . . . is never an entity separable from the individuals who compose it. No individual can arrive even at the threshold of his potentialities without a culture in which he participates. Conversely, no civilization has in it any element which in the last analysis is not the contribution of an individual. Where else could any trait come from except from the behaviour of a man or a woman or a child?

It is largely because of the traditional acceptance of a conflict between society and the individual, that emphasis upon cultural behaviour is so often interpreted as a denial of the autonomy of the individual. The reading of Sumner's *Folkways*[4] usually rouses a protest at the limitations such an interpretation places upon the scope and initiative of the individual. Anthropology is often believed to be a counsel of despair which makes untenable a beneficent human illusion. But no anthropologist with a background of experience of other cultures has ever believed that individuals were automatons, mechanically carrying out the decrees of their civilization. No culture yet observed has been able to eradicate the differences in the temperaments of the persons who compose it. It is always a give-and-take. The problem of the individual is not clarified by stressing the antagonism between culture and the individual, but by stressing their mutual reinforcement. This rapport is so close that it is not possible to discuss patterns of culture without considering specifically their relation to individual psychology.

We have seen that any society selects some segment of the arc of possible human behaviour, and in so far as it achieves integration its institutions tend to further the expression of its selected segment and to inhibit opposite expressions. But these opposite expressions are the congenial responses, nevertheless, of a certain proportion of the carriers of the culture. We have already discussed the reasons for believing that this selection is primarily cultural and not biological. We cannot, therefore, even on theoretical grounds imagine that all the congenial responses of all its people will be equally served by the institutions of any culture. To understand the behaviour of the individual, it is not merely necessary to relate his personal life-history to his endowments, and to measure these against an arbitrarily selected normality. It is necessary also to relate his congenial responses to the behaviour that is singled out in the institutions of his culture.

5

4. **Sumner's** *Folkways:* William Graham Sumner (1840–1910) was an American sociologist and Yale University professor. His 1907 book, *Folkways*, describes the way that cultures construct certain absolute values and beliefs, which are woven into the patterns of everyday life so that children internalize them from a very young age.

The vast proportion of all individuals who are born into any society always and whatever the idiosyncrasies of its institutions, assume, as we have seen, the behaviour dictated by that society. This fact is always interpreted by the carriers of that culture as being due to the fact that their particular institutions reflect an ultimate and universal sanity. The actual reason is quite different. Most people are shaped to the form of their culture because of the enormous malleability of their original endowment. They are plastic to the moulding force of the society into which they are born. It does not matter whether, with the Northwest Coast, it requires delusions of self-reference, or with our own civilization the amassing of possessions. In any case the great mass of individuals take quite readily the form that is presented to them.

They do not all, however, find it equally congenial, and those are favoured and fortunate whose potentialities most nearly coincide with the type of behaviour selected by their society. Those who, in a situation in which they are frustrated, naturally seek ways of putting the occasion out of sight as expeditiously as possible are well served in Pueblo culture. Southwest institutions, as we have seen, minimize the situations in which serious frustration can arise, and when it cannot be avoided, as in death, they provide means to put it behind them with all speed.

On the other hand, those who react to frustration as to an insult and whose first thought is to get even are amply provided for on the Northwest Coast. They may extend their native reaction to situations in which their paddle breaks or their canoe overturns or to the loss of relatives by death. They rise from their first reaction of sulking to thrust back in return, to "fight" with property or with weapons. Those who can assuage despair by the act of bringing shame to others can register freely and without conflict in this society, because their proclivities are deeply channelled in their culture. In Dobu those whose first impulse is to select a victim and project their misery upon him in procedures of punishment are equally fortunate. . . .

The individuals we have so far discussed . . . illustrate the dilemma of the individual whose congenial drives are not provided for in the institutions of his culture. This dilemma becomes of psychiatric importance when the behaviour in question is regarded as categorically abnormal in a society. Western civilization tends to regard even a mild homosexual as an abnormal. The clinical picture of homosexuality stresses the neuroses and psychoses to which it gives rise, and emphasizes almost equally the inadequate functioning of the invert and his behaviour. We have only to turn to other cultures, however, to realize that homosexuals have by no means been uniformly inadequate to the social situation. They have not always failed to function. In some societies they have even been especially acclaimed. Plato's *Republic* is, of course, the most convincing statement of the honourable estate of homosexuality. It is presented as a major means to the good life, and Plato's high ethical evaluation of this response was upheld in the customary behaviour of Greece at that period.

The American Indians do not make Plato's high moral claims for homosexuality, but homosexuals are often regarded as exceptionally able. In most of North America

10

there exists the institution of the *berdache*, as the French called them. These men-women were men who at puberty or thereafter took the dress and the occupations of women. Sometimes they married other men and lived with them. Sometimes they were men with no inversion, persons of weak sexual endowment who chose this role to avoid the jeers of the women. The berdaches were never regarded as of first-rate supernatural power, as similar men-women were in Siberia, but rather as leaders in women's occupations, good healers in certain diseases, or, among certain tribes, as the genial organizers of social affairs. They were usually, in spite of the manner in which they were accepted, regarded with a certain embarrassment. It was thought slightly ridiculous to address as "she" a person who was known to be a man and who, as in Zuñi, would be buried on the men's side of the cemetery. But they were socially placed. The emphasis in most tribes was upon the fact that men who took over women's occupations excelled by reason of their strength and initiative and were therefore leaders in women's techniques and in the accumulation of those forms of property made by women. One of the best known of all the Zuñis of a generation ago was the man-woman We-wha, who was, in the words of his friend, Mrs. Stevenson, "certainly the strongest person in Zuñi, both mentally and physically." His remarkable memory for ritual made him a chief personage on ceremonial occasions, and his strength and intelligence made him a leader in all kinds of crafts.

The men-women of Zuñi are not all strong, self-reliant personages. Some of them take this refuge to protect themselves against their inability to take part in men's activities. One is almost a simpleton, and one, hardly more than a little boy, has delicate features like a girl's. There are obviously several reasons why a person becomes a berdache in Zuñi, but whatever the reason, men who have chosen openly to assume women's dress have the same chance as any other persons to establish themselves as functioning members of the society. Their response is socially recognized. If they have native ability, they can give it scope; if they are weak creatures, they fail in terms of their weakness of character, not in terms of their inversion.

The Indian institution of the berdache was most strongly developed on the plains. The Dakota had a saying "fine possessions like a berdache's," and it was the epitome of praise for any woman's household possessions. A berdache had two strings to his bow, he was supreme in women's techniques, and he could also support his *ménage*[5] by the man's activity of hunting. Therefore no one was richer. When especially fine beadwork or dressed skins were desired for ceremonial occasions, the berdache's work was sought in preference to any other's. It was his social adequacy that was stressed above all else. As in Zuñi, the attitude toward him is ambivalent and touched with malaise in the face of a recognized incongruity. Social scorn, however, was visited not upon the berdache but upon the man who lived with him. The latter was regarded as a weak man who had chosen an easy berth instead of the recognized goals of their culture; he did not contribute to the household, which was already a model for all households through the

---

5. **Ménage:** household.

sole efforts of the berdache. His sexual adjustment was not singled out in the judgment that was passed upon him, but in terms of his economic adjustment he was an outcast.

When the homosexual response is regarded as a perversion, however, the invert is immediately exposed to all the conflicts to which aberrants are always exposed. His guilt, his sense of inadequacy, his failures, are consequences of the disrepute which social tradition visits upon him; and few people can achieve a satisfactory life unsupported by the standards of the society. The adjustments that society demands of them would strain any man's vitality, and the consequences of this conflict we identify with their homosexuality.

Trance is a similar abnormality in our society. Even a very mild mystic is aberrant in Western civilization. In order to study trance or catalepsy[6] within our own social groups, we have to go to the case histories of the abnormal. Therefore the correlation between trance experience and the neurotic and psychotic seems perfect. As in the case of the homosexual, however, it is a local correlation characteristic of our century. Even in our own cultural background other eras give different results. In the Middle Ages when Catholicism made the ecstatic experience the mark of sainthood, the trance experience was greatly valued, and those to whom the response was congenial, instead of being overwhelmed by a catastrophe as in our century, were given confidence in the pursuit of their careers. It was a validation of ambitions, not a stigma of insanity. Individuals who were susceptible to trance, therefore, succeeded or failed in terms of their native capacities, but since trance experience was highly valued, a great leader was very likely to be capable of it.

Among primitive peoples, trance and catalepsy have been honoured in the extreme. Some of the Indian tribes of California accorded prestige principally to those who passed through certain trance experiences. Not all of these tribes believed that it was exclusively women who were so blessed, but among the Shasta this was the convention. Their shamans were women, and they were accorded the greatest prestige in the community. They were chosen because of their constitutional liability to trance and allied manifestations. One day the woman who was so destined, while she was about her usual work, fell suddenly to the ground. She had heard a voice speaking to her in tones of the greatest intensity. Turning, she had seen a man with drawn bow and arrow. He commanded her to sing on pain of being shot through the heart by his arrow, but under the stress of the experience she fell senseless. Her family gathered. She was lying rigidly, hardly breathing. They knew that for some time she had had dreams of a special character which indicated a shamanistic calling, dreams of escaping grizzly bears, falling off cliffs or trees, or of being surrounded by swarms of yellow-jackets. The community knew therefore what to expect. After a few hours the woman began to moan gently and to roll about upon the ground, trembling violently. She was supposed to be repeating the song which she had been told to sing and which during the trance had been taught her by the spirit. As she revived, her moaning became more

15

6. **Catalepsy:** a condition characterized by a lack of awareness of one's surroundings.

and more clearly the spirit's song until at last she called out the name of the spirit itself, and immediately blood oozed from her mouth.

When the woman had come to herself after the first encounter with her spirit, she danced that night her first initiatory shaman's dance. For three nights she danced, holding herself by a rope that was swung from the ceiling. On the third night she had to receive in her body her power from the spirit. She was dancing, and as she felt the approach of the moment she called out, "He will shoot me, he will shoot me." Her friends stood close, for when she reeled in a kind of cataleptic seizure, they had to seize her before she fell or she would die. From this time on she had in her body a visible materialization of her spirit's power, an icicle-like object which in her dances thereafter she would exhibit, producing it from one part of her body and returning it to another part. From this time on she continued to validate her supernatural power by further cataleptic demonstrations, and she was called upon in great emergencies of life and death, for curing and for divination and for counsel. She became, in other words, by this procedure a woman of great power and importance.

It is clear that, far from regarding cataleptic seizures as blots upon the family escutcheon[7] and as evidences of dreaded disease, cultural approval had seized upon them and made of them the pathway to authority over one's fellows. They were the outstanding characteristic of the most respected social type, the type which functioned with most honour and reward in the community. It was precisely the cataleptic individuals who in this culture were singled out for authority and leadership.

The possible usefulness of "abnormal" types in a social structure, provided they are types that are culturally selected by that group, is illustrated from every part of the world. The shamans of Siberia dominate their communities. According to the ideas of these peoples, they are individuals who by submission to the will of the spirits have been cured of a grievous illness—the onset of the seizures—and have acquired by this means great supernatural power and incomparable vigour and health. Some, during the period of the call, are violently insane for several years; others irresponsible to the point where they have to be constantly watched lest they wander off in the snow and freeze to death; others ill and emaciated to the point of death, sometimes with bloody sweat. It is the shamanistic practice which constitutes their cure, and the extreme exertion of a Siberian séance leaves them, they claim, rested and able to enter immediately upon a similar performance. Cataleptic seizures are regarded as an essential part of any shamanistic performance. . . .

It is clear that culture may value and make socially available even highly unstable human types. If it chooses to treat their peculiarities as the most valued variants of human behaviour, the individuals in question will rise to the occasion and perform their social roles without reference to our usual ideas of the types who can make social adjustments and those who cannot. Those who function inadequately in any society are not those with certain fixed "abnormal" traits, but may well be those

20

7. **Escutcheon:** coat of arms, here used to mean reputation.

whose responses have received no support in the institutions of their culture. The weakness of these aberrants is in great measure illusory. It springs, not from the fact that they are lacking in necessary vigour, but that they are individuals whose native responses are not reaffirmed by society. They are, as Sapir[8] phrases it, "alienated from an impossible world."

The person unsupported by the standards of his time and place and left naked to the winds of ridicule has been unforgettably drawn in European literature in the figure of Don Quixote. Cervantes turned upon a tradition still honoured in the abstract the limelight of a changed set of practical standards, and his poor old man, the orthodox upholder of the romantic chivalry of another generation, became a simpleton. The windmills with which he tilted were the serious antagonists of a hardly vanished world, but to tilt with them when the world no longer called them serious was to rave. He loved his Dulcinea in the best traditional manner of chivalry, but another version of love was fashionable for the moment, and his fervour was counted to him for madness. . . .

We have been considering individuals from the point of view of their ability to function adequately in their society. This adequate functioning is one of the ways in which normality is clinically defined. It is also defined in terms of fixed symptoms, and the tendency is to identify normality with the statistically average. In practice this average is one arrived at in the laboratory, and deviations from it are defined as abnormal.

From the point of view of a single culture this procedure is very useful. It shows the clinical picture of the civilization and gives considerable information about its socially approved behaviour. To generalize this as an absolute normal, however, is a different matter. As we have seen, the range of normality in different cultures does not coincide. Some, like Zuñi and the Kwakiutl, are so far removed from each other that they overlap only slightly. The statistically determined normal on the Northwest Coast would be far outside the extreme boundaries of abnormality in the Pueblos. The normal Kwakiutl rivalry contest would only be understood as madness in Zuñi, and the traditional Zuñi indifference to dominance and the humiliation of others would be the fatuousness of a simpleton in a man of noble family on the Northwest Coast. Aberrant behaviour in either culture could never be determined in relation to any least common denominator of behaviour. Any society, according to its major preoccupations, may increase and intensify even hysterical, epileptic, or paranoid symptoms, at the same time relying socially in a greater and greater degree upon the very individuals who display them.

This fact is important in psychiatry because it makes clear another group of abnormals which probably exists in every culture: the abnormals who represent the extreme development of the local cultural type. This group is socially in the opposite

8. **Sapir:** Edward Sapir (1884–1939) was a linguist and a close friend of Ruth Benedict. He is best known for his contribution to the Sapir-Whorf hypothesis, which claims that people's ways of understanding the world are strongly shaped by the structure of their language.

situation from the group we have discussed, those whose responses are at variance with their cultural standards. Society, instead of exposing the former group at every point, supports them in their furthest aberrations. They have a licence which they may almost endlessly exploit. For this reason these persons almost never fall within the scope of any contemporary psychiatry. They are unlikely to be described even in the most careful manuals of the generation that fosters them. Yet from the point of view of another generation or culture they are ordinarily the most bizarre of the psychopathic types of the period.

The Puritan divines of New England in the eighteenth century were the last persons whom contemporary opinion in the colonies regarded as psychopathic. Few prestige groups in any culture have been allowed such complete intellectual and emotional dictatorship as they were. They were the voice of God. Yet to a modern observer it is they, not the confused and tormented women they put to death as witches, who were the psychoneurotics of Puritan New England. A sense of guilt as extreme as they portrayed and demanded both in their own conversion experiences and in those of their converts is found in a slightly saner civilization only in institutions for mental diseases. They admitted no salvation without a conviction of sin that prostrated the victim, sometimes for years, with remorse and terrible anguish. It was the duty of the minister to put the fear of hell into the heart of even the youngest child, and to exact of every convert emotional acceptance of his damnation if God saw fit to damn him. It does not matter where we turn among the records of New England Puritan churches of this period, whether to those dealing with witches or with unsaved children not yet in their teens or with such themes as damnation and predestination, we are faced with the fact that the group of people who carried out to the greatest extreme and in the fullest honour the cultural doctrine of the moment are by the slightly altered standards of our generation the victims of intolerable aberrations. From the point of view of a comparative psychiatry they fall in the category of the abnormal.

In our own generation extreme forms of ego-gratification are culturally supported in a similar fashion. Arrogant and unbridled egoists as family men, as officers of the law and in business, have been again and again portrayed by novelists and dramatists, and they are familiar in every community. Like the behaviour of Puritan divines, their courses of action are often more asocial than those of the inmates of penitentiaries. In terms of the suffering and frustration that they spread about them there is probably no comparison. There is very possibly at least as great a degree of mental warping. Yet they are entrusted with positions of great influence and importance and are as a rule fathers of families. Their impress both upon their own children and upon the structure of our society is indelible. They are not described in our manuals of psychiatry because they are supported by every tenet of our civilization. They are sure of themselves in real life in a way that is possible only to those who are oriented to the points of the compass laid down in their own culture. Nevertheless a future psychiatry may well ransack our novels and letters and public records for illumination upon a type of abnormality to which it would not otherwise give credence. In every society it is among this very group of the culturally encouraged and fortified that some of the most extreme types of human behaviour are fostered.

Social thinking at the present time has no more important task before it than that of taking adequate account of cultural relativity. In the fields of both sociology and psychology the implications are fundamental, and modern thought about contacts of peoples and about our changing standards is greatly in need of sane and scientific direction. The sophisticated modern temper has made of social relativity, even in the small area which it has recognized, a doctrine of despair. It has pointed out its incongruity with the orthodox dreams of permanence and ideality and with the individual's illusions of autonomy. It has argued that if human experience must give up these, the nutshell of existence is empty. But to interpret our dilemma in these terms is to be guilty of an anachronism. It is only the inevitable cultural lag that makes us insist that the old must be discovered again in the new, that there is no solution but to find the old certainty and stability in the new plasticity. The recognition of cultural relativity carries with it its own values, which need not be those of the absolutist philosophies. It challenges customary opinions and causes those who have been bred to them acute discomfort. It rouses pessimism because it throws old formulae into confusion, not because it contains anything intrinsically difficult. As soon as the new opinion is embraced as customary belief, it will be another trusted bulwark of the good life. We shall arrive then at a more realistic social faith, accepting as grounds of hope and as new bases for tolerance the coexisting and equally valid patterns of life which mankind has created for itself from the raw materials of existence.

UNDERSTANDING THE TEXT

1. According to Benedict, what is the relationship between the individual and society? Should the concepts of "individual" and "society" be opposite or separate? How does the individual factor into the concept of society, and vice versa?

2. What relationship between the individual and culture does Benedict reject? Why does she believe individuals wrongly assume that their culture is against them? What does Benedict claim concerning the average person's perception of laws and authority and other instruments of culture?

3. Does Benedict argue that people are locked into a fate dictated by the boundaries of their culture? Does her interpretation of culture allow room for individuals to express themselves? Why, according to Benedict, do some people see anthropology as "a counsel of despair"? Does she agree?

4. What happens, in Benedict's analysis, to people within a culture whose natural inclinations are not valued by that culture? What kinds of people does your own culture perceive in this way?

5. How does Benedict argue by analogy throughout the selection? How does she employ examples and counterexamples to prove her thesis?

6. Why does Benedict bring up homosexuality? How have different cultures perceived homosexual relationships? How did Benedict's culture perceive such relationships?

7. What kind of people does Benedict identify as the "psychopathic types of the period"? Can you cite historical examples of people who were extremely successful in their own cultures but would be considered crazy today?

8. What does Benedict mean by "cultural relativity"? Why does she believe that it is important to view cultures through a relativistic lens?

MAKING CONNECTIONS

1. How does Benedict's view of human nature compare with other views presented in this chapter? Would she agree, for example, that the various biological factors outlined by Wilson (p. 356) are universal to the human condition?

2. How might Benedict respond to Hobbes's concept (p. 94) of a "state of nature" in which no cultural rules influenced human behavior? Is such a state possible, in Benedict's view?

3. Compare Benedict's view of culture with Margaret Mead's in "Warfare: An Invention—Not a Biological Necessity" (p. 500). What assumptions about human nature is each anthropologist working from?

4. In other chapters of *Patterns of Culture*, Benedict argues that the environment in which a culture develops strongly influences its values. She suggests, for example, that the Dobu are extremely competitive because they live in an area where food is scarce and that the Zuñi have no taboos against female adultery because their villages have traditionally had fewer women than men. How do such arguments show the influence of Darwin's principle of natural selection (p. 314)?

WRITING ABOUT THE TEXT

1. Imagine you are an anthropologist from another planet examining the "primitive" culture of Americans. Write an essay describing American values and social institutions from the perspective of such an observer.

2. How has your culture shaped you? What are some things you do, say, or believe that have directly resulted from the society you were born into? What tenets of your society have you rejected? How does your personal nature work within the standards of your society? Write an essay reflecting on these questions.

3. Write a rebuttal to Benedict's assertion that other cultures should be observed without an imposition of the observer's values. Would it be possible, or even wise, for you to view such cultural practices as slavery, cannibalism, human sacrifice, or female genital mutilation from a value-neutral perspective?

4. Compare Benedict's view of human nature to Hobbes's (p. 94) or Wilson's (p. 356). Explain what elements of a human being would be considered "natural" by one of these writers and "cultural" by Benedict.

NICHOLAS CARR
A Thing Like Me
[2010]

NICHOLAS CARR (b. 1959) is an American journalist and technology writer. After receiving degrees from Dartmouth College and Harvard University, he worked at the *Harvard Business Review*, where he became the executive editor. In 2003, he published an article in that journal entitled "IT Doesn't Matter," arguing that, once a technology becomes universal in the business world, individual businesses no longer derive any competitive advantages from using that technology (because everybody else is using it, too). This became the theme of Carr's first book, *Does IT Matter?* (2004). In his second book, *The Big Switch: Rewiring the World from Edison to Google* (2008), Carr examined the rise of internet-based cloud computing, which, Carr believes, will transform society by permitting a high level of collaboration among people who need never meet in person.

Carr's third book, *The Shallows: What the Internet Is Doing to Our Brains*, became a national bestseller in 2011 and was a finalist for the Pulitzer Prize. In *The Shallows*, Carr invoked current research on the phenomenon of neuroplasticity, the process by which our brains actually rewire themselves in order to best harness the information available in our environment. In an oral culture, for example, the brain will dedicate the bulk of its excess capacity to the long-term memory that allows people to remember the historical and scientific facts necessary for them to survive. When writing was invented, brains had to rewire themselves to master print literacy. The rise of the internet, Carr believes, will transform human cognition in similar ways, as the cognitive skills necessary to master it are different than those necessary to navigate a library and read books.

In all of his writings, Carr consistently balances enthusiasm for new technologies with warnings about their unintended social consequences. Following in the footsteps of Marshall McLuhan (1911–1980), an influential Canadian philosopher and communication theorist, he sees computing technologies as tools with the power to reshape nearly every aspect of society—a transition that involves both gains and losses to different people and groups. Though we can rarely stop new technologies from taking hold in society once they have been introduced, Carr believes that we must acknowledge, and try to compensate for, the things that any technology causes us to lose.

"A Thing Like Me" is the final chapter in *The Shallows*. In it, Carr builds on an anecdote about Friedrich Nietzsche (1844–1900) that he includes earlier in the book. In 1882, Nietzsche became unable to write by hand due to illness and purchased one of the first typewriters, the Malling-Hansen Writing Ball. Nietzsche was so impressed with the typewriter and the way that it allowed him to resume writing that he wrote an ode to it, beginning, "The writing ball is a thing like me." Carr uses this story to illustrate the way that people often merge their own personalities with the tools that allow them to extend their abilities—a process that, he believes, has already begun to happen in the Internet Age. In this section, Carr uses a similar rhetorical strategy, drawing his arguments from a striking historical narrative about human responses to a piece of technology.

It was one of the odder episodes in the history of computer science, yet also one of the more telling. Over the course of a few months in 1964 and 1965, Joseph Weizenbaum, a forty-one-year-old computer scientist at the Massachusetts Institute of Technology, wrote a software application for parsing written language, which he programmed to run on the university's new time-sharing system. A student, sitting at one of the system's terminals, would type a sentence into the computer, and Weizenbaum's program, following a set of simple rules about English grammar, would identify a salient word or phrase in the sentence and analyze the syntactical context in which it was used. The program would then, following another set of rules, transform the sentence into a new sentence that had the appearance of being a response to the original. The computer-generated sentence would appear almost instantly on the student's terminal, giving the illusion of a conversation.

In a January 1966 paper introducing his program, Weizenbaum provided an example of how it worked. If a person typed the sentence "I am very unhappy these days," the computer would need only know that the phrase "I am" typically comes before a description of the speaker's current situation or state of mind. The computer could then recast the sentence into the reply "How long have you been very unhappy these days?" The program worked, Weizenbaum explained, by first applying "a kind of template to the original sentence, one part of which matched the two words 'I am' and the remainder [of which] isolated the words 'very unhappy these days.'" It then used an algorithmic "reassembly kit," tailored to the template, that included a rule specifying that "any sentence of the form 'I am BLAH'" should be "transformed to 'How long have you been BLAH,' independently of the meaning of BLAH."

Weizenbaum's application was a product of its time. During the 1950s and '60s, the enthusiasm for computers, software programming, and artificial intelligence gave rise not only to the idea that the human brain is a type of computer but to the sense that human language is the output of one of the algorithms running inside that computer. As David Golumbia explains in *The Cultural Logic of Computation*, a new breed of "computational linguists," led by Weizenbaum's MIT colleague Noam Chomsky, posited that the form of the "natural language" that people speak and write reflects "the operation of the computer inside the human mind that performs all linguistic operations." In a 1958 article in the journal *Information and Control*, Chomsky had written that "one possible method for describing a grammar is in terms of a program for a universal Turing machine. What made the computationalist theory so compelling was that it came wrapped in a seductive "penumbra of technological newness," writes Golumbia. It offered a "mechanic clarity," replacing language's human "messiness" with "a clean internal computer." By reverse-engineering the way people talk, you could discover language's underlying code, which you could then replicate as software.

Weizenbaum named his program ELIZA, after Eliza Doolittle, the cockney flower girl who, in George Bernard Shaw's *Pygmalion*, learns to speak proper English under the tutelage of the haughty phonetics professor Henry Higgins. To make the simulated conversations a little more interesting, Weizenbaum also gave his artificial interlocutor a persona—that of a Rogerian psychotherapist.[1] The choice, as he explained in his paper, was a pragmatic one. Using a technique developed by the psychologist Carl Rogers in the 1940s, Rogerian therapists pretended, in their conversations with patients, to have no understanding of the world. For the most part, they simply parroted their patients' statements back to them in the form of banal, open-ended questions or comments. Knowing that the naïveté was a pose, the patients were free to attribute to their therapists "all sorts of background knowledge, insights and reasoning ability." The Rogerian persona, Weizenbaum recognized, had "a crucial psychological utility" for ELIZA: it suggested that the program's vacuity masked some sort of real intelligence.

Weizenbaum provided a transcript of part of an exchange between ELIZA and a   5
young woman who had been an early tester of the program (the machine's responses are in italic type):

> Men are all alike.
> *In what way?*
> They're always bugging us about something or other.
> *Can you think of a specific example?*
> Well, my boyfriend made me come here.
> *Your boyfriend made you come here.*
> He says I'm depressed much of the time.
> *I am sorry to hear you are depressed.*
> It's true. I am unhappy.
> *Do you think coming here will help you to be not unhappy?*
> I need some help, that much seems certain.
> *What would it mean to you if you got some help?*
> Perhaps I could learn to get along with my mother.
> *Tell me more about your family.*
> My mother takes care of me.
> *Who else in your family takes care of you?*
> My father.

1. **Carl Rogers:** American psychologist (1902–1987) who was influential in developing the counseling strategy of asking open-ended questions and encouraging patients to reflect on their own answers.

Your father.
You are like my father in some ways.
What resemblance do you see?
You are not very aggressive but I think you don't want me to notice that.
What makes you think I am not very aggressive?
You don't argue with me.
Why do you think I don't argue with you?
You are afraid of me.
Does it please you to believe I am afraid of you?
My father is afraid of everybody.

In commenting on his creation, which he acknowledged to be a modest and even slightly silly contribution to the fledgling field of natural-language processing, Weizenbaum observed how easy it is for computer programmers to make machines "behave in wondrous ways, often sufficient to dazzle even the most experienced observer." But as soon as a program's "inner workings are explained in language sufficiently plain to induce understanding," he continued, "its magic crumbles away; it stands revealed as a mere collection of procedures, each quite comprehensible. The observer says to himself 'I could have written that.'" The program goes "from the shelf marked 'intelligent' to that reserved for curios."

But Weizenbaum, like Henry Higgins, was soon to have his equilibrium disturbed. ELIZA quickly found fame on the MIT campus, becoming a mainstay of lectures and presentations about computing and time-sharing. It was among the first software programs able to demonstrate the power and speed of computers in a way that laymen could easily grasp. You didn't need a background in mathematics, much less computer science, to chat with ELIZA. Copies of the program proliferated at other schools as well. Then the press took notice, and ELIZA became, as Weizenbaum later put it, "a national plaything." While he was surprised by the public's interest in his program, what shocked him was how quickly and deeply people using the software "became emotionally involved with the computer," talking to it as if it were an actual person. They "would, after conversing with it for a time, insist, in spite of my explanations, that the machine really understood them." Even his secretary, who had watched him write the code for ELIZA "and surely knew it to be merely a computer program," was seduced. After a few moments using the software at a terminal in Weizenbaum's office, she asked the professor to leave the room because she was embarrassed by the intimacy of the conversation. "What I had not realized," said Weizenbaum, "is that extremely short exposures to a relatively simple computer program could induce powerful delusional thinking in quite normal people."

Things were about to get stranger still. Distinguished psychiatrists and scientists began to suggest, with considerable enthusiasm, that the program could play a valuable role in actually treating the ill and the disturbed. In an article in the *Journal of Nervous and Mental Disease*, three prominent research psychiatrists wrote that ELIZA, with a bit of tweaking, could be "a therapeutic tool which can be made widely available to mental hospitals and psychiatric centers suffering a shortage of therapists." Thanks to the "time-sharing capabilities of modern and future computers, several hundred patients an hour could be handled by a computer system designed for this purpose." Writing in *Natural History*, the prominent astrophysicist Carl Sagan expressed equal excitement about ELIZA's potential. He foresaw the development of "a network of computer therapeutic terminals, something like arrays of large telephone booths, in which, for a few dollars a session, we would be able to talk with an attentive, tested, and largely non-directive psychotherapist."

In his paper "Computing Machinery and Intelligence," Alan Turing[2] had grappled with the question "Can machines think?" He proposed a simple experiment for judging whether a computer could be said to be intelligent, which he called "the imitation game" but which soon came to be known as the Turing test. It involved having a person, the "interrogator," sit at a computer terminal in an otherwise empty room and engage in a typed conversation with two other people, one an actual person and the other a computer pretending to be a person. If the interrogator was unable to distinguish the computer from the real person, then the computer, argued Turing, could be considered intelligent. The ability to conjure a plausible self out of words would signal the arrival of a true thinking machine.

To converse with ELIZA was to engage in a variation on the Turing test. But, as 10 Weizenbaum was astonished to discover, the people who "talked" with his program had little interest in making rational, objective judgments about the identity of ELIZA. They *wanted* to believe that ELIZA was a thinking machine. They *wanted* to imbue ELIZA with human qualities—even when they were well aware that ELIZA was nothing more than a computer program following simple and rather obvious instructions. The Turing test, it turned out, was as much a test of the way human beings think as of the way machines think. In their *Journal of Nervous and Mental Disease* article, the three psychiatrists hadn't just suggested that ELIZA could serve as a substitute for a real therapist They went on to argue, in circular fashion, that a psychotherapist was in essence a kind of computer: "A human therapist can be viewed as an information processor and decision maker with a set of decision rules which are closely linked to short-range and long-range goals." In simulating a human being, however clumsily, ELIZA encouraged human beings to think of themselves as simulations of computers.

The reaction to the software unnerved Weizenbaum. It planted in his mind a question he had never before asked himself but that would preoccupy him for many years: "What is it about the computer that has brought the view of man as a machine to a new level of plausibility?" In 1976, a decade after ELIZA's debut, he provided

---

2. **Alan Turing:** British mathematician and cryptologist (1912–1954) who was an influential pioneer in computer science.

an answer in his book *Computer Power and Human Reason*. To understand the effects of a computer, he argued, you had to see the machine in the context of mankind's past intellectual technologies, the long succession of tools that, like the map and the clock, transformed nature and altered "man's perception of reality." Such technologies become part of "the very stuff out of which man builds his world." Once adopted, they can never be abandoned, at least not without plunging society into "great confusion and possibly utter chaos." An intellectual technology, he wrote, "becomes an indispensable component of any structure once it is so thoroughly integrated with the structure, so enmeshed in various vital substructures, that it can no longer be factored out without fatally impairing the whole structure."

That fact, almost "a tautology," helps explain how our dependence on digital computers grew steadily and seemingly inexorably after the machines were invented at the end of the Second World War. "The computer was not a prerequisite to the survival of modern society in the post-war period and beyond," Weizenbaum argued; "its enthusiastic, uncritical embrace by the most 'progressive' elements of American government, business, and industry made it a resource essential to society's survival *in the form* that the computer itself had been instrumental in shaping." He knew from his experience with time-sharing networks that the role of computers would expand beyond the automation of governmental and industrial processes. Computers would come to mediate the activities that define people's everyday lives—how they learn, how they think, how they socialize. What the history of intellectual technologies shows us, he warned, is that "the introduction of computers into some complex human activities may constitute an irreversible commitment." Our intellectual and social lives may, like our industrial routines, come to reflect the form that the computer imposes on them.

What makes us most human, Weizenbaum had come to believe, is what is least computable about us—the connections between our mind and our body, the experiences that shape our memory and our thinking, our capacity for emotion and empathy. The great danger we face as we become more intimately involved with our computers—as we come to experience more of our lives through the disembodied symbols flickering across our screens—is that we'll begin to lose our humanness, to sacrifice the very qualities that separate us from machines. The only way to avoid that fate, Weizenbaum wrote, is to have the self-awareness and the courage to refuse to delegate to computers the most human of our mental activities and intellectual pursuits, particularly "tasks that demand wisdom."

In addition to being a learned treatise on the workings of computers and software, Weizenbaum's book was a cri de coeur,[3] a computer programmer's passionate and at times self-righteous examination of the limits of his profession. The book did not endear the author to his peers. After it came out, Weizenbaum was spurned as a heretic by leading computer scientists, particularly those pursuing artificial intelligence. John McCarthy, one of the organizers of the original Dartmouth AI conference, spoke

---

3. **Cri de coeur:** a cry from the heart.

for many technologists when, in a mocking review, he dismissed *Computer Power and Human Reason* as "an unreasonable book" and scolded Weizenbaum for unscientific "moralizing." Outside the data-processing field, the book caused only a brief stir. It appeared just as the first personal computers were making the leap from hobbyists' workbenches to mass production. The public, primed for the start of a buying spree that would put computers into most every office, home, and school in the land, was in no mood to entertain an apostate's doubts.

When a carpenter picks up a hammer, the hammer becomes, so far as his brain is   15
concerned, part of his hand. When a soldier raises a pair of binoculars to his face, his brain sees through a new set of eyes, adapting instantaneously to a very different field of view. The experiments on pliers-wielding monkeys revealed how readily the plastic primate brain can incorporate tools into its sensory maps, making the artificial feel natural. In the human brain, that capacity has advanced far beyond what's seen in even our closest primate cousins. Our ability to meld with all manner of tools is one of the qualities that most distinguishes us as a species. In combination with our superior cognitive skills, it's what makes us so good at using new technologies. It's also what makes us so good at inventing them. Our brains can imagine the mechanics and the benefits of using a new device before that device even exists. The evolution of our extraordinary mental capacity to blur the boundary between the internal and the external, the body and the instrument, was, says University of Oregon neuroscientist Scott Frey, "no doubt a fundamental step in the development of technology."

The tight bonds we form with our tools go both ways. Even as our technologies become extensions of ourselves, we become extensions of our technologies. When the carpenter takes his hammer into his hand, he can use that hand to do only what a hammer can do. The hand becomes an implement for pounding and pulling nails. When the soldier puts the binoculars to his eyes, he can see only what the lenses allow him to see. His field of view lengthens, but he becomes blind to what's nearby. Nietzsche's experience with his typewriter provides a particularly good illustration of the way technologies exert their influence on us. Not only did the philosopher come to imagine that his writing ball was "a thing like me"; he also sensed that he was becoming a thing like it, that his typewriter was shaping his thoughts. T. S. Eliot had a similar experience when he went from writing his poems and essays by hand to typing them. "Composing on the typewriter," he wrote in a 1916 letter to Conrad Aiken, "I find that I am sloughing off all my long sentences which I used to dote upon. Short, staccato, like modern French prose. The typewriter makes for lucidity, but I am not sure that it encourages subtlety."

Every tool imposes limitations even as it opens possibilities. The more we use it, the more we mold ourselves to its form and function. That explains why, after working with a word processor for a time, I began to lose my facility for writing and editing in longhand. My experience, I later learned, was not uncommon. "People who write on a computer are often at a loss when they have to write by hand," Norman Doidge reports. Their ability "to translate thoughts into cursive writing" diminishes as they become used to tapping keys and watching letters appear as if by magic on a screen." Today, with kids using keyboards and keypads from a very young age and schools discontinuing penmanship lessons, there is mounting evidence that the ability to write in cursive script is disappearing altogether from our culture. It's becoming a lost art. "We shape our tools," observed the Jesuit priest and media scholar John Culkin in 1967, "and thereafter they shape us."

Marshall McLuhan,[4] who was Culkin's intellectual mentor, elucidated the ways our technologies at once strengthen and sap us. In one of the most perceptive, if least remarked, passages in *Understanding Media*, McLuhan wrote that our tools end up "numbing" whatever part of our body they "amplify." When we extend some part of ourselves artificially, we also distance ourselves from the amplified part and its natural functions. When the power loom was invented, weavers could manufacture far more cloth during the course of a workday than they'd been able to make by hand, but they sacrificed some of their manual dexterity, not to mention some of their "feel" for fabric. Their fingers, in McLuhan's terms, became numb. Farmers, similarly, lost some of their feel for the soil when they began using mechanical harrows and plows. Today's industrial farm worker, sitting in his air-conditioned cage atop a gargantuan tractor, rarely touches the soil at all—though in a single day he can till a field that his hoe-wielding forebear could not have turned in a month. When we're behind the wheel of our car, we can go a far greater distance than we could cover on foot, but we lose the walker's intimate connection to the land.

As McLuhan acknowledged, he was far from the first to observe technology's numbing effect. It's an ancient idea, one that was given perhaps its most eloquent and ominous expression by the Old Testament psalmist:

> Their idols are silver and gold,
> The work of men's hands.
> They have mouths, but they speak not;
> Eyes have they, but they see not;
> They have ears, but they hear not:
> Noses have they, but they smell not;
> They have hands, but they handle not;
> Feet have they, but they walk not;
> Neither speak they through their throat.
> They that make them are like unto them;
> So is every one that trusteth in them.[5]

4. **Marshall McLuhan:** Influential Canadian philosopher and communication theorist (1911–1980).

5. **Psalms 115:** 4–8 (King James Version of the Bible)

The price we pay to assume technology's power is alienation. The toll can be par-   20
ticularly high with our intellectual technologies. The tools of the mind amplify and
in turn numb the most intimate, the most human, of our natural capacities—those
for reason, perception, memory, emotion. The mechanical clock, for all the blessings it bestowed, removed us from the natural flow of time. When Lewis Mumford
described how modern clocks helped "create the belief in an independent world of
mathematically measurable sequences," he also stressed that, as a consequence, clocks
"disassociated time from human events."[6] Weizenbaum, building on Mumford's point,
argued that the conception of the world that emerged from timekeeping instruments
"was and remains an impoverished version of the older one, for it rests on a rejection
of those direct experiences that formed the basis for, and indeed constituted, the old
reality." In deciding when to eat, to work, to sleep, to wake up, we stopped listening
to our senses and started obeying the clock. We became a lot more scientific, but we
became a bit more mechanical as well.

Even a tool as seemingly simple and benign as the map had a numbing effect.
Our ancestors' navigational skills were amplified enormously by the cartographer's
art. For the first time, people could confidently traverse lands and seas they'd never
seen before—an advance that spurred a history-making expansion of exploration,
trade, and warfare. But their native ability to comprehend a landscape, to create a
richly detailed mental map of their surroundings, weakened. The map's abstract,
two-dimensional representation of space interposed itself between the map reader
and his perception of the actual land. As we can infer from recent studies of the
brain, the loss must have had a physical component. When people came to rely on
maps rather than their own bearings, they would have experienced a diminishment
of the area of their hippocampus devoted to spatial representation. The numbing
would have occurred deep in their neurons.

We're likely going through another such adaptation today as we come to depend on
computerized GPS devices to shepherd us around. Eleanor Maguire, the neuroscientist
who led the study of the brains of London taxi drivers, worries that satellite navigation
could have "a big effect" on cabbies' neurons. "We very much hope they don't start
using it," she says, speaking on behalf of her team of researchers. "We believe [the hip-
pocampal] area of the brain increased in grey matter volume because of the huge amount
of data [the drivers] have to memorize. If they all start using GPS, that knowledge base
will be less and possibly affect the brain changes we are seeing." The cabbies would
be freed from the hard work of learning the city's roads, but they would also lose the
distinctive mental benefits of that training. Their brains would become less interesting.

In explaining how technologies numb the very faculties they amplify, to the point
even of "autoamputation," McLuhan was not trying to romanticize society as it existed

6. **Lewis Mumford:** American historian and philosopher (1895–1990) whose influential book *Tech-
nics and Civilization* (1934) discusses the ways that clocks and other inventions shaped the way that
people thought about themselves.

before the invention of maps or clocks or power looms. Alienation, he understood, is an inevitable by-product of the use of technology. Whenever we use a tool to exert greater control over the outside world, we change our relationship with that world. Control can be wielded only from a psychological distance. In some cases, alienation is precisely what gives a tool its value. We build houses and sew Gore-Tex jackets because we *want* to be alienated from the wind and the rain and the cold. We build public sewers because we *want* to maintain a healthy distance from our own filth. Nature isn't our enemy, but neither is it our friend. McLuhan's point was that an honest appraisal of any new technology, or of progress in general, requires a sensitivity to what's lost as well as what's gained. We shouldn't allow the glories of technology to blind our inner watchdog to the possibility that we've numbed an essential part of our self.

UNDERSTANDING THE TEXT

1. What point is Carr making with the story about Joseph Weizenbaum and the ELIZA computer program? What do the reactions that people had to ELIZA suggest about human nature?

2. Why does Carr believe that people attributed special intelligence to a program that asked seemingly unintelligent questions?

3. What is a "Turing Test"? How well do you think a program like ELIZA would do in such a test under experimental conditions?

4. What other technologies does Carr point out as examples of tools that changed the way human beings think and perceive themselves? Why does he think that the computer will bring about the same kinds of changes?

5. How does Carr believe that tools shape human cognition and behavior? What kinds of limitations do tools impose as a consequence of the limitations they remove?

6. How does Carr's quotation from Psalms 115 support his argument? What "technology" is discussed in this biblical poem?

7. Why, according to Carr, do researchers think it would be a bad thing for taxi drivers to use GPS devices?

MAKING CONNECTIONS

1. Does Carr have a view of the brain that is similar to John Locke's view in "Of Ideas" (p. 100)? Is "neuroplasticity" the same thing as a "blank slate"?

2. Can you relate Carr's view of technology use to Margaret Mead's view (p. 500) that war is a human invention and not an innate part of human psychology? In what way might war be a tool in the same way that the internet is a tool?

3. In what ways do Zeynep Tufekci's views of the role of social networking (p. 225) confirm Carr's predictions? In what ways might they fail to do so? How does the tool of social networking alter the way we understand ourselves and our relationships to others?

WRITING ABOUT THE TEXT

1. Think of an important tool or invention that Carr does not mention in this selection and write a paper about how it has shaped human behavior and cognition.

2. Examine the technologies that you use in your everyday life and compare them to the technologies of your parents and grandparents. Show how different technological tools create different assumptions about the proper way to live.

3. Write a paper comparing the "nature v. nurture" assumptions in the selections by Carr, Benedict (p. 500), and Wilson (p. 356). To what degree does each thinker believe that environment affects human psychology?

DANIEL KAHNEMAN
from *Thinking, Fast and Slow*
[2011]

DANIEL KAHNEMAN (b. 1934) is an Israeli-American psychologist and professor emeritus at Princeton University. Kahneman was born in Tel Aviv in 1934 and grew up in Paris. During the Nazi occupation of France (1940–1944), he and his family lived in constant fear of persecution because of their Jewish identity. When the war ended, they immigrated to the newly created nation of Israel. Kahneman received a bachelor's degree from the Hebrew University of Jerusalem in 1954, and in 1958 moved to the United States to pursue a Ph.D. in psychology from the University of California at Berkeley. He has held positions at a number of universities, including Hebrew University, the University of British Columbia, and the University of California at Berkeley before moving to Princeton in 1993.

Though a psychologist, Kahneman was awarded the Nobel Memorial Prize in Economics in 2002 for his theories about the way people make decisions in uncertain conditions. Kahneman's work demonstrated the flaws in traditional economic theories that assume consumers will always act rationally. The human mind, Kahneman argued, contains a number of built-in irrational biases that prevent us from acting like the rational consumers that our traditional economic theories assume us to be.

In 2011, Kahneman compiled the results of much of his life's academic work into a book aimed at general readers, *Thinking, Fast and Slow*, which became a bestseller. The book's overall argument is that the human mind has two different systems for processing information. The first system is fast, effortless, instinctive, emotional, and largely subconscious. The second system is slow, logical, difficult, plodding, and the product of conscious effort. According to Kahneman, we are unable to avoid certain cognitive biases because so much of our thinking happens automatically in ways that do not activate the logical centers of our brain.

The following example comes from the first chapter of *Thinking, Fast and Slow*. Here, Kahneman introduces the two cognitive systems, which are the centerpieces of his book, as though they were characters in a play. Rather than simply explaining the two systems, he uses a series of images and puzzles to activate both systems in the minds of his readers: a picture of a scowling woman, for example, immediately activates our System 1 mechanism for judging people's moods, while a math problem that we cannot solve quickly forces us to move into System 2 and begin the slower work of figuring it out. These images and problems become rhetorically powerful as they allow the reader to engage firsthand with the two systems he describes.

To observe your mind in automatic mode, glance at the image below.

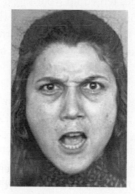

Figure 1

Your experience as you look at the woman's face seamlessly combines what we normally call seeing and intuitive thinking. As surely and quickly as you saw that the young woman's hair is dark, you knew she is angry. Furthermore, what you saw extended into the future. You sensed that this woman is about to say some very unkind words, probably in a loud and strident voice. A premonition of what she was going to do next came to mind automatically and effortlessly. You did not intend to assess her mood or to anticipate what she might do, and your reaction to the picture did not have the feel of something you did. It just happened to you. It was an instance of fast thinking.

Now look at the following problem:

$$17 \times 24$$

You knew immediately that this is a multiplication problem, and probably knew that you could solve it, with paper and pencil, if not without. You also had some vague intuitive knowledge of the range of possible results. You would be quick to recognize that both 12,609 and 123 are implausible. Without spending some time on the problem, however, you would not be certain that the answer is not 568. A precise solution did not come to mind, and you felt that you could choose whether or not to engage in the computation. If you have not done so yet, you should attempt the multiplication problem now, completing at least part of it.

You experienced slow thinking as you proceeded through a sequence of steps. You first retrieved from memory the cognitive program for multiplication that you learned in school, then you implemented it. Carrying out the computation was a strain. You felt the burden of holding much material in memory, as you needed to keep track of where you were and of where you were going, while holding on to the intermediate result. The process was mental work: deliberate, effortful, and orderly—a prototype

5

of slow thinking. The computation was not only an event in your mind; your body was also involved. Your muscles tensed up, your blood pressure rose, and your heart rate increased. Someone looking closely at your eyes while you tackled this problem would have seen your pupils dilate. Your pupils contracted back to normal size as soon as you ended your work—when you found the answer (which is 408, by the way) or when you gave up.

TWO SYSTEMS

Psychologists have been intensely interested for several decades in the two modes of thinking evoked by the picture of the angry woman and by the multiplication problem, and have offered many labels for them. I adopt terms originally proposed by the psychologists Keith Stanovich and Richard West, and will refer to two systems in the mind, System 1 and System 2.

- *System 1* operates automatically and quickly, with little or no effort and no sense of voluntary control.
- *System 2* allocates attention to the effortful mental activities that demand it, including complex computations. The operations of System 2 are often associated with the subjective experience of agency, choice, and concentration.

The labels of System 1 and System 2 are widely used in psychology, but I go further than most.in this book, which you can read as a psychodrama with two characters.

When we think of ourselves, we identify with System 2, the conscious, reasoning self that has beliefs, makes choices, and decides what to think about and what to do. Although System 2 believes itself to be where the action is, the automatic System 1 is the hero of the book. I describe System 1 as effortlessly originating impressions and feelings that are the main sources of the explicit beliefs and deliberate choices of System 2. The automatic operations of System 1 generate surprisingly complex patterns of ideas, but only the slower System 2 can construct thoughts in an orderly series of steps. I also describe circumstances in which System 2 takes over, overruling the freewheeling impulses and associations of System 1. You will be invited to think of the two systems as agents with their individual abilities, limitations, and functions.

In rough order of complexity, here are some examples of the automatic activities that are attributed lo System I:

- Detect that one object is more distant than another.
- Orient to the source of a sudden sound.
- Complete the phrase "bread and . . ."
- Make a "disgust face" when shown a horrible picture.
- Detect hostility in a voice.

- Answer to 2 + 2 = ?
- Read words on large billboards.
- Drive a car on an empty road.
- Find a strong move in chess (if you are a chess master).
- Understand simple sentences.
- Recognize that a "meek and tidy soul with a passion for detail" resembles an occupational stereotype.

All these mental events belong with the angry woman—they occur automatically and require little or no effort. The capabilities of System 1 include innate skills that we share with other animals. We are born prepared to perceive the world around us, recognize objects, orient attention, avoid losses, and fear spiders. Other mental activities become fast and automatic through prolonged practice. System 1 has learned associations between ideas (the capital of France?); it has also learned skills such as reading and understanding nuances of social situations. Some skills, such as finding strong chess moves, are acquired only by specialized experts. Others are widely shared. Detecting the similarity of a personality sketch to an occupational stereotype requires broad knowledge of the language and the culture, which most of us possess. The knowledge is stored in memory and accessed without intention and without effort.

Several of the mental actions in the list are completely involuntary. You cannot refrain from understanding simple sentences in your own language or from orienting to a loud unexpected sound, nor can you prevent yourself from knowing that 2 + 2 = 4 or from thinking of Paris when the capital of France is mentioned. Other activities, such as chewing, are susceptible to voluntary control but normally run on automatic pilot. The control of attention is shared by the two systems. Orienting to a loud sound is normally an involuntary operation of System 1, which immediately mobilizes the voluntary attention of System 2. You may be able to resist turning toward the source of a loud and offensive comment at a crowded party, but even if your head does not move, your attention is initially directed to it, at least for a while. However, attention can be moved away from an unwanted focus, primarily by focusing intently on another target.

The highly diverse operations of System 2 have one feature in common: they require attention and are disrupted when attention is drawn away. Here are some examples:

- Brace for the starter gun in a race.
- Focus attention on the clowns in the circus.
- Focus on the voice of a particular person in a crowded and noisy room.
- Look for a woman with white hair.
- Search memory to identify a surprising sound.
- Maintain a faster walking speed than is natural for you.

- Monitor the appropriateness of your behavior in a social situation.
- Count the occurrences of the letter *a* in a page of text.
- Tell someone your phone number.
- Park in a narrow space (for most people except garage attendants).
- Compare two washing machines for overall value.
- Fill out a tax form.
- Check the validity of a complex logical argument.

In all these situations you must pay attention, and you will perform less well, or not at all, if you are not ready or if your attention is directed inappropriately. System 2 has some ability to change the way System 1 works, by programming the normally automatic functions of attention and memory. When waiting for a relative at a busy train station, for example, you can set yourself at will to look for a white-haired woman or a bearded man, and thereby increase the likelihood of detecting your relative from a distance. You can set your memory to search for capital cities that start with N or for French existentialist novels. And when you rent a car at London's Heathrow Airport, the attendant will probably remind you that "we drive on the left side of the road over here." In all these cases, you are asked to do something that does not come naturally, and you will find that the consistent maintenance of a set requires continuous exertion of at least some effort.

The often-used phrase "pay attention" is apt: you dispose of a limited budget of attention that you can allocate to activities, and if you try to go beyond your budget, you will fail. It is the mark of effortful activities that they interfere with each other, which is why it is difficult or impossible to conduct several at once. You could not compute the product of 17×24 while making a left turn into dense traffic, and you certainly should not try. You can do several things at once, but only if they are easy and undemanding. You are probably safe carrying on a conversation with a passenger while driving on an empty highway, and many parents have discovered, perhaps with some guilt, that they can read a story to a child while thinking of something else.

Everyone has some awareness of the limited capacity of attention, and our social behavior makes allowances for these limitations. When the driver of a car is overtaking a truck on a narrow road, for example, adult passengers quite sensibly stop talking. They know that distracting the driver is not a good idea, and they also suspect that he is temporarily deaf and will not hear what they say.

Intense focusing on a task can make people effectively blind, even to stimuli that normally attract attention. The most dramatic demonstration was offered by Christopher Chabris and Daniel Simons in their book *The Invisible Gorilla*. They constructed a short film of two teams passing basketballs, one team wearing white shirts, the other wearing black. The viewers of the film are instructed to count the number of passes made by the white team, ignoring the black players. This task is difficult and completely absorbing. Halfway through the video, a woman wearing a   15 gorilla suit appears, crosses the court, thumps her chest, and moves on. The gorilla is in view for 9 seconds. Many thousands of people have seen the video, and about half of them do not notice anything unusual. It is the counting task—and especially the instruction to ignore one of the teams—that causes the blindness. No one who watches the video without that task would miss the gorilla. Seeing and orienting are automatic functions of System 1, but they depend on the allocation of some attention to the relevant stimulus. The authors note that the most remarkable observation of their study is that people find its results very surprising. Indeed, the viewers who fail to see the gorilla are initially sure that it was not there—they cannot imagine missing such a striking event. The gorilla study illustrates two important facts about our minds: we can be blind to the obvious, and we are also blind to our blindness.

Plot Synopsis

The interaction of the two systems is a recurrent theme of the book, and a brief synopsis of the plot is in order. In the story I will tell, Systems 1 and 2 are both active whenever we are awake. System 1 runs automatically and System 2 is normally in a comfortable low-effort mode, in which only a fraction of its capacity is engaged. System 1 continuously generates suggestions for System 2: impressions, intuitions, intentions, and feelings. If endorsed by System 2, impressions and intuitions turn into beliefs, and impulses turn into voluntary actions. When all goes smoothly, which is most of the time, System 2 adopts the suggestions of System 1 with little or no modification. You generally believe your impressions and act on your desires, and that is fine—usually.

When System 1 runs into difficulty, it calls on System 2 to support more detailed and specific processing that may solve the problem of the moment. System 2 is mobilized when a question arises for which System 1 does not offer an answer, as probably happened to you when you encountered the multiplication problem 17 × 24. You can also feel a surge of conscious attention whenever you are surprised. System 2 is activated when an event is detected that violates the model of the world that System 1 maintains. In that world, lamps do not jump, cats do not bark, and gorillas do not cross basketball courts. The gorilla experiment demonstrates that some attention is needed for the surprising stimulus to be detected. Surprise then activates and orients your attention: you will stare, and you will search your memory for a story that makes sense of the surprising event. System 2 is also credited with the continuous monitoring of your own behavior—the control that keeps you polite when you are angry, and alert when you are driving at night. System 2 is mobilized to increased effort when it detects an error about to be made. Remember a time when you almost blurted out an offensive remark and note how hard you worked to restore control. In summary, most of what you (your System 2) think and do originates in your System 1, but System 2 takes over when things get difficult, and it normally has the last word.

The division of labor between System 1 and System 2 is highly efficient: it minimizes effort and optimizes performance. The arrangement works well most of the time because System 1 is generally very good at what it does: its models of familiar situations are accurate, its short-term predictions are usually accurate as well, and its initial reactions to challenges are swift and generally appropriate. System 1 has biases, however, systematic errors that it is prone to make in specified circumstances. As we shall see, it sometimes answers easier questions than the one it was asked, and it has little understanding of logic and statistics. One further limitation of System 1 is that it cannot be turned off. If you are shown a word on the screen in a language you know, you will read it—unless your attention is totally focused elsewhere.

Conflict

Figure 2 is a variant of a classic experiment that produces a conflict between the two systems. You should try the exercise before reading on.

Your first task is to go down both columns, calling out whether each word is printed in lowercase or in uppercase. When you are done with the first task, go down both columns again, saying whether each word is printed to the left or to the right of center by saying (or whispering to yourself) "LEFT" or "RIGHT."

LEFT		upper	
	left	lower	
right			LOWER
RIGHT		upper	
	RIGHT	UPPER	
	left		lower
LEFT			LOWER
	right	upper	

Figure 2

You were almost certainly successful in saying the correct words in both tasks, and you surely discovered that some parts of each task were much easier than others. When you identified upper- and lowercase, the left-hand column was easy and the right-hand column caused you to slow down and perhaps to stammer or stumble. When you named the position of words, the left-hand column was difficult and the right-hand column was much easier.

These tasks engage System 2, because saying "upper/lower" or "right/left" is not what you routinely do when looking down a column of words. One of the things you did to set yourself for the task was to program your memory so that the relevant words (*upper* and *lower* for the first task) were "on the tip of your tongue." The prioritizing of the chosen words is effective and the mild temptation to read other words

20

was fairly easy to resist when you went through the first column. But the second column was different, because it contained words for which you were set, and you could not ignore them. You were mostly able to respond correctly, but overcoming the competing response was a strain, and it slowed you down. You experienced a conflict between a task that you intended to carry out and an automatic response that interfered with it.

Conflict between an automatic reaction and an intention to control it is common in our lives. We are all familiar with the experience of trying not to stare at the oddly dressed couple at the neighboring table in a restaurant. We also know what it is like to force our attention on a boring book, when we constantly find ourselves returning to the point at which the reading lost its meaning. Where winters are hard, many drivers have memories of their car skidding out of control on the ice and of the struggle to follow well-rehearsed instructions that negate what they would naturally do: "Steer into the skid, and whatever you do, do not touch the brakes!" And every human being has had the experience of *not* telling someone to go to hell. One of the tasks of System 2 is to overcome the impulses of System 1. In other words, System 2 is in charge of self-control.

Illusions

To appreciate the autonomy of System 1, as well as the distinction between impressions and beliefs, take a good look at Figure 3.

This picture is unremarkable: two horizontal lines of different lengths, with fins appended, pointing in different directions. The bottom line is obviously longer than the one above it. That is what we all see, and we naturally believe what we see. If you have already encountered this image, however, you recognize it as the famous Müller-Lyer illusion. As you can easily confirm by measuring them with a ruler, the horizontal lines are in fact identical in length.

Now that you have measured the lines, you—your System 2, the conscious being you call "I"—have a new belief: you *know* that the lines are equally long.

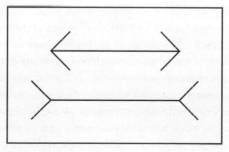

Figure 3

If asked about their length, you will say what you know. But you still *see* the bottom line as longer. You have chosen to believe the measurement, but you cannot prevent System 1 from doing its thing; you cannot decide to see the lines as equal, although you know they are. To resist the illusion, there is only one thing you can do: you must learn to mistrust your impressions of the length of lines when fins are attached to them. To implement that rule, you must be able to recognize the illusory pattern and recall what you know about it. If you can do this, you will never again be fooled by the Müller-Lyer illusion. But you will still see one line as longer than the other.

Not all illusions are visual. There are illusions of thought, which we call *cognitive illusions*. As a graduate student, I attended some courses on the art and science of psychotherapy. During one of these lectures, our teacher imparted a morsel of clinical wisdom. This is what he told us: "You will from time to time meet a patient who shares a disturbing tale of multiple mistakes in his previous treatment. He has been seen by several clinicians, and all failed him. The patient can lucidly describe how his therapists misunderstood him, but he has quickly perceived that you are different. You share the same feeling, are convinced that you understand him, and will be able to help." At this point my teacher raised his voice as he said, "Do not even *think* of taking on this patient! Throw him out of the office! He is most likely a psychopath and you will not be able to help him."

Many years later I learned that the teacher had warned us against psychopathic charm, and the leading authority in the study of psychopathy confirmed that the teacher's advice was sound. The analogy to the Müller-Lyer illusion is close. What we were being taught was not how to feel about that patient. Our teacher took it for granted that the sympathy we would feel for the patient would not be under our control; it would arise from System 1. Furthermore, we were not being taught to be generally suspicious of our feelings about patients. We were told that a strong attraction to a patient with a repeated history of failed treatment is a danger sign—like the fins on the parallel lines. It is an illusion—a cognitive illusion—and I (System 2) was taught how to recognize it and advised not to believe it or act on it.

The question that is most often asked about cognitive illusions is whether they can be overcome. The message of these examples is not encouraging. Because System 1 operates automatically and cannot be turned off at will, errors of intuitive thought are often difficult to prevent. Biases cannot always be avoided, because System 2 may have no clue to the error. Even when cues to likely errors are available, errors can be prevented only by the enhanced monitoring and effortful activity of System 2. As a way to live your life, however, continuous vigilance is not necessarily good, and it is certainly impractical. Constantly questioning our own thinking would be impossibly tedious, and System 2 is much too slow and inefficient to serve as a substitute for System 1 in making routine decisions. The best we can do is a compromise: learn to recognize situations in which mistakes are likely and try harder to avoid significant mistakes when the stakes are high.

UNDERSTANDING THE TEXT

1. How do the opening examples—the picture and the math problem—work to illustrate System 1 and System 2? Do you feel that you understand both of these systems after working through these examples?

2. Why does Kahneman talk about System 1 and System 2 as characters in a play? What element of the relationship between these two cognitive processes does he illuminate with this metaphor?

3. Which system can be equated with "paying attention"? How does the concept of "attention" figure into Kahneman's theory?

4. How does Kahneman use the example of the "invisible gorilla"? What is demonstrated by the fact that many people, when working on a cognitively demanding task, are unable to perceive a gorilla on a basketball court?

5. How, in Kahneman's view, does System 2 process information from System 1? How are our quick judgments incorporated into our logical thinking?

6. What does the optical illusion on p. 141 demonstrate? How are "cognitive illusions" similar to "optical illusions"? How can we best compensate for the mistakes that cognitive illusions lead us into?

MAKING CONNECTIONS

1. How might the thought processes Kahneman describes as System 1 be related to the Jungian view of the archetype (p. 108)?

2. How does Kahneman's System 2 correspond to the neurologically plastic mind that Nicholas Carr describes in "A Thing Like Me" (p. 123)? Do you think that System 2 can adapt in the same way?

3. What are the best ways to convince somebody by appealing to System 1? How about by appealing to System 2? Which of Kahneman's systems would you appeal to if you wanted to convince somebody of something they did not already believe? Would Kahneman answer this question the same way that Wayne Booth (p. 198) would?

4. Which elements of System 1 might have provided evolutionary advantages in the model that Edward Wilson explains in "The Fitness of Human Nature"(p. 356)?

WRITING ABOUT THE TEXT

1. Compare and contrast Kahneman's two systems, emphasizing how arguments can be structured to appeal to each system.

2. Examine several optical illusions other than the one on p. 141 and explain how they trick the mind. How do these illusions appeal to System 1 and cause us to see things incorrectly?

3. Write a paragraph about a controversial topic designed to appeal to System 1. Then write another version of the same paragraph designed to appeal to System 2. After writing both paragraphs, reflect on the way that your own understanding of "persuasion" changed from one paragraph to the next.

3

⬜

LANGUAGE AND RHETORIC

How Do We Use Language to Communicate Persuasively?

Rhetoric is useful . . . because things that are true and things that
are just have a natural tendency to prevail over their opposites.
—*Aristotle*

The DISCIPLINE OF RHETORIC includes all the elements involved in using language persuasively. Rhetoricians study logic, style, audience awareness, methods of delivery, strategies for generating ideas, models of organization, and many other topics related to the creation of persuasive arguments. In short, rhetoric covers precisely the things that most college students learn about in composition classes. Indeed, most colleges and universities that offer courses in writing and in teaching others how to write do so in a program or department called Rhetoric and Composition.

The roots of rhetoric stretch back to the fifth century BCE in Athens, Greece, the world's first democracy. We begin this chapter with an illustration and text of one of the founding myths of Athens, as illustrated by an anonymous Athenian painter and told by the great poet Aeschylus. In this myth, Athena, the goddess for whom the city is named, secures the cooperation of the Furies—dangerous immortals who were preventing her from establishing the city—by using her rhetorical skills to persuade them to abandon their objections. While nearly every other city or state in Greece traced its roots back to spectacular acts of violence, Athens alone claimed to have been founded by an act of persuasion.

And persuasion remained at the heart of the Athenian city-state. The Athenians' democratic system included a forum for debating issues and voting on them, which in turn produced one of the world's first marketplaces for persuasive speaking. People were willing to pay large sums of money to be instructed in the art of writing and delivering persuasive speeches that could help them gain support for their ideas.

The traveling teachers who came to Athens to meet this new need were collectively known as the Sophists. Sophists taught their students how to win arguments, and they believed that a speech's success was measured by persuasiveness, rather than inherent justice or truthfulness. They found many willing students, but they also earned the enmity of another group of teachers—philosophers, such as Socrates and Plato, who believed that seeking truth was far more important than learning techniques of persuasion.

Very few of the Sophists' writings have survived, but several of Plato's major dialogues fictionally dramatize debates between Sophists and Socrates. This chapter includes a selection from *Gorgias*, the most famous of these dialogues. In it Socrates compels Gorgias, the most successful Sophist of his day, to admit that the study of rhetoric can only mimic genuine philosophy. The arguments against rhetoric that Plato outlines—that it produces no knowledge and that it shows contempt for truth—have followed the study of rhetoric for millennia and are answered, in different forms, by all the readings in this chapter that follow. An example of the kind of rhetoric that Plato despised is found in Pericles's "The Funeral Oration," which celebrates Athens and asks its citizens to make every sacrifice necessary to keep it free.

The first rebuttal to Plato, which remains one of the most influential, comes from his own student Aristotle. In his treatise *Rhetoric*, Aristotle uses a Platonic argument to refute Plato's dismissal of rhetoric. "Rhetoric is useful," he argues, "because things that are true and things that are just have a natural tendency to prevail over their opposites." For Aristotle, truth is inherently superior and will always prevail in equal contests. Since those making bad arguments study rhetoric, Aristotle reasons, those who make good arguments must study it too; otherwise the contest will not be equal. Aristotle saw rhetoric as valuable far beyond its function in political deliberations, in judicial affairs, public celebrations, and community speeches. Understanding the basic principles of persuasion, he believed, was part of being an educated member of a society.

The next group of readings comes from the medieval and early modern periods. In the first, Augustine, the Bishop of Hippo and one of the greatest philosophers of the early Middle Ages, argues that those who defend true principles must learn the art of rhetoric so that they are not defeated by those who advocate false ones. In the next reading, the Mexican poet and nun Sor Juana Inés de la Cruz argues that both women and men have a responsibility to study true principles and good books.

After these ancient and early modern readings, the chapter fast forwards to the twentieth century, where the study of language and rhetoric has been vital to the emergence of modern culture and contemporary educational institutions. The first selection from the twentieth century, Wayne Booth's "The Rhetorical Stance," argues that the art of rhetoric requires writers to maintain a delicate balance between what they want to say, the expectations of their audience, and their own strengths and weaknesses as writers. This definition of rhetoric has since been widely adopted.

The chapter ends with three contemporary discussions of language and rhetoric. In "How to Tame a Wild Tongue," the Chicana writer Gloria Anzaldúa argues that robbing people of their native tongue is equivalent to robbing them of their dignity and political rights. In her Nobel Prize acceptance speech, novelist Toni Morrison explains that with the great power of language comes an equally great responsibility to use it wisely. And finally, in "Networked Politics," the Turkish writer and scholar Zeynep Tufekci explores the way that rhetoric works on the social media platforms that now dominate communication across the world.

Language and rhetoric are integral parts of modern life. Most people today do not give speeches in great assemblies, but most write memos and emails, and engage in debate. All of these acts are fundamentally rhetorical: they involve a writer, an audience, and an act of persuasion. What forms of persuasion are most effective? What moral responsibilities come with persuading other people to help you accomplish your goals? When does language become a tool of ignorance and oppression rather than of education and liberation? These questions have been with us since the days of the Athenian democracy, and they remain vital to the health of our society.

AESCHYLUS

The Eumenides

[458 BCE]

THE ATHENIAN PLAYWRIGHT AESCHYLUS (circa 525–circa 455 BCE) is often described as the father of Greek tragedy. He is the first of the three great tragedians—the others being Sophocles (circa 497–circa 406 BCE) and Euripides (circa 480–circa 406 BCE)—whose plays have survived and are still regularly performed all over the world. Scholars estimate that Aeschylus wrote between seventy and ninety plays, only seven of which have survived.

Aeschylus's most famous works are the three plays of *The Oresteia*, which center on Agamemnon, a leader of the Greek soldiers, and the ten-year siege known as the Trojan War. According to legend, Agamemnon sailed to Troy to recapture the most beautiful woman in all of Greece, Helen, who had been seduced and spirited away by the Trojan prince, Paris. After a long battle, the Greeks defeated the Trojans and burned their city to the ground.

Before setting out for Troy, in order to please the gods and secure favorable winds for the journey, Agamemnon sacrificed his daughter. *Agamemnon*, the first play in the trilogy, takes place ten years later when Agamemnon returns to his home in triumph. His wife, Clytemnestra, has never forgiven him for killing their daughter, and she plots to have him murdered upon his return. The second play, *The Libation Bearers*, dramatizes the horrible dilemma faced by Agamemnon's son, Orestes. Under Greek law and custom, Orestes must avenge his father's death, which, in this case, requires him to commit one of the worst sins imaginable: killing his own mother.

The following selection is drawn from *The Eumenides*, the final play in *The Oresteia*. When the play begins, Orestes is being tormented by the Furies, the divine beings charged with driving to madness those who commit terrible acts of violence. The Furies serve as both the Chorus—a group of characters that speak in unison and in the first person to comment on the action occurring in the play—and antagonist. They argue that as one who has killed his mother, Orestes is subject to their jurisdiction and should be tormented until he goes mad. But Orestes is protected by the Greek gods Athena and Apollo. Apollo believes that they can browbeat the Furies into submission with physical force. Athena, however, knows that she can persuade them through argument.

As an Olympian goddess, Athena has more power than the Furies, but not enough to prevent them from destroying her city of Athens, which she is in the process of establishing. She therefore appoints a jury of Athenian citizens to try the case. Athena eventually wins over the Furies and they become the Eumenides, or "Kindly Ones" of Athens. Athena's strategy for dealing with this situation has become a classic example of how to achieve victory through persuasion when it cannot be obtained through physical force.

The text in this selection is accompanied by a drawing on a Grecian urn depicting the action of the play. Orestes is shown seated, holding the sword that he used to kill his mother. Apollo, with Athena behind him, stands over Orestes holding a sacrificial pig, whose blood, according to Greek religion, rids one of guilt. The Furies are asleep to the side, but the ghost of Clytemnestra is trying to awaken them to do their duty and persecute Orestes. This painting identifies those elements of the text that its original audience considered most important and therefore serves as one of the earliest commentaries on the play.

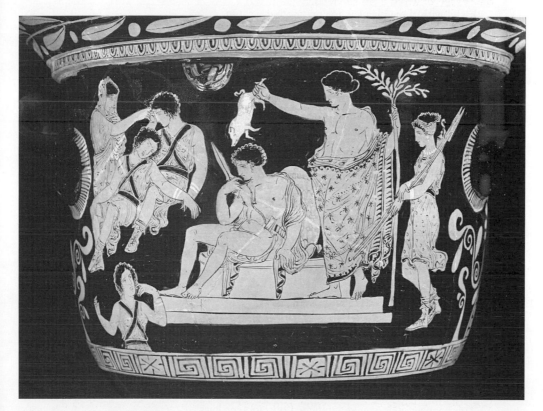

ORESTEIA, circa 380–370 BCE.
Louvre, Paris / Erich Lessing/Art Resource.

ATHENA
The numbers of the votes are equal—thus,
this man's acquitted of the murder charge.[1]

ORESTES
O Pallas Athena,[2] you've saved my house.
I'd lost my homeland—now you give it back,
and anyone in Greece can say, "This man   5
is once again an Argive,[3] occupying
his father's property, thanks to Pallas,
thanks to Apollo, and thanks to Zeus,
third god and all-fulfilling saviour."
Faced with these pleaders for my mother's cause,   10
Zeus chose to honour my father's death.
Now I'll go home. But first I make this oath
to your land and people for all time to come—
never will an Argive leader march in here
with spears arrayed against you. If he does,   15
in violation of this oath of mine,
from the grave we'll see his effort fails.
We'll bring him bad luck, trouble on the march,
send birds of evil omen over him.
He'll regret the pains his campaign brings him.   20
But all those who keep this oath, who honour
for all time Athena's city, allies
who fight on its behalf, such citizens
we'll treat with greater favour and good will.
And so farewell to you, Athena,   25
farewell to those who guard your city.
In struggles with your enemies, I hope
you catch them in a stranglehold, win out,
and gain the spear denoting victory.

[Apollo and Orestes leave. The Furies move to surround Athena]

CHORUS
You younger gods, you've wrenched our ancient laws   30
out of my grasp, then stamped them underfoot.

This translation has been prepared by Ian Johnston of Malaspina University College, Nanaimo, British Columbia, Canada.
1. **The numbers of the votes are equal:** To judge between Orestes and the Furies, Athena organizes a jury of Athenian citizens to decide his fate. The jury ties and Athena votes in favor of acquittal.
2. **Pallas Athena:** The more formal name for the goddess Athena.
3. **Argive:** Greek.

You heap on us dishonourable contempt.
Now my anger turns against this land
I'll spread my poisons—how it's going to pay,
when I release this venom in my heart   35
to ease my grief. I'll saturate this ground.
It won't survive. From it disease will grow,
infecting leaves and children—that's justice.
Sterility will spread across the land,
contaminate the soil, destroy mankind.   40
What can I do now but scream out in pain?
The citizens make fun of us, the Furies.
How can we put up with such indignity,
daughters of Night disgracefully abused,
dishonoured, shamed, our powers cast aside?   45

ATHENA
Let me persuade you not to spurn this trial.
You've not been beaten—the votes were fair,
the numbers equal, no disgrace to you.
But we received clear evidence from Zeus.
The one who spoke the oracle declared   50
Orestes should not suffer for his act.
So don't be vengeful, breathing anger
on this land and drenching it with showers,
whose drops, like spears, will kill the seeds,
and blast its fruitfulness. I promise you   55
in all righteousness you'll have your place,
a subterranean cavern, yours by right.
Beside the hearth you'll sit on glittering thrones,
worshipped with reverence by my citizens.

CHORUS
You younger gods, you've wrenched our ancient laws   60
out of my grasp, then stamped them underfoot.
You heap on us dishonourable contempt.
Now my anger turns against this land
I'll spread my poisons—how it's going to pay,
when I release this venom in my heart   65
to ease my grief. I'll saturate this ground.
It won't survive. From it disease will grow,
infecting leaves and children—that's justice.
Sterility will spread across the land,

contaminate the soil, destroy mankind.   70
What can I do now but scream out in pain?
The citizens make fun of us, the Furies.
How can we put up with such indignity,
daughters of Night disgracefully abused,
shamed, dishonoured, our powers cast aside?   75

ATHENA
But you've not lost honour—you're goddesses.
Don't let your anger lead you to excess,
to blast this land of men past remedy.
I have faith in Zeus. Why must I mention that?
Well, I'm the only god who knows the keys   80
to Zeus' arsenal where he keeps sealed
his lightning bolt. But there's no need for that.
Accept my argument. Don't let rash tongues
hurl threats against this land, condemning it
to sterile fruitlessness. Ease your anger.   85
Let your fury's black and bitter waves recede.
You can live with me, receive full honours.
The first fruits of this fertile land are yours,
forever, all those offerings for heirs,
for marriages—from now on they're yours.   90
With all this, you'll praise what I'm advising.

CHORUS
Such suffering for me.
My ancient wisdom
driven underground,
despised, dishonoured.   95
The shame, my shame.
This pure rage I breathe
consumes me utterly.
What sinks under my ribs
and pains my heart?   100

O Night, my mother,
the cunning of those gods,
too hard to overcome,
takes all my ancient powers,
and leaves me nothing.   105

ATHENA
I'll bear with your rage, for you are older,
and thus your wisdom far exceeds my own.
But Zeus gave me a fine intelligence as well.
So let me tell you this—if you leave here,
for this land you'll feel a lover's yearning.   110
As time goes on, my citizens will win
increasing honour, and you, on your thrones,
seated outside the house of Erechtheus,[4]
a place of honour, will win more respect
from lines of men and women filing past   115
than you could find in all the world beyond.
So cast no stones for bloodshed on this land,
my realm. Do not corrupt our youthful hearts,
intoxicating them with rage, like wine,
or rip the heart out of a fighting cock   120
to set it in my people, giving them
a thirst for reckless internecine war.
Let them fight wars abroad, without restraint
in those men driven by a lust for fame.
I want no birds who fight their wars at home.   125
That's what I offer you. It's yours to take.
Do good things, receive good things in honour.
Take your place in a land the gods all love.

CHORUS
Such suffering for me—
my ancient wisdom   130
driven underground,
despised, dishonoured.
The shame, my shame.
This pure rage I breathe
consumes me utterly.   135
What sinks under my ribs
and pains my heart?

O Night, my mother,
the cunning of those gods,
too hard to overcome,   140

4. **Erechtheus:** The Erectheum, or "House of Erechtheus," was a prominent temple on the north side of the Acropolis, the famous hilltop in Athens where Athena's temple was located.

takes all my ancient powers,
and leaves me nothing.

ATHENA
I'll not tire of telling you your gifts,
so you can never lodge complaints that I,
a newer god, or men who guard this land   145
failed to revere such ancient goddesses
and cast you out in exile from our city.
No. But if you respect Persuasion,
holding in reverence that sacred power
whose soothing spell sits on my tongue,   150
then you should stay. If that's not your wish,
it would be unjust to vent your anger
on this city, injuring its people,
enraged at them from spite. It's up to you—
take your allotted portion of this land,   155
justly entitled to your share of honour.

CHORUS LEADER
Queen Athena, this place you say is ours,
what exactly is it?

ATHENA
                        One free of pain,
without anxieties. Why not accept?   160

CHORUS LEADER
If I do, what honours would I get?

ATHENA
Without you no house can thrive.

CHORUS LEADER
You'd do this? You'd grant me that much power?

ATHENA
I will. Together we'll enrich the lives
of all who worship us.   165

CHORUS LEADER
                        This promise you make—
you'll hold to it forever?

ATHENA
Yes. I don't say anything I don't fulfill.

CHORUS LEADER
Your magic's doing its work, it seems—   170
I feel my rage diminish.

ATHENA
Then stay.
In this land you'll win more friends.

CHORUS LEADER
Let me speak out a blessing on the land.
Tell me what I might say.

ATHENA
Speak nothing   175
of brutal victories—only blessings
stemming from the earth, the ocean depths,
the heavens. Let gusting winds caress the land
in glorious sunlight, our herds and harvests
overflow with plenty, so they never fail   180
our citizens in time to come, whose seed
will last forever. Let their prosperity
match how well they worship you. I love
these righteous men, the way a gardener loves
his growing plants, this race now free of grief.   185
These things are yours to give. For my part,
I'll see this city wins triumphal fame
in deadly wars where men seek glory,
so all men celebrate victorious Athens.

CHORUS
Then we'll accept this home   190
and live here with Athena.
We'll never harm a place
which she and Ares[5]
and all-powerful Zeus
hold as a fortress of the gods,   195

5. **Ares:** In Greek mythology, the god of war.

this glorious altar, the shield
for all the gods of Greece.
I make this prayer for Athens,
prophesying fine things for her—
bounteous happy harvests
bursting from the earth,
beneath a radiant sun.

UNDERSTANDING THE TEXT

1. What is the Furies' primary concern after the verdict?

2. Why does Athena remind them that Orestes was acquitted after a fair vote?

3. The Furies repeat the same words in each of their first two speeches. What might this mean? Do they show any evidence of having heard Athena's first response?

4. How does Athena combine threats with promises of rewards? How effective is this combination?

5. At one point, Athena tells the Furies "your wisdom far exceeds my own" (p. 153). Do you think she believes this? What advantage does she gain in complimenting them in this way?

6. Which arguments finally convince the Furies to accept Athena's offer and become part of the city she is creating?

7. What elements of the story are captured in the vase painting? How does it symbolically represent the action of the narrative?

MAKING CONNECTIONS

1. How do Athena's speeches incorporate the three elements of Wayne Booth's "rhetorical position" (p. 198): the character of the speaker, the needs of the audience, and the subject matter? Would Burke say that she communicated effectively?

2. How are Athena's attempts to reconcile the Furies to the jury's decision similar to the actions of the Truth and Reconciliation Committee described in Desmond Tutu's "Nuremberg or National Amnesia: A Third Way" (p. 450). Are Tutu's motivations for pursuing reconciliation similar to Athena's? Why or why not?

3. Compare the symbolism in the vase painting of "The Oresteia" with that in "Liberty Leading the People" (p. 494). Are there similarities in the ways that the artists represent argument through images?

WRITING ABOUT THE TEXT

1. Compare the way that Athena treats her opponents with the way politicians treat their political opponents today. Are there elements of Athena's strategy that could improve contemporary political discourse?

2. Explain how *The Eumenides* reflects the concerns of people living in the world's first democracy. What elements of democratic government does the text comment upon? Discuss instances of modern democracies grappling with some of the same issues that Aeschylus commented on 2,500 years ago.

3. Examine Athena's speeches to the Furies as examples of Machiavellian *realpolitik* (p. 405). Does she combine incentives and disincentives in a way that Machiavelli would see as appropriate?

PERICLES
The Funeral Oration
[431 BCE]

IN 431 BCE, war broke out between the two most powerful military alliances in the region of Greece: the Delian League, an alliance of Greek city-states led by Athens, and the Peloponnesian League, a similar alliance led by Sparta. The contrast between the two principal city-states could not have been greater. Athens was the world's only democracy. It had an elected assembly, a profitable export (olive oil), a powerful military, and a thriving culture. Sparta, on the other hand, was a rigidly controlled dictatorship in which all citizens were trained exclusively for war. The Peloponnesian War between these two city-states and their allies lasted from 431 to 404 BCE, ending with the total defeat of the Athenians and a profound reshaping of the Greek world.

The leader of Athens at the outbreak of the war was Pericles (495–429 BCE), who was a skilled orator, a dedicated patron of the arts, and a passionate defender of Athenian democracy. His rule is often seen as both a political and cultural high point, a time in which the city produced such luminaries as the playwrights Aristophanes, Sophocles, Euripides, and Aeschylus and the philosopher Socrates. However, many historians also see Pericles as a primary instigator of the Peloponnesian War and the subsequent collapse of the Athenian Empire. Pericles is, therefore, remembered for both creating and helping to destroy the golden age of Athenian civilization.

Much of what historians know about this period comes from *History of the Peloponnesian War* by the Athenian general Thucydides (circa 460–circa 395 BCE). Thucydides was an eyewitness to the events that he chronicled, and most scholars believe that his account is essentially objective, though occasionally pro-Athenian. Along with his own narrative of the war and analysis of its causes, Thucydides included dozens of speeches by both Athenians and Spartans involved in the war. The most famous of these speeches is "The Funeral Oration of Pericles," which Pericles delivered at an annual ceremony to honor Athens's war dead. Here, Pericles departs from the traditional formula for such speeches—rather than simply praising the dead, as was expected of such orations, Pericles praises the city of Athens, condemns its enemies, and makes the case for continuing the war.

One of the most intriguing speculations about the funeral oration is that it was written not by Pericles but by a woman named Aspasia of Miletus. Aspasia's exact status is the subject of much debate. She has been alternately labeled a prostitute, a mistress, and a wife to Pericles. But her influence upon him and his speeches has been commented on by, among others, Plato, Xenophon, Plutarch, and Cicero. In his dialogue "Menexenus" (circa 380 BCE), Plato includes a somewhat satirical version of the funeral oration that he attributes directly to Aspasia. The actual involvement of Aspasia in this speech, or in any of Pericles's speeches, is subject to much debate, but the philosophical tradition contains at least some reasonable speculation that the brains behind Athens's greatest statesman may have been a woman.

Pericles's speech provides a good example of the appeal to emotion. The primary emotion that he appeals to is patriotism, the love of one's country. Pericles introduces this topic early on and he uses the superiority of Athens as an organizing principle of the speech.

Most of those who have spoken before me on this occasion have praised the man who added this oration to our customs because it gives honor to those who have died in the wars; yet I would have thought it sufficient that those who have shown their mettle in action should also receive their honor in an action, as now you see they have, in this burial performed for them at public expense, so that the virtue of many does not depend on whether one person is believed to have spoken well or poorly. It is a hard matter to speak in due measure when there is no firm consensus about the truth. A hearer who is favorable and knows what was done will perhaps think that a eulogy falls short of what he wants to hear and knows to be true; while an ignorant one will find some of the praise to be exaggerated, especially if he hears of anything beyond his own talent—because that would make him envious. Hearing another man praised is bearable only so long as the hearer thinks he could himself have done what he hears. But if a speaker goes beyond that, the hearer soon becomes envious and ceases to believe. Since our ancestors have thought it good, however, I too should follow the custom and endeavor to answer to the desires and opinions of every one of you, as far as I can.

I will begin with our ancestors, since it is both just and fitting that they be given the honor of remembrance at such a time. Because they have always lived in this land, they have so far always handed it down in liberty through their valor to successive generations up to now. They deserve praise; but our fathers deserve even more, for with great toil they acquired our present empire in addition to what they had received, and they delivered it in turn to the present generation. We ourselves who are here now in the prime of life have expanded most parts of the empire; and we have furnished the city with everything it needs to be self-sufficient both in peace and in war. The acts of war by which all this was attained, the valiant deeds of arms that we and our fathers performed against foreign or Greek invaders—these I will pass over, to avoid making a long speech on a subject with which you are well acquainted. But the customs that brought us to this point, the form of government and the way of life that have made our city great—these I shall disclose before I turn to praise the dead. I think these subjects are quite suitable for the occasion, and the whole gathering of citizens and guests will profit by hearing them discussed.

We have a form of government that does not try to imitate the laws of our neighboring states. We are more an example to others, than they to us. In name, it is called a democracy, because it is managed not for a few people, but for the majority. Still, although we have equality at law for everyone here in private disputes, we do not let our system of rotating public offices undermine our judgment of a candidate's virtue; and no one is held back by poverty or because his reputation is not well known, as long as he can do good service to the city. We are free and generous not only in our public activities as citizens, but also in our daily lives: there is no suspicion in our dealings with one another, and we are not offended by our neighbor for following his own pleasure. We do not cast on anyone the censorious looks that—though they are no punishment—are nevertheless painful. We live together without taking offense on private matters; and as for public affairs, we respect the law greatly and fear to violate it, since we are obedient to those in office at any time, and also to the laws—especially to those laws that were made to help people who have suffered an injustice, and to the unwritten laws that bring shame on their transgressors by the agreement of all.

Moreover, we have provided many ways to give our minds recreation from labor: 5
we have instituted regular contests and sacrifices throughout the year, while the attractive furnishings of our private homes give us daily delight and expel sadness. The greatness of our city has caused all things from all parts of the earth to be imported here, so that we enjoy the products of other nations with no less familiarity than we do our own.

Then, too, we differ from our enemies in preparing for war: we leave our city open to all; and we have never expelled strangers in order to prevent them from learning or seeing things that, if they were not hidden, might give an advantage to the enemy. We do not rely on secret preparation and deceit so much as on our own courage in action. And as for education, our enemies train to be men from early youth by rigorous exercise, while we live a more relaxed life and still take on dangers as great as they do.

The evidence for this is that the Lacedaemonians[1] do not invade our country by themselves, but with the aid of all their allies; when we invade our neighbors, however, we usually overcome them by ourselves without difficulty, even though we are fighting on hostile ground against people who are defending their own homes. Besides, no enemy has yet faced our whole force at once, because at the same time we are busy with our navy and sending men by land to many different places. But when our enemies run into part of our forces and get the better of them, they boast that they have beaten our whole force; and when they are defeated, they claim they were beaten by all of us. We are willing to go into danger with easy minds and natural courage rather than through rigorous training and laws, and that gives us an advantage: we'll never weaken ourselves in advance by preparing for future troubles, but we'll turn out to be no less daring in action than those who are always training hard. In this, as in other things, our city is worthy of admiration.

1. **Lacedaemonians:** inhabitants of Laconia, a city-state on the southern coast of Greece.

We are lovers of nobility with restraint, and lovers of wisdom without any softening of character. We use wealth as an opportunity for action, rather than for boastful speeches. And as for poverty, we think there is no shame in confessing it; what is shameful is doing nothing to escape it. Moreover, the very men who take care of public affairs look after their own at the same time; and even those who are devoted to their own businesses know enough about the city's affairs. For we alone think that a man who does not take part in public affairs is good for nothing, while others only say he is "minding his own business." We are the ones who develop policy, or at least decide what is to be done; for we believe that what spoils action is not speeches, but going into action without first being instructed through speeches. In this too we excel over others: ours is the bravery of people who think through what they will take in hand, and discuss it thoroughly; with other men, ignorance makes them brave and thinking makes them cowards. But the people who most deserve to be judged tough-minded are those who know exactly what terrors or pleasures lie ahead, and are not turned away from danger by that knowledge. Again we are opposite to most men in matters of virtue:[2] we win our friends by doing them favors, rather than by accepting favors from them. A person who does a good turn is a more faithful friend: his goodwill towards the recipient preserves his feeling that he should do more; but the friendship of a person who has to return a good deed is dull and flat, because he knows he will be merely paying a debt—rather than doing a favor—when he shows his virtue in return. So that we alone do good to others not after calculating the profit, but fearlessly and in the confidence of our freedom.

In sum, I say that our city as a whole is a lesson for Greece, and that each of us presents himself as a self-sufficient individual, disposed to the widest possible diversity of actions, with every grace and great versatility. This is not merely a boast in words for the occasion, but the truth in fact, as the power of this city, which we have obtained by having this character, makes evident.

For Athens is the only power now that is greater than her fame when it comes to the test. Only in the case of Athens can enemies never be upset over the quality of those who defeat them when they invade; only in our empire can subject states never complain that their rulers are unworthy. We are proving our power with strong evidence, and we are not without witnesses: we shall be the admiration of people now and in the future. We do not need Homer, or anyone else, to praise our power with words that bring delight for a moment, when the truth will refute his assumptions about what was done. For we have compelled all seas and all lands to be open to us by our daring; and we have set up eternal monuments on all sides, of our setbacks as well as of our accomplishments.

10

---

2. **Virtue:** *areté*. This traditionally involved doing good to one's friends and harm to one's enemies; that is why Pericles uses the concept here to introduce the topic of friendship among cities. [Translator's note]

Such is the city for which these men fought valiantly and died, in the firm belief that it should never be destroyed, and for which every man of you who is left should be willing to endure distress.

That is why I have spoken at such length concerning the city in general, to show you that the stakes are not the same, between us and the enemy—for their city is not like ours in any way—and, at the same time, to bring evidence to back up the eulogy of these men for whom I speak.³ The greatest part of their praise has already been delivered, for it was their virtues, and the virtues of men like them, that made what I praised in the city so beautiful. Not many Greeks have done deeds that are obviously equal to their own reputations, but these men have. The present end these men have met is, I think, either the first indication, or the final confirmation, of a life of virtue. And even those who were inferior in other ways deserve to have their faults overshadowed by their courageous deaths in war for the sake of their country. Their good actions have wiped out the memory of any wrong they have done, and they have produced more public good than private harm. None of them became a coward because he set a higher value on enjoying the wealth that he had; none of them put off the terrible day of his death in hopes that he might overcome his poverty and attain riches. Their longing to punish their enemies was stronger than this; and because they believed this to be the most honorable sort of danger, they chose to punish their enemies at this risk, and to let everything else go. The uncertainty of success they entrusted to hope; but for that which was before their eyes they decided to rely on themselves in action. They believed that this choice entailed resistance and suffering, rather than surrender and safety; they ran away from the word of shame, and stood up in action at risk of their lives. And so, in the one brief moment allotted them, at the peak of their fame and not in fear, they departed.

Such were these men, worthy of their country. And you who remain may pray for a safer fortune, but you must resolve to be no less daring in your intentions against the enemy. Do not weigh the good they have done on the basis of one speech. Any long-winded orator could tell you how much good lies in resisting our enemies; but you already know this. Look instead at the power our city shows in action every day, and so become lovers of Athens. When the power of the city seems great to you, consider then that this was purchased by valiant men who knew their duty and kept their honor in battle, by men who were resolved to contribute the most noble gift to their city: even if they should fail in their attempt, at least they would leave their fine character [areté] to the city. For in giving their lives for the common good, each man won praise for himself that will never grow old; and the monument that awaits them is the most splendid—not where they are buried, but where their glory is laid up to be remembered forever, whenever the time comes for speech or action. For to famous men, all the earth is a monument,

---

3. **These men for whom I speak:** the war dead being honored at the funeral.

and their virtues are attested not only by inscriptions on stone at home; but an unwritten record of the mind lives on for each of them, even in foreign lands, better than any gravestone.

Try to be like these men, therefore: realize that happiness lies in liberty, and liberty in valor, and do not hold back from the dangers of war. Miserable men, who have no hope of prosperity, do not have a just reason to be generous with their lives; no, it is rather those who face the danger of a complete reversal of fortune for whom defeat would make the biggest difference: they are the ones who should risk their lives. Any man of intelligence will hold that death, when it comes unperceived to a man at full strength and with hope for his country, is not so bitter as miserable defeat for a man grown soft.

That is why I offer you, who are here as parents of these men, consolation rather than a lament. You know your lives teem with all sorts of calamities, and that it is good fortune for anyone to draw a glorious end for his lot, as these men have done. While your lot was grief, theirs was a life that was happy as long as it lasted. I know it is a hard matter to dissuade you from sorrow, when you will often be reminded by the good fortune of others of the joys you once had; for sorrow is not for the want of a good never tasted, but for the loss of a good we have been used to having. Yet those of you who are of an age to have children may bear this loss in the hope of having more. On a personal level new children will help some of you forget those who are no more; while the city will gain doubly by this, in population and insecurity. It is not possible for people to give fair and just advice to the state, if they are not exposing their own children to the same danger when they advance a risky policy. As for you who are past having children, you are to think of the greater part of your life as pure profit, while the part that remains is short and its burden lightened by the glory of these men. For the love of honor is the one thing that never grows old, and useless old age takes delight not in gathering wealth (as some say), but in being honored.

As for you who are the children or the brothers of these men, I see that you will have considerable competition. Everyone is used to praising the dead, so that even extreme virtue will scarcely win you a reputation equal to theirs, but it will fall a little short. That is because people envy the living as competing with them, but they honor those who are not in their way, and their good will towards the dead is free of rivalry.

And now, since I must say something about feminine virtue, I shall express it in this brief admonition to you who are now widows: your glory is great if you do not fall beneath the natural condition of your sex, and if you have as little fame among men as is possible, whether for virtue or by way of reproach.

Thus I have delivered, according to custom, what was appropriate in a speech, while those men who are buried here have already been honored by their own actions. It remains to maintain their children at the expense of the city until they grow up. This benefit is the city's victory garland for them and for those they leave

15

behind after such contests as these, because the city that gives the greatest rewards for virtue has the finest citizens.

So now, when everyone has mourned for his own, you may go.

UNDERSTANDING THE TEXT

1. Read the first three paragraphs of Pericles's speech and consider the way he frames the introduction. How does he introduce his major ideas? How effective is the introduction?

2. Why does Pericles spend so much time praising Athens, its form of government, and its culture? What does this suggest about his real motives in making this speech?

3. What difference does Pericles see between the way Athens prepares for war and the way its neighbors do? Why is this difference important to the speech?

4. Pericles tries throughout his speech to increase the hostility of his audience towards Sparta. Find several passages where he does this and explain the effect each would have on the audience and why.

5. How does Pericles distinguish himself from "long winded orators"? Why does he say so little about the men whose funeral he is speaking at?

6. What advice does Pericles give to women? Might anything in this passage confirm Plato's argument that it was Aspasia, a woman, who wrote the oration for Pericles to give? Explain.

MAKING CONNECTIONS

1. Both "The Funeral Oration" and the Women of World War II Memorial (p. 514) were intended to honor soldiers killed in war. With this purpose in mind, what similarities can you find between the two texts?

2. Compare the way that Pericles treats war with the way that George Orwell does in "Pacifism and the War" (p. 508). Does Pericles treat the enemies of Athens the same way that Orwell treats the threat of fascism? Explain. Which argument do you find most persuasive? Why?

3. Does Pericles use rhetoric the same way that, according to Plato, dishonest Sophists such as Gorgias do (p. 166)? Is there anything in the text that suggests that Pericles might not believe what he is saying? Explain.

WRITING ABOUT THE TEXT

1. Write an essay in which you argue for or against the theory that Aspasia actually wrote "The Funeral Oration." Use passages from the text to support your claim.

2. How does Pericles appeal to emotion and logic in his argument? Write an essay in which you analyze his appeals to each, citing specific passages to support your analysis.

3. Write an essay in which you compare and contrast the assumptions about war in "The Funeral Oration" with those in *Guernica* (p. 497), *Liberty Leading the People* (p. 494), or "Against War" (p. 488). Analyze each text to determine what it says about war, and use passages from the texts (or descriptions of the images) to support your claim.

4. Examine a twentieth-century speech by a political leader at a time of war and compare it to Pericles' funeral oration, delivered during the Peloponnesian War. Be sure to identify and account for both similarities and differences.

PLATO
from *Gorgias*
[380 BCE]

PLATO (CIRCA 428–348 or 347 BCE), one of the greatest philosophers of the ancient world, came of age during an era of almost perpetual warfare. In 431 BCE, the Peloponnesian War between his native Athens and the militaristic city-state of Sparta began. The war lasted for twenty-seven years, during which time Plato grew up in an aristocratic family and became a disciple of the Greek philosopher Socrates. When the war ended in Athens's total defeat, the Athenian assembly tried and executed Socrates, who had been one of the war's strongest critics. Officially, Socrates was charged with impiety and corrupting the young, but Plato felt that his mentor had been executed because he had spent years engaging the city's people in conversations designed to unmask their foolishness and hypocrisy. Plato recorded Socrates' trial in his *Apology*.

The war and Socrates's execution affected Plato deeply; he saw both as fruits of Athens's unwise government, in which an assembly of ordinary men made decisions that affected the entire state. Masterminded by a few very persuasive speakers who managed to build consensus within the assembly, these events made Plato especially suspicious of the art of rhetoric, which, he felt, focused on persuasion at the expense of truth. He believed that important questions should be decided by wise leaders and not be subjected to public debate and popular vote.

For Plato, the figures that symbolized rhetoric's dangers were the Sophists, a group of teachers—most of them foreign—who had set up successful schools of rhetoric in Athens. Sophists often taught that the truth of a situation depended on one's perspective, that any argument could be effective if presented well, and that "winning" a debate was more important than discovering the truth. All of these views were anathema to Plato, who believed that the most important thing in life was to discover the truth.

The Sicilian rhetorician Gorgias (circa 483–circa 376 BCE) was one of the most successful Sophists in Athens. His major discourse, *On Nature or the Non-Existent*, has not survived, but accounts indicate that it argued against the possibility of knowing, or communicating, anything. Although Plato's dialogue *Gorgias* is a debate between Socrates and Gorgias about the relative merits of philosophy and rhetoric, such a conversation probably never occurred; Plato often expressed his ideas through fictional dialogues that echoed the kind of persistent questioning for which Socrates was famous. This format is especially apt for the *Gorgias*, in which Plato focuses on the ultimate purpose of dialogue.

Plato's rhetorical strategy in *Gorgias*, as in most of his dialogues, is to place his own argument in Socrates's mouth while summarizing his opponent's argument in the person of Gorgias. This strategy can be very effective, but Plato has often been criticized for turning characters such as Gorgias into straw men for his own rhetorical ends.

What are we to call you, and what is the art which you profess?

Gor. Rhetoric, Socrates, is my art.

Soc. Then I am to call you a rhetorician?

Gor. Yes, Socrates, and a good one too, if you would call me that which, in Homeric language, "I boast myself to be."

Soc. I should wish to do so.   5

Gor. Then pray do.

Soc. And are we to say that you are able to make other men rhetoricians?

Gor. Yes, that is exactly what I profess to make them, not only at Athens, but in all places.

Soc. And will you continue to ask and answer questions, Gorgias, as we are at present doing and reserve for another occasion the longer mode of speech which Polus[1] was attempting? Will you keep your promise, and answer shortly the questions which are asked of you?

Gor. Some answers, Socrates, are of necessity longer; but I will do my best to   10
make them as short as possible; for a part of my profession is that I can be as short as any one.

Soc. That is what is wanted, Gorgias; exhibit the shorter method now, and the longer one at some other time.

Gor. Well, I will; and you will certainly say, that you never heard a man use fewer words.

Soc. Very good then; as you profess to be a rhetorician, and a maker of rhetoricians, let me ask you, with what is rhetoric concerned: I might ask with what is weaving concerned, and you would reply (would you not?), with the making of garments?

Gor. Yes.

Soc. And music is concerned with the composition of melodies?   15

Gor. It is.

Soc. By Herè,[2] Gorgias, I admire the surpassing brevity of your answers.

Gor. Yes, Socrates, I do think myself good at that.

Soc. I am glad to hear it; answer me in like manner about rhetoric: with what is rhetoric concerned?

Gor. With discourse.   20

Soc. What sort of discourse, Gorgias?—such discourse as would teach the sick under what treatment they might get well?

Gor. No.

---

1. **Polus:** a student of Gorgias and a minor character in the Gorgias.

2. **Herè:** Hera, in Greek mythology the wife of
Zeus and queen of the gods.

Soc. Then rhetoric does not treat of all kinds of discourse?

Gor. Certainly not.

Soc. And yet rhetoric makes men able to speak?   25

Gor. Yes.

Soc. And to understand that about which they speak?

Gor. Of course.

Soc. But does not the art of medicine, which we were just now mentioning, also make men able to understand and speak about the sick?

Gor. Certainly.   30

Soc. Then medicine also treats of discourse?

Gor. Yes.

Soc. Of discourse concerning diseases?

Gor. Just so.

Soc. And does not gymnastic[3] also treat of discourse concerning the good or evil   35
condition of the body?

Gor. Very true.

Soc. And the same, Gorgias, is true of the other arts:—all of them treat of discourse concerning the subjects with which they severally have to do.

Gor. Clearly.

Soc. Then why, if you call rhetoric the art which treats of discourse, and all the other arts treat of discourse, do you not call them arts of rhetoric?

Gor. Because, Socrates, the knowledge of the other arts has only to do with some   40
sort of external action, as of the hand; but there is no such action of the hand in rhetoric which works and takes effect only through the medium of discourse. And therefore I am justified in saying that rhetoric treats of discourse.

Soc. I am not sure whether I entirely understand you, but I dare say I shall soon know better; please to answer me a question:—you would allow that there are arts?

Gor. Yes.

Soc. As to the arts generally, they are for the most part concerned with doing, and require little or no speaking; in painting, and statuary, and many other arts, the work may proceed in silence; and of such arts I suppose you would say that they do not come within the province of rhetoric.

Gor. You perfectly conceive my meaning, Socrates.

Soc. But there are other arts which work wholly through the medium of language,   45
and require either no action or very little, as, for example, the arts of arithmetic, of calculation, of geometry, and of playing draughts; in some of these speech is pretty nearly co-extensive with action, but in most of them the verbal element is greater— they depend wholly on words for their efficacy and power: and I take your meaning to be that rhetoric is an art of this latter sort?

Gor. Exactly.

3. **Gymnastic:** the general science of exercise and physical education.

Soc. And yet I do not believe that you really mean to call any of these arts rhetoric; although the precise expression which you used was, that rhetoric is an art which works and takes effect only through the medium of discourse; and an adversary who wished to be captious might say, "And so, Gorgias, you call arithmetic rhetoric." But I do not think that you really call arithmetic rhetoric any more than geometry would be so called by you.

Gor. You are quite right, Socrates, in your apprehension of my meaning.

Soc. Well, then, let me now have the rest of my answer:—seeing that rhetoric is one of those arts which works mainly by the use of words and there are other arts which also use words tell me what is that quality in words with which rhetoric is concerned:—Suppose that a person asks me about some of the arts which I was mentioning just now; he might say, "Socrates, what is arithmetic?" and I should reply to him, as you replied to me, that arithmetic is one of those arts which take effect through words. And then he would proceed to ask, "Words about what?" and I should reply, Words about odd and even numbers, and how many there are of each. And if he asked again, "What is the art of calculation?" I should say, That also is one of the arts which is concerned wholly with words. And if he further said, "Concerned with what?" I should say, like the clerks in the assembly, "as aforesaid" of arithmetic, but with a difference, the difference being that the art of calculation considers not only the quantities of odd and even numbers, but also their numerical relations to themselves and to one another. And suppose, again, I were to say that astronomy is only words—he would ask, "Words about what, Socrates?" and I should answer, that astronomy tells us about the motions of the stars and sun and moon, and their relative swiftness.

Gor. You would be quite right, Socrates.   50

Soc. And now let us have from you, Gorgias, the truth about rhetoric: which you would admit (would you not?) to be one of those arts which act always and fulfil all their ends through the medium of words?

Gor. True.

Soc. Words which do what? I should ask. To what class of things do the words which rhetoric uses relate?

Gor. To the greatest, Socrates, and the best of human things.

Soc. That again, Gorgias, is ambiguous; I am still in the dark: for which are the   55
greatest and best of human things? I dare say that you have heard men singing at feasts the old drinking song, in which the singers enumerate the goods of life, first health, beauty next, thirdly, as the writer of the song says, wealth honestly obtained.

Gor. Yes, I know the song; but what is your drift?

Soc. I mean to say, that the producers of those things which the author of the song praises, that is to say, the physician, the trainer, the money-maker, will at once come to you, and first the physician will say: "O Socrates, Gorgias is deceiving you, for my art is concerned with the greatest good of men and not his." And when I ask, Who are you? he will reply, "I am a physician." What do you mean? I shall say.

Do you mean that your art produces the greatest good? "Certainly," he will answer, "for is not health the greatest good? What greater good can men have, Socrates?" And after him the trainer will come and say, "I too, Socrates, shall be greatly surprised if Gorgias can show more good of his art than I can show of mine." To him again I shall say, Who are you, honest friend, and what is your business? "I am a trainer," he will reply, "and my business is to make men beautiful and strong in body." When I have done with the trainer, there arrives the money-maker, and he, as I expect, will utterly despise them all. "Consider, Socrates," he will say, "whether Gorgias or any one else can produce any greater good than wealth." Well, you and I say to him, and are you a creator of wealth? "Yes," he replies. And who are you? "A money-maker." And do you consider wealth to be the greatest good of man? "Of course," will be his reply. And we shall rejoin: Yes; but our friend Gorgias contends that his art produces a greater good than yours. And then he will be sure to go on and asks, "What good? Let Gorgias answer." Now I want you, Gorgias, to imagine that this question is asked of you by them and by me; What is that which, as you say, is the greatest good of man, and of which you are the creator? Answer us.

Gor. That good, Socrates, which is truly the greatest, being that which gives to men freedom in their own persons, and to individuals the power of ruling over others in their several states.

Soc. And what would you consider this to be?

Gor. What is there greater than the word which persuades the judges in the courts, or the senators in the council, or the citizens in the assembly, or at any other political meeting?—if you have the power of uttering this word, you will have the physician your slave, and the trainer your slave, and the money-maker of whom you talk will be found to gather treasures, not for himself, but for you who are able to speak and to persuade the multitude. 60

Soc. Now I think, Gorgias, that you have very accurately explained what you conceive to be the art of rhetoric; and you mean to say, if I am not mistaken, that rhetoric is the artificer of persuasion, having this and no other business, and that this is her crown and end. Do you know any other effect of rhetoric over and above that of producing persuasion?

Gor. No: the definition seems to me very fair, Socrates; for persuasion is the chief end of rhetoric.

Soc. Then hear me, Gorgias, for I am quite sure that if there ever was a man who entered on the discussion of a matter from a pure love of knowing the truth, I am such a one, and I should say the same of you.

Gor. What is coming, Socrates?

Soc. I will tell you: I am very well aware that I do not know what, according to you, is the exact nature, or what are the topics of that persuasion of which you speak, and which is given by rhetoric; although I have a suspicion about both the one and the other. And I am going to ask—what is this power of persuasion which is given by rhetoric, and about what? But why, if I have a suspicion, do I ask instead 65 of telling you? Not for your sake, but in order that the argument may proceed in such a manner as is most likely to set forth the truth. And I would have you observe, that I am right in asking this further question: If I asked, "What sort of a painter is Zeuxis?"[4] and you said, "The painter of figures," should I not be right in asking, "What kind of figures, and where do you find them?"

Gor. Certainly.

Soc. And the reason for asking this second question would be, that there are other painters besides, who paint many other figures?

Gor. True.

Soc. But if there had been no one but Zeuxis who painted them, then you would have answered very well?

Gor. Quite so.   70

Soc. Now I want to know about rhetoric in the same way;—is rhetoric the only art which brings persuasion, or do other arts have the same effect? I mean to say—Does he who teaches anything persuade men of that which he teaches or not?

Gor. He persuades, Socrates,—there can be no mistake about that.

Soc. Again, if we take the arts of which we were just now speaking:—do not arithmetic and the arithmeticians teach us the properties of number?

Gor. Certainly.

Soc. And therefore persuade us of them?   75

Gor. Yes.

Soc. Then arithmetic as well as rhetoric is an artificer of persuasion?

Gor. Clearly.

Soc. And if any one asks us what sort of persuasion, and about what,—we shall answer, persuasion which teaches the quantity of odd and even; and we shall be able to show that all the other arts of which we were just now speaking are artificers of persuasion, and of what sort, and about what.

Gor. Very true.   80

Soc. Then rhetoric is not the only artificer of persuasion?

Gor. True.

Soc. Seeing, then, that not only rhetoric works by persuasion, but that other arts do the same, as in the case of the painter, a question has arisen which is a very fair one: Of what persuasion is rhetoric the artificer, and about what?—is not that a fair way of putting the question?

Gor. I think so.

Soc. Then, if you approve the question, Gorgias, what is the answer?   85

Gor. I answer, Socrates, that rhetoric is the art of persuasion in courts of law and other assemblies, as I was just now saying, and about the just and unjust.

Soc. And that, Gorgias, was what I was suspecting to be your notion; yet I would not have you wonder if by-and-by I am found repeating a seemingly plain question; for

---

4. **Zeuxis:** a well-known painter from the Greek city of Ephesus.

I ask not in order to confute you, but as I was saying that the argument may proceed consecutively, and that we may not get the habit of anticipating and suspecting the meaning of one another's words; I would have you develop your own views in your own way, whatever may be your hypothesis.

Gor. I think that you are quite right, Socrates.

Soc. Then let me raise another question; there is such a thing as "having learned"?

Gor. Yes.   90

Soc. And there is also "having believed"?

Gor. Yes.

Soc. And is the "having learned" the same as "having believed," and are learning and belief the same things?

Gor. In my judgment, Socrates, they are not the same.[5]

Soc. And your judgment is right, as you may ascertain in this way:—If a person   95
were to say to you, "Is there, Gorgias, a false belief as well as a true?"—you would reply, if I am not mistaken, that there is.

Gor. Yes.

Soc. Well, but is there a false knowledge as well as a true?

Gor. No.

Soc. No, indeed; and this again proves that knowledge and belief differ.

Gor. Very true.   100

Soc. And yet those who have learned as well as those who have believed are persuaded?

Gor. Just so.

Soc. Shall we then assume two sorts of persuasion,—one which is the source of belief without knowledge, as the other is of knowledge?

Gor. By all means.

Soc. And which sort of persuasion does rhetoric create in courts of law and other   105
assemblies about the just and unjust, the sort of persuasion which gives belief without knowledge, or that which gives knowledge?

Gor. Clearly, Socrates, that which only gives belief.

Soc. Then rhetoric, as would appear, is the artificer of a persuasion which creates belief about the just and unjust, but gives no instruction about them?

Gor. True.

Soc. And the rhetorician does not instruct the courts of law or other assemblies about things just and unjust, but he creates belief about them; for no one can be supposed to instruct such a vast multitude about such high matters in a short time?

Gor. Certainly not.   110

Soc. Come, then, and let us see what we really mean about rhetoric; for I do not know what my own meaning is as yet. When the assembly meets to elect a physician

---

5. The historical Gorgias probably would not have conceded this point so easily, as he is said to have taught that nothing is ultimately knowable.

or a shipwright or any other craftsman, will the rhetorician be taken into counsel? Surely not. For at every election he ought to be chosen who is most skilled; and, again, when walls have to be built or harbours or docks to be constructed, not the rhetorician but the master workman will advise; or when generals have to be chosen and an order of battle arranged, or a proposition taken, then the military will advise and not the rhetoricians: what do you say, Gorgias? Since you profess to be a rhetorician and a maker of rhetoricians, I cannot do better than learn the nature of your art from you. And here let me assure you that I have your interest in view as well as my own. For likely enough some one or other of the young men present might desire to become your pupil, and in fact I see some, and a good many too, who have this wish, but they would be too modest to question you. And therefore when you are interrogated by me, I would have you imagine that you are interrogated by them. "What is the use of coming to you, Gorgias?" they will say—"about what will you teach us to advise the state?—about the just and unjust only, or about those other things also which Socrates has just mentioned?" How will you answer them?

Gor. I like your way of leading us on, Socrates, and I will endeavour to reveal to you the whole nature of rhetoric. You must have heard, I think, that the docks and the walls of the Athenians and the plan of the harbour were devised in accordance with the counsels, partly of Themistocles, and partly of Pericles,[6] and not at the suggestion of the builders.

Soc. Such is the tradition, Gorgias, about Themistocles; and I myself heard the speech of Pericles when he advised us about the middle wall.

Gor. And you will observe, Socrates, that when a decision has to be given in such matters the rhetoricians are the advisers; they are the men who win their point.

Soc. I had that in my admiring mind, Gorgias, when I asked what is the nature of rhetoric, which always appears to me, when I look at the matter in this way, to be a marvel of greatness.

Gor. A marvel, indeed, Socrates, if you only knew how rhetoric comprehends and holds under her sway all the inferior arts. Let me offer you a striking example of this. On several occasions I have been with my brother Herodicus or some other physician to see one of his patients, who would not allow the physician to give him medicine, or apply a knife or hot iron to him; and I have persuaded him to do for me what he would not do for the physician just by the use of rhetoric. And I say that if a rhetorician and a physician were to go to any city, and had there to argue in the Ecclesia[7] or any other assembly as to which of them should be elected state-physician, the physician would have no chance; but he who could speak would

115

6. **Pericles:** the leader of Athens (495–429 BCE) during much of its golden age and a major proponent of the Peloponnesian War. **Themistocles:** the Athenian leader (circa 524–circa 460 BCE) who masterminded the naval victory over the Persian Empire in 480 BCE, which established Athens as a regional power.

7. **Ecclesia:** the Athenian Assembly, which, in Plato's day, consisted of more than forty thousand citizens.

be chosen if he wished; and in a contest with a man of any other profession the rhetorician more than any one would have the power of getting himself chosen, for he can speak more persuasively to the multitude than any of them, and on any subject. Such is the nature and power of the art of rhetoric! And yet, Socrates, rhetoric should be used like any other competitive art, not against everybody—the rhetorician ought not to abuse his strength any more than a pugilist or pancratiast or other master of fence;[8] because he has powers which are more than a match either for friend or enemy, he ought not therefore to strike, stab, or slay his friends. Suppose a man to have been trained in the palestra[9] and to be a skilful boxer—he in the fulness of his strength goes and strikes his father or mother or one of his familiars or friends; but that is no reason why the trainers or fencing-masters should be held in detestation or banished from the city—surely not. For they taught their art for a good purpose, to be used against enemies and evil-doers, in self-defence not in aggression, and others have perverted their instructions, and turned to a bad use their own strength and skill. But not on this account are the teachers bad, neither is the art in fault, or bad in itself; I should rather say that those who make a bad use of the art are to blame. And the same argument holds good of rhetoric; for the rhetorician can speak against all men and upon any subject—in short, he can persuade the multitude better than any other man of anything which he pleases, but he should not therefore seek to defraud the physician or any other artist of his reputation merely because he has the power; he ought to use rhetoric fairly, as he would also use his athletic powers. And if after having become a rhetorician he makes a bad use of his strength and skill, his instructor surely ought not on that account to be held in detestation or banished. For he was intended by his teacher to make a good use of his instructions, but he abuses them. And therefore he is the person who ought to be held in detestation, banished, and put to death, and not his instructor.[10]

Soc. You, Gorgias, like myself, have had great experience of disputations, and you must have observed, I think, that they do not always terminate in mutual edification, or in the definition by either party of the subjects which they are discussing; but disagreements are apt to arise—somebody says that another has not spoken truly or clearly; and then they get into a passion and begin to quarrel, both parties conceiving that their opponents are arguing from personal feeling only

---

8. **Master of fence:** fencing master. **Pugilist or pancratiast:** Pugilists were the ancient equivalent of boxers; pancratiasts practiced *pankration*, a Greek martial art featured in the early Olympic games.

9. **Palestra:** a public training ground for wrestling and other athletic events.

10. Gorgias's defense of rhetoric here repeats the defense that the Athenian orator Isocrates

(436–338 BCE) makes in his rhetorical tract *Antidosis*. Thus it was probably standard to argue that, as a tool, rhetoric was morally neutral and could be used for good or bad. Plato would not have been impressed by such a defense—he believed that something must be actively good to be morally justified.

and jealousy of themselves, not from any interest in the question at issue. And sometimes they will go on abusing one another until the company at last are quite vexed at themselves for ever listening to such fellows. Why do I say this? Why, because I cannot help feeling that you are now saying what is not quite consistent or accordant with what you were saying at first about rhetoric. And I am afraid to point this out to you, lest you should think that I have some animosity against you, and that I speak, not for the sake of discovering the truth, but from jealousy of you. Now if you are one of my sort, I should like to cross-examine you, but if not I will let you alone. And what is my sort? you will ask. I am one of those who are very willing to be refuted if I say anything which is not true, and very willing to refute any one else who says what is not true, and quite as ready to be refuted as to refute; for I hold that this is the greater gain of the two, just as the gain is greater of being cured of a very great evil than of curing another. For I imagine that there is no evil which a man can endure so great as an erroneous opinion about the matters of which we are speaking; and if you claim to be one of my sort, let us have the discussion out, but if you would rather have done, no matter—let us make an end of it.

UNDERSTANDING THE TEXT

1. How does Gorgias initially define "rhetoric"? To what redefinition does Socrates lead him? Why does Socrates not simply state his redefinition—what does he gain by drawing it out of Gorgias?

2. What other subjects besides rhetoric does Socrates claim to be focused on persuasion? What is the difference between these subjects and rhetoric, according to the dialogue?

3. Explain the distinction that Socrates draws between "knowledge" and "belief." Which one is the province of rhetoric? Which, then, is the subject of philosophy? Do you agree with Socrates that all kinds of persuasion create either knowledge or belief? Why or why not?

4. What major defense of rhetoric does Gorgias offer? Do you agree with his reasoning? Why or why not?

5. Are the words that Plato puts into Gorgias's mouth strong enough to represent an actual argument? At which points is Gorgias's position at its strongest, and at which points is it at its weakest?

MAKING CONNECTIONS

1. Would Plato agree with Aristotle's assertion (p. 177) that good arguments naturally tend to prevail over bad ones? Would Plato agree with Aristotle's implicit assumption that rhetoric should be studied so that good arguments can compete on the same grounds as bad ones? Explain your answers.

2. In what ways does Plato see language as exercising a destructive power? Compare his perspective to the views of Augustine (p. 184) and Toni Morrison (p. 217) about the power of language.

3. Compare Plato's attack on rhetorical manipulation with Wayne Booth's concept of "the advertiser's stance" (p. 198). Are the two authors' points the same? Explain.

WRITING ABOUT THE TEXT

1. Use Socrates's arguments against rhetoric to analyze a television commercial or other advertisement. In what ways might the advertiser have focused on persuasion at the expense of truth? Does the advertisement seem aimed at producing knowledge or belief?

2. Defend the teaching of rhetoric on the grounds that knowing how to be persuasive increases one's ability to do good. Perhaps draw on the examples of historical figures (Mohandas Gandhi or Martin Luther King Jr., for instance) who accomplished great things because of their ability to persuade others.

3. Analyze Plato's rhetorical use of the dialogue form. How does the format of a fictional debate affect the persuasiveness of Plato's argument? How might Plato reconcile his use of rhetoric with the opposition to rhetoric that he expresses in *Gorgias*?

ARISTOTLE
from *Rhetoric*
[350 BCE]

THE PHILOSOPHER ARISTOTLE (384–322 BCE) began his career as a brilliant student in Plato's Academy. However, his views often clashed with those of Plato and other students, and after Plato's death (in 348 or 347 BCE), he left Athens and eventually became the private tutor of Prince Alexander of Macedon, later known as Alexander the Great. When he returned to Athens in 355 BCE, Aristotle founded his own school, the Lyceum, where he taught philosophy, natural science, and rhetoric.

Contemporary references indicate that Aristotle composed as many as 150 treatises on a wide variety of subjects (though many of these were probably detailed lecture notes taken by students at the Lyceum). The thirty surviving treatises cover such topics as logic, ethics, physics, metaphysics, politics, literature, and rhetoric and lay the foundations of Western reasoning. Unlike Plato, whose writings focus on the mind and the world of ideal forms, Aristotle focuses on the tangible realities of the external world. Also, while Plato's arguments tend to be *prescriptive*, or to advocate positions and points of view, Aristotle's writings are mostly *descriptive*, describing, organizing, and classifying their subjects.

Plato's and Aristotle's distinct approaches to philosophy can be seen clearly in their different approaches to rhetoric. Plato's *Gorgias* is an argument about the value of rhetoric, which he condemns as an inferior and dangerous counterfeit of philosophy. Aristotle's *Rhetoric*, on the other hand, concerns the practice of rhetoric. In it, he classifies different kinds of arguments, appeals, and tools that can form the basis for persuasive arguments. Much like the Sophists, Aristotle acknowledges that rhetoric can be either helpful or harmful, depending on how it is used. Unlike the Sophists, however, he believes that rhetoric inherently favors moral and just arguments because "things that are true and things that are just have a natural tendency to prevail over their opposites."

The first two chapters of Aristotle's *Rhetoric* are presented here. In the first part of this selection, Aristotle explains the usefulness of rhetoric. Rhetoric forms the counterpart of what he calls "dialectic"—while rhetoric is public speaking designed to persuade, dialectic is a more private philosophical dialogue designed to uncover the truth. In the second part of the selection, Aristotle establishes three categories of persuasive appeal: pathos (appeals to emotion), logos (appeals to logic and reasoning), and ethos (appeals based on the character of the speaker).

Aristotle's own rhetorical style highlights the deductive reasoning for which he was famous. Aristotle typically starts with a statement of general principle and then applies it to specific instances. He also spends a great deal of time dividing and classifying phenomena.

1

Rhetoric is the counterpart of Dialectic.[1] Both alike are concerned with such things as come, more or less, within the general ken of all men and belong to no definite science. Accordingly all men make use, more or less, of both; for to a certain extent all men attempt to discuss statements and to maintain them, to defend themselves and to attack others. Ordinary people do this either at random or through practice and from acquired habit. Both ways being possible, the subject can plainly be handled systematically, for it is possible to inquire the reason why some speakers succeed through practice and others spontaneously; and every one will at once agree that such an inquiry is the function of an art.

Now, the framers of the current treatises on rhetoric[2] have constructed but a small portion of that art. The modes of persuasion are the only true constituents of the art: everything else is merely accessory. These writers, however, say nothing about enthymemes,[3] which are the substance of rhetorical persuasion, but deal mainly with non-essentials. The arousing of prejudice, pity, anger, and similar emotions has nothing to do with the essential facts, but is merely a personal appeal to the man who is judging the case. Consequently if the rules for trials which are now laid down in some states—especially in well-governed states—were applied everywhere, such people would have nothing to say. All men, no doubt, *think* that the laws should prescribe such rules, but some, as in the court of Areopagus,[4] give practical effect to their thoughts and forbid talk about non-essentials. This is sound law and custom. It is not right to pervert the judge by moving him to anger or envy or pity—one might as well warp a carpenter's rule before using it. Again, a litigant has clearly nothing to do but to show that the alleged fact is so or is not so, that it has or has not happened. As to whether a thing is important or unimportant, just or unjust, the judge must surely refuse to take his instructions from the litigants: he must decide for himself all such points as the law-giver has not already defined for him.

Now, it is of great moment that well-drawn laws should themselves define all the points they possibly can and leave as few as may be to the decision of the judges; and this for several reasons. First, to find one man, or a few men, who are sensible persons and capable of legislating and administering justice is easier than to find a large number. Next, laws are made after long consideration, whereas decisions in the courts are given at short notice, which makes it hard for those who try the case to

1. **Dialectic:** discussion, specifically philosophical discussion that aims to uncover truth rather than persuade. Aristotle's use of the term differs somewhat from Hegel's (see p. 678).
2. **Current treatises on rhetoric:** the works of Sophists such as Gorgias, Isocrates, and Protagoras.
3. **Enthymemes:** In Aristotle's terms, an "enthymeme" was the basic unit of an argument: a conclusion attached to a single supporting premise, with other premises merely implied. A rough modern equivalent is the "thesis statement."
4. **Areopagus:** Athens's "Hill of Ares," where murder trials were held in Aristotle's time.

satisfy the claims of justice and expediency. The weightiest reason of all is that the decision of the lawgiver is not particular but prospective and general, whereas members of the assembly and the jury find it *their* duty to decide on definite cases brought before them. They will often have allowed themselves to be so much influenced by feelings of friendship or hatred or self-interest that they lose any clear vision of the truth and have their judgement obscured by considerations of personal pleasure or pain. In general, then, the judge should, we say, be allowed to decide as few things as possible. But questions as to whether something has happened or has not happened, will be or will not be, is or is not, must of necessity be left to the judge, since the lawgiver cannot foresee them. If this is so, it is evident that any one who lays down rules about other matters, such as what must be the contents of the 'introduction' or the 'narration' or any of the other divisions of a speech, is theorizing about non-essentials as if they belonged to the art. The only question with which these writers here deal is how to put the judge into a given frame of mind. About the orator's proper modes of persuasion they have nothing to tell us; nothing, that is, about how to gain skill in enthymemes.

Hence it comes that, although the same systematic principles apply to political as to forensic oratory,[5] and although the former is a nobler business, and fitter for a citizen, than that which concerns the relations of private individuals, these authors say nothing about political oratory, but try, one and all, to write treatises on the way to plead in court. The reason for this is that in political oratory there is less inducement to talk about non-essentials. Political oratory is less given to unscrupulous practices than forensic, because it treats of wider issues. In a political debate the man who is forming a judgement is making a decision about his own vital interests. There is no need, therefore, to prove anything except that the facts are what the supporter of a measure maintains they are. In forensic oratory this is not enough; to conciliate the listener is what pays here. It is other people's affairs that are to be decided, so that the judges, intent on their own satisfaction and listening with partiality, surrender themselves to the disputants instead of judging between them. Hence in many places, as we have said already, irrelevant speaking is forbidden in the law-courts: in the public assembly those who have to form a judgement are themselves well able to guard against that.

It is clear, then, that rhetorical study, in its strict sense, is concerned with the modes of persuasion. Persuasion is clearly a sort of demonstration, since we are most fully persuaded when we consider a thing to have been demonstrated. The orator's demonstration is an enthymeme, and this is, in general, the most effective of the modes of persuasion. The enthymeme is a sort of syllogism,[6] and the consideration of syllogisms of all kinds, without distinction, is the business of dialectic, either of dialectic as a whole or of one of its branches. It follows plainly, therefore, that he who is best able to see how and from what elements a syllogism is produced will also

5

5. **Forensic oratory:** arguments designed to establish facts from the past, especially as they relate to guilt or innocence in a criminal trial.

6. **Syllogism:** see p. 652.

be best skilled in the enthymeme, when he has further learnt what its subject-matter is and in what respects it differs from the syllogism of strict logic. The true and the approximately true are apprehended by the same faculty; it may also be noted that men have a sufficient natural instinct for what is true, and usually do arrive at the truth. Hence the man who makes a good guess at truth is likely to make a good guess at probabilities.

It has now been shown that the ordinary writers on rhetoric treat of non-essentials; it has also been shown why they have inclined more towards the forensic branch of oratory.

Rhetoric is useful (1) because things that are true and things that are just have a natural tendency to prevail over their opposites, so that if the decisions of judges are not what they ought to be, the defeat must be due to the speakers themselves, and they must be blamed accordingly. Moreover, (2) before some audiences not even the possession of the exactest knowledge will make it easy for what we say to produce conviction. For argument based on knowledge implies instruction, and there are people whom one cannot instruct. Here, then, we must use, as our modes of persuasion and argument, notions possessed by everybody, as we observed in the *Topics*[7] when dealing with the way to handle a popular audience. Further, (3) we must be able to employ persuasion, just as strict reasoning can be employed, on opposite sides of a question, not in order that we may in practice employ it in both ways (for we must not make people believe what is wrong), but in order that we may see clearly what the facts are, and that, if another man argues unfairly, we on our part may be able to confute him. No other of the arts draws opposite conclusions: dialectic and rhetoric alone do this. Both these arts draw opposite conclusions impartially. Nevertheless, the underlying facts do not lend themselves equally well to the contrary views. No; things that are true and things that are better are, by their nature, practically always easier to prove and easier to believe in. Again, (4) it is absurd to hold that a man ought to be ashamed of being unable to defend himself with his limbs, but not of being unable to defend himself with speech and reason, when the use of rational speech is more distinctive of a human being than the use of his limbs. And if it be objected that one who uses such power of speech unjustly might do great harm, *that* is a charge which may be made in common against all good things except virtue, and above all against the things that are most useful, as strength, health, wealth, generalship. A man can confer the greatest of benefits by a right use of these, and inflict the greatest of injuries by using them wrongly.

It is clear, then, that rhetoric is not bound up with a single definite class of subjects, but is as universal as dialectic; it is clear, also, that it is useful. It is clear, further, that its function is not simply to succeed in persuading, but rather to discover the means of coming as near such success as the circumstances of each particular

7. *Topics:* one of Aristotle's six known works on logic, which form a collective work called the *Organon.*

case allow. In this it resembles all other arts. For example, it is not the function of medicine simply to make a man quite healthy, but to put him as far as may be on the road to health; it is possible to give excellent treatment even to those who can never enjoy sound health. Furthermore, it is plain that it is the function of one and the same art to discern the real and the apparent means of persuasion, just as it is the function of dialectic to discern the real and the apparent syllogism. What makes a man a 'sophist' is not his faculty, but his moral purpose. In rhetoric, however, the term 'rhetorician' may describe either the speaker's knowledge of the art, or his moral purpose. In dialectic it is different: a man is a 'sophist' because he has a certain kind of moral purpose, a 'dialectician' in respect, not of his moral purpose, but of his faculty.

Let us now try to give some account of the systematic principles of Rhetoric itself—of the right method and means of succeeding in the object we set before us. We must make as it were a fresh start, and before going further define what rhetoric is.

2

Rhetoric may be defined as the faculty of observing in any given case the available   10 means of persuasion. This is not a function of any other art. Every other art can instruct or persuade about its own particular subject-matter; for instance, medicine about what is healthy and unhealthy, geometry about the properties of magnitudes, arithmetic about numbers, and the same is true of the other arts and sciences. But rhetoric we look upon as the power of observing the means of persuasion on almost any subject presented to us; and that is why we say that, in its technical character, it is not concerned with any special or definite class of subjects.

Of the modes of persuasion some belong strictly to the art of rhetoric and some do not. By the latter I mean such things as are not supplied by the speaker but are there are the outset—witnesses, evidence given under torture, written contracts, and so on. By the former I mean such as we can ourselves construct by means of the principles of rhetoric. The one kind has merely to be used, the other has to be invented.

Of the modes of persuasion furnished by the spoken word there are three kinds. The first kind depends on the personal character of the speaker; the second on putting the audience into a certain frame of mind; the third on the proof, or apparent proof, provided by the words of the speech itself. Persuasion is achieved by the speaker's personal character when the speech is so spoken as to make us think him credible. We believe good men more fully and more readily than others: this is true generally whatever the question is, and absolutely true where exact certainty is impossible and opinions are divided. This kind of persuasion, like the others, should be achieved by what the speaker says, not by what people think of his character before he begins to speak. It is not true, as some writers assume in their treatises on rhetoric, that the personal goodness revealed by the speaker contributes nothing to his power of persuasion; on the contrary, his character may almost be called the most effective means of persuasion he possesses. Secondly, persuasion may come through the hearers, when the speech stirs their emotions. Our judgements when we are pleased and friendly are not the same as when we are pained and hostile. It is towards producing these effects, as we maintain, that present-day writers on rhetoric direct the whole of their efforts. This subject shall be treated in detail when we come to speak of the emotions. Thirdly, persuasion is effected through the speech itself when we have proved a truth or an apparent truth by means of the persuasive arguments suitable to the case in question.

There are, then, these three means of effecting persuasion. The man who is to be in command of them must, it is clear, be able (1) to reason logically, (2) to understand human character and goodness in their various forms, and (3) to understand the emotions—that is, to name them and describe them, to know their causes and the way in which they are excited. It thus appears that rhetoric is an offshoot of dialectic and also of ethical studies. Ethical studies may fairly be called political; and for this reason rhetoric masquerades as political science, and the professors of it as political experts—sometimes from want of education, sometimes from ostentation, sometimes owing to other human failings. As a matter of fact, it is a branch of dialectic and similar to it, as we said at the outset. Neither rhetoric nor dialectic is the scientific study of any one separate subject: both are faculties for providing arguments. This is perhaps a sufficient account of their scope and of how they are related to each other.

UNDERSTANDING THE TEXT

1. What, according to Aristotle, is rhetoric's primary purpose?

2. What does Aristotle consider the hallmarks of "well-drawn laws"? Do you agree with this assertion? Why or why not?

3. How does Aristotle differentiate between a "Sophist" and a "rhetorician"? Can one employ rhetoric without being a Sophist?

4. What are Aristotle's three means of persuasion? What specific skills does each method require? Which method do you consider the most persuasive, and why?

MAKING CONNECTIONS

1. Compare Aristotle's defense of rhetoric with the one made by Gorgias in Plato's *Gorgias* (p. 166). Which of Gorgias's ideas does Aristotle echo? How does his position differ from Gorgias's?

2. How might Wayne Booth (p. 198) respond to Aristotle's assertion that the strongest arguments will always prevail? Cite passages from "The Rhetorical Stance" in your reply.

3. How do Aristotle's views of the natural superiority of true arguments compare with the warnings given by Toni Morrison (p. 217) about the destructive power of speech?

WRITING ABOUT THE TEXT

1. Select a text that was written specifically to persuade—such as Martin Luther King Jr.'s "Letter from Birmingham Jail" (p. 425) or Rachel Carson's "The Obligation to Endure" (p. 328)—and analyze its use of Aristotle's three means of persuasion. How effective are the text's appeals to logic, appeals to emotion, and appeals based on the character of the speaker?

2. Write an essay in which you agree or disagree with Aristotle's assertion that "things that are true and things that are just have a natural tendency to prevail over their opposites." In your experience, do morally sound, factually correct arguments generally prevail in public discourse?

3. Compare Aristotle's and Plato's (p. 166) views on rhetoric. What underlying assumptions might have contributed to their very different ideas about the art of persuasion?

AUGUSTINE
from *On Christian Doctrine*
[426]

IN 397, AUGUSTINE (354–430), a newly appointed bishop in the Algerian city of Hippo, shocked his followers by writing a candid autobiography of his early life. Raised Christian, Augustine abandoned the faith for a series of sexual and philosophical adventures that he recounts in great detail in his *Confessions*. At the age of 31, Augustine reconverted to Christianity and, shortly thereafter, began a career in the church that would last until his death in 430 at the age of 76.

Augustine of Hippo was one of the most prolific writers in the early Christian church, and he was indisputably its greatest theologian. Well trained in Greek and Roman philosophy, he formulated his own, uniquely Christian answers to many of the enduring questions of his day. He wrote dozens of books and tracts that helped to establish Christian doctrine in the fifth century and refute the various Christian heresies that had split the early church into competing factions. Soon after his death, Augustine was proclaimed a saint by popular decree. In 1298, he was officially declared one of the first four "Doctors of the Church" by Pope Boniface VIII.

Before his conversion, Augustine trained as a rhetorician and taught rhetoric in Carthage and Rome before accepting a prestigious professorship in Milan. His most famous treatment of rhetoric is the four-volume *On Christian Doctrine*—a work designed to teach Christians how to read and talk to others about the Bible. The first three books were published in 397, soon after Augustine became a bishop. The fourth was added nearly thirty years later in 426, by which time he was the most famous writer in the Christian world.

The following selection has been taken from Book IV of *On Christian Doctrine*. Here, Augustine gently rebuts those Christians who see rhetoric as a pagan artifact that should be eschewed. Rhetoric can be used to prove both truth and falsehood, Augustine argues, and it would be unwise to concede the most useful persuasive tools to those with evil intentions "while the defenders of truth are ignorant of that art." Augustine announces at the beginning of the selection, however, that he does not intend to provide his readers with rules that they can follow to become more persuasive. Rather, he insists, they should read and listen to the most eloquent Christians and imitate what they see.

1. This work of ours entitled *On Christian Doctrine* was at the beginning divided into two parts. For after the Prologue in which I replied to those who would criticize it, I wrote, "There are two things necessary to the treatment of the Scriptures: a way of discovering those things which are to be understood, and a way of teaching what we have learned. We shall speak first of discovery and second of teaching." Since

we have already said much concerning discovery and devoted three books to that one part, with the help of God we shall say a few things concerning teaching, so that, if possible, we shall conclude everything with one book and thus complete the whole work in four books.

I

2. But first in these preliminary remarks I must thwart the expectation of those readers who think that I shall give the rules of rhetoric here which I learned and taught in the secular schools. And I admonish them not to expect such rules from me, not that they have no utility, but because, if they have any, it should be sought elsewhere if perhaps some good man has the opportunity to learn them. But he should not expect these rules from me, either in this work or in any other.

II

3. For since by means of the art of rhetoric both truth and falsehood are urged, who would dare to say that truth should stand in the person of its defenders unarmed against lying, so that they who wish to urge falsehoods may know how to make their listeners benevolent, or attentive, or docile in their presentation, while the defenders of truth are ignorant of that art? Should they speak briefly, clearly, and plausibly while the defenders of truth speak so that they tire their listeners, make themselves difficult to understand and what they have to say dubious? Should they oppose the truth with fallacious arguments and assert falsehoods, while the defenders of truth have no ability either to defend the truth or to oppose the false? Should they, urging the minds of their listeners into error, ardently exhort them, moving them by speech so that they terrify, sadden, and exhilarate them, while the defenders of truth are sluggish, cold, and somnolent? Who is so foolish as to think this to be wisdom? While the faculty of eloquence, which is of great value in urging either evil or justice, is in itself indifferent, why should it not be obtained for the uses of the good in the service of truth if the evil usurp it for the winning of perverse and vain causes in defense of iniquity and error?

III

4. But whatever observations and rules concerning this matter there may be, in accordance with which one acquires through exercise and habit a most skillful use of vocabulary and plentiful verbal ornaments, are established by what is called eloquence or oratory. Those who are able to do so quickly, having set aside an

appropriate period of time, should learn them at a proper and convenient age out-side of these writings of mine. For the masters of Roman eloquence themselves did not hesitate to say that, unless one can learn this art quickly, he can hardly learn it at all. Why should we inquire whether this is true? For even if these rules can sometimes be learned by those who are slow, we do not hold them to be of such importance that we would wish mature and grave men to spend their time learning them. It is enough that they be the concern of youths; nor should they concern all of those whom we wish to educate for the utility of the Church, but only those who are not pursuing some more urgent study, or one which obviously ought to take precedence over this one. For those with acute and eager minds more readily learn eloquence by reading and hearing the eloquent than by following the rules of eloquence. There is no lack of ecclesiastical literature, including that outside of the canon established in a place of secure authority, which, if read by a capable man, even though he is interested more in what is said than in the eloquence with which it is said, will imbue him with that eloquence while he is studying. And he will learn eloquence especially if he gains practice by writing, dictating, or speak-ing what he has learned according to the rule of piety and faith. But if capacity of this kind to learn eloquence is lacking, the rules of rhetoric will not be understood, nor will it help any if they are in some small measure understood after great labor. Even those who have learned these rules and speak fluently and eloquently cannot be aware of the fact that they are applying them while they are speaking unless they are discussing the rules themselves; indeed, I think that there is hardly a single eloquent man who can both speak well and think of the rules of eloquence while he is speaking. And we should beware lest what should be said escape us while we are thinking of the artistry of the discourse. Moreover, in the speeches and sayings of the eloquent, the precepts of eloquence are found to have been fulfilled, although the speakers did not think of them in order to be eloquent or while they were being eloquent, and they were eloquent whether they had learned the rules or never come in contact with them. They fulfilled them because they were eloquent; they did not apply them that they might be eloquent.

5. Therefore, since infants are not taught to speak except by learning the expres-sions of speakers, why can men not be made eloquent, not by teaching them the rules of eloquence, but by having them read and hear the expressions of the eloquent and imitate them in so far as they are able to follow them? Have we not seen examples of this being done? For we know many men ignorant of the rules of eloquence who are more eloquent than many who have learned them; but we know of no one who is eloquent without having read or heard the disputations and sayings of the eloquent. For boys do not need the art of grammar which teaches correct speech if they have the opportunity to grow up and live among men who speak correctly. Without know-ing any of the names of the errors, they criticize and avoid anything erroneous they hear spoken on the basis of their own habits of speech, just as city dwellers, even if they are illiterate, criticize the speech of rustics.

IV

6. Thus the expositor and teacher of the Divine Scripture, the defender of right faith and the enemy of error, should both teach the good and extirpate the evil. And in this labor of words, he should conciliate those who are opposed, arouse those who are remiss, and teach those ignorant of his subject what is occurring and what they should expect. But when he has either found his listeners to be benevolent, attentive, and docile, or has caused them to be so, other aims are to be carried out as the cause requires. If those who hear are to be taught, exposition must be composed, if it is needed, that they may become acquainted with the subject at hand. In order that those things which are doubtful may be made certain, they must be reasoned out with the use of evidence. But if those who hear are to be moved rather than taught, so that they may not be sluggish in putting what they know into practice and so that they may fully accept those things which they acknowledge to be true, there is need for greater powers of speaking. Here entreaties and reproofs, exhortations and rebukes, and whatever other devices are necessary to move minds must be used.

7. And almost all men who make use of eloquence do not cease to do all of those things which I have mentioned.

UNDERSTANDING THE TEXT

1. Why does Augustine seem to react so strongly against the "secular" rhetoricians, even as he is using many of their ideas? Does he seem to be overstating his opposition to them?

2. Why does Augustine believe that Christians should learn how to argue persuasively? What consequences might follow if Christians are untrained in rhetoric while pagans and heretics are well versed in it?

3. Why does Augustine believe that people cannot learn to be persuasive by reading other people's theories of how to be persuasive? What does he recommend instead?

4. Why does Augustine say that people should read "ecclesiastical literature" to find models of good rhetoric? Why does he exclude other kinds of persuasive texts?

5. What should the objectives of Christian teaching be, according to Augustine? What role does rhetoric play in achieving these objectives?

MAKING CONNECTIONS

1. Both Augustine and Wayne Booth (p. 198) write about the difficulty of teaching people how to be persuasive by explaining rules and concepts. Do the two agree on the best way to solve this problem? Where do they agree and where do they disagree?

2. Throughout this selection, Augustine appears to be addressing a reluctance in the Christian community to study secular topics such as rhetoric and persuasion, topics that Augustine himself believes are important to understand. How do his arguments

compare to those that Sor Juana Inés de la Cruz (p. 189) makes about allowing women to study secular branches of knowledge?

3. The great medieval theologian Thomas Aquinas was deeply influenced by the writings of Augustine. Read Aquinas's argument on war from *Summa Theologica* (p. 483) and assess whether or not it could be considered Christian rhetoric of the sort that Augustine advocates in this passage.

WRITING ABOUT THE TEXT

1. Evaluate Augustine's contention that rhetoric can be better learned by imitation than by following rules. Do you think he is correct? Does it apply to other fields of study as well? What might be the limitations of this approach to education?

2. Compare Augustine's view of rhetoric to Plato's (p. 166). Augustine believes that rhetoric can be used for good or for bad, while Plato believes that it is inherently dangerous and likely to lead to deception. Who do you think is right? Why?

SOR JUANA INÉS DE LA CRUZ
from *La Respuesta*
[1691]

JUANA INÉS DE ASBAJE Y RAMÍREZ DE SANTILLANA (1651–1695) was born near Mexico City. At the time, all of present-day Mexico was part of the Spanish colony called New Spain. Juana was the illegitimate daughter of a prominent Spanish officer. She was raised by her mother, the daughter of a prominent local farmer, and grandparents, and by all accounts was an intellectual prodigy from a very young age. While still a child, she learned Greek and Latin from the books in her grandfather's library and began writing poetry in both Spanish and the Mexican Aztec language.

By her teens, Juana was known throughout New Spain as a writer and poet. She attracted the patronage of the viceroy of New Spain, Antonio Sebastián de Toledo, who had her poems published throughout the colony and in Spain. As a woman in a highly patriarchal society, however, she had very few opportunities to continue her education except through the church. In 1669, she entered the Order of Saint Jerome, a cloistered order of nuns, where she became Sor (Sister) Juana Inés de la Cruz.

Sor Juana Inés de la Cruz is remembered today as one of Mexico's greatest poets and national treasures. Her picture is on the widely circulated 200 peso bill (worth about 15 U.S. dollars), and statues of her have been erected in public spaces throughout the country. In her own lifetime, though, she faced constant censure from a religious establishment that did not believe that women had the right to an education.

La Respuesta ("The Answer") is addressed to a fictional fellow sister, Sor Filota, but is actually a response to the bishop of Puebla, Manuel Fernández de Santa Cruz, who had recently reprimanded her for having published comments critical of a male Portuguese priest. In her response, Sor Juana describes her own education and upbringing and attributes her desire to learn and write to God. She also argues that women, like men, need to study subjects in many different fields if they are to understand the Holy Scriptures and the teachings of the church, and she points to many great women of the Bible and of classical antiquity who served God and society by becoming learned. Like most writers of her day, Sor Juana bases most of her rhetoric on appeals to the authority of scripture and on logical conclusions that can be drawn using reason from sacred texts.

My most illustrious *señora*, dear lady. It has not been my will, my poor health, or my justifiable apprehension that for so many days delayed my response. How could I write, considering that at my very first step my clumsy pen encountered two obstructions in its path? The first (and, for me, the most uncompromising) is to know how to reply to your most learned, most prudent, most holy, and most loving letter. For I recall that when Saint Thomas, the Angelic Doctor of Scholasticism, was asked about his silence regarding his teacher Albertus Magnus,[1] he replied that he had not spoken because he knew no words worthy of Albertus. With so much greater reason, must not I too be silent? Not, like the Saint, out of humility, but because in reality I know nothing I can say that is worthy of you. The second obstruction is to know how to express my appreciation for a favor as unexpected as extreme, for having my scribblings printed, a gift so immeasurable as to surpass my most ambitious aspiration, my most fervent desire, which even as an entity of reason never entered my thoughts. Yours was a kindness, finally, of such magnitude that words cannot express my gratitude, a kindness exceeding the bounds of appreciation, as great as it was unexpected—which is as Quintilian[2] said: *aspirations engender minor glory; benefices, major.* To such a degree as to impose silence on the receiver.

When the blessedly sterile—that she might miraculously become fecund—Mother of John the Baptist saw in her house such an extraordinary visitor as the Mother of the Word,[3] her reason became clouded and her speech deserted her; and thus, in the place of thanks, she burst out with doubts and questions: *And whence is to me [that the mother of my Lord should come to me?]* And whence cometh such a thing to *me*? And so also it fell to Saul when he found himself the chosen, the annointed, King of Israel: *Am I not a son of Jemini, of the least tribe of Israel, and my kindred the last among all the families of the tribe of Benjamin? Why then hast thou spoken this word to me?* And thus say I, most honorable lady. Why do I receive such favor? By chance, am I other than an humble nun, the lowliest creature of the world, the most unworthy to occupy your attention? "Wherefore then speakest thou so to me?" "And whence is this to me?" Nor to the first obstruction do I have any response other than I am little worthy of your eyes; nor to the second, other than wonder, in the stead of thanks, saying that I am not capable of thanking you for the smallest part of that which I owe you. . . . And, in truth, I have written nothing except when compelled and constrained, and then only to give pleasure to others; not alone without pleasure of my own, but with absolute repugnance, for I have never deemed myself one who has any worth in letters or the wit necessity demands of one who would write; and thus my customary response to those who press me, above all in sacred matters, is, what capacity of reason have I? what application? what resources? what rudimentary knowledge of such matters beyond that of the most superficial scholarly degrees? Leave these matters to those who understand them; I wish no quarrel with the

1. **Saint Thomas:** Thomas Aquinas (1225–1274), Italian theologian, friar, and author of *Summa Theologica* (p. 483); **Albertus Magnus:** German philosopher, scholar, and Dominican friar (1193–1280) who was Thomas Aquinas's teacher.

2. **Quintilian:** Marcus Fabius Quintilianus (circa 35–circa 100), an influential Roman rhetorician and author of *Institutio Oratorio*.

3. **Mother of the Word:** Mary, the mother of Christ, whose visit to her cousin Elizabeth, the mother of John the Baptist, is recorded in Luke 1:39–56.

Holy Office, for I am ignorant, and I tremble that I may express some proposition that will cause offense or twist the true meaning of some scripture. I do not study to write, even less to teach—which in one like myself were unseemly pride—but only to the end that if I study, I will be ignorant of less. This is my response, and these are my feelings.

I have never written of my own choice, but at the urging of others, to whom with reason I might say, *You have compelled me.* But one truth I shall not deny (first, because it is well-known to all, and second, because although it has not worked in my favor, God has granted me the mercy of loving truth above all else), which is that from the moment I was first illuminated by the light of reason, my inclination toward letters has been so vehement, so overpowering, that not even the admonitions of others—and I have suffered many—nor my own meditations—and they have not been few—have been sufficient to cause me to forswear this natural impulse that God placed in me: the Lord God knows why, and for what purpose. And He knows that I have prayed that He dim the light of my reason, leaving only that which is needed to keep His Law, for there are those who would say that all else is unwanted in a woman, and there are even those who would hold that such knowledge does injury. And my Holy Father knows too that as I have been unable to achieve this (my prayer has not been answered), I have sought to veil the light of my reason—along with my name—and to offer it up only to Him who bestowed it upon me, and He knows that none other was the cause for my entering into Religion, notwithstanding that the spiritual exercises and company of a community were repugnant to the freedom and quiet I desired for my studious endeavors. And later, in that community, the Lord God knows—and, in the world, only the one who must know—how diligently I sought to obscure my name, and how this was not permitted, saying it was temptation: and so it would have been. If it were in my power, lady, to repay you in some part what I owe you, it might be done by telling you this thing which has never before passed my lips, except to be spoken to the one who should hear it. It is my hope that by having opened wide to you the doors of my heart, by having made patent to you its most deeply-hidden secrets, you will deem my confidence not unworthy of the debt I owe to your most august person and to your most uncommon favors.

Continuing the narration of my inclinations, of which I wish to give you a thorough account, I will tell you that I was not yet three years old when my mother determined to send one of my elder sisters to learn to read at a school for girls we call the *Amigas.* Affection, and mischief, caused me to follow her, and when I observed how she was being taught her lessons I was so inflamed with the desire to know how to read, that deceiving—for so I knew it to be—the mistress, I told her that my mother had meant for me to have lessons too. She did not believe it, as it was little to be believed, but, to humor me, she acceded. I continued to go there, and she continued to teach me, but now, as experience had disabused her, with all seriousness; and I learned so quickly that before my mother knew of it I could already read, for my teacher had kept it from her in order to reveal the surprise and reap the reward at one and the same time. And

I, you may be sure, kept the secret, fearing that I would be whipped for having acted without permission. The woman who taught me, may God bless and keep her, is still alive and can bear witness to all I say. I also remember that in those days, my tastes being those common to that age, I abstained from eating cheese because I had heard that it made one slow of wits, for in me the desire for learning was stronger than the desire for eating—as powerful as that is in children. When later, being six or seven, and having learned how to read and write, along with all the other skills of needle-work and household arts that girls learn, it came to my attention that in Mexico City there were Schools, and a University, in which one studied the sciences. The moment I heard this, I began to plague my mother with insistent and importunate pleas: she should dress me in boy's clothing and send me to Mexico City to live with relatives, to study and be tutored at the University. She would not permit it, and she was wise, but I assuaged my disappointment by reading the many and varied books belonging to my grandfather, and there were not enough punishments, nor reprimands, to prevent me from reading: so that when I came to the city many marveled, not so much at my natural wit, as at my memory, and at the amount of learning I had mastered at an age when many have scarcely learned to speak well.

I began to study Latin grammar—in all, I believe, I had no more than 20 lessons— 5 and so intense was my concern that though among women (especially a woman in the flower of her youth) the natural adornment of one's hair is held in such high esteem, I cut off mine to the breadth of some four to six fingers, measuring the place it had reached, and imposing upon myself the condition that if by the time it had again grown to that length I had not learned such and such a thing I had set for myself to learn while my hair was growing, I would again cut it off as punishment for being so slow-witted. And it did happen that my hair grew out and still I had not learned what I had set for myself—because my hair grew quickly and I learned slowly—and in fact I did cut it in punishment for such stupidity: for there seemed to me no cause for a head to be adorned with hair and naked of learning—which was the more desired embellishment. And so I entered the religious order, knowing that life there entailed certain conditions (I refer to superficial, and not fundamental, regards) most repugnant to my nature; but given the total antipathy I felt for marriage, I deemed convent life the least unsuitable and the most honorable I could elect if I were to insure my salvation. Working against that end, first (as, finally, the most important) was the matter of all the trivial aspects of my nature which nourished my pride, such as wishing to live alone, and wishing to have no obligatory occupa-tion that would inhibit the freedom of my studies, nor the sounds of a community that would intrude upon the peaceful silence of my books. These desires caused me to falter some while in my decision, until certain learned persons enlightened me, explaining that they were temptation, and, with divine favor, I overcame them, and took upon myself the state which now so unworthily I hold. I believed that I was fleeing from myself, but—wretch that I am!—I brought with me my worst enemy, my inclination, which I do not know whether to consider a gift or a punishment from Heaven, for once dimmed and encumbered by the many activities common to Religion, that inclination exploded in me like gunpowder, proving how *privation is the source of appetite*. . . .

And so I continued, as I have said, directing the course of my studies toward the peak of Sacred Theology, it seeming necessary to me, in order to scale those heights, to climb the steps of the human sciences and arts; for how could one undertake the study of the Queen of Science[4] if first one had not come to know her servants?

How, without Logic, could I be apprised of the general and specific way in which the Holy Scripture is written? How, without Rhetoric, could I understand its figures, its tropes, its locutions? How, without Physics, so many innate questions concerning the nature of animals, their sacrifices, wherein exist so many symbols, many already declared, many still to be discovered? How should I know whether Saul's being refreshed by the sound of David's harp was due to the virtue and natural power of Music, or to a transcendent power God wished to place in David? How, without Arithmetic, could one understand the computations of the years, days, months, hours, those mysterious weeks communicated by Gabriel to Daniel, and others for whose understanding one must know the nature, concordance, and properties of numbers? How, without Geometry, could one measure the Holy Arc of the Covenant and the Holy City of Jerusalem, whose mysterious measures are foursquare in their dimensions, as well as the miraculous proportions of all their parts? How, without Architecture, could one know the great Temple of Solomon, of which God Himself was the Author who conceived the disposition and the design, and the Wise King but the overseer who executed it, of which temple there was no foundation without mystery, no column without symbolism, no cornice without allusion, no architrave without significance; and similarly others of its parts, of which the least fillet was never intended solely for the service and complement of Art, but as symbol of greater things? How, without great knowledge of the laws and parts of which History is comprised, could one understand historical Books? Or those recapitulations in which many times what happened first is seen in the narrated account to have happened later? How, without great learning in Canon and Civil Law, could one understand Legal Books? How, without great erudition, could one apprehend the secular histories of which the Holy Scripture makes mention, such as the many customs of the Gentiles, their many rites, their many ways of speaking? How without the abundant laws and lessons of the Holy Fathers could one understand the obscure lesson of the Prophets? And without being expert in Music, how could one understand the exquisite precision of the musical proportions that grace so many Scriptures. . . .

How then should I—so lacking in virtue and so poorly read—find courage to write? But as I had acquired the rudiments of learning, I continued to study ceaselessly diverse subjects, having for none any particular inclination, but for all in general; and having studied some more than others was not owing to preference, but to the

4. **Queen of Sciences:** theology.

chance that more books on certain subjects had fallen into my hands, causing the election of them through no discretion of my own. . . .

This manner of reflection has always been my habit, and is quite beyond my will to control; on the contrary, I am wont to become vexed that my intellect makes me weary; and I believed that it was so with everyone, as well as making verses, until experience taught me otherwise; and it is so strong in me this nature, or custom, that I look at nothing without giving it further examination. Once in my presence two young girls were spinning a top and scarcely had I seen the motion and the figure described, when I began, out of this madness of mine, to meditate on the effortless *motus*[5] of the spherical form, and how the impulse persisted even when free and independent of its cause—for the top continued to dance even at some distance from the child's hand, which was the causal force. And not content with this, I had flour brought and sprinkled about, so that as the top danced one might learn whether these were perfect circles it described with its movement; and I found that they were not, but, rather, spiral lines that lost their circularity as the impetus declined. Other girls sat playing at spillikins (surely the most frivolous game that children play):[6] I walked closer to observe the figures they formed, and seeing that by chance three lay in a triangle, I set to joining one with another, recalling that this was said to be the form of the mysterious ring of Solomon[7] in which he was able to see the distant splendor and images of the Holy Trinity, by virtue of which the ring worked such prodigies and marvels. And the same shape was said to form David's harp, and that is why Saul was refreshed at its sound; and harps today largely conserve that shape.

And what shall I tell you, lady, of the natural secrets I have discovered while   10 cooking? I see that an egg holds together and fries in butter or in oil, but, on the contrary, in syrup shrivels into shreds; observe that to keep sugar in a liquid state one need only add a drop or two of water in which a quince or other bitter fruit has been soaked; observe that the yolk and the white of one egg are so dissimilar that each with sugar produces a result not obtainable with both together. I do not wish to weary you with such inconsequential matters, and make mention of them only to give you full notice of my nature, for I believe they will be occasion for laughter. But, lady, as women, what wisdom may be ours if not the philosophies of the kitchen? Lupercio Leonardo[8] spoke well when he said: how well one may philosophize when preparing dinner. And I often say, when observing these trivial details: had Aristotle prepared victuals, he would have written more. And pursuing the manner of my cogitations, I tell you that this process is so continuous in me that I have no need for books.

5. **Motus:** motions
6. **Spillikins:** also called "jackstraws" or "pickup sticks," a game in which children use a straw or a stick to pick up another one from a pile without moving any of the others in that pile.
7. **Ring of Solomon:** according to legend, a signet ring owned by Solomon that gave him certain magical powers including (depending on the source) summoning demons, commanding djinn, talking to animals, and working alchemical transformations. Sor Juana imputes to it the power to see God's kingdom.
8. **Lupercio Leonardo:** Spanish poet and playwright (1559–1613).

And on one occasion, when because of a grave upset of the stomach the physicians forbade me to study, I passed thus some days, but then I proposed that it would be less harmful if they allowed me books, because so vigorous and vehement were my cogitations that my spirit was consumed more greatly in a quarter of an hour than in four days' studying books. And thus they were persuaded to allow me to read. And moreover, lady, not even have my dreams been excluded from this ceaseless agitation of my imagination; indeed, in dreams it is wont to work more freely and less encumbered, collating with greater clarity and calm the gleanings of the day, arguing and making verses, of which I could offer you an extended catalogue, as well as of some arguments and inventions that I have better achieved sleeping than awake. I relinquish this subject in order not to tire you, for the above is sufficient to allow your discretion and acuity to penetrate perfectly and perceive my nature, as well as the beginnings, the methods, and the present state of my studies.

Even, lady, were these merits (and I see them celebrated as such in men), they would not have been so in me, for I cannot but study. If they are fault, then, for the same reasons, I believe I have none. Nevertheless, I live always with so little confidence in myself that neither in my study, nor in any other thing, do I trust my judgment; and thus I remit the decision to your sovereign genius, submitting myself to whatever sentence you may bestow, without controversy, without reluctance, for I have wished here only to present you with a simple narration of my inclination toward letters.

I confess, too, that though it is true, as I have stated, that I had no need of books, it is nonetheless also true that they have been no little inspiration, in divine as in human letters. Because I find a Debbora administering the law, both military and political, and governing a people among whom there were many learned men. I find a most wise Queen of Saba, so learned that she dares to challenge with hard questions the wisdom of the greatest of all wise men, without being reprimanded for doing so, but, rather, as a consequence, to judge unbelievers. I see many and illustrious women; some blessed with the gift of prophecy, like Abigail, others of persuasion, like Esther; others with pity, like Rehab; others with perserverance, like Anna, the mother of Samuel; and an infinite number of others, with diverse gifts and virtues.[9]

If I again turn to the Gentiles, the first I encounter are the Sibyls, those women chosen by God to prophesy the principal mysteries of our Faith, and with learned and elegant verses that surpass admiration. . . . An Aspasia Milesia, who taught philosophy and rhetoric, and who was a teacher of the philosopher Pericles. An Hypatia, who taught astrology, and studied many years in Alexandria. A Leontium, a Greek woman, who questioned the philosopher Theophrastus, and convinced him. A Jucia, a Corinna, a Cornelia; and, finally, a great throng of women deserving

9. **Debbora, Queen of S[he]ba, Abigail, Esther, Rehab, [H]anna:** women in the Old Testament who are presented as wise, knowledgeable, or powerful.

to be named, some as Greeks, some as muses, some as seers; for all were nothing more than learned women, held, and celebrated—and venerated as well—as such by antiquity. . . . [10]

If, most venerable lady, the tone of this letter may not have seemed right and proper, I ask forgiveness for its homely familiarity, and the less than seemly respect in which by treating you as a nun, one of my sisters, I have lost sight of the remoteness of your most illustrious person; which, had I seen you without your veil, would never have occurred; but you in all your prudence and mercy will supplement or amend the language, and if you find unsuitable the *Vos* of the address I have employed, believing that for the reverence I owe you, Your Reverence seemed little reverent, modify it in whatever manner seems appropriate to your due, for I have not dared exceed the limits of your custom, nor transgress the boundary of your modesty.

And hold me in your grace, and entreat for me divine grace, of which the Lord   15
God grant you large measure, and keep you, as I pray Him, and am needful. From this convent of our Father Saint Jerome in Mexico City, the first day of the month of March of sixteen hundred and ninety-one. Allow me to kiss your hand, your most favored.

UNDERSTANDING THE TEXT

1. Why do you think that Sor Juana addresses *La Respuesta* to a fictional sister instead of to the bishop who had criticized her?

2. Why does Sor Juana say that she studies? Why does she say that she writes?

3. According to Sor Juana, why did she enter religious life? What kinds of things did she sacrifice to do so?

4. Why does Sor Juana request that her mother allow her to dress in boys' clothing? What might this tell us about the culture in which she lived?

5. Sor Juana argues that one cannot understand the teachings of God (which women were encouraged to do) without understanding philosophy, science, history, mathematics, and nearly every other area of study. How does this claim affect her argument?

6. One of the most famous quotations from *La Respuesta* is the following: "Had Aristotle prepared victuals, he would have written more." What do you think she means by this? How is it related to her argument that one needs to study many things to understand one thing well?

MAKING CONNECTIONS

1. Compare Sor Juana's letter with that of Martin Luther King Jr.'s "Letter from Birmingham Jail" (p. 425). What common themes emerge in the two letters?

10. **Aspasia, Hypatia, Leontium, Jucia, Corinna, Cornelia:** women from Greek and Roman antiquity who exercised power using their wisdom and judgment.

2. Compare Sor Juana's view of a woman's role in the church with Christine de Pizan's (p. 397) view of a woman's role in the state. Would you consider both positions to be early examples of feminism?

3. Is Sor Juana ultimately making the same argument that Virginia Woolf makes in "Shakespeare's Sister" (p. 46)? What are the main similarities between the two arguments? What are the main differences?

WRITING ABOUT THE TEXT

1. Analyze *La Respuesta* as a feminist argument. How does Sor Juana frame the issue of women studying? Are her arguments persuasive?

2. Compare Sor Juana's story of learning how to read with Frederick Douglass's experiences in *Learning to Read* (p. 24). How are they similar? How are they different?

3. Choose a field of study—either your major or a field that you would like to study—and explain how it connects to other fields. Do you think that Sor Juana is correct in arguing that studying theology requires one to understand many other things? Is this true of any field of study? Why or why not?

WAYNE BOOTH
The Rhetorical Stance
[1963]

WAYNE BOOTH (1921–2005) was one of the most influential American literary critics of the twentieth century. Born in American Fork, Utah, Booth received his undergraduate degree from Brigham Young University in 1944 and a Ph.D. in English from the University of Chicago in 1950. In 1962, he joined the English faculty at the University of Chicago, where he taught until his retirement in 1992. At the time of his death in 2005, he was a Professor Emeritus of English at the University of Chicago.

Booth's most important contribution to literary criticism—a field in the humanities concerned with the analysis and interpretation of literature—was to combine the study of literature with the study of rhetoric. For much of the twentieth century, literary criticism was dominated by the New Critics, who chose to view a literary work as an isolated unit that could be divorced from the intentions of its author and the historical background of its construction. In his landmark book, *The Rhetoric of Fiction* (1961), Booth argues that narrative is always a form of rhetoric in which a specific author attempts to persuade a specific audience of a particular argument.

"The Rhetorical Stance" was originally given as an address to the College Conference on Composition and Communication and was published in that society's journal in 1963. In this speech, Booth argues that it is possible, but difficult, to teach the art of persuasion, which he sees as a combination of three factors: 1) mastery of the subject matter one is speaking about; 2) an understanding of the audience one is addressing; and 3) a concern with the voice and character of the communicator. For Booth, one who pays constant attention to all three of these factors is adopting "the rhetorical stance."

Booth contrasts the rhetorical stance to two other stances that writers and speakers can adopt, both of which ignore some part of the rhetorical equation. The first of these, the "pedant's stance," relies exclusively on mastery. Unlike the rhetor, the pedant attempts to persuade others with the sheer force of his or her knowledge, which invariably leads to resentment rather than persuasion. The second stance, "the advertiser's stance," seeks to persuade without knowledge or understanding. The person taking this stance resorts to attention-getting gimmicks and strong statements but does nothing to indicate understanding of the issues involved.

In "The Rhetorical Stance," Wayne Booth advocates a way of writing that keeps the different aspects of the rhetorical situation—the speaker, the audience, and the subject—in balance. He models this approach in his own writing by constantly invoking, or appealing to, the three different elements of the rhetorical stance.

Last fall, I had an advanced graduate student, bright, energetic, well-informed, whose papers were almost unreadable. He managed to be pretentious, dull, and disorganized in his paper on *Emma*, and pretentious, dull, and disorganized on *Madame Bovary*. On *The Golden Bowl*[1] he was all these and obscure as well. Then one day, toward the end of term, he cornered me after class and said, "You know, I think you were all wrong about Robbe-Grillet's *Jealousy* today."[2] We didn't have time to discuss it, so I suggested that he write me a note about it. Five hours later I found in my faculty box a four-page polemic, unpretentious, stimulating, organized, convincing. Here was a man who had taught freshman composition for several years and who was incapable of committing any of the more obvious errors that we think of as characteristic of bad writing. Yet he could not write a decent sentence, paragraph, or paper until his rhetorical problem was solved—until, that is, he had found a definition of his audience, his argument, and his own proper tone of voice.

The word "rhetoric" is one of those catch-all terms that can easily raise trouble when our backs are turned. As it regains a popularity that it once seemed permanently to have lost, its meanings seem to range all the way from something like "the whole art of writing on any subject," as in Kenneth Burke's[3] *The Rhetoric of Religion*, through "the special arts of persuasion," on down to fairly narrow notions about rhetorical figures and devices. And of course we still have with us the meaning of "empty bombast," as in the phrase "merely rhetorical."

I suppose that the question of the role of rhetoric in the English course is meaningless if we think of rhetoric in either its broadest or its narrowest meanings. No English course could avoid dealing with rhetoric in Burke's sense, under whatever name, and on the other hand nobody would ever advocate anything so questionable as teaching "mere rhetoric." But if we settle on the following, traditional, definition, some real questions are raised: "Rhetoric is the art of finding and employing the most effective means of persuasion on any subject, considered independently of intellectual mastery of that subject." As the students say, "Prof. X knows his stuff but he doesn't know how to put it across." If rhetoric is thought of as the art of "putting it across," considered as quite distinct from mastering an "it" in the first place, we are immediately landed in a bramble bush of controversy. Is there such an art? If so, what does it consist of? Does it have a content of its own? Can it be taught? Should it be taught? If it should, how do we go about it, head on or obliquely? . . .

The case against the isolability and teachability of rhetoric may look at first like a good one. Nobody writes rhetoric, just as nobody ever writes writing. What we write and speak is always *this* discussion of the decline of railroading and *that* discussion

---

1. *Emma, Madame Bovary, The Golden Bowl:* novels by Jane Austen (1775–1817), Gustave Flaubert (1821–1880), and Henry James (1843–1916), respectively.

2. **Robbe-Grillet's** *Jealousy:* 1957 novel by Alain Robbe-Grillet (1922–2008), a French writer and film director.
3. **Kenneth Burke:** American rhetorician and literary critic (1897–1993).

of Pope's[4] couplets and the other argument for abolishing the poll-tax or for getting rhetoric back into English studies.

We can also admit that like all the arts, the art of rhetoric is at best very chancy, only partly amenable to systematic teaching; as we are all painfully aware when our 1:00 section goes miserably and our 2:00 section of the same course is a delight, our own rhetoric is not entirely under control. Successful rhetoricians are to some extent like poets, born, not made. They are also dependent on years of practice and experience. And we can finally admit that even the firmest of principles about writing cannot be taught in the same sense that elementary logic or arithmetic or French can be taught. In my first year of teaching, I had a student who started his first two essays with a swear word. When I suggested that perhaps the third paper ought to start with something else, he protested that his high school teacher had taught him always to catch the reader's attention. Now the teacher was right, but the application of even such a firm principle requires reserves of tact that were somewhat beyond my freshman.

But with all of the reservations made, surely the charge that the art of persuasion cannot in any sense be taught is baseless. I cannot think that anyone who has ever read Aristotle's *Rhetoric* or, say, Whateley's *Elements of Rhetoric*[5] could seriously make the charge. There is more than enough in these and the other traditional rhetorics to provide structure and content for a year-long course. I believe that such a course, when planned and carried through with intelligence and flexibility, can be one of the most important of all educational experiences. But it seems obvious that the arts of persuasion cannot be learned in one year, that a good teacher will continue to teach them regardless of his subject matter, and that we as English teachers have a special responsibility at all levels to get certain basic rhetorical principles into all of our writing assignments. When I think back over the experiences which have had any actual effect on my writing, I find the great good fortune of a splendid freshman course, taught by a man who believed in what he was doing, but I also find a collection of other experiences quite unconnected with a specific writing course. I remember the instructor in psychology who pencilled one word after a peculiarly pretentious paper of mine: *bull*. I remember the day when P. A. Christensen[6] talked with me about my Chaucer paper, and made me understand that my failure to use effective transitions was not simply a technical fault but a fundamental block in my effort to get him to see my meaning. His off-the-cuff pronouncement that I should never let myself write a sentence that was not in some way explicitly attached to preceding and following sentences meant far more to me at that moment, when I had something I wanted to say, than it could have meant as part of a pattern of such

4. **Pope:** Alexander Pope (1688–1744) was an English poet.
5. **Whateley's *Elements of Rhetoric*:** influential nineteenth-century textbook by British scholar and rhetorician Richard Whateley (1787–1863). **Aristotle's *Rhetoric*:** see p. 177.
6. **P. A. Christensen:** English professor (1888–1968) at Brigham Young University from 1927 to 1965.

rules offered in a writing course. Similarly, I can remember the devastating lessons about my bad writing that Ronald Crane[7] could teach with a simple question mark on a graduate seminar paper, or a pencilled "Evidence for this?" or "Why this section here?" or "Everybody says so. Is it true?". . .

The common ingredient that I find in all of the writing I admire—excluding for now novels, plays and poems—is something that I shall reluctantly call the rhetorical stance, a stance which depends on discovering and maintaining in any writing situation a proper balance among the three elements that are at work in any communicative effort: the available arguments about the subject itself, the interests and peculiarities of the audience, and the voice, the implied character, of the speaker. I should like to suggest that it is this balance, this rhetorical stance, difficult as it is to describe, that is our main goal as teachers of rhetoric. Our ideal graduate will strike this balance automatically in any writing that he considers finished. Though he may never come to the point of finding the balance easily, he will know that it is what makes the difference between effective communication and mere wasted effort.

What I mean by the true rhetorician's stance can perhaps best be seen by contrasting it with two or three corruptions, unbalanced stances often assumed by people who think they are practicing the arts of persuasion.

The first I'll call the pedant's stance; it consists of ignoring or underplaying the personal relationship of speaker and audience and depending entirely on statements about a subject—that is, the notion of a job to be done for a particular audience is left out. It is a virtue, of course, to respect the bare truth of one's subject, and there may even be some subjects which in their very nature define an audience and a rhetorical purpose so that adequacy to the subject can be the whole art of presentation. For example, an article on "The relation of the ontological and teleological proofs," in a recent *Journal of Religion*, requires a minimum of adaptation of argument to audience. But most subjects do not in themselves imply in any necessary way a purpose and an audience and hence a speaker's tone. The writer who assumes that it is enough merely to write an exposition of what he happens to know on the subject will produce the kind of essay that soils our scholarly journals, written not for readers but for bibliographies.

In my first year of teaching I taught a whole unit on "exposition" without ever   10
suggesting, so far as I can remember, that the students ask themselves what their expositions were *for*. So they wrote expositions like this one—I've saved it, to teach me toleration of my colleagues: the title is "Family relations in More's *Utopia*." "In this theme I would like to discuss some of the relationships with the family which Thomas More elaborates and sets forth in his book, *Utopia*. The first thing that I would like to discuss about family relations is that overpopulation, according to More, is a just cause of war." And so on. Can you hear that student sneering at me, in this opening? What he is saying is something like "you ask for a meaningless paper,

---

7. **Ronald Crane:** English professor (1886–1967) at the University of Chicago and founder of the "Chicago School" of literary criticism.

I give you a meaningless paper." He knows that he has no audience except me. He knows that I don't want to read his summary of family relations in *Utopia*, and he knows that I know that he therefore has no rhetorical purpose. Because he has not been led to see a question which he considers worth answering, or an audience that could possibly care one way or the other, the paper is worse than no paper at all, even though it has no grammatical or spelling errors and is organized right down the line, one, two, three. . . .

This first perversion, then, springs from ignoring the audience or overreliance on the pure subject. The second, which might be called the advertiser's stance, comes from *under*valuing the subject and overvaluing pure effect: how to win friends and influence people.

Some of our best freshman texts—Sheridan Baker's *The Practical Stylist*, for example—allow themselves on occasion to suggest that to be controversial or argumentative, to stir up an audience is an end in itself. Sharpen the controversial edge, one of them says, and the clear implication is that one should do so even if the truth of the subject is honed off in the process. This perversion is probably in the long run a more serious threat in our society than the danger of ignoring the audience. In the time of audience-reaction meters and pre-tested plays and novels, it is not easy to convince students of the old Platonic truth that good persuasion is honest persuasion, or even of the old Aristotelian truth that the good rhetorician must be master of his subject, no matter how dishonest he may decide ultimately to be. Having told them that good writers always to some degree accommodate their arguments to the audience, it is hard to explain the difference between justified accommodation—say changing *point one* to the final position—and the kind of accommodation that fills our popular magazines, in which the very substance of what is said is accommodated to some preconception of what will sell. "The publication of *Eros* [magazine] represents a major breakthrough in the battle for the liberation of the human spirit."

At a dinner about a month ago I sat between the wife of a famous civil rights lawyer and an advertising consultant. "I saw the article on your book yesterday in the Daily News," she said, "but I didn't even finish it. The title of your book scared me off. Why did you ever choose such a terrible title? Nobody would buy a book with a title like that." The man on my right, whom I'll call Mr. Kinches, overhearing my feeble reply, plunged into a conversation with her, over my torn and bleeding corpse. "Now with my *last* book," he said, "I listed 20 possible titles and then tested them out on 400 businessmen. The one I chose was voted for by 90 percent of the businessmen." "That's what I was just saying to Mr. Booth," she said. "A book title ought to grab you, and *rhetoric* is not going to grab anybody." "Right," he said. "My *last* book sold 50,000 copies already; I don't know how this one will do, but I polled 200 businessmen on the table of contents, and . . ."

At one point I did manage to ask him whether the title he chose really fit the book. "Not quite as well as one or two of the others," he admitted, "but that doesn't matter, you know. If the book is designed right, so that the first chapter pulls them in, and you *keep* 'em in, who's going to gripe about a little inaccuracy in the title?"

Well, rhetoric is the art of persuading, not the art [of] seeming to persuade by   15
giving everything away at the start. It presupposes that one has a purpose concerning a subject which itself cannot be fundamentally modified by the desire to persuade. If Edmund Burke[8] had decided that he could win more votes in Parliament by choosing the other side—as he most certainly could have done—we would hardly hail this party-switch a master stroke of rhetoric. If Churchill[9] had offered the British "peace in our time," with some laughs thrown in, because opinion polls had shown that more Britishers were "grabbed" by these than by blood, sweat, and tears, we could hardly call his decision a sign of rhetorical skill. . . .

Now obviously the habit of seeking this balance is not the only thing we have to teach under the heading of rhetoric. But I think that everything worth teaching under that heading finds its justification finally in that balance. Much of what is now considered irrelevant or dull can, in fact, be brought to life when teachers and students know what they are seeking. Churchill reports that the most valuable training he ever received in rhetoric was in the diagramming of sentences. Think of it! Yet the diagramming of a sentence, regardless of the grammatical system, can be a live subject as soon as one asks not simply "How is this sentence put together?" but rather "Why is it put together in this way?" or "Could the rhetorical balance and hence the desired persuasion be better achieved by writing it differently?"

As a nation we are reputed to write very badly. As a nation, I would say, we are more inclined to the perversions of rhetoric than to the rhetorical balance. Regardless of what we do about this or that course in the curriculum, our mandate would seem to be, then, to lead more of our students than we now do to care about and practice the true arts of persuasion.

UNDERSTANDING THE TEXT

1. In Booth's introductory example about his graduate student, what inspired this student to write with persuasive power and adopt the rhetorical stance?

2. What various definitions of "rhetoric" does Booth discuss? Which definition does he settle on? Why?

3. Does Booth believe that rhetoric and persuasion can be taught, or does he see them as innate talents that people either have or do not have?

4. What sorts of things does Booth think English teachers should teach in composition classes? What kinds of assignments does he think composition teachers should give?

8. **Edmund Burke:** Anglo-Irish writer, philosopher, and politician (1729–1797). See p. 256.
9. **Churchill:** Winston Churchill British politician and statesman (1874–1965) who was prime minister of the United Kingdom during most of World War II.

5. What advice does Booth recall from his own teachers? What did they teach him about the nature of persuasion?

6. What three elements go into what Booth describes as "the rhetorical stance?" Can you paraphrase this principle in your own words?

7. Briefly define the "pedant's stance" and the "advertiser's stance." In what ways do these stances disrupt the balance of the rhetorical stance?

MAKING CONNECTIONS

1. Both Booth and Augustine question the effectiveness of teaching rhetoric or persuasion by teaching guidelines or principles. Compare the conclusions that both men reach.

2. Compare Booth's view of rhetoric with that of Gorgias in Plato's *Gorgias* (p. 166). Would Plato agree with the three parts of the rhetorical stance that Booth outlines?

3. How does Booth's view of the role of a teacher compare with that of Hsün Tzu in "Encouraging Learning" (p. 5)? How might Booth describe the latter's view of the appropriate way to teach students?

WRITING ABOUT THE TEXT

1. Describe the three "stances" that Booth discusses in this essay. Give examples of each stance from your own experience or from contemporary public discourse.

2. Analyze Wayne Booth's understanding of the term "rhetoric." Explain how his definition of this term differs from those of other authors in this chapter, such as Plato (p. 166), Aristotle (p. 177), or Augustine (p. 184).

3. Argue for or against the assertion that rhetoric, or the ability to persuade others, can be taught through guidelines and procedures. Consider some of the principles in the "Guide to Reading and Writing" section of this book (p. 603) and explain whether or not you think they can actually help people become more persuasive.

GLORIA ANZALDÚA
How to Tame a Wild Tongue
[1987]

FOR THE MEXICAN AMERICAN writer Gloria Anzaldúa (1942–2004), "borderlands" is a concept with many levels of meaning. Literally, it refers to the border between the United States and Mexico. But borderlands also exist wherever different cultures, languages, value systems, or sexual identities come into contact with each other. "Borderlands," she writes, "are physically present wherever two or more cultures edge each other, where people of different races occupy the same territory, where under, lower, middle and upper classes touch, where the space between two individuals shrinks with intimacy."

Anzaldúa spent most of her life positioned on the borderlands that became such an important image in her work. She was born and raised in the Rio Grande Valley of southern Texas. Most of the members of her family were farm laborers, and neither of her parents attended high school, but she excelled in school and became the first in her family to attend college. She received degrees from Pan American University and the University of Texas at Austin and, in 1972, went to teach children of migrant families. During this time, she also edited several important volumes of essays by women of color. She taught English, women's studies, and cultural studies at Georgetown University, the University of Colorado, and the University of California at Santa Cruz.

In her most influential work, *Borderlands/La Frontera: The New Mestiza* (1987), Anzaldúa proposes that borderlands of all kinds give birth to a category of person she refers to as the *mestiza*, or "mixture." The *mestiza* exists between cultures, fully embracing—and fully embraced by—neither. For Anzaldúa, borderland culture must be considered distinct from and equal to the cultures that combine to produce it. The chapter included here, "How to Tame a Wild Tongue," is a kind of mestiza, as Anzaldúa blends styles, genres, and even languages to produce a written text that cannot be reduced to single categories: it is at once English and Spanish, poetry and prose, narrative and analysis, academic and autobiographical. It deals specifically with the languages of the borderlands. Mestizos usually speak multiple languages; Anzaldúa's languages include not only Standard English and Standard Spanish but also various dialects that have emerged out of the collision of the two. Because language is a primary part of a person's identity, Anzaldúa insists, it is vital to validate all of the languages that people speak and claim as their own. In an academic context, this means allowing people to speak and write in their native tongues and trying to understand others by learning their languages rather than by forcing them to learn ours. To ignore the imperative need that people have to speak, write, and create in their native tongues, Anzaldúa claims, is an act of violence.

Rhetorically, Anzaldúa works toward a synthesis of two different positions: the view that Americans should all speak English and the view that all people of Mexican descent should speak Spanish. The Chicanola language, like its speakers, is both a linguistic and an ideological synthesis.

"We're going to have to control your tongue," the dentist says, pulling out all the metal from my mouth. Silver bits plop and tinkle into the basin. My mouth is a motherlode.

The dentist is cleaning out my roots. I get a whiff of the stench when I gasp. "I can't cap that tooth yet, you're still draining," he says.

"We're going to have to do something about your tongue," I hear the anger rising in his voice. My tongue keeps pushing out the wads of cotton, pushing back the drills, the long thin needles. "I've never seen anything as strong or as stubborn," he says. And I think, how do you tame a wild tongue, train it to be quiet, how do you bridle and saddle it? How do you make it lie down?

> Who is to say that robbing a people of
> its language is less violent than war?
> —RAY GWYN SMITH[1]

I remember being caught speaking Spanish at recess—that was good for three licks on the knuckles with a sharp ruler. I remember being sent to the corner of the classroom for "talking back" to the Anglo teacher when all I was trying to do was tell her how to pronounce my name. "If you want to be American, speak 'American.' If you don't like it, go back to Mexico where you belong."

"I want you to speak English. *Pa' hallar buen trabajo tienes que saber hablar el inglés bien. Qué vale toda tu educación si todavía hablas inglés con un* 'accent,'"[2] my mother would say, mortified that I spoke English like a Mexican. At Pan American University, I, and all Chicano students were required to take two speech classes. Their purpose: to get rid of our accents.

Attacks on one's form of expression with the intent to censor are a violation of the First Amendment. *El Anglo con cara de inocente nos arrancó la lengua.* Wild tongues can't be tamed, they can only be cut out.

Overcoming the Tradition of Silence

Ahogadas, escupimos el oscuro.
Peleando con nuestra propia sombra
el silencio nos sepulta.

All notes are the author's unless otherwise indicated.
1. Ray Gwyn Smith, *Moorland Is Cold Country,* unpublished book.

2. At the author's request, all Spanish phrases in the text have been left untranslated. [Editor's note]

En boca cerrada no entran moscas. "Flies don't enter a closed mouth" is a saying I kept hearing when I was a child. *Ser habladora* was to be a gossip and a liar, to talk too much. *Muchachitas bien criadas*, well-bred girls don't answer back. *Es una falta de respeto* to talk back to one's mother or father. I remember one of the sins I'd recite to the priest in the confession box the few times I went to confession: talking back to my mother, *hablar pa' 'tras, repelar. Hocicona, repelona, chismosa*, having a big mouth, questioning, carrying tales are all signs of being *mal criada*. In my culture they are all words that are derogatory if applied to women—I've never heard them applied to men.

The first time I heard two women, a Puerto Rican and a Cuban, say the word "*nosotras*," I was shocked. I had not known the word existed. Chicanas use *nosotros* whether we're male or female. We are robbed of our female being by the masculine plural. Language is a male discourse.

> And our tongues have become
> dry   the wilderness has
> dried out our tongues   and
> we have forgotten speech.
> —IRENA KLEPFISZ[3]

Even our own people, other Spanish speakers *nos quieren poner candados en la boca.* They would hold us back with their bag of *reglas de academia.*

Oyé como ladra: el lenguaje de la frontera

> Quien tiene boca se equivoca.
> —MEXICAN SAYING

"*Pocho*, cultural traitor, you're speaking the oppressor's language by speaking English, you're ruining the Spanish language," I have been accused by various Latinos and Latinas. Chicano Spanish is considered by the purist and by most Latinos deficient, a mutilation of Spanish.   10

But Chicano Spanish is a border tongue which developed naturally. Change, *evolución, enriquecimiento de palabras nuevas por invención o adopción* have created variants of Chicano Spanish, *un nuevo lenguaje. Un lenguaje que corresponde a un modo de vivir.* Chicano Spanish is not incorrect, it is a living language.

For a people who are neither Spanish nor live in a country in which Spanish is the first language; for a people who live in a country in which English is the

3. Irena Klepfisz, "*Di rayze aheym*/The Journey Home," in *The Tribe of Dina: A Jewish Women's Anthology*, Melanie Kaye/Kantrowitz and Irena Klepfisz, eds. (Montpelier, VT: Sinister Wisdom Books, 1986), 49.

reigning tongue but who are not Anglo; for a people who cannot entirely identify with either standard (formal, Castillian) Spanish nor standard English, what recourse is left to them but to create their own language? A language which they can connect their identity to, one capable of communicating the realities and values true to themselves—a language with terms that are neither *español ni inglés*, but both. We speak a patois, a forked tongue, a variation of two languages.

Chicano Spanish sprang out of the Chicanos' need to identify ourselves as a distinct people. We needed a language with which we could communicate with ourselves, a secret language. For some of us, language is a homeland closer than the Southwest—for many Chicanos today live in the Midwest and the East. And because we are a complex, heterogeneous people, we speak many languages. Some of the languages we speak are:

1. Standard English
2. Working class and slang English
3. Standard Spanish
4. Standard Mexican Spanish
5. North Mexican Spanish dialect
6. Chicano Spanish (Texas, New Mexico, Arizona and California have regional variations)
7. Tex-Mex
8. *Pachuco* (called *caló*)

My "home" tongues are the languages I speak with my sister and brothers, with my friends. They are the last five listed, with 6 and 7 being closest to my heart. From school, the media and job situations, I've picked up standard and working class English. From Mamagrande Locha and from reading Spanish and Mexican literature, I've picked up Standard Spanish and Standard Mexican Spanish. From *los recién llegados*, Mexican immigrants, and *braceros*, I learned the North Mexican dialect. With Mexicans I'll try to speak either Standard Mexican Spanish or the North Mexican dialect. From my parents and Chicanos living in the Valley, I picked up Chicano Texas Spanish, and I speak it with my mom, younger brother (who married a Mexican and who rarely mixes Spanish with English), aunts and older relatives.

With Chicanas from *Nuevo México* or *Arizona* I will speak Chicano Spanish a little, but often they don't understand what I'm saying. With most California Chicanas I speak entirely in English (unless I forget). When I first moved to San Francisco, I'd rattle off something in Spanish, unintentionally embarrassing them. Often it is only with another Chicana *tejana* that I can talk freely.   15

Words distorted by English are known as anglicisms or *pochismos*. The *pocho* is an anglicized Mexican or American of Mexican origin who speaks Spanish with an accent characteristic of North Americans and who distorts and reconstructs the language according to the influence of English.[4] Tex-Mex, or Spanglish, comes most naturally to me. I may switch back and forth from English to Spanish in the same sentence or in the same word. With my sister and my brother Nune and with Chicano *tejano* contemporaries I speak in Tex-Mex.

From kids and people my own age I picked up *Pachuco*. Pachuco (the language of the zoot suiters) is a language of rebellion, both against Standard Spanish and Standard English. It is a secret language. Adults of the culture and outsiders cannot understand it. It is made up of slang words from both English and Spanish. *Ruca* means girl or woman, *vato* means guy or dude, *chale* means no, *simón* means yes, *churro* is sure, talk is *periquiar*, *pigionear* means petting, *que gacho* means how nerdy, *ponte águila* means watch out, death is called *la pelona*. Through lack of practice and not having others who can speak it, I've lost most of the *Pachuco* tongue.

Chicano Spanish

Chicanos, after 250 years of Spanish/Anglo colonization, have developed significant differences in the Spanish we speak. We collapse two adjacent vowels into a single syllable and sometimes shift the stress in certain words such as *maíz/maiz, cohete/cuete*. We leave out certain consonants when they appear between vowels: *lado/lao, mojado/mojao*. Chicanos from South Texas pronounce *f* as *j* as in *jue* (*fue*). Chicanos use "archaisms," words that are no longer in the Spanish language, words that have been evolved out. We say *semos, truje, haiga, ansina*, and *naiden*. We retain the "archaic" *j*, as in *jalar*, that derives from an earlier *h* (the French *halar* or the Germanic *halon* which was lost to standard Spanish in the 16th century), but which is still found in several regional dialects such as the one spoken in South Texas. (Due to geography, Chicanos from the Valley of South Texas were cut off linguistically from other Spanish speakers. We tend to use words that the Spaniards brought over from Medieval Spain. The majority of the Spanish colonizers in Mexico and the Southwest came from Extremadura—Hernán Cortés was one of them—and Andalucía. Andalucians pronounce *ll* like a *y*, and their *d*'s tend to be absorbed by adjacent vowels: *tirado* becomes *tirao*. They brought *el lenguaje popular, dialectos y regionalismos*.[5])

Chicanos and other Spanish speakers also shift *ll* to *y* and *z* to *s*.[6] We leave out initial syllables, saying *tar* for *estar*, *toy* for *estoy*, *hora* for *ahora* (*cubanos* and *puertorriqueños* also leave out initial letters of some words). We also leave out the final syllable such as *pa* for *para*. The intervocalic *y*, the *ll* as in *tortilla, ella, botella*, gets replaced by *tortia* or *tortiya, ea, botea*. We add an additional syllable at the

4. R. C. Ortega, *Dialectología del Barrio*, trans. Hortencia S. Alwan (Los Angeles, CA: R. C. Ortega Publisher & Bookseller, 1977), 132.
5. Eduardo Hernandéz-Chávez, Andrew D. Cohen, and Anthony F. Beltramo, *El Lenguaje de los Chicanos: Regional and Social Characteristics of Language Used by Mexican Americans* (Arlington, VA: Center for Applied Linguistics, 1975), 39.
6. Hernandéz-Chávez, xvii.

beginning of certain words: *atocar* for *tocar*, *agastar* for *gastar*. Sometimes we'll say *lavaste las vacijas*, other times *lavates* (substituting the *ates* verb endings for the *aste*).

We use anglicisms, words borrowed from English: *bola* from ball, *carpeta* from   20
carpet, *máchina de lavar* (instead of *lavadora*) from washing machine. Tex-Mex argot, created by adding a Spanish sound at the beginning or end of an English word such as *cookiar* for cook, *watchar* for watch, *parkiar* for park, and *rapiar* for rape, is the result of the pressures on Spanish speakers to adapt to English.

We don't use the word *vosotros/as* or its accompanying verb form. We don't say *claro* (to mean yes), *imagínate*, or *me emociona*, unless we picked up Spanish from Latinas, out of a book or in a classroom. Other Spanish-speaking groups are going through the same, or similar, development in their Spanish.

Linguistic Terrorism

Desleguadas. Somos los del español deficiente. We are your linguistic nightmare, your linguistic aberration, your linguistic *mestisaje*, the subject of your *burla*. Because we speak with tongues of fire we are culturally crucified. Racially, culturally and linguistically *somos huérfanos*—we speak an orphan tongue.

Chicanas who grew up speaking Chicano Spanish have internalized the belief that we speak poor Spanish. It is illegitimate, a bastard language. And because we internalize how our language has been used against us by the dominant culture, we use our language differences against each other.

Chicana feminists often skirt around each other with suspicion and hesitation. For the longest time I couldn't figure it out. Then it dawned on me. To be close to another Chicana is like looking into the mirror. We are afraid of what we'll see there. *Pena.* Shame. Low estimation of self. In childhood we are told that our language is wrong. Repeated attacks on our native tongue diminish our sense of self. The attacks continue throughout our lives.

Chicanas feel uncomfortable talking in Spanish to Latinas, afraid of their censure. Their language was not outlawed in their countries. They had a whole lifetime of being immersed in their native tongue; generations, centuries in which Spanish was a first language, taught in school, heard on radio and TV, and read in the newspaper.

If a person, Chicana or Latina, has a low estimation of my native tongue, she   25
also has a low estimation of me. Often with *mexicanas y latinas* we'll speak English as a neutral language. Even among Chicanas, we tend to speak English at parties or conferences. Yet, at the same time, we're afraid the other will think we're *agringadas* because we don't speak Chicano Spanish. We oppress each other trying to out-Chicano each other, vying to be the "real" Chicanas, to speak like Chicanos. There is no one Chicano language just as there is no one Chicano experience. A monolingual

Chicana whose first language is English or Spanish is just as much a Chicana as one who speaks several variants of Spanish. A Chicana from Michigan or Chicago or Detroit is just as much a Chicana as one from the Southwest. Chicano Spanish is as diverse linguistically as it is regionally.

By the end of this century, Spanish speakers will comprise the biggest minority group in the U.S., a country where students in high schools and colleges are encouraged to take French classes because French is considered more "cultured." But for a language to remain alive it must be used.[7] By the end of this century English, and not Spanish, will be the mother tongue of most Chicanos and Latinos.

So, if you want to really hurt me, talk badly about my language. Ethnic identity is twin skin to linguistic identity—I am my language. Until I can take pride in my language, I cannot take pride in myself. Until I can accept as legitimate Chicano Texas Spanish, Tex-Mex and all the other languages I speak, I cannot accept the legitimacy of myself. Until I am free to write bilingually and to switch codes without having always to translate, while I still have to speak English or Spanish when I would rather speak Spanglish, and as long as I have to accommodate the English speakers rather than having them accommodate me, my tongue will be illegitimate.

I will no longer be made to feel ashamed of existing. I will have my voice: Indian, Spanish, white. I will have my serpent's tongue—my woman's voice, my sexual voice, my poet's voice. I will overcome the tradition of silence.

> My fingers
> move sly against your palm
> Like women everywhere, we speak in code. . . .
> —MELANIE KAYE/KANTROWITZ[8]

"*Vistas*," *corridos*, *y comida*: My Native Tongue

In the 1960s, I read my first Chicano novel. It was *City of Night* by John Rechy, a gay Texan, son of a Scottish father and a Mexican mother. For days I walked around in stunned amazement that a Chicano could write and could get published. When I read *I Am Joaquín*[9] I was surprised to see a bilingual book by a Chicano in print. When I saw poetry written in Tex-Mex for the first time, a feeling of pure joy flashed through me. I felt like we really existed as a people. In 1971, when I started teaching High School English to Chicano students, I tried to supplement the required texts with

7. Irena Klepfisz, "Secular Jewish Identity: Yidishkayt in America," in *The Tribe of Dina*, Kay/Kantrowitz and Klepfisz, eds., 43.
8. Melanie Kaye / Kantrowitz, "Sign," in *We Speak in Code: Poems and Other Writings* (Pittsburgh, PA: Motheroot Publications, Inc., 1980), 85.

9. Rodolfo Gonzales, *I Am Joaquín/Yo Soy Joaquín* (New York, NY: Bantam Books, 1972). It was first published in 1967.

works by Chicanos, only to be reprimanded and forbidden to do so by the principal. He claimed that I was supposed to teach "American" and English literature. At the risk of being fired, I swore my students to secrecy and slipped in Chicano short stories, poems, a play. In graduate school, while working toward a Ph.D., I had to "argue" with one advisor after the other, semester after semester, before I was allowed to make Chicano literature an area of focus.

Even before I read books by Chicanos or Mexicans, it was the Mexican movies 30 I saw at the drive-in—the Thursday night special of $1.00 a carload—that gave me a sense of belonging. "*Vámonos a las vistas*," my mother would call out and we'd all—grandmother, brothers, sister and cousins—squeeze into the car. We'd wolf down cheese and bologna white bread sandwiches while watching Pedro Infante in melodramatic tearjerkers like *Nosotros los pobres*, the first "real" Mexican movie (that was not an imitation of European movies). I remember seeing *Cuando los hijos se van* and surmising that all Mexican movies played up the love a mother has for her children and what ungrateful sons and daughters suffer when they are not devoted to their mothers. I remember the singing-type "westerns" of Jorge Negrete and Miquel Aceves Mejía. When watching Mexican movies, I felt a sense of homecoming as well as alienation. People who were to amount to something didn't go to Mexican movies, or *bailes* or tune their radios to *bolero*, *racherita*, and *corrido* music.

The whole time I was growing up, there was *norteño* music sometimes called North Mexican border music, or Tex-Mex music, or Chicano music, or *cantina* (bar) music. I grew up listening to *conjuntos*, three- or four-piece bands made up of folk musicians playing guitar, *bajo sexto*, drums and button accordion, which Chicanos had borrowed from the German immigrants who had come to Central Texas and Mexico to farm and build breweries. In the Rio Grande Valley, Steve Jordan and Little Joe Hernández were popular, and Flaco Jiménez was the accordian king. The rhythms of Tex-Mex music are those of the polka, also adapted from the Germans, who in turn had borrowed the polka from the Czechs and Bohemians.

I remember the hot, sultry evenings when *corridos*—songs of love and death on the Texas-Mexican borderlands—reverberated out of cheap amplifiers from the local *cantinas* and wafted in through my bedroom window.

Corridos first became widely used along the South Texas/Mexican border during the early conflict between Chicanos and Anglos. The *corridos* are usually about Mexican heroes who do valiant deeds against the Anglo oppressors. Pancho Villa's song, "*La cucaracha*," is the most famous one. *Corridos* of John F. Kennedy and his death are still very popular in the Valley. Older Chicanos remember Lydia Mendoza, one of the great border *corrido* singers who was called *la Gloria de Tejas*. Her "*El tango negro*," sung during the Great Depression, made her a singer of the people. The ever-present *corridos* narrated one hundred years of border history, bringing news of events as well as entertaining. These folk musicians and folk songs are our chief cultural mythmakers, and they made our hard lives seem bearable.

I grew up feeling ambivalent about our music. Country-western and rock-and-roll had more status. In the 50s and 60s, for the slightly educated and *agringado* Chicanos, there existed a sense of shame at being caught listening to our music. Yet I couldn't stop my feet from thumping to the music, could not stop humming the words, nor hide from myself the exhilaration I felt when I heard it.

There are more subtle ways that we internalize identification, especially in the   35
forms of images and emotions. For me food and certain smells are tied to my identity, to my homeland. Woodsmoke curling up to an immense blue sky; woodsmoke perfuming my grandmother's clothes, her skin. The stench of cow manure and the yellow patches on the ground; the crack of a .22 rifle and the reek of cordite. Homemade white cheese sizzling in a pan, melting inside a folded *tortilla*. My sister Hilda's hot, spicy *menudo*, *chile colorado* making it deep red, pieces of *panza* and hominy floating on top. My brother Carito barbequing *fajitas* in the backyard. Even now and 3,000 miles away, I can see my mother spicing the ground beef, pork and venison with *chile*. My mouth salivates at the thought of the hot steaming *tamales* I would be eating if I were home.

Si le pregunta a mi mamá, "¿Qué eres?"

> "Identity is the essential core of who
> we are as individuals, the conscious
> experience of the self inside."
> —KAUFMAN[10]

Nosotros los Chicanos straddle the borderlands. On one side of us, we are constantly exposed to the Spanish of the Mexicans, on the other side we hear the Anglos' incessant clamoring so that we forget our language. Among ourselves we don't say *nosotros los americanos, o nosotros los españoles, o nosotros los hispanos*. We say *nosotros los mexicanos* (by *mexicanos* we do not mean citizens of Mexico; we do not mean a national identity, but a racial one). We distinguish between *mexicanos del otro lado* and *mexicanos de este lado*. Deep in our hearts we believe that being Mexican has nothing to do with which country one lives in. Being Mexican is a state of soul—not one of mind, not one of citizenship. Neither eagle nor serpent, but both. And like the ocean, neither animal respects borders.

10. Kaufman, Gershen. *Shame: The Power of Caring* (Cambridge, Mass.: Schenkman Books, Inc., 1980), 68.

Dime con quien andas y te diré quien eres.
(Tell me who your friends are and I'll tell you who you are.)
—MEXICAN SAYING

Si le preguntas a mi mamá, "¿Qué eres?" te dirá, "Soy mexicana." My brothers and sister say the same. I sometimes will answer *"soy mexicana"* and at others will say *"soy Chicana" o "soy tejana."* But I identified as *"Raza"* before I ever identified as *"mexicana"* or "Chicana."

As a culture, we call ourselves Spanish when referring to ourselves as a linguistic group and when copping out. It is then that we forget our predominant Indian genes. We are 70–80% Indian.[11] We call ourselves Hispanic[12] or Spanish-American or Latin American or Latin when linking ourselves to other Spanish-speaking peoples of the Western hemisphere and when copping out. We call ourselves Mexican-American[13] to signify we are neither Mexican nor American, but more the noun "American" than the adjective "Mexican" (and when copping out).

Chicanos and other people of color suffer economically for not acculturating. This voluntary (yet forced) alienation makes for psychological conflict, a kind of dual identity—we don't identify with the Anglo-American cultural values and we don't totally identify with the Mexican cultural values. We are a synergy of two cultures with various degrees of Mexicanness or Angloness. I have so internalized the borderland conflict that sometimes I feel like one cancels out the other and we are zero, nothing, no one. *A veces no soy nada ni nadie. Pero hasta cuando no lo soy, lo soy.*

When not copping out, when we know we are more than nothing, we call our- 40 selves Mexican, referring to race and ancestry; *mestizo* when affirming both our Indian and Spanish (but we hardly ever own our Black ancestry); Chicano when referring to a politically aware people born and/or raised in the U.S.; *Raza* when referring to Chicanos; *tejanos* when we are Chicanos from Texas.

Chicanos did not know we were a people until 1965 when Cesar Chavez and the farmworkers united and *I Am Joaquín* was published and *la Raza Unida* party was formed in Texas. With that recognition, we became a distinct people. Something momentous happened to the Chicano soul—we became aware of our reality and acquired a name and a language (Chicano Spanish) that reflected that reality. Now that we had a name, some of the fragmented pieces began to fall together—who we were, what we were, how we had evolved. We began to get glimpses of what we might eventually become.

Yet the struggle of identities continues, the struggle of borders is our reality still. One day the inner struggle will cease and a true integration take place. In the meantime, *tenémos que hacer la lucha. ¿Quién está protegiendo los ranchos de mi gente?*

11. Chávez, 88–90.
12. "Hispanic" is derived from *Hispanis* (*España*, a name given to the Iberian Peninsula in ancient times when it was a part of the Roman Empire) and is a term designated by the U.S. government to make it easier to handle us on paper.
13. The Treaty of Guadalupe Hidalgo created the Mexican-American in 1848.

¿Quién está tratando de cerrar la fisura entre la india y el blanco en nuestra sangre? El Chicano, si, el Chicano que anda como un ladrón en su propia casa.

Los Chicanos, how patient we seem, how very patient. There is the quiet of the Indian about us.[14] We know how to survive. When other races have given up their tongue, we've kept ours. We know what it is to live under the hammer blow of the dominant *norteamericano* culture. But more than we count the blows, we count the days the weeks the years the centuries the eons until the white laws and commerce and customs will rot in the deserts they've created, lie bleached. *Humildes* yet proud, *quietos* yet wild, *nosotros los mexicanos-Chicanos* will walk by the crumbling ashes as we go about our business. Stubborn, persevering, impenetrable as stone, yet possessing a malleability that renders us unbreakable, we, the *mestizas* and *mestizos,* will remain.

UNDERSTANDING THE TEXT

1. What is the effect of the mixture of English and Spanish in the text? How does this style of writing reinforce Gloria Anzaldúa's point?

2. According to Anzaldúa, how do the parents and teachers of Chicano children try to convince them not to speak in their native tongues? Have you encountered pressures or arguments like this?

3. What does Anzaldúa mean by "Chicano/a"? What geographical and political connotations does the word, as she uses it, take on?

4. What does Anzaldúa mean by "linguistic terrorism"? Why does she consider attacks on a language similar to attacks on a person?

5. What role did literature play in Anzaldúa's development of her Chicana identity? How might a body of literature create a separate identity for a group of people?

6. In what situations, according to Anzaldúa, are Chicanos/as "copping out"?

MAKING CONNECTIONS

1. Compare Anzaldúa's experiences growing up in an environment hostile to her language with Alice Walker's (p. 271) story of growing up in an environment hostile to her physical appearance.

2. Compare the way that Anzaldúa describes Chicano/a identity with the way that Octavio Paz describes Mexican identity in "The Day of the Dead" (p. 575). How are the two portrayals similar?

3. Both Anzaldúa and Frederick Douglass (p. 24) write about the role of literacy in promoting tolerance and social justice. Where do their opinions differ?

14. Anglos, in order to alleviate their guilt for dispossessing the Chicano, stressed the Spanish part of us and perpetrated the myth of the Spanish Southwest. We have accepted the fiction that we are Hispanic, that is Spanish, in order to accommodate ourselves to the dominant culture and its abhorrence of Indians. Chávez, 88–91.

WRITING ABOUT THE TEXT

1. Write an essay in which you make an argument for the kind of educational philosophy that can be derived from "How to Tame a Wild Tongue." How should teachers respond to students who speak "borderland" languages?

2. Respond to the arguments that Anzaldúa cites in favor of learning a country's dominant language. Are getting a good job and becoming successful worth the price of suppressing or even silencing one's identity? How might Anzaldúa respond to the charge that her advice could keep people from succeeding in the United States?

3. Compare Anzaldúa's arguments for the inclusion of a marginalized group with those of Martin Luther King Jr. (p. 425). What are the strengths and weaknesses of their rhetorical approaches?

4. One of Anzaldúa's key points is that people employ different "languages" within their different cultures and subcultures. Discuss how a group that you belong to (racial, national, religious, occupational, etc.) uses a unique language.

TONI MORRISON
Nobel Lecture
[1993]

TONI MORRISON was born in Lorain, Ohio, in 1931. She studied English at Howard University from 1949 to 1953, and in 1955 she received a master's degree in English from Cornell University with a thesis on the work of William Faulkner and Virginia Woolf—authors who would later influence her own work substantially. Morrison taught English at Texas Southern University and Howard University before moving to New York City in 1964 to work as an editor at Random House.

Morrison's first novel, *The Bluest Eye*, was published in 1970. Two huge critical successes followed: *Sula* (1975), which was nominated for a National Book Award, and *Song of Solomon* (1977), which won the National Book Critics Circle Award. Her biggest commercial and critical success, however, came in 1987 with *Beloved*, the haunting story of an escaped slave that won the Pulitzer Prize for Fiction. To date, over her forty-year career, Morrison has published ten novels, several books of nonfiction, and many essays and works of literary criticism.

Morrison was awarded the Nobel Prize for Literature in 1993. In her acceptance speech, reprinted here, she explains her work as a writer within the context of a well-known African folktale about a wise woman who is confronted by two children wanting to know whether a bird that one of them holds is living or dead. Morrison weaves this story throughout her speech, constantly reinterpreting it in different frameworks to advance her argument. In all of her interpretations, the bird represents language, the old woman represents a writer, and the children represent the members of the culture that the writer addresses. The old woman's answer to the children, "It is in your hands," points out the great responsibility that we have to the language that has been entrusted to our care.

The folktale at the heart of Morrison's speech functions rhetorically much as the parables of Jesus do in the New Testament. The tale creates an analogy that serves as scaffolding for her observations. Morrison, though, repeatedly revises and reinterprets the meaning of her parable—and by doing so adds a new layer of meaning about the ambiguous nature of narrative itself.

"Once upon a time there was an old woman. Blind but wise." Or was it an old man? A guru, perhaps. Or a griot soothing restless children. I have heard this story, or one exactly like it, in the lore of several cultures.

"Once upon a time there was an old woman. Blind. Wise."

In the version I know the woman is the daughter of slaves, black, American, and lives alone in a small house outside of town. Her reputation for wisdom is without peer and without question. Among her people she is both the law and its transgression.

The honor she is paid and the awe in which she is held reach beyond her neighborhood to places far away; to the city where the intelligence of rural prophets is the source of much amusement.

One day the woman is visited by some young people who seem to be bent on disproving her clairvoyance and showing her up for the fraud they believe she is. Their plan is simple: they enter her house and ask the one question the answer to which rides solely on her differences from them, a difference they regard as a profound disability: her blindness. They stand before her, and one of them says, "Old woman, I hold in my hand a bird. Tell me whether it is living or dead."

She does not answer, and the question is repeated. "Is the bird I am holding   5 living or dead?"

Still she doesn't answer. She is blind and cannot see her visitors, let alone what is in their hands. She does not know their color, gender or homeland. She only knows their motive.

The old woman's silence is so long, the young people have trouble holding their laughter.

Finally she speaks and her voice is soft but stern. "I don't know," she says. "I don't know whether the bird you are holding is dead or alive, but what I do know is that it is in your hands. It is in your hands."

Her answer can be taken to mean: if it is dead, you have either found it that way or you have killed it. If it is alive, you can still kill it. Whether it is to stay alive, it is your decision. Whatever the case, it is your responsibility.

For parading their power and her helplessness, the young visitors are reprimanded,   10 told they are responsible not only for the act of mockery but also for the small bundle of life sacrificed to achieve its aims. The blind woman shifts attention away from assertions of power to the instrument through which that power is exercised.

Speculation on what (other than its own frail body) that bird-in-the-hand might signify has always been attractive to me, but especially so now thinking, as I have been, about the work I do that has brought me to this company. So I choose to read the bird as language and the woman as a practiced writer. She is worried about how the language she dreams in, given to her at birth, is handled, put into service, even withheld from her for certain nefarious purposes. Being a writer she thinks of language partly as a system, partly as a living thing over which one has control, but mostly as agency—as an act with consequences. So the question the children put to her: "Is it living or dead?" is not unreal because she thinks of language as susceptible to death, erasure; certainly imperiled and salvageable only by an effort of the will. She believes that if the bird in the hands of her visitors is dead the custodians are responsible for the corpse. For her a dead language is not only one no longer spoken or written, it is unyielding language content to admire its own paralysis. Like statist language,[1] censored and censoring. Ruthless in its policing

1. **Statist language:** language produced by a government, with connotations of authoritarianism or propaganda.

duties, it has no desire or purpose other than maintaining the free range of its own narcotic narcissism, its own exclusivity and dominance. However moribund, it is not without effect for it actively thwarts the intellect, stalls conscience, suppresses human potential. Unreceptive to interrogation, it cannot form or tolerate new ideas, shape other thoughts, tell another story, fill baffling silences. Official language smitheryed[2] to sanction ignorance and preserve privilege is a suit of armor polished to shocking glitter, a husk from which the knight departed long ago. Yet there it is: dumb, predatory, sentimental. Exciting reverence in schoolchildren, providing shelter for despots, summoning false memories of stability, harmony among the public.

She is convinced that when language dies, out of carelessness, disuse, indifference and absence of esteem, or killed by fiat, not only she herself, but all users and makers are accountable for its demise. In her country children have bitten their tongues off and use bullets instead to iterate the voice of speechlessness, of disabled and disabling language, of language adults have abandoned altogether as a device for grappling with meaning, providing guidance, or expressing love. But she knows tongue-suicide is not only the choice of children. It is common among the infantile heads of state and power merchants whose evacuated language leaves them with no access to what is left of their human instincts for they speak only to those who obey, or in order to force obedience.

The systematic looting of language can be recognized by the tendency of its users to forgo its nuanced, complex, mid-wifery properties for menace and subjugation. Oppressive language does more than represent violence; it is violence; does more than represent the limits of knowledge; it limits knowledge. Whether it is obscuring state language or the faux-language of mindless media; whether it is the proud but calcified language of the academy or the commodity driven language of science; whether it is the malign language of law-without-ethics, or language designed for the estrangement of minorities, hiding its racist plunder in its literary cheek—it must be rejected, altered and exposed. It is the language that drinks blood, laps vulnerabilities, tucks its fascist boots under crinolines of respectability and patriotism as it moves relentlessly toward the bottom line and the bottomed-out mind. Sexist language, racist language, theistic language—all are typical of the policing languages of mastery, and cannot, do not permit new knowledge or encourage the mutual exchange of ideas.

The old woman is keenly aware that no intellectual mercenary, nor insatiable dictator, no paid-for politician or demagogue; no counterfeit journalist would be persuaded by her thoughts. There is and will be rousing language to keep citizens armed and arming; slaughtered and slaughtering in the malls, courthouses, post offices, playgrounds, bedrooms and boulevards; stirring, memorializing language to mask the pity and waste of needless death. There will be more diplomatic language to countenance rape, torture, assassination. There is and will be more seductive, mutant

2. **Smitheryed:** connected, as if in a blacksmith's forge.

language designed to throttle women, to pack their throats like paté-producing geese with their own unsayable, transgressive words; there will be more of the language of surveillance disguised as research; of politics and history calculated to render the suffering of millions mute; language glamorized to thrill the dissatisfied and bereft into assaulting their neighbors; arrogant pseudo-empirical language crafted to lock creative people into cages of inferiority and hopelessness.

Underneath the eloquence, the glamor, the scholarly associations, however stir-   15
ring or seductive, the heart of such language is languishing, or perhaps not beating at all—if the bird is already dead.

She has thought about what could have been the intellectual history of any discipline if it had not insisted upon, or been forced into, the waste of time and life that rationalizations for and representation of dominance required—lethal discourses of exclusion blocking access to cognition for both the excluder and the excluded.

The conventional wisdom of the Tower of Babel[3] story is that the collapse was a misfortune. That it was the distraction, or the weight of many languages that precipitated the tower's failed architecture. That one monolithic language would have expedited the building and heaven would have been reached. Whose heaven, she wonders? And what kind? Perhaps the achievement of Paradise was premature, a little hasty if no one could take the time to understand other languages, other views, other narratives period. Had they, the heaven they imagined might have been found at their feet. Complicated, demanding, yes, but a view of heaven as life; not heaven as post-life.

She would not want to leave her young visitors with the impression that language should be forced to stay alive merely to be. The vitality of language lies in its ability to limn the actual, imagined and possible lives of its speakers, readers, writers. Although its poise is sometimes in displacing experience it is not a substitute for it. It arcs toward the place where meaning may lie. When a President of the United States thought about the graveyard his country had become, and said, "The world will little note nor long remember what we say here. But it will never forget what they did here,"[4] his simple words are exhilarating in their life-sustaining properties because they refused to encapsulate the reality of 600,000 dead men in a cataclysmic race war. Refusing to monumentalize, disdaining the "final word," the precise "summing up," acknowledging their "poor power to add or detract," his words signal deference to the uncapturability of the life it mourns. It is the deference that moves her, that recognition that language can never live up to life once and for all. Nor should it. Language can never "pin down" slavery, genocide, war. Nor should it yearn for the arrogance to be able to do so. Its force, its felicity is in its reach toward the ineffable.

Be it grand or slender, burrowing, blasting, or refusing to sanctify; whether it laughs out loud or is a cry without an alphabet, the choice word, the chosen silence,

3. **Tower of Babel:** In Genesis 11:1–9, the people of earth build a huge tower in the city of Babylon to try to reach God. As a punishment, God separates their single language into a multitude of languages, so that they cannot understand each other.
4. **"The world . . . they did here:** from Lincoln's Gettysburg Address.

unmolested language surges toward knowledge, not its destruction. But who does not know of literature banned because it is interrogative; discredited because it is critical; erased because alternate? And how many are outraged by the thought of a self-ravaged tongue?

Word-work is sublime, she thinks, because it is generative; it makes meaning that secures our difference, our human difference—the way in which we are like no other life.   20

We die. That may be the meaning of life. But we do language. That may be the measure of our lives.

"Once upon a time, . . ." visitors ask an old woman a question. Who are they, these children? What did they make of that encounter? What did they hear in those final words: "The bird is in your hands"? A sentence that gestures towards possibility or one that drops a latch? Perhaps what the children heard was "It's not my problem. I am old, female, black, blind. What wisdom I have now is in knowing I cannot help you. The future of language is yours."

They stand there. Suppose nothing was in their hands? Suppose the visit was only a ruse, a trick to get to be spoken to, taken seriously as they have not been before? A chance to interrupt, to violate the adult world, its miasma of discourse about them, for them, but never to them? Urgent questions are at stake, including the one they have asked: "Is the bird we hold living or dead?" Perhaps the question meant: "Could someone tell us what is life? What is death?" No trick at all; no silliness. A straightforward question worthy of the attention of a wise one. An old one. And if the old and wise who have lived life and faced death cannot describe either, who can?

But she does not; she keeps her secret; her good opinion of herself; her gnomic pronouncements; her art without commitment. She keeps her distance, enforces it and retreats into the singularity of isolation, in sophisticated, privileged space.

Nothing, no word follows her declaration of transfer. That silence is deep, deeper   25
than the meaning available in the words she has spoken. It shivers, this silence, and the children, annoyed, fill it with language invented on the spot.

"Is there no speech," they ask her, "no words you can give us that helps us break through your dossier of failures? Through the education you have just given us that is no education at all because we are paying close attention to what you have done as well as to what you have said? To the barrier you have erected between generosity and wisdom?

"We have no bird in our hands, living or dead. We have only you and our important question. Is the nothing in our hands something you could not bear to contemplate, to even guess? Don't you remember being young when language was magic without meaning? When what you could say, could not mean? When the invisible was what imagination strove to see? When questions and demands for answers burned so brightly you trembled with fury at not knowing?

"Do we have to begin consciousness with a battle heroines and heroes like you have already fought and lost leaving us with nothing in our hands except what you have imagined is there? Your answer is artful, but its artfulness embarrasses us and ought to embarrass you. Your answer is indecent in its self-congratulation. A made-for-television script that makes no sense if there is nothing in our hands.

"Why didn't you reach out, touch us with your soft fingers, delay the sound bite, the lesson, until you knew who we were? Did you so despise our trick, our modus operandi you could not see that we were baffled about how to get your attention? We are young. Unripe. We have heard all our short lives that we have to be responsible. What could that possibly mean in the catastrophe this world has become; where, as a poet said, "nothing needs to be exposed since it is already barefaced." Our inheritance is an affront. You want us to have your old, blank eyes and see only cruelty and mediocrity. Do you think we are stupid enough to perjure ourselves again and again with the fiction of nationhood? How dare you talk to us of duty when we stand waist deep in the toxin of your past?

"You trivialize us and trivialize the bird that is not in our hands. Is there no   30 context for our lives? No song, no literature, no poem full of vitamins, no history connected to experience that you can pass along to help us start strong? You are an adult. The old one, the wise one. Stop thinking about saving your face. Think of our lives and tell us your particularized world. Make up a story. Narrative is radical, creating us at the very moment it is being created. We will not blame you if your reach exceeds your grasp; if love so ignites your words they go down in flames and nothing is left but their scald. Or if, with the reticence of a surgeon's hands, your words suture only the places where blood might flow. We know you can never do it properly—once and for all. Passion is never enough; neither is skill. But try. For our sake and yours forget your name in the street; tell us what the world has been to you in the dark places and in the light. Don't tell us what to believe, what to fear. Show us belief's wide skirt and the stitch that unravels fear's caul. You, old woman, blessed with blindness, can speak the language that tells us what only language can: how to see without pictures. Language alone protects us from the scariness of things with no names. Language alone is meditation.

"Tell us what it is to be a woman so that we may know what it is to be a man. What moves at the margin. What it is to have no home in this place. To be set adrift from the one you knew. What it is to live at the edge of towns that cannot bear your company.

"Tell us about ships turned away from shorelines at Easter, placenta in a field. Tell us about a wagonload of slaves, how they sang so softly their breath was indistinguishable from the falling snow. How they knew from the hunch of the nearest shoulder that the next stop would be their last. How, with hands prayered in their sex, they thought of heat, then sun. Lifting their faces as though it was there for the taking. Turning as though there for the taking. They stop at an inn. The driver and his mate go in with the lamp leaving them humming in the dark. The horse's void steams into the snow beneath its hooves and its hiss and melt are the envy of the freezing slaves.

"The inn door opens: a girl and a boy step away from its light. They climb into the wagon bed. The boy will have a gun in three years, but now he carries a lamp and a jug of warm cider. They pass it from mouth to mouth. The girl offers bread, pieces of meat and something more: a glance into the eyes of the one she serves. One helping for each man, two for each woman. And a look. They look back. The next stop will be their last. But not this one. This one is warmed."

It's quiet again when the children finish speaking, until the woman breaks into the silence.

"Finally," she says, "I trust you now. I trust you with the bird that is not in your   35 hands because you have truly caught it. Look. How lovely it is, this thing we have done—together."

UNDERSTANDING THE TEXT

1. What is the moral of the story that Toni Morrison begins with? Why does she choose this particular story? Why does she stress that different regions of Africa have different versions of the story?

2. Morrison says that "children have bitten their tongues off and use bullets instead." In what ways might violence replace language as a way of dealing with others?

3. How, according to Morrison, can language be used to oppress and subjugate people? What other, more noble purposes of language does she suggest?

4. For Morrison, what is the difference between "living language" and "dead language"? How does this difference parallel the living or dead bird in the story that frames her speech?

5. Why does Morrison devote so much time at the end of her speech to the possibility that the children in her tale do not have a bird in their hand at all? How would this change the traditional moral of the story? What point about the possibilities of language does she make with this change?

MAKING CONNECTIONS

1. Contrast Morrison's views on the abuse of language with those of Plato (p. 166) and Gloria Anzaldúa (p. 205). How might each of these authors' backgrounds have shaped their perceptions of language? Explain.

2. Would Frederick Douglass (p. 24) have agreed with Morrison's view that language can be used for violence and oppression? What are the characteristics of language used in these ways?

WRITING ABOUT THE TEXT

1. Write an essay in which you analyze the connection between language and violence. Refer to Morrison's text and to one other text in this chapter in your essay. You might

also include anecdotes from your own life, facts, statistics, expert testimony, and other forms of evidence you can uncover during research.

2. Write an essay in which you analyze Morrison's use of an African folktale in this speech. Explain how this story functions as an introduction, a conclusion, and evidence for a claim, and evaluate its effectiveness in each role.

3. Listen to Morrison's speech online—it's available on the Nobel Prize website, nobelprize.org—and read it again carefully. Then, write an essay in which you explain how the experience of hearing the speech is different from the experience of reading it. In your essay, consider how these differences might be related to the differences between oral and written narrative that Morrison and others discuss.

ZEYNEP TUFEKCI
Networked Politics from Tahrir to Taksim:
Is There a Social Media–Fueled
Protest Style?
[2013]

ZEYNEP TUFEKCI is an assistant professor of information and library science, with an affiliate appointment in sociology, at the University of North Carolina at Chapel Hill. Her work focuses on the interactions between technology and social, cultural, and political dynamics. Tufekci is a leading scholar of both social media and social movements, and her work on recent uprisings in the United States, Egypt, and Turkey has helped to clarify the problems and possibilities of using sites like Facebook and Twitter to organize popular revolts.

The present article originally appeared as a post on dmlcentral, a blog sponsored by the Digital Media and Learning Research Hub, whose mission is to "advance research in the service of a more equitable, participatory, and effective ecosystem of learning keyed to the digital and networked era." In this blog post, Professor Tufekci examines the common features of four mass protest movements across the world in which social media sites like Facebook and Twitter played an important role:

- The #Jan 25 protests in Egypt, which began on January 25, 2011, and led to the ousting of Egyptian president Hosni Mubarak five months later.
- The #M15 movement in Spain, which began on May 15, 2011, with demonstrations simultaneously arising in 58 Spanish cities. Protesters demanded social and economic changes such as addressing high unemployment rates and reversing cuts to social spending.
- The #Occupy Wall Street movement in the United States, which began in September 2011 when protesters camped out in New York City's Zuccotti Park and spoke out against corporate power, financial corruption, and the unequal distribution of wealth.
- The #Occupygezi movement in Turkey, which began in May 2013 as a demonstration against proposed plans to replace Taksim Gezi Park with a shopping mall, but which grew to encompass protests against police violence, corporate control of the government, and the curtailing of civil rights.

Though these mass protest movements had very different causes, motives, and outcomes, they were all made possible by social media networks, which informed people about the initial protests, alerted millions to the activities of the protesters, and helped to shape the publicity that the movements received. Exploring these developments, Tufekci addresses the rhetorical potential and limitations of social media outlets.

Protesters from one of the world's richest countries, one of the world's oldest autocracies, and one of the world's rising developing countries walk into . . . a public space, use Twitter extensively, and capture global attention to their movement and their hashtag.

From "#Occupy Wall Street" in the United States to the #M15 movement in Spain, from Tahrir Square and #Jan 25 in Egypt, to Taksim Square and #occupygezi in Turkey, there have been a variety of social movements that, while coming from strikingly different backgrounds and contexts, also share structural and stylistic elements. In this post, I'd like to offer some preliminary analyses of this emergent type of what I'm calling "networked movements."

To be clear, I am not attempting to analyze every aspect of these movements—no movement or revolution is simple or reducible to a single cause—nor is it identical to any other. Nor do I claim that this is an exhaustive or final list of their characteristics. However, we now have enough examples to try to make sense of common elements to these seemingly disparate social media–fueled movements.

There are also other interesting political commonalities to these movements, including their use of durable presence in public space as a form of protest, anti-authoritarianism as a uniting ideology, an "anti-political" stance among participants, the participation and key role played by "lumpen"[1] elements such as soccer fans, the importance of anger towards cronyism, police repression as a spark and uniting theme, to name a few. Hence, this post is an attempt to take a bite out of a complex topic with a special focus on social media and organizational styles of networked movements:

1. Lack of organized, institutional leadership. None of these movements has identifiable institutional leadership, either in institutional form or as spokespersons. This is quite a striking change from the traditional, common (though not exclusive) form of movements of the 20th century.

This is not to say that these movements are flat or lack prominent persons or a hierarchy of influence or attention. There are structures, hierarchy, informal leadership and other elements of leadership in all these movements. However, there is no NAACP or trade-union or political party that has control over, or the ability to speak for them and there is no formalized mechanism of representation—or decision making.

This, of course, creates advantages and disadvantages in terms of long-term politics. Since these movements have no recognized representation, they cannot be co-opted or negotiated away behind closed doors. (In his book, *Revolution 2.0*, Wael Ghonim[2] recounts how Mubarak's top officials tried to negotiate an end to the demonstrations with him. He could only chuckle as he had no such power).

However, in the same vein, since these movements have no recognized representation, it is difficult for them to develop a coherent and delimited set of policies,

5

---

1. **"lumpen":** people who are alienated from their society and, often, from the social class to which they would normally belong.

2. **Wael Ghonim:** Egyptian activist and computer engineer who created the Facebook page "We Are All Khaled Saeed" (see note 5).

demands or make any significant gains that go beyond providing a strong refusal to a particular event, leader or framing. This leads to my next point.

2. Organized around a "no" not a "go." Existing social media structures allow for easier collective action around shared grievances to "stop" or "oppose" something (downfall of Mubarak, stopping a government's overreach, etc.) rather than strategic action geared towards obtaining and sustaining political power. This is probably why these movements don't make as much long-term impact as their size and power would suggest. (They do have impacts, of course, but often not proportional to their size.)

Not only has the world not moved towards more "participatory democracy" as opposed to "representative democracy," the current trend globally has been otherwise. Even mere representative democracy has been eroding as moneyed interests have expanded their power over more and more areas of politics and the public sphere. Hence, we see an outburst of "participatory refusal," which does not necessarily expand into either addressing or opposing failing parts of representative democracy. Instead, these demonstrations seem to be unable to break out of a "no." 10

It is also easier to use social media to communicate a message or an image of refusal or dissent rather than convey complicated arguments. The closest example to a mass participatory online environment that tries to negotiate complex outcomes is Wikipedia. While wildly successful in some ways, research also shows Wikipedia to be run by relatively small numbers of highly influential people who are spectacularly good mostly at providing a certain, narrow outcome (eg., a summary of existing sources on a topic, the depth and quality of which varies, depending in part on the amount of conflict over the topic).

There needs to be a lot more "practical" research into what and how online platforms could contribute to positive civic outcomes through participation, negotiation, and solution generation, especially for complex problems. By research, I mean creation, trial, error and study rather than merely examining existing forms—as these are clearly not enough.

3. A feeling of lack of institutional outlet. In all these cases, there has been a failure of both oppositional politics as well as mainstream media. Protesters repeatedly state they have felt a lack of outlets to express their dissent. In the case of Egypt, this was because elections were rigged and politics banned.

In Turkey, the media has cowered and opposition parties are spectacularly incompetent. During the height of the most recent protests, CNN Turkey alternated between showing documentaries on penguins, and then a cooking show. At a particularly low moment, CNN Turkey was showing a documentary about a popular Turkish volunteer search and rescue team, AKUT, while AKUT members were out in the streets providing medical aid to protesters and AKUT founder Nasuk Masruhi lay in a hospital after both his legs were broken by police.

The failure of media and institutional outlet carries over to a country like the United States as well. In the Occupy movement in the US, there also was a widespread feeling among #occupy participants that the government and the media 15 were at the hands of the moneyed interests and the corrupt. For example, look at this chart about mentions of the word "inequality" in major US media before and after Occupy:

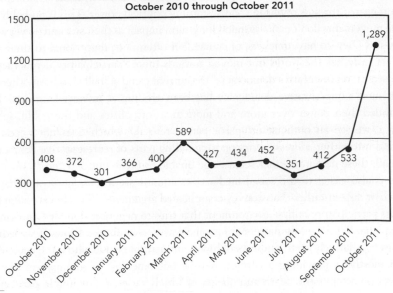

Number of articles with the word "inequality" in U.S. newspapers—October 2010 through October 2011

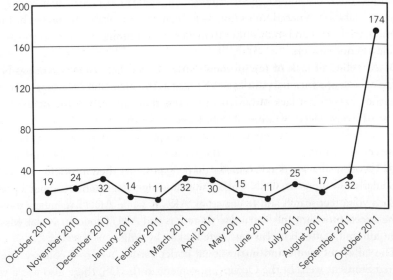

Number of articles with phrase "richest one percent" in U.S. newspapers—October 2010 through October 2011

Source: Lexis/Nexis

At the time, the grave effects of the economic crisis could be seen in historically high unemployment and underemployment. Yet, most US media were covering economics mainly from the point of view of a very small minority of people who were concerned with inflation and levels of public debt and taxation on the rich—all of which are more of a concern to [the] wealthy and to bondholders rather than to the struggling middle and working classes.

The feeling of lack of institutional outlet also, crucially, includes political parties. In Turkey, Spain and the United States (representative democracies), opposition parties and parliaments have been seen as incompetent, corrupt or uninterested in issues that concerned broad swaths of the public. This failure and sense of non-representation, of course, varies according to context but is nonetheless shared in all these movements.

4. Non-activist participation. Most previous big demonstrations before #occupygezi in Turkey were attended by experienced protesters. In contrast, the 2013 protests in Turkey are being attended by large numbers of people who have probably never been in a protest before. It has induded participation from residents in their homes (banging pots and pans, turning lights on and off) on a scale that is unprecedented in Turkey in the post 1980 coup era. Tahrir protests 2011, Tunisia December 2010, Gezi 2013 drew large numbers of non-activists. My own study of Tahrir participants (a non-random sample) similarly found a great many who had never attended a protest before.

Occupy, too, attracted a mix of seasoned activists as well as many participants who seemed drawn to the action partly because it was seen as "more than politics."

5. External attention. Social media allows for bypassing domestic choke-points of censorship and reach for global attention. This was crucial in the Arab Spring (and we know many people tweeting about it were outside the region which, in my view, makes Twitter more powerful in its effects, not less).

In fact, just as in the Arab Spring, there have been moments in Turkey where international coverage of the protests was better than the domestic counterparts.

In all these cases, social media sources provided more comprehensive and more timely coverage of the events. Of course, the lack of institutional media reporting inside the country also had insidious effects in that it was difficult to keep in check unfounded and inflammatory rumors that ricocheted around online social networks.

6. Social media as structuring the narrative. In all these protests, we see that social media allows a crowd-sourced, participatory, but also often social media–savvy, activist-led structuring of the meta-narrative, as well as the shaping of the collective grievances. Stories we tell about politics are incredibly important in shaping that very politics, and social media has opened a new, complicated path in which meta-narratives[3] about political actions emerge and coalesce.

3. **meta-narrative:** a comprehensive way of describing something that accounts for all of the smaller narratives comprised by it.

Many of the "network analyses" based on social network analyses methods have missed this crucial aspect of the narrative shaping power of social media as it cannot be seen merely by scraping a billion tweets and making a colorful "spaghetti" map[4] of the network. What has emerged is that Twitter, Facebook and online social networks are the new mass, participatory, open, but also UNFLAT spaces of uneven influence where narratives conflict, coalesce and then are rebroadcast and recirculated by mass media.

In short, Twitter is the new spin room for the 21st century.   25

7. Breaking of pluralistic ignorance and altering of collective action dynamics. Revolutions, political upheavals, and large movements are quite hard to predict, but once they happen, they seem inevitable. Then there is a lot of hand-wringing on why they weren't predicted before by analysts and observers. (A classic case is the 1979 Iranian revolution which everyone should have seen coming but nobody did).

This is not because all analysts and political observers are idiots but because of a particular characteristic of large-scale social upheaval, especially in repressive environments. Many such events break through when "pluralistic ignorance"—i.e., the idea that you are the only one, or one of few, with a particular view—is broken. This can happen via a public mass action which can be a street demonstration or a Facebook page proclaiming "we are all Khaled Saeed."[5]

In other words, many people keep their true preferences private, or speak only with a few trusted people, thinking either that they are a minority or that if they speak up, they will be one of only a few and thus meet with massive repression. Once this dam breaks, however, the dissent explodes. Thus, it's easy to predict that there is a lot of pressure on this dam; however, it is hard to predict when and where it will break.

The key conceptual issue here is not digital versus non-digital but visibility, accessibility and signaling power. Street demonstrations, in that regard, are a form of social media in that they are powerful to the degree that they allow citizens to signal a plurality to their fellow citizens, and to help break pluralist ignorance. Overall, social media are altering mechanisms of collective action in societies and we have just begun to understand this fundamental shift.

8. Not easily steerable towards complex, strategic political action. The com-   30
bination of the above factors makes social media–fueled protests very powerful and consequential in some dimensions and somewhat ephemeral and weak in others.

While social media–fueled collective action lacks the affordances of politics and the institutional capital that political parties and NGOs can provide, they can be very

---

4. **"spaghetti" map:** a chart showing the geographical connections between different parts of a process.

5. **Khaled Saeed:** a young Egyptian man who was killed while in police custody in June 2010.

The Facebook page "We Are All Khaled Saeed" was a major precursor to the 2011 protests in Egypt.

good at drawing red lines and organizing and gathering attention to a loud "NO!" (i.e., Mubarak, SOPA/PIPA, Gezi Parki demolition). However, such movements seem usually unable to translate their power into a next step which directly impacts policy, law or regulation through elections or parliament.

This partly stems from the lack of representative power within the movement. During Occupy, for example, the protests were almost shut down at one point not because of police, or Zuccotti Park's owners' actions but because the protesters were unable to contain a few people among them who wanted to continue drumming around the clock. The neighborhood almost evicted them themselves—the crisis was averted at the last minute. Lack of representational power has meant that movements have little capacity to direct their own participants towards any tactical steps or strategic steps.

Whether there will emerge new platforms and ways of organizing enabled by online media remains to be seen; however, as of now, this is where this nascent phenomenon stands.

UNDERSTANDING THE TEXT

1. According to Tufekci what are the primary benefits of social media as it relates to political protests? What does she see as social media's drawbacks?

2. Tufekci identifies Wikipedia as the best example of a "mass participatory online environment that tries to negotiate complex outcomes." What does she say makes Wikipedia work? Is this something that protest organizers can duplicate?

3. Why does Tufekci believe that protests organized through social media outlets attract non-activist participants? Why are people who are not otherwise politically active motivated to attend demonstrations that they read about on social media sites?

4. How do social media sites shape the narrative of a protest event? Do social media sites have the same kind of opinion-shaping influence today that mainstream news sites do?

5. What does Tufekci mean by the term "pluralistic ignorance"? How do social media sites help people overcome this problem?

MAKING CONNECTIONS

1. Compare the mass movements that Tufekci talks about with the Green Belt movement in Kenya described by Wangari Mathaai (p. 363) or the democracy movement in Burma described by Aung San Suu Kyi (p. 442). What does the presence of social media add to a political protest movement?

2. How does Tufekci's understanding of social connectedness compare with Nicholas Carr's in "A Thing Like Me" (p. 123)? Are the two writers equally skeptical of some aspects of internet culture?

WRITING ABOUT THE TEXT

1. Explore your own reactions to political and social discussions on social media. Discuss any ways that you have, or could imagine, engaging in political discourse over the internet.

2. Conduct your own research on one of the four protest movements that Zeynep Tufekci addresses in this selection. Give a brief description of the movement and explore the ways that it has relied on social media.

3. Construct an argument about the rhetorical potential of social media. Look at the ways different sites such as Facebook, Twitter, and YouTube shape our reactions to political events. Explore both the advantages and disadvantages to a public discourse conducted primarily online.

4

THE ARTS

Why Do Humans Create Art?

What distinguishes a work of art from all other mental activity is just the fact that its language is understood by all, and that it infects all without distinction.
—Leo Tolstoy

THE MAKING OF ART is a human preoccupation. Paintings in caves and broken musical instruments left by the earliest civilizations in historical record are a testament to their attraction to art and music. Every culture ever studied has expressed itself artistically in music, poetry, painting, dance, and storytelling. Human beings have always spent a considerable share of their resources surrounding themselves with things they consider beautiful.

It is almost impossible to explain our love of art in evolutionary terms. Drawing pictures and telling fictional stories do not, seemingly, help us to survive or reproduce. As Oscar Wilde writes in his famous preface to *The Picture of Dorian Gray*, "all art is quite useless." In fact, the time and attention that early humans spent making cave paintings and bone flutes could have been spent more productively in hunting animals and gathering resources necessary for survival. Though other animals engage in behaviors that resemble artistic expression—such as the elaborate songs of some bird species or the carefully synchronized movements of schools of fish—we can always demonstrate that these activities are biologically useful.

Just as humans in every culture have been drawn to create works of art, philosophers in every culture have been compelled to explain them. Aesthetics is the branch of philosophy that deals with questions of art and beauty. Many of the greatest thinkers in world history have written about aesthetics. Plato's *Symposium*, for example, presents a series of monologues about beauty and the human mind. *The Analects of Confucius* considers the power of music to shape human behavior. And Aristotle's *Poetics* explores the psychology of dramatic literature.

The first two selections in this chapter deal with the aesthetics of music. In the first of these, "Against Music," the ancient Chinese philosopher Mo Tzu argues against the prevailing Confucian consensus of his day. Confucius held that music was a powerful moral force with its rhythms and tempos reinforcing the value of highly regulated personal behavior. Mo Tzu, on the other hand, sees music as a waste of resources that could be better used providing food and shelter to needy people. For Mo Tzu, the only aesthetic principle worth discussing is the principle of utility.

In the next selection, the philosopher Boethius, living during the final days of the Roman Empire, argues that music's powerful influence on the human mind gives it the potential for both good and bad. Following Plato (and echoing Confucius), he explains that some modes of music are "prudent and modest" and influence people to be prudent and modest as well. Other kinds of music are lascivious and disorderly and can lead to the moral decline of entire societies.

Another group of selections is concerned with visual art. Johannes Vermeer's *Study of a Young Woman* is a 350-year-old masterpiece from the Golden Age of Dutch painting. The second, Lisa Yuskavage's *Babie I*, is a modern painting from a contemporary feminist artist. The two works are in many ways strikingly similar in their conception of feminine beauty: both artists eschew traditional notions of beauty and focus instead on the facial features and characteristics that make their subjects interesting and unique. Complementing these images is Alice Walker's essay "Beauty: When the Other Dancer Is the Self," a deeply personal narrative of how a disfiguring childhood accident changed the author's self-image.

Two other selections in this chapter contemplate the craft of writing. In a reading from the medieval Japanese masterpiece *The Tale of Genji*, Lady Murasaki Shikibu explains the practical value of narrative fiction. In a much later essay, the Russian novelist Leo Tolstoy, author of such masterpieces as *War and Peace* and *Anna Karenina*, argues that literature, and art in general, can be considered great only if it is understood by the majority of people in the world.

The final category of readings in the chapter speaks to aesthetic issues generally and can be applied to music, art, and literature. Edmund Burke's classic treatise *A Philosophical Enquiry into the Origins of Our Ideas of the Sublime and Beautiful* maintains that "sublime" images—those that evoke feelings of terror and fear—are more aesthetically compelling to us than things that are merely beautiful; William Blake's illustrated poem "The Tyger" provides an example of this kind of sublimity. In the final selection, professor Elaine Scarry argues that the symmetry we find in beautiful images helps us to understand the principles upon which just social systems can be based.

The selections in this chapter represent only a small sample of the ways we can find and create meaning through artistic expression. Each reading, along with the images that accompany it, tries to understand humanity itself through the universal drive to create and appreciate works of art.

MO TZU
Against Music
[CIRCA 425 BCE]

MO TZU (CIRCA 470–CIRCA 391 BCE) holds a unique position in the canon of classical Chinese philosophers known as the hundred schools, which flourished from the sixth to the third century BCE. He opposed and ridiculed both the Confucians, who he believed were overly concerned with ritual, and the Legalists, whom he saw as totalitarian and immoral. Though he had many followers during his lifetime and in the three centuries after his death, his influence steadily declined as Confucianism, rather than Moism, became the principal ethical philosophy of the Chinese state.

Mo Tzu is best known for his philosophy of "universal love," which advocated a general, impartial concern for all of humanity, with no person held in higher regard than any other. This idea rankled the Confucians of his day because it implied that the most honored relationships in Chinese culture—those between sons and their fathers and between younger and older brothers—were no more important than relationships between strangers. Mo Tzu taught that the chief value of love lay in its universality and that family ties, which he saw as mere accidents of birth, did not make people more worthy of this love.

Only slightly less disconcerting to Confucians were Mo Tzu's writings against music. Confucian orthodoxy saw ritual music as a force for good; they believed it helped to organize thoughts and regulate behavior. Mo Tzu, however, disapproved of the fact that, in ancient China, music and its benefits were limited to an extremely small number of people, namely the very wealthy. Musical instruments were expensive to manufacture, trained musicians were rare, and musical celebrations were usually accompanied by elaborate dancing and expensive feasts, all of which made "music" virtually synonymous with "luxury."

At the center of "Against Music," part 1 of which follows, are two assertions: that artistic pursuits such as music are not useful to society, and that people should not be forced to pay—with their tax dollars—for artistic programs that do not benefit them directly. Today, the first assertion often comes up in discussions about core curricula (for example, should art and music classes be required for elementary school students?). The second surfaces just as frequently in discussions about government funding for the arts through programs such as the National Endowment for the Arts and the National Endowment for the Humanities.

Mo Tzu employs several rhetorical strategies in this selection. He argues through examples, close analysis, and appeals to authority. His most direct argument, however, is a simple deductive syllogism given in the first paragraph: benevolent men should promote what is beneficial; music is not beneficial; therefore, benevolent men should not promote music.

It is the business of the benevolent man to seek to promote what is beneficial to the world, to eliminate what is harmful, and to provide a model for the world. What benefits men he will carry out; what does not benefit men he will leave alone. Moreover, when the benevolent man plans for the benefit of the world, he does not consider merely what will please the eye, delight the ear, gratify the mouth, and give ease to the body. If in order to gratify the senses he has to deprive the people of the wealth needed for their food and clothing, then the benevolent man will not do so. Therefore Mo Tzu condemns music,[1] not because the sound of the great bells and rolling drums, the zithers and pipes, is not delightful; not because the sight of the carvings and ornaments is not beautiful, not because the taste of the fried and broiled meats is not delicious; and not because lofty towers, broad pavilions, and secluded halls are not comfortable to live in. But though the body finds comfort, the mouth gratification, the eye pleasure, and the ear delight, yet if we examine the matter, we will find that such things are not in accordance with the ways of the sage kings, and if we consider the welfare of the world we will find that they bring no benefit to the common people. Therefore Mo Tzu said: Making music is wrong!

Now if the rulers and ministers want musical instruments to use in their government activities, they cannot extract them from the sea water, like salt, or dig them out of the ground, like ore. Inevitably, therefore, they must lay heavy taxes upon the common people before they can enjoy the sound of great bells, rolling drums, zithers, and pipes. In ancient times the sage kings likewise laid heavy taxes on the people, but this was for the purpose of making boats and carts, and when they were completed and people asked, "What are these for?" the sage kings replied, "The boats are for use on water, and the carts for use on land, so that gentlemen may rest their feet and laborers spare their shoulders." So the common people paid their taxes and levies and did not dare to grumble. Why? Because they knew that the taxes would be used for the benefit of the people. Now if musical instruments were also used for the benefit of the people, I would not venture to condemn them. Indeed, if they were as useful as the boats and carts of the sage kings, I would certainly not venture to condemn them.

There are three things the people worry about: that when they are hungry they will have no food, when they are cold they will have no clothing, and when they are weary they will have no rest. These are the three great worries of the people. Now let us try sounding the great bells, striking the rolling drums, strumming the zithers, blowing the pipes, and waving the shields and axes in the war dance. Does this do anything to provide food and clothing for the people? I hardly think so. But let us leave that point for the moment.

The translator's footnotes have been omitted. Bracketed insertions are the translator's.

1. **Music:** Mo Tzu means not only singing and playing instruments but also the dancing, banquets, and other expensive entertainments that went along with the enjoyment of music by wealthy people in ancient China.

Now there are great states that attack small ones, and great families that molest small ones. The strong oppress the weak, the many tyrannize the few, the cunning deceive the stupid, the eminent lord it over the humble, and bandits and thieves rise up on all sides and cannot be suppressed. Now let us try sounding the great bells, striking the rolling drums, strumming the zithers, blowing the pipes, and waving the shields and axes in the war dance. Does this do anything to rescue the world from chaos and restore it to order? I hardly think so. Therefore Mo Tzu said: If you try to promote what is beneficial to the world and eliminate what is harmful by laying heavy taxes on the people for the purpose of making bells, drums, zithers, and pipes, you will get nowhere. So Mo Tzu said: Making music is wrong!

Now the rulers and ministers, seated in their lofty towers and broad pavil-   5
ions, look about them, and there are the bells, hanging like huge cauldrons. But unless the bells are struck, how can the rulers get any delight out of them? Therefore it is obvious that the rulers must have someone to strike the bells. But they cannot employ old men or young boys, since their eyes and ears are not keen enough and their arms are not strong, and they cannot make the sounds harmonious or see to strike the bells front and back. Therefore the rulers must have young people in their prime, whose eyes and ears are keen and whose arms are so strong that they can make the sounds harmonious and see to strike the bells front and back. If they employ young men, then they will be taking them away from their plowing and planting, and if they employ young women, they will be taking them away from their weaving and spinning. Yet the rulers and ministers will have their music, though their music-making interferes to such an extent with the people's efforts to produce food and clothing! Therefore Mo Tzu said: Making music is wrong!

Now let us suppose that the great bells, rolling drums, zithers, and pipes have all been provided. Still if the rulers and ministers sit quietly all alone and listen to the performance, how can they get any delight out of it? Therefore it is obvious that they must listen in the company of others, either humble men or gentlemen. If they listen in the company of gentlemen, then they will be keeping the gentlemen from attending to affairs of state, while if they listen in the company of humble men, they will be keeping the humble men from pursuing their tasks. Yet the rulers and ministers will have their music, though their music-making interferes to such an extent with the people's efforts to produce food and clothing! Therefore Mo Tzu said: Making music is wrong!

In former times Duke K'ang of Ch'i [404–379 BCE] loved the music of the Wan dance. The Wan dancers cannot wear robes of cheap cloth or eat coarse food, for it is said that unless they have the finest food and drink, their faces and complexions will not be fit to look at, and unless they have beautiful clothing, their figures and movements will not be worth watching. Therefore the Wan dancers ate only millet and meat,[2] and wore only robes of patterned and embroidered silk. They did nothing to help produce food or clothing, but lived entirely off the efforts of others. Yet the rulers and ministers will have their music, though their music-making interferes to such an extent with the people's efforts to produce food and clothing! Therefore Mo Tzu said: Making music is wrong!

Now man is basically different from the beasts, birds, and insects. The beasts, birds, and insects have feathers and fur for their robes and coats, hoofs and claws for their leggings and shoes, and grass and water for their food and drink. Therefore the male need not plow or plant, the female need not weave or spin, and still they have plenty of food and clothing. But man is different from such creatures. If a man exerts his strength, he may live, but if he does not, he cannot live. If the gentlemen do not diligently attend to affairs of state, the government will fall into disorder, and if humble men do not diligently pursue their tasks, there will not be enough wealth and goods.

If the gentlemen of the world do not believe what I say, then let us try enumerating the various duties of the people of the world and see how music interferes with them. The rulers and ministers must appear at court early and retire late, hearing lawsuits and attending to affairs of government—this is their duty. The gentlemen must exhaust the strength of their limbs and employ to the fullest the wisdom of their minds, directing bureaus within the government and abroad, collecting taxes on the barriers and markets and on the resources of the hills, forests, lakes, and fish weirs,[3] so that the granaries and treasuries will be full—this is their duty. The farmers must leave home early and return late, sowing seed, planting trees, and gathering large crops of vegetables and grain—this is their duty. Women must rise early and go to bed late, spinning, weaving, producing large quantities of hemp, silk, and other fibers, and preparing cloth—this is their duty. Now if those who occupy the position of rulers and ministers are fond of music and spend their time listening to it, then they will not be able to appear at court early and retire late, or hear lawsuits and attend to affairs of government, and as a result the state will fall into disorder and its altars of the soil and grain will be in danger. If those who occupy the position of gentlemen are fond of music and spend their time listening to it, then they will be unable to exhaust the strength of their limbs and employ to the fullest the wisdom of their minds in directing bureaus within the government and abroad, collecting taxes on the barriers and markets and on the resources of the hills, forests, lakes, and fish weirs, in order to fill the granaries and treasuries, and as a result the granaries and treasuries will not be filled. If those who occupy the position of farmers are fond of music and spend their time listening to it, then they will be unable to leave

2. **Millet and meat:** Meals composed solely of millet, a cereal grain, and meat would have been considered extremely luxurious by most Chinese in Mo Tzu's time.

3. **Fish weirs:** fenced-in areas in bodies of water, used to trap large quantities of migrating fish.

home early and return late, sowing seed, planting trees, and gathering large crops of vegetables and grain, and as a result there will be a lack of vegetables and grain. If women are fond of music and spend their time listening to it, then they will be unable to rise early and go to bed late, spinning, weaving, producing large quantities of hemp, silk, and other fibers, and preparing cloth, and as a result there will not be enough cloth. If you ask what it is that has caused the ruler to neglect the affairs of government and the humble man to neglect his tasks, the answer is music. Therefore Mo Tzu said: Making music is wrong!

How do we know that this is so? The proof is found among the books of the for-   10
mer kings, in Tang's "Code of Punishment," where it says: "Constant dancing in the palace—this is the way of shamans! As a punishment, gentlemen shall be fined two measures of silk, but for common men the line shall be two hundred pieces of yellow silk." It also says: "Alas, all this dancing! The sound of the pipes is loud and clear. The Lord on High does not aid him, and the nine districts[4] are lost to him. The Lord on High does not approve him, but sends down a hundred misfortunes. His house will be destroyed." If we examine the reason why he lost the nine districts, we will find that it was because he idly spent his time arranging elaborate musical performances.

The "Wu kuan"[5] says: "Ch'i gave himself up to pleasure and music, eating and drinking in the fields. Ch'iang-ch'iang, the flutes and chimes sounded in unison! He drowned himself in wine and behaved indecently by eating in the fields. Splendid was the Wan dance, but Heaven clearly heard the sound and Heaven did not approve." So it was not approved by Heaven and the spirits above, and brought no benefit to the people below.

Therefore Mo Tzu said: If the rulers, ministers, and gentlemen of the world truly desire to promote what is beneficial to the world and eliminate what is harmful, they must prohibit and put a stop to this thing called music!

UNDERSTANDING THE TEXT

1. What does Mo Tzu mean by "music"? What aspects of contemporary Western culture might fit into Mo Tzu's overall category of "music"?

2. Why does Mo Tzu begin the essay by acknowledging the delight and pleasure that music brings? What effect does this acknowledgment have on his ethos (p. 663)?

3. According to Mo Tzu, what are the people's three primary concerns? How does he believe music will prevent people from performing their duties and therefore hurt the well-being of the entire community? Are his arguments reasonable? How so?

4. How might music affect government? What might then happen to the state?

5. What difference between humans and animals does Mo Tzu use to support his argument?

4. **Nine districts:** according to legend, the nine provinces of China in the distant past, which Mo Tzu would have considered "ancient."

5. **"Wu kuan":** an ancient Chinese text known to Mo Tzu but now lost.

6. What kinds of activities does Mo Tzu claim are useful to society? Do you agree with his assessment? Why or why not?

MAKING CONNECTIONS

1. What ideas about beauty does Mo Tzu's "Against Music" imply? Is it possible under his assumptions to say that something is beautiful unless it has some practical value to it? How would Mo Tzu's ideas about beauty and usefulness compare to those of Tolstoy (p. 265), who argued that nothing can be truly beautiful unless it can be universally comprehended?

2. Compare Mo Tzu's views on beauty and justice to those of Elaine Scarry (p. 279). How does each of them see the connection between a work of art and a more just society?

3. How might advocates of a broad liberal education, such as Seneca (p. 13) and John Henry Newman (p. 31), defend music against Mo Tzu's charges?

WRITING ABOUT THE TEXT

1. Think of something in your own culture that is comparable to what music was for Mo Tzu—an expensive luxury item or service that only the wealthy can afford. Make an argument in the style of "Against Music" that society should not be required to devote time or money to this item or service.

2. Write an essay agreeing or disagreeing with Mo Tzu's argument that beautiful things can be morally justified only if they promote some social good. Is it possible to find positive moral value in a thing simply because it is beautiful?

3. Drawing on Mo Tzu's arguments, refute or defend the proposition that colleges and universities should require students to study art, music, literature, and other liberal arts that do not have an immediately obvious social or industrial purpose. Consider the arguments of Seneca (p. 13) and John Henry Newman (p. 31) as you make your argument.

BOETHIUS
from *Of Music*
[CIRCA 500]

ANICIUS MANLIUS SEVERINUS BOETHIUS (circa 480–circa 524 CE) has been called both the first medieval philosopher and the last philosopher of the Roman world. Born in Rome shortly after the fall of the Western Roman Empire, Boethius came from a family of prominent Roman Christians, including two emperors and one pope. Though Rome had come under control of the Ostrogoths (the Eastern branch of the Germanic tribe known as the Goths), who set up their kingdom in post-Roman Italy, Roman educational and political institutions did not disappear all at once. Boethius and other members of his family held positions under the Ostrogothic king, Theodoric the Great.

Boethius was a philosophical prodigy who came to the attention of Rome's rulers at a young age. By the time he was twenty-five, he was a member of the Roman Senate, and at thirty he was appointed Consul of Rome. In 522 CE, at the age of forty-two, he was appointed *magister officiorum*, effectively the head of the Roman government—a position that he used to try to improve religious ties between the Christian churches of Rome and Constantinople, who had different views about the authority of the Pope and the role of government in religion. Through these efforts, however, he ran afoul of Theodoric, who imprisoned him for treason in 523 CE and had him executed a year later.

While in prison, Boethius wrote his most famous work, *The Consolation of Philosophy*, which became one of the most important philosophical works of the early Middle Ages. In addition to this work, he composed (we are not exactly sure when) treatises on rhetoric, arithmetic, theology, and music. The reading in this chapter is drawn from his book *De institutione musica*, or "Of Music," a study of the forms of music common in the Greek and Roman worlds and their influence on human psychology. *Of Music* became an important resource for preserving Greek theories of music during the Middle Ages, including an understanding of the seven musical "modes" or note progressions that formed the basis of Greek musical composition.

In this selection, Boethius argues, following Plato, that human beings are naturally attracted to music, which gives it the potential to produce both great good and great evil. Music that is orderly and harmonious can help people to be more logical and prudent, while music that is chaotic and violent can lead people toward immoral thoughts and behavior. Because music has the potential to exercise great influence on its listeners, those in the church and the government responsible for protecting the morals of the people must pay close attention to the kinds of music promoted and made available by the state.

Throughout this reading, Boethius uses historical narratives and analogies to illustrate his claims, investing them with the authority of ancient Greek philosophers such as Pythagoras, Empedocles, and Plato.

An ability to perceive through the senses is so spontaneously and naturally present in certain living creatures that an animal without senses cannot be imagined. But a knowledge and clear perception of these senses themselves is not so easily acquired, even with an investigation of the mind. It is obvious that we use our senses in perceiving sensible objects. But what is the exact nature of these senses in connection with which we carry out our actions? And what is the actual property of these objects sensed? The answers to these questions are not so obvious; and they cannot become clear to anyone unless the contemplation of these things is guided by a comprehensive investigation of reality.

Now sight is present in all mortals. But whether we see by images coming to the eye or by rays sent out from the eye to the object seen, this problem is in doubt to the learned,[1] although the common man is not conscious of doubt. Again if someone sees a triangle or square, he can easily identify it by sight. But what is the essence of a triangle or a square? This he must learn from a mathematician.

The same thing can be said of the other senses, especially concerning aural perception. For the sense of hearing can apprehend sounds in such a way that it not only judges them and recognizes their differences, but it very often takes pleasure in them if they are in the form of sweet and well-ordered modes, whereas it finds displeasure if the sounds heard are unordered and incoherent. Thus it follows that, since there are four mathematical disciplines,[2] the others are concerned with the investigation of truth, whereas music is related not only to speculation but to morality as well. For nothing is more consistent with human nature than to be soothed by sweet modes and disturbed by their opposites. And this affective quality of music is not peculiar to certain professions or ages, but it is common to all professions; and infants, youths and old people as well are so naturally attuned to the musical modes by a certain spontaneous affection that there is no age at all that is not delighted by sweet song. Thus we can begin to understand that apt doctrine of Plato which holds that the soul of the universe is united by a musical concord.[3] For when we compare that which is coherently and harmoniously joined together in sound—that is, that which gives us pleasure—so we come to recognize that we ourselves are united according to this same principle of similarity. For similarity is pleasing, whereas dissimilarity is unpleasant and contrary.

1. **This problem is in doubt to the learned:** There was a vigorous debate among ancient philosophers between two different theories of human visual perception: Some, such as Euclid and Ptolemy, believed that rays of light came from the eyes and illuminated objects by intersecting with them; others, such as Galen and Aristotle, held that objects emitted particles of some kind that were received by the eyes.

2. **Four mathematical disciplines:** The ancient Greeks divided mathematics into four sub-fields—arithmetic, geometry, astronomy, and music. Music was considered mathematical because it was governed by observable, quantifiable laws of harmony.

3. **A musical concord:** In his dialogue "Timaeus," Plato argued that the universe was modelled on the same principles of harmony and balance that form the basis of musical compositions.

From this same principle radical changes in one's character also occur. A lascivious mind takes pleasure in the more lascivious modes or is often softened and moved upon hearing them. On the other hand, a more violent mind finds pleasure in the more exciting modes or will become excited when it hears them. This is the reason that the musical modes were named after certain peoples, such as the "Lydian" mode, and the "Thrygian"[4] mode; for the modes are named after the people that find pleasure in them. A people will find pleasure in a mode resembling its own character, and thus a sensitive people cannot be united by or find pleasure in a severe mode, nor a severe people in a sensitive mode. But, as has been said, similarity causes love and pleasure. Thus Plato held that we should be extremely cautious in this matter, lest some change in music of good moral character should occur. He also said that there is no greater ruin for the morals of a community than the gradual perversion of a prudent and modest music. For the minds of those hearing the perverted music immediately submit to it, little by little depart from their character, and retain no vestige of justice or honesty. This will occur if either the lascivious modes bring something immodest into the minds of the people or if the more violent modes implant something warlike and savage.

For there is no greater path whereby instruction comes to the mind than through the ear. Therefore when rhythms and modes enter the mind by this path, there can be no doubt that they affect and remold the mind into their own character. This fact can be recognized in various peoples. For those peoples which have a more violent nature delight in the more severe modes of the Thracians.[5] Gentler peoples, on the other hand, delight in more moderate modes, although in these times this almost never occurs. Indeed today the human race is lascivious and effeminate, and thus it is entertained totally by the representational and theatrical modes. Music was prudent and modest when it was performed on simple instruments; but since it has come to be performed in various ways with many changes, it has lost its mode of gravity and virtue, and having almost fallen into a state of disgrace, it preserves almost nothing of its ancient splendor. For this reason Plato prescribed that boys must not be trained in all modes but only in those which are vigorous and simple. Moreover, it should be especially remembered that if some melody or mode is altered in some way, even if this alteration is only the slightest change, the fresh change will not be immediately noticed; but after some time it will cause a great difference and will sink down through the ears into the soul itself. Thus Plato held that the state ought to see that only music of the highest moral character and prudence be composed, and that it should be modest, simple and masculine, rather than effeminate, violent or fickle. . . .

5

4. **Lydian and Thrygian modes:** The Lydian and Thrygian (also called Phrygian) were two of the seven standard Greek musical "modes," or note progressions used as the basis for musical composition. Greek theory held that each of the modes invoked different moods and emotions, some of which were more desirable in certain times and places than others. The ancient Greek Lydian mode used a modern major scale, and the Phrygian mode used a modern minor scale. 5. **Thracians:** the non-Greek tribes to the northeast of ancient Greece, roughly in present-day Bulgaria.

It is common knowledge that song has calmed rages many times and that it has often worked wonders on affections of either the body or the spirit. For who does not know that Pythagoras[6] calmed a drunk adolescent of Taormine who had become incited under the influence of the Phrygian mode, and that Pythagoras further restored this boy to his rightful senses, all by means of a spondaic melody?[7] For one night this frenzied youth was about to set fire to the house of a rival who had locked himself in the house with a whore. Now that same night Pythagoras was out contemplating the course of the heavens, as was his usual custom. When he learned that this youth under the influence of the Phrygian mode would not be stopped from his crime, even by the admonitions of his friends, he ordered that the mode be changed; and thus Pythagoras restored the frenzied mind of the boy to a state of absolute calm. . . .

But to give briefly some similar examples, Terpander and Arion of Methymna saved the citizens of Lesbos and Ionia from very serious illnesses by the aid of song. Moreover, in this same way Ismenias the Theban is said to have cured all the maladies of the many Boeotians, who were suffering from sciatica. Similarly it is said that Empedocles had the mode of singing altered when an infuriated youth attacked one of his guests with a sword for having insulted his father; and by this means he tempered the wrath of the youth.[8]

The power of the musical discipline was so evident to the ancient students of philosophy that the Pythagoreans would employ certain melodies when they wanted to forget their daily cares in sleep, and, upon hearing these, a mild and quiet slumber would fall upon them. In the same manner, upon awakening, they would purge the stupor and confusion of sleep with certain other melodies; for these ancients knew that the total structure of our soul and body consists of musical harmony. For the very pulse of the heart itself is determined by the state and disposition of the body. Democritus[9] is said to have told this to the physician Hippocrates, who came to treat Democritus when he was being held in custody by his fellow townsmen because they thought he was a lunatic.

6. **Pythagoras of Samos:** an ancient Greek philosopher and mathematician (circa 570–circa 495 BCE) best known for his geometrical theorem that the square of the hypotenuse of a triangle is equal to the sum of the square of the other two sides.

7. **Spondaic melody:** a melody based on consistent, equally stressed sounds that was generally considered one of the most somber musical forms.

8. **Terpander of Antissa:** a seventh-century BCE poet and musician and reputed founder of Greek music; **Arion of Methymna** was a poet of the same period credited with inventing the dithyramb, a form of hymn sung to Dionysus, the god of wine and merrymaking; **Ismenias** was a Theban politician in the fourth century BCE, shortly after the end of the Peloponnesian War; **Empedocles** was a prominent pre-Socratic philosopher in the fifth century BCE.

9. **Democritus:** ancient Greek philosopher (circa. 460–circa 370 BCE) and one of the first people to postulate that all matter was composed of atoms; **Hippocrates**, prominent Greek physician (circa 460–circa 370 BCE) often considered the father of modern medicine.

But why have I said all this? Because there can be no doubt that the unity of our body and soul seems to be somehow determined by the same proportions that join together and unite the harmonious inflections of music, as our subsequent discussion will demonstrate. Hence it happens that sweet melodies even delight infants, whereas a harsh and rough sound will interrupt their pleasure. Indeed this reaction to various types of music is experienced by both sexes, and by people of all ages; for although they may differ in their actions, they are nevertheless united as one in the pleasure of music.

UNDERSTANDING THE TEXT

1. Why does Boethius begin the essay by writing about other senses, especially sight, before introducing the topic of music? What kinds of connections do you think he wants us to draw between how we perceive music and how we perceive things visually?

2. What about music, according to Boethius, gives us pleasure? What kinds of music should produce the most pleasure? What kinds should produce the least?

3. Why does Boethius say that music is related to morality? How can music make people more or less moral? What definition of "morality" does he imply in this argument?

4. What kinds of modern music might Boethius view as "lascivious"? As "prudent and modest"?

5. Do you agree with Boethius's assertion that "there is no greater path whereby instruction comes to the mind than through the ear"? What kinds of things can music (without words) teach us? What effect does adding words to music have on its ability to instruct?

6. What kinds of music does Boethius (following Plato) believe that a state should promote? What kinds should it discourage? Why?

7. What is the purpose of the story of Taormine and Pythagoras that Boethius recounts in paragraph 6? How do the other stories that he tells support his argument?

8. Ultimately, what connection does Boethius draw between music and human nature? In what ways can music teach us about ourselves? Do you agree?

MAKING CONNECTIONS

1. Both Boethius and Elaine Scarry (p. 279) argue that there is a connection between beauty and morality. How are their arguments similar? How are they different? Would Scarry accept the idea that the human mind is drawn toward certain kinds of sounds that represent order and harmony?

2. Boethius argues that people are naturally drawn to "sweet and well-ordered modes" of music but can be swayed to more violent and corrupt forms. What assumptions about human nature lie behind this assertion? Would Boethius agree more with Mencius's view of human nature (p. 78) or Hsün Tzu's (p. 84)?

3. Music was one of the liberal arts most prized by Seneca (p. 13). In what ways does Boethius confirm Seneca's view of the value of purely intellectual pursuits? Are there areas in which Boethius and Seneca might disagree?

WRITING ABOUT THE TEXT

1. Write an essay in which you agree or disagree with Boethius's assertion that "there is no greater path whereby instruction comes to the mind than through the ear." Consider whether this has been true in your education. Consider the differences between visual, auditory, and kinesthetic learning styles as you write your essay.

2. Choose one song that you find "prudent and modest" and another that you find "violent" or "lascivious." Examine the properties of both songs in light of Boethius's arguments. Do you accept his connection between the kinds of music a person likes and his or her personal character?

3. Compare or contrast Boethius's understanding of beauty with that of Edmund Burke (p. 256). What emotions does Boethius associate with beautiful things? How about Burke? What might account for the differences in their emphasis?

LADY MURASAKI SHIKIBU
On the Art of the Novel
[ELEVENTH CENTURY]

THE IMPERIAL COURT of Heian Japan, where Lady Murasaki Shikibu (circa 978–circa 1014 or 1025) spent most of her life, was unlike any other capital in the world's history. By 1000, the court included the entire city of Kyoto—nearly 100,000 people—and was governed by an absolute monarch with the emperor as ruler. The emperor was usually a young boy who pursued his own pleasures while his grandfather or father-in-law—almost always a member of the powerful Fujiwara clan—ruled behind the scenes. Emperors were routinely "encouraged" to abdicate while still relatively young in favor of other young men with Fujiwara wives and mothers.

Lady Murasaki Shikibu came from a minor branch of the Fujiwara family, a powerful Japanese clan. After a very early marriage, she became a personal assistant to the empress. As such, she had firsthand experience with the domestic politics of Heian Japan—a world of poetry, pomp, and sexual conquest. Though the women of the court were not taught Chinese character script, or *kanji*, used for official correspondence, Lady Murasaki and other women did learn a simpler script, *hiragana*, which was much more suitable for sustained works of prose.

Between 1000 and 1012, Lady Murasaki wrote *Genji Monogatari*, or *The Tale of Genji*, one of the longest sustained prose narratives in world literature. Initially, the work circulated around the Imperial court, where it found great favor. Soon after Lady Murasaki's death, it was recognized as an important work, and it has long been considered one of the greatest classics of Japanese literature. This story focuses on the life of Genji, a fictional "shining prince" of the Heian court. He is the son of an emperor and a low-ranking concubine. Officially this makes him a commoner, but his wit, good looks, and impeccable manners endear him to the emperor, and, more importantly for the story, the ladies of the court.

The Tale of Genji contains 54 chapters that cover Genji's life from his birth to his death and beyond. Each chapter stands alone as an episode in the main character's life, but there are also recurring themes and conflicts that tie the work together as a whole. Most of the chapters revolve around Genji's many love affairs and sexual intrigues.

The following selection, "On the Art of the Novel," comes from Chapter 19 of *The Tale of Genji*. In this passage, Genji discusses the function of prose literature with his adopted daughter, Tamakatsura. He initially teases her for her fascination with romance novels, and then gives his own theories about the popularity of fiction and the ways that it should be constructed. For a thousand years, critics and readers alike have seen this passage as Lady Murasaki's description of her own craft as a writer. This passage is rhetorically notable because it couches the author's own aesthetic philosophy in both the larger narrative of *The Tale of Genji* and the specific dialogue between Genji and Tamakatsura.

One day Genji, going around with a number of romances which he had promised to lend, came to Tamakatsura's[1] room and found her, as usual, hardly able to lift her eyes from the book in front of her. "Really, you are incurable," he said, laughing. "I sometimes think that young ladies exist for no other purpose than to provide purveyors of the absurd and improbable with a market for their wares. I am sure that the book you are now so intent upon is full of the wildest nonsense. Yet knowing this all the time, you are completely captivated by its extravagances and follow them with the utmost excitement: why, here you are on this hot day, so hard at work that, though I am sure you have not the least idea of it, your hair is in the most extraordinary tangle. . . . But there; I know quite well that these old tales are indispensable during such weather as this. How else would you all manage to get through the day? Now for a confession. I too have lately been studying these books and have, I must tell you, been amazed by the delight which they have given me. There is, it seems, an art of so fitting each part of the narrative into the next that, though all is mere invention, the reader is persuaded that such things might easily have happened and is as deeply moved as though they were actually going on around him. We may know with one part of our minds that every incident has been invented for the express purpose of impressing us; but (if the plot is constructed with the requisite skill) we may all the while in another part of our minds be burning with indignation at the wrongs endured by some wholly imaginary princess. Or again we may be persuaded by a writer's eloquence into accepting the crudest absurdities, our judgment being as it were dazzled by sheer splendor of language.

"I have lately sometimes stopped and listened to one of our young people reading out loud to her companions and have been amazed at the advances which this art of fiction is now making. How do you suppose that our new writers come by this talent? It used to be thought that the authors of successful romances were merely particularly untruthful people whose imaginations had been stimulated by constantly inventing plausible lies. But that is clearly unfair." . . . "Perhaps," she said, "only people who are themselves much occupied in practicing deception have the habit of thus dipping below the surface. I can assure you that for my part, when I read a story, I always accept it as an account of something that has really and actually happened."

So saying she pushed away from her book which she had been copying. Genji continued: "So you see as a matter of fact I think far better of this art than I have led you to suppose. Even its practical value is immense. Without it what should we

---

1. **Tamakatsura:** the daughter of Genji's friend, Tō No Chūjō, by a woman who later became Genji's concubine. By this chapter, Genji has adopted Tamakatsura and treats her as his own daughter.

know of how people lived in the past, from the Age of the Gods down to the present day? For history books such as the *Chronicles of Japan*[2] show us only one small corner of life; whereas these diaries and romances which I see piled around you contain, I am sure, the most minute information about all sorts of people's private affairs.". . . He smiled, and went on: "But I have a theory of my own about what this art of the novel is, and how it came into being. To begin with, it does not simply consist in the author's telling a story about the adventures of some other person. On the contrary, it happens because the storyteller's own experience of men and things, whether for good or ill—not only what he has passed through himself, but even events which he has only witnessed or been told of—has moved him to an emotion so passionate that he can no longer keep it shut up in his heart. Again and again something in his own life or in that around him will seem to the writer so important that he cannot bear to let it pass into oblivion. There must never come a time, he feels, when men do not know about it. That is my view of how this art arose.

"Clearly then, it is no part of the storyteller's craft to describe only what is good or beautiful. Sometimes, of course, virtue will be his theme, and he may then make such play with it as he will. But he is just as likely to have been struck by numerous examples of vice and folly in the world around him, and about them he has exactly the same feelings as about the pre-eminently good deeds which he encounters: they are more important and must all be garnered in. Thus anything whatsoever may become the subject of a novel, provided only that it happens in this mundane life and not in some fairyland beyond our human ken.

"The outward forms of this art will not of course be everywhere the same. At the court of China and in other foreign lands both the genius of the writers and their actual methods of composition are necessarily very different from ours; and even here in Japan the art of storytelling has in course of time undergone great changes. There will, too, always be a distinction between the lighter and the more serious forms of fiction. . . . Well, I have said enough to show that when at the beginning of our conversation I spoke of romances as though they were mere frivolous fabrications, I was only teasing you. Some people have taken exception on moral grounds to an art in which the perfect and imperfect are set side by side. But even in the discourses which Buddha in his bounty allowed to be recorded, certain passages contain what the learned call *Upāya* or Adapted Truth[3]—a fact that has led some superficial persons to doubt whether a doctrine so inconsistent with itself could possibly command

5

2. **Chronicles of Japan:** The *Nihon Shoki*, or *Chronicles of Japan*, gives a history of Japan from the mythical past through the eighth century. It was completed in 720, nearly three hundred years before *The Tale of Genji*.
3. **Upāya:** a Sanskrit word meaning "pedagogy," but usually translated as "expedient means."

According to the principle of *upāya*, the Buddhist teacher should adapt the lesson to the needs of the audience, focusing on the larger goal of enlightenment rather than on any particular doctrine.

our credence. Even in the scriptures of the Greater Vehicle[4] there are, I confess, many such instances. We may indeed go so far as to say that there is an actual mixture of Truth and Error. But the purpose of these holy writings, namely the compassing of our Salvation, remains always the same. So too, I think, may it be said that the art of fiction must not lose our allegiance because, in the pursuit of the main purpose to which I have alluded above, it sets virtue by the side of vice, or mingles wisdom with folly. Viewed in this light the novel is seen to be not, as is usually supposed, a mixture of useful truth with idle invention, but something which at every stage and in every part has a definite and serious purpose."

UNDERSTANDING THE TEXT

1. Why might have Lady Murasaki chosen to use the male prince Genji to advance her own argument instead of one of the female characters whose position in the court would be closer to her own? What is the rhetorical effect of the novel's main male character making these arguments?

2. According to Genji, what kinds of reactions can we have to a fictional narrative? Are these reactions ever contradictory? Which of these reactions are primarily emotional and which are primarily intellectual?

3. What connection does Genji draw between telling lies and writing fiction? Does Tamakatsura agree? Which position does the author herself seem to hold?

4. What does Genji suggest is the value of fiction as compared to the value of history? Can fictional stories illuminate elements of the past that are not available through reading history books and primary public documents?

5. Briefly summarize Genji's theory of why storytellers write. What forces compel the novelist or fiction writer to tell a story? Do you think that this is a plausible theory?

6. Why does Genji believe that "it is no part of the storyteller's craft to describe only what is good or beautiful"? What does he see as the connection between literature and morality?

7. What is Genji's point in comparing romance novels to the discourses of the Buddha? What is similar about the two kinds of works? How does he use the authority of scripture to legitimize fictional narratives?

4. **Scriptures of the Greater Vehicle:** "Greater Vehicle" is a literal translation of *Mahāyāna*, one of the two branches of Buddhism. Mahāyāna Buddhism is distinguished from the older branch, *Theravāda*.

MAKING CONNECTIONS

1. How do the values toward art in *The Tale of Genji* compare to those found in Bashō's *Narrow Road to the Interior* (p. 300), one of the other great works in the Japanese tradition? Does Basho's decision to set his haiku in a narrative have anything to do with the kind of narrative persuasion that Genji discusses here?

2. Compare Lady Murasaki's view of the purpose of art to that of Leo Tolstoy (p. 265). Would Genji agree that the best forms of art and literature are those that can be most easily understood by everyone?

3. Contrast the dialogue between Genji and Tamakatsura with the Socratic dialogue in Plato's *Gorgias* (p. 166). Does Genji lead his interlocutor to a point of view in the same way that Socrates does?

WRITING ABOUT THE TEXT

1. Analyze the connection between truth and fiction in this excerpt from *The Tale of Genji*. Analyze the positions of both Genji and Tamakatsura and explain which view you find most compelling and why.

2. Defend modern science fiction or fantasy fiction against Genji's claim that literature should only take place in "mundane life and not in some fairyland beyond our human ken." Argue that a wildly speculative work of literature can still have value. Support your arguments with concrete examples.

3. Compare or contrast a work of historical nonfiction with a work of historical fiction that covers the same events. Use this comparison to evaluate Genji's claim that fiction can sometimes express historical truths in a way that historical texts cannot.

JOHANNES VERMEER
Study of a Young Woman
[CIRCA 1665–67]

JOHANNES VERMEER (1632–1675) is now recognized as one of the most important figures of the Dutch Golden Age—a period of intense artistic activity that included the work of such notable figures as Rembrandt, Frans Hals, and Jan de Bray. Still, he was only modestly successful in his lifetime, and virtually unknown in the centuries thereafter. Vermeer's artistic output lagged behind that of his contemporaries, which caused him to be overlooked until the nineteenth century. Today, only thirty-four existing paintings have been definitively credited to Vermeer, but among these are such universally acclaimed masterpieces as *The Milkmaid*, *The Geographer*, and *Girl with a Pearl Earring*.

Study of a Young Woman is often grouped with *Girl with a Pearl Earring*, which may have originally been its companion piece. Both paintings are examples of a Dutch form of painting called the "tronie." A tronie, derived from the Dutch word for "face," is a painting of the head and face of a figure thought to be unusual or striking. Unlike formal portraits, which they resemble, tronies were not commissioned or sold to their subjects. The models for these paintings were usually anonymous and, hence, unknown to us today.

Several elements of *Study of a Young Woman* have puzzled art critics for centuries. For one thing, the subject is not conventionally beautiful, which has caused some scholars to speculate that the work might have been commissioned as a portrait or that it could even have been Vermeer's own daughter. Another puzzling fact for some critics is that this painting lacks the kind of background for which Vermeer was well known. Still, both of these elements are consistent with the tronie form, which sought to go beyond the physical beauty of its model and explore aspects of character not always visible through artistic representation.

The Metropolitan Museum of Art (where the painting is currently housed) explains Vermeer's motivations thus: "Although a live model must have been employed, the artist's goal was not portraiture but a study of character and expression. Dutch pictures of this type (tronies) often feature curious costumes and artistic effects, such as the fall of light on fine fabrics, soft skin, or a pearl earring." For Vermeer, then, it can be said that the most important task of the artist is to use his or her medium to create something beautiful through art, rather than simply to reproduce conventional forms of beauty.

JOHANNES VERMEER
Study of a Young Woman, circa 1665–67 (oil on canvas).
Metropolitan Museum of Art, New York / Wikimedia Commons and Art Resource.
See p.C–4 in the color insert for a full-color reproduction of this image.

UNDERSTANDING THE TEXT

1. Do you agree with the critics who say that the subject of *Study of a Young Woman* is not "conventionally beautiful"? Why or why not?

2. The primary function of the tronie was to capture an interesting or unique human face. Do you believe that *Study of a Young Woman* succeeds in this regard?

3. Another function of the tronie form was to display interesting or exotic costumes, such as the scarf that the young woman is wearing. How does this costuming influence your interpretation of the picture?

4. How does the dark background affect the way that you understand the picture? What effect does Vermeer create by removing any recognizable forms from the background of the painting?

MAKING CONNECTIONS

1. Compare *Study of a Young Woman* with Lisa Yuskavage's *Babie I* (p. 286). Explore how both paintings use and subvert traditional ideas of female attractiveness.

2. Are there elements of *Study of a Young Woman* that Edmund Burke (p. 256) might consider to be "sublime"? Think especially about the way that darkness and light are configured in the painting.

3. Compare the underlying idea of beauty in the painting to that in Alice Walker's feminist essay "Beauty: When the Other Dancer Is the Self" (p. 271). How are the two conceptions of beauty the same? How are they different?

WRITING ABOUT THE TEXT

1. Analyze the way that light and darkness are used in *Study of a Young Woman*. Look at the backgrounds of other Vermeer paintings and make an argument about why he makes the background of this painting dark without any perceivable objects in the background.

2. Some art historians believe that the model in *Study of a Young Woman* is the same figure from *Girl with a Pearl Earring* and that the first painting is an earlier version of the second. Find a copy of *Girl with a Pearl Earring* online and argue for or against this hypothesis.

3. Use *Study of a Young Woman* and two or three other artworks in *Reading the World*—such as *Babie I* (p. 286), *Liberty Leading the People* (p. 494), or Athena in *The Oresteia* (p. 148)—to make an argument about the way feminine beauty is depicted in art.

EDMUND BURKE

from *The Sublime and Beautiful*

[1757]

EDMUND BURKE (1729–1797) was an Irish philosopher and politician who served in the British Parliament during the eighteenth century. In the 1770s, he gained notoriety in Great Britain for his public support of the American colonies in their conflict with England. In later years, he became even better known for his opposition to the French Revolution, which he outlined in his most famous book, *Reflections on the Revolution in France* (1790). In *Reflections*, Burke argued that social change, when necessary, should occur gradually in a way that does not destroy the fabric of a society—an argument that has become central to modern conservatism in Europe and the United States.

Before entering politics, Burke made his living by writing works of historical and philosophical criticism. It was during this time that he wrote his influential treatise *A Philosophical Enquiry into the Origin of Our Ideas of the Sublime and Beautiful*, a sustained meditation on human aesthetic responses. For the purpose of his argument, Burke divided aesthetic objects into two kinds: the beautiful, which give us emotional pleasure by evoking positive feelings; and the sublime, which overwhelm our consciousness with their largeness, power, and capacity for destruction.

For Burke, sublime objects have a greater potential to move us emotionally because they are based on our primal instinct to fear what can kill us. When such fear-inspiring phenomena are contained at a safe distance, they retain their power to overwhelm our emotions even though we know intellectually that they pose no real danger. This is why we derive such pleasure from things like roller coasters, horror movies, and dangerous animals at the zoo.

Burke's idea of the sublime had a tremendous influence on English literature of the Romantic period, and especially on writers such as William Blake (p. 262), Samuel Taylor Coleridge, Mary Wollstonecraft Shelley, and Lord Byron. The works of these writers are full of things that Burke would consider sublime: expansive landscapes, wild animals, terrifying monsters, immense spaces, and supernatural evil. Governed largely by Burke's theories, the Romantics believed that it was better to overwhelm readers with immensity and terror than merely entertain them with pleasing images and well-constructed verses.

A major rhetorical device that Burke uses in this selection is proof by example. His argument consists of organizing and explaining a phenomenon that most people are already familiar with, providing relatable examples in the belief that his audience will have already felt the emotions that he describes as "sublime." Evidence of Burke's influence can still be observed today in the huge market for scary books and horror movies designed to frighten their audiences from the relative safety of living rooms and movie theaters.

The passion caused by the great and sublime in nature, when those causes operate most powerfully, is astonishment; and astonishment is that state of the soul, in which all its motions are suspended, with some degree of horror. In this case the mind is so entirely filled with its object, that it cannot entertain any other, nor by consequence reason on that object which employs it. Hence arises the great power of the sublime, that, far from being produced by them, it anticipates our reasonings, and hurries us on by an irresistible force. Astonishment, as I have said, is the effect of the sublime in its highest degree; the inferior effects are admiration, reverence, and respect.

No passion so effectually robs the mind of all its powers of acting and reasoning as *fear*. For fear being an apprehension of pain or death, it operates in a manner that resembles actual pain. Whatever therefore is terrible, with regard to sight, is sublime too, whether this cause of terror be endued with greatness of dimensions or not; for it is impossible to look on anything as trifling, or contemptible, that may be dangerous. There are many animals, who though far from being large, are yet capable of raising ideas of the sublime, because they are considered as objects of terror. As serpents and poisonous animals of almost all kinds. And to things of great dimensions, if we annex an adventitious idea of terror, they become without comparison greater. A level plain of a vast extent on land, is certainly no mean idea; the prospect of such a plain may be as extensive as a prospect of the ocean: but can it ever fill the mind with anything so great as the ocean itself? This is owing to several causes; but it is owing to none more than this, that the ocean is an object of no small terror. Indeed, terror is in all cases whatsoever, either more openly or latently, the ruling principle of the sublime. Several languages bear a strong testimony to the affinity of these ideas. They frequently use the same word, to signify indifferently the modes of astonishment or admiration, and those of terror.

To make anything very terrible, obscurity seems in general to be necessary. When we know the full extent of any danger, when we can accustom our eyes to it, a great deal of the apprehension vanishes. Every one will be sensible of this, who considers how greatly night adds to our dread, in all cases of danger, and how much the notions of ghosts and goblins, of which none can form clear ideas, affect minds which give credit to the popular tales concerning such sorts of beings. Those despotic governments, which are founded on the passions of men, and principally upon the passion of fear, keep their chief as much as may be from the public eye. The policy has been the same in many cases of religion. Almost all the heathen temples were dark. Even in the barbarous temples of the Americans at this day, they keep their idol in a dark part of the hut, which is consecrated to his worship. For this purpose too the Druids[1] performed all their ceremonies in the bosom of the darkest woods, and in the shade of the oldest and most spreading oaks. . . .

It is one thing to make an idea clear, and another to make it *affecting* to the imagination. If I make a drawing of a palace, or a temple, or a landscape, I present a very clear idea of those objects; but then (allowing for the effect of imitation, which is something) my picture can at most affect only as the palace, temple, or landscape would have affected in the reality. On the other hand, the most lively and spirited verbal description I can give raises a very obscure and imperfect *idea* of such objects; but then it is in my power to raise a stronger *emotion* by the description than I could do by the best painting. This experience constantly evinces. The proper manner of conveying the *affections* of the mind from one to another, is by words; there is a great insufficiency in all other methods of communication; and so far is a clearness of imagery from being absolutely necessary to an influence upon the passions, that they may be considerably operated upon, without presenting any image at all, by certain sounds adapted to that purpose; of which we have a sufficient proof in the acknowledged and powerful effects of instrumental music. In reality, a great clearness helps but little towards affecting the passions, as it is in some sort an enemy to all enthusiasms whatsoever. . . .

Besides those things which *directly* suggest the idea of danger, and those which produce a similar effect from a mechanical cause,[2] I know of nothing sublime, which is not some modification of power. And this branch rises, as naturally as the other two branches, from terror, the common stock of everything that is sublime. The idea of power, at first view, seems of the class of those indifferent ones, which may equally belong to pain or to pleasure. But in reality, the affection, arising from the idea of vast power, is extremely remote from that neutral character.

For first, we must remember, that the idea of pain, in its highest degree, is much stronger than the highest degree of pleasure; and that it preserves the same superiority through all the subordinate gradations. From hence it is, that where the chances for equal degrees of suffering or enjoyment are in any sort equal, the idea of the suffering must always be prevalent. And indeed the ideas of pain, and, above all, of death, are so very affecting, that whilst we remain in the presence of whatever is supposed to have the power of inflicting either, it is impossible to be perfectly free from terror. Again, we know by experience, that, for the enjoyment of pleasure, no great efforts of power are at all necessary; nay, we know, that such efforts would go a great way towards destroying our satisfaction: for pleasure must be stolen, and not forced upon us; pleasure follows the will; and therefore we are generally affected with it by many things of a force greatly inferior to our own.

But pain is always inflicted by a power in some way superior, because we never submit to pain willingly. So that strength, violence, pain, and terror, are ideas that

5

1. **Druids:** priests of the Celtic people who were early inhabitants of present-day Britain and France.

2. **Mechanical cause:** an automatic, unconscious response.

rush in upon the mind together. Look at a man, or any other animal of prodigious strength, and what is your idea before reflection? Is it that this strength will be subservient to you, to your ease, to your pleasure, to your interest in any sense? No; the emotion you feel is, lest this enormous strength should be employed to the purposes of rapine and destruction. That power derives all its sublimity from the terror with which it is generally accompanied, will appear evidently from its effect in the very few cases, in which it may be possible to strip a considerable degree of strength of its ability to hurt. When you do this, you spoil it of everything sublime, and it immediately becomes contemptible.

An ox is a creature of vast strength; but he is an innocent creature, extremely serviceable, and not at all dangerous; for which reason the idea of an ox is by no means grand. A bull is strong too: but his strength is of another kind; often very destructive, seldom (at least amongst us) of any use in our business; the idea of a bull is therefore great, and it has frequently a place in sublime descriptions, and elevating comparisons. Let us look at another strong animal, in the two distinct lights in which we may consider him. The horse in the light of a useful beast, fit for the plough, the road, the draft; in every social, useful light, the horse has nothing sublime: but is it thus that we are affected with him, *whose neck is clothed with thunder, the glory of whose nostrils is terrible, who swalloweth the ground with fierceness and rage, neither believeth that it is the sound of the trumpet?*[3] In this description, the useful character of the horse entirely disappears, and the terrible and sublime blaze out together.

We have continually about us animals of a strength that is considerable, but not pernicious. Amongst these we never look for the sublime; it comes upon us in the gloomy forest, and in the howling wilderness, in the form of the lion, the tiger, the panther, or rhinoceros. Whenever strength is only useful, and employed for our benefit or our pleasure, then it is never sublime: for nothing can act agreeably to us, that does not act in conformity to our will; but to act agreeably to our will, it must be subject to us, and therefore can never be the cause of a grand and commanding conception. . . .

Greatness of dimension is a powerful cause of the sublime. This is too evident, and the observation too common, to need any illustration: it is not so common to consider in what ways greatness of dimension, vastness of extent or quantity, has the most striking effect. For certainly, there are ways and modes, wherein the same quantity of extension shall produce greater effects than it is found to do in others. Extension is either in length, height, or depth. Of these the length strikes least; an hundred yards of even ground will never work such an effect as a tower an hundred yards high, or a rock or mountain of that altitude. I am apt to imagine likewise, that height is less grand than depth; and that we are more struck at looking down

10

---

3. **"Whose neck is clothed with thunder . . . the sound of the trumpet":** Burke is paraphrasing, not directly quoting, Job 39: 19–25, a passage in which God challenges Job by asking him if he created horses and gave them their attributes. The importance for Burke is that the horse is described as something wild, and therefore sublime, instead of as a domestic beast.

from a precipice, than looking up at an object of equal height; but of that I am not very positive.

A perpendicular has more force in forming the sublime, than an inclined plane; and the effects of a rugged and broken surface seem stronger than where it is smooth and polished. It would carry us out of our way to enter in this place into the cause of these appearances; but certain it is they afford a large and fruitful field of speculation. However, it may not be amiss to add to these remarks upon magnitude, that, as the great extreme of dimension is sublime, so the last extreme of littleness is in some measure sublime likewise: when we attend to the infinite divisibility of matter, when we pursue animal life into these excessively small, and yet organized beings, that escape the nicest inquisition of the sense; when we push our discoveries yet downward, and consider those creatures so many degrees yet smaller, and the still diminishing scale of existence, in tracing which the imagination is lost as well as the sense; we become amazed and confounded at the wonders of minuteness; nor can we distinguish in its effects this extreme of littleness from the vast itself. For division must be infinite as well as addition; because the idea of a perfect unity can no more be arrived at, than that of a complete whole, to which nothing may be added.

Another source of the sublime is infinity; if it does not rather belong to the last. Infinity has a tendency to fill the mind with that sort of delightful horror, which is the most genuine effect and truest test of the sublime. There are scarce any things which can become the objects of our senses, that are really and in their own nature infinite. But the eye not being able to perceive the bounds of many things, they seem to be infinite, and they produce the same effects as if they were really so. We are deceived in the like manner, if the parts of some large object are so continued to any indefinite number, that the imagination meets no check which may hinder its extending them at pleasure.

Whenever we repeat any idea frequently, the mind, by a sort of mechanism, repeats it long after the first cause has ceased to operate. After whirling about, when we sit down, the objects about us still seem to whirl. After a long succession of noises, as the fall of waters, or the beating of forge-hammers, the hammers beat and the water roars in the imagination long after the first sounds have ceased to affect it; and they die away at last by gradations which are scarcely perceptible. If you hold up a straight pole, with your eye to one end, it will seem extended to a length almost incredible. Place a number of uniform and equi-distant marks on this pole, they will cause the same deception, and seem multiplied without end. The senses, strongly affected in some one manner, cannot quickly change their tenor, or adapt themselves to other things; but they continue in their old channel until the strength of the first mover decays. This is the reason of an appearance very frequent in madmen; that they remain whole days and nights, sometimes whole years, in the constant repetition of some remark, some complaint, or song; which having struck powerfully on their disordered imagination in the beginning of their frenzy, every repetition reinforces it with new strength; and the hurry of their spirits, unrestrained by the curb of reason, continues it to the end of their lives.

UNDERSTANDING THE TEXT

1. What sublime aspects of nature does Burke describe to begin this passage? Why does he begin by writing about nature in a work that is supposedly about art?

2. What does Burke see as the emotional effect of fear? How does our mind react when presented with something immediately dangerous? In what way is this an aesthetic feeling?

3. Why does Burke point out the way that different languages equate fear and astonishment? How does this linguistic analysis count as evidence of a claim?

4. What is the emotional effect of obscurity? Why do people tend to be more afraid of what they can't see than of what they can see? How might an awareness of this fear be useful to an artist or writer?

5. Why does Burke point out that the idea of pain is stronger than the idea of pleasure? How is this relevant to his overall argument?

6. What does Burke see as the difference between powerful animals that have been domesticated and equally powerful animals that have not? What does he say is the fundamental difference between an ox and a bull?

7. How do the concepts of vastness and infinity produce the sublime? How are these concepts related to fear or power?

MAKING CONNECTIONS

1. How might you use Burke's idea of the sublime to describe William Blake's painting and poem "The Tyger" (p. 262)? Are there specific references to the sublime in Blake's poem?

2. Does Burke see the natural world in the same way that Bashō (p. 300) does? Do the objects of Basho's haiku appear to be the kinds of things that Burke would describe as "sublime"?

3. In what ways are the images in Carl Jung's The Red Book (p. 108) sublime? Does Jung's view of human nature equate with Burke's?

WRITING ABOUT THE TEXT

1. Explain, in your own words, why Burke feels that sublime images have more aesthetic power than beautiful ones. Evaluate the effectiveness of his argument. Do you agree, disagree, or agree and disagree?

2. Choose a book or movie from the horror genre and use Burke's theory of the sublime to explain its appeal. Look specifically for elements that Burke lists, such as terror, obscurity, power, magnificence, and infinity.

3. Analyze either the selection from Jung's The Red Book (p. 108), Picasso's Guernica (p. 497), or Blake's drawing of "The Tyger" (p. 262) as an example of the sublime. What element(s) of the image give it power?

WILLIAM BLAKE
The Tyger
[1794]

POET, PAINTER, PRINTMAKER, and prophet, William Blake (1757–1827) has consistently defied critics' attempts to place him into categories. During his lifetime, Blake made a modest living engraving books; his illustrations for Dante's *Inferno* and the Book of Job are among his most famous and historically significant contributions to English literature and history. Additionally, he illustrated and published his own books of poetry and prose meditations that he referred to as "prophecies," such as *The Marriage of Heaven and Hell* (1793) and *Jerusalem* (1820).

Blake saw himself as the modern equivalent of an Old Testament prophet. He was hostile to organized religion and specifically to Christianity, which he saw as a religion that took the most vital elements of human nature—sexuality, creativity, and individual expression—and proscribed them as "Satanic." Blake believed that, to fulfill their potential, human beings had to fully develop what Christians called the "angelic" and "demonic" elements of their natures. In *The Marriage of Heaven and Hell*, Blake famously argues that Milton's *Paradise Lost* is a great poem because Milton "was of the devil's party without knowing it."

Blake's most famous poetic works are the two books *The Songs of Innocence* (1794) and *The Songs of Experience* (1794). The first of these books features, as its title suggests, sweet, innocent expressions of faith from the perspective of a young child. The most famous of these, "The Lamb," affirms Christ as the Good Shepherd—a common image in the New Testament—and is often included in Christian sermons and literary anthologies. The second group of poems, however, is narrated by the voice of an experienced poet who understands that the child's voice is naïve and incomplete. Many of the poems in *The Songs of Experience* are specifically intended to accompany poems in *The Songs of Innocence*.

"The Tyger," the most famous of Blake's works, is a companion poem to "The Lamb." The former poem asks, "Little Lamb, who made thee[?]" and answers with allusions to Christ, who "calls himself a Lamb." "The Tyger," on the other hand, abounds with Satanic and infernal images—yet asks the same basic question: "What immortal hand or eye, could frame thy fearful symmetry?" The poet answers with a rhetorical question: "Did he who made the lamb make thee?" If the answer is yes, then we must acknowledge that God is a very different creature than the New Testament leads us to believe.

Both *The Songs of Innocence* and *The Songs of Experience* were published as illustrated manuscripts with Blake's own illustrations. In Blake's view, the illustrations were as important to the overall rhetorical effect of the poem as the words themselves. Both are reprinted here.

42

The Tyger

Tyger Tyger, burning bright,
In the forests of the night !
What immortal hand or eye.
Could frame thy fearful symmetry?

In what distant deeps or skies
Burnt the fire of thine eyes !
On what wings dare he aspire?
What the hand, dare seize the fire?

And what shoulder, & what art,
Could twist the sinews of thy heart?
And when thy heart began to beat,
What dread hand? & what dread feet?

What the hammer? what the chain,
In what furnace was thy brain?
What the anvil? what dread grasp,
Dare its deadly terrors clasp?

When the stars threw down their spears
And water'd heaven with their tears :
Did he smile his work to see?
Did he who made the Lamb make thee?

Tyger Tyger burning bright,
In the forests of the night :
What immortal hand or eye
Dare frame thy fearful symmetry?

WILLIAM BLAKE

The Tyger, 1794 (relief etchings printed in orange-brown).

Metropolitan Museum of Art, New York / Wikimedia Commons.

See p. C–5 in the color insert for a full-color reproduction of this image.

UNDERSTANDING THE TEXT

1. How do Blake's illustrations and hand-lettered text affect the way that you read "The Tyger"?

2. Almost all of the lines of "The Tyger" are phrased as questions, and all of the questions are related to the overall question of the poem. What do you think that overarching question is?

3. Look at all of the words in the poem that associate the tiger with fire. What is the effect of this extended metaphor?

4. "The Tyger" was originally intended to be a companion poem to "The Lamb." Blake alludes to this earlier poem in the line "Did he who made the Lamb make thee?" What do you see as the point of this question?

5. The last stanza of "The Tyger" repeats the first stanza almost verbatim. Only one word changes: "What immortal hand or eye / Could frame thy fearful symmetry?" changes to "What immortal hand or eye / **Dare** frame thy fearful symmetry?" How does this slight difference reframe the overall question that the poem is asking?

MAKING CONNECTIONS

1. Examine "The Tyger" in light of the arguments about human nature found in Mencius's "Man's Nature Is Good" (p. 78) and Hsün Tzu's "Man's Nature Is Evil" (p. 84). Is the tiger of the poem good, evil, or something outside of this dichotomy?

2. How do both Blake in "The Tyger" and William Paley in *Natural Theology* (p. 311) use the existence of a creation to draw conclusions about the creator?

WRITING ABOUT THE TEXT

1. Analyze "The Tyger" as a painting that happens to include words instead of a poem that happens to be accompanied by an illustration. How does your view of the work change?

2. Look up the text and image of Blake's poem "The Lamb" online. Write an essay analyzing "The Tyger" as a response to, and companion for, "The Lamb."

3. Apply Edmund Burke's arguments about the sublime (p. 256) to "The Tyger." What elements of the sublime can you see in Blake's poem?

LEO TOLSTOY
from *What Is Art?*
[1896]

COUNT LEO TOLSTOY (1828–1910) is the author of what many consider the two greatest novels ever written: *War and Peace* (1869) and *Anna Karenina* (1877). Born into a noble family, Tolstoy followed the typical career path of a young aristocrat in czarist Russia. This included nearly failing in his early studies, dropping out of college, racking up huge gambling debts, joining the army, and later marrying and starting a family.

As an army officer and later as a world traveler, Tolstoy had the opportunity to experience both the best and the worst of European culture. Through his friendships with such influential French figures as the novelist Victor Hugo and the political theorist Pierre-Joseph Proudhon, he developed a strong interest in both prose fiction and the plight of the poor. When he returned to Russia, he began to write. His early novels were primarily autobiographical, but, by 1869, he had developed his craft well enough to produce *War and Peace*.

As his social consciousness continued to develop, Tolstoy grew uncomfortable in his roles as privileged aristocrat and famous author. In 1881, deeply influenced by both the New Testament and the writings of European socialists such as Proudhon, Tolstoy experienced a religious conversion to "Christian anarchism"—a religion largely of his own design that rejected the authority of secular governments and advocated strict nonviolence, severe aestheticism, and care of the poor. Toward the end of his life, much to the dismay of his wife and their thirteen children, Tolstoy renounced the copyrights on his novels and changed his will to leave his estate to his serfs.

From the time of his conversion until his death in 1910, Tolstoy spent much of his time working the fields as a peasant and writing both fiction and nonfiction promoting Christian anarchism. Tolstoy's later works include *The Death of Ivan Ilyich* (1886), a novella about a dying man who finds meaning in his life only in the minutes before his death, and *The Kingdom of God Is Within You* (1894), a meditation on nonviolence that profoundly influenced Mohandas Gandhi (p. 560), with whom Tolstoy briefly corresponded during the final months of his life.

The selection in this chapter is taken from the book-length essay *What Is Art?* (1897), Tolstoy's most complete elaboration of his post-conversion aesthetic theory. In this selection, Tolstoy criticizes the popular belief among intellectuals that "great" art must be incomprehensible to average people. Tolstoy argues quite the reverse; only art that can be universally appreciated deserves to be called great.

As soon as ever the art of the upper classes separated itself from universal art, a conviction arose that art may be art and yet be incomprehensible to the masses. And as soon as this position was admitted, it had inevitably to be admitted also that art may be intelligible only to the very smallest number of the elect, and, eventually, to two, or to one, of our nearest friends, or to oneself alone, which is practically what is being said by modern artists: "I create and understand myself, and if any one does not understand me, so much the worse for him."

The assertion that art may be good art and at the same time incomprehensible to a great number of people is extremely unjust, and its consequences are ruinous to art itself; but at the same time it is so common and has so eaten into our conceptions that it is impossible sufficiently to elucidate all the absurdity of it.

Nothing is more common than to hear it said of reputed works of art that they are very good but very difficult to understand. We are quite used to such assertions, and yet to say that a work of art is good but incomprehensible to the majority of men is the same as saying of some kind of food that it is very good, but that most people can't eat it. The majority of men may not like rotten cheese or putrefying grouse—dishes esteemed by people with perverted tastes; but bread and fruit are only good when they please the majority of men. And it is the same with art. Perverted art may not please the majority of men, but good art always pleases everyone.

It is said that the very best works of art are such that they cannot be understood by the mass, but are accessible only to the elect who are prepared to understand these great works. But if the majority of men do not understand, the knowledge necessary to enable them to understand should be taught and explained to them. But it turns out that there is no such knowledge, that the works cannot be explained, and that those who say the majority do not understand good works of art still do not explain those works but only tell us that, in order to understand them, one must read, and see, and hear these same works over and over again. But this is not to explain; it is only to habituate! And people may habituate themselves to anything, even to the very worst things. As people may habituate themselves to bad food, to spirits, tobacco, and opium, just in the same way they may habituate themselves to bad art—and that is exactly what is being done.

Moreover, it cannot be said that the majority of people lack the taste to esteem the highest works of art. The majority always has understood, and still understands, what we also recognize as being the very best art: the epic of Genesis,[1] the gospel parables, folk legends, fairy tales, and folk songs are understood by all. How can it be that the majority has suddenly lost its capacity to understand what is high in our art?

Of a speech it may be said that it is admirable, but incomprehensible to those who do not know the language in which it is delivered. A speech delivered in

5

---

1. **Genesis:** the first book of both the Hebrew Bible and the Christian Old Testament. Genesis contains the stories of Adam and Eve, Noah's Ark, Abraham, Isaac, Jacob, and Joseph.

Chinese may be excellent and may yet remain incomprehensible to me if I do not know Chinese; but what distinguishes a work of art from all other mental activity is just the fact that its language is understood by all, and that it infects all without distinction. The tears and laughter of a Chinese infect me just as the laughter and tears of a Russian; and it is the same with painting and music and poetry when it is translated into a language I understand. The songs of a Kirghiz[2] or of a Japanese touch me, though in a lesser degree than they touch a Kirghiz or a Japanese. I am also touched by Japanese painting, Indian architecture, and Arabian stories. If I am but little touched by a Japanese song and a Chinese novel, it is not that I do not understand these productions but that I know and am accustomed to higher works of art. It is not because their art is above me. Great works of art are only great because they are accessible and comprehensible to everyone. The story of Joseph translated into the Chinese language, touches a Chinese. The story of Sakya Muni[3] touches us. And there are, and must be, buildings, pictures, statues, and music of similar power. So that, if art fails to move men, it cannot be said that this is due to the spectators' or hearers' lack of understanding; but the conclusion to be drawn may and should be that such art is either bad art or is not art at all.

Art is differentiated from activity of the understanding, which demands preparation and a certain sequence of knowledge (so that one cannot learn trigonometry before knowing geometry), by the fact that it acts on people independently of their state of development and education, that the charm of a picture, sounds, or of forms, infects any man whatever his plane of development.

The business of art lies just in this—to make that understood and felt which, in the form of an argument, might be incomprehensible and inaccessible. Usually it seems to the recipient of a truly artistic impression that he knew the thing before but had been unable to express it.

And such has always been the nature of good, supreme art; the *Iliad*, the *Odyssey*,[4] the stories of Isaac, Jacob, and Joseph, the Hebrew prophets, the psalms, the gospel parables, the story of Sakya Muni, and the hymns of the Vedas[5] all transmit very elevated feelings and are nevertheless quite comprehensible now to us, educated or uneducated, as they were comprehensible to the men of those times, long ago, who were even less educated than our laborers. People talk about incomprehensibility; but if art is the transmission of feelings flowing from man's religious perception, how can a feeling be incomprehensible which is founded on religion, i.e., on man's relation to God? Such art should be, and has actually always been, comprehensible to everybody because every man's relation to God is one and the same. And therefore

2. **Kirghiz:** a central Asian people who live mainly in China and the Kyrgyz Republic. The Kirghiz were absorbed into the Russian Empire in 1876, about 20 years before Tolstoy wrote *What Is Art?*

3. **Sakya Muni:** another name for the Buddha.

4. **The *Iliad* and the *Odyssey*:** ancient Greek epic poems written in the seventh or eighth century BCE and attributed to the poet Homer.

5. **Vedas:** ancient Sanskrit texts considered sacred to Hinduism.

the churches and the images in them are always comprehensible to everyone. The hindrance to understanding the best and highest feelings (as is said in the gospel) does not at all lie in deficiency of development or learning, but, on the contrary, in false development and false learning. A good and lofty work of art may be incomprehensible, but not to simple, unperverted peasant laborers (all that is highest is understood by them)—it may be, and often is, unintelligible to erudite, perverted people destitute of religion. And this continually occurs in our society in which the highest feelings are simply not understood. For instance, I know people who consider themselves most refined and who say that they do not understand the poetry of love to one's neighbor, of self-sacrifice, or of chastity.

So good, great, universal, religious art may be incomprehensible to a small circle   10
of spoiled people but certainly not to any large number of plain men.

Art cannot be incomprehensible to the great masses only because it is very good—as artists of our day are fond of telling us. Rather we are bound to conclude that this art is unintelligible to the great masses only because it is very bad art, or even is not art at all. So that the favorite argument (naïvely accepted by the cultured crowd), that in order to feel art one has first to understand it (which really only means habituate oneself to it), is the truest indication that what we are asked to understand by such a method is either very bad, exclusive art, or is not art at all.

People say that works of art do not please the people because they are incapable of understanding them. But if the aim of works of art is to infect people with the emotion the artist has experienced, how can one talk about not understanding?

A man of the people reads a book, sees a picture, hears a play or a symphony, and is touched by no feeling. He is told that this is because he cannot understand. People promise to let a man see a certain show; he enters and sees nothing. He is told that this is because his sight is not prepared for this show. But the man well knows that he sees quite well, and if he does not see what people promised to show him, he only concludes (as is quite just) that those who undertook to show him the spectacle have not fulfilled their engagement. And it is perfectly just for a man who does feel the influence of some works of art to come to this conclusion concerning artists who do not, by their works, evoke feeling in him. To say that the reason a man is not touched by my art is because he is still too stupid, besides being very self-conceited and also rude, is to reverse the roles and for the sick to send the hale to bed.

Voltaire said that "*Tous les genres sont bons, hors le genre ennuyeux;*"[6] but with even more right one may say of art that *tous les genres sont bons, hors celui qu'on ne comprend pas*, or *qui ne produit pas son effet*[7] for of what value is an article which fails to do that for which it was intended?

Mark this above all: if only it be admitted that art may be art and yet be unintelligible to anyone of sound mind, there is no reason why any circle of perverted people

6. **Tous . . . ennuyeux [translator's note]:** All styles are good except the boring style.

7. **Tous . . . effet [translator's note]:** All styles are good except that which is not understood, or which fails to produce its effect.

should not compose works tickling their own perverted feelings and comprehensible to no one but themselves and call it "art," as is actually being done by the so-called Decadents.[8]

The direction art has taken may be compared to placing on a large circle other circles, smaller and smaller, until a cone is formed, the apex of which is no longer a circle at all. That is what has happened to the art of our times.

UNDERSTANDING THE TEXT

1. What does Tolstoy see as the effect of separate art forms for the upper classes and the lower classes? What is Tolstoy's attitude toward the upper classes and the intellectual elite?

2. What is the point of Tolstoy's comparison between a work of art and a food item? What deeper comparison does he make here about the purpose of art?

3. What is the difference between understanding something and habituating oneself to something? What examples does Tolstoy use to illustrate this distinction?

4. What stories does Tolstoy use as examples of "great art"? Do you agree with the examples that he chooses?

5. What relationship does Tolstoy see between art and religion? Why does he believe that "a good and lofty work of art" may be unintelligible to "erudite, perverted people destitute of religion"?

MAKING CONNECTIONS

1. Both Tolstoy in *What Is Art?* and Mo Tzu in "Against Music" (p. 236) criticize artistic expression that can only be enjoyed by the elite. Yet Tolstoy is a strong advocate of art, while Mo Tzu believes that music has no place in a society. What underlying differences between the two men's philosophies might be responsible for this difference?

2. Mohandas Gandhi (p. 560) frequently cited Tolstoy as one of his greatest influences. Can you see connections between Tolstoy's view of art and Gandhi's view of economic justice?

3. Compare the underlying assumptions of Tolstoy's *What Is Art?* with those of Hsun Tzü in "Encouraging Learning" (p. 5). Does Tolstoy believe that education is necessary to make people able to appreciate important things?

8. **Decadents:** a late nineteenth-century movement in art and literature—including such figures as Charles Baudelaire in France and Oscar Wilde in England—that focused on works of art as completely divorced from ethical questions.

WRITING ABOUT THE TEXT

1. Write a paper that analyzes Tolstoy's underlying assumptions about the purposes of art. Explain what art should and should not try to do, in the framework that he articulates in this selection.

2. Support or refute Tolstoy's main assertion that great art can be understood by everybody. You may consider whether or not education can increase people's understanding and appreciation of art, music, and literature.

3. Choose a work of art that has been especially influential in your life. It can be a book, painting, movie, television program, or popular song. Analyze this work from Tolstoy's perspective. Would he call it "great" art? Why or why not?

ALICE WALKER
Beauty: When the Other Dancer Is the Self
[1983]

ALICE WALKER is an American novelist, poet, essayist, and political activist. She was born in 1944 in rural Georgia during racial segregation. Her parents were share-croppers and manual laborers whose deep faith in the power of education made school a priority for their children. Walker attended Spelman College in Atlanta and Sarah Lawrence College in New York. After graduating from Sarah Lawrence in 1965, she dedicated herself both to her writing career and to the civil rights movement in the South, where segregation and legalized discrimination were still common throughout state and local jurisdictions.

During the 1970s, Walker published several novels and collections of poetry, both well received. In 1983, she became the first African American woman to win the Pulitzer Prize for fiction for her novel *The Color Purple*, since adapted into a successful movie and Broadway musical. The success of *The Color Purple* secured Walker's reputation as a major American writer, and she has continued to write both fiction and poetry while remaining active in civil rights and antiwar causes in the United States and elsewhere.

The essay reprinted here, "Beauty: When the Other Dancer Is the Self," was first published in the collection *In Search of Our Mothers' Gardens*, Walker's follow-up to *The Color Purple*. In this essay, she recounts an accident that occurred when she was eight years old. While Walker and her brothers were playing "Cowboys and Indians," one brother shot her in the eye with a BB gun and convinced her to report it to her parents as an accident with a stray wire. Because the family was extremely poor, they waited a full week to take Alice to a doctor, by which time it was too late to save the eye or to prevent the buildup of substantial scar tissue.

In this personal narrative, Walker's essay explores one of the central questions of this chapter—"what makes something beautiful." She describes her life before and after the accident, using the present tense throughout as a rhetorical device to emphasize the permanent impact that past images have had on the way she views herself.

It is a bright summer day in 1947. My father, a fat, funny man with beautiful eyes and a subversive wit, is trying to decide which of his eight children he will take with him to the county fair. My mother, of course, will not go. She is knocked out from getting most of us ready: I hold my neck stiff against the pressure of her knuckles as she hastily completes the braiding and then beribboning of my hair.

My father is the driver for the rich old white lady up the road. Her name is Miss Mey. She owns all the land for miles around, as well as the house in which we live. All I remember about her is that she once offered to pay my mother thirty-five cents for cleaning her house, raking up piles of her magnolia leaves, and washing her family's clothes, and that my mother—she of no money, eight children, and a chronic earache—refused it. But I do not think of this in 1947. I am two and a half years old. I want to go everywhere my daddy goes. I am excited at the prospect of riding in a car. Someone has told me fairs are fun. That there is room in the car for only three of us doesn't faze me at all. Whirling happily in my starchy frock, showing off my biscuit-polished patent-leather shoes and lavender socks, tossing my head in a way that makes my ribbons bounce, I stand, hands on hips, before my father. "Take me, Daddy," I say with assurance; "I'm the prettiest!"

Later, it does not surprise me to find myself in Miss Mey's shiny black car, sharing the back seat with the other lucky ones. Does not surprise me that I thoroughly enjoy the fair. At home that night I tell the unlucky ones all I can remember about the merry-go-round, the man who eats live chickens, and the teddy bears, until they say: that's enough, baby Alice. Shut up now, and go to sleep.

It is Easter Sunday, 1950. I am dressed in a green, flocked, scalloped-hem dress (handmade by my adoring sister, Ruth) that has its own smooth satin petticoat and tiny hot-pink roses tucked into each scallop. My shoes, new T-strap patent leather, again highly biscuit-polished. I am six years old and have learned one of the longest Easter speeches to be heard that day, totally unlike the speech I said when I was two: "Easter lilies/pure and white/blossom in/the morning light." When I rise to give my speech I do so on a great wave of love and pride and expectation. People in the church stop rustling their new crinolines. They seem to hold their breath. I can tell they admire my dress, but it is my spirit, bordering on sassiness (womanishness), they secretly applaud.

"That girl's a little *mess*," they whisper to each other, pleased.

Naturally I say my speech without stammer or pause, unlike those who stutter, stammer, or, worst of all, forget. This is before the word "beautiful" exists in people's vocabulary, but "Oh, isn't she the *cutest* thing!" frequently floats my way. "And got so much sense!" they gratefully add . . . for which thoughtful addition I thank them to this day.

It was great fun being cute. But then, one day, it ended.

I am eight years old and a tomboy. I have a cowboy hat, cowboy boots, checkered shirt and pants, all red. My playmates are my brothers, two and four years older than I. Their colors are black and green, the only difference in the way we are dressed. On Saturday nights we all go to the picture show, even my mother; Westerns are her favorite kind of movie. Back home, "on the ranch," we pretend we are Tom Mix, Hopalong Cassidy, Lash LaRue (we've even named one of our dogs Lash LaRue); we chase each other for hours rustling cattle, being outlaws, delivering damsels from distress. Then my parents decide to buy my brothers guns. These are not "real" guns.

5

They shoot "BBs," copper pellets my brothers say will kill birds. Because I am a girl, I do not get a gun. Instantly I am relegated to the position of Indian. Now there appears a great distance between us. They shoot and shoot at everything with their new guns. I try to keep up with my bow and arrows.

One day while I am standing on top of our makeshift "garage"—pieces of tin nailed across some poles—holding my bow and arrow and looking out toward the fields, I feel an incredible blow in my right eye. I look down just in time to see my brother lower his gun.

Both brothers rush to my side. My eye stings, and I cover it with my hand. "If you   10 tell," they say, "we will get a whipping. You don't want that to happen, do you?" I do not. "Here is a piece of wire," says the older brother, picking it up from the roof; "say you stepped on one end of it and the other flew up and hit you." The pain is beginning to start. "Yes," I say, "Yes, I will say that is what happened." If I do not say this is what happened, I know my brothers will find ways to make me wish I had. But now I will say anything that gets me to my mother.

Confronted by our parents we stick to the lie agreed upon. They place me on a bench on the porch and I close my left eye while they examine the right. There is a tree growing from underneath the porch that climbs past the railing to the roof. It is the last thing my right eye sees. I watch as its trunk, its branches, and then its leaves are blotted out by the rising blood.

I am in shock. First there is intense fever, which my father tries to break using lily leaves bound around my head. Then there are chills; my mother tries to get me to eat soup. Eventually, I do not know how, my parents learn what has happened. A week after the "accident" they take me to see a doctor. "Why did you wait so long to come?" he asks, looking into my eye and shaking his head. "Eyes are sympathetic," he says. "If one is blind, the other will likely become blind too."

This comment of the doctor's terrifies me. But it is really how I look that bothers me most. Where the BB pellet struck there is a glob of whitish scar tissue, a hideous cataract, on my eye. Now when I stare at people—a favorite pastime, up to now—they will stare back. Not at the "cute" little girl, but at her scar. For six years I do not stare at anyone, because I do not raise my head.

Years later, in the throes of a mid-life crisis, I ask my mother and sister whether I changed after the "accident." "No," they say, puzzled. "What do you mean?"

What do I mean?   15

I am eight, and, for the first time, doing poorly in school, where I have been something of a whiz since I was four. We have just moved to the place where the "accident" occurred. We do not know any of the people around us because this is a different county. The only time I see the friends I knew is when we go back to our old church. The new school is the former state penitentiary. It is a large stone building, cold and drafty, crammed to overflowing with boisterous, ill-disciplined children. On the third floor there is a huge circular imprint of some partition that has been torn out.

"What used to be here?" I ask a sullen girl next to me on our way past it to lunch.

"The electric chair," says she.

At night I have nightmares about the electric chair, and about all the people reputedly "fried" in it. I am afraid of the school, where all the students seem to be budding criminals.

"What's the matter with your eye?" they ask, critically.   20

When I don't answer (I cannot decide whether it was an "accident" or not), they shove me, insist on a fight.

My brother, the one who created the story about the wire, comes to my rescue. But then brags so much about "protecting" me, I become sick.

After months of torture at the school, my parents decide to send me back to our old community, to my old school. I live with my grandparents and the teacher they board. But there is no room for Phoebe, my cat. By the time my grandparents decide there is room, and I ask for my cat, she cannot be found. Miss Yarborough, the boarding teacher, takes me under her wing, and begins to teach me to play the piano. But soon she marries an African—a "prince," she says—and is whisked away to his continent.

At my old school there is at least one teacher who loves me. She is the teacher who "knew me before I was born" and bought my first baby clothes. It is she who makes life bearable. It is her presence that finally helps me turn on the one child at the school who continually calls me "one-eyed bitch." One day I simply grab him by his coat and beat him until I am satisfied. It is my teacher who tells me my mother is ill.

My mother is lying in bed in the middle of the day, something I have never seen.   25
She is in too much pain to speak. She has an abscess in her ear. I stand looking down on her, knowing that if she dies, I cannot live. She is being treated with warm oils and hot bricks held against her cheek. Finally a doctor comes. But I must go back to my grandparents' house. The weeks pass but I am hardly aware of it. All I know is that my mother might die, my father is not so jolly, my brothers still have their guns, and I am the one sent away from home.

"You did not change," they say.

Did I imagine the anguish of never looking up?

I am twelve. When relatives come to visit I hide in my room. My cousin Brenda, just my age, whose father works in the post office and whose mother is a nurse, comes to find me. "Hello," she says. And then she asks, looking at my recent school picture, which I did not want taken, and on which the "glob," as I think of it, is clearly visible, "You still can't see out of that eye?"

"No," I say, and flop back on the bed over my book.

That night, as I do almost every night, I abuse my eye. I rant and rave at it, in   30
front of the mirror. I plead with it to clear up before morning. I tell it I hate and despise it. I do not pray for sight. I pray for beauty.

"You did not change," they say.

I am fourteen and baby-sitting for my brother Bill, who lives in Boston. He is my favorite brother and there is a strong bond between us. Understanding my feelings of shame and ugliness he and his wife take me to a local hospital, where the "glob" is removed by a doctor named O. Henry. There is still a small bluish crater where the scar tissue was, but the ugly white stuff is gone. Almost immediately I become a different person from the girl who does not raise her head. Or so I think. Now that I've raised my head I win the boyfriend of my dreams. Now that I've raised my head I have plenty of friends. Now that I've raised my head classwork comes from my lips as faultlessly as Easter speeches did, and I leave high school as valedictorian, most popular student, and *queen*, hardly believing my luck. Ironically, the girl who was voted most beautiful in our class (and was) was later shot twice through the chest by a male companion, using a "real" gun, while she was pregnant. But that's another story in itself. Or is it?

"You did not change," they say.

It is now thirty years since the "accident." A beautiful journalist comes to visit and to interview me. She is going to write a cover story for her magazine that focuses on my latest book. "Decide how you want to look on the cover," she says. "Glamorous, or whatever."

Never mind "glamorous," it is the "whatever" that I hear. Suddenly all I can   35
think of is whether I will get enough sleep the night before the photography session: if I don't, my eye will be tired and wander, as blind eyes will.

At night in bed with my lover I think up reasons why I should not appear on the cover of a magazine. "My meanest critics will say I've sold out," I say. "My family will now realize I write scandalous books."

"But what's the real reason you don't want to do this?" he asks.

"Because in all probability," I say in a rush, "my eye won't be straight."

"It will be straight enough," he says. Then, "Besides, I thought you'd made your peace with that."

And I suddenly remember that I have.   40

I remember:

I am talking to my brother Jimmy, asking if he remembers anything unusual about the day I was shot. He does not know I consider that day the last time my father, with his sweet home remedy of cool lily leaves, chose me, and that I suffered and raged inside because of this. "Well," he says, "all I remember is standing by the side of the highway with Daddy, trying to flag down a car. A white man stopped, but when Daddy said he needed somebody to take his little girl to the doctor, he drove off."

I remember:

I am in the desert for the first time. I fall totally in love with it. I am so over-whelmed by its beauty, I confront for the first time, consciously, the meaning of the doctor's words years ago: "Eyes are sympathetic. If one is blind, the other will likely become blind too." I realize I have dashed about the world madly, looking at this, looking at that, storing up images against the fading of the light. *But I might have missed seeing the desert!* The shock of that possibility—and gratitude for over twenty-five years of sight—sends me literally to my knees. Poem after poem comes—which is perhaps how poets pray.

On Sight

I am so thankful I have seen
The Desert
And the creatures in the desert
And the desert Itself.

The desert has its own moon
Which I have seen
With my own eye.
There is no flag on it.

Trees of the desert have arms
All of which are always up
That is because the moon is up
The sun is up

Also the sky
The stars
Clouds
None with flags.

If there were flags, I doubt
the trees would point.
Would you?

But mostly, I remember this: 45

I am twenty-seven, and my baby daughter is almost three. Since her birth I have worried about her discovery that her mother's eyes are different from other people's. Will she be embarrassed? I think. What will she say? Every day she watches a television program called "Big Blue Marble." It begins with a picture of the earth as it appears from the moon. It is bluish, a little battered-looking, but full of light, with whitish clouds swirling around it. Every time I see it I weep with love, as if it is a picture of Grandma's house. One day when I am putting Rebecca down for her nap, she suddenly focuses on my eye. Something inside me cringes, gets ready to try to protect myself. All children are cruel about physical differences, I know from experience, and that they don't always mean to be is another matter. I assume Rebecca will be the same.

But no-o-o-o. She studies my face intently as we stand, her inside and me outside her crib. She even holds my face maternally between her dimpled little hands. Then, looking every bit as serious and lawyerlike as her father, she says, as if it may just possibly have slipped my attention: "Mommy, there's a *world* in your eye." (As in, "Don't be alarmed, or do anything crazy.") And then, gently, but with great interest: "Mommy, where did you *get* that world in your eye?"

For the most part, the pain left then. (So what, if my brothers grew up to buy even more powerful pellet guns for their sons and to carry real guns themselves. So what, if a young "Morehouse man"[1] once nearly fell off the steps of Trevor Arnett Library because he thought my eyes were blue.) Crying and laughing I ran to the bathroom, while Rebecca mumbled and sang herself off to sleep. Yes indeed, I realized, looking into the mirror. There *was* a world in my eye. And I saw that it was possible to love it: that in fact, for all it had taught me of shame and anger and inner vision, I *did* love it. Even to see it drifting out of orbit in boredom, or rolling up out of fatigue, not to mention floating back at attention in excitement (bearing witness, a friend has called it), deeply suitable to my personality, and even characteristic of me.

That night I dream I am dancing to Stevie Wonder's[2] song "Always" (the name of the song is really "As," but I hear it as "Always"). As I dance, whirling and joyous, happier than I've ever been in my life, another bright-faced dancer joins me. We dance and kiss each other and hold each other through the night. The other dancer has obviously come through all right, as I have done. She is beautiful, whole and free. And she is also me.

UNDERSTANDING THE TEXT

1. How does Walker describe her family in the opening paragraphs? What social position does the family occupy? What kind of internal family dynamics does she describe?

2. Why do her brothers ask her not to tell their parents how her eye was injured? Why does she comply with the request?

3. Why does Alice begin to have problems in school and with her social group after the "accident"? Are these caused by other people's reactions to her, by a change in the way that she views herself, or both?

4. Why do Alice's parents and family members later insist that she did not change after the accident? What might this tell us about the nature of the changes?

5. What is the point of Walker's brief narrative about seeing the desert? How does this affect the imagery of the overall narrative?

1. **"Morehouse Man":** student at Morehouse College in Atlanta, an all-male, historically black college close to Spelman, the all-women's historically black college that Walker attended.

2. **Stevie Wonder:** a popular singer, songwriter, and producer (b. 1950) who achieved great success in music despite being blind from birth.

6. How does Walker's own daughter reframe the question of the beauty (or lack thereof) in her eye?

7. How do you interpret the title of the essay, "Beauty: When the Other Dancer Is the Self"? What "dance" is Walker referring to?

MAKING CONNECTIONS

1. One theme of Walker's essay is the importance of accepting imperfections in ourselves and in others. Examine the paintings in this section by Vermeer and Yusksavage as examples of this same theme—how are they similar? How are they different?

2. How might "Beauty: When the Other Dancer Is the Self" fit into the model of storytelling that Toni Morrison articulates in her "Nobel Lecture" (p. 217)? Compare the following two symbols: the eye in Walker's essay, and the bird in Morrison's.

3. How might Joseph Stiglitz (p. 594) interpret the substandard medical care that Walker received as a child in rural Georgia? Would he see this lack of care as a logical outgrowth of the economic inequality that he examines?

WRITING ABOUT THE TEXT

1. Write a personal essay in the style of "Beauty: When the Other Dancer Is the Self." Use present-tense constructions to narrate the way that you learned something important over various stages of your life.

2. Explore the function of beauty in "Beauty: When the Other Dancer Is the Self." Look at the various ways beauty is defined in different parts of the essay, and consider how Walker's race and gender influenced these definitions.

ELAINE SCARRY
from *On Beauty and Being Just*
[1999]

ELAINE SCARRY (B. 1946) is the Walter M. Cabot Professor of Aesthetics and the General Theory of Value at Harvard University, where she teaches courses in English and American literature. Her first book, *The Body in Pain* (1985), is a sustained meditation on torture and the political and cultural dimensions of human suffering. It has become a classic work of cultural criticism—a form of analysis that uses techniques developed to read written texts in order to understand historical and cultural events. In recent years, Scarry has applied her analytical methods to current events in the United States. Since the World Trade Center attacks of September 11, 2001, she has written three books on national defense and political decision-making.

The following selection comes from the book *On Beauty and Being Just* (1999), in which Scarry sets out to rehabilitate theoretical discussions of beauty in the humanities. As she argues, while academics who study such things as music, art, and literature are constantly surrounded with beautiful things, they have been prevented from focusing on beauty per se by two pervasive political arguments. First, political critics have argued that discussing beauty distracts people from social injustices. And second, many feminists have argued that focusing on something beautiful or someone's beauty objectifies the thing or person by converting it into an object of our pleasure.

In response to these criticisms, Scarry argues that beauty can help us become more just. The word "fair," she observes, can mean either "attractive" or "just"—and this is more than simply a linguistic coincidence. Both concepts rely on the idea of symmetry. Beautiful objects (and people) are usually so considered because they are evenly proportioned. Similarly, a society can be considered just when its people are treated equally and resources are distributed evenly.

On Beauty and Being Just uses two powerful rhetorical techniques. First, Scarry invokes the authority of such philosophical figures as Plato, Boethius, and Augustine in support of her position. Even more importantly, she creates a chain of deductive arguments to bolster the following assertion: when we study and learn how to appreciate beautiful objects, we train ourselves to think about the world in terms that will lead us to greater justice.

Fairness as "A Symmetry of Everyone's Relation to One Another"

One day I ran into a friend, and when he asked me what I was doing, I said I was trying to explain how beauty leads us to justice. (It happens that this friend is a philosopher and an economist who has spent many years inquiring into the relation between famine and forms of procedural justice such as freedom of the press. He also tracked demographic figures in Asia and North Africa that revealed more than one hundred million missing women and showed a long-standing practice of neglecting the health of girls.) Without pausing, he responded that he remembered being a child in India and coming upon Aristotle's statement that justice was a perfect cube: he had been completely baffled by the statement, except he knew it had something to do with equality in all directions.

Happening to find myself sometime later walking beside another friend, and again pressed to describe what I was up to, I said I was showing that beauty assists us in getting to justice, and—perhaps because the subject seemed out of keeping with the morning's seaside glee—I for some reason added, "But *you* surely don't believe this." (He is a political philosopher who inquires into the nature of deliberative processes, and has established a series of alternative models for ethics; he served in British intelligence during the Second World War and in the Foreign Office during the period of the Marshall Plan.[1]) "No," he agreed, still laughing, and high above the cresting waves, for we were walking on a steep dune, he cited with delight a proclamation about beauty's inevitable descent into bohemia. "Except, of course," he added, turning suddenly serious, and holding out his two large hands, "analogically"[2] by what they share: balance and the weighing of both sides."

The speed and immediacy with which Amartya Sen and Stuart Hampshire[3] spoke is indicative of the almost self-evident character of the argument that will be made here: that beautiful things give rise to the notion of distribution, to a lifesaving reciprocity, to fairness not just in the sense of loveliness of aspect but in the sense of "a symmetry of everyone's relation to one another."

When we speak about beauty, attention sometimes falls on the beautiful object, at other times on the perceiver's cognitive act of beholding the beautiful thing, and at still other times on the creative act that is prompted by one's being in the presence of what is beautiful. The invitation to ethical fairness can be found at each of these three sites. . . .

When we begin at the first of the three sites—the site of the beautiful object   5
itself—it is clear that the attribute most steadily singled out over the centuries has been "symmetry." Some eras single it out almost to the exclusion of all else (remarkably, one such period is the decade of the 1990s), whereas others insist that it is not symmetry alone but symmetry companioned by departures and exceptions from itself that makes a piece of music, a face, or a landscape beautiful (as in the

1. **Marshall Plan:** an American initiative to provide economic aid to European countries after the devastation of World War II, and to promote capitalism and democracy in the region. Named after then-Secretary of State, George Marshall, the operation was in effect from April 1948 to December 1951.

2. **Analogically:** through analogy.
3. **Amartya Sen:** a Nobel Prize–winning economist (b. 1933) from India whose research focuses on social justice; **Stuart Hampshire:** a British moral philosopher (1914–2004). Both were colleagues of Elaine Scarry at Harvard.

nineteenth-century romantic modification of the principles of eighteenth-century neoclassicism). The feature, despite these variations in emphasis, never ceases to be, even in eras that strive to depart from it, the single most enduringly recognized attribute. But what happens when we move from the sphere of aesthetics to the sphere of justice? Here symmetry remains key, particularly in accounts of distributive justice[4] and fairness "as a symmetry of everyone's relation to one another." It was this shared feature of beauty and justice that Amartya Sen saluted in the figure of the cube, equidistant in all directions, and that Stuart Hampshire again saluted in the figure of scales, equally weighted in both directions.

But why should we not just accept Hampshire's formulation that this is an "analogy," a feature they share, rather than the much stronger formulation, that it is the very symmetry of beauty which leads us to, or somehow assists us in discovering, the symmetry that eventually comes into place in the realm of justice? One answer is this: in periods when a human community is too young to have yet had time to create justice, as well as in periods when justice has been taken away, beautiful things (which do not rely on us to create them but come on their own and have never been absent from a human community) hold steadily visible the manifest good of equality and balance.

Which of the many early writers—such as Parmenides Plato, Boethius[5], each of whom saw the sphere, because equidistant in all directions, as the most perfect of shapes—shall we call on for illustration? Here is Augustine[6] thinking about musical rhythm in the sixth book of *De Musica*. He is not setting forth an attribute of distributive justice; he is not recommending that medieval hierarchies be overthrown and replaced by democracies; yet present to his mind—as present to the mind of the writers of scores of other ancient treatises on cubes, spheres—is a conviction that equality is the heart of beauty, that equality is pleasure-bearing, and that (most important in the shift we are seeking to undertake from beauty to justice) equality is the morally highest and best feature of the world. In other words, equality is set forth as the thing of all things to be aspired to:

> The higher things are those in which equality resides, supreme, unshaken, unchangeable, eternal.

> This rhythm [that, like certain principles of arithmetic, can be elicited from a person who has never before been tutored in it] is immutable and eternal, with no inequality possible in it. Therefore it must come from God.

---

4. **Distributive justice:** an understanding of justice that focuses on the equitable distribution of resources across society.
5. **Boethius:** a philosopher in the late-Roman/early-Medieval period (circa 480–524) who wrote a famous treatise on music (p. 242). **Parmenides:** a pre-Socratic Greek philosopher (fifth century BCE) and author of the early treatise "On Nature." **Plato:** ancient Greek philosopher (circa 427–347 BCE) who wrote about both beauty and justice (p. 166).
6. **Augustine of Hippo:** early Christian bishop and theologian (354–430) (p. 184).

Beautiful things please by proportion, *numero*, . . . equality is not found only in sounds for the ear and in bodily movements, but also in visible forms, in which hitherto equality has been identified with beauty even more customarily than in sounds.

It is easy to love colours, musical sounds, *voces*, cakes, roses and the body's soft, smooth surface, *corpora leniter mollia*. In all of them the soul is in quest of nothing except equality and similitude.

Water is a unity, all the more beautiful and transparent on account of a yet greater similitude of its parts . . . on guard over its order and its security. Air has still greater unity and internal regularity than water. Finally the sky . . . has the greatest well-being.

Can we, could Augustine, did any reader, ever emerge from this cascade of paragraphs—of which only a small filigree is given here—without having their yearning for, their commitment to, equality intensified? No claim is being made here about the length of time—a year, a century, a millennium—it might take for the same equality to inhere in social relations. All that is claimed is that the aspiration to political, social, and economic equality has already entered the world in the beauty-loving treatises of the classical and Christian periods, as has the readiness to recognize it as beautiful if and when it should arrive in the world.

To return, then, to the question of whether the symmetry in beauty and that in justice are analogous, or whether instead the first leads to the second, the answer already proposed can be restated and expanded through Augustine's idiom. Imagine, then, a world that has blue sky, musical sounds, cakes, roses, and the body's soft, smooth surface; and now imagine further that this world also has a set of just social arrangements and laws that (like Augustine's water) by their very consistency stand guard over and secure themselves. The equality residing in the song-filled sky light and the equality residing in the legal arrangements need not be spoken about as anything other than analogous, especially since the laws (both written and applied with a consistency across all persons) are now themselves beautiful. But remembering there was a time antecedent to the institution of these laws, and recognizing also that this community will be very lucky if, in its ongoing existence through future history, there never comes an era when its legal system for a brief period deteriorates, we can perceive that ongoing work is actively carried out by the continued existence of a locus of aspiration: the evening skies, the dawn chorus of roosters and mourning doves, the wild rose that, with the sweet pea, uses even prison walls to climb on. In the absence of its counterpart, one term of an analogy actively calls out for its missing fellow; it presses on us to bring its counterpart into existence, acts as a lever in the direction of justice. An analogy is inert and at rest only if both terms are present in the world; when one term is absent, the other becomes an active conspirator for the exile's return.

But there is also a second way in which even in a community that has both fair   10 skies and fair legal arrangements, the sky still assists us. For the symmetry, equality, and self-sameness of the sky are present to the senses, whereas the symmetry, equality, and self-sameness of the just social arrangements are not. In the young worlds and in the lapsed worlds, justice was not available to the senses for the simple reason that justice was not in the world. But even when justice comes into the world, it is not ordinarily sensorially available. Even once it has been instantiated, it is seldom available to sensory apprehension, because it is dispersed out over too large a field (an entire town or entire country), and because it consists of innumerable actions, almost none of which are occurring simultaneously. If I step out my front door, I can see the four petals of each mother-of-pearl poppy, like small signal flags: two up, two down; three up, one down; all four up; all four down. I cannot see that around the corner a traffic rule is being followed; I cannot see that over on the other side of town, the same traffic rule is being followed. It is not that the following of the traffic rule is not material: it is that its justice, which is not in a solitary location but in a consistency across all locations and in the resulting absence of injury, is not sensorially visible, as are the blades of the poppy, even though each of its component members (each car, each driver, each road surface with its white dividing line, each blinking light) is surely as material as the fragile poppy. It is the very exigencies of materiality, the susceptibility of the world to injury, that require justice, yet justice itself is outside the compass of our sensory powers.

Now it is true that once a law or constitutional principle is formulated that protects the arrangement, the sentence can be taken in in a single visual or acousti-cal glance; and this is one of the great powers of bestowing on a diffuse principle a doctrinal location. Having a phrase at hand—"the First Amendment," "the Fourth Amendment"—gathers into itself what is, though material, outside the bounds of sensory perception. Sometimes it may even happen that a just legal principle has the good fortune to be formulated in a sentence whose sensory features reinforce the availability of the principle to perception: "We hold these truths to be self-evident, that all men are created equal. . . ." The sentence scans. The cadence of its opening sequence of monosyllables shifts suddenly forward to the polysyllabic "self-evident," the rapidity of completion adrenalizing the line, as though performing its own claim (it sounds self-verifying). The table has been cleared for the principle about to be announced. Now the sentence starts over with the stark sequence of monosyllables ("that all men are") and the faster-paced, polysyllabic, self-verifying "created equal." The repeated cadence enables each half of the sentence to authorize the other. Who is the "we" empowered to declare certain sentences true and self-evident? the "we" who count themselves as one another's equals. We more often speak of beau-tiful laws than of beautiful social arrangements because the laws, even when only pieces of language, have a sensory compression that the diffusely scattered social arrangements do not have, and it is this availability to the senses that is also one of the key features of beauty. . . .

When aesthetic fairness and ethical fairness are both present to perception, their shared commitment to equality can be seen as merely an analogy, for it may truly be said that when both terms of an analogy are present, the analogy is inert. It asks nothing more of us than that we occasionally notice it. But when one term ceases to be visible (either because it is not present, or because it is present but dispersed beyond our sensory field), then the analogy ceases to be inert: the term that is present becomes pressing, active, insistent, calling out for, directing our attention toward, what is absent. I describe this, focusing on touch, as a weight or lever, but ancient and medieval philosophers always referred to it acoustically: beauty is a call.

UNDERSTANDING THE TEXT

1. What perspectives do the two friends that Scarry mentions in the beginning of this selection add to her understanding of beauty and justice? Why do you think she introduces these perspectives to begin this section of her essay?

2. What are the "three sites" that our attention falls upon when speaking of a beautiful object? How do these sites provide different perspectives on beauty?

3. What role does the notion of symmetry play in our understanding of beauty? What role does the same notion play in our understanding of justice?

4. Why does Scarry believe that symmetry in beauty and symmetry in justice are connected by more than just analogy? Does she believe that they are ultimately the same thing?

5. Why does Scarry quote Augustine's treatise on music? What is the rhetorical effect of quoting an ancient Christian philosopher to establish the connection between beauty and justice?

6. Why does Scarry suggest that societies will always perceive symmetry through beauty before they have a concept of justice? What is the primary example that she uses to explain this point?

MAKING CONNECTIONS

1. How is Scarry's concept of symmetry similar to William Blake's concept of "fearful symmetry" in "The Tyger" (p. 262)? How do they both use the idea that our senses are pleased by symmetrical things?

2. Scarry references Boethius (p. 242) as an ancient figure who perceived beauty as symmetry. What underlying principles about the role of art do Scarry and Boethius share?

3. Does Scarry's view of distributive justice—or the belief that resources should be distributed fairly across the social spectrum—support Tolstoy's view that great art must be understandable by everybody (p. 265)? Would Tolstoy accept that some people have more exposure to beauty—and therefore to justice—than other people?

WRITING ABOUT THE TEXT

1. Analyze the claims that Scarry makes and the support that she offers for those claims. Focus especially on her claim that symmetry is important to both beauty and justice and that the definition of "symmetry" is essentially the same in both contexts.

2. Consider what kinds of empirical evidence might prove (or disprove) Scarry's claim that people who pay attention to questions of beauty learn how to be more just. Write a paper testing this claim against the evidence that you gather.

3. Explore the connections between beauty and justice in the essays by Scarry, Mo Tzu (p. 236), and Boethius (p. 242). Look for areas of agreement and disagreement among the three authors.

LISA YUSKAVAGE
Babie I
[2003]

LISA YUSKAVAGE (B. 1962) is a contemporary American painter based in New York City. She was born in Pennsylvania and educated at Temple University and Yale University, where she received a Master of Fine Arts degree in 1986. Nearly all of Yuskavage's paintings feature women, often nude, in exaggerated poses or with physically impossible features. Art critics see the cartoonish, fanciful nature of her subjects as a criticism of the unrealistic images of female sexuality that modern culture creates.

A 1999 article in the *New York Times* described Yuskavage's paintings as "provocative depictions of loose, blasé women in colors that glow or sometimes scream." The article continues to summarize the reaction of most art critics to Yuskavage's work:

> Critics have described the works, usually in praise, as "anatomically impossible bimbos, nymphets and other female travesties" and "demonically distorted Kewpie-doll women" that are "perversely entertaining" and "visual spectacles." Ms. Yuskavage once said she captured the "far-out extension" of male sex fantasies. To question prevailing views about women and sex is not enough; she wants a reaction, as so many artists of her generation do.

Babie I communicates many of Yuskavage's standard themes through the subject's facial expressions—a plainly dressed young woman clutches a partially wilted bouquet of flowers to her chest. She frowns nervously and glances off to her right as if waiting for something or someone to show up. Her facial features, though exaggerated, do not project a conventional image of beauty.

LISA YUSKAVAGE
Babie I, 2003 (oil on linen).
David Zwirner Art Gallery, New York & London / Courtesy of the artist and David Zwirner.
See p. C–6 in the color insert for a full-color reproduction of this image.

UNDERSTANDING THE TEXT

1. What adjectives would you use to describe the girl in the picture? Would you consider her beautiful, plain, nervous, unattractive, or would you use other words altogether?

2. Is it significant that her name (according to the title) is "Babie"—a misspelling of the common diminutive "Baby"?

3. What feeling do the background colors of the painting create? How do the background and foreground colors blend together? Does the girl appear to blend into the background in any way?

4. Why do you think that the girl is glancing to the side? Is there someone she is waiting for or something that she is expecting to happen? Use your imagination as to what you think this may be.

5. What do the flowers that she is holding represent? Why does the bouquet appear to be falling apart?

MAKING CONNECTIONS

1. Would *Babie I* fit the definition of a "tronie" that Vermeer used when painting *Study of a Young Woman* (p. 253)? Why or why not? How are the two paintings similar? How are they different?

2. What do you see as the underlying understanding of "beauty" in *Babie I*? How is this similar to or different than the understanding of beauty in "Beauty: When the Other Dancer Is the Self" (p. 271)?

WRITING ABOUT THE TEXT

1. Use your imagination to tell the story of the girl in the painting. Give her a character and a set of motivations, and explain where she is, why she is there, and what she might be expecting to happen next.

2. Compare or contrast *Babie I* with Vermeer's *Study of a Young Woman*. Explain the way both artists approach their subjects and the understanding of female beauty that each painting seems to convey.

5

SCIENCE AND NATURE

How Can We Best Understand the Natural World?

> The book of nature is a fine and large piece of tapestry rolled up, which we are not able to see all at once, but must be content to wait for the discovery of its beauty and symmetry little by little, as it gradually comes to be more and more unfolded, or displayed.
>
> —*Robert Boyle*

Robert Boyle (1627–1691), often referred to as the "father of chemistry," lived during one of the most exciting periods of scientific discovery in the history of the world. During the sixteenth and seventeenth centuries, towering intellectual figures like Boyle, Nicolaus Copernicus, Galileo Galilei, Johannes Keppler, and Sir Isaac Newton redefined our understanding of the natural world. The kind of science to which these thinkers devoted their lives—a science that draws conclusions based on observation and analysis—defined what we now call the Scientific Revolution.

Along with being excellent scientists, many of these great figures were also theologians. In their religious writings, they spoke often of God's "two books"—the Bible, which contained revealed truth, and "The Book of Nature," which contained deep mysteries and profound truths about the natural world. The idea of a "book of nature"—a natural world that can be read and understood like a written text—is traceable as far back as the ancient world and the works of such figures as Galen, Hypocrites, and Aristotle, who spent their lives observing the world and cataloguing the things that they found. The line from these thinkers to the Scientific Revolution is neither straight nor direct. But after a lot of fits and starts, and a long period in which religious belief often prevented scientific inquiry, the ideas of the ancients were revived and extended, producing an explosion of scientific knowledge that still persists today.

The selections in this chapter all, in one way or another, attempt to explain how to read the Book of Nature; that is, how to understand the natural world. The readings begin with the ancient Roman poet and philosopher Lucretius, who argued that the world was composed of extremely small particles whose constant motions and interactions with each other produced different forms of matter—a radical view in its own day that is now completely accepted in ours.

Following Lucretius are two very different selections from the time of the Scientific Revolution. The first of these comes from the work of the great Japanese poet, Matsuo Bashō, who walked around much of the perimeter of Japan in the 1680s and composed brief haiku poems describing the natural world. For Bashō, it was poetry, rather than scientific experimentation, that best helped humans to "read" the natural world. The second selection is a famous painting from England, Joseph Wright of Derby's *An Experiment on a Bird in the Air Pump*, which depicts a scientific experiment conducted in a dark room as a variety of spectators react to both the science and spectacle of the experiment.

The next two readings, which come from the eighteenth century, sum up one of the most important paradigm shifts in the history of science. William Paley's introduction to his book *Natural Theology* argues that the great work of creation can only be understood as the work of an equally great creator. Just as we would assume the existence of a watchmaker if we came upon a well-made watch in the forest, we must assume the existence of God when we study the intricate beauty of the world. This view held sway throughout Europe until the publication of the next selection, Charles Darwin's *On the Origin of Species*, which laid out a completely natural process—evolution by natural selection—capable of creating all life on earth.

The remainder of the readings in this chapter come from the twentieth century. "The Obligation to Endure," a chapter from Rachel Carson's *Silent Spring*, is one of the foundational texts of the modern environmental movement. Carson uses the theory of evolution to explain how insects adapt to deadly pesticides, greatly diminishing the pesticide's value for insect control while poisoning many other parts of the environment. This selection is followed by Karl Popper's seminal essay, "Science as Falsification," which explains that the fundamental operation of the scientific method is not to prove things true, but to try to prove things false. Barry Commoner's selection in this chapter, "The Four Laws of Ecology," is drawn from his 1971 book *The Closing Circle*. Commoner was one of the first scientists in the world to identify as an "ecologist," one who studies the ways that different parts of our environment are connected. Following Commoner is Edward O. Wilson, a biologist and two-time Pulitzer Prize–winning science writer. His essay, "The Fitness of Human Nature," attempts to understand the evolutionary foundations of human behavior.

The last two selections come from women in developing countries who have worked tirelessly to change the ways that their contemporaries view humans' relationship to nature. In "Foresters without Diplomas," Wangari Maathai, the founder of the Green Belt Movement in Kenya and winner of the Nobel Peace Prize, describes the beginnings of her work organizing African women to plant trees and reverse deforestation in the region. And in "Soil, Not Oil," Indian scientist and activist Vandana Shiva argues that genuine justice in the world will require us all to cultivate a different understanding of our relationship to nature—and to each other.

The unifying theme of the selections in this chapter is the drive to understand the natural world on its own terms and to negotiate our relationship with that natural world in ways that can be sustained far into the future. The poets, artists, scientists, and activists gathered here all share this fundamental concern with how best to understand—and respect—nature. They have been asking questions about how we understand our world for a very long time, the answers to which are still being debated today.

LUCRETIUS
from *De Rerum Natura*
[FIRST CENTURY BCE]

WE KNOW VERY LITTLE about Titus Lucretius Carus except that he lived in the first century BCE, that his works were well regarded by his contemporaries, and that he wrote one of the most important poems known to humankind. This poem, *De Rerum Natura*, was unheard of until 1417, when an Italian scholar named Poggio Bracciolini discovered the only surviving manuscript in a German monastery and brought it to the attention of the world.

De Rerum Natura—which has been translated into English variously as *The Nature of Things, The Nature of the Universe,* and *The Way Things Are*—is at once a great poem and a profound work of physics. Lucretius followed the ancient philosophy of Epicureanism, which held that the universe was controlled by natural laws, not divine whims, and that people produce unnecessary misery by trying to decipher and live by the rules of the various gods, objects of worship in the ancient world. The founder of this philosophy, Epicurus, believed that the greatest good in life was pleasure, by which he meant not the satisfaction of carnal appetites but the deep pleasure that comes with understanding how the natural world works.

In his long poem, Lucretius sets out to explain the workings of the natural world by using the important Epicurean concept of "atoms"—indescribably small bits of matter that compose everything in the universe. For twenty-first century students, the theory of atoms seems logical; for medieval European Christians, however, it was heresy. Explaining everything in material terms eliminated the need for divine intervention, and insisting on pleasure as the primary purpose of human beings cast doubt on all of the social institutions devoted to pleasing the gods. As the ideas found in *De Rerum Natura* began to circulate and take root, they contributed both to the Renaissance that marked the end of the medieval period in Europe, and to the Scientific Revolution that began in the seventeenth century and profoundly shaped the modern world.

The following selection comes from the Second Book of *De Rerum Natura*. Here, Lucretius explains the motion of atoms and introduces his famous concept of "the swerve" (*clinamen* in Latin). According to Lucretius, all atoms are in motion all the time. Their natural tendency is to move down, because they have weight, but they can be propelled upward by external forces such as great gusts of wind. They mostly move up and down in straight lines, but "they swerve a little." These minute swerves are responsible for everything new that happens in the universe, as they introduce an element of unpredictability into an otherwise determined system. Nobody can predict what might happen when atoms swerve, and this uncertainty makes anything possible.

This observation might seem simple, but its immense influence on modern scientific thought is the subject of *The Swerve*, a recent Pulitzer Prize–winning book by Harvard professor Stephen Greenblatt, which discusses the rediscovery of *De Rerum Natura* and its influence on the European Renaissance. According to Greenblatt, the discovery of the only surviving copy of Lucretius's poem in the early fifteenth century was itself a "swerve"—an imperceptible and unlikely change in fortune that had profound consequences for the world.

The selection excerpted here comes from Rolfe Humphries's 1968 translation titled *The Way Things Are*. Unlike the many modern prose translations of *De Rerum Natura*, Humphries preserves Lucretius's original intention to work in poetry, which establishes scientific arguments with both the force of its ideas and the beauty of its language.

> If you think
> Atoms can stop their course, refrain from movement,
> And by cessation cause new kinds of motion,
> You are far astray indeed. Since there is void
> Through which they move, all fundamental motes[1]   5
> Must be impelled, either by their own weight
> Or by some force outside them. When they strike
> Each other, they bounce off; no wonder, either,
> Since they are absolute solid, all compact,
> With nothing back of them to block their path.   10
> To help you see more clearly that all atoms
> Are always moving, just remember this:
> There is no bottom to the universe,
> No place for basic particles to rest,
> Since space is infinite, unlimited,   15
> Reaching beyond all bounds, in all directions,
> As time and time again I have shown you proof.
> Therefore, of course, no atom ever rests
> Coming through void, but always drives, is driven
> In various ways, and their collisions cause,   20
> As the case may be, greater or less rebound.
> When they are held in thickest combination,
> At closer intervals, with the space between
> More hindered by their interlock of figure,
> These give us rock, or adamant[2], or iron,   25

1 **Motes:** small particles; the term "fundamental motes" refers to atoms, but later in this selection, Lucretius will use "motes" to refer to the small particles of dust that are visible in a house when sunlight streams through the window.

2. **Adamant:** a legendary rock said to be the hardest substance on earth. Today, the word is used as an adjective to describe someone who is firm in a belief or desire.

Things of that nature, (Not very many kinds
Go wandering little and lonely through the void.)
There are some whose alternate meetings, partings, are
At greater intervals; from these we are given
Thin air, the shining sunlight. Many more   30
Have been kept out of any combination,
Nowhere conjoin. Before our eyes we have
An illustration. If you look sometimes,
You see the motes all dancing, as the sun
Streams through the shutters into a dark room.   35
Look!—there they go, like armies in maneuver
Whose little squadrons charge, retreat, join, part,
From this you can deduce that on a scale
Oh, infinitely smaller, beyond your sight,
Similar turbulence whirls. A little thing   40
Can often show us what a great one's like,
And that's not all the story, either. Watch!—
Those motes in the sunlight, by their restlessness,
Tell you there's motion, hidden and unseen,
In what seems solid matter. As they bounce,   45
Change course, come back, here, there, and every which way,
You may be sure this restlessness is given
By their essential core, atomic essence,
From just these first-beginnings. They are moved
By their own inner impulse first, and then   50
Such groups as form with just a few together,
Only a little bigger than their units,
Are moved by unseen blows from these: in turn
They shove along the somewhat larger masses.
So, motion comes from first-beginnings, grows   55
By slow degrees till we can see the process,
Just as we see the dancing motes in the sunlight,
But cannot see what urge compels the dancing.

Now then—what kind of speed does matter have?
The answer, Memmius,[3] won't take very long.   60
When dawn bathes earth with morning light, and birds,
All kinds of them, flying through pathless woods,
Fill all the delicate air with liquid song,
How suddenly at such a time the sun

3. **Memmius:** Gaius Memmius, a Roman poet and statesman to whom Lucretius dedicated *De Rerum Natura.*

Clothes everything with light! This we can see,   65
And so can all men, plain before their eyes.
But the sun's warmth and that calm light come on
Not through an empty void; their course is set
More slowly, as if they parted waves of air
The way a swimmer does. Not one by one   70
Do the tiny particles of heat proceed,
But rather *en masse*, get in each other's way,
At times, and are also blocked by outside force.
All this combines to make them go more slowly.
It does not work this way with single atoms   75
Which go along through empty void, unchecked
By opposition. They have their parts, of course,
But they are single units; they drive on,
Resistless, toward their first direction's impulse,
And they must be of marvelous speed, beyond   80
The speed of light, surpassing far the sweep
Of lightning in split seconds through the sky—
Impossible to follow every atom,
To see complete their order, action, system.

Some people do not know how matter works.   85
They think that nature needs the will of the gods
To fit the seasons of the year so nicely
To human needs, to bring to birth the crops
And other blessings, which our guide to life,
The radiance of pleasure, makes us crave   90
Through Venus'[4] agency. To be sure, we breed
To keep the race alive, but to think that gods
Have organized all things for the sake of men
Is nothing but a lot of foolishness.
I might not know a thing about the atoms,   95
But this much I can say, from what I see
Of heaven's ways and many other features:
The nature of the world just could not be
A product of the gods' devising; no,
There are too many things the matter with it.   100
I'll give you further details, Memmius, later.
Now to get on with further explanation
Concerning motion.

4. **Venus:** Roman goddess of love and beauty.

                        The first point to make
Is, no internal force can make things rise   105
Or force them upward. Don't be fooled by sparks:
I know they rise, increase, grow upward; crops
Act the same way, and trees, although their weight
Exerts a downward pull. We must not think,
When fires go leaping toward the roofs of houses,   110
And the swift flames lick out at beams and timbers,
That they do this of their own will entirely,
Without the urge of pressure from below.
Blood acts the same way, spurting from our bodies,
Arterial jets, a scarlet-colored fountain,   115
And don't you see how violently water
Geysers beams and timbers? The deeper we shove them,
The harder we push them down, all might and main—
With just that energy water shoots them back,
Heaving them up till they leap clear into air.   120
Yet, I suppose, we have no doubt all things,
So far as in them lies, are carried down
Through empty space. So flames, through wafts of air,
Must rise, impelled, although their weight fights back
To bring them downward. Don't you see the torches   125
Of the night sky draw their long fiery trails
Wherever nature gives them passageway?
Don't you see stars and meteors fall to earth?
Even the sun from heaven's height rains heat,
Sows fields with light. From heaven to earth descends   130
Downward the course of heat. Watch lightning flash
Across the countering winds; now here, now there,
Dart the cloud-riving fires; most often, though,
The bolts drive down to earth.

                        I'd have you know   135
That while these particles come mostly down,
Straight down of their own weight through void, at times—
No one knows when or where—they swerve a little,
Not much, but just enough for us to say
They change direction. Were this not the case,   140
All things would fall straight down, like drops of rain,
Through utter void, no birth-shock would emerge
Out of collision, nothing be created.

If anyone thinks heavier bodies fall
More swiftly in their downward plunge, and thus   145
Fall on the lighter ones, and by this impact
Cause generation, he is very wrong.
To be sure, whatever falls through air or water
Goes faster in proportion to its weight,
For air's a frailer element than water.   150
Neither imposes quite the same delay
On all things passing through them, though both yield
More quickly to the heavier. But void
Can never hold up anything at all,
Never; its very essence is to yield.   155
So all things, though their weights may differ, drive
Through unresisting void at the same rate,
With the same speed. No heavier ones can catch
The lighter from above, nor downward strike
Such blows as might effect the variance   160
In motion nature gives to things. There must,
I emphasize, there has to be, a swerve
No more than minimal, for otherwise
We'd seem to predicate a slanting motion,
But this the facts refute. It's obvious,   165
It's clear to see, that substances don't sidle,
Fall sidewise, hurtling downward; but whose eyes
Are quick enough to see they never veer
With almost infinitesimal deviation?

If cause forever follows after cause   170
In infinite, undeviating sequence
And a new motion always has to come
Out of an old one, by fixed law; if atoms
Do not, by swerving, cause new moves which break
The laws of fate; if cause forever follows,   175
In infinite sequence, cause—where would we get
This free will that we have, wrested from fate,
By which we go ahead, each one of us,
Wherever our pleasures urge? Don't we also swerve
At no fixed time or place, but as our purpose   180
Directs us? There's no doubt each man's will
Initiates action, and this prompting stirs
Our limbs to movement. When the gates fly open,

No racehorse breaks as quickly as he wants to,
For the whole body of matter must be aroused,   185
Inspired to follow what the mind desires;
So, you can see, motion begins with will
Of heart or mind, and from that will moves on
Through all the framework. This is not the same
As our advance when we are prodded on   190
Or shoved along by someone else's force.
Under those circumstances, it is clear
That all our substance moves against our will,
Violence-driven, till our purpose checks it.
A foreign force often propels men on,   195
Makes them go forward, hurries them pell-mell.
Yet you see, don't you, something in ourselves
Can offer this force resistance, fight against it,
And this resistance has sufficient power
To permeate the body, to check the course,   200
To bring it to a halt? In atoms also
There has to be some other cause for motion
Beyond extrinsic thrust or native weight,
And this third force is resident in us
Since we know *nothing can be born of nothing.*   205
It is weight that stops all things from being caused
By blows, by outer force. Well then (you ask)
What keeps the mind from having inside itself
Some such compulsiveness in all its doings,
What keeps it from being matter's absolute slave?   210
The answer is, that our free-will derives
From just that ever-so-slight atomic swerve
At no fixed time, at no fixed place whatever.

UNDERSTANDING THE TEXT

1. Which elements of Lucretius's theory of atoms correspond to scientific principles you have learned in school? Which elements do not?

2. Why does Lucretius talk about dust particles in the sunlight? What does he hope to illustrate with this example?

3. According to Lucretius, what causes people to see the world as the creation of divine beings? Does Lucretius dispute the existence of gods? If not, what roles does he assign to them?

4. The principal argument Lucretius makes against a god-created world is that "there are too many things the matter with it." What does he mean by this statement? Do you agree?

5. What causes atoms to swerve? What are the consequences of their swerving? What is the connection between atomic swerving and human free will?

MAKING CONNECTIONS

1. How does Lucretius's view of the role of divine beings in the world's affairs compare with William Paley's (p. 311)? Is there an element of the "watchmaker god" in *De Rerum Natura*?

2. Compare the statements that Lucretius makes about the interconnectedness of all things with those by Rachel Carson (p. 328) and Barry Commoner (p. 344) about ecology.

3. Lucretius is very careful to argue that the mechanical operation of the universe does not mean that all events are determined—there is, he claims, such a thing as free will. How does this view of free will compare with that of Ruth Benedict in *Patterns of Culture* (p. 112)?

WRITING ABOUT THE TEXT

1. Evaluate Lucretius's statement that "the nature of the world just could not be / A product of the gods' devising; no, There are too many things the matter with it." Do you agree, disagree, or agree and disagree with this statement? Use examples from this text and one or two others of your choice to support your argument.

2. Examine the notion of free will in Lucretius's poem. Explain how he sees free will and randomness emerging from purely mechanical operations and compare his view with that of William Paley (p. 311).

MATSUO BASHŌ
The Narrow Road to the Interior
[1689]

JAPAN'S MOST FAMOUS and beloved poet Matsuo Bashō(1644–1694) was born to parents likely to have been low-ranking members of the samurai, or the aristocratic class. The teenage Bashō worked as a servant to a wealthy samurai named Tōdō Yoshitada, who was also a poet and encouraged Bashō to study the classics. When Tōdō died unexpectedly in 1666, Bashō renounced the samurai life and dedicated himself to poetry.

Bashō soon became well known throughout Japan for his simple, direct use of haiku, the seventeen-syllable verse form that characterized Japanese poetry in this period. A passionate student of Chinese poetry, Bashō incorporated the ideas and styles of the major Tang Dynasty poets—Li Po, Tu Fu, and Po Chü-i—with whom he was intimately familiar. He eventually ended up in the capital city of Edo (present-day Tokyo) where he became a full-time teacher of poetry and an acknowledged haiku master.

In the spring of 1689, Bashō took one of the most famous walking tours in all of human history. At a time when very few people travelled the roads alone for fear of bandits and wild beasts, he and a companion left from the safety of Edo and walked more than 1,700 miles around the Japanese mainland, visiting the sites that earlier poets had described and writing poetry at every stop. When Bashō returned, he published *Oku no Hosomichi*, or *The Narrow Road to the Interior*—a combination of prose and haiku poetry that has become one of the most important classics of Japanese literature.

The following excerpts from *The Narrow Road to the Interior* showcase Bashō's effortless blend of evocative prose and sparse haiku verse. Unlike Western poetry, which frequently employs symbolism and metaphors, Bashō's verses are short and concrete, almost never using these rhetorical devices. Bashō is said to have taught his students that the greatness of a poem lay in its ordinariness—its ability to reproduce the most important elements of a common experience or feeling using only a few uncomplicated words. It is in this sense, and perhaps no other, that we can call *The Narrow Road to the Interior* an "ordinary" book.

The moon and sun are eternal travelers. Even the years wander on. A lifetime adrift in a boat, or in old age leading a tired horse into the years, every day is a journey, and the journey itself is home. From the earliest times there have always been some who perished along the road. Still I have always been drawn by windblown clouds into dreams of a lifetime of wandering. Coming home from a year's walking tour of the coast last autumn, I swept the cobwebs from my hut on the banks of the

Sumida[1] just in time for New Year, but by the time spring mists began to rise from the fields, I longed to cross the Shirakawa Barrier[2] into the Northern Interior. Drawn by the wanderer-spirit Dōsojin,[3] I couldn't concentrate on things. Mending my cotton pants, sewing a new strap on my bamboo hat, I daydreamed. Rubbing moxa into my legs to strengthen them, I dreamed a bright moon rising over Matsushima.[4] So I placed my house in another's hands and moved to my patron Mr. Sampū's summer house in preparation for my journey. And I left a verse by my door:

> Even this grass hut
> may be transformed
> into a doll's house[5]

Very early on the twenty-seventh morning of the third moon, under a predawn haze, transparent moon barely visible, Mount Fuji just a shadow, I set out under the cherry blossoms of Ueno and Yanaka. When would I see them again? A few old friends had gathered in the night and followed along far enough to see me off from the boat. Getting off at Senju, I felt three thousand miles rushing through my heart, the whole world only a dream. I saw it through farewell tears.

> Spring passes
> and the birds cry out—tears
> in the eyes of fishes

With these first words from my brush, I started. Those who remain behind watch the shadow of a traveler's back disappear. . . .

On the first day of the fourth moon, climbed to visit the shrines on a mountain once called Two Wildernesses, renamed by Kūkar when he dedicated the shrine. Perhaps he saw a thousand years into the future, this shrine under sacred skies, his compassion endlessly scattered through the eight directions, falling equally, peaceably, on all four classes of people. The greater the glory, the less these words can say.

> Ah—speechless before
> these budding green spring leaves
> in blazing sunlight

---

1. **Sumida:** a river that flows through Tokyo.
2. **Shirakawa Barrier:** a fortified border between the "civilized" southern region of Japan and the wilder Oku region to which Bashō was traveling.
3. **Dōsojin:** In the Sinto religion, dōsojin were benevolent spirits who protected travelers.
4. **Matsushima:** a group of 260 small islands off the coast of Japan.
5. When translated into English, the haiku does not always maintain the seventeen-syllable form of the original Japanese poem.

Mount Kurokami still clothed in snow, faint in the mist, Sora wrote:

> Head shaven
> at Black Hair Mountain
> we change into summer clothes

Sora was named Kawai Sogoro.[6] Sora's his nom de plume. At my old home—called   10
Bashō-an [plantain tree hermitage]—he carried water and wood. Anticipating the
pleasures of seeing Matsushima and Kisakata, we agreed to share the journey, pleasure
and hardship alike. The morning we started, he put on Buddhist robes, shaved his
head, and changed his name to Sogo, the Enlightened. So the "changing clothes"
in his poem is pregnant with meaning.

A hundred yards uphill, the waterfall plunged a hundred feet from its cavern in
the ridge, filling into a basin made by a thousand stones. Crouched in the cavern
behind the falls, looking out, I understood why it's called Urami-no-Taki [View-
from-behind-Falls]

> Stopped awhile
> inside a waterfall—
> summer retreat begins

* * *

After all the breathtaking views of rivers and mountains, lands and seas, after everything we'd seen, thoughts of seeing Kisakata's famous bay still made my heart begin
to race. Twenty miles north of Sakata Harbor, as we walked the sandy shore beneath
mountains where sea winds wander, a storm came up at dusk and covered Mount
Chokai in mist and rain reminiscent of Su Tung-p'o's famous poem.[7] We made our
way in the dark, hoping for a break in the weather, groping on until we found a
fisherman's shack. By dawn the sky had cleared, sun dancing on the harbor. We
took a boat for Kisakata, stopping by the priest Nōin's island retreat, honoring his
three-year seclusion. On the opposite shore we saw the ancient cherry tree Saigyō[8]
saw reflected and immortalized, "Fishermen row over blossoms."

Near the shore, Empress Jingū's tomb.[9] And Kammanju Temple. Did the empress
ever visit? Why is she buried here?

Sitting in the temple chamber with the blinds raised, we saw the whole lagoon,   15
Mount Chōkai holding up the heavens inverted on the water. To the west the road

---

6. **Sora (Kawai Sogoro):** Bashō's disciple and
traveling companion for the entire journey. It
was traditional for poets at this time to adopt a
"poetry name" to use when circulating or publishing their poems.
7. **Su Tung-p'o:** major Chinese poet (1037–
1101) of the Sung Dynasty.

8. **Saigyō:** Heian Dynasty Japanese poet (1118–
1190) whom Bashō considered a major influence
on his own style.
9. **Empress Jingū:** legendary Japanese empress
of the third century.

leads to the Muyamuya Barrier; to the east it curves along a bank toward Akita; to the north, the sea comes in on tide flats at Shiogoshi. The whole lagoon, though only a mile or so across, reminds one of Matsushima, although Matsushima seems much more contented, whereas Kisakata seems bereaved. A sadness maybe in its sense of isolation here where nature's darker spirits hide—like a strange and beautiful woman whose heart has been broken.

> Kisakata rain:
> the legendary beauty Seishi
> wrapped in sleeping leaves

> At the Shallows
> the long-legged crane cool,
> stepping in the sea

Sora wrote:

> Kisakata Festival—
> at holy feasts, what specialties
> do the locals eat?

The merchant Teiji from Minō Province wrote: 20

> Fishermen sit
> on their shutters on the sand
> enjoying cool evening

Sora found an osprey nest in the rocks:

> May the ocean resist
> violating the vows
> of the osprey's nest

After several days, clouds gathering over the North Road, we left Sakata reluctantly, aching at the thought of a hundred thirty miles to the provincial capital of Kaga. We crossed the Nezu Barrier into Echigo Province, and from there went on to Ichiburi Barrier in Etchu, restating our resolve all along the way. Through nine hellish days of heat and rain, all my old maladies tormenting me again, feverish and weak, I could not write.

> Altair meets Vega   25
> tomorrow—Tanabata—
> already the night is changed

High over wild seas
surrounding Sado Island—
the River of Heaven

Today we came through places with names like Children-Desert-Parents, Lost Children, Send-Back-the-Dog, Turn-Back-the-Horse, some of the most fearsomely dangerous places in all the North Country. And well named. Weakened and exhausted,
I went to bed early, but was roused by the voices of two young women in the room
next door. Then an old man's voice joined theirs. They were prostitutes from
Niigata in Echigo Province and were on their way to Ise Shrine in the south, the
old man seeing them off at this barrier, Ichiburi. He would turn back to Niigata in
the morning, carrying their letters home. One girl quoted the *Shinkokinshū* poem,
"On the beach where white waves fall, / we all wander like children into every
circumstance, / carried forward every day . . ." And as they bemoaned their fate in
life, I fell asleep.

In the morning, preparing to leave, they came to ask directions. "May we follow
along behind?" they asked. "We're lost and not a little fearful. Your robes bring the
spirit of the Buddha to our journey." They had mistaken us for priests. "Our way
includes detours and retreats," I told them. "But follow anyone on this road and the
gods will see you through." I hated to leave them in tears, and thought about them
hard for a long time after we left. I told Sora, and he wrote down:

Under one roof,
courtesans and monks asleep—
moon and bush clover

We managed to cross all "forty-eight rapids" of the Kurobe River on our way to the
bay of Nago. Although it was no longer spring, we thought even an autumn visit
to the wisteria at Tako—made famous in the *Man'yōshū*—worth the trouble, and
asked the way: "Five miles down the coast, then up and over a mountain. A few
fishermen's shacks, but no lodging, no place even to camp." It sounded so difficult,
we pushed on instead into the province of Kaga.

Fragrance of rice
as we pass by—to the right,
Ariso Sea

We crossed Mount Unohana and Kurikara Valley at noon on the fifteenth day of
the seventh moon and entered Kanazawa, where we took rooms at an inn with a
merchant from Osaka, a Mr. Kasho, who was in town to attend memorial services
for the haiku poet Isshō, locally renowned for his verse and devotion to craft. The
poet's elder brother served as host, the poet having died last winter. . . .

After supper, I set out for Fukui, five miles down the road, the way made difficult by falling dark. An old recluse named Tōsai lived somewhere around here. More than ten years had passed since he came to visit me in Edo. Was he still alive? I was told he still lived near town, a small, weathered house just off the road, lost in tangles of gourdvines growing under cypress. I found the gate and knocked. A lonely-looking woman answered. "Where do you come from, honorable priest? The master has gone to visit friends." Probably his wife, she looked like she'd stepped right out of *Genji*.[10]

I found Tōsai and stayed two days before deciding to leave to see the full moon at Tsuruga Harbor. Tōsai, enthused, tied up his robes in his sash, and we set off with him serving as guide.

Mount Shifane faded behind us and Mount Hina began to appear. We crossed   35
Asamuzu Bridge and saw the legendary "reeds of Tamae" in bloom. We crossed Uguisu Barrier at Yuno-o Pass and passed by the ruins of Hiuchi Castle. On Returning Hill we heard the first wild geese of autumn. We arrived at Tsuruga Harbor on the evening of the fou[r]teenth day of the eighth moon. The harbor moonlight was marvelously bright.

I asked at the inn, "Will we have this view tomorrow night?" The innkeeper said, "Can't guarantee weather in Koshiji. It may be clear, but then again it may turn overcast. It may rain." We drank sake with the innkeeper, then paid a late visit to the Kei Myōjin Shrine honoring the second-century Emperor Chūai. A great spirituality—moonlight in pines, white sands like a touch of frost. In ancient times Yugyō, the second high priest, himself cleared away the grounds, carried stones, and built drains. To this day, people carry sands to the shrine. "*Yugyō-no-sunamochi*," the innkeeper explained, "Yugyō's sand-bringing."

> Transparent moonlight,
> just as it shone when Yugyō
> carried sand to the shrine

On the fifteenth, just as the innkeeper predicted, it rained:

> A harvest moon, but
> true North Country weather—
> nothing to view

The sky cleared the morning of the sixteenth. I sailed to Iro Beach a dozen miles   40
away and gathered several colorful shells with a Mr. Tenya, who provided a box lunch

---

10. *Genji: The Tale of Genji*, written by Lady Murasaki Shikibu in the eleventh century, was one of the classic prose narratives of the Japanese tradition (see p. 248).

and sake and even invited his servants. Tail winds got us there in a hurry. A few fishermen's shacks dotted the beach, and the tiny Hokke temple was disheveled. We drank tea and hot sake, lost in a sweeping sense of isolation as dusk came on.

> Loneliness greater
> than *Genji's* Suma Beach:
> the shores of autumn

> Wave after wave
> mixes tiny seashells with
> bush clover flowers

Tōsai wrote a record of our afternoon and left it at the temple.

A disciple, Rotsū had come to Tsuruga to travel with me to Mino Province. We rode horses into the castle town of Ōgaki. Sora returned from Ise, joined by Etsujin, also riding a horse. We gathered at the home of Jokō, a retired samurai. Lord Zensen, the Keikou men, and other friends arrived by day and night, all to welcome me as though I'd come back from the dead. A wealth of affection!

Still exhausted and weakened from my long journey, on the sixth day of the dark-   45
est month, I felt moved to visit Ise Shrine, where a twenty-one-year Rededication Ceremony was about to get underway. At the beach, in the boat, I wrote:

> Clam ripped from its shell,
> I move on to Futami Bay:
> passing autumn.

UNDERSTANDING THE TEXT

1. How do the haiku verses complement or set off the prose narrative? Do you think that Bashō is successful at distilling into poetry the experiences he describes in prose?

2. How does Bashō invoke earlier poets? Why is it significant to him that some of the sites he visits on his journey were described in earlier classic poems?

3. Bashō himself believed that linked verses—when one haiku verse follows another— were his most important contribution to the haiku form. How do linking verses compare to a single verse in representing the author's experience?

4. Why might Bashō and Sora have travelled dressed as Buddhist priests? Does knowing this affect your understanding of the prose narrative?

5. In what way does the text use the physical journey of Bashō and Sora as a metaphor for a spiritual journey? What role do the haiku verses play in this spiritual journey?

MAKING CONNECTIONS

1. Bashō's poetry is deeply infused with the Buddhist idea that everything in nature is connected to everything else. How does this understanding compare with Barry Commoner's ecological understanding of nature (p. 344)?

2. Does the narrative style of *The Narrow Road to the Interior* correspond to the ideal writing style that Lady Murasaki describes in "The Art of the Novel" (p. 248)? Do these two texts expound similar aesthetic ideals?

3. What elements of Bashō's journey might Edmund Burke consider "sublime"? What things seem to fill Bashō with awe?

WRITING ABOUT THE TEXT

1. Perhaps the most famous quotation from *The Narrow Road of the Interior* appears at the beginning: "Every day is a journey, and the journey itself is home." Write a brief essay interpreting this line.

2. Choose one passage from *The Narrow Road to the Interior* that ends with a haiku and analyze its rhetorical function within the prose narrative. Examine what the haiku verse adds to the prose and how it changes the way that you understand Bashō's experience.

3. Write a narrative in the style of *The Narrow Road to the Interior*—using prose and haiku—in which you describe a trip that you have taken recently.

JOSEPH WRIGHT OF DERBY

An Experiment on a Bird in the Air Pump

[1768]

PERHAPS MORE THAN any other painter of his day, Joseph Wright (1734–1797) made science the subject of art. Born in the English town of Derby, Wright studied in London with the well-known painter Thomas Hudson (1701–1779) before returning to his native town and adopting its name as part of his official signature. His paintings often centered around scientific and industrial contraptions that were unfamiliar to his audience, such as the "orrey," or model solar system, which is the subject of his 1766 painting *A Philosopher Lecturing on the Orrey*. In his paintings, he often attempted to capture the transition from an unscientific worldview to a scientific one.

An Experiment on a Bird in the Air Pump is one of Joseph Wright of Derby's most famous paintings and one of the most recognizable artistic images of the Scientific Revolution. In the painting, a scientist is using an air pump to create a vacuum in a small glass container holding a bird, which, deprived of oxygen, is going into convulsions. The crowd gathered for the experiment displays a range of reactions, from horror to intense interest to complete indifference.

The experiment does not seem to serve any valid scientific purpose. Though even before this time air pumps had been used by the English physicist and chemist Robert Boyle (1627–1691) and others in important research, this experiment takes place not in a laboratory or another controlled environment that would allow it to yield useful data but in a private home, apparently for entertainment. The spectators are not students or colleagues of the scientist, and the exotic bird in the container—a cockatoo—is not well suited for this kind of experiment: it is far too rare and expensive to use as a research subject. The entire display seems designed as a scientific-themed sideshow with no real value for the production or dissemination of knowledge. Both the experiment and the reactions of the crowd work allegorically to capture a number of contradictory attitudes about science during the eighteenth century.

JOSEPH WRIGHT OF DERBY
An Experiment on a Bird in the Air Pump, 1768 (oil on canvas).
National Gallery, London, UK / Bridgeman Art Library.
See p. C–7 in the color insert for a full-color reproduction of this image.

UNDERSTANDING THE TEXT

1. How does each spectator project or represent a possible opinion about science?

2. Does the scientist seem more like an experimenter or a showman? What might Joseph Wright of Derby be suggesting about science through this figure?

3. Why does the painting focus on an act of cruelty that does not seem to have any scientific value?

4. How does the lighting of the picture function symbolically? What is the symbolic significance of the candle on the table?

5. Why is the servant lowering the curtain? How might this act figure into the symbolic drama?

6. What overall view of scientific experimentation, progress, and technology comes through in the painting?

MAKING CONNECTIONS

1. Compare the scientist in *An Experiment on a Bird in the Air Pump* with Liberty in *Liberty Leading the People* (p. 494). If both figures symbolize revolutions, one scientific and one political, could both paintings be considered "revolutionary"?

2. *An Experiment on a Bird in the Air Pump* dates from about the same time as Hogarth's *Gin Lane* (p. 548). Compare these works' treatments of the Scientific and Industrial Revolutions and of those revolutions' effects on society.

WRITING ABOUT THE TEXT

1. Using *An Experiment on a Bird in the Air Pump* as a model, choose a contemporary scientific discovery or new field of inquiry, such as cloning, genetic engineering, or virtual reality, and propose an allegorical artwork conveying that phenomenon and responses to it.

2. Translate the symbolism in *An Experiment on a Bird in the Air Pump*—the use of light and darkness, the figures, the allegorical significance—into words.

3. Consider *An Experiment on a Bird in the Air Pump* in terms of research involving animals, which sometimes results in injury or death. Is the acquisition of knowledge always worth the costs?

4. How might Wright's portrayal of the scientist as entertainer apply to contemporary scientists? Read and contrast media portraits of, for example, laboratory researchers and the authors of books that popularize scientific ideas. Does showmanship invalidate good science?

WILLIAM PALEY
from *Natural Theology*
[1802]

WILLIAM PALEY (1743–1805) was born in Peterborough, England, where his father was a schoolmaster. He studied at Christ's College of Cambridge University and was later elected to be a fellow there, where he taught a course on moral philosophy. He later published his lectures in book form as *Principles of Moral and Political Philosophy* (1786), which became required reading at Cambridge and was one of the bestselling works of philosophy in Britain.

But it was in the field of Christian apologetics—the branch of theology devoted to making factual, historical, or scientific arguments for the truth of Christianity—that Paley was to make his greatest mark. His book *View of the Evidences of Christianity* (1794) was required reading for all students at Cambridge well into the twentieth century. Among its most fervent admirers was the young Charles Darwin, who studied at Christ's College in the 1820s. The popularity of this book led Paley to receive several prestigious ecclesiastical appointments.

Paley's most famous book, and the one that would shape debates between science and religion for more than 200 years, is *Natural Theology* (1802). In it, Paley argues that all of creation points to a benevolent creator who wants human beings to be happy. He argues for the existence of a creator using God's creations as evidence. The selection here—the most famous passage in the book—argues that a traveler discovering a watch on the ground would immediately assume that somebody had created it. Similarly, when we consider the true complexities of nature, we must assume the existence of a creator of the world.

Like most of the ideas in *Natural Theology*, the notion of God as a watchmaker did not originate with William Paley. Eighteenth-century deists such as Thomas Jefferson had employed the imagery of a watchmaker or clockmaker God for years. But Paley excelled in identifying the strongest arguments, stripping them of unnecessary commentary, and presenting them to common readers as brief, understandable, and rhetorically powerful. As such, his work offers the most powerful argument for the existence of God to come out of Enlightenment Europe.

State of the Argument

In crossing a heath, suppose I pitched my foot against a *stone*, and were asked how the stone came to be there, I might possibly answer, that for any thing I knew to the contrary it had lain there for ever; nor would it, perhaps, be very easy to show the absurdity of this answer. But suppose I had found a *watch* upon the ground, and it should be inquired how the watch happened to be in that place, I should hardly think of the answer which I had before given, that for any thing I knew the watch might have always been there. Yet why should not this answer serve for the watch as well as for the stone; why is it not as admissible in the second case as in the first? For this reason, and for no other, namely, that when we come to inspect the watch, we perceive—what we could not discover in the stone—that its several parts are framed and put together for a purpose, *e.g.* that they are so formed and adjusted as to produce motion, and that motion so regulated as to point out the hour of the day; that if the different parts had been differently shaped from what they are, or placed after any other manner or in any other order than that in which they are placed, either no motion at all would have been carried on in the machine, or none which would have answered the use that is now served by it. To reckon up a few of the plainest of these parts and of their offices, all tending to one result: We see a cylindrical box containing a coiled elastic spring, which, by its endeavor to relax itself, turns round the box. We next observe a flexible chain—artificially wrought for the sake of flexure—communicating the action of the spring from the box to the fusee. We then find a series of wheels, the teeth of which catch in and apply to each other, conducting the motion from the fusee to the balance and from the balance to the pointer, and at the same time, by the size and shape of those wheels, so regulating that motion as to terminate in causing an index, by an equable and measured progression, to pass over a given space in a given time. We take notice that the wheels are made of brass, in order to keep them from rust; the springs of steel, no other metal being so elastic; that over the face of the watch there is placed a glass, a material employed in no other part of the work, but in the room of which, if there had been any other than a transparent substance, the hour could not be seen without opening the case. This mechanism being observed—it requires indeed an examination of the instrument, and perhaps some previous knowledge of the subject, to perceive and understand it; but being once, as we have said, observed and understood, the inference we think is inevitable, that the watch must have had a maker—that there must have existed, at some time and at some place or other, an artificer or artificers who formed it for the purpose which we find it actually to answer, who comprehended its construction and designed its use.

UNDERSTANDING THE TEXT

1. Why does Paley first talk about finding a stone and then discuss finding a watch? What is the rhetorical effect of the contrast between the stone and the watch?

2. What are the essential characteristics of the watch that set it apart from a natural object such as a stone?

3. What kinds of knowledge does one need to have in order to understand the purpose of a watch? What kinds of comparable knowledge does one need to understand the workings of nature?

4. Do you agree with Paley's conclusion, that the existence of a watch implies the exist-
    ence of a watchmaker? Do you agree with the implied conclusion that the existence
    of the world implies a God? Why or why not?

MAKING CONNECTIONS

1. Compare Paley's view of nature with Lucretius's view of natural harmony (p. 292).
    Where would Lucretius be most likely to disagree with Paley?

2. Charles Darwin was an admirer of Paley's work, yet *Origin of Species* (p. 314) is now
    often presented as a refutation of *Natural Theology*. Do you believe that the views of
    Darwin and Paley can be reconciled?

WRITING ABOUT THE TEXT

1. Compare and contrast Lucretius's opinion that there is too much wrong with the
    world for it to have been made by the gods (p. 292) with Paley's opinion that the
    world shows too much evidence of design not to have been made by a god. Write
    a paper supporting one of these views and disagreeing with the other, and explain
    your reasoning.

2. Compare the way that Paley uses a parable to make a point with the way that Jesus
    uses parables in the New Testament (p. 541) or Plato uses allegories in "The Speech
    of Aristophanes" (p. 74). Explain the rhetorical value of using stories and examples to
    prove a point.

3. Write a research paper that explores the current debate about teaching evolution
    and intelligent design in public schools. Trace the way that current theories of intel-
    ligent design relate to the theories of William Paley and his contemporaries.

CHARLES DARWIN

from *Natural Selection; or, the Survival of the Fittest*

[1859]

THOUGH CHARLES DARWIN (1809–1882) was one of the most famous naturalists in world history, he originally studied theology and medicine. After an unremarkable undergraduate career at Cambridge University, he took the job of ship's naturalist on the H.M.S. *Beagle*, a scientific survey vessel that from 1831 to 1836 charted navigable waters throughout South America, the Pacific Islands, and Australia. At some points on this journey, Darwin observed enormous variations in species in environments that were separated from each other by only a few miles. These variations inspired him to formulate a theory of how organisms might evolve through time to adapt to their environment.

Contrary to popular belief, Darwin did not originate the theory of evolution. Many scientists in Darwin's time accepted the idea that organisms evolved through gradual changes over time, but they did not understand the mechanism that produced those changes. Before Darwin, the most widely accepted theory was that of the French naturalist Jean-Baptiste Lamarck (1744–1829), who speculated that organisms acquired slight useful modifications during their lifetimes and passed them on to their offspring, resulting in gradual change over time.

Darwin, however, theorized that changes in a species resulted from a mechanism that he called "natural selection." Working from the understanding that variations exist in all species, Darwin reasoned that naturally occurring variations within species sometimes give an organism distinct advantages in the competition for resources. These advantages might help the organism find food or defend itself from predators, thus allowing it to survive long enough to reproduce; or they might help the organism attract a mate or disseminate its seeds. In either case, an organism with an advantageous variation will have more reproductive success, and that variation will eventually become a more prominent characteristic of the species.

Darwin was influenced by the work of Thomas Malthus, whose "Essay on the Principle of Population" argued that people tend to produce more offspring than local resources can support. He also benefited from the work of nineteenth-century geologists such as Sir Charles Lyell (1797–1875), who demonstrated that the earth was millions of times older than had previously been imagined. Darwin understood that his work would be opposed by those who believed that God created all the individual species of plants and animals—including human beings—and these concerns probably influenced his decision to delay the publication of his theories until more than twenty years after he formulated them. Though his book *The Origin of Species*—of which "Natural Selection" is the fourth chapter—encountered resistance on religious grounds when it was published, and continues to do so today in some places, the scientific community has accepted natural selection as the mechanism by which organisms on Earth adapt and change.

Unlike the earlier writers in this chapter, who make deductive arguments about nature by beginning with general principles derived from religious or classical sources, Darwin's arguments are primarily inductive. He begins with specific observations about nature that have not been sufficiently explained in previous theories and then draws general principles from those observations to create a new explanation.

How will the struggle for existence . . . act in regard to variation? Can the principle of selection, which . . . is so potent in the hands of man, apply under nature? I think we shall see that it can act most efficiently. Let the endless number of slight variations and individual differences occurring in our domestic productions, and, in a lesser degree, in those under nature, be borne in mind; as well as the strength of the hereditary tendency. Under domestication, it may be truly said that the whole organisation becomes in some degree plastic. But the variability, which we almost universally meet with in our domestic productions, is not directly produced, as Hooker and Asa Gray[1] have well remarked, by man; he can neither originate varieties, nor prevent their occurrence; he can preserve and accumulate such as do occur. Unintentionally he exposes organic beings to new and changing conditions of life, and variability ensues; but similar changes of conditions might and do occur under nature. Let it also be borne in mind how infinitely complex and close-fitting are the mutual relations of all organic beings to each other and to their physical conditions of life; and consequently what infinitely varied diversities of structure might be of use to each being under changing conditions of life. Can it, then, be thought improbable, seeing that variations useful to man have undoubtedly occurred, that other variations useful in some way to each being in the great and complex battle of life, should occur in the course of many successive generations? If such do occur, can we doubt (remembering that many more individuals are born than can possibly survive) that individuals having any advantage, however slight, over others, would have the best chance of surviving and of procreating their kind? On the other hand, we may feel sure that any variation in the least degree injurious would be rigidly destroyed. This preservation of favourable individual differences and variations, and the destruction of those which are injurious, I have called Natural Selection, or the Survival of the Fittest. Variations neither useful nor injurious would not be affected by natural selection, and would be left either a fluctuating element, as perhaps we see in certain polymorphic species,[2] or would ultimately become fixed, owing to the nature of the organism and the nature of the conditions.

1. **Hooker and Asa Gray:** Sir Joseph Dalton Hooker (1817–1911) was an English botanist; Asa Gray (1810–1888) was an American botanist and a professor at Harvard University. Both were friends of Darwin and early champions of the theory of evolution by natural selection.

2. **Polymorphic species:** species in which an individual changes form during its lifetime, such as frogs and butterflies.

Several writers have misapprehended or objected to the term Natural Selection. Some have even imagined that natural selection induces variability, whereas it implies only the preservation of such variations as arise and are beneficial to the being under its conditions of life. No one objects to agriculturists speaking of the potent effects of man's selection; and in this case the individual differences given by nature, which man for some object selects, must of necessity first occur. Others have objected that the term selection implies conscious choice in the animals which become modified; and it has even been urged that, as plants have no volition, natural selection is not applicable to them! In the literal sense of the word, no doubt, natural selection is a false term; but who ever objected to chemists speaking of the elective affinities[3] of the various elements?—and yet an acid cannot strictly be said to elect the base with which it in preference combines. It has been said that I speak of natural selection as an active power or Deity; but who objects to an author speaking of the attraction of gravity as ruling the movements of the planets? Every one knows what is meant and is implied by such metaphorical expressions; and they are almost necessary for brevity. So again it is difficult to avoid personifying the word Nature; but I mean by Nature, only the aggregate action and product of many natural laws, and by laws the sequence of events as ascertained by us. With a little familiarity such superficial objections will be forgotten.

We shall best understand the probable course of natural selection by taking the case of a country undergoing some slight physical change, for instance, of climate. The proportional numbers of its inhabitants will almost immediately undergo a change, and some species will probably become extinct. We may conclude, from what we have seen of the intimate and complex manner in which the inhabitants of each country are bound together, that any change in the numerical proportions of the inhabitants, independently of the change of climate itself, would seriously affect the others. If the country were open on its borders, new forms would certainly immigrate, and this would likewise seriously disturb the relations of some of the former inhabitants. Let it be remembered how powerful the influence of a single introduced tree or mammal has been shown to be. But in the case of an island, or of a country partly surrounded by barriers, into which new and better adapted forms could not freely enter, we should then have places in the economy of nature which would assuredly be better filled up, if some of the original inhabitants were in some manner modified; for, had the area been open to immigration, these same places would have been seized on by intruders. In such cases, slight modifications, which in any way favoured the individuals of any species, by better adapting them to their altered conditions, would tend to be preserved; and natural selection would have free scope for the work of improvement.

3. **Elective affinities:** a term from eighteenth- and early-nineteenth-century chemistry regarding chemical compounds that interacted with each other only in certain circumstances. Darwin's point is that, like this term, "natural selection" can be taken to attribute humanlike qualities to abstract nature, but in both cases the attribute of intentional selection or election is simply a metaphor.

We have good reason to believe . . . that changes in the conditions of life give a tendency to increased variability; and in the foregoing cases the conditions have changed, and this would manifestly be favourable to natural selection, by affording a better chance of the occurrence of profitable variations. Unless such occur, natural selection can do nothing. Under the term of "variations," it must never be forgotten that mere individual differences are included. As man can produce a great result with his domestic animals and plants by adding up in any given direction individual differences, so could natural selection, but far more easily from having incomparably longer time for action. Nor do I believe that any great physical change, as of climate, or any unusual degree of isolation to check immigration, is necessary in order that new and unoccupied places should be left, for natural selection to fill up by improving some of the varying inhabitants. For as all the inhabitants of each country are struggling together with nicely balanced forces, extremely slight modifications in the structure or habits of one species would often give it an advantage over others; and still further modifications of the same kind would often still further increase the advantage, as long as the species continued under the same conditions of life and profited by similar means of subsistence and defence. No country can be named in which all the native inhabitants are now so perfectly adapted to each other and to the physical conditions under which they live, that none of them could be still better adapted or improved; for in all countries, the natives have been so far conquered by naturalised productions, that they have allowed some foreigners to take firm possession of the land. And as foreigners have thus in every country beaten some of the natives, we may safely conclude that the natives might have been modified with advantage, so as to have better resisted the intruders.

As man can produce, and certainly has produced, a great result by his methodical and unconscious means of selection, what may not natural selection effect? Man can act only on external and visible characters: Nature, if I may be allowed to personify the natural preservation or survival of the fittest, cares nothing for appearances, except in so far as they are useful to any being. She can act on every internal organ, on every shade of constitutional difference, on the whole machinery of life. Man selects only for his own good: Nature only for that of the being which she tends. Every selected character is fully exercised by her, as is implied by the fact of their selection. Man keeps the natives of many climates in the same country; he seldom exercises each selected character in some peculiar and fitting manner; he feeds a long and a short beaked pigeon on the same food; he does not exercise a long-backed or long-legged quadruped in any peculiar manner; he exposes sheep with long and short wool to the same climate. He does not allow the most vigorous males to struggle for the females. He does not rigidly destroy all inferior animals, but protects during each varying season, as far as lies in his power, all his productions. He often begins his selection by some half-monstrous form; or at least by some modification prominent enough to catch the eye or to be plainly useful to him. Under Nature, the slightest

5

differences of structure or constitution may well turn the nicely balanced scale in the struggle for life, and so be preserved. How fleeting are the wishes and efforts of man! how short his time! and consequently how poor will be his results, compared with those accumulated by Nature during whole geological periods! Can we wonder, then, that Nature's productions should be far "truer" in character than man's productions; that they should be infinitely better adapted to the most complex conditions of life, and should plainly bear the stamp of far higher workmanship?

It may metaphorically be said that natural selection is daily and hourly scrutinising, throughout the world, the slightest variations; rejecting those that are bad, preserving and adding up all that are good; silently and insensibly working, *whenever and wherever opportunity offers*, at the improvement of each organic being in relation to its organic and inorganic conditions of life. We see nothing of these slow changes in progress, until the hand of time has marked the lapse of ages, and then so imperfect is our view into long-past geological ages, that we see only that the forms of life are now different from what they formerly were.

In order that any great amount of modification should be effected in a species, a variety when once formed must again, perhaps after a long interval of time, vary or present individual differences of the same favourable nature as before; and these must be again preserved, and so onwards step by step. Seeing that individual differences of the same kind perpetually recur, this can hardly be considered as an unwarrantable assumption. But whether it is true, we can judge only by seeing how far the hypothesis accords with and explains the general phenomena of nature. On the other hand, the ordinary belief that the amount of possible variation is a strictly limited quantity is likewise a simple assumption.

Although natural selection can act only through and for the good of each being, yet characters and structures, which we are apt to consider as of very trifling importance, may thus be acted on. When we see leaf-eating insects green, and bark-feeders mottled-grey; the alpine ptarmigan[4] white in winter, the red-grouse the colour of heather, we must believe that these tints are of service to these birds and insects in preserving them from danger. Grouse, if not destroyed at some period of their lives, would increase in countless numbers; they are known to suffer largely from birds of prey; and hawks are guided by eyesight to their prey—so much so, that on parts of the Continent persons are warned not to keep white pigeons, as being the most liable to destruction. Hence natural selection might be effective in giving the proper colour to each kind of grouse, and in keeping that colour, when once acquired, true and constant. Nor ought we to think that the occasional destruction of an animal of any particular colour would produce little effect: we should remember how essential it is in a flock of white sheep to destroy a lamb with the faintest trace of black. We have seen how the colour of the hogs, which feed on the

4. **Ptarmigan:** a bird, belonging to the grouse family, that lives mainly in cold climates; members of the species have various colors during most of the year, but all turn white during the winter, enabling them to blend in with snow.

"paint-root"[5] in Virginia, determines whether they shall live or die. In plants, the down on the fruit and the colour of the flesh are considered by botanists as characters of the most trifling importance; yet we hear from an excellent horticulturist, Downing,[6] that in the United States, smooth-skinned fruits suffer far more from a beetle, a Curculio,[7] than those with down; that purple plums suffer far more from a certain disease than yellow plums; whereas another disease attacks yellow-fleshed peaches far more than those with other coloured flesh. If, with all the aids of art, these slight differences make a great difference in cultivating the several varieties, assuredly, in a state of nature, where the trees would have to struggle with other trees, and with a host of enemies, such differences would effectually settle which variety, whether a smooth or downy, a yellow or purple fleshed fruit, should succeed.

In looking at many small points of difference between species, which, as far as our ignorance permits us to judge, seem quite unimportant, we must not forget that climate, food, &c., have no doubt produced some direct effect. It is also necessary to bear in mind that, owing to the law of correlation, when one part varies, and the variations are accumulated through natural selection, other modifications, often of the most unexpected nature, will ensue.

As we see that those variations which, under domestication, appear at any   10 particular period of life, tend to reappear in the offspring at the same period;—for instance, in the shape, size, and flavour of the seeds of the many varieties of our culinary and agricultural plants; in the caterpillar and cocoon stages of the varieties of the silk-worm; in the eggs of poultry, and in the colour of the down of their chickens; in the horns of our sheep and cattle when nearly adult;—so in a state of nature natural selection will be enabled to act on and modify organic beings at any age, by the accumulation of variations profitable at that age, and by their inheritance at a corresponding age. If it profit a plant to have its seeds more and more widely disseminated by the wind, I can see no greater difficulty in this being effected through natural selection, than in the cotton-planter increasing and improving by selection the down in the pods on his cotton-trees. Natural selection may modify and adapt the larva of an insect to a score of contingencies, wholly different from those which concern the mature insect; and these modifications may affect, through correlation, the structure of the adult. So, conversely, modifications in the adult may affect the structure of the larva; but in all cases natural selection will ensure that they shall not be injurious: for if they were so, the species would become extinct.

5. **Paint-root:** a plant that grows in marshy areas along the eastern coast of North America. According to some evidence with which Darwin was familiar, the plant is poisonous to pigs with light skin but edible by those with dark skin, causing most of the pigs in the regions where the plant grows to be dark.

6. **Downing:** Andrew Jackson Downing (1815–1852), American landscaper and horticulturalist.

7. **Curculio:** a type of snout beetle that causes significant damage in peach, plum, cherry, and apple orchards in the United States.

Natural selection will modify the structure of the young in relation to the parent, and of the parent in relation to the young. In social animals it will adapt the structure of each individual for the benefit of the whole community; if the community profits by the selected change. What natural selection cannot do, is to modify the structure of one species, without giving it any advantage, for the good of another species; and though statements to this effect may be found in works of natural history, I cannot find one case which will bear investigation. A structure used only once in an animal's life, if of high importance to it, might be modified to any extent by natural selection; for instance, the great jaws possessed by certain insects, used exclusively for opening the cocoon—or the hard tip to the beak of unhatched birds, used for breaking the egg. It has been asserted, that of the best short-beaked tumbler-pigeons a greater number perish in the egg than are able to get out of it; so that fanciers assist in the act of hatching. Now if nature had to make the beak of a full-grown pigeon very short for the bird's own advantage, the process of modification would be very slow, and there would be simultaneously the most rigorous selection of all the young birds within the egg, which had the most powerful and hardest beaks, for all with weak beaks would inevitably perish; or, more delicate and more easily broken shells might be selected, the thickness of the shell being known to vary like every other structure.

It may be well here to remark that with all beings there must be much fortuitous destruction, which can have little or no influence on the course of natural selection. For instance a vast number of eggs or seeds are annually devoured, and these could be modified through natural selection only if they varied in some manner which protected them from their enemies. Yet many of these eggs or seeds would perhaps, if not destroyed, have yielded individuals better adapted to their conditions of life than any of those which happened to survive. So again a vast number of mature animals and plants, whether or not they be the best adapted to their conditions, must be annually destroyed by accidental causes, which would not be in the least degree mitigated by certain changes of structure or constitution which would in other ways be beneficial to the species. But let the destruction of the adults be ever so heavy, if the number which can exist in any district be not wholly kept down by such causes,—or again let the destruction of eggs or seeds be so great that only a hundredth or a thousandth part are developed,—yet of those which do survive, the best adapted individuals, supposing that there is any variability in a favourable direction, will tend to propagate their kind in larger numbers than the less well adapted. If the numbers be wholly kept down by the causes just indicated, as will often have been the case, natural selection will be powerless in certain beneficial directions; but this is no valid objection to its efficiency at other times and in other ways; for we are far from having any reason to suppose that many species ever undergo modification and improvement at the same time in the same area.

Sexual Selection

Inasmuch as peculiarities often appear under domestication in one sex and become hereditarily attached to that sex, so no doubt it will be under nature. Thus it is rendered possible for the two sexes to be modified through natural selection in relation to different habits of life, as is sometimes the case, or for one sex to be modified in relation to the other sex, as commonly occurs. This leads me to say a few words on what I have called Sexual Selection. This form of selection depends, not on a struggle for existence in relation to other organic beings or to external conditions, but on a struggle between the individuals of one sex, generally the males, for the possession of the other sex. The result is not death to the unsuccessful competitor, but few or no offspring. Sexual selection is, therefore, less rigorous than natural selection. Generally, the most vigorous males, those which are best fitted for their places in nature, will leave most progeny. But in many cases, victory depends not so much on general vigor, as on having special weapons, confined to the male sex. A hornless stag or spurless cock would have a poor chance of leaving numerous offspring. Sexual selection, by always allowing the victor to breed, might surely give indomitable courage, length to the spur, and strength to the wing to strike in the spurred leg, in nearly the same manner as does the brutal cock-fighter by the careful selection of his best cocks. How low in the scale of nature the law of battle descends, I know not; male alligators have been described as fighting, bellowing, and whirling round, like Indians in a war-dance, for the possession of the females; male salmons have been observed fighting all day long; male stag-beetles sometimes bear wounds from the huge mandibles of other males; the males of certain hymenopterous insects[8] have been frequently seen by that inimitable observer M. Fabre,[9] fighting for a particular female who sits by, an apparently unconcerned beholder of the struggle, and then retires with the conqueror. The war is, perhaps, severest between the males of polygamous animals, and these seem oftenest provided with special weapons. The males of carnivorous animals are already well armed; though to them and to others, special means of defence may be given through means of sexual selection, as the mane of the lion, and the hooked jaw to the male salmon; for the shield may be as important for victory, as the sword or spear.

Amongst birds, the contest is often of a more peaceful character. All those who have attended to the subject, believe that there is the severest rivalry between the males of many species to attract, by singing, the females. The rock-thrush of Guiana, birds of paradise, and some others, congregate; and successive males display with the most elaborate care, and show off in the best manner, their gorgeous plumage; they likewise perform strange antics before the females, which,

8. **Hymenopterous insects:** members of the hymenoptera order, which includes wasps, bees, and ants.

9. **M. Fabre:** Jean-Henri Fabre (1823–1915), French botanist and etymologist.

standing by as spectators, at last choose the most attractive partner. Those who have closely attended to birds in confinement well know that they often take individual preferences and dislikes: thus Sir R. Heron[10] has described how a pied[11] peacock was eminently attractive to all his hen birds. I cannot here enter on the necessary details; but if man can in a short time give beauty and an elegant carriage to his bantams, according to his standard of beauty, I can see no good reason to doubt that female birds, by selecting, during thousands of generations, the most melodious or beautiful males according to their standard of beauty, might produce a marked effect. Some well-known laws, with respect to the plumage of male and female birds, in comparison with the plumage of the young, can partly be explained through the action of sexual selection on variations occurring at different ages, and transmitted to the males alone or to both sexes at corresponding ages; but I have not space here to enter on this subject.

Thus it is, as I believe, that when the males and females of any animal have the   15
same general habits of life, but differ in structure, colour, or ornament, such differences have been mainly caused by sexual selection: that is, by individual males having had, in successive generations, some slight advantage over other males, in their weapons, means of defence, or charms, which they have transmitted to their male offspring alone. Yet, I would not wish to attribute all sexual differences to this agency: for we see in our domestic animals peculiarities arising and becoming attached to the male sex, which apparently have not been augmented through selection by man. The tuft of hair on the breast of the wild turkey-cock cannot be of any use, and it is doubtful whether it can be ornamental in the eyes of the female bird;—indeed, had the tuft appeared under domestication, it would have been called a monstrosity.

Illustrations of the Action of Natural Selection, or the Survival of the Fittest

In order to make it clear how, as I believe, natural selection acts, I must beg permission to give one or two imaginary illustrations. Let us take the case of a wolf, which preys on various animals, securing some by craft, some by strength, and some by fleetness; and let us suppose that the fleetest prey, a deer for instance, had from any change in the country increased in numbers, or that other prey had decreased in numbers, during that season of the year when the wolf was hardest pressed for food. Under such circumstances the swiftest and slimmest wolves would have the best chance of surviving and so be preserved or selected,—provided always that they retained strength to master their prey at this or some other period of the year, when they were compelled to prey on other animals. I can see no more reason to doubt that

10. **Sir R. Heron:** Sir Robert Heron (1765–1854), an English politician with whom Darwin maintained a correspondence.

11. **Pied:** spotted, patched.

this would be the result, than that man should be able to improve the fleetness of his greyhounds by careful and methodical selection, or by that kind of unconscious selection which follows from each man trying to keep the best dogs without any thought of modifying the breed. I may add, that, according to Mr. Pierce, there are two varieties of the wolf inhabiting the Catskill Mountains, in the United States, one with a light greyhound-like form, which pursues deer, and the other more bulky, with shorter legs, which more frequently attacks the shepherd's flocks. . . .

It may be worth while to give another and more complex illustration of the action of natural selection. Certain plants excrete sweet juice, apparently for the sake of eliminating something injurious from the sap: this is effected, for instance, by glands at the base of the stipules in some Leguminosæ,[12] and at the backs of the leaves of the common laurel. This juice, though small in quantity, is greedily sought by insects; but their visits do not in any way benefit the plant. Now, let us suppose that the juice or nectar was excreted from the inside of the flowers of a certain number of plants of any species. Insects in seeking the nectar would get dusted with pollen, and would often transport it from one flower to another. The flowers of two distinct individuals of the same species would thus get crossed; and the act of crossing, as can be fully proved, gives rise to vigorous seedlings which consequently would have the best chance of flourishing and surviving. The plants which produced flowers with the largest glands or nectaries, excreting most nectar, would oftenest be visited by insects, and would oftenest be crossed; and so in the long-run would gain the upper hand and form a local variety. The flowers, also, which had their stamens and pistils[13] placed, in relation to the size and habits of the particular insects which visited them, so as to favour in any degree the transportal of the pollen, would likewise be favoured. We might have taken the case of insects visiting flowers for the sake of collecting pollen instead of nectar; and as pollen is formed for the sole purpose of fertilisation, its destruction appears to be a simple loss to the plant; yet if a little pollen were carried, at first occasionally and then habitually, by the pollen-devouring insects from flower to flower, and a cross thus effected, although nine-tenths of the pollen were destroyed it might still be a great gain to the plant to be thus robbed; and the individuals which produced more and more pollen, and had larger anthers, would be selected.

When our plant, by the above process long continued, had been rendered highly attractive to insects, they would, unintentionally on their part, regularly carry pollen from flower to flower; and that they do this effectually, I could easily show by many striking facts. I will give only one, as likewise illustrating one step in the separation of the sexes of plants. Some holly-trees bear only male flowers, which have four

---

12. **Leguminosæ:** a family of plants that includes more than eighteen thousand species, the most well-known of which are beans, peas, soybeans, lentils, alfalfa, and clover. **Stipules:** small outgrowths on the base of a leaf.

13. **Stamens and pistils:** parts of the reproductive system of plants. The **stamen** is the male organ that produces pollen; the **pistil** is the female organ that receives pollen; the **anther** (below) is part of the stamen that contains the pollen.

stamens producing a rather small quantity of pollen, and a rudimentary pistil: other holly-trees bear only female flowers; these have a full-sized pistil, and four stamens with shrivelled anthers, in which not a grain of pollen can be detected. Having found a female tree exactly sixty yards from a male tree, I put the stigmas of twenty flowers, taken from different branches, under the microscope, and on all, without exception, there were a few pollen-grains, and on some a profusion. As the wind had set for several days from the female to the male tree, the pollen could not thus have been carried. The weather had been cold and boisterous, and therefore not favourable to bees, nevertheless every female flower which I examined had been effectually fertilised by the bees, which had flown from tree to tree in search of nectar. But to return to our imaginary case: as soon as the plant had been rendered so highly attractive to insects that pollen was regularly carried from flower to flower, another process might commence. No naturalist doubts the advantage of what has been called the "physiological division of labour"; hence we may believe that it would be advantageous to a plant to produce stamens alone in one flower or on one whole plant, and pistils alone in another flower or on another plant. In plants under culture and placed under new conditions of life, sometimes the male organs and sometimes the female organs become more or less impotent; now if we suppose this to occur in ever so slight a degree under nature, then, as pollen is already carried regularly from flower to flower, and as a more complete separation of the sexes of our plant would be advantageous on the principle of the division of labour, individuals with this tendency more and more increased, would be continually favoured or selected, until at last a complete separation of the sexes might be effected. It would take up too much space to show the various steps, through dimorphism and other means, by which the separation of the sexes in plants of various kinds is apparently now in progress; but I may add that some of the species of holly in North America, are, according to Asa Gray, in an exactly intermediate condition, or, as he expresses it, are more or less diœciously polygamous.[14]

Let us now turn to the nectar-feeding insects; we may suppose the plant, of which we have been slowly increasing the nectar by continued selection, to be a common plant; and that certain insects depended in main part on its nectar for food. I could give many facts showing how anxious bees are to save time: for instance, their habit of cutting holes and sucking the nectar at the bases of certain flowers, which, with a very little more trouble, they can enter by the mouth. Bearing such facts in mind, it may be believed that under certain circumstances individual differences in the curvature or length of the proboscis, &c., too slight to be appreciated by us, might profit a bee or other insect, so that certain individuals would be able to obtain their food more quickly than others; and thus the communities to which they belonged would flourish and throw off many swarms inheriting the same peculiarities. The tubes

14. **Diœciously:** referring to a characteristic within plant species of having the male and female reproductive parts carried separately by different plants. **Dimorphism:** the existence of two distinctive forms within the same species.

of the corolla of the common red and incarnate clovers (Trifolium pratense and incarnatum) do not on a hasty glance appear to differ in length; yet the hive-bee can easily suck the nectar out of the incarnate clover, but not out of the common red clover, which is visited by humble-bees alone; so that whole fields of red clover offer in vain an abundant supply of precious nectar to the hive-bee. That this nectar is much liked by the hive-bee is certain; for I have repeatedly seen, but only in the autumn, many hive-bees sucking the flowers through holes bitten in the base of the tube by humble-bees. The difference in the length of the corolla in the two kinds of clover, which determines the visits of the hive-bee, must be very trifling; for I have been assured that when red clover has been mown, the flowers of the second crop are somewhat smaller, and that these are visited by many hive-bees. I do not know whether this statement is accurate; nor whether another published statement can be trusted, namely, that the Ligurian bee which is generally considered a mere variety of the common hive-bee, and which freely crosses with it, is able to reach and suck the nectar of the red clover. Thus, in a country where this kind of clover abounded, it might be a great advantage to the hive-bee to have a slightly longer or differently constructed proboscis. On the other hand, as the fertility of this clover absolutely depends on bees visiting the flowers, if humble-bees were to become rare in any country, it might be a great advantage to the plant to have a shorter or more deeply divided corolla, so that the hive-bees should be enabled to suck its flowers. Thus I can understand how a flower and a bee might slowly become, either simultaneously or one after the other, modified and adapted to each other in the most perfect manner, by the continued preservation of all the individuals which presented slight deviations of structure mutually favourable to each other.

I am well aware that this doctrine of natural selection, exemplified in the above imaginary instances, is open to the same objections which were first urged against Sir Charles Lyell's[15] noble views on "the modern changes of the earth, as illustrative of geology"; but we now seldom hear the agencies which we see still at work, spoken of as trifling or insignificant, when used in explaining the excavation of the deepest valleys or the formation of long lines of inland cliffs. Natural selection acts only by the preservation and accumulation of small inherited modifications, each profitable to the preserved being; and as modern geology has almost banished such views as the excavation of a great valley by a single diluvial[16] wave, so will natural selection banish the belief of the continued creation of new organic beings, or of any great and sudden modification in their structure.

20

15. **Sir Charles Lyell:** English geologist (1797–1875), whose book *Principles of Geology* postulated that the earth was millions, rather than thousands, of years old. Lyell claimed that great changes in the earth's structure resulted from natural forces acting gradually over long periods of time.

16. **Diluvial:** relating to a flood. Darwin here alludes to the Christian belief that major geological changes in the earth can be attributed to the great flood described in the Book of Genesis.

UNDERSTANDING THE TEXT

1. Why, according to Charles Darwin, is natural variation within species important to evolution? What would happen to a species if all of its members were born with uniform characteristics?

2. Why does Darwin believe that very slight advantages increase an organism's chances to survive? What other factors make this the case? Do you agree?

3. How would natural selection operate without any directive will? What would the selection process entail?

4. What does Darwin mean by "man selects only for his own good"? How does such selection support Darwin's theory?

5. What examples does Darwin give of characteristics that help organisms survive in specific environments? How might an advantage in one environment become a disadvantage in another environment?

6. What does Darwin mean by "sexual selection"? How does this process differ from the kinds of selection that he refers to earlier? Why does he say that it is "less rigorous than natural selection"?

7. What kinds of potential objections does Darwin refer to in the final paragraph of this selection? How do the objections that he expects to be raised against his work resemble those that were raised against Lyell's ideas?

8. Analyze Darwin's use of evidence to prove his points. How effectively do his examples support his argument?

MAKING CONNECTIONS

1. Elsewhere, Darwin reports that Thomas Malthus's "Essay on the Principle of Population" (p. 552) started him thinking about natural selection. How does Darwin draw on Malthus's ideas, especially concerning the competition for resources?

2. How does Darwin's view of the natural world compare with Hobbes's view of the state of nature (p. 94)?

3. How does the concept of natural selection compare with Ruth Benedict's assertions about character traits and culture (p. 112)? In what sense are cultures and societies "environments" that shape their members through natural selection? At what point does such an analogy break down?

4. How is Garrett Hardin's argument in "Lifeboat Ethics" (p. 582) consistent with the theory of natural selection? What role does overpopulation play in the "survival of the fittest"?

WRITING ABOUT THE TEXT

1. Some nineteenth-century commentators argued that the poor are not well-adapted to survive, that perhaps their poverty is a result of their poor adaptation. Does the theory of natural selection support this interpretation? Or is a society's tendency

to support its poorer members an evolutionary advantage, increasing that society's ability to survive? Consider such questions in an essay on poverty and Darwinian theory.

2. Compare Darwin's use of the word "nature" with its uses by Rachel Carson (p. 328), William Paley (p. 311), and Barry Commoner (p. 344). How do subtle differences in the definition of this word lead to very different kinds of arguments?

3. Research the current controversy over teaching evolution in public schools and write an essay outlining the arguments posed by the advocates of the theory of "intelligent design." Is this theory compatible with the theory of natural selection? Why or why not?

RACHEL CARSON
The Obligation to Endure
[1962]

BEFORE SHE TOOK up the problem of chemical pesticides in *Silent Spring*, Rachel Carson (1907–1964) was already a respected scientist and a bestselling author. After earning a master's degree in zoology from Johns Hopkins University in 1932, she spent her early career as an aquatic biologist with the U.S. Bureau of Fisheries and its later incarnation as the Fish and Wildlife Service. In 1949, she rose to the position of chief editor of publications for the Fish and Wildlife Service and published three books about the ocean: *Under the Sea-Wind* (1941), *The Sea Around Us* (1951), and *The Edge of the Sea* (1955). The second of these books won the National Book Award and sold so many copies that Carson was able to give up her job and devote her time to writing.

With the publication of her most famous work, *Silent Spring*, Carson took on the unfamiliar role of social activist. The book began as a magazine article about the environmental impact of pesticides, especially of the compound dichlorodiphenyltrichloroethane, better known as DDT. During and after World War II, DDT had been used throughout the world to control insects, remove disease threats, and increase food production. Carson traced the poisonous effects of DDT and other pesticides through the ecosystem, beginning with plants and insects and moving to fish, birds, wildlife, domestic animals, and finally to people, for whom, Carson argued, DDT was a carcinogen.

When the book was published, the chemical pesticide industry launched a major counterstrike aimed at discrediting Carson. Despite their attack, the book became a phenomenal bestseller and caused millions of Americans to consider the effects of chemicals on their environment. Furthermore, it caused many to reevaluate their faith in technology, scientific progress, and the role of government in protecting their interests.

Carson died of breast cancer in 1964 before she could see the effect of her work on the world. In 1972, largely because of *Silent Spring*, the Environmental Protection Agency banned the use of DDT. In 1980, Carson was posthumously awarded the Presidential Medal of Freedom. And in 1999, the Modern Library Editorial Board ranked *Silent Spring* as one of the most important nonfiction books of the twentieth century.

Carson's accomplishment in *Silent Spring*, the second chapter of which follows, goes beyond exposing the dangers of pesticides. The portrait that she created of a deeply interconnected natural world, where changes to one species have far-reaching, unforeseen consequences for the entire ecological system, struck a deep chord with her readers and even changed their perception of nature. Today, many consider the publication of *Silent Spring* to mark the beginning of the modern environmental movement.

Carson's claim about the dangers of chemicals is primarily supported by facts and statistics. She links together a series of historical and scientific facts to focus readers' attention on the negative consequences of using chemicals—chemicals previously viewed by many in only a positive light.

The history of life on earth has been a history of interaction between living things and their surroundings. To a large extent, the physical form and the habits of the earth's vegetation and its animal life have been molded by the environment. Considering the whole span of earthly time, the opposite effect, in which life actually modifies its surroundings, has been relatively slight. Only within the moment of time represented by the present century has one species—man—acquired significant power to alter the nature of his world.

During the past quarter century this power has not only increased to one of disturbing magnitude but it has changed in character. The most alarming of all man's assaults upon the environment is the contamination of air, earth, rivers, and sea with dangerous and even lethal materials. This pollution is for the most part irrecoverable; the chain of evil it initiates not only in the world that must support life but in living tissues is for the most part irreversible. In this now universal contamination of the environment, chemicals are the sinister and little-recognized partners of radiation in changing the very nature of the world—the very nature of its life. Strontium 90, released through nuclear explosions into the air, comes to earth in rain or drifts down as fallout, lodges in soil, enters into the grass or corn or wheat grown there, and in time takes up its abode in the bones of a human being, there to remain until his death. Similarly, chemicals sprayed on croplands or forests or gardens lie long in soil, entering into living organisms, passing from one to another in a chain of poisoning and death. Or they pass mysteriously by underground streams until they emerge and, through the alchemy of air and sunlight, combine into new forms that kill vegetation, sicken cattle, and work unknown harm on those who drink from once pure wells. As Albert Schweitzer[1] has said, "Man can hardly even recognize the devils of his own creation."

It took hundreds of millions of years to produce the life that now inhabits the earth—eons of time in which that developing and evolving and diversifying life reached a state of adjustment and balance with its surroundings. The environment, rigorously shaping and directing the life it supported, contained elements that were hostile as well as supporting. Certain rocks gave out dangerous radiation; even within the light of the sun, from which all life draws its energy, there were short-wave radiations with power to injure. Given time—time not in years but in millennia—life

1. **Albert Schweitzer:** German-Alsatian theologian, philosopher, music scholar, and physician (1875–1965), who won the Nobel Peace Prize in 1952 for his lifelong devotion to providing medical services in Africa.

adjusts, and a balance has been reached. For time is the essential ingredient; but in the modern world there is no time.

The rapidity of change and the speed with which new situations are created follow the impetuous and heedless pace of man rather than the deliberate pace of nature. Radiation is no longer merely the background radiation of rocks, the bombardment of cosmic rays, the ultraviolet of the sun that have existed before there was any life on earth; radiation is now the unnatural creation of man's tampering with the atom. The chemicals to which life is asked to make its adjustment are no longer merely the calcium and silica and copper and all the rest of the minerals washed out of the rocks and carried in rivers to the sea; they are the synthetic creations of man's inventive mind, brewed in his laboratories, and having no counterparts in nature.

To adjust to these chemicals would require time on the scale that is nature's; it would require not merely the years of a man's life but the life of generations. And even this, were it by some miracle possible, would be futile, for the new chemicals come from our laboratories in an endless stream; almost five hundred annually find their way into actual use in the United States alone. The figure is staggering and its implications are not easily grasped—500 new chemicals to which the bodies of men and animals are required somehow to adapt each year, chemicals totally outside the limits of biologic experience.

Among them are many that are used in man's war against nature. Since the mid-1940's over 200 basic chemicals have been created for use in killing insects, weeds, rodents, and other organisms described in the modern vernacular as "pests"; and they are sold under several thousand different brand names.

These sprays, dusts, and aerosols are now applied almost universally to farms, gardens, forests, and homes—nonselective chemicals that have the power to kill every insect, the "good" and the "bad," to still the song of birds and the leaping of fish in the streams, to coat the leaves with a deadly film, and to linger on in soil—all this though the intended target may be only a few weeds or insects. Can anyone believe it is possible to lay down such a barrage of poisons on the surface of the earth without making it unfit for all life? They should not be called "insecticides," but "biocides."

The whole process of spraying seems caught up in an endless spiral. Since DDT was released for civilian use, a process of escalation has been going on in which ever more toxic materials must be found. This has happened because insects, in a triumphant vindication of Darwin's principle of the survival of the fittest, have evolved super races immune to the particular insecticide used, hence a deadlier one has always to be developed—and then a deadlier one than that. It has happened also because, for reasons to be described later, destructive insects often undergo a "flareback," or resurgence, after spraying, in numbers greater than before. Thus the chemical war is never won, and all life is caught in its violent crossfire.

Along with the possibility of the extinction of mankind by nuclear war, the central problem of our age has therefore become the contamination of man's total environment with such substances of incredible potential for harm—substances that accumulate in the tissues of plants and animals and even penetrate the germ cells to shatter or alter the very material of heredity upon which the shape of the future depends.

Some would-be architects of our future look toward a time when it will be pos-   10 sible to alter the human germ plasm by design. But we may easily be doing so now by inadvertence, for many chemicals, like radiation, bring about gene mutations. It is ironic to think that man might determine his own future by something so seemingly trivial as the choice of an insect spray.

All this has been risked—for what? Future historians may well be amazed by our distorted sense of proportion. How could intelligent beings seek to control a few unwanted species by a method that contaminated the entire environment and brought the threat of disease and death even to their own kind? Yet this is precisely what we have done. We have done it, moreover, for reasons that collapse the moment we examine them. We are told that the enormous and expanding use of pesticides is necessary to maintain farm production. Yet is our real problem not one of *over-production?* Our farms, despite measures to remove acreages from production and to pay farmers *not* to produce, have yielded such a staggering excess of crops that the American taxpayer in 1962 is paying out more than one billion dollars a year as the total carrying cost of the surplus-food storage program. And is the situation helped when one branch of the Agriculture Department tries to reduce production while another states, as it did in 1958, "It is believed generally that reduction of crop acreages under provisions of the Soil Bank will stimulate interest in use of chemicals to obtain maximum production on the land retained in crops."

All this is not to say there is no insect problem and no need of control. I am saying, rather, that control must be geared to realities, not to mythical situations, and that the methods employed must be such that they do not destroy us along with the insects.

The problem whose attempted solution has brought such a train of disaster in its wake is an accompaniment of our modern way of life. Long before the age of man, insects inhabited the earth—a group of extraordinarily varied and adaptable beings. Over the course of time since man's advent, a small percentage of the more than half a million species of insects have come into conflict with human welfare in two principal ways: as competitors for the food supply and as carriers of human disease.

Disease-carrying insects become important where human beings are crowded together, especially under conditions where sanitation is poor, as in time of natural disaster or war or in situations of extreme poverty and deprivation. Then control of some sort becomes necessary. It is a sobering fact, however, as we shall presently see, that the method of massive chemical control has had only limited success, and also threatens to worsen the very conditions it is intended to curb.

Under primitive agricultural conditions the farmer had few insect problems.   15 These arose with the intensification of agriculture—the devotion of immense acreages to a single crop. Such a system set the stage for explosive increases in specific insect populations. Single-crop farming does not take advantage of the principles by which nature works; it is agriculture as an engineer might conceive it to be. Nature has introduced great variety into the landscape, but man has displayed a passion for simplifying it. Thus he undoes the built-in checks and balances by which nature holds the species within bounds. One important natural check is a limit on the amount of suitable habitat for each species. Obviously then, an insect that lives on wheat can build up its population to much higher levels on a farm devoted to wheat than on one in which wheat is intermingled with other crops to which the insect is not adapted.

The same thing happens in other situations. A generation or more ago, the towns of large areas of the United States lined their streets with the noble elm tree. Now the beauty they hopefully created is threatened with complete destruction as disease sweeps through the elms, carried by a beetle that would have only limited chance to build up large populations and to spread from tree to tree if the elms were only occasional trees in a richly diversified planting.

Another factor in the modern insect problem is one that must be viewed against a background of geologic and human history: the spreading of thousands of different kinds of organisms from their native homes to invade new territories. This worldwide migration has been studied and graphically described by the British ecologist Charles Elton in his recent book *The Ecology of Invasions*. During the Cretaceous Period, some hundred million years ago, flooding seas cut many land bridges between continents and living things found themselves confined in what Elton calls "colossal separate nature reserves." There, isolated from others of their kind, they developed many new species. When some of the land masses were joined again, about 15 million years ago, these species began to move out into new territories—a movement that is not only still in progress but is now receiving considerable assistance from man.

The importation of plants is the primary agent in the modern spread of species, for animals have almost invariably gone along with the plants, quarantine being a comparatively recent and not completely effective innovation. The United States Office of Plant Introduction alone has introduced almost 200,000 species and varieties of plants from all over the world. Nearly half of the 180 or so major insect enemies of plants in the United States are accidental imports from abroad, and most of them have come as hitchhikers on plants.

In new territory, out of reach of the restraining hand of the natural enemies that kept down its numbers in its native land, an invading plant or animal is able to become enormously abundant. Thus it is no accident that our most troublesome insects are introduced species.

These invasions, both the naturally occurring and those dependent on human   20
assistance, are likely to continue indefinitely. Quarantine and massive chemical campaigns are only extremely expensive ways of buying time. We are faced, according to Dr. Elton, "with a life-and-death need not just to find new technological

means of suppressing this plant or that animal"; instead we need the basic knowledge of animal populations and their relations to their surroundings that will "promote an even balance and damp down the explosive power of outbreaks and new invasions."

Much of the necessary knowledge is now available but we do not use it. We train ecologists in our universities and even employ them in our governmental agencies but we seldom take their advice. We allow the chemical death rain to fall as though there were no alternative, whereas in fact there are many, and our ingenuity could soon discover many more if given opportunity.

Have we fallen into a mesmerized state that makes us accept as inevitable that which is inferior or detrimental, as though having lost the will or the vision to demand that which is good? Such thinking, in the words of the ecologist Paul Shepard, "idealizes life with only its head out of water, inches above the limits of toleration of the corruption of its own environment . . . Why should we tolerate a diet of weak poisons, a home in insipid surroundings, a circle of acquaintances who are not quite our enemies, the noise of motors with just enough relief to prevent insanity? Who would want to live in a world which is just not quite fatal?"

Yet such a world is pressed upon us. The crusade to create a chemically sterile, insect-free world seems to have engendered a fanatic zeal on the part of many specialists and most of the so-called control agencies. On every hand there is evidence that those engaged in spraying operations exercise a ruthless power. "The regulatory entomologists . . . function as prosecutor, judge and jury, tax assessor and collector and sheriff to enforce their own orders," said Connecticut entomologist Neely Turner. The most flagrant abuses go unchecked in both state and federal agencies.

It is not my contention that chemical insecticides must never be used. I do contend that we have put poisonous and biologically potent chemicals indiscriminately into the hands of persons largely or wholly ignorant of their potentials for harm. We have subjected enormous numbers of people to contact with these poisons, without their consent and often without their knowledge. If the Bill of Rights contains no guarantee that a citizen shall be secure against lethal poisons distributed either by private individuals or by public officials, it is surely only because our forefathers, despite their considerable wisdom and foresight, could conceive of no such problem.

I contend, furthermore, that we have allowed these chemicals to be used with   25
little or no advance investigation of their effect on soil, water, wildlife, and man himself. Future generations are unlikely to condone our lack of prudent concern for the integrity of the natural world that supports all life.

There is still very limited awareness of the nature of the threat. This is an era of specialists, each of whom sees his own problem and is unaware of or intolerant of the larger frame into which it fits. It is also an era dominated by industry, in which the right to make a dollar at whatever cost is seldom challenged. When the public protests, confronted with some obvious evidence of damaging results of pesticide applications, it is fed little tranquilizing pills of half truth. We urgently need an end to these false assurances, to the sugar coating of unpalatable facts. It is the public that is being asked to assume the risks that the insect controllers calculate. The public must decide whether it wishes to continue on the present road, and it can do so only when in full possession of the facts. In the words of Jean Rostand,[2] "The obligation to endure gives us the right to know."

UNDERSTANDING THE TEXT

1. What "power" have human beings recently acquired that, according to Rachel Carson, makes the current time period unique in the history of life on Earth?

2. What does Carson mean by "in the modern world there is no time"?

3. What happens when insects adapt to pesticides in their environment? Could any pesticide, theoretically, not result in an increased tolerance for that pesticide among insects? Why or why not?

4. What arguments in favor of pesticide use does Carson anticipate? How does she build responses to these arguments into her treatment of the issues?

5. What role does single-crop farming play in the rise of insect populations? Why is it dangerous, in Carson's view, to limit diversity in specific natural areas?

6. Which of the dangers and mysteries of pesticide use does Carson object to most?

MAKING CONNECTIONS

1. How do large increases in human populations create conditions in which insects and other forms of life must be controlled? How does Malthus anticipate these kinds of problems in his "Essay on the Principle of Population" (p. 552)?

2. Exactly how does Darwin's principle of natural selection (p. 314) explain insects' adaptation to pesticides?

3. How have Carson's views of nature influenced later environmental writers such as Barry Commoner (p. 344) and Vandana Shiva (p. 374)?

WRITING ABOUT THE TEXT

1. Conducting extra research as necessary, describe an environmental threat to the ecosystem in the area in which you live. How are the lives of insects, birds, fish, animals, and plants connected to each other, and how are they threatened?

2. Analyze Carson's use of evidence in this selection. What claims does she make, and how effectively does she support each one?

2. **Jean Rostand:** French biologist and playwright (1894–1977).

3. The international accord on pesticides reached in Stockholm, Sweden, in 2004 contains this "malaria exception" in its restriction of DDT:

    > The Stockholm Convention on Persistent Organic Pollutants (POPs) recognizes that in some countries, especially those in sub-Saharan Africa, DDT remains an important tool in the war against malaria. Countries that ratify the Convention may continue using DDT for controlling mosquitoes that spread malaria. Thus, the Convention will not increase the likelihood that people will be infected with malaria.

    Many environmental groups opposed this exception, but supporters argued that DDT had already prevented hundreds of millions of people from dying of malaria and that, if its use were entirely eliminated, the human costs in some of the world's poorest countries would be severe. Write an essay supporting or opposing this exception, based on the case against DDT that Carson outlines in "The Obligation to Endure."

KARL POPPER

from *Science as Falsification*

[1963]

KARL POPPER (1902–1994) was one of the twentieth century's best-known and important philosophers of science. He was born in Vienna in 1902 to a German-Jewish family that had converted to the Lutheran Church before he was born. In 1918, at the age of sixteen, he entered the University of Vienna and studied mathematics, physics, and psychology with the intention of becoming an elementary or secondary school teacher. In 1928, he received a Ph.D. in psychology and began teaching mathematics and physics to secondary students in Austria. While teaching, he wrote his first book, *The Logic of Scientific Discovery* (1934).

In 1936, Popper left Austria for England, fearing the rise of Nazism and increased persecution of Jews. A year later, he accepted an academic position in New Zealand, where he stayed for ten years. In 1946, he returned to England and accepted a position teaching philosophy at the prestigious London School of Economics. He continued to publish books in both political philosophy and the philosophy of science, earning a reputation as one of the most important philosophers of the twentieth century. In 1965, he was knighted by Queen Elizabeth II, and in 1976, he was elected a fellow of the Royal Society of England.

Popper's most important contribution to science was his redefinition of the scientific method. Since the beginning of the Scientific Revolution in the sixteenth century, science had been understood as a method for testing and proving various theories and hypotheses. Popper felt that this concept of the scientific method made it very easy for nonscientific and pseudoscientific theories like palm reading and astrology to claim scientific status. Since it is always possible to read events and results as confirmations of a theory, he reasoned, the prevailing scientific model gave no way of distinguishing between science and folklore.

Popper ultimately concluded that a genuine scientific theory must make predictions that can be tested by other scientists, who must try to prove the theory false. Theories that cannot be disproved can be considered conditionally true until such time as they are proved false. In the essay presented below, which is based on a lecture that he first delivered as part of a course on contemporary British philosophy at Cambridge in 1953, Popper offers his clearest explanation of the nature of science as a process of falsification.

Science: Conjectures and Refutations

Mr. Turnbull had predicted evil consequences, . . . and
was now doing the best in his power to bring about
the verification of his own prophecies.

Anthony Trollope

I

When I received the list of participants in this course and realized that I had been asked to speak to philosophical colleagues I thought, after some hesitation and con-sultation, that you would probably prefer me to speak about those problems which interest me most, and about those developments with which I am most intimately acquainted. I therefore decided to do what I have never done before: to give you a report on my own work in the philosophy of science, since the autumn of 1919 when I first began to grapple with the problem, '*When should a theory be ranked as scientific?*' or '*Is there a criterion for the scientific character or status of a theory?*'

The problem which troubled me at the time was neither, 'When is a theory true?' nor, 'When is a theory acceptable?' My problem was different. I *wished to distinguish between science and pseudo-science*; knowing very well that science often errs, and that pseudo-science may happen to stumble on the truth.

I knew, of course, the most widely accepted answer to my problem: that science is distinguished from pseudo-science—or from 'metaphysics'—by its *empirical method*, which is essentially *inductive*, proceeding from observation or experiment. But this did not satisfy me. On the contrary, I often formulated my problem as one of dis-tinguishing between a genuinely empirical method and a non-empirical or even a pseudo-empirical method—that is to say, a method which, although it appeals to observation and experiment, nevertheless does not come up to scientific standards. The latter method may be exemplified by astrology, with its stupendous mass of empirical evidence based on observation—on horoscopes and on biographies.

But as it was not the example of astrology which led me to my problem I should perhaps briefly describe the atmosphere in which my problem arose and the examples by which it was stimulated. After the collapse of the Austrian Empire[1] there had been a revolution in Austria: the air was full of revolutionary slogans and ideas, and new and often wild theories. Among the theories which interested me Einstein's theory of relativity was no doubt by far the most important. Three others were Marx's theory of history, Freud's psycho-analysis, and Alfred Adler's[2] so-called 'individual psychology'.

---

1. **Austrian Empire:** the Austro-Hungarian Empire, composed of the Austrian Empire and the Kingdom of Hungary, collapsed after being defeated in World War I.

2. **Alfred Adler:** Austrian psychologist (1870–1937) with whom Popper studied at the University of Vienna.

There was a lot of popular nonsense talked about these theories, and especially   5
about relativity (as still happens even today), but I was fortunate in those who
introduced me to the study of this theory. We all—the small circle of students to
which I belonged—were thrilled with the result of Eddington's[3] eclipse observations which in 1919 brought the first important confirmation of Einstein's theory of
gravitation. It was a great experience for us, and one which had a lasting influence
on my intellectual development.

The three other theories I have mentioned were also widely discussed among students at that time. I myself happened to come into personal contact with Alfred
Adler, and even to co-operate with him in his social work among the children and
young people in the working-class districts of Vienna where he had established social
guidance clinics.

It was during the summer of 1919 that I began to feel more and more dissatisfied with these three theories—the Marxist theory of history, psychoanalysis, and
individual psychology; and I began to feel dubious about their claims to scientific
status. My problem perhaps first took the simple form, 'What is wrong with Marxism,
psycho-analysis, and individual psychology? Why are they so different from physical
theories, from Newton's theory, and especially from the theory of relativity?'

To make this contrast clear I should explain that few of us at the time would
have said that we believed in the *truth* of Einstein's theory of gravitation. This shows
that it was not my doubting the *truth* of those other three theories which bothered
me, but something else. Yet neither was it that I merely felt mathematical physics
to be more *exact* than the sociological or psychological type of theory. Thus what
worried me was neither the problem of truth, at that stage at least, nor the problem
of exactness or measurability. It was rather that I felt that these other three theories,
though posing as sciences, had in fact more in common with primitive myths than
with science; that they resembled astrology rather than astronomy.

I found that those of my friends who were admirers of Marx, Freud, and Adler, were
impressed by a number of points common to these theories, and especially by their
apparent *explanatory power*. These theories appeared to be able to explain practically
everything that happened within the fields to which they referred. The study of any
of them seemed to have the effect of an intellectual conversion or revelation, opening
your eyes to a new truth hidden from those not yet initiated. Once your eyes were thus
opened you saw confirming instances everywhere: the world was full of *verifications* of
the theory. Whatever happened always confirmed it. Thus its truth appeared manifest;
and unbelievers were clearly people who did not want to see the manifest truth; who
refused to see it, either because it was against their class interest, or because of their
repressions which were still 'un-analysed' and crying out for treatment.

The most characteristic element in this situation seemed to me the incessant   10
stream of confirmations, of observations which 'verified' the theories in question; and

3. **Eddington:** Arthur Eddington (1882–1944). British physicist who, in 1919, used his observations of
a solar eclipse to confirm Einstein's prediction that the light around the sun should be bent by gravity.

this point was constantly emphasized by their adherents. A Marxist could not open a newspaper without finding on every page confirming evidence for his interpretation of history; not only in the news, but also in its presentation—which revealed the class bias of the paper—and especially of course in what the paper did *not* say. The Freudian analysts emphasized that their theories were constantly verified by their 'clinical observations'. As for Adler, I was much impressed by a personal experience. Once, in 1919, I reported to him a case which to me did not seem particularly Adlerian, but which he found no difficulty in analysing in terms of his theory of inferiority feelings, although he had not even seen the child. Slightly shocked, I asked him how he could be so sure. 'Because of my thousandfold experience', he replied; whereupon I could not help saying: 'And with this new case, I suppose, your experience has become thousand-and-one-fold.'

What I had in mind was that his previous observations may not have been much sounder than this new one; that each in its turn had been interpreted in the light of 'previous experience', and at the same time counted as additional confirmation. What, I asked myself, did it confirm? No more than that a case could be interpreted in the light of the theory. But this meant very little, I reflected, since every conceivable case could be interpreted in the light of Adler's theory, or equally of Freud's. I may illustrate this by two very different examples of human behaviour: that of a man who pushes a child into the water with the intention of drowning it; and that of a man who sacrifices his life in an attempt to save the child. Each of these two cases can be explained with equal ease in Freudian and in Adlerian terms. According to Freud the first man suffered from repression (say, of some component of his Oedipus complex), while the second man had achieved sublimation. According to Adler the first man suffered from feelings of inferiority (producing perhaps the need to prove to himself that he dared to commit some crime), and so did the second man (whose need was to prove to himself that he dared to rescue the child). I could not think of any human behaviour which could not be interpreted in terms of either theory. It was precisely this fact—that they always fitted, that they were always confirmed—which in the eyes of their admirers constituted the strongest argument in favour of these theories. It began to dawn on me that this apparent strength was in fact their weakness.

With Einstein's theory the situation was strikingly different. Take one typical instance—Einstein's prediction, just then confirmed by the findings of Eddington's expedition. Einstein's gravitational theory had led to the result that light must be attracted by heavy bodies (such as the sun), precisely as material bodies were attracted. As a consequence it could be calculated that light from a distant fixed star whose apparent position was close to the sun would reach the earth from such a direction that the star would seem to be slightly shifted away from the sun; or, in other words, that stars close to the sun would look as if they had moved a little away from the sun, and from one another. This is a thing which cannot normally be observed since such stars are rendered invisible in daytime by the sun's overwhelming brightness; but during an eclipse it is possible to take photographs of them. If the same constellation is photographed at night one can measure the distances on the two photographs, and check the predicted effect.

Now the impressive thing about this case is the *risk* involved in a prediction of this kind. If observation shows that the predicted effect is definitely absent, then the theory is simply refuted. The theory is *incompatible with certain possible results of observation*—in fact with results which everybody before Einstein would have expected. This is quite different from the situation I have previously described, when it turned out that the theories in question were compatible with the most divergent human behaviour, so that it was practically impossible to describe any human behaviour that might not be claimed to be a verification of these theories.

These considerations led me in the winter of 1919–20 to conclusions which I may now reformulate as follows.

(1) It is easy to obtain confirmations, or verifications, for nearly every theory—if   15
we look for confirmations.

(2) Confirmations should count only if they are the result of *risky predictions*; that is to say, if, unenlightened by the theory in question, we should have expected an event which was incompatible with the theory—an event which would have refuted the theory.

(3) Every 'good' scientific theory is a prohibition: it forbids certain things to happen. The more a theory forbids, the better it is.

(4) A theory which is not refutable by any conceivable event is nonscientific. Irrefutability is not a virtue of a theory (as people often think) but a vice.

(5) Every genuine *test* of a theory is an attempt to falsify it, or to refute it. Testability is falsifiability; but there are degrees of testability: some theories are more testable, more exposed to refutation, than others; they take, as it were, greater risks.

(6) Confirming evidence should not count *except when it is the result of a genuine*   20
test of the theory; and this means that it can be presented as a serious but unsuccessful attempt to falsify the theory. (I now speak in such cases of 'corroborating evidence'.)

(7) Some genuinely testable theories, when found to be false, are still upheld by their admirers—for example by introducing *ad hoc* some auxiliary assumption, or by re-interpreting the theory *ad hoc* in such a way that it escapes refutation. Such a procedure is always possible, but it rescues the theory from refutation only at the price of destroying, or at least lowering, its scientific status. (I later described such a rescuing operation as a *'conventionalist twist'* or a *'conventionalist stratagem'*.)

One can sum up all this by saying that *the criterion of the scientific status of a theory is its falsifiability, or refutability, or testability*.

II

I may perhaps exemplify this with the help of the various theories so far mentioned. Einstein's theory of gravitation clearly satisfied the criterion of falsifiability. Even if our measuring instruments at the time did not allow us to pronounce on the results of the tests with complete assurance, there was clearly a possibility of refuting the theory.

Astrology did not pass the test. Astrologers were greatly impressed, and misled, by what they believed to be confirming evidence—so much so that they were quite unimpressed by any unfavourable evidence. Moreover, by making their interpretations and prophecies sufficiently vague they were able to explain away anything that might have been a refutation of the theory had the theory and the prophecies been more precise. In order to escape falsification they destroyed the testability of their theory. It is a typical soothsayer's trick to predict things so vaguely that the predictions can hardly fail: that they become irrefutable.

The Marxist theory of history, in spite of the serious efforts of some of its founders and followers, ultimately adopted this soothsaying practice. In some of its earlier formulations (for example in Marx's analysis of the character of the 'coming social revolution') their predictions were testable, and in fact falsified. Yet instead of accepting the refutations the followers of Marx re-interpreted both the theory and the evidence in order to make them agree. In this way they rescued the theory from refutation; but they did so at the price of adopting a device which made it irrefutable. They thus gave a 'conventionalist twist' to the theory; and by this stratagem they destroyed its much advertised claim to scientific status.

The two psycho-analytic theories were in a different class. They were simply non-testable, irrefutable. There was no conceivable human behaviour which could contradict them. This does not mean that Freud and Adler were not seeing certain things correctly: I personally do not doubt that much of what they say is of considerable importance, and may well play its part one day in a psychological science which is testable. But it does mean that those 'clinical observations' which analysts naively believe confirm their theory cannot do this any more than the daily confirmations which astrologers find in their practice. And as for Freud's epic of the Ego, the Super-ego, and the Id,[4] no substantially stronger claim to scientific status can be made for it than for Homer's collected stories from Olympus. These theories describe some facts, but in the manner of myths. They contain most interesting psychological suggestions, but not in a testable form.

At the same time I realized that such myths may be developed, and become testable; that historically speaking all—or very nearly all—scientific theories originate from myths, and that a myth may contain important anticipations of scientific theories. Examples are Empedocles' theory of evolution by trial and error, or Parmenides' myth of the unchanging block universe in which nothing ever happens and which, if we add another dimension, becomes Einstein's block universe (in which, too, nothing ever happens, since everything is, four-dimensionally speaking, determined and laid

1. **Freud's epic of the Ego, the Super-ego, and the Id:** according to Freud in his book *The Ego and the Id*, the human mind consists of three elements: the id, which drives people to seek pleasure; the super-ego, which drives them to follow the social and moral codes of their culture; and the ego, which must negotiate between the demands of the id and the superego in order to make decisions about how to behave.

25

down from the beginning). I thus felt that if a theory is found to be non-scientific, or 'metaphysical' (as we might say), it is not thereby found to be unimportant, or insignificant, or 'meaningless', or 'nonsensical'. But it cannot claim to be backed by empirical evidence in the scientific sense—although it may easily be, in some genetic sense, the 'result of observation'.

(There were a great many other theories of this pre-scientific or pseudo-scientific character, some of them, unfortunately, as influential as the Marxist interpretation of history; for example, the racialist interpretation of history—another of those impressive and all-explanatory theories which act upon weak minds like revelations.)

Thus the problem which I tried to solve by proposing the criterion of falsifiability was neither a problem of meaningfulness or significance, nor a problem of truth or acceptability. It was the problem of drawing a line (as well as this can be done) between the statements, or systems of statements, of the empirical sciences, and all other statements—whether they are of a religious or of a metaphysical character, or simply pseudo-scientific. Years later—it must have been in 1928 or 1929—I called this first problem of mine the '*problem of demarcation*'. The criterion of falsifiability is a solution to this problem of demarcation, for it says that statements or systems of statements, in order to be ranked as scientific, must be capable of conflicting with possible, or conceivable, observations.

UNDERSTANDING THE TEXT

1. What question does Popper say he was trying to answer when he first conceived of his theory of science as falsification? What factors led him to ask this question?

2. How did the theories of Marx, Freud, Adler, and Einstein influence Popper in his quest to understand the scientific method? Which of these four theories does he consider pseudoscience? Which does he consider genuinely scientific?

3. What is the difference between the explanatory power of a theory and its scientific reliability? Why, according to Popper, do so many pseudoscientific theories seem to be able to explain so much?

4. What is the point of Popper's story about his conversation with Alfred Adler? Does the story reinforce the main point of the essay?

5. What is the main difference between Einstein's theories and those of Marx, Freud, and Adler? What makes Einstein's ideas "scientific"?

6. What does Popper mean by a "risky prediction"?

MAKING CONNECTIONS

1. Apply Popper's ideas to the scientific arguments of Lucretius (p. 292) or William Paley (p. 311). Does either of these other scientists generate falsifiable hypotheses?

2. How does Popper's understanding of science compare with Richard Feynman's (p. 53)?

3. How is Popper's understanding of evidence different from the deductive method employed by Thomas Aquinas (p. 483)? Can Popper's model properly be called "inductive" (see p. 655)?

WRITING ABOUT THE TEXT

1. Examine the phrenology chart on p. 105. Write a paper explaining how the theory represented by this chart could be tested. Does phrenology contain any falsifiable claims?

2. Use Popper's idea of falsification to examine a scientific controversy, such as climate change or intelligent design theory. Which claims in the debate are falsifiable? Which are not?

BARRY COMMONER
The Four Laws of Ecology
[1971]

BARRY COMMONER (1917–2012), a leading ecologist and environmental activist, and one of the founders of the environmental movement in the United States, was born in Brooklyn, New York. He studied zoology at Columbia University as an undergraduate and then attended Harvard University, where he received a Ph.D. in 1941. After a short stint in the army during World War II, he joined the faculty of Washington University in St. Louis, where he taught courses in botany and plant physiology for more than thirty years.

Commoner combined academic research with political activism throughout his career. In the 1950s, he became a vocal opponent of above-ground nuclear testing, which the United States and the Soviet Union conducted during the Cold War, and which he saw as having an extremely negative effect on the world's ecosystems. He also wrote extensively on the connection between poverty and overpopulation. Unlike Garrett Hardin (p. 344), who believed that wealthy nations should refuse to give even minimal food aid to poorer, overpopulated countries, Commoner believed that poverty caused overpopulation and that industrialized nations could only address the root of the problem by radically redistributing the world's wealth.

In 1979, Commoner founded the Citizens Party, an organization that he hoped would serve as the political arm of the environmental movement. In 1980, he ran for president of the United States under the party's banner, receiving more than 200,000 votes and becoming the first minor-party candidate to qualify for federal matching funds. After the election, Commoner returned to his native New York City and spent the rest of his career at Queens College, where he was still listed as a senior scientist when he died in 2012 at the age of ninety-five.

Commoner is best known as one of the founders of the science of ecology, or the study of the ways that different natural systems are connected to each other. His bestselling book *The Closing Circle* (1971) has become a standard reference point in that field. In this book, he argues that the laws of ecology are as absolute and inflexible as the laws of physics and that the nations of the world must align their policies with those laws or pay a steep price. The example presented here, "The Four Laws of Ecology," offers four ironclad principles that, Commoner believes, should become the basis of all economic and social policy.

To survive on the earth, human beings require the stable, continuing existence of a suitable environment. Yet the evidence is overwhelming that the way in which we now live on the earth is driving its thin, life-supporting skin, and ourselves with it, to destruction. To understand this calamity, we need to begin with a close look at the nature of the environment itself. Most of us find this a difficult thing to do, for there is a kind of ambiguity in our relation to the environment. Biologically, human beings *participate* in the environmental system as subsidiary parts of the whole. Yet, human society is designed to *exploit* the environment as a whole, to produce wealth. The paradoxical role we play in the natural environment—at once participant and exploiter—distorts our perception of it.

Among primitive people, a person is seen as a dependent part of nature, a frail reed in a harsh world governed by natural laws that must be obeyed if he is to survive. Pressed by this need, primitive peoples can achieve a remarkable knowledge of their environment. The African Bushman[1] lives in one of the most stringent habitats on earth; food and water are scarce, and the weather is extreme. The Bushman survives because he has an incredibly intimate understanding of this environment. A Bushman can, for example, return after many months and miles of travel to find a single underground tuber, noted in his previous wanderings, when he needs it for his water supply in the dry season.

We who call ourselves advanced seem to have escaped from this kind of dependence on the environment. The Bushman must squeeze water from a searched-out tuber; we get ours by the turn of a tap. Instead of trackless terrain, we have the grid of city streets. Instead of seeking the sun's heat when we need it, or shunning it when it is too strong, we warm and cool ourselves with man-made machines. All this leads us to believe that we have made our own environment and no longer depend on the one provided by nature. In the eager search for the benefits of modern science and technology we have become enticed into a nearly fatal illusion: that through our machines we have at last escaped from dependence on the natural environment.

A good place to experience this illusion is a jet airplane. Safely seated on a plastic cushion, carried in a winged aluminum tube, streaking miles above the earth, through air nearly thin enough to boil the blood, at a speed that seems to make the sun stand still, it is easy to believe that we have conquered nature and have escaped from the ancient bondage to air, water, and soil.

But the illusion is easily shattered, for like the people it carries, the airplane is itself a creature of the earth's 'environment'. Its engines burn fuel and oxygen produced by the earth's green plants. Traced a few steps back, every part of the craft is equally dependent on the environment. The steel came from smelters fed with coal, water, and oxygen—all nature's products. The aluminum was refined from ore using electricity, again produced by combustion of fuel and oxygen or generated by falling water. For every pound of plastic in the plane's interior, we must reckon

5

1. **African Bushman:** a member of one of several hunter-gatherer tribes in the Southern region of Africa. This term is now considered to be pejorative and is normally replaced with "San people" in academic writing.

that some amount of coal was needed to produce the power used to manufacture it. For every manufactured part, gallons of pure water were used. Without the earth's natural environmental constituents—oxygen, water, fuel—the airplane, like man, could not exist.

The environment makes up a huge, enormously complex living machine that forms a thin dynamic layer on the earth's surface, and every human activity depends on the integrity and the proper functioning of this machine. Without the photosynthetic activity of green plants, there would be no oxygen for our engines, smelters, and furnaces, let alone support for human and animal life. Without the action of the plants, animals, and microorganisms that live in them, we could have no pure water in our lakes and rivers. Without the biological processes that have gone on in the soil for thousands of years, we would have neither food crops, oil, nor coal. This machine is our biological capital, the basic apparatus on which our total productivity depends. If we destroy it, our most advanced technology will become useless and any economic and political system that depends on it will founder. The environmental crisis is a signal of this approaching catastrophe. . . .

In broad outline, these are the environmental cycles which govern the behavior of the three great global systems: the air, the water, and the soil. Within each of them live many thousands of different species of living things. Each species is suited to its particular environmental niche, and each, through its life processes, affects the physical and chemical properties of its immediate environment.

Each living species is also linked to many others. These links are bewildering in their variety and marvelous in their intricate detail. An animal, such as a deer may depend on plants for food; the plants depend on the action of soil bacteria for their nutrients; the bacteria in turn live on the organic wastes dropped by the animal on the soil. At the same time, the deer is food for the mountain lion. Insects may live on the juices of plants or gather pollen from their flowers. Other insects suck blood from animals. Bacteria may live on the internal tissues of animals and plants. Fungi degrade the bodies of dead plants and animals. All this, many times multiplied and organized species by species in intricate, precise relationships, makes up the vast network of life on the earth.

The science that studies these relationships and the processes linking each living thing to the physical and chemical environment is *ecology*. It is the science of planetary housekeeping. For the environment is, so to speak, the house created on the earth *by* living things *for* living things. It is a young science and much of what it teaches has been learned from only small segments of the whole network of life on the earth. Ecology has not yet explicitly developed the kind of cohesive, simplifying generalizations exemplified by, say, the laws of physics. Nevertheless there are a number of generalizations that are already evident in what we now know about the ecosphere and that can be organized into a kind of informal set of "laws of ecology." These are described in what follows.

The First Law of Ecology:
Everything Is Connected to Everything Else

Some of the evidence that leads to this generalization has already been discussed. It   10
reflects the existence of the elaborate network of interconnections in the ecosphere:
among different living organisms, and between populations, species, and individual
organisms and their physicochemical surroundings.

The single fact that an ecosystem consists of multiple interconnected parts, which
act on one another, has some surprising consequences. Our ability to picture the
behavior of such systems has been helped considerably by the development, even
more recent than ecology, of the science of cybernetics. We owe the basic concept,
and the word itself, to the inventive mind of the late Norbert Wiener.[2]

The word "cybernetics" derives from the Greek word for helmsman; it is concerned
with cycles of events that steer, or govern, the behavior of a system. The helmsman is
part of a system that also includes the compass, the rudder, and the ship. If the ship
veers off the chosen compass course, the change shows up in the movement of the
compass needle. Observed and interpreted by the helmsman this event determines
a subsequent one: the helmsman turns the rudder, which swings the ship back to its
original course. When this happens, the compass needle returns to its original, on-
course position and the cycle is complete. If the helmsman turns the rudder too far in
response to a small deflection of the compass needle, the excess swing of the ship shows
up in the compass—which signals the helmsman to correct his overreaction by an
opposite movement. Thus the operation of this cycle stabilizes the course of the ship.

In quite a similar way, stabilizing cybernetic relations are built into an ecological
cycle. Consider, for example, the fresh-water ecological cycle: fish—organic waste—
bacteria of decay—inorganic products—algae—fish. Suppose that due to unusually
warm summer weather there is a rapid growth of algae. This depletes the supply of
inorganic nutrients so that two sectors of the cycle, algae and nutrients, are out of
balance, but in opposite directions. The operation of the ecological cycle, like that
of the ship, soon brings the situation back into balance. For the excess in algae
increases the ease with which fish can feed on them; this reduces the algal population, increases fish waste production, and eventually leads to an increased level of
nutrients when the waste decays. Thus, the levels of algae and nutrients tend to
return to their original balanced position.

In such cybernetic systems the course is not maintained by rigid control, but
flexibly. Thus the ship does not move unwaveringly on its path, but actually follows
it in a wavelike motion that swings equally to both sides of the true course. The
frequency of these swings depends on the relative speeds of the various steps in the
cycle, such as the rate at which the ship responds to the rudder.

2. **Norbert Wiener:** American mathematician and philosopher (1894–1964).

Ecological systems exhibit similar cycles, although these are often obscured by the   15
effects of daily or seasonal variations in weather and environmental agents. The most
famous examples of such ecological oscillations are the periodic fluctuations of the size
of fur-bearing animal populations. For example, from trapping records in Canada it is
known that the populations of rabbits and lynx follow ten-year fluctuations. When
there are many rabbits the lynx prosper; the rising population of lynx increasingly rav-
ages the rabbit population, reducing it; as the latter become scarce, there is insufficient
food to support the now numerous lynx; as the lynx begin to die off, the rabbits are less
fiercely hunted and increase in number. And so on. These oscillations are built into the
operation of the simple cycle, in which the lynx population is positively related to the
number of rabbits and the rabbit population is negatively related to the number of lynx.

In such an oscillating system there is always the danger that the whole system
will collapse when an oscillation swings so wide of the balance point that the system
can no longer compensate for it. Suppose, for example, in one particular swing of
the rabbit—lynx cycle, the lynx manage to eat *all* the rabbits (or, for that matter,
all but one). Now the rabbit population can no longer reproduce. As usual, the
lynx begin to starve as the rabbits are consumed; but this time the drop in the lynx
population is not followed by an increase in rabbits. The lynx then die off. The
entire rabbit—lynx system collapses.

This is similar to the ecological collapse which accompanies what is called
"eutrophication."[3] If the nutrient level of the water becomes so high as to stimulate the rapid growth of algae, the dense algal population cannot be long sustained
because of the intrinsic limitations of photosynthetic efficiency. As the thickness
of the algal layer in the water increases, the light required for photosynthesis that
can reach the lower parts of the algal layer becomes sharply diminished, so that
any strong overgrowth of algae very quickly dies back, releasing organic debris. The
organic matter level may then become so great that its decay totally depletes the
oxygen content of the water. The bacteria of decay then die off, for they must have
oxygen to survive. The entire aquatic cycle collapses.

The dynamic behavior of a cybernetic system—for example, the frequency of its
natural oscillations, the speed with which it responds to external changes, and its
over-all rate of operation—depends on the relative rates of its constituent steps. In
the ship system, the compass needle swings in fractions of a second; the helmsman's
reaction takes some seconds; the ship responds over a time of minutes. These different
reaction times interact to produce, for example, the ship's characteristic oscillation
frequency around its true course.

In the aquatic ecosystem, each biological step also has a characteristic reaction
time, which depends on the metabolic and reproductive rates of the organisms
involved. The time to produce a new generation of fish may be some months; of algae,

3. **Eutrophication:** the biological process in which the dissolved nutrients in a body of water stimulate the growth of plant life, which, in turn, depletes the amount of dissolved oxygen.

a matter of days; decay bacteria can reproduce in a few hours. The metabolic rates of these organisms—that is, the rates at which they use nutrients, consume oxygen, or produce waste—is inversely related to their size. If the metabolic rate of a fish is 1, the algal rate is about 100, and the bacterial rate about 10,000.

If the entire cyclical system is to remain in balance, the over-all rate of turnover   20
must be governed by the slowest step—in this case, the growth and metabolism of the fish. Any external effect that forces part of the cycle to operate faster than the over-all rate leads to trouble. So, for example, the rate of waste production by fish determines the rate of bacterial decay and the rate of oxygen consumption due to that decay. In a balanced situation, enough oxygen is produced by the algae and enters from the air to support the decay bacteria. Suppose that the rate at which organic waste enters the cycle is increased artificially, for example, by dumping sewage into the water. Now the decay bacteria are supplied with organic waste at a much higher level than usual; because of their rapid metabolism they are able to act quickly on the increased organic load. As a result, the rate of oxygen consumption by the decay bacteria can easily exceed the rate of oxygen production by the algae (and its rate of entry from the air) so that the oxygen level goes to zero and the system collapses. Thus, the rates of the separate processes in the cycle are a natural state of balance which is maintained only so long as there are no external intrusions on the system. When such an effect originates outside the cycle, it is not controlled by the self-governing cyclical relations and is a threat to the stability of the whole system.

Ecosystems differ considerably in their rate characteristics and therefore vary a great deal in the speed with which they react to changed situations or approach the point of collapse. For example, aquatic ecosystems turn over much faster than soil ecosystems. Thus, an acre of richly populated marine shoreline or an acre of fish pond produces about seven times as much organic material as an acre of alfalfa annually. The slow turnover of the soil cycle is due to the rather low rate of one of its many steps—the release of nutrient from the soil's organic store, which is very much slower than the comparable step in aquatic systems.

The amount of stress which an ecosystem can absorb before it is driven to collapse is also a result of its various interconnections and their relative speeds of response. The more complex the ecosystem, the more successfully it can resist a stress. For example, in the rabbit–lynx system, if the lynx had an alternative source of food they might survive the sudden depletion of rabbits. In this way, branching—which establishes alternative pathways—increases the resistance of an ecosystem to stress. Most ecosystems are so complex that the cycles are not simple circular paths, but are crisscrossed with branches to form a network or a fabric of interconnections. Like a net, in which each knot is connected to others by several strands, such a fabric can resist collapse better than a simple, unbranched circle of threads—which if . cut anywhere breaks down as a whole. Environmental pollution is often a sign that ecological links have been cut and that the ecosystem has been artificially simplified and made more vulnerable to stress and to final collapse.

The feedback characteristics of ecosystems result in amplification and intensification processes of considerable magnitude. For example, the fact that in food chains small organisms are eaten by bigger ones and the latter by still bigger ones inevitably results in the concentration of certain environmental constituents in the bodies of the largest organisms at the top of the food chain. Smaller organisms always exhibit much higher metabolic rates than larger ones, so that the amount of their food which is oxidized relative to the amount incorporated into the body of the organism is thereby greater. Consequently, an animal at the top of the food chain depends on the consumption of an enormously greater mass of the bodies of organisms lower down in the food chain. Therefore, any *non*metabolized material present in the lower organisms of this chain will become concentrated in the body of the top one. Thus, if the concentration of DDT[4] (which is not readily metabolized) in the soil is 1 unit, earthworms living in the soil will achieve a concentration of from 10 to 40 units, and in woodcocks feeding on the earthworms the DDT level will rise to about 200 units.

All this results from a simple fact about ecosystems—everything is connected to everything else: the system is stabilized by its dynamic self-compensating properties; these same properties, if overstressed, can lead to a dramatic collapse; the complexity of the ecological network and its intrinsic rate of turnover determine how much it can be stressed, and for how long, without collapsing; the ecological network is an amplifier, so that a small perturbation in one place may have large, distant, long-delayed effects.

The Second Law of Ecology:
Everything Must Go Somewhere

This is, of course, simply a somewhat informal restatement of a basic law of physics— 25 that matter is indestructible. Applied to ecology, the law emphasizes that in nature there is no such thing as "waste." In every natural system, what is excreted by one organism as waste is taken up by another as food. Animals release carbon dioxide as a respiratory waste; this is an essential nutrient for green plants. Plants excrete oxygen, which is used by animals. Animal organic wastes nourish the bacteria of decay. Their wastes, inorganic materials such as nitràte, phosphate, and carbon dioxide, become algal nutrients.

A persistent effort to answer the question "Where does it go?" can yield a surprising amount of valuable information about an ecosystem. Consider, for example, the fate of a household item which contains mercury—a substance with environmental effects that have just recently surfaced. A dry-cell battery containing mercury is purchased, used to the point of exhaustion, and then "thrown out." But where does it really go? First it is placed in a container of rubbish; this is collected and taken to an incinerator. Here the mercury is heated; this produces mercury vapor which is

---

4. **DDT:** Dichlorodiphenyltrichloroethane, a common pesticide discussed in Rachel Carson's *Silent Spring* (p. 328).

emitted by the incinerator stack, and mercury *vapor* is toxic. Mercury vapor is carried by the wind, eventually brought to earth in rain or snow. Entering a mountain lake, let us say, the mercury condenses and sinks to the bottom. Here it is acted on by bacteria which convert it to methyl mercury. This is soluble and taken up by fish; since it is not metabolized, the mercury accumulates in the organs and flesh of the fish. The fish is caught and eaten by a man and the mercury becomes deposited in his organs, where it might be harmful. And so on.

This is an effective way to trace out an ecological path. It is also an excellent way to counteract the prevalent notion that something which is regarded as useless simply "goes away" when it is discarded. Nothing "goes away"; it is simply transferred from place to place, converted from one molecular form to another, acting on the life processes of any organism in which it becomes, for a time, lodged. One of the chief reasons for the present environmental crisis is that great amounts of materials have been extracted from the earth, converted into new forms, and discharged into the environment without taking into account that "everything has to go somewhere." The result, too often, is the accumulation of harmful amounts of material in places where, in nature, they do not belong.

The Third Law of Ecology:
Nature Knows Best

In my experience this principle is likely to encounter considerable resistance, for it appears to contradict a deeply held idea about the unique competence of human beings. One of the most pervasive features of modern technology is the notion that it is intended to "improve on nature"—to provide food, clothing, shelter, and means of communication and expression which are superior to those available to man in nature. Stated baldly, the third law of ecology holds that any major man-made change in a natural system is likely to be *detrimental* to that system. This is a rather extreme claim; nevertheless I believe it has a good deal of merit if understood in a properly defined context.

I have found it useful to explain this principle by means of an analogy. Suppose you were to open the back of your watch, close your eyes, and poke a pencil into the exposed works. The almost certain result would be damage to the watch. Nevertheless, this result is not *absolutely* certain. There is some finite possibility that the watch was out of adjustment and that the random thrust of the pencil happened to make the precise change needed to improve it. However, this outcome is exceedingly improbable. The question at issue is: why? The answer is self-evident: there is a very considerable amount of what technologists now call "research and development" (or, more familiarly, "R & D") behind the watch. This means that over the years numerous watchmakers, each taught by a predecessor, have tried out a huge variety of detailed arrangements of watch works, have discarded those that are not compatible with the over-all operation of the system and retained the better features. In effect, the watch mechanism, as it now exists, represents a very restricted selection, from among an enormous variety of possible arrangements of component parts, of a singular organization of the watch works. Any random change made in the watch is likely to fall into the very large class of inconsistent, or harmful, arrangements which have been tried out in past watch-making experience and discarded. One might say, as a law of watches, that "the watchmaker knows best."

There is a close, and very meaningful, analogy in biological systems. It is possible   30 to induce a certain range of random, inherited changes in a living thing by treating it with an agent, such as x-irradiation, that increases the frequency of mutations. Generally, exposure to x-rays increases the frequency of all mutations which have been observed, albeit very infrequently, in nature and can therefore be regarded as *possible* changes. What is significant, for our purpose, is the universal observation that when mutation frequency is enhanced by x-rays or other means, nearly all the mutations are harmful to the organisms and the great majority so damaging as to kill the organism before it is fully formed.

In other words, like the watch, a living organism that is forced to sustain a random change in its organization is almost certain to be damaged rather than improved. And in both cases, the explanation is the same—a great deal of "R & D." In effect there are some two to three billion years of "R & D" behind every living thing. In that time, a staggering number of new individual living things have been produced, affording in each case the opportunity to try out the suitability of some random genetic change. If the change damages the viability of the organism, it is likely to kill it before the change can be passed on to future generations. In this way, living things accumulate a complex organization of compatible parts; those possible arrangements that are not compatible with the whole are screened out over the long course of evolution. Thus, the structure of a present living thing or the organization of a current natural ecosystem is likely to be "best" in the sense that it has been so heavily screened for disadvantageous components that any new one is very likely to be worse than the present ones.

This principle is particularly relevant to the field of organic chemistry. Living things are composed of many thousands of different organic compounds, and it is sometimes imagined that at least some of these might be improved upon if they were replaced by some man-made variant of the natural substance. The third law of ecology suggests that the artificial introduction of an organic compound that does not occur in nature, but is man-made and is nevertheless active in a living system, is very likely to be harmful.

This is due to the fact that the varieties of chemical substances actually found in living things are vastly more restricted than the *possible* varieties. A striking illustration is that if one molecule each of all the possible types of proteins were made, they would together weigh more than the observable universe. Obviously there are a fantastically large number of protein types that are *not* made by living cells. And on the basis of the foregoing, one would reason that many of these possible protein types were once formed in some particular living things, found to be harmful, and rejected through the death of the experiment. In the same way, living cells synthesize fatty acids (a type of organic molecule that contains carbon chains of various lengths) with even-numbered carbon chain lengths (i.e., 4, 6, 8, etc., carbons), but no fatty acids with odd-numbered carbon chain lengths. This suggests that the latter have once been tried out and found wanting. Similarly, organic compounds that contain attached nitrogen and oxygen atoms are singularly rare in living things. This should warn us that the artificial introduction of substances of this type would be dangerous. This is indeed the case, for such substances are usually toxic and frequently carcinogenic. And, I would suppose from the fact that DDT is nowhere found in nature, that somewhere, at some time in the past, some unfortunate cell synthesized this molecule—and died.

One of the striking facts about the chemistry of living systems is that for every organic substance produced by a living organism, there exists, somewhere in nature, an enzyme capable of breaking that substance down. In effect, no organic substance is synthesized unless there is provision for its degradation; recycling is thus enforced. Thus, when a new man-made organic substance is synthesized with a molecular structure that departs significantly from the types which occur in nature, it is probable that no degradative enzyme exists, and the material tends to accumulate.

Given these considerations, it would be prudent, I believe, to regard every man-made organic chemical *not* found in nature which has a strong action on any one organism as potentially dangerous to other forms of life. Operationally, this view means that all man-made organic compounds that are at all active biologically ought to be treated as we do drugs, or rather as we *should* treat them—prudently, cautiously. Such caution or prudence is, of course, impossible when billions of pounds of the substance are produced and broadly disseminated into the ecosystem where it can reach and affect numerous organisms not under our observation. Yet this is precisely what we have done with detergents, insecticides, and herbicides. The often catastrophic results lend considerable force to the view that "Nature knows best."   35

The Fourth Law of Ecology:
There Is No Such Thing as a Free Lunch

In my experience, this idea has proven so illuminating for environmental problems that I have borrowed it from its original source, economics. The "law" derives from a story that economists like to tell about an oil-rich potentate who decided that his new wealth needed the guidance of economic science. Accordingly he ordered his advisers, on pain of death, to produce a set of volumes containing all the wisdom of economics. When the tomes arrived, the potentate was impatient and again issued an order—to reduce all the knowledge of economics to a single volume. The story goes on in this vein, as such stories will, until the advisers are required, if they are to survive, to reduce the totality of economic science to a single sentence. This is the origin of the "free lunch" law.

In ecology, as in economics, the law is intended to warn that every gain is won at some cost. In a way, this ecological law embodies the previous three laws. Because the global ecosystem is a connected whole, in which nothing can be gained or lost and which is not subject to over-all improvement, anything extracted from it by human effort must be replaced. Payment of this price cannot be avoided; it can only be delayed. The present environmental crisis is a warning that we have delayed nearly too long.

The preceding pages provide a view of the web of life on the earth. An effort has been made to develop this view from available facts, through logical relations, into a set of comprehensive generalizations. In other words, the effort has been scientific.

Nevertheless, it is difficult to ignore the embarrassing fact that the final generalizations which emerge from all this—the four laws of ecology—are ideas that have been widely held by many people without any scientific analysis or professional authorization. The complex web in which all life is enmeshed, and man's place in it, are clearly—and beautifully—described in the poems of Walt Whitman. A great deal about the interplay of the physical features of the environment and the creatures that inhabit it can be learned from *Moby Dick*. Mark Twain is not only a marvelous source of wisdom about the nature of the environment of the United States from the Mississippi westward, but also a rather incisive critic of the irrelevance of science which loses connection to the realities of life. As the critic Leo Marx reminds us, "Anyone familiar with the work of the classic American writers (I am thinking of men like Cooper, Emerson, Thoreau, Melville, Whitman, and Mark Twain) is likely to have developed an interest in what we recently have learned to call ecology."

Unfortunately, this literary heritage has not been enough to save us from ecological disaster. After all, every American technician, industrialist, agriculturalist, or public official who has condoned or participated in the assault on the environment has read at least some of Cooper, Emerson, Thoreau, Melville, Whitman, and Mark Twain. Many of them are campers, bird-watchers, or avid fishermen, and therefore to some degree personally aware of the natural processes that the science of ecology hopes to elucidate. Nevertheless, most of them were taken unawares by the environmental crisis, failing to understand, apparently, that Thoreau's woods, Mark Twain's rivers, and Melville's oceans are *today* under attack.

40

The rising miasma of pollution has helped us to achieve this understanding. For, in Leo Marx's[5] words, "The current environmental crisis has in a sense put a literal, factual, often quantifiable base under this poetic idea [i.e., the need for human harmony with nature]." This is perhaps the major value of the effort to show that the simple generalizations which have already emerged from perceptive human contact with the natural world have a valid base in the facts and principles of a science, ecology. Thus linked to science, these ideas become tools for restoring the damage inflicted on nature by the environmental crisis.

In the woods around Walden Pond or on the reaches of the Mississippi, most of the information needed to understand the natural world can be gained by personal

5. **Leo Marx:** American literary and cultural critic (b. 1919) and author of *The Machine in the Garden* (1964).

experience. In the world of nuclear bombs, smog, and foul water, environmental understanding needs help from the scientist.

UNDERSTANDING THE TEXT

1. Summarize Commoner's four laws of ecology in your own words. What are these laws? Are they provable and absolute the way that the laws of physics are?

2. How does Commoner define "cybernetics"? What is the connection between a cybernetic system and an ecosystem?

3. What keeps ecosystems in balance? Is it possible for an ecosystem to become so unbalanced that it stops functioning? How?

4. What does Commoner mean by "eutrophication"? How can it contribute to the collapse of an ecosystem?

5. What determines the amount of stress that a system can absorb? What happens when a system is no longer able to absorb stress?

6. Why does Commoner say that there is no such thing as waste? What happens to the materials that we commonly refer to as waste substances?

7. Is human intervention always detrimental to an ecosystem? Why is it more likely to be detrimental than beneficial?

MAKING CONNECTIONS

1. How would Charles Darwin (p. 314) interpret the rabbit–lynx dynamic that Commoner discusses? Is Commoner ultimately explaining an evolutionary system?

2. Do Commoner's observations about DDT confirm or challenge the assertions of Rachel Carson (p. 328)? Would Carson agree that DDT moves up the food chain?

3. Like William Paley (p. 311), Commoner uses the metaphor of a watch to describe the natural world. In what ways are the two watch metaphors similar? How are they different?

WRITING ABOUT THE TEXT

1 Examine an ecosystem you are familiar with, such as a local park or waterway. Choose five or six elements of this ecosystem and explain, using Commoner's terms, how all of these elements are related to each other.

2. Select one of Commoner's four laws of ecology and try to falsify it (Popper, p. 336). Think of ways that the law might not be universally applicable and, therefore, not really a "law" in the scientific sense.

3. Use Commoner's four laws of ecology to analyze one of the following readings: Rachel Carson's "The Obligation to Endure" (p. 328), Wangari Maathai's "Foresters Without Diplomas" (p. 363), or Vandana Shiva's "Soil, not Oil" (p. 374).

EDWARD O. WILSON
The Fitness of Human Nature

[1998]

IN HIS LONG career as a teacher, writer, and researcher, Edward Osborn Wilson (b. 1929) has become one of America's most renowned, and controversial, scientists. Trained as an entomologist, Wilson's early work on ants and other social insects helped to explain why these creatures act in ways that humans consider altruistic. His 1971 book *The Insect Societies* remains a classic in the field of entymology. In 1990, Wilson teamed with German scientist Bert Hölldobler (b. 1936) to produce *The Ants*, an encyclopedic, 740-page analysis of ant behavior that won the 1991 Pulitzer Prize.

After years of scholarly work on the biological basis of insect society, Wilson began to explore ways that biology influences social behavior in other species, including human beings. In his 1976 book *Sociobiology*, he examined biologically based social interaction throughout the animal kingdom. The final chapter explores ways that natural selection might have influenced such human traits as love, loyalty, friendship, and faith. *Sociobiology* ignited a firestorm of controversy across the political spectrum. Conservatives denounced Wilson for assaulting the dignity of human beings by explaining our most cherished beliefs in biological terms. Progressives, on the other hand—led by Wilson's Harvard University colleagues Stephen Jay Gould and Richard Lewontin—felt that Wilson's ideas opened the door to racist and sexist beliefs about the nature of human beings, a charge that Wilson vehemently denied.

In 1979, Wilson received a second Pulitzer Prize for his book *Human Nature*, which advances the ideas about human evolution that he set forth in *Sociobiology*. Over the past thirty years, sociobiological ideas have become increasingly accepted by natural and social scientists alike. Current disciplines such as evolutionary psychology, evolutionary anthropology, population genetics, and even Darwinian literary criticism all trace their core ideas back to Wilson's initial work on sociobiology.

The selection here is taken from Wilson's 1998 book *Consilience: The Unity of Knowledge*. The word *consilience* means "jumping together," and Wilson uses this concept to frame his argument that a correct understanding of human biology—and of natural selection—can unify all branches of knowledge into a single, coherent area of study. By understanding the way that our minds evolved, Wilson believes, we can form better and more useful ideas about psychology, sociology, economics, politics, art, music, literature, religion, and any other area of study that involves human beings.

Wilson builds his argument in this chapter on a simple deductive proposition: if the process of natural selection has determined all complex biological functions, and the human brain contains complex biological functions, then natural selection must have determined the operations of the human brain.

What is human nature? It is not the genes, which prescribe it, or culture, its ultimate product. Rather, human nature is something else for which we have only begun to find ready expression. It is the epigenetic rules,[1] the hereditary regularities of mental development that bias cultural evolution in one direction as opposed to another, and thus connect the genes to culture. . . .

By expressing gene-culture coevolution in such a simple manner, I have no wish either to overwork the metaphor of the selfish gene[2] or to minimize the creative powers of the mind. After all, the genes prescribing the epigenetic rules of brain and behavior are only segments of giant molecules. They feel nothing, care for nothing, intend nothing. Their role is simply to trigger the sequences of chemical reactions within the highly structured fertilized cell that orchestrate epigenesis. Their writ extends to the levels of molecule, cell, and organ. . . . The brain is a product of the very highest levels of biological order, which are constrained by epigenetic rules implicit in the organism's anatomy and physiology. Working in a chaotic flood of environmental stimuli, it sees and listens, learns, plans its own future. By that means the brain determines the fate of the genes that prescribed it. Across evolutionary time, the aggregate choices of many brains determine the Darwinian fate of everything human—the genes, the epigenetic rules, the communicating minds, and the culture.

Brains that choose wisely possess superior Darwinian fitness, meaning that statistically they survive longer and leave more offspring than brains that choose badly. That generalization by itself, commonly telescoped into the phrase "survival of the fittest," sounds like a tautology—the fit survive and those who survive are fit—yet it expresses a powerful generative process well documented in nature. During hundreds of millennia of Paleolithic history, the genes prescribing certain human epigenetic rules increased and spread at the expense of others through the species by means of natural selection. By that laborious process human nature assembled itself.

1. **Epigenetic rules:** In biology, "epigenetic" refers to a change in an organism that takes place without a change in the underlying DNA. Wilson uses the term "epigenetic rule" to refer to a set of instructions passed through the genes that triggers some kind of response when certain environmental conditions are met. The human ability to learn language, for example, is a consequence of an epigenetic rule. People do not inherit any knowledge of a specific language, but they are born with the ability to acquire language at a very young age if they are in a language-saturated environment.

2. **Selfish gene:** *The Selfish Gene* is a 1976 book by Richard Dawkins that argues for a gene-centered view of evolution. The "selfish gene" metaphor does not refer to a gene for selfish behavior, but to a view of natural selection that sees each gene in the body as a "replicator," whose primary function is to make copies of itself that survive into the next generation. Genes that contribute to an organism's ability to survive and reproduce achieve this end. The "selfish gene" theory of evolution is at odds with the organism-centered view of evolution, held by Stephen Jay Gould and others, which sees the whole organism, rather than individual genes, as the primary unit affected by natural selection.

What is truly unique about human evolution, as opposed say to chimpanzee or wolf evolution, is that a large part of the environment shaping it has been cultural. Therefore, construction of a special environment is what culture does to the behavioral genes. Members of past generations who used their culture to best advantage, like foragers gleaning food from a surrounding forest, enjoyed the greatest Darwinian advantage. During prehistory their genes multiplied, changing brain circuitry and behavior traits bit by bit to construct human nature as it exists today. Historical accident played a role in the assembly, and there were many particular expressions of the epigenetic rules that proved self-destructive. But by and large, natural selection, sustained and averaged over long periods of time, was the driving force of human evolution. Human nature is adaptive, or at least was at the time of its genetic origin. . . .

To take behavioral genes into account therefore seems a prudent step when assessing human behavior. Sociobiology (or Darwinian anthropology, or evolutionary psychology, or whatever more politically acceptable term one chooses to call it) offers a key link in the attempt to explain the biological foundation of human nature. By asking questions framed in evolutionary theory, it has already steered research in anthropology and psychology in new directions. Its major research strategy in human studies has been to work from the first principles of population genetics and reproductive biology to predict the forms of social behavior that confer the greatest Darwinian fitness. The predictions are then tested with data taken from ethnographic archives and historical records, as well as from fresh field studies explicitly designed for the purpose. Some of the tests are conducted on preliterate and other traditional societies, whose conservative social practices are likely to resemble most closely those of Paleolithic ancestors. A very few societies in Australia, New Guinea, and South America in fact still have stone-age cultures, which is why anthropologists find them especially interesting. Other tests are conducted with data from modern societies, where fast-evolving cultural norms may no longer be optimally fit. In all these studies a full array of analytic techniques is brought to bear. They include multiple competing hypotheses, mathematical models, statistical analysis, and even the reconstruction of the histories of memes and cultural conventions by the same quantitative procedures used to trace the evolution of genes and species.

In the past quarter-century, human sociobiology has grown into a large and technically complex subject. Nevertheless, it is possible to reduce its primary evolutionary principles to some basic categories, which I will now briefly summarize.

Kin selection is the natural selection of genes based on their effects on individuals carrying them plus the effects the presence of the genes has on all the genetic relatives of the individuals, including parents, children, siblings, cousins, and others who still live and are capable either of reproducing or of affecting the reproduction of blood relatives. Kin selection is especially important in the origin of altruistic behavior. Consider two sisters, who share half their genes by virtue of having the same father and mother. One sacrifices her life, or at least remains childless, in order to help her sister. As a result the sister raises more than twice as many children as she would have otherwise. Since half of her genes are identical to those of her generous sister, the loss in genetic fitness is more than made up by the altruistic nature of the sacrifice. If such actions are predisposed by genes and occur commonly, the genes can spread through the population, even though they induce individuals to surrender personal advantage

From this simple premise and elaborations of it have come a wealth of predictions about patterns of altruism, patriotism, ethnicity, inheritance rules, adoption practices, and infanticide. Many are novel, and most have held up well under testing.

Parental investment is behavior toward offspring that increases the fitness of the latter at the cost of the parent's ability to invest in other offspring. The different patterns of investment have consequences for the fitness of the genes that predispose individuals to select the patterns. Choose one, and you leave more offspring; choose another, and you leave fewer offspring. The idea has given rise to a biologically based "family theory," spinning off new insights on sex ratios, marriage contracts, parent-offspring conflict, grief at the loss of a child, child abuse, and infanticide. . . .

Mating strategy is influenced by the cardinal fact that women have more at stake in   10
sexual activity than men, because of the limited age span in which they can reproduce and the heavy investment required of them with each child conceived. One egg, to put the matter in elemental terms, is hugely more valuable than a single sperm, which must compete with millions of other sperm for the egg. The achievement of pregnancy closes off further breeding opportunity of the mother for a substantial fraction of her remaining reproductive life, whereas the father has the physical capacity to inseminate another woman almost immediately. With considerable success, the nuances of this concept have been used by scientists to predict patterns of mate choice and courtship, relative degrees of sexual permissiveness, paternity anxiety, treatment of women as resources, and polygyny (multiple wives, which in the past at least has been an accepted arrangement in three-quarters of societies around the world). The optimum sexual instinct of men, to put the matter in the now familiar formula of popular literature, is to be assertive and ruttish, while that of women is to be coy and selective. Men are expected to be more drawn than women to pornography and prostitution. And in courtship, men are predicted to stress exclusive sexual access and guarantees of paternity, while women consistently emphasize commitment of resources and material security.

Status is central to all complex mammal societies, humanity included. To say that people generally seek status, whether by rank, class, or wealth, is to sum up a large part of the catalogue of human social behavior. In traditional societies genetic fitness of individuals is generally but not universally correlated with status. In chiefdoms and despotic states especially, dominant males have easy access to multiple women and produce more children, often in spectacular disproportion. Throughout history, despots (absolute rulers with arbitrary powers of life and death over their subjects) commanded access to hundreds or even thousands of women. Some states used explicit rules of distribution, as in Inca Peru, where by law petty chiefs were given seven women, governors of a hundred people eight, leaders of a thousand people fifteen, and lords and kings no fewer than seven hundred. Commoners took what was left over. The fathering of children was commensurately lopsided. In modern industrial states, the relationship between status and genetic fitness is more ambiguous. The data show that high male status is correlated with greater longevity and copulation with more women, but not necessarily the fathering of more children.

Territorial expansion and defense by tribes and their modern equivalents the nation states is a cultural universal. The contribution to survival and future reproductive potential, especially of tribal leaders, is overwhelming, and so is the warlike imperative of tribal defense. "Our country!" declared Commodore Stephen Decatur, hard-fighting hero of the War of 1812, "may she always be right; but our country, right or wrong." (Personal aggressiveness has its Darwinian limits, however; Decatur was killed in a duel in 1820.)

Biologists have determined that territoriality is not unavoidable during social evolution. It is apparently entirely absent in many animal species. The territorial instinct arises during evolution when some vital resource serves as a "density-dependent factor." That is, the growth of population density is slowed incrementally by an increasing shortage of food, water, nest sites, or the entire local terrain available to individuals searching for these resources. Death rates increase or birth rates decrease, or both, until the two rates come more or less into balance and population density levels off. Under such circumstances animal species tend to evolve territorial behavior. The theoretical explanation is that individuals hereditarily predisposed to defend private resources for themselves and their social group pass more genes on to the next generation.

In contrast, the growth of other species is not leveled off by limiting resources but by rising amounts of emigration, disease, or predation. When such alternative density-dependent factors are paramount, and resource control is therefore not required, territorial defense usually does not evolve as a hereditary response.

Humanity is decidedly a territorial species. Since the control of limiting resources has been a matter of life and death through millennia of evolutionary time, territorial aggression is widespread and reaction to it often murderous. It is comforting to say that war, being cultural in origin, can be avoided. Unfortunately, that bit of conventional wisdom is only a half truth. It is more nearly correct—and far more prudent—to say that war arises from both genes and culture and can best be avoided by a thorough understanding of the manner in which these two modes of heredity interact within different historical contexts.

Contractual agreement so thoroughly pervades human social behavior, virtually like the air we breathe, that it attracts no special notice—until it goes bad. Yet it deserves focused scientific research for the following reason. All mammals, including humans, form societies based on a conjunction of selfish interests. Unlike the worker castes of ants and other social insects, they resist committing their bodies and services to the common good. Rather, they devote their energies to their own welfare and that of close kin. For mammals, social life is a contrivance to enhance personal survival and reproductive success. As a consequence, societies of nonhuman mammalian species are far less organized than the insect societies. They depend on a combination of dominance hierarchies, rapidly shifting alliances, and blood ties. Human beings have loosened this constraint and improved social organization by extending kinshiplike ties to others through long-term contracts.

Contract formation is more than a cultural universal. It is a human trait as characteristic of our species as language and abstract thought, having been constructed from both instinct and high intelligence. Thanks to ground-breaking experiments by the psychologists Leda Cosmides and John Tooby at the University of California at Santa Barbara, we know that contract formation is not simply the product of a single rational faculty that operates equally across all agreements made among bargaining parties. Instead, one capacity, the detection of cheating, is developed to exceptional levels of sharpness and rapid calculation. Cheater detection stands out in acuity from mere error detection and the assessment of altruistic intent on the part of others. It is furthermore triggered as a computation procedure only when the cost and benefits of a social contract are specified. More than error, more than good deeds, and more even than the margin of profit, the possibility of cheating by others attracts attention. It excites emotion and serves as the principal source of hostile gossip and moralistic aggression by which the integrity of the political economy is maintained.

UNDERSTANDING THE TEXT

1. How does Wilson characterize the interaction between genes and culture—or, in the terms made familiar by earlier debates, between nature and nurture? How do "epigenetic rules" bridge the gap between these two sides?

2. According to Wilson, what role has natural selection played in the development of human psychology? Does he see any difference at all between the evolution of the mind and the evolution of the body?

3. How, according to Wilson, has human evolution been different from the evolution of any other species? What accounts for this key difference?

4. How have scientists such as Wilson gathered evidence for theories about human behavior in primitive conditions?

5. What does Wilson mean by the term "kin selection"? What evolutionary factors have led people to feel altruistic toward members of their own family?

6. What are the basic differences in mating strategies between males and females? How have these differences, according to Wilson, led to certain differences between male and female human nature?

7. Why, according to Wilson, are humans tribal and territorial? Are these traits that can be altered, or does Wilson present them as inherent parts of our psychological makeup? Explain.

8. What does Wilson say lies behind the human desire to cooperate and make agreements with other human beings? Why do we act altruistically toward people who are not closely related to us and do not therefore carry any of our genes?

MAKING CONNECTIONS

1. How does Wilson use the arguments of Charles Darwin in *Origin of Species* (p. 314)? Are his arguments about the evolution of human psychology consistent with Darwin's principles of evolution generally? Explain.

2. Do Wilson's theories tend to support Mencius's positive view of human nature (p. 78) or Hsün Tzu's more negative view (p. 84)? How might supporters of either of these theories appeal to biological or evolutionary evidence to support their claims?

3. How might biological evidence support or refute Thomas Hobbes's view of the state of nature as a state of perpetual war (p. 94)?

4. Would Wilson agree with Margaret Mead's view that warfare is a learned behavior rather than a biological imperative (p. 500)? What would Wilson single out as the basis of aggressive behavior in humans?

WRITING ABOUT THE TEXT

1. Compare or contrast Wilson's views on the interaction between nature and culture with those of Ruth Benedict in "The Individual and the Pattern of Culture" (p. 112).

2. Choose one of Wilson's categories of human behavior (kin selection, mating strategies, etc.) and use it as the basis for analyzing a book or a movie of your choice. You might, for example, examine the differences between male and female courtship strategies in a romantic comedy or the underlying reasons for violence in a war movie or historical epic.

3. Refute Wilson's argument that human behavior has a biological basis by arguing that humans don't behave as we would expect from the evolutionary factors that Wilson names. Include several examples in your response.

WANGARI MAATHAI
Foresters without Diplomas
[2006]

WANGARI MAATHAI (1940–2011) was a Kenyan educator, activist, and politician. After studying biology in the United States, she returned to Kenya and received a Ph.D. in veterinary anatomy from the University of Nairobi in 1971. There she became the first female professor in the Department of Veterinary Anatomy.

Maathai is best known as the founder of Kenya's Green Belt Movement, an organization that trains women to plant trees in order to obtain a renewable fuel source and to combat both deforestation and soil erosion. Since it was formed in 1977, the Green Belt Movement has employed more than 30,000 women and has planted more than 51 million trees. Her involvement with the organization brought Maathai to national and international prominence and, increasingly, into conflict with the Kenyan government.

In the 1980s and 1990s, Maathai became an important part of Kenya's pro-democracy movement, which pressured the single-party government to allow competitive elections. She also played an important role in the coalition opposed to the powerful Kenya African National Union (KANU) Party. In 2002, the opposition parties finally succeeded in ousting the ruling party, and Maathai was elected to Parliament with 98 percent of the vote in her district. She held this position until her death in 2011 from ovarian cancer.

In 2004, Wangari Maathai became the first African woman ever to win the Nobel Peace Prize. In awarding her the prize, the Nobel Committee praised "her contribution to sustainable development, democracy and peace." The selection here, "Foresters without Diplomas," is drawn from Maathai's 2007 memoir *Unbowed*. In this selection, she explains the factors that led to her conclusion that planting trees would be the best way to solve many of the problems in her country. As she narrates the events leading to the founding of the Green Belt Movement, she uses stories to illustrate that women can be empowered to solve some of the most complicated environmental problems of our day.

A great river always begins somewhere. Often it starts as a tiny spring bubbling up from a crack in the soil, just like the little stream on my family's land in Ihithe,[1] which starts where the roots of the fig tree broke through the rocks beneath the ground. But for the stream to grow into a river, it must meet other tributaries and join them as it heads for a lake or the sea. So, when people learn about my life and the work of the Green Belt Movement and ask me "Why trees?," the truth of the

---

1. **Ihithe:** a village in the Nyeri District of Central Kenya.

matter is that the question has many answers. The essential one was that I reacted to a set of problems by focusing on what could be done. As it turned out, the idea that sprang from my roots merged with other sources of knowledge and action to form a confluence that grew bigger than I would ever have imagined.

In the early 1970s, in addition to my work at the University of Nairobi, I was involved with a number of civic organizations, including the Nairobi branch of the Kenya Red Cross of which I became director in 1973, and the Kenya Association of University Women. Many of these organizations had been founded by the British and staffed almost entirely by the wives of colonial officials. After independence,[2] Africans gradually replaced the white women. Educated Kenyan women, of whom there were still very few in the early 1970s, were often asked to volunteer their time in positions of leadership.

I was invited to join the local board of the Environment Liaison Centre. The Centre had been established in 1974 by a group of international environmental organizations to ensure the participation of civil society groups (also known as nongovernmental organizations, or NGOs) in the work of the United Nations Environment Programme (UNEP), whose headquarters were established in Nairobi. UNEP, the first (and only) UN agency devoted to environmental issues and the only one headquartered in the developing world, was launched following the first United Nations global conference on the environment, held in Stockholm in 1972. The Stockholm conference helped raise awareness of the realities of environmental degradation in Africa and other regions, even though many developing countries' governments didn't agree with the solutions to the environmental crisis put forth by the industrialized nations, which they viewed as seeking to inhibit the development of poor countries.

Most of the originators of the Environment Liaison Centre (now called the Environment Liaison Centre International) were from Europe, North America, and Asia, and felt it was important for local people—Kenyans—to serve as "alternate," or local, board members. I was one of the few women members of the local board and became an alternate for Huey Johnson of the Resource Renewal Institute in California. Huey became a good friend and supporter and remains so to this day.

For me, a biologist who had grown up in a rural area where our daily lives depended on the health of the environment, the issues raised at the Liaison Centre were not completely strange. For example, when we discussed biological diversity, my study of genetics was relevant. But a great deal of the information I was exposed to through meetings at UNEP, books and articles, and discussions with people working in environmental NGOs in different countries was new to me. Much of it dealt with natural sciences from a holistic perspective. Through the Liaison Centre, a whole different world opened up to me. In time, my colleagues elected me chair of the local board, a position I was to hold for more than ten years. I became so preoccupied with my voluntary work with the Liaison Centre that it almost became my second full-time career!

5

2. **Independence:** Kenya received its independence from Great Britain in 1963.

Another stream that contributed to my growing environmental awareness was academic. In the early 1970s, Kenya was the best producer of livestock products in East Africa. At the university I participated in research in veterinary medicine in an effort to keep domestic animals healthy and productive, not just in Kenya but throughout the region. Consequently, I undertook postdoctoral research on the life cycle of a parasite responsible for East Coast fever, a disease fatal to imported hybrid cattle that is spread through brown ear ticks. Local bovines are almost immune to the disease. I collected hundreds of the ticks from the cattle, incised them through the salivary glands (where the parasite lodged), cut them up for microscopic observation, and produced thousands of slides.

While I was in the rural areas outside Nairobi collecting the ticks, I noticed that the rivers would rush down the hillsides and along paths and roads when it rained, and that they were muddy with silt. This was very different from when I was growing up. "That is soil erosion," I remember thinking to myself. "We must do something about that." I also observed that the cows were so skinny that I could count their ribs. There was little grass or other fodder for them to eat where they grazed, and during the dry season much of the grass lacked nutrients.

The people, too, looked undernourished and poor and the vegetation in their fields was scanty. The soils in the fields weren't performing as they should because their nutrient value had been depleted. It became clear to me through these observations that Kenya's and the whole region's livestock industry was threatened more by environmental degradation than by either the ticks in the cows' ears or the parasites in the ticks' salivary glands.

When I went home to visit my family in Nyeri, I had another indication of the changes under way around us. I saw rivers silted with topsoil, much of which was coming from the forest where plantations of commercial trees had replaced indigenous forest. I noticed that much of the land that had been covered by trees, bushes, and grasses when I was growing up had been replaced by tea and coffee.

I also learned that someone had acquired the piece of land where the fig tree I was   10
in awe of as a child had stood. The new owner perceived the tree to be a nuisance because it took up too much space and he felled it to make room to grow tea. By then I understood the connection between the tree and water, so it did not surprise me that when the fig tree was cut down, the stream where I had played with the tadpoles dried up. My children would never be able to play with the frogs' eggs as I had or simply to enjoy the cool, clear water of that stream. I mourned the loss of that tree. I profoundly appreciated the wisdom of my people, and how generations of women had passed on to their daughters the cultural tradition of leaving the fig trees in place. I was expected to pass it on to my children, too.

Whatever the original inspiration for not cutting these trees, people in that region had been spared landslides, as the strong roots of the fig trees held the soil together in the steep mountains. They also had abundant, clean water. But by the early 1970s, landslides were becoming common and sources of clean water for drinking were becoming scarce. Ironically, the area where the fig tree of my childhood once stood always remained a patch of bare ground where nothing grew. It was as if the land rejected anything but the fig tree itself.

Another tributary of knowledge consisted of the women themselves, who brought the urgency of the situation home to me. By the early 1970s, I was a member of the National Council of Women of Kenya (NCWK). The NCWK was founded in 1964 as an umbrella organization to unify women's groups, both large and small, throughout Kenya, with membership drawn from urban and rural areas. The leadership consisted of women who were successful in their business, professional, or religious lives and they gave one another moral support in whatever sphere they were involved.

At a seminar organized by the NCWK, a woman researcher presented the results of a study she had done, which found that children in the central region of Kenya were suffering from diseases associated with malnutrition. This was an eye-opener for me, since that is where I come from and I knew from personal experience that the central region was one of the most fertile in Kenya. But times had changed. Many farmers had converted practically all of their land into growing coffee and tea to sell in the international market. These "cash crops" were occupying land previously used to produce food for people to eat.

Consequently, women were feeding their families processed foods like white bread, maize flour, and white rice, all of which are high in carbohydrates but relatively low in vitamins, proteins, and minerals. Cooking these foods consumed less energy than the foods I had eaten as a child, and this made them attractive and practical, because available firewood for cooking was limited due to deforestation in the region. Instead, women were using as fuel materials left over from the harvest, such as corn stems and husks. This shortage of firewood, the researcher concluded, was leading directly to malnutrition as people's diets changed in response. The most vulnerable were children and the elderly.

These facts troubled me, not least because they seemed so contrary to my experiences as a child—when there was more than enough food, the food itself was nutritious and wholesome, people were healthy and strong, and there was always enough firewood to cook with. I remembered how the colonial administration had cleared the indigenous forests and replaced them with plantations of exotic trees for the timber industry. After independence, Kenyan farmers had cleared more natural forests to create space to grow coffee and tea. Until now, however, I had not fully appreciated the multiple costs of these activities.

Although the leadership of the NCWK was generally elite and urban, we were concerned with the social and economic status of the majority of our members, who were poor, rural women. We worried about their access to clean water and firewood, how they would feed their children, pay their school fees, and afford clothing, and we wondered what we could do to ease their burdens. We had a choice: We could either sit in an ivory tower wondering how so many people could be so poor and

15

not be working to change their situation, or we could try to help them escape the vicious cycle they found themselves in. This was not a remote problem for us. The rural areas were where our mothers and sisters still lived. We owed it to them to do all we could.

At the same time, women in other countries throughout the world were recognizing the need to make changes in their own communities and bring their perspectives and experiences to the global arena, and their political leaders were giving them increasing space to do so. In June 1975, to coincide with the International Women's Year, 133 governments and about 4,000 women from around the world gathered in Mexico City for the first UN conference on women.

In the two years leading up to the women's conference, at both the Environment Liaison Centre and the NCWK, we were asking ourselves what our agenda should be for Mexico City. The NCWK held a number of seminars at which we heard from various constituencies, including women from the rural areas. These women confirmed what the researcher's study had suggested. They didn't have enough wood for fuel or fencing, fodder for their livestock, water to cook with or drink, or enough for themselves or their families to eat.

As I sat listening to the women talk about water, energy, and nutrition, I could see that everything they lacked depended on the environment. These women were laying out their agenda. When the representatives of the NCWK returned from the Mexico City conference (I was unable to go because there were not sufficient funds), they carried the same message: We needed to do something about water and energy. The conference participants had also concluded that the world needed to address the realities of rural women, their poverty, the overall lack of development, and the state of the environment that sustained them.

It suddenly became clear. Not only was the livestock industry threatened by a   20
deteriorating environment, but I, my children, my students, my fellow citizens, and my entire country would pay the price. The connection between the symptoms of environmental degradation and their causes—deforestation, devegetation, unsustainable agriculture, and soil loss—were self-evident. Something had to be done. We could not just deal with the manifestations of the problems. We had to get to the root causes of those problems.

Now, it is one thing to understand the issues. It is quite another to do something about them. But I have always been interested in finding solutions. This is, I believe, a result of my education as well as my time in America: to think of what can be done rather than worrying about what cannot. I didn't sit down and ask myself, "Now let me see; what shall I do?" It just came to me: "Why not plant trees?" The trees would provide a supply of wood that would enable women to cook nutritious foods. They would also have wood for fencing and fodder for cattle and goats. The trees would offer shade for humans and animals, protect watersheds and bind the soil, and, if they were fruit trees, provide food. They would also heal the land by bringing back birds and small animals and regenerate the vitality of the earth.

This is how the Green Belt Movement began. The rest of it perhaps was sheer luck: If I'd picked something other than trees my efforts might have failed, and I may have remained at the University of Nairobi as a professor and now be retired and enjoying my pension. But that wouldn't have been half as interesting. When I reflect on the years leading to the creation of the Green Belt Movement and the years of its emergence and growth, it also seems no coincidence that it was nurtured during the time the global women's movement was taking off, or that it flourished during the decade for women (1976–1985) the United Nations declared in Mexico City.

By 1975, I already had an idea of how I might go about encouraging the planting of trees because of events that were happening simultaneously in my personal life. In spite of his defeat in 1969, my husband's appetite for politics had not diminished. In 1974 he decided to run for Parliament again for the same constituency, Lang'ata, that he had contested five years earlier. I supported this decision and worked very hard to make sure that this time he won. This was a tall order since I was still working full time at the university and we now had three children, including a newborn, Muta. Nevertheless, we worked together and separately on the campaign trail, visiting people and talking to them about their aspirations. We were a young and highly educated couple, and I could see how much hope people were investing in us. They believed we could make a difference in their lives.

By this time, unemployment had become a major issue for Kenya and lack of jobs was one of the voters' main concerns. In the course of the campaign, Mwangi[3] promised that he would create more employment for people if they voted for him. This worried me a lot. When I make a promise, I expect to keep it, and if I cannot deliver something, then I do not promise that I will. But Mwangi kept on saying that jobs would be found. "Where will he get these jobs from?" I thought to myself. "There are no jobs these days." We couldn't simply knock on doors and ask people to give the voters jobs. Many of them had no academic qualifications or marketable skills and were illiterate. It simply wasn't possible.

But I have never been interested in what is not possible. "I'm going to plan," I said   25
to myself. "I'm going to make sure these people have jobs, or they will never vote for us again, because we've broken our promise." When Mwangi won the election, I was proud of his achievement. I was in the speaker's gallery when he took his oath of office and was genuinely happy for him. I knew that he was happy, too; he was now an honorable member of Parliament. After he had taken his oath of office, I raised the issue of his promises. "What are you going to do with all the people you promised the jobs to?" I asked. "That was the campaign," he replied. "Now we are in Parliament."

"But they might not vote for us the next time," I urged him to remember.

"Don't worry, they won't remember."

3. **Mwangi:** Mwangi Maathai, a Kenyan politician and Wangari Maathai's husband.

I couldn't believe what I was hearing. "Excuse me?" I cried. "Of course, they'll remember! How can we face these people in another campaign? How can we walk around asking for their votes? Don't you think they'll ask, 'Where are those jobs you promised?'" Mwangi told me not to worry. But I did. I refused to accept that we should break our promises so easily. Soon after, I launched a business that I hoped could provide many jobs and would incorporate the planting of trees. I called it Envirocare Ltd.

Now, Lang'ata constituency contained many of the richest as well as some of the poorest parts of the city, including a section of the expansive Kibera slum. The wealthy areas consisted of huge estates with many large and luxuriant gardens. To me these gardens never looked well maintained, even though the owners of the estates employed servants to look after them throughout the year. I thought that I could change that. My idea was simple: Why not bring a whole army of men and women into these gardens and let them do everything that needed to be done, in one day? The owner of the house would come home to find his garden looking perfect and he would need only to call us again when his hedges needed trimming or his flowerbeds required tending or new trees needed to be planted. Furthermore, the owner could enjoy his garden by himself, without having servants wandering around it each day.

Envirocare would employ people from the poor part of Mwangi's constituency, who needed jobs, to keep happy the richer members of the constituency, who could afford to employ them. They would also plant seedlings in parts of the city that were bare of trees. In the process we would create a beautiful Nairobi! It seemed to me a perfect solution, and I thought the wealthy people would support it. Envirocare would be located in our house, and my idea was that, in addition to providing employment, it would become a forum through which Mwangi and I could listen and respond to the concerns of his constituents. . . .

30

By late 1977, news of the tree-planting initiatives had spread throughout the NCWK networks and soon farmers, schools, and churches were eager to set up their own programs. That was the beginning of communities themselves taking ownership of Green Belt Movement initiatives, and I have insisted on working this way ever since. It was gratifying that after so many disappointments, my idea was taking off. But it was still an extracurricular activity for me, on top of my job at the university, my other affiliations, and raising my children.

Luckily, I enjoyed using my potential and I had a lot of energy: Then, I could move like a gazelle; nowadays my legs are giving way. I also had a woman who helped me take care of the children and worked around the house. It was, nonetheless, difficult for me to be in so many places: I was organizing and instructing and, when we decided to establish our own tree nurseries, I went out in the field with the foresters and created them.

With the tree planting taking root, work and expenses increased. I was constantly asking friends and others to sponsor trees. Luckily, we were beginning to get support from institutions. I managed to get some money from the NCWK, and the Canadian ambassador to Kenya gave us a car for the project activities, while Mobil Oil (Kenya) was one of the few companies that responded to my requests for funds. It provided a grant that allowed us to establish another tree nursery in Nairobi.

Within months, the tree-planting program became so popular that the NCWK was overwhelmed by the demand for seedlings. So I paid a visit to the government's chief conservator of forests, Onesimus Mburu, and told him our plans. We were thinking big: We wanted to plant a tree for every person in Kenya—at that time, a total of fifteen million. We even had a slogan: "One person, one tree."

Mr. Mburu burst into laughter. "You can have all the seedlings you like," he replied. "And you can have them free of charge." Now it is obvious that he didn't believe that we would ever exceed his supply of seedlings. However, only a few months later, this is exactly what happened. "You'll have to pay for them," he told me when I asked for more. "You are taking too many seedlings from the foresters." Then it was my turn to laugh. We could not possibly afford to pay for as many as we needed. We still needed the trees, however, and it was getting increasingly difficult to get them from the Department of Forests. Although the foresters had been supportive at the beginning, I sensed some professional jealousy creeping in as the women became more efficient at planting trees.

Initially, we had distributed seedlings through individual farmers and groups of women who went to the nearest forester in their region to take seedlings, and the NCWK would compensate the Department of Forests for them. However, we soon had to change this policy, partly because the foresters raised fast-growing exotic species and not native trees, which grow more slowly but are better for long-term environmental health. Many of the sites from which women had to collect the seedlings were far from their farms and they usually needed a way to bring their seedlings home. Complicating things further was the fact that the foresters didn't have money or vehicles to transport the women to and from the nurseries to collect the trees. In addition, when the trees were taken from the nurseries they lost a lot of soil because they were virtually uprooted. This meant a lot of seedlings died before they could be planted.

Our solution was to create our own supply of trees. Most of the seedlings we grew were indigenous, although a few communities did plant exotic species, which they liked because they grew very quickly. We organized meetings where foresters talked to the women about how to run their own nurseries. But these were difficult encounters. The foresters didn't understand why I was trying to teach rural women how to plant trees. "You need a professional," they told me. "You need people with diplomas to plant trees." But, I learned, professionals can make simple things complicated. They told the women about the gradient of the land and the entry point of the sun's rays, the depth of the seedbed, the content of the gravel, the type of

35

soil, and all the specialized tools and inputs needed to run a successful tree nursery! Naturally, this was more than the women, nearly all of whom were poor and illiterate, could handle or even needed.

What the foresters were saying didn't seem right to me. You might need a diploma to understand a tree's growth and what the content of the seedling was, but I didn't believe the women needed all the technical knowledge the foresters were dispensing to plant trees successfully. All they needed to know was how to put the seedling in the soil and help it grow, and that didn't seem too hard. Anybody can dig a hole, put a tree in it, water it, and nurture it.

In any case, these women were farmers. They were putting things in the ground and watching them grow all the time. Like them, I too had seen and planted seeds ever since I was a child. So I advised the women to look at the seedlings in a different way. "I don't think you need a diploma to plant a tree," I told them. "Use your woman sense. These tree seedlings are very much like the seeds you deal with—beans and maize and millet—every day. Put them in the soil. If they're good, they'll germinate. If they're not, they won't. Simple."

And this is what they did. The good ones germinated and the bad ones didn't, and the ones that did looked exactly like the trees planted by the foresters! This showed us we were on the right track. Soon the women started showing one another, and before we knew it tree nurseries were springing up on farms and public land around the country. These women were our "foresters without diplomas."

As we went along, we constantly examined what we were doing, looking to change what didn't work as well as it could and refine what did and make it even more effective. At first, we gave the women seeds, but that made the women too dependent on us. It also meant that we'd be growing the same kinds of trees around the country. Just as we did not want exotic species instead of native trees, we also wanted, as in nature, a diversity of species and not millions of the same trees spread across Kenya. So we told the women to collect seeds in the forests and their fields and try to grow trees native to their area. We also encouraged them to experiment with different ways of ensuring the seedlings' survival. In addition, we gave the women containers to retain the soil around the seedlings as they grew and when they were transplanted.

Not surprisingly, the women were incredibly resourceful. They used the technology they had available and they used it well. Sometimes they laid their seedbeds on the ground and sometimes they filled broken pots with soil and placed them in a high spot out of reach of their chickens and goats, who might eat the growing trees. The women also used old pots or cans with holes punched in them to water their seedlings. I encouraged this innovation and constantly asked them to think of new ways to do things and not wait for some "official assessment" to take place.

We also gave the women an incentive. "Whenever a seedling that you have raised is planted," I told them, "the movement will compensate you." This was a small amount—the equivalent then of four U.S. cents a tree—but it provided a lot

40

of motivation. After all, these were poor women who, even though they were work-ing all the time—tending crops and livestock, gathering firewood, carrying water, cooking, taking care of their children—had few options for paid employment.

To help the women progress in a way they could handle, we developed a procedure with ten steps, from forming a group, locating a site for a tree nursery, and report-ing on their progress to planting trees and following up to make sure they survived. "Do the first step," I said. "If you do the first step and you succeed, let us know. Then move to the second step and the third. By the time you get to the tenth step we'll bring you your money. You'll have done a good job.

After the women had planted seedlings on their own farms, I suggested that   45 they go to surrounding areas and convince others to plant trees. This was a break-through, because it was now communities empowering one another for their own needs and benefit. In this way, step by step, the process replicated itself several thousand times. As women and communities increased their efforts, we encouraged them to plant seedlings in rows of at least a thousand trees to form green "belts" that would restore to the earth its cloth of green. This is how the name Green Belt Movement began to be used. Not only did the "belts" hold the soil in place and provide shade and windbreaks but they also re-created habitat and enhanced the beauty of the landscape.

Although I was a highly educated woman, it did not seem odd to me to be working with my hands, often with my knees on the ground, alongside rural women. Some politicians and others in the 1980s and 1990s ridiculed me for doing so. But I had no problem with it, and the rural women both accepted and appreciated that I was working with them to improve their lives and the environment. After all, I was a child of the same soil.

Education, if it means anything, should not take people away from the land, but instill in them even more respect for it, because educated people are in a position to understand what is being lost. The future of the planet concerns all of us, and all of us should do what we can to protect it. As I told the foresters, and the women, you don't need a diploma to plant a tree.

UNDERSTANDING THE TEXT

1. What is the first symptom of environmental degradation that Maathai notices? What effects does she attribute to this form of degradation?

2. How are deforestation, soil erosion, malnutrition in cattle, lack of clean water, and malnutrition in children all related to each other? How can planting trees alleviate these problems?

3. What has been the effect on the Kenyan population of farmers replacing food crops with "cash crops"—like coffee—that can be sold on the international market?

4. What does Maathai say happens when families do not have access to wood from local sources?

5. Why does Maathai believe that the women of the Green Belt Movement need to create their own nurseries and gather their own seeds instead of using available resources?

6. What kinds of knowledge do the women of Kenya bring to the Green Belt Movement? How does their knowledge compare to the knowledge of those who are experts in forestry?

MAKING CONNECTIONS

1. Discuss the connections that Maathai sees between various environmental factors in terms of Barry Commoner's four laws of ecology (p. 344).

2. How does Maathai compare the kinds of knowledge that women gain in their own gardens with the kind that foresters receive in their formal schooling? How does this compare to the two kinds of knowledge that Richard Feynman discusses in "O Americano Outra Vez" (p. 53)?

3. Compare and contrast Wangari Maathai, Aung San Suu Kyi (p. 442), and Vandana Shiva (p. 374) as political activists. How are their principles or philosophies similar? How are they different?

WRITING ABOUT THE TEXT

1. Use the effects of deforestation that Wangari Maathai describes as the basis for a discussion of the ecological consequences of isolated actions. Use the readings by Carson (p. 328), Commoner (p. 344), and Shiva (p. 374) as further evidence for your argument.

2. Compare the kinds of knowledge that the women of the Green Belt Movement hold with those of the professional foresters.

3. Compare the philosophies of Wangari Maathai's Green Belt Movement and Vandana Shiva's Navdanya movement. How are the two movements similar? How are they different?

VANDANA SHIVA
from *Soil, Not Oil*
[2008]

DR. VANDANA SHIVA was born in India in 1952. She holds an M.A. in the history of science from the University of Guelph in Ontario, Canada, and a Ph.D. in physics from the University of Western Ontario. Shiva is the founder of the Research Foundation for Science, Technology, and Ecology (RFSTE) in Uttar Pradesh, a province in northern India. This, in turn, led to the creation of Navdanya ("nine crops" and "new gift"), a group that promotes organic farming, establishes seed banks, and lobbies against genetically modified foods.

Shiva has become one of the world's most well-known ecologists. She has written more than twenty books and lectured around the world on topics such as food security, globalization, biodiversity, sustainability, and women's rights. She has also served as a policy advisor to national and local governments in India, Italy, Spain, and Bhutan and has won dozens of awards for her writing, speaking, and activism. In 2003, *Time* magazine named her an "Environmental Hero."

The reading excerpted here comes from Shiva's 2008 book *Soil, Not Oil: Environmental Justice in an Age of Climate Crisis*. In it, she argues that current levels of fossil fuel consumption are both unsustainable and ecologically destructive, since there is not enough available energy on Earth for all people to consume it at the rate of the wealthiest countries. To create sustainable communities, the world needs to shift from an "industrial paradigm," which defines progress as moving more and more people to a high-level consumption of fossil-based carbon, to a "biodiversity paradigm" which meets energy needs with renewable, plant-based carbon.

Necessarily, this kind of paradigm shift will mean a world in which people travel less, work differently, and eat different kinds of foods. As Shiva points out, however, many people in the world already live and work close to home and eat food that they grow themselves. Rather than trying to push these communities into an industrial paradigm, industrialized nations should work to protect these communities' ways of life, learn from them, and emulate their consumption patterns.

Much of Shiva's rhetorical power comes from the way that she defines familiar terms in new ways. In this reading she encourages readers to think of the terms "equity" and "democracy" not merely in the context of human relationships, but as applicable as well to how we treat the earth itself and the generations of people who have yet to be born.

The climate crisis is at its roots a consequence of human beings having gone astray from the ecological path of living with justice and sustainability. It is a consequence of forgetting that we are earth citizens. It is acting like we are kids in a supermarket with limitless appetites for consumption and falsely imagining that the corporations that stock the supermarkets have unlimited energy warehouses. The real problem is the conflict between the economic laws that have reduced the planet and society to a supermarket where everything is for sale and the ecological laws that maintain the planet's ecological functions and social laws that distribute nature's goods and services equitably. The real problem is a global economy that has created a planetary ecological imbalance.

If these are the real problems, then the real solution cannot be replacing fossil fuels with other non-sustainable sources to power the same systems. The real solution must be to search for right living, for well-being, and for joy, while simultaneously reducing consumption. In Indian philosophy, right living is "dharma"—the bridge between resources, *arth*, and human needs, *kama*. Dharma is therefore based on the sustainable and just use of resources for fulfilling needs. Ecological balance and social justice are intrinsic to right livelihood, to dharma. "Dharanath dharma ucyat"—that which sustains all species of life and helps maintain harmonious relationship among them is "dharma." That which disturbs the balance of the earth and her species is "adharma."

Equity is about fair share. There are currently two paradigms of equity. One sets the overconsumption and waste of rich industrial societies as the model and measure of being human, being developed. Equity is presented as the entire world being pushed to that level of resource and energy consumption. However, this version of equity would need five planets. This non-sustainable paradigm inevitably produces inequity. Shall we choose a non-sustainable paradigm in which we affirm an equal right to pollute or a sustainable paradigm in which we affirm an equal responsibility to *not* pollute.

Earth Democracy and ecological equity recognize that because the planet's resources and capacity to renew resources are limited, a reduction in energy and resource consumption of the rich is necessary for all to have access to land and water, food and fiber, air and energy. In an ecological paradigm, what works against Gaia works against the poor and works against future generations, and what works for Gaia works for the poor and for the future.[1]

We need to define equity on the same ecological parameters locally and globally. If communities in India are resisting displacement and uprooting, if they define and experience their lives in the forest or small farms as the terms of their material and spiritual well-being, respecting their rights and freedoms is the first step toward equity. Equity needs to be grounded in the earth, in people's struggles and movements, not dropped in as an abstraction from remote conference halls. Those who would uproot farmers say the life of a peasant is "undignified." Those who would uproot indigenous people define life in a forest as "below the dignity line." Dignity is an experience and consequence of self-organization and sovereignty, of sufficiency and satisfaction.

1. **Gaia:** according to Greek legend, the personification of Earth, often used as a synonym for Earth itself.

I have never found working the soil or lighting a wood fire lacking in dignity. It is disposability that robs people of their dignity and selfhood. That is why movements against displacement are so intense and widespread in contemporary India.

Real solutions will come from breaking free of the crippling world of mechanistic assumptions, industrial methods of producing goods with high energy and resource costs, and market mechanisms that make high-cost products appear cheap on supermarket shelves.

The eco-imperialist response to the climate crisis is to grab the remaining resources of the planet, close the remaining spaces of freedom, and use the worst form of militarized violence to exterminate people's rights and people themselves when they get in the way of an insatiable economy's resource appropriation, driven by the insatiable greed of corporations.

There is another response—that of Earth Democracy.

Earth Democracy recognizes that if the survival of our species is threatened, maintaining our ability to live on the planet is the only intelligent response. Chasing economic growth while ecosystems collapse is a sign of stupidity, not wisdom. Earth Democracy calls for a systemic and inclusive response to the climate crisis, not the fragmented and self-serving response that corporations and rich countries are making. Earth Democracy allows us to break free of the global supermarket of commodification and consumerism, which is destroying our food, our farms, our homes, our towns, and our planet. It allows us to re-imbed our eating and drinking, our moving and working, into our local ecosystems and local cultures, enriching our lives while lowering our consumption without impoverishing others. In Earth Democracy, everything is interconnected. To address the pollution of the atmosphere, we do not have to limit ourselves to changes in the atmosphere. We can change agriculture; we can change the way we design buildings and towns; we can change the way we shop.

In Earth Democracy, solutions will not come from the corporations and governments that have raped the planet and destroyed peoples' lives. Solutions are coming from those who know how to live lightly, who have never had an oil addiction, who do not define the good life as "shop till you drop," but rather define it as looking after the living earth and their living community. Those who are being treated as disposable in the dominant system, which is pushing the planet's ecosystems to collapse and our species to extinction, carry the knowledge and values, the cultures and skills, that give humanity a chance for survival.

To mitigate and adapt to climate change we need to stop the assault on small farmers and indigenous communities, to defend their rights to their land and territory, to see them not as remnants of our past but as the path for our future.

Earth Democracy begins and ends with Gaia's laws—the law of renewability, the law of conservation, the law of entropy, the law of diversity. In Earth Democracy, all beings and all peoples are equal, and all beings and all communities have rights to the resources of the earth for their sustenance.

10

In Earth Democracy, the solution to the climate crisis begins with the cultures and communities who have not contributed to it.

Earth Democracy is based on equal rights of all beings to ecological space, including atmospheric space. The atmosphere is an ecological commons. Climate justice demands that this commons not be enclosed by a handful of polluters. Climate justice also demands that people be compensated for the impact of climate chaos caused by the actions of others. But above all, climate justice demands that every person, every community, every society have the freedom to create and defend economies that cause no harm to the climate or to other people.

To prevent climate chaos and to avoid further increases in emissions we must stop the   15
coercion of trade liberalization and rewrite the rules of trade to favor the local. WTO[2] rules and World Bank structural adjustment programs are robbing sustainable local economies and sustainable communities of their freedom to be sustainable. Compelling them to import food from thousands of miles away and preventing them from having safeguards that protect the local are—in terms of climate change—ecological crimes.

Earth Democracy generates a radical shift in our paradigms and in our patterns of production. It offers real solutions to resource exhaustion, peak oil, climate change, disposability of people, and the erosion of democracy.

Climate change and the two carbon economies: Biodiversity vs Fossil Fuels

Reductionism seems to have become the habit of the contemporary human mind. We are increasingly talking of climate change in the context of "the carbon economy." We refer to "zero carbon" and "no carbon" as if carbon exists only in fossilized form under the ground. We forget that the cellulose of plants is primarily carbon. Humus in the soil is mostly carbon. Vegetation in the forests is mostly carbon. It is living carbon. It is part of the cycle of life.

The problem is not carbon *per se*, but our increasing use of fossil carbon that was formed over millions of years. Today the world burns 400 years' worth of this accumulated biological matter every year, three to four times more than in 1956. While plants are a renewable resource, fossil carbon for our purposes is not. It will take millions of years to renew the earth's supply of coal and oil.

Before the industrial revolution, there were 580 billions tons of carbon in the atmosphere. Today there are 750 billion tons. That accumulation, the result of burning fossil fuels, is causing the climate change crisis. Humanity needs to solve this problem if we are to survive. It is the other carbon economy, the renewable carbon embodied in biodiversity, that offers the solution.

Our dependence on fossil fuels has broken us out of nature's renewable carbon   20
cycle. Our dependence on fossil fuels has fossilized our thinking.

2. **WTO:** World Trade Organization.

Biodiversity is the alternative to fossil carbon. Everything that we derive from the petrochemical industry has an alternative in the realm of biodiversity. The synthetic fertilizers and pesticides, the chemical dyes, the sources of mobility and energy, all of these have sustainable alternatives in the plant and animal world. In place of nitrogen fertilizers, we have nitrogen-fixing leguminous crops and biomass recycled by earthworms (vermi-compost) or microorganisms (compost). In place of synthetic dyes, we have vegetable dyes. In place of the automobile, we have the camel, the horse, the bullock, the donkey, the elephant, and the bicycle.

Climate change is a consequence of the transition from biodiversity based on renewable carbon economies to a fossil fuel-based non-renewable carbon economy. This was the transition called the industrial revolution.

While climate change, combined with peak oil and the end of cheap oil, is creating an ecological imperative for a post-oil, post–fossil fuel, postindustrial economy, the industrial paradigm is still the guiding force for the search for a transition pathway beyond oil.

That's because industrialization has also become a cultural paradigm for measuring human progress. We want a post-oil world but do not have the courage to envisage a postindustrial world. As a result, we cling to the infrastructure of the energy-intensive fossil fuel economy and try and run it on substitutes such as nuclear power and biofuels. Dirty nuclear power is being redefined as "clean energy." Non-sustainable production of biodiesel and biofuel is being welcomed as a "green" option.

Humanity is playing these tricks with itself and the planet because we are locked   25
into the industrial paradigm. Our ideas of the good life are based on production and consumption patterns that the use of fossil fuels gave rise to. We cling to these patterns without reflecting on the fact that they have become a human addiction only over the past 50 years and that maintaining this short term, non-sustainable pattern of living for another 50 years comes at the risk of wiping out millions of species and destroying the very conditions for human survival on the planet. We think of well-being only in terms of human beings, and more accurately, only in terms of human beings over the next 50 years. We are sacrificing the rights of other species and the welfare of future generations.

To move beyond oil, we must move beyond our addiction to a certain model of human progress and human well-being. To move beyond oil, we must reestablish partnerships with other species. To move beyond oil, we must reestablish the other carbon economy, a renewable economy based on biodiversity.

Renewable carbon and biodiversity redefine progress. They redefine development. They redefine "developed," "developing," and "underdeveloped." In the fossil fuel paradigm, to be developed is to be industrialized—to have industrialized food and clothing, shelter and mobility, ignoring the social costs of displacing people from work and the ecological costs of polluting the atmosphere and destabilizing the climate. In the fossil fuel paradigm, to be under-developed is to have non-industrial, fossil-free systems of producing our food and clothing, of providing our shelter and mobility.

In the biodiversity paradigm, to be developed is to be able to leave ecological space for other species, for all people and future generations of humans. To be underdeveloped is to usurp the ecological space of other species and communities, to pollute the atmosphere, and to threaten the planet.

We need to change our mind before we can change our world. This cultural transition is at the heart of making an energy transition to an age beyond oil. What blocks the transition is a cultural paradigm that perceives industrialization as progress combined with false ideas of productivity and efficiency. We have been made to believe that industrialization of agriculture is necessary to produce more food. This is not at all true. Biodiverse ecological farming produces more and better food than the most energy- and chemical-intensive agriculture. We have been made to falsely believe that cities designed for automobiles provide more effective mobility to meet our daily needs than cities designed for pedestrians and cyclists.

Vested interests who gain from the sale of fertilizers and diesel, cars and trucks, have brainwashed us to believe that chemical fertilizers and cars mean progress. We have been reduced to buyers of their non-sustainable products rather than creators of sustainable, cooperative partnerships—both within human society and with other species and the earth as a whole.   30

The biodiversity economy is the sustainable alternative to the fossil fuel economy. The shift from fossil fuel-driven to biodiversity-supported systems reduces green-house gas emissions by emitting less and absorbing more CO_2. Above all, because the impacts of atmospheric pollution will continue even if we do reduce emissions, we need to create biodiverse ecosystems and economies because only they offer the potential to adapt to an unpredictable climate. And only biodiverse systems provide alternatives that everyone can afford. We need to return to the renewable carbon cycle of biodiversity. We need to create a carbon democracy so that all beings have their just share of useful carbon, and no one is burdened with carrying an unjust share of climate impacts due to carbon pollution.

UNDERSTANDING THE TEXT

1. What does Shiva call the "real problem" in the world today? What are some of the other problems that are symptoms, or consequences, of this problem?

2. What does "dharma" mean? How does Shiva use this ancient Indian concept to talk about different ways of life and patterns of consumption?

3. Why does Shiva believe it is important to respect the lifestyle choices of those who live in rural communities, forestlands, and small farms?

4. How does Shiva define "Earth Democracy"? Is Earth Democracy compatible with political democracy?

5. What are the two kinds of carbon that Shiva discusses? Why is one kind more suited to human consumption than the other?

6. What solutions does Shiva see for the world's ecological problems? What has to happen before these solutions can be effective?

MAKING CONNECTIONS

1. How does Shiva's view of ecology compare with that of Barry Commoner (p. 344)? Can you see Commoner's "Four Laws of Ecology" in her arguments?

2. Compare Shiva's view of democracy with Aung San Suu Kyi's in "In Quest of Democracy" (p. 442). How are their definitions similar? How are they different?

3. Compare Shiva's view of industrialization with Gandhi's view of "economic progress" (p. 560). What assumptions are shared by these two thinkers writing almost a hundred years apart?

WRITING ABOUT THE TEXT

1. Analyze the way that Shiva uses strategic definitions of terms like "industrialization," "equity," and "democracy" in her argument. To what extent does she define these terms as others do?

2. Compare the efforts of Wangari Maathai in Kenya (p. 363) and Vandana Shiva in India to create sustainable communities. What role do you think gender plays in their vision?

3. Support or oppose Shiva's assertion that trade liberalization is a form of coercion. In what ways might additional trade opportunities help people in rural economies?

6

□

LAW AND GOVERNMENT

What Is the Role of Law and Government in Society?

> . . . to bring about the rule of righteousness
> in the land, to destroy the wicked and the evil-doers;
> so that the strong should not harm the weak . . .
> —*Hammurabi's Code*

HAMMURABI'S CODE, the first known set of laws in history, was written in Babylon nearly thirty-eight hundred years ago, but its preface still sounds startlingly familiar. Before giving his list of laws, fines, and penalties, Hammurabi, the king of Meso-potamia and founder of the Babylonian Empire, states the purpose of his Code: "to bring about the rule of righteousness in the land, to destroy the wicked and the evil-doers; so that the strong should not harm the weak; so that I should rule over the black-headed people like Shamash, and enlighten the land, to further the well-being of mankind." We need make only a few surface changes in this and it sounds like the stated purpose of the Constitution of the United States, as set forth in its famous Preamble: to "establish justice, insure domestic tranquility, provide for the common defense, promote the general welfare, and secure the blessings of liberty to ourselves and our posterity." Many of the ideal functions of law and government have remained remarkably constant over the course of recorded history.

The fact that one of the oldest writings in history is a fully developed legal code testifies to the inseparability of law and civilization. According to social con-tract theorists (such as Thomas Hobbes, whose work *Leviathan* is excerpted in the previous chapter), society begins when people band together to protect themselves from conquest and their property from theft. Only societies with established laws, and with the governmental power necessary to enforce these laws, can provide the protection that people seek.

The first reading in this chapter comes from Lao Tzu's *Tao Te Ching*, a work of ancient Chinese philosophy. Written during a time of civil war and great upheaval, the *Tao Te Ching* presents good government as the result of aggressive non-action. The forces of the universe act independently of human striving, Lao Tzu insists, and the role of government is to recognize and adapt to these forces rather than to alter or direct them. This placed Lao Tzu and his followers in direct opposition to the philosophy of Confucianism, which believed that government had the responsibility to structure society and encourage virtuous behavior.

Among the Western readings included in this chapter are complementary excerpts from Christine de Pizan's *The Treasure of the City of Ladies* and Niccolò Machiavelli's *The Prince*, both written toward the end of the Middle Ages in Europe. In these texts, Christine and Machiavelli focus on effective leadership, that is, on the practical nature of governing rather than on its moral aspects. This is especially true of Machiavelli, whose name, since the publication of *The Prince*, has been inextricably associated with cynical, opportunistic, amoral political maneuvering. Such maneuvering is often viewed in connection with *realpolitik* (from the German, meaning "realistic politics" or "the politics of reality"), politics based on practicality and not ideals or ethics.

Images can also prompt questions about law and government. When you look at a magazine, read the news online, or watch television, you might see a political cartoon; an arresting photograph of a peaceful (or violent) demonstration by a mass of civilians; or the leader of a country delivering a speech. Whom or what is the cartoon criticizing? How does a popular demonstration change the way we see the government of the country where the protest is taking place? And how does the leader appear behind the podium—confident? Concerned? Fearful? The sole image in this chapter is an illustration by Abraham Bosse that appeared in Thomas Hobbes's *Leviathan* (an excerpt of which appears in Chapter 2). Here we see a royal figure whose body is composed entirely of his countrymen, a symbol for the Enlightenment understanding of sovereignty. The figure holds both a sword and a religious staff, suggesting that true sovereignty requires mastery of both realms. This view contrasts sharply with the view of American founding father James Madison in "Memorial and Remonstrance Against Religious Assessments," which argues that a strong and truly free society must maintain a strong separation between church and state.

We then move to Martin Luther King Jr.'s "Letter from Birmingham Jail," which describes the philosophy of "civil disobedience," or the belief that one is not obliged to submit to an unjust law. However, rather than proposing revolution— that is, a violent renegotiation of the social contract—King argues that even while refusing to obey an unjust law, one should respect legal authority by accepting the consequences of that disobedience. This argument, driven by King's passionate commitment, became the driving force of America's civil rights movement in the 1960s.

A commitment to peaceful reform also animates two of the final readings of this chapter. The first of these comes from Burmese democracy advocate Aung San Suu Kyi, who was elected prime minister in an open election and then put under house arrest by a military dictatorship. After spending most of the time between 1989 and 2010 under house arrest, Suu Kyi was finally released in November of 2010. In 2012, she was elected to a seat in Burma's Parliament. The second reading comes from Archbishop Desmond Tutu, a South African democracy advocate during the apartheid era who played a major role in his country's transition to democracy.

The final selection in the chapter comes from a speech by Barack Obama during his 2008 presidential campaign. In this speech, Obama talks about the progress that the United States has made since the time of Martin Luther King Jr. and the civil rights movement, and about the progress that we still need to make before King's dream, and the promise of "a more perfect union," can be realized.

The potential for any government structure to protect or abuse its citizens makes it imperative to pose the crucial questions about law and government, justice and citizenship, that are presented only briefly in this chapter. There has always been agreement on the broad outlines of what a good government should do: protect people from both external and internal violence, provide the conditions necessary for human activity to flourish, and create a stable environment where people can live their lives in relative peace and security. Still, while these basic goals have been acknowledged for thousands of years, it has taken human societies a long time to put them into practice in ways that benefit all people. We have made progress on many fronts, but there is still work to do. As Martin Luther King Jr. observed at a crucial moment in the civil rights movement, quoting the Civil War–era abolitionist Theodore Parker, "the arc of the moral universe is long, but it bends toward justice."

LAO TZU
from the *Tao Te Ching*
[600–400 BCE]

WHEN THE MIGHTY Chou Dynasty collapsed, in about 770 BCE, ancient China dissolved into seven small states. Between 475 and 221 BCE, these states fought furiously with each other, each attempting to reunify China under its banner. This "Period of Warring States" was also, not coincidentally, a golden age of Chinese political thought. Hundreds of philosophers, representing dozens of different schools of thought, emerged during this time to propose answers to the burning question of the day: what is the best system of government under which we can reunify China?

Of all of the proposed solutions, however, none was as simple—or as radical—as that offered by the Taoists: maybe, they suggested, China should not be unified. If nature or fate had divided the old empire into separate states, then why not let them remain separate? This political philosophy is consistent with the founding text of Taoism, the *Tao Te Ching*.

Very little is known about the origin of this short collection. Some of the verses appear to have been engraved on stones as early as 300 BCE, but not until the Han Dynasty (206 BCE–220 CE) was the *Tao Te Ching* referred to in other texts. However, authorship of the volume is traditionally attributed to an ancient sage, Lao Tzu ("the Old Master," or "the Old Boy"), around 600 BCE. According to the legend, Lao Tzu, disgusted with the Chinese and their inability to learn, planned to ride off forever on a yak. On his way out of town, he hastily wrote the *Tao Te Ching* to give his disciples something to remember him by.

The overall argument of the *Tao Te Ching* is that human beings constitute a small part of a much larger whole, referred to as "the Tao," or "the Way." Humans cannot change the Way; it goes on with or without our presence. We can, however, work to bring our lives in accordance with its principles. For the Taoist, the world is a great river, and we are all floating on rafts. We can spend our efforts trying to row upstream, making ourselves miserable in the process, or we can relax, make sure that our raft points downstream, and enjoy wherever the river takes us. As a political philosophy, Taoism translates into a minimal approach to governing. Rulers lead most successfully when they give up ambition; they should not make changes simply for the sake of making changes; and they should govern in a way that works with, rather than against, the natural order of the universe.

The *Tao Te Ching's* rhetorical style combines two major strategies: short, declarative statements and intentional contradictions. The first of these strategies creates memorable phrases, while the second, much like the Hegelian dialectic, forces us to create our own reconciliations of the supposed contradictions.

17

In ancient times
The people knew that they had rulers.
Then they loved and praised them,
Then they feared them,
Then they despised them.

The rulers did not trust the people,
The people did not trust the rulers.

The rulers were grave, their words were precious.
The people having finished their work,
    and brought it to a successful issue, said:—
        "We are sufficient in ourselves."[1] . . .

19

If the people renounce self-control and reject wisdom,
Let them gain simplicity and purity.

If the people renounce duty to man and reject right conduct,
Let them return to filial piety deep, deep in the heart.

If they renounce skill and leave off search for profit,
Let them rob and by violence take possession of spiritual life.

These three things do not help our progress.
Therefore now let us seek
To perceive simplicity,
To conserve beauty in the heart,
To curb selfishness and to have few desires. . . .

29

If you desire to gain the kingdom by action,
I see that you will not succeed.
The kingdom is a spiritual vessel,
It cannot be gained by action.

The translator's footnotes have been omitted. The original title of the translation, *Tao Teh King*, has been changed to the more familiar *Tao Te Ching*. The Chinese word *tao* has generally been rendered as "the Way," and "Teh" has been rendered as "Te" throughout.

1. **"We are sufficient in ourselves":** that is, "We did not need the ruler." According to Lao Tzu, the actions of the most effective leaders are not even noticed by the people, who see them as simply the results of nature.

He who acts, destroys it.
He who grasps, loses it.

Therefore behold the animals:
　　Some go in front, others follow;
　　Some are warm, others are cold;
　　Some are strong, others are feeble;
　　Some keep moving, others are still.

That is why the self-controlled man
　　puts away excess,
　　he puts away egotism,
　　he puts away easy living.

30

He who would help a Ruler of men by the Way
Does not take soldiers to give strength to the kingdom.
His service is well rewarded.

Where troops dwell, there grow thorns and briers.
After great wars, there follow bad years.

He who loves, bears fruit unceasingly,
He does not dare to conquer by strength.
He bears fruit, but not with assertiveness,
He bears fruit, but not with boastfulness,
He bears fruit, but not with meanness,
He bears fruit, but not to obtain it for himself,
He bears fruit, but not to shew his strength.

Man is great and strong, then he is old,
In this he is not of the Way.
If he is not of the Way
He quickly will perish. . . .

33

He who knows men is wise,
He who knows himself can see clearly.

He who conquers men has strength,
He who conquers himself has power.
He who knows that he has enough is rich,
He who acts with energy has a strong will.

He who fails not to find the Self shall endure,
He who dies, but does not perish, shall endure for ever. . . .

35

Hold fast the idea of "The Great,"
Then all men will be drawn to you.
They will come to you and receive no hurt,
But rest, peace and great calm.

When you provide music and exquisite food
The traveller will stay with you gladly.
When the Way flows out from you to him
By his palate he does not detect its savour,
By his eyes he cannot perceive it,
By his ears he cannot hear it,
But in using it he finds it to be inexhaustible.

36

If you desire to breathe deeply,
   you must first empty the lungs.
If you desire to be strong,
   you must first learn to be weak.
If you desire to be in a lofty position,
   you must first learn to take a lowly position.
If you desire to be enriched by gifts,
   you must first give away all that you have.
This is called concealment and enlightenment.

The soft overcomes the hard.
The weak overcomes the strong.
Fish cannot swim safely in shallow waters.
The secrets of government of a kingdom
   should not be revealed to the people. . . .

38

To assume virtue without being really virtuous
   is to be virtuous from duty;
To be less virtuous, yet not to lose real virtue,
   is to be virtuous from Inner Life.

Supreme virtue comes through activity of Inner Life;
    then let us actively seek Inner Life.
To be less virtuous and to practise it,
    let us be active in the performance of duty.

To assume benevolence and practise it
    let us actively seek Inner Life.
To assume right conduct and practise it
    let us be active in the performance of duty.
To assume expediency and practise it is to find that no one honours it;
    then it bares the arm, and asserts itself by force.

Therefore, when the Way is lost, follow Virtue;
    when virtue is lost, follow benevolence;
    when benevolence is lost, follow right conduct;
    when right conduct is lost, follow expediency.

Those who are Masters of expediency
    have in the heart only the shadow of faith,
    and in the mind only confusion.

Those who are Leaders of politeness
    have only the husk of the Way,
    which is the source of ignorance.

That is why the greatest of the Masters
    abide in the real,
    they do not abide in the shadow.
They hold to the fruit,
    they do not hold to the husk.
Therefore they put away the latter
    and take hold of the former. . . .

46

When the Way was manifested to men,
Horses were used for cultivating the fields.

When the Way was hid within Itself,
War horses were reared on the frontiers.

There is no sin greater than desire,
There is no misfortune greater than discontent,
There is no calamity greater than the wish to acquire,
Therefore to be satisfied is an everlasting sufficiency. . . .

49

The Heart of the self-controlled man
   is always in the Inner Kingdom.
He draws the hearts of all men into his Heart.

If a man is good, he blesses him;
If a man is not good, still he blesses him with the Blessing of Te.[2]
If a man is faithful, he is faithful to him;
If a man is not faithful, still he is faithful to him with the Faithfulness of Te.

The self-controlled man dwells in the world.
Patiently and persistently
He brings the whole world into active community of Heart.

All men turn their ears and their eyes towards him.
They are all the children of the self-controlled man. . . .

57

To govern a kingdom, use righteousness.
To conduct a war, use strategy.
To be a true world-ruler, be occupied with Inner Life.

How do I know that this is so?
By this:—
   The more restrictive the laws,
      the poorer the people.
   The more machinery used,
      the more trouble in a kingdom.
   The more clever and skillful the people,
      the more do they make artificial things.
   The more the laws are in evidence,
      the more do thieves and robbers abound.

That is why the self-controlled man says:—
   If I act from Inner Life
      the people will become transformed in themselves.
   If I love stillness
      the people will become righteous in themselves.

2. **Te:** in the philosophy of the *Tao Te Ching*, the counterpart of "Tao." Whereas "Tao" is the universal way of nature, "Te" is the ability of an individual to live according to the "Tao." "Te" is normally translated into English as either "virtue" or "power," and it contains elements of both concepts.

If I am occupied with Inner Life
　　the people will become enriched in themselves.
If I love the Inner Life
　　the people will become pure in themselves.

58

If the government is from the heart
　　the people will be richer and richer.
If the government is full of restrictions
　　the people will be poorer and poorer.

Miserable! you rely upon coming happiness.
Happy! you crouch under dread of coming misery.
You may know the end from the beginning.

If a ruler is in line with Inner Life
　　his strategy will come right,
　　his bad luck will become good,
　　and the people will be astonished.
　　Things have been so for a long time.

That is why the self-controlled man
　　is just and hurts no one,
　　is disinterested and does no wrong,
　　is true and takes no licence;
　　he shines, and offends not by his brightness. . . .

60

Govern a great State
As you would cook a small fish (do it gently).

When the Way is manifest in the world
Evil spirits have no power.

When evil spirits have no power
They cannot hurt men.

Evil spirits cannot hurt men.
The self-controlled man does not hurt men.
The Master also does not hurt men.
Therefore they unite in manifesting Te. . . .

61

A great kingdom, lowly like running water,
  is the Meeting-place of the world.
It is the feminine quality of the world.
The feminine quality always overcomes the
  masculine by stillness.
In order to be still, we must become lowly.

Therefore, if a great kingdom is lowly towards a little kingdom
  it will take possession of the little kingdom.
If a little kingdom is lowly towards a great kingdom
  it will take possession of the great kingdom.
So the one becomes lowly in order to conquer,
The other is lowly and yet it conquers.

If a great kingdom only desires to unify and nourish men,
If a small kingdom only desires to enter in and serve men,
Then the Master, in each case, shall obtain his desire.

He who is great ought to be lowly. . . .

62

He who has the Way is the refuge of all beings.
He is the treasure of the good man,
He is the support of the man who is not good.

Beautiful words through the Way gain power,
Man by following it gains steadfastness in action,
But, by the evil man, its possession is ignored.

The Son of Heaven sits enthroned,
His three Ministers are appointed.
One carries in his hand a tablet of jade;
Another is followed by a mounted retinue.
But the one who is most valued
  sits quietly, and offers as his gift the Way.

How was the Way prized by men of Old?
Daily they sought for it.
They found it, hid within the Self.
It gives a way of escape to the guilty.
Therefore it is prized by all men. . . .

65

Of Old, he who was active in the Way
    did not use it to make people enlightened,
    but to make them more kind.

If people are difficult to govern
    it is because they have too much knowledge.

Therefore if you govern a kingdom by knowledge,
    you will be an oppressor of the kingdom.

But if you govern a kingdom by wisdom,
    you will give happiness to the kingdom.

If you know and do these things
    you will be a pattern for men.

Knowledge of how to be always a pattern for men
    is called profound Te.

Profound Te is in the very source of life,
    it pervades the utmost limits of life,
    it returns and dwells in every being.

When fully manifested,
    it unites all beings in a great harmony.

66

The Rivers and the Seas (because they seek a lowly place)
    are Lords of a hundred valleys.
Let your love flow, seek a lowly place,
    you will be Lord of a hundred valleys.

That is why
    if the self-controlled man desires to exalt the people,
    in his speech he must take a lowly place;
    if he desires to put the people first,
    he must put himself after them.

Thus, though he dwells above them,
    the people are not burdened by him.
Though he is placed before them,
    the people are not obstructed by him,

Therefore men serve him gladly,
    they do not tire in serving him.
Because he does not strive,
    no one in the world can strive against him. . . .

74

If the people do not fear death,
How then can you frighten them by death?

But if you cause the people continually to fear death,
And if one of them becomes a great criminal,
Can you take hold of him and slay him?

Would you dare to do this?
There is always one, the Executioner, who kills men.

But, on the contrary, if you kill as if you were Executioner,
It would be as if you tried to do the work of a Master Carpenter.

In attempting to do the work of a Master Carpenter,
Few there be who do not wound their own hands.

75

The people are hungry.
Because they who are over the food tax it heavily
That is why the people are hungry.

The people are difficult to govern.
Because the rulers trust in possessions and activities,
That is why the people are difficult to govern.

The people make light of death.
Because they work hard in order to save their life,
That is why they make light of death.

A Master indeed is he whose life-activities are from within.
He excels all men in his appreciation of Life. . . .

79

To harmonise great enemies
We must possess that which far surpasses enmity.

We must be able to be at peace
In order to be active in Love.

That is why the self-controlled man
   holds the left-hand portion of the contract,
   but does not insist upon the other man producing his portion.

He who is virtuous may rule by a contract,
He whose virtue is within may rule by destroying it.

Akin to the Way is Inner Life.
A constant giver is the man who loves.

80

Take a small kingdom and few people,
Cause ten or a hundred of them to carry weapons,
But not to use them.

Cause the people to fear death,
Do not let them travel far,
Though they may have boats and carriages,
Let them use them only within the kingdom.
Though they may have soldiers in uniform,
Let them parade only within the kingdom.
Cause the people again to have knotted cords,
And to use them (instead of the written character).

Their food would be sweet,
Their clothing would be beautiful in their own eyes,
Their dwellings would be resting-places,
They would love simple ways.

If another kingdom were so near
That they could hear the sounds of dogs and fowls,
They would not come into mutual contact
Until they all grew old and died. . . .

UNDERSTANDING THE TEXT

1. How does paradox function in the *Tao Te Ching*? What is the rhetorical effect
   of presenting concepts as integrally connected to their opposites? What overall
   philosophy does this support?

2. Why does Lao Tzu advocate a leader who shows no ambition and takes no action? Is it always necessary for a leader to act, or is it possible to be a good leader by simply allowing things to happen on their own?

3. What does Lao Tzu mean by "the Inner Life"? In what contexts does he generally employ this phrase? How is it related to "the Way"?

4. Why is having too many desires presented as a crime? How would having desires make following the *Tao Te Ching's* other suggestions difficult? According to the *Tao Te Ching*, what makes desire the root of all unrest?

5. Which qualities does Lao Tzu label as "feminine"? Which does he label as "masculine"? How do these two sets of qualities interact?

6. What does it mean for a ruler to take the "lower position"? What metaphors does Lao Tzu use to get this point across?

MAKING CONNECTIONS

1. How does Lao Tzu's view of government differ from Machiavelli's (p. 405)? What are the major differences between the ideal Taoist ruler and the Machiavellian "Prince"?

2. For many centuries, Taoism and Confucianism have represented opposite poles of Chinese thought: while Confucians attempt to control human nature through rigid adherence to rites and rituals, Taoists assert that nature cannot be controlled or restrained. With these ideas in mind, compare the passages from the *Tao Te Ching* with the selection by either Mencius (p. 78) or Hsün Tzu (p. 84).

3. In what ways might the *Tao Te Ching* have influenced Sun Tzu's *The Art of War* (p. 479)?

4. Can you detect in the *Tao Te Ching* an environmentalist ethic? Would a contemporary environmentalist, such as Rachel Carson (p. 328) or Wangari Maathai (p. 363), agree with Lao Tzu's opinion that the natural world should simply be left alone? Explain.

WRITING ABOUT THE TEXT

1. To explore the political philosophy of the *Tao Te Ching*, choose a contemporary government and imagine the changes it would have to make in order to follow Taoist principles.

2. Analyze the paradox of "leading without doing anything." Explain how a leader could be effective simply by allowing a natural flow rather than by making changes or inventing programs.

3. The translation of the *Tao Te Ching* included here is from 1922. Try modernizing one passage, using your own words. Is it possible to use contemporary language and examples and still preserve the meaning?

4. Refute or support the *Tao Te Ching*'s assertion that desires are disastrous, using historical examples to back up your argument. How does desire relate to ambition? How would Lao Tzu view ambition within government?

CHRISTINE DE PIZAN

from *The Treasure of the City of Ladies*

[1405]

BORN IN VENICE, Christine de Pizan (circa 1365–circa 1430) spent much of her early life at the court of the French king Charles V, where her father was the court physician and an esteemed astrologer. She was married at a young age to a court official and had three children. When King Charles died, in 1380, her father and her husband lost their positions at court and much of their financial support. After the deaths of her father around 1387 and her husband around 1390, Christine was left to raise her children without the advantage of position or money. She responded by writing poetry and dedicating it to the rich and powerful in hopes of attracting patronage—an occupation well established for men of her education and family background but almost unheard of for women. She succeeded nonetheless, becoming the first woman in the history of France to earn a living through her writing.

Within ten years, Christine had acquired a substantial following. Rather than continuing to write pleasant poems praising wealthy patrons, however, she turned to writing philosophy and social commentary. Her first book in this vein was *Letter to the God of Love* (1399), an attack on the immorality and misogyny of Guillaume de Lorris and Jean de Meun's *The Romance of the Rose*, one of the most popular French poems of the Middle Ages. In 1404, she wrote a utopian treatise, *The Book of the City of Ladies*, which was modeled partly on Augustine's *City of God*. *The Book of the City of Ladies* chronicled the historical oppression of women, defended the female sex against charges of inferiority, and imagined a city in which women were authors, inventors, rulers, and religious leaders and participated fully in the life of the community.

Whereas *The Book of the City of Ladies* addressed the world as it might have become, her follow-up, *The Treasure of the City of Ladies* (1405), sometimes called *The Book of the Three Virtues*, dealt with the world as it was. If the earlier book looked back to Augustine for its inspiration, the later book anticipated the work of Niccolò Machiavelli, whose advice to princes in 1513 lacked the soft edges, but not the essential pragmatism, of Christine's advice to queens, princesses, ladies of rank, and women of substantial fortunes. Christine argues that such women—and the way that they behave in public ceremonies and in private conversations with their husbands—are essential to the prosperity of the state.

Christine's rhetoric relies primarily on her ethos—both the ethos that she constructs in the text as a gentle, knowledgable participant in civic affairs and the ethos that she brings to the text as a poet and a noblewoman.

16. The Fifth Teaching of Prudence, which Is How the Wise Princess Will Try Her Best to Be in Favour with, and Have the Good Wishes of, All Classes of Her Subjects.

As it is fitting for the wise and prudent princess to wish to regulate her actions so that she seeks and follows all the paths that honour demands, she will want for this reason (which is the fifth teaching) to enjoy the favour of the clergy and to be on good terms with persons in religious orders, leaders of the Church, prelates and councillors, as well as the middle classes and even the common people. No one can be surprised that we say she should especially cultivate these people more than the barons and nobles. The reason for this is that we suppose that she already associates with barons and nobles, for it would be according to the common custom for her to be acquainted with them. She wishes to be in favour with the above-mentioned persons for two reasons.

The first is so that the good and devout will pray to God for her, and the second is that she may be praised by them in their sermons and homilies so that, if the need arises, their voices and words can be a shield and defence against the rumours and reports of her slanderous enemies and can negate them. By this strategy she will have more of her husband's love and also that of the common people, who will hear good things about their lady, and also she may be supported by the most powerful people in an emergency. She will find out which of the clerks and scholars, those in religious orders as well as others, will be the most useful and of the greatest authority and in whom and in whose word people place the most confidence. Those persons will inspire the others with confidence in her. She will speak to them all very amiably and want to have their advice and make use of it. She will sometimes ask them to dinner at her court, together with her confessor and the people of her chapel, who will all be honourable people. She will accord them great honour and will wish them to be honoured by her household, which is a very seemly thing, for truly those who are ennobled by learning ought to be honoured. She will do them all the good in her power and contribute to their colleges and monasteries.

Although almsgiving[1] should be done secretly (the reason for this is so that the person who gives them may not be puffed up with pride about it, for that is a mortal sin), if she did not feel any pride in her heart, it would be better to give publicly than in secret, because she would set a good example to others. Whoever does it in this frame of mind doubles her merit and does well. This wise lady who knows how to protect herself from this vice will indeed wish that the gifts and alms that

---

1. **Almsgiving:** making charitable contributions. According to Jesus's Sermon on the Mount, almsgiving should always be done in secret, so as to avoid public displays of charity that are designed to bring recognition to the giver. Matthew 6:2–3 states: "Therefore when thou doest thine alms, do not sound a trumpet before thee, as the hypocrites do in the synagogues and in the streets, that they may have glory of men. Verily I say unto you, They have their reward. But when thou doest alms, let not thy left hand know what thy right hand doeth."

she gives in this way will be known and recorded (if they are notable, such as for rebuilding churches and monasteries or some other necessary thing) in perpetual memory on tablets in their churches so that the people will pray to God for her. Or her name may appear on other lists of benefactors, or her gifts may be announced publicly. Others will follow her example and give similarly, and by their actions they will gain a good reputation. It may seem that she has a small streak of hypocrisy or that she is getting a name for it, yet it may be called a "just hypocrisy", so to speak, for it strives towards good and the avoidance of evil. We do not mean that under cover of almsgiving they ought to commit evil deeds and sin, nor that great vanity ought to arise in their hearts. Certainly being "hypocritical" in the cause of good will not offend any person who desires honour. We repeat that this kind of "just hypocrisy" is almost necessary, especially to princes and princesses who must rule over others and to whom more reverence is due than to other people. As for that, it is written in the book of Valerius[2] that formerly princes claimed that they were descended from the gods so that their subjects would hold them in greater reverence and fear them more.

The wise lady will wish her husband's counsellors to think well of her, be they prelates, chancellors or others. She will command them to come to her. She will receive them honourably and speak to them intelligently. As best she can, she will try to be worthy of their great esteem. This approach will be valuable to her in several ways. They will praise her good sense and conduct, which they will regard as outstanding. If it happens that any envious person wishes to intrigue against her, they will not allow any decisions to be made to her prejudice. They will dissuade the prince if he has been misinformed by any other people. If she desired anything to be discussed in council they would be more friendly and favourable to her.

In addition, this lady will wish to have the good will of the clergy, who become embroiled with the "common causes" of the people, as we say in Paris, with advocates in Parliament and elsewhere. She will wish to see such defenders of causes on certain days, the leaders and principal men among them and the other most notable ones. She will confer with them amiably and want them to understand her honourable position. She will do this not so that she may speak to them from motives of vengeance, but so that they should perceive the effect of her conduct and great knowledge. To have such a custom can be valuable for the increase of her honour and praise. The reason for this is that she will wish all sorts and conditions of the legal fraternity, the leading citizens of towns and cities in her husband's jurisdiction, and also great merchants and even some of the most respectable artisans to come to her from time to time. She will welcome them warmly and try hard to be well regarded by them, so that if she were to have any difficulty and if she needed some ready money, these merchants, being well disposed towards her, would gladly help her. If she must borrow and if she wishes

2. **Book of Valerius:** Valerius Antias was a Roman historian in the first century BCE.

to honour her commitments, she ought to render payment without fail on the appointed day. If she always keeps her word sincerely and unswervingly, people will consequently believe in it.

While we have been telling in this chapter how the wise princess ought to be well regarded by her subjects, it could seem wrong to some readers to say such a pointless thing. They might think that it was not the princess's business to court her subjects, but rather she ought to command her pleasures boldly, and her subjects ought to obey and take pains to court *her* love and not the other way around, or otherwise they will not be subjects and she the mistress. But to this we will reply that, with no disrespect to the speakers, it is appropriate to do this, not only for princesses but for princes. There are many reasons, but we will discuss only two, for this matter could be enlarged upon much more. The first reason is that although the prince may be lord and master of his subjects, the subjects nevertheless make the lord and not the lord the subjects. They would very much more easily find someone who would take them on as subjects (if they wished to overthrow him) than he would find people who would receive him as lord! And for this reason, and also because he would not be able to overcome them by himself if they rebelled against him (and even if he then had the power to destroy them, he would forbear to do it), he must necessarily keep their affection, not by harshness but in such a way that from this love comes fear, or otherwise his authority is in peril. The common proverb is quite true that avers, "There is no lord of a land who is hated by his men." As for keeping their affection, truly one who sincerely wishes to be called "lord" could do nothing more sensible, for he could have neither city nor fortress of such a great defensive strength and power as the love and benevolence of true subjects.

The other reason is that, supposing that the subjects feel good will towards the prince and princess, if they never have the courage to go freely to their rulers and if they have never been invited to do so, it would not be their place to begin. Therefore, the prince or princess ought to make the overture. It is perfectly natural for the subjects to celebrate this with great joy and consider themselves quite honoured by it. It ought to double their love and loyalty, and they will then find still more kindness from their rulers. Speaking on this subject, a wise man has said that there is nothing that wins over the hearts of a ruler's subjects more nor that draws them to their lord so much as when they find gentleness and kindness in him, such as is written of a good emperor who said that he wished to behave towards his subjects in such a manner that they themselves would desire him to be their emperor. Bearing this firmly in mind, the wise princess will sometimes invite the wives to visit her, and she will make them very welcome and speak to everyone so amiably that they will be very content and praise her wisdom. Her whole court will celebrate their lyings-in and the weddings of their children, and the princess will wish the women to be in the company of ladies and damsels. From all this she will acquire much love from all men and women. . . .

18. The Seventh Teaching Describes How the Wise Princess Will Keep a Careful Eye on Her Revenues and Finances and on the State of Her Court.

The seventh teaching of Prudence to the wise princess is that she will carefully look after her revenue and her expenditure, which not only princes and princesses ought to consider, but likewise all people who wish their lives to be regulated by wisdom. She herself will feel no shame in wishing to know the sum of her revenues or payments; on certain days she will have her collectors and the administrators of her finances do their accounts in her presence. She will want to know how the masters of her household govern their staffs, command their underlings and distribute food. In the same way the princess will want to be familiar with other departments of her court. She will want to know that all her officers, whether great or little, are prudent, lead a good life and are the true gentlemen that she takes them for. If she finds out the contrary, she will immediately dismiss them.

She will want to know what the household expenses are. She will want to know what has been bought for her out of her funds from merchants and from her subjects, and she will command that the bills be fully paid on a certain day, for she will certainly not want the curses or the ill will of creditors. She will wish to owe nothing; she will prefer to manage with less and to spend her money more moderately. She will not permit anyone to take anything from the people against their will or at an unfair price, and she will stipulate that her staff must pay promptly and not oblige the poor people of the villages and other places, at great expense and trouble, to come time and time again to deliver a memorandum of a debt to her private apartments or to her finance officers before they are paid. She will not want her treasurers or stewards to be liars, as is the common custom, nor to put the people off with hollow promises and one delay after another.

This wise lady will organize the management of her revenues in the following manner. She will divide her income into five parts. The first will be the portion that she wants to devote to alms and give to the poor. The second part is her household expenses: she will know what the total amounts to—indeed, if need be, she should find out what it is and request her husband not to settle the accounts without involving her in the transaction. The third part is for payment to her officers and women servants. The fourth is for gifts to strangers or others who are particularly deserving of them. And the fifth part she will save and use when she decides to spend something on herself for jewels, gowns and other clothing. Each portion of the amount will be what she sees that she can afford according to her revenue. By means of this rule she will be able to keep her affairs orderly and without confusion, nor will she lack money to fulfill any of the above-mentioned items. For this reason she needs to have some ready money in reserve, and that would not be possible if she had indulged in lavish expenditure and waste.

In this manner the princess will be able to follow the above seven teachings of Prudence, with the other virtues. These things are not at all hard to do, but rather are agreeable and pleasant provided that she is sincere and that she had made something of a habit of them. The wise lady will be able to acquire glory, renown and great honour in this world and eventually in Paradise, which is promised to those who live virtuously.

19. How the Wise Princess Ought to Extend Largesse and Liberality.

As we have spoken at some length about the other virtues appropriate to princesses and we have touched only briefly on a suitable generosity in gifts outside her ordinary expenditure, and as it is out of the ordinary and is something about which a princess ought to be informed, we will now treat it at greater length.

The wise princess wishing to be without reproach will take special care that neither the vice of meanness and avarice may be seen in her, nor foolish generosity, which is no less a vice. Therefore, she will distribute these gifts with great discretion and prudence, for munificence is one of the things that most magnifies the reputation of great lords and ladies. John of Salisbury[3] proves this in *Polycraticus* (book three, chapter twenty-four) by demonstrating that the virtue of generosity is necessary for those who rule over public affairs. For example, Titus,[4] the noble emperor, acquired such renown through his generosity that he was known as the benefit, the relief and the help of all persons. He loved this virtue of largesse so much that the day he had not given any gift he could not be happy. In this way he acquired the general favour and love of everyone.

The wise lady will demonstrate her generosity like this: if she has the power to give, and she learns that some foreign gentlemen or other people have lost much of their wealth through long imprisonment or ransom or are suffering great penury, she will help them with her own resources very willingly and liberally as a matter of course, according to her ability. As largesse does not consist only in material gifts, as a wise man has said, but also in comforting words, she will comfort them with hopes for a better future. This comfort will perhaps do them as much good as, or even more good than, the money that she gives them, for it is very agreeable to any person when a prince or princess comforts him, even just in words.

If this lady sees any gentleman, be he knight or squire, of good courage who has a great desire to increase his honour but does not have much money to outfit himself properly, and if she sees that it is worth while to help him, the gentle lady will do so, for she has within her all good impulses for honour and gentility and for always encouraging noble and valiant actions. And thus in various situations that may arise

15

---

3. **John of Salisbury:** English philosopher and bishop of Chartres (1115 or 1120–1180). His *Polycraticus, or The Statesman's Book* was an important work of medieval political theory.

4. **Titus:** Roman emperor (39–81 CE) who gained fame by providing generous relief efforts after the city of Pompeii was destroyed by the eruption of Mount Vesuvius in 79 CE.

this lady will extend wise and well-considered largesse. And if any great lords give her presents or gifts she will reward the messengers so generously that they will have cause to rejoice. She will give more to foreigners than to other people so that in their country they may mention her generosity to their lords. She will want her stewards to deliver the gifts promptly. If great ladies give her presents, she will send them some of her jewels and fine things, but more generously. If a poor or simple person does her any service or kindly presents her with some curiosity, she will consider the abilities of the person and his or her social position and the importance of the service, or the value, beauty or novelty of the gift, according to the case. Whatever the remuneration is, she will give it so abundantly that the person will rejoice. Furthermore, she will receive the thing with such a delighted expression that it will be half the payment by itself.

She will certainly not do what we saw happen once, something that we thought was deplorable at a sophisticated court of a prince or princess. A person was summoned there who was considered wise, so that the court might hear and learn his knowledge. He attended the court several times and everyone felt greatly satisfied with his deeds and his counsel. As a result of his knowledge he did the ruler certain just, good and laudable services that were worthy of commendation and reward. At the same time another person frequented this same court who had the reputation of being a buffoon and was in the habit of entertaining the lords and ladies with jests and stories of what everyone was doing everywhere and with worthless chatter in the way of mockery and jokes. It was decided that they both be remunerated, and so gifts were given both to the person who was reputed to be wise and who had deserved them because of his knowledge and to the person reputed to be a fool who had done nothing but tell his jokes. A gift was given to this buffoon that was valued at forty *écus* and to the other a gift worth twelve *écus*. When we three sisters, Reason, Rectitude,[5] and Justice, saw this, we hid our faces with shame at seeing such improper valuation and such blind ignorance in a court that is supposed to be famous. We were ashamed not for the value of the gifts but for the relative esteem for the persons and their deeds. The wise princess will not behave in this way and will not have to do with foolish people or those who imitate the ways of this court. Neither will she have much time for worthless things, nor will she offer her gifts for them, but to the virtuous and to those who have done something worth while.

UNDERSTANDING THE TEXT

1. What does Christine suggest a "wise and prudent" princess should do to establish and keep order in her kingdom? How do personal relations between royalty and subjects factor into government processes? How is amiability between the two classes important in maintaining order and peace?

---

5. **Rectitude:** righteousness. Reason, Rectitude, and Justice are the three "goddess" figures at the heart of *The Book of the City of Ladies*.

2. Why does Christine advise princesses to give charitable contributions publicly if they can do so without pride? How does she use this formulation to get around the scriptural injunction to give alms in secret?

3. In what ways does Christine construct an ethos (p. 663) that suggests both knowledge and trustworthiness? What other personal characteristics does her writing style suggest?

4. What role does Christine believe that a woman should play in her husband's government? Why is it important that "her husband's counsellors . . . think well of her"?

5. Are the aims of "the wise princess" completely selfish? Would her attempts to be "well regarded by her subjects" remain effective, even if they are motivated by self-interest? What are her reasons for "courting" her subjects? Is this reasoning sound?

6. Why is it important for a princess to understand household finances? What correlation does Christine suggest between a well-run household and a well-run state?

7. Why should a princess cultivate a reputation for generosity? What are the advantages of such a reputation, both to the state and to her personally?

MAKING CONNECTIONS

1. How does the advice that Christine gives to princesses compare with the advice that Niccolò Machiavelli gives to princes (p. 405)? Can *The Treasure of the City of Ladies* be considered realpolitik (p. 405)? Why or why not?

2. How does Christine believe that Christian principles should influence government? How do her views compare with those of another Christian thinker, Thomas Aquinas (p. 483)?

3. How does Christine's feminism compare with that of Virginia Woolf (p. 46) and Gloria Anzaldúa (p. 205)? According to each thinker, what strategies can women in male-dominated societies use to make their voices heard?

WRITING ABOUT THE TEXT

1. Argue for or against Christine de Pizan's notion of "just hypocrisy." Is it possible to accomplish a noble end through evil means? Why or why not?

2. Compare the advice of Christine de Pizan and Niccolò Machiavelli (p. 405).

3. Write an essay arguing that Christine de Pizan should be considered a feminist, because she advocates an expanded role for women in public life, or an antifeminist, because she treats women as subordinate to their husbands.

4. Examine the role of appearance (versus reality) in *The Treasure of the City of Ladies*. Which, for Christine de Pizan, is more important: for a princess to be good or for a princess to be considered good?

NICCOLÒ MACHIAVELLI
from *The Prince*
[1513]

FOR NEARLY FIVE HUNDRED YEARS, Niccolò Machiavelli (1469–1527), his book *The Prince*, and the adjective "Machiavellian" have been associated with dishonesty, underhandedness, political maneuvering, and the philosophy that "the end justifies the means." These associations, while carrying an element of truth, have too often been used to dismiss one of the most perceptive works ever written about the way that power works in a political state.

Machiavelli was deeply concerned with the stability of governments, a natural result of the political climate of his native Italy. During his lifetime, Italy had no central government and was divided into city-states, which were constantly at war with each other. Machiavelli, a loyal Florentine, believed that Florence had the potential to unite the other Italian states under its banner.

His devotion to Florence led to a successful career in public service. At a young age, Machiavelli achieved distinction as a Florentine ambassador to the courts of Europe. He wrote a series of insightful reports on foreign governments and thus gained great influence with the government that he served; and he observed countless instances of the damaging effects of weak leaders, unstable governments, and revolutions, experiences that directly shaped the advice he gave to rulers in *The Prince*. Despite its modern reputation for advising ruthlessness, guile, and secrecy, *The Prince* was intended to help rulers work for good by staying in power longer—a stable government, Machiavelli argues, would be able to prevent the misery caused by warfare and civic unrest. Ironically, Machiavelli did not write *The Prince* until the Republic of Florence had fallen and been replaced by the powerful autocrat Lorenzo de' Medici (1449–1492). Machiavelli dedicated *The Prince* to the new ruler in an attempt to earn his favor, but he was unsuccessful and forced to retire.

The Prince begins with the premise that political power is exercised in the real world and must therefore take into account the unsavory characteristics of real human beings: ambition, cruelty, greed, gullibility, and incompetence. This approach to politics is now known as "realpolitik" and is more associated with Machiavelli than with any other figure in history.

Unlike almost every well-known political theorist who preceded him, Machiavelli does not attempt to instruct rulers how to be moral. He attempts, rather, to show them how to be effective—how to accumulate, exercise, and maintain power. For Machiavelli, this means that, at times, rulers must be cruel, dishonest, duplicitous, and manipulative. Those who loosen their holds on power and focus on enjoying the fruits of power or the luxury of position will not, in the long run, succeed—their principalities will experience misrule, even chaos.

Machiavelli's arguments are inductive in nature and generally proceed from historical examples. Throughout *The Prince*, Machiavelli studies the lives of successful leaders and from them generalizes the ideal qualities of princes.

Chapter XV

Concerning Things for which Men, and Especially Princes, Are Praised or Blamed

It remains now to see what ought to be the rules of conduct for a prince towards subject and friends. And as I know that many have written on this point, I expect I shall be considered presumptuous in mentioning it again, especially as in discussing it I shall depart from the methods of other people. But, it being my intention to write a thing which shall be useful to him who apprehends it, it appears to me more appropriate to follow up the real truth of a matter than the imagination of it; for many have pictured republics and principalities which in fact have never been known or seen, because how one lives is so far distant from how one ought to live, that he who neglects what is done for what ought to be done, sooner effects his ruin than his preservation; for a man who wishes to act entirely up to his professions of virtue soon meets with what destroys him among so much that is evil.

Hence it is necessary for a prince wishing to hold his own to know how to do wrong, and to make use of it or not according to necessity. Therefore, putting on one side imaginary things concerning a prince, and discussing those which are real, I say that all men when they are spoken of, and chiefly princes for being more highly placed, are remarkable for some of those qualities which bring them either blame or praise; and thus it is that one is reputed liberal, another miserly, using a Tuscan[1] term (because an avaricious person in our language is still he who desires to possess by robbery, whilst we call one miserly who deprives himself too much of the use of his own); one is reputed generous, one rapacious; one cruel, one compassionate; one faithless, another faithful; one effeminate and cowardly, another bold and brave; one affable, another haughty; one lascivious, another chaste; one sincere, another cunning; one hard, another easy; one grave, another frivolous; one religious, another unbelieving, and the like. And I know that every one will confess that it would be most praiseworthy in a prince to exhibit all the above qualities that are considered good; but because they can neither be entirely possessed nor observed, for human conditions do not permit it, it is necessary for him to be sufficiently prudent that he may know how to avoid the reproach of those vices which would lose him his state; and also to keep himself, if it be possible, from those which would not lose him it; but this not being possible, he may with less hesitation abandon himself to them. And again, he need not make himself uneasy at incurring a reproach for those vices without which the state can only be saved with difficulty, for if everything is considered carefully, it will be found that something which looks like

---

1. **Tuscan:** from Tuscany, the region in central Italy that includes Florence. **Liberal:** The term here means generous, rather than politically progressive.

virtue, if followed, would be his ruin; whilst something else, which looks like vice, yet followed brings him security and prosperity.

Chapter XVI

Concerning Liberality and Meanness

Commencing then with the first of the above-named characteristics, I say that it would be well to be reputed liberal. Nevertheless, liberality exercised in a way that does not bring you the reputation for it, injures you; for if one exercises it honestly and as it should be exercised, it may not become known, and you will not avoid the reproach of its opposite. Therefore, any one wishing to maintain among men the name of liberal is obliged to avoid no attribute of magnificence; so that a prince thus inclined will consume in such acts all his property, and will be compelled in the end, if he wish to maintain the name of liberal, to unduly weigh down his people, and tax them, and do everything he can to get money. This will soon make him odious to his subjects, and becoming poor he will be little valued by anyone; thus, with his liberality, having offended many and rewarded few, he is affected by the very first trouble and imperilled by whatever may be the first danger; recognizing this himself, and wishing to draw back from it, he runs at once into the reproach of being miserly.

Therefore, a prince, not being able to exercise this virtue of liberality in such a way that it is recognized, except to his cost, if he is wise he ought not to fear the reputation of being mean, for in time he will come to be more considered than if liberal, seeing that with his economy his revenues are enough, that he can defend himself against all attacks, and is able to engage in enterprises without burdening his people; thus it comes to pass that he exercises liberality towards all from whom he does not take, who are numberless, and meanness towards those to whom he does not give, who are few.

We have not seen great things done in our time except by those who have been considered mean; the rest have failed. Pope Julius the Second was assisted in reaching the papacy by a reputation for liberality, yet he did not strive afterwards to keep it up, when he made war on the King of France; and he made many wars without imposing any extraordinary tax on his subjects, for he supplied his additional expenses out of his long thriftiness. The present King of Spain[2] would not have undertaken or conquered in so many enterprises if he had been reputed liberal. A prince, therefore, provided that he has not to rob his subjects, that he can defend himself, that he does not become poor and abject, that he is not forced

5

2. **Present King of Spain:** King Ferdinand II (1452–1516), who united the kingdoms of Castile and Aragon through his marriage to Isabella and defeated the last Islamic stronghold in Spain, the kingdom of Grenada. Ferdinand also commissioned Christopher Columbus's first expedition, thus paving the way for Spain's conquests of the New World.

to become rapacious, ought to hold of little account a reputation for being mean, for it is one of those vices which will enable him to govern.

And if any one should say: Caesar obtained empire by liberality, and many others have reached the highest positions by having been liberal, and by being considered so, I answer: Either you are a prince in fact, or in a way to become one. In the first case this liberality is dangerous, in the second it is very necessary to be considered liberal; and Caesar was one of those who wished to become pre-eminent in Rome; but if he had survived after becoming so, and had not moderated his expenses, he would have destroyed his government. And if anyone should reply: Many have been princes, and have done great things with armies, who have been considered very liberal, I reply: Either a prince spends that which is his own or his subjects' or else that of others. In the first case he ought to be sparing, in the second he ought not to neglect any opportunity for liberality. And to the prince who goes forth with his army, supporting it by pillage, sack, and extortion, handling that which belongs to others, this liberality is necessary, otherwise he would not be followed by soldiers. And of that which is neither yours nor your subjects' you can be a ready giver, as were Cyrus, Caesar, and Alexander; because it does not take away your reputation if you squander that of others, but adds to it; it is only squandering your own that injures you.

And there is nothing wastes so rapidly as liberality, for even whilst you exercise it you lose the power to do so, and so become either poor or despised, or else, in avoiding poverty, rapacious and hated. And a prince should guard himself, above all things, against being despised and hated; and liberality leads you to both. Therefore it is wiser to have a reputation for meanness which brings reproach without hatred, than to be compelled through seeking a reputation for liberality to incur a name for rapacity which begets reproach with hatred.

Chapter XVII

Concerning Cruelty and Clemency, and Whether It Is Better to Be Loved than Feared

Coming now to the other qualities mentioned above, I say that every prince ought to desire to be considered clement and not cruel. Nevertheless he ought to take care not to misuse this clemency. Cesare Borgia was considered cruel; notwithstanding, his cruelty reconciled the Romagna, unified it, and restored it to peace and loyalty.[3]

3. **Cesare Borgia:** the son of Rodrigo Borgia (1431–1503), who became Pope Alexander VI in 1492. Alexander was an intensely political pope, bent on increasing the power of the papacy and the extent of papal lands, and Cesare Borgia (1475 or 1476–1507) led a sustained attempt, with his father's help, to unify the central Italian states known as the **Romagna** into a single political entity. Machiavelli greatly admired Borgia, and some scholars have argued that he is the model "prince" that Machiavelli had in mind throughout the work.

And if this be rightly considered, he will be seen to have been much more merciful than the Florentine people, who, to avoid a reputation for cruelty, permitted Pistoia to be destroyed. Therefore a prince, so long as he keeps his subjects united and loyal, ought not to mind the reproach of cruelty; because with a few examples he will be more merciful than those who, through too much mercy, allow disorders to arise, from which follow murders or robberies; for these are wont to injure the whole people, whilst those executions which originate with a prince offend the individual only.

And of all princes, it is impossible for the new prince to avoid the imputation of cruelty, owing to new states being full of dangers. . . . Nevertheless he ought to be slow to believe and to act, nor should he himself show fear, but proceed in a temperate manner with prudence and humanity, so that too much confidence may not make him incautious and too much distrust render him intolerable.

Upon this a question arises: whether it be better to be loved than feared or feared   10
than loved? It may be answered that one should wish to be both, but, because it is difficult to unite them in one person, it is much safer to be feared than loved, when, of the two, either must be dispensed with. Because this is to be asserted in general of men, that they are ungrateful, fickle, false, cowardly, covetous, and as long as you succeed they are yours entirely; they will offer you their blood, property, life, and children, as is said above, when the need is far distant; but when it approaches they turn against you. And that prince who, relying entirely on their promises, has neglected other precautions, is ruined; because friendships that are obtained by payments, and not by greatness or nobility of mind, may indeed be earned, but they are not secured, and in time of need cannot be relied upon; and men have less scruple in offending one who is beloved than one who is feared, for love is preserved by the link of obligation which, owing to the baseness of men, is broken at every opportunity for their advantage; but fear preserves you by a dread of punishment which never fails.

Nevertheless a prince ought to inspire fear in such a way that, if he does not win love, he avoids hatred; because he can endure very well being feared whilst he is not hated, which will always be as long as he abstains from the property of his citizens and subjects and from their women. But when it is necessary for him to proceed against the life of someone, he must do it on proper justification and for manifest cause, but above all things he must keep his hands off the property of others, because men more quickly forget the death of their father than the loss of their patrimony. Besides, pretexts for taking away the property are never wanting; for he who has once begun to live by robbery will always find pretexts for seizing what belongs to others; but reasons for taking life, on the contrary, are more difficult to find and sooner lapse. But when a prince is with his army, and has under control a multitude of soldiers, then it is quite necessary for him to disregard the reputation of cruelty, for without it he would never hold his army united or disposed to its duties.

Among the wonderful deeds of Hannibal[4] this one is enumerated: that having led an enormous army, composed of many various races of men, to fight in foreign lands, no dissensions arose either among them or against the prince, whether in his bad or in his good fortune. This arose from nothing else than his inhuman cruelty, which, with his boundless valour, made him revered and terrible in the sight of his soldiers, but without that cruelty, his other virtues were not sufficient to produce this effect. And shortsighted writers admire his deeds from one point of view and from another condemn the principal cause of them. That it is true his other virtues would not have been sufficient for him may be proved by the case of Scipio,[5] that most excellent man, not only of his own times but within the memory of man, against whom, nevertheless, his army rebelled in Spain; this arose from nothing but his too great forbearance, which gave his soldiers more licence than is consistent with military discipline. For this he was upbraided in the Senate by Fabius Maximus, and called the corrupter of the Roman soldiery. The Locrians were laid waste by a legate of Scipio, yet they were not avenged by him, nor was the insolence of the legate[6] punished, owing entirely to his easy nature. Insomuch that someone in the Senate, wishing to excuse him, said there were many men who knew much better how not to err than to correct the errors of others. This disposition, if he had been continued in the command, would have destroyed in time the fame and glory of Scipio; but, he being under the control of the Senate, this injurious characteristic not only concealed itself, but contributed to his glory.

Returning to the question of being feared or loved, I come to the conclusion that, men loving according to their own will and fearing according to that of the prince, a wise prince should establish himself on that which is in his own control and not in that of others; he must endeavour only to avoid hatred, as is noted.

Chapter XVIII

Concerning the Way in which Princes Should Keep Faith

Everyone admits how praiseworthy it is in a prince to keep faith, and to live with integrity and not with craft. Nevertheless our experience has been that those princes who have done great things have held good faith of little account, and have known how to circumvent the intellect of men by craft, and in the end have overcome those who have relied on their word. You must know there are two ways of contesting, the one by the law, the other by force; the first method is proper to men, the second

4. **Hannibal:** legendary Carthaginian general (247–circa 183 BCE), who defeated the Romans in 218 BCE by leading an army of nearly forty thousand men across the Alps—a feat that no one believed possible—and catching the Romans completely off guard.

5. **Scipio:** the name of a Roman family that included two generals, father and son, who fought against Hannibal during the Second Punic War. Machiavelli refers here to the younger of the two, Scipio Africanus Major (236–184 or 183 BCE), the general who finally defeated Hannibal in 202 BCE.

6. **Legate:** assistant to a Roman general. **Locrians:** inhabitants of the ancient Greek region of Locris.

to beasts; but because the first is frequently not sufficient, it is necessary to have recourse to the second. Therefore it is necessary for a prince to understand how to avail himself of the beast and the man. This has been figuratively taught to princes by ancient writers, who describe how Achilles and many other princes of old were given to the Centaur Chiron[7] to nurse, who brought them up in his discipline; which means solely that, as they had for a teacher one who was half beast and half man, so it is necessary for a prince to know how to make use of both natures, and that one without the other is not durable. A prince, therefore, being compelled knowingly to adopt the beast, ought to choose the fox and the lion; because the lion cannot defend himself against snares and the fox cannot defend himself against wolves. Therefore, it is necessary to be a fox to discover the snares and a lion to terrify the wolves. Those who rely simply on the lion do not understand what they are about. Therefore a wise lord cannot, nor ought he to, keep faith when such observance may be turned against him, and when the reasons that caused him to pledge it exist no longer. If men were entirely good this precept would not hold, but because they are bad, and will not keep faith with you, you too are not bound to observe it with them. Nor will there ever be wanting to a prince legitimate reasons to excuse this nonobservance. Of this endless modern examples could be given, showing how many treaties and engagements have been made void and of no effect through the faithlessness of princes; and he who has known best how to employ the fox has succeeded best.

But it is necessary to know well how to disguise this characteristic, and to be a great pretender and dissembler; and men are so simple, and so subject to present necessities, that he who seeks to deceive will always find someone who will allow himself to be deceived. One recent example I cannot pass over in silence. Alexander VI did nothing else but deceive men, nor ever thought of doing otherwise, and he always found victims; for there never was a man who had greater power in asserting, or who with greater oaths would affirm a thing, yet would observe it less; nevertheless his deceits always succeeded according to his wishes, because he well understood this side of mankind. 15

Therefore it is unnecessary for a prince to have all the good qualities I have enumerated, but it is very necessary to appear to have them. And I shall dare to say this also, that to have them and always to observe them is injurious, and that to appear to have them is useful; to appear merciful, faithful, humane, religious, upright, and to be so, but with a mind so framed that should you require not to be so, you may be able and know how to change to the opposite.

And you have to understand this, that a prince, especially a new one, cannot observe all those things for which men are esteemed, being often forced, in order to maintain the state, to act contrary to faith, friendship, humanity, and religion. Therefore it is necessary for him to have a mind ready to turn itself accordingly as the winds and

7. **Centaur Chiron:** In Greek mythology, Chiron the Centaur (half-horse, half-man) was a gifted tutor whose pupils included many heroes of ancient Greece, including Achilles, the great hero of the Trojan War.

variations of fortune force it, yet, as I have said above, not to diverge from the good if he can avoid doing so, but, if compelled, then to know how to set about it.

For this reason a prince ought to take care that he never lets anything slip from his lips that is not replete with the above-named five qualities, that he may appear to him who sees and hears him altogether merciful, faithful, humane, upright, and religious. There is nothing more necessary to appear to have than this last quality, inasmuch as men judge generally more by the eye than by the hand, because it belongs to everybody to see you, to few to come in touch with you. Every one sees what you appear to be, few really know what you are, and those few dare not oppose themselves to the opinion of the many, who have the majesty of the state to defend them; and in the actions of all men, and especially of princes, which it is not prudent to challenge, one judges by the result.

For that reason, let a prince have the credit of conquering and holding his state, the means will always be considered honest, and he will be praised by everybody; because the vulgar are always taken by what a thing seems to be and by what comes of it; and in the world there are only the vulgar, for the few find a place there only when the many have no ground to rest on.

One prince of the present time, whom it is not well to name, never preaches   20
anything else but peace and good faith, and to both he is most hostile, and either, if he had kept it, would have deprived him of reputation and kingdom many a time.

UNDERSTANDING THE TEXT

1. Why must a prince "know how to do wrong"? What connection, if any, does Machiavelli see between ethics and politics?

2. How does Machiavelli justify being "miserly" as a leader? List the major reasons for this assertion: "And a prince should guard himself, above all things, against being despised and hated; and liberality leads you to both."

3. Why does Machiavelli reason that it is better for a prince to be feared than loved? How is cruelty a motivating force to keep order? What restraints does he put on inflicting fear? Why does he name these limits?

4. How does Machiavelli use the analogies of the fox and the lion as part of his argument? What qualities of a leader does each represent? How does the ideal leader combine these qualities?

5. Do you believe that Machiavelli is correct in his estimation that having a reputation for good character traits is actually better than having those character traits? What is the difference, in political terms, between reputation and reality?

6. Why are the historical references to past rulers important to Machiavelli's argument? What points of his argument concerning the essential duality of a leader do these stories illustrate?

MAKING CONNECTIONS

1. How does Machiavelli employ the "just hypocrisy" argument that Christine de Pizan (p. 397) also proposes? Are the two operating from the same basic presumptions?

2. How does Machiavelli instruct princes to deal with the negative aspects of human nature, such as lust, greed, ambition, and dishonesty? How does he instruct princes to deal with the more positive aspects of human nature, such as trust, loyalty, and a willingness to believe in the good of others? Is it possible to deduce from *The Prince* a sense of Machiavelli's overall conception of human nature?

3. How does Machiavelli's pragmatism compare to that of Sun Tzu in *The Art of War* (p. 476)? The two types have often been grouped as examples of "win at any cost" thinking. Do you agree? Explain.

4. Does Machiavelli's approach to leadership suggest a kind of natural selection comparable to what Darwin saw in nature (p. 314)? Are political leaders subject to the same "survival of the fittest" rules that pervade the natural world? Why or why not?

WRITING ABOUT THE TEXT

1. Consider whether Machiavelli's idea that it is better for a ruler to be feared than loved applies to contemporary politics. Does the emergence of democracy in many parts of the world alter this equation? If so, how so? If not, why not?

2. Examine the underlying ethical structure of Machiavelli's argument that the goal of political stability justifies cruelty, deception, and hypocrisy. Do you believe that this is true? Do the peace and prosperity brought about by political stability justify the kind of leadership that Machiavelli proposes?

3. Compare the concepts of human nature in Hobbes's *Leviathan* (p. 94) with those in Machiavelli's *The Prince* (p. 405).

4. Rebut Machiavelli's argument that effective leadership requires duplicity. Cite examples of cases in which honesty and straightforwardness have produced strong and effective leaders.

5. Examine Machiavelli's use of historical examples. Is he ultimately writing a prescriptive argument (one that instructs rulers how they should exercise power most effectively) or a descriptive argument (one that simply describes how power has been exercised effectively in the past)?

ABRAHAM BOSSE

Frontispiece of Thomas Hobbes's Leviathan

[1651]

ARTIST AND PRINTMAKER Abraham Bosse (1602–1676) was born in Paris to German immigrant parents. After an apprenticeship with Melchior Tavernier, a well-known Belgian illustrator and publisher, Bosse began his career as a book illustrator, eventually becoming one of the most influential and imitated French artists of the seventeenth century. Though Bosse worked occasionally in watercolors, most of his works were etchings on copper plates, a printmaking process to which he made important technical contributions. In his lifetime, he produced more than 1,600 etches, most of them illustrations for books, but some of which became popular as stand-alone works of art.

In 1651, Bosse collaborated with the English philosopher Thomas Hobbes to produce the frontispiece—the page opposite the title page in a book—for Hobbes's major book, *Leviathan* (p. 94), which was published by the well-known London publisher Andrew Crooke. Hobbes spent most of that troubled period in France, where he interacted frequently with the Royalist exiles—supporters of King Charles I who were forced into exile after they were defeated by the armies of Oliver Cromwell during the English Civil War that lasted from 1642 to 1651. The Civil War so profoundly disturbed Hobbes that he felt compelled to respond to them with a detailed theory of the civil state, which he called the "Leviathan." The Leviathan state, Hobbes argued, was the only power capable of preventing the "war of all against all" that would occur if human beings were left to their own natures.

Hobbes collaborated extensively with Bosse on the design for the frontispiece, which, he believed, should compress the major arguments of the book into a single, unforgettable image. The etching is dominated by a giant crowned figure whose body is composed entirely of other people. This is Hobbes's great metaphor for sovereignty in a Leviathan state. The sovereign is a single person, but that person's sovereignty comprises the natural sovereignty of all the people, which they voluntarily cede to the state in exchange for the civil peace that allows them to maximize their own happiness.

The sovereign holds both a sword, the symbol of military force, and a crosier, an emblem of religious authority—the two chief forms of power that Hobbes believed resided in the sovereign. At the top of the etching is a Latin inscription from the Book of Job describing the sea-monster Leviathan, for whom Hobbes named his most important concept: *"Non est potestas Super Terram quae Comparetur"* ("There is no power on earth to be compared to him"). Hobbes believed that this image would capture the primary argument of his book: a powerful sovereign can create a safe and orderly society when supported by the people of the state. But when people rebel against a legitimately constituted authority—as many of Hobbes's countrymen did in the 1640s—they jeopardize the entire body politic of which they are a part.

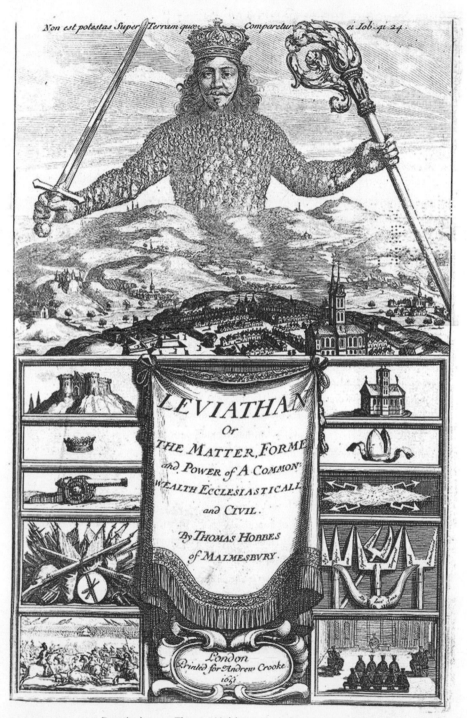

ABRAHAM BOSSE Frontispiece to Thomas Hobbes's *Leviathan*, 1651 (etching on copper plate). Wikimedia Commons.

UNDERSTANDING THE TEXT

1. Hobbes believed that people entered into a "social contract" with their governments in which they exchange certain natural freedoms in exchange for specific protections. How do you think this image might illustrate such a social contract?

2. What does it mean that the sovereign in the image holds symbols of both military and religious power? How might Hobbes have seen both of these kinds of power as tools that the sovereign can use to produce a stable state?

3. Explain how the quotation from the Book of Job—"There is no power on earth compared to him"—characterizes the kind of state that Hobbes advocated. Why, according to Hobbes, must the sovereign of such a state have incomparable power?

4. Identify the ten objects in the lower portion of the engraving. How do they support the engraving's central argument?

MAKING CONNECTIONS

1. Read the excerpt from *Leviathan* (p. 94) in Chapter 2 and explain the different ways it relates to the Bosse drawing.

2. Contrast the importance of religion to the civil state, as indicated by the sovereign holding the religious crosier, with James Madison's belief (p. 417) that the civil government should be completely impartial to religion. Why do you think that Madison and Hobbes disagreed on this issue?

3. How would nonviolent civil disobedience of the kind advocated by Martin Luther King Jr. in *Letter from Birmingham Jail* (p. 425) fit into Hobbes's Leviathan state? Is it possible to disagree with a sovereign without rejecting his or her sovereignty?

4. Compare the abstract "Sovereign" in this etching with the "Liberty" figure in Delacroix's "Liberty Leading the People" (p. 494). How do both images create allegories through their central figures?

WRITING ABOUT THE TEXT

1. Examine the rhetorical power of images using the frontispiece of *Leviathan* and one other image from this book. Explain how images can frame arguments and make assertions visually, and compare this to other ways of making the same arguments.

2. Define "sovereignty" as you believe it should apply to societies and governments. From where do you think governments draw their legitimate authority? Compare your view to the Hobbesian view portrayed in the frontispiece.

3. Analyze the use of a particular set of symbols (i.e., crowns, military implements, religious icons) in both the upper and the lower portion of the frontispiece. Explain how these symbols work with the larger symbolic structure of the work.

JAMES MADISON
Memorial and Remonstrance against
Religious Assessments
[1785]

JAMES MADISON (1751–1836) wore many hats during the founding of the United States of America, and he did more to shape and ratify the Constitution than any other person in the Republic. He led the charge for a Constitutional Convention in 1787 to revise the Articles of Confederation, and he wrote the initial document that delegates used as a working draft. When the Convention ended, Madison joined Alexander Hamilton to write the *Federalist Papers*, which refuted the arguments of the many colonists who felt that the government created by the Constitution was too powerful and would lead to the kind of tyranny they experienced under British rule. As soon as the Constitution was ratified, Madison became the legislative force behind the Bill of Rights. Once the new government was in place, Madison served for many years as a leader in the House of Representatives before becoming Thomas Jefferson's secretary of state and then, finally, the fourth president of the United States from 1809 to1817.

Before Madison ever became involved in national politics, however, he served as a member of the Virginia House of Delegates, to which he was first elected in 1776 at the age of twenty-five. During his first term he became an ally of Thomas Jefferson, and the two worked on Jefferson's signature piece of legislation in the Virginia assembly, the Virginia Statute for Religious Freedom—a radical document for its time. It disestablished the Anglican Church in Virginia, guaranteed full religious freedom to all citizens, and called for a complete separation of church and state. The statute was defeated in 1779 and, soon after, Jefferson was appointed the United States Minister to France, where he remained until 1789.

In 1785, however, Madison had an opportunity to revive Jefferson's religious freedom bill when Patrick Henry, then governor of Virginia, introduced a bill to use tax revenues to subsidize churches and other religious organizations. Henry's bill was cross-denominational—it allowed taxpayers to direct their tax subsidies to the religious organization of their choice—but it violated the strict church–state separation that both Madison and Jefferson believed to be essential to a free society. Madison successfully led the opposition to Henry's bill and then brought Jefferson's Statute for Religious Freedom back to the floor, where it passed by a wide margin.

In the midst of the Virginia debate over a religious tax, Madison wrote a brief pamphlet for the general public—who could pressure their representatives in Congress—outlining his views. "Memorial and Remonstrance against Religious Assessments" is a reminder ("memorial") to Virginians of the tyrannies they experienced under the

European system of state religions, and a "remonstrance," or forcible protest, against any kind of mixing of church and state. For Madison, the only position that a civil government can take towards religion is "non-cognizance," that is, not recognizing religion at all. When the state does this, Madison believed, religious ideas can circulate in an intellectual free market where the best ones will naturally flourish.

"Memorial and Remonstrance against Religious Assessments" is organized like a legislative resolution, with a series of clauses giving the rationale for the resolution (each beginning with "because") and a final, succinct statement of the main point. You'll notice that certain nouns are capitalized and others are not; while eighteenth-century usage dictated this punctuation, it was falling into disuse and used haphazardly by the time Madison wrote "Memorial." The pamphlet helped Madison secure passage of Jefferson's Declaration of Religious Freedom in Virginia, and it is one of our clearest glimpses of how Madison, the principal author of both the Constitution and the Bill of Rights, conceived of the relationship between church and state in a free republic.

To the Honorable the General Assembly of the Commonwealth of Virginia

We the subscribers, citizens of the said Commonwealth, having taken into serious consideration, a Bill printed by order of the last Session of General Assembly, entitled "A Bill establishing a provision for Teachers of the Christian Religion,"[1] and conceiving that the same if finally armed with the sanctions of a law, will be a dangerous abuse of power, are bound as faithful members of a free State to remonstrate against it, and to declare the reasons by which we are determined. We remonstrate against the said Bill,

1. Because we hold it for a fundamental and undeniable truth, "that religion or the duty which we owe to our Creator and the manner of discharging it, can be directed only by reason and conviction, not by force or violence." The Religion then of every man must be left to the conviction and conscience of every man; and it is the right of every man to exercise it as these may dictate. This right is in its nature an unalienable right. It is unalienable, because the opinions of men, depending only on the evidence contemplated by their own minds cannot follow the dictates of other men: It is unalienable also, because what is here a right towards men, is a duty towards the Creator. It is the duty of every man to render to the Creator such homage and such only as he believes to be acceptable to him. This duty is precedent, both in order of time and in degree of obligation, to the claims of Civil Society.[2] Before any man

1. **"A Bill establishing a provision for Teachers of the Christian Religion":** the title of Patrick Henry's bill to subsidize religious organizations with a special tax.

2. **Civil Society:** the portion of society that is subject to the law or the regulation of the state.

can be considered as a member of Civil Society, he must be considered as a subject of the Governour of the Universe.[3] And if a member of Civil Society, do it with a saving of his allegiance to the Universal Sovereign. We maintain therefore that in matters of Religion, no man's right is abridged by the institution of Civil Society and that Religion is wholly exempt from its cognizance.[4] True it is, that no other rule exists, by which any question which may divide a Society, can be ultimately determined, but the will of the majority; but it is also true that the majority may trespass on the rights of the minority.

2. Because Religion be exempt from the authority of the Society at large, still less can it be subject to that of the Legislative Body. The latter are but the creatures and vicegerents of the former. Their jurisdiction is both derivative and limited: it is limited with regard to the co-ordinate departments, more necessarily is it limited with regard to the constituents. The preservation of a free Government requires not merely, that the metes and bounds[5] which separate each department of power be invariably maintained; but more especially that neither of them be suffered to overleap the great Barrier which defends the rights of the people. The Rulers who are guilty of such an encroachment, exceed the commission from which they derive their authority, and are Tyrants. The People who submit to it are governed by laws made neither by themselves nor by an authority derived from them, and are slaves.

3. Because it is proper to take alarm at the first experiment on our liberties. We hold this prudent jealousy to be the first duty of Citizens, and one of the noblest characteristics of the late Revolution.[6] The free men of America did not wait till usurped power had strengthened itself by exercise, and entangled the question in precedents. They saw all the consequences in the principle, and they avoided the consequences by denying the principle. We revere this lesson too much soon to forget it. Who does not see that the same authority which can establish Christianity, in exclusion of all other Religions, may establish with the same ease any particular sect of Christians, in exclusion of all other Sects? that the same authority which can force a citizen to contribute three pence only of his property for the support of any one establishment, may force him to conform to any other establishment in all cases whatsoever?

4. Because the Bill violates the equality which ought to be the basis of every law, and which is more indispensible, in proportion as the validity or expediency of any law is more liable to be impeached. If "all men are by nature equally free and independent," all men are to be considered as entering into Society on equal conditions; as relinquishing no more, and therefore retaining no less, one than another, of their natural rights. Above all are they to be considered as retaining an "equal title to the

---

3. **Governour of the Universe:** God.
4. **Cognizance:** recognition.
5. **Metes and bounds:** standard eighteenth-century surveying term to denote boundary lines.

6. **Late Revolution:** the American Revolution.

free exercise of Religion according to the dictates of Conscience."[7] "Whilst we assert for ourselves a freedom to embrace, to profess and to observe the Religion which we believe to be of divine origin, we cannot deny an equal freedom to those whose minds have not yet yielded to the evidence which has convinced us. If this freedom be abused, it is an offence against God, not against man: To God, therefore, not to man, must an account of it be rendered. As the Bill violates equality by subjecting some to peculiar burdens, so it violates the same principle, by granting to others peculiar exemptions. Are the Quakers and Menonists[8] the only sects who think a compulsive support of their Religions unnecessary and unwarrantable? Can their piety alone be entrusted with the care of public worship? Ought their Religions to be endowed above all others with extraordinary privileges by which proselytes may be enticed from all others? We think too favorably of the justice and good sense of these denominations to believe that they either covet pre-eminences over their fellow citizens or that they will be seduced by them from the common opposition to the measure.

5. Because the Bill implies either that the Civil Magistrate[9] is a competent Judge of Religious Truth; or that he may employ Religion as an engine of Civil policy. The first is an arrogant pretension falsified by the contradictory opinions of Rulers in all ages, and throughout the world: the second an unhallowed perversion of the means of salvation.

6. Because the establishment proposed by the Bill is not requisite for the support of the Christian Religion. To say that it is, is a contradiction to the Christian Religion itself, for every page of it disavows a dependence on the powers of this world: it is a contradiction to fact; for it is known that this Religion both existed and flourished, not only without the support of human laws, but in spite of every opposition from them, and not only during the period of miraculous aid, but long after it had been left to its own evidence and the ordinary care of Providence. Nay, it is a contradiction in terms; for a Religion not invented by human policy, must have pre-existed and been supported, before it was established by human policy. It is moreover to weaken in those who profess this Religion a pious confidence in its innate excellence and the patronage of its Author, and to foster in those who still reject it, a suspicion that its friends are too conscious of its fallacies to trust it to its own merits.

7. Because experience witnesseth that ecclesiastical establishments, instead of maintaining the purity and efficacy of Religion, have had a contrary operation. During almost fifteen centuries has the legal establishment of Christianity been

7. **"Equal title to the free exercise of Religion according to the dictates of Conscience":** a direct quotation, along with **"all men are by nature free and independent"** from the Virginia Declaration of Rights adopted in June of 1776 and used as a model for the Declaration of Independence in July of 1776.

8. **Quakers and Mennonites:** conscientious objectors to military service who were exempt from military service and, therefore, according to some, should have been subject to additional taxation. They were among the most vocal opponents of Henry's bill.

9. **Civil Magistrate:** any secular political leader.

on trial. What have been its fruits? More or less in all places, pride and indolence in the Clergy, ignorance and servility in the laity, in both, superstition, bigotry and persecution. Enquire of the Teachers of Christianity for the ages in which it appeared in its greatest lustre; those of every sect, point to the ages prior to its incorporation with Civil policy. Propose a restoration of this primitive State in which its Teachers depended on the voluntary rewards of their flocks, many of them predict its downfall. On which Side ought their testimony to have greatest weight, when for or when against their interest?

8. Because the establishment in question is not necessary for the support of Civil Government.[10] If it be urged as necessary for the support of Civil Government only as it is a means of supporting Religion, and it be not necessary for the latter purpose, it cannot be necessary for the former. If Religion be not within the cognizance of Civil Government how can its legal establishment be necessary to Civil Government? What influence in fact have ecclesiastical establishments had on Civil Society? In some instances they have been seen to erect a spiritual tyranny on the ruins of the Civil authority; in many instances they have been seen upholding the thrones of political tyranny: in no instance have they been seen the guardians of the liberties of the people. Rulers who wished to subvert the public liberty, may have found an established Clergy convenient auxiliaries. A just Government instituted to secure & perpetuate it needs them not. Such a Government will be best supported by protecting every Citizen in the enjoyment of his Religion with the same equal hand which protects his person and his property; by neither invading the equal rights of any Sect, nor suffering any Sect to invade those of another.

9. Because the proposed establishment is a departure from the generous policy, which, offering an Asylum to the persecuted and oppressed of every Nation and Religion, promised a lustre to our country, and an accession to the number of its citizens. What a melancholy mark is the Bill of sudden degeneracy? Instead of holding forth an Asylum to the persecuted, it is itself a signal of persecution. It degrades from the equal rank of Citizens all those whose opinions in Religion do not bend to those of the Legislative authority. Distant as it may be in its present form from the Inquisition, it differs from it only in degree. The one is the first step, the other the last in the career of intolerance. The magnanimous sufferer under this cruel scourge in foreign Regions, must view the Bill as a Beacon on our Coast,[11] warning him to seek some other haven, where liberty and philanthrophy in their due extent, may offer a more certain repose from his Troubles.

10. Because it will have a like tendency to banish our Citizens. The allurements presented by other situations are every day thinning their number. To superadd a fresh motive to emigration by revoking the liberty which they now enjoy, would be the same species of folly which has dishonoured and depopulated flourishing kingdoms.

---

10. **Civil Government:** any secular government.
11. **Beacon on our Coast:** the signal from a lighthouse warning of danger. Here, Madison means that the Bill for religious assessment would cause people to avoid moving to Virginia, thinking it hostile to those seeking freedom.

11. Because it will destroy that moderation and harmony which the forbearance of our laws to intermeddle with Religion has produced among its several sects. Torrents of blood have been spilt in the old world,[12] by vain attempts of the secular arm, to extinguish Religious discord, by proscribing all difference in Religious opinion. Time has at length revealed the true remedy. Every relaxation of narrow and rigorous policy, wherever it has been tried, has been found to assuage the disease. The American Theatre[13] has exhibited proofs that equal and compleat[14] liberty, if it does not wholly eradicate it, sufficiently destroys its malignant influence on the health and prosperity of the State. If with the salutary effects of this system under our own eyes, we begin to contract the bounds of Religious freedom, we know no name that will too severely reproach our folly. At least let warning be taken at the first fruits of the threatened innovation. The very appearance of the Bill has transformed "that Christian forbearance, love and charity," which of late mutually prevailed, into animosities and jealousies, which may not soon be appeased. What mischiefs may not be dreaded, should this enemy to the public quiet be armed with the force of a law?

12. Because the policy of the Bill is adverse to the diffusion of the light of Christianity. The first wish of those who enjoy this precious gift ought to be that it may be imparted to the whole race of mankind. Compare the number of those who have as yet received it with the number still remaining under the dominion of false Religions; and how small is the former! Does the policy of the Bill tend to lessen the disproportion? No; it at once discourages those who are strangers to the light of revelation from coming into the Region of it; and countenances by example the nations who continue in darkness, in shutting out those who might convey it to them. Instead of Levelling as far as possible, every obstacle to the victorious progress of Truth, the Bill with an ignoble and unchristian timidity would circumscribe it with a wall of defence against the encroachments of error.

13. Because attempts to enforce by legal sanctions, acts obnoxious to so great a proportion of Citizens, tend to enervate the laws in general, and to slacken the bands of Society. If it be difficult to execute any law which is not generally deemed necessary or salutary, what must be the case, where it is deemed invalid and dangerous? And what may be the effect of so striking an example of impotency in the Government, on its general authority?

14. Because a measure of such singular magnitude and delicacy ought not to be imposed, without the clearest evidence that it is called for by a majority of citizens, and no satisfactory method is yet proposed by which the voice of the majority in this case may be determined, or its influence secured. "The people of the respective counties are indeed requested to signify their opinion respecting the adoption of the Bill to the next Session of Assembly." But the representation must be made

---

12. **Old world:** Europe, especially France and Great Britain.

13. **American Theatre:** the American colonies.

14. **Compleat:** complete.

equal, before the voice either of the Representatives or of the Counties will be that of the people. Our hope is that neither of the former will, after due consideration, espouse the dangerous principle of the Bill. Should the event disappoint us, it will still leave us in full confidence, that a fair appeal to the latter will reverse the sentence against our liberties.

Because finally, "the equal right of every citizen to the free exercise of his Religion according to the dictates of conscience" is held by the same tenure with all our other rights. If we recur to its origin, it is equally the gift of nature; if we weigh its importance, it cannot be less dear to us; if we consult the "Declaration of those rights which pertain to the good people of Virginia, as the basis and foundation of Government," it is enumerated with equal solemnity, or rather studied emphasis. Either then, we must say, that the Will of the Legislature is the only measure of their authority; and that in the plenitude of this authority, they may sweep away all our fundamental rights; or, that they are bound to leave this particular right untouched and sacred: Either we must say, that they may controul the freedom of the press, may abolish the Trial by Jury, may swallow up the Executive and Judiciary Powers of the State; nay that they may despoil us of our very right of suffrage, and erect themselves into an independent and hereditary Assembly or, we must say, that they have no authority to enact into the law the Bill under consideration.

We the Subscribers say, that the General Assembly of this Commonwealth have no such authority: And that no effort may be omitted on our part against so dangerous an usurpation, we oppose to it, this remonstrance; earnestly praying, as we are in duty bound, that the Supreme Lawgiver of the Universe, by illuminating those to whom it is addressed, may on the one hand, turn their Councils from every act which would affront his holy prerogative, or violate the trust committed to them: and on the other, guide them into every measure which may be worthy of his blessing, may redound to their own praise, and may establish more firmly the liberties, the prosperity and the happiness of the Commonwealth.

UNDERSTANDING THE TEXT

1. Why is it significant to Madison that a person's relationship with God exists prior to that person's relationship with the government?

2. Why does Madison bring up the possibility of the majority trespassing on the rights of the minority? How might this occur if the state recognizes religion?

3. How does Madison treat non-Christians and those who practice no religion at all? Does he believe that it is acceptable to support Christianity generally as long as individual denominations are not given any preference?

4. How does Madison counter the argument that requiring small donations to religious causes through taxation does not constitute religious establishment?

5. How does Madison see governmental support of religion as potentially damaging to the aims of religions themselves? How is such support damaging to the governments that support religions?

6. Over the past 1500 years, what have been the outcomes of governments that support Christianity, according to Madison? How has this made the Christian religion something different than it was originally designed to be?

7. How does Madison see the freedom of religion in relation to other rights and freedoms? How would passing a law that limited some people's freedom to choose their religion affect the framework that guarantees all of the other rights to the people of Virginia?

MAKING CONNECTIONS

1. How might Madison's concept of the separation of church and state be considered part of the minimalist form of government advocated by the *Tao Te Ching* (p. 384)? Does Madison suggest that leaders should avoid interfering with the natural order of things the way that a Taoist might?

2. How do Madison's views of religious toleration compare with the other kinds of toleration discussed by Simone Weil (p. 571), Martin Luther King Jr. (p. 425), Barack Obama (p. 460), and Vandana Shiva (p. 374)?

3. What is similar and what is different in the way that James Madison and Martha Nussbaum (p. 61) see the idea of democracy?

WRITING ABOUT THE TEXT

1. Write a paper that examines Madison's fourteen major points and determine which are the most relevant today. Are some no longer pertinent to our society?

2. Apply Madison's argument to a current debate involving questions of church and state, such as religious displays on public property, prayers at state-sanctioned events, or taxpayer subsidies of religious education.

3. Write your own argument about the proper role of religion in the public sphere. Look at both historical and contemporary debates to determine how governments should treat religions and vice versa.

MARTIN LUTHER KING JR.

Letter from Birmingham Jail

[1963]

IN THE FIRST HALF OF THE TWENTIETH CENTURY, "Jim Crow" laws ensured that whites and blacks in America remained segregated in all areas of public life—on buses, on railroads, in schools, in restaurants, and elsewhere. However, in 1954, the Supreme Court ruled in the case of *Brown v. Board of Education of Topeka* that separating students of different races into different schools was unconstitutional. That decision signaled the beginning of the end of the segregation laws. In the following years, schools across the country would be integrated, followed by other public facilities and public transportation.

The Reverend Martin Luther King Jr. (1929–1968) gained wide exposure as a civil rights leader in 1955, when, while serving as a pastor in Montgomery, Alabama, he led a boycott against that city's bus lines that resulted in their desegregation the following year. In 1957, after the success of the bus boycott, King founded the Southern Christian Leadership Conference (SCLC) and began a series of nonviolent campaigns aimed at ending racial segregation across the South. In 1963, the SCLC led a series of highly publicized protests and demonstrations in Birmingham, Alabama, that proved to be one of the turning points in the struggle for civil rights.

King, who was well versed in the philosophy and practice of nonviolent civil disobedience, understood that one powerful application of this philosophy was to disobey unjust laws publicly and to accept the consequences of that disobedience. Consequently, when a local judge issued a blatantly unconstitutional injunction that forbade King and others from engaging in protest activities, he defied the order and went to jail. While in jail, he read, with dismay, an open letter from eight moderate, white clergymen in Birmingham condemning the demonstrations as "unwise and untimely . . . extreme measures [that were] led . . . by outsiders." In its conclusion, the letter states, "We . . . urge our own Negro community to withdraw support from these demonstrations, and to unite locally in working peacefully for a better Birmingham. When rights are consistently denied, a cause should be pressed in the courts and in negotiations among local leaders, and not in the streets. We appeal to both our white and Negro citizenry to observe the principles of law and order and common sense."

King was disheartened by this rebuke from the very Christian and Jewish leaders he had hoped would support his cause. He used their letter as the platform for what would become one of the most famous arguments for civil disobedience ever written: his "Letter from Birmingham Jail." Because he wrote this response to fellow members of the clergy, and because he rooted his activism in Christianity, King bases his argument firmly in the Judeo-Christian tradition. He invokes passages from both the Old and New Testaments to support two different propositions: that segregation is unjust in the eyes of God, and that the Judeo-Christian tradition allows, and even at times requires, disobedience to unjust laws.

The "Letter from Birmingham Jail" is dated April 16, 1963. King could not send the letter directly to those it addressed; friends had to smuggle it out of the jail in pieces and reassemble it later. The letter was included in King's book *Why We Can't Wait*, which was published in 1964, the year that King became, at thirty-five, the youngest person ever to be awarded the Nobel Prize for Peace.

The "Letter from Birmingham Jail" has long been considered a casebook of different rhetorical approaches. King takes great pains to establish the ethos of a trusted and knowledgeable member of the clergy, but he also makes powerful appeals to justice and fairness, and his arguments about just and unjust laws give an excellent example of deductive reasoning in action.

My Dear Fellow Clergymen,

While confined here in the Birmingham city jail, I came across your recent statement calling our present activities "unwise and untimely." Seldom, if ever, do I pause to answer criticism of my work and ideas. If I sought to answer all of the criticisms that cross my desk, my secretaries would be engaged in little else in the course of the day, and I would have no time for constructive work. But since I feel that you are men of genuine good will and your criticisms are sincerely set forth, I would like to answer your statement in what I hope will be patient and reasonable terms.

I think I should give the reason for my being in Birmingham, since you have been influenced by the argument of "outsiders coming in." I have the honor of serving as president of the Southern Christian Leadership Conference, an organization operating in every southern state, with headquarters in Atlanta, Georgia. We have some eighty-five affiliate organizations all across the South—one being the Alabama Christian Movement for Human Rights. Whenever necessary and possible we share staff, educational and financial resources with our affiliates. Several months ago our local affiliate here in Birmingham invited us to be on call to engage in a nonviolent direct-action program if such were deemed necessary. We readily consented and when the hour came we lived up to our promises. So I am here, along with several members of my staff, because we were invited here. I am here because I have basic organizational ties here.

Beyond this, I am in Birmingham because injustice is here. Just as the eighth century prophets[1] left their little villages and carried their "thus saith the Lord" far beyond the boundaries of their hometowns; and just as the Apostle Paul left his little village of Tarsus and carried the gospel of Jesus Christ to practically every hamlet and city of the Graeco-Roman world, I too am compelled to carry the gospel of

1. **Eighth century prophets:** a group of Hebrew prophets—including Isaiah, Amos, Hosea, Jonah, and Elijah—who preached against idolatry. Like King and the Southern Christian Leadership Conference, these prophets were often seen as "outside agitators" by the people they preached to.

freedom beyond my particular hometown. Like Paul, I must constantly respond to the Macedonian call for aid.[2]

Moreover, I am cognizant of the interrelatedness of all communities and states. I cannot sit idly by in Atlanta and not be concerned about what happens in Birmingham. Injustice anywhere is a threat to justice everywhere. We are caught in an inescapable network of mutuality, tied in a single garment of destiny. Whatever affects one directly affects all indirectly. Never again can we afford to live with the narrow, provincial "outside agitator" idea. Anyone who lives in the United States can never be considered an outsider anywhere in this country.

You deplore the demonstrations that are presently taking place in Birmingham.   5
But I am sorry that your statement did not express a similar concern for the conditions that brought the demonstrations into being. I am sure that each of you would want to go beyond the superficial social analyst who looks merely at effects, and does not grapple with underlying causes. I would not hesitate to say that it is unfortunate that so-called demonstrations are taking place in Birmingham at this time, but I would say in more emphatic terms that it is even more unfortunate that the white power structure of this city left the Negro community with no other alternative.

In any nonviolent campaign there are four basic steps. (1) collection of the facts to determine whether injustices are alive, (2) negotiation, (3) self-purification, and (4) direct action. We have gone through all of these steps in Birmingham. There can be no gainsaying of the fact that racial injustice engulfs this community.

Birmingham is probably the most thoroughly segregated city in the United States. Its ugly record of police brutality is known in every section of this country. Its injust treatment of Negroes in the courts is a notorious reality. There have been more unsolved bombings of Negro homes and churches in Birmingham than any city in this nation. These are the hard, brutal and unbelievable facts. On the basis of these conditions Negro leaders sought to negotiate with the city fathers. But the political leaders consistently refused to engage in good faith negotiation.

Then came the opportunity last September to talk with some of the leaders of the economic community. In these negotiating sessions certain promises were made by the merchants—such as the promise to remove the humiliating racial signs from the stores. On the basis of these promises Rev. Shuttlesworth[3] and the leaders of the

---

2. **Macedonian call for aid:** Paul was an early Christian missionary who established Christian congregations in many of the major cities of the Roman Empire, such as Corinth, Galatia, Philippi, Thessalonica, and Rome itself. Much of the latter part of the New Testament consists of Paul's letters to these various congregations. Macedonia was a region of the Roman Empire north of Greece, in which several of these congregations were located. The Macedonian call refers to a vision that Paul had, which is described in Acts 16:9–10: "And a vision appeared to Paul in the night; There stood a man of Macedonia, and prayed him, saying, Come over into Macedonia, and help us. And after he had seen the vision, immediately we endeavoured to go into Macedonia, assuredly gathering that the Lord had called us for to preach the gospel unto them."

3. **Rev. Shuttlesworth:** The Reverend Fred Shuttlesworth (b. 1922) was one of the cofounders, with King, of the SCLC.

Alabama Christian Movement for Human Rights agreed to call a moratorium on any type of demonstrations. As the weeks and months unfolded we realized that we were the victims of a broken promise. The signs remained. Like so many experiences of the past we were confronted with blasted hopes, and the dark shadow of a deep disappointment settled upon us. So we had no alternative except that of preparing for direct action, whereby we would present our very bodies as a means of laying our case before the conscience of the local and national community. We were not unmindful of the difficulties involved. So we decided to go through a process of self-purification. We started having workshops on nonviolence and repeatedly asked ourselves the questions, "Are you able to accept blows without retaliating?" "Are you able to endure the ordeals of jail?" We decided to set our direct-action program around the Easter season, realizing that with the exception of Christmas, this was the largest shopping period of the year. Knowing that a strong economic withdrawal program would be the by-product of direct action, we felt that this was the best time to bring pressure on the merchants for the needed changes. Then it occurred to us that the March election was ahead and so we speedily decided to postpone action until after election day. When we discovered that Mr. Connor[4] was in the run-off, we decided again to postpone action so that the demonstrations could not be used to cloud the issues. At this time we agreed to begin our nonviolent witness the day after the run-off.

This reveals that we did not move irresponsibly into direct action. We too wanted to see Mr. Connor defeated; so we went through postponement after postponement to aid in this community need. After this we felt that direct action could be delayed no longer.

You may well ask, "Why direct action? Why sit-ins, marches, etc.? Isn't negotia-   10
tion a better path?" You are exactly right in your call for negotiation. Indeed, this is the purpose of direct action. Nonviolent direct action seeks to create such a crisis and establish such creative tension that a community that has constantly refused to negotiate is forced to confront the issue. It seeks so to dramatize the issue that it can no longer be ignored. I just referred to the creation of tension as a part of the work of the nonviolent resister. This may sound rather shocking. But I must confess that I am not afraid of the word tension. I have earnestly worked and preached against violent tension, but there is a type of constructive nonviolent tension that is neces-sary for growth. Just as Socrates felt that it was necessary to create a tension in the mind so that individuals could rise from the bondage of myths and half-truths to the unfettered realm of creative analysis and objective appraisal, we must see the need of having nonviolent gadflies to create the kind of tension in society that will help

4. **Mr. Connor:** Theophilus Eugene "Bull" Connor (1897–1973), a police commissioner in Birmingham, was noted for using vicious methods—including fire hoses and police dogs—to suppress civil rights demonstrations. Images of Connor using these tactics on peaceful demon-strators in Birmingham were broadcast all over the world, generating an outrage that helped pass the 1963 and 1964 Civil Rights Acts.

men to rise from the dark depths of prejudice and racism to the majestic heights of understanding and brotherhood. So the purpose of the direct action is to create a situation so crisis-packed that it will inevitably open the door to negotiation. We, therefore, concur with you in your call for negotiation. Too long has our beloved Southland been bogged down in the tragic attempt to live in monologue rather than dialogue.

One of the basic points in your statement is that our acts are untimely. Some have asked, "Why didn't you give the new administration time to act?" The only answer that I can give to this inquiry is that the new administration must be prodded about as much as the outgoing one before it acts. We will be sadly mistaken if we feel that the election of Mr. Boutwell[5] will bring the millennium to Birmingham. While Mr. Boutwell is much more articulate and gentle than Mr. Connor, they are both segregationists, dedicated to the task of maintaining the status quo. The hope I see in Mr. Boutwell is that he will be reasonable enough to see the futility of massive resistance to desegregation. But he will not see this without pressure from the devotees of civil rights. My friends, I must say to you that we have not made a single gain in civil rights without determined legal and nonviolent pressure. History is the long and tragic story of the fact that privileged groups seldom give up their privileges voluntarily. Individuals may see the moral light and voluntarily give up their unjust posture; but as Reinhold Niebuhr has reminded us, groups are more immoral than individuals.[6]

We know through painful experience that freedom is never voluntarily given by the oppressor; it must be demanded by the oppressed. Frankly, I have never yet engaged in a direct action movement that was "well-timed," according to the timetable of those who have not suffered unduly from the disease of segregation. For years now I have heard the word "Wait!" It rings in the ear of every Negro with a piercing familiarity. This "Wait" has almost always meant "Never." It has been a tranquilizing thalidomide,[7] relieving the emotional stress for a moment, only to give birth to an ill-formed infant of frustration. We must come to see with the distinguished jurist of yesterday that "justice too long delayed is justice denied." We have waited for more than 340 years for our constitutional and God-given rights. The nations of Asia and Africa are moving with jetlike speed toward the goal of political independence, and we still creep at horse and buggy pace toward the gaining of a cup of coffee at a lunch counter. I guess it is easy for those who have never felt the stinging darts of segregation to say, "Wait." But when you have seen vicious mobs lynch your mothers and fathers at will and drown your sisters and brothers at whim; when you have seen hate-filled policemen curse, kick, brutalize and even

5. **Mr. Boutwell:** Albert Boutwell (1904–1978) defeated Bull Connor in the 1963 race for mayor of Birmingham.
6. **Reinhold Niebuhr:** American Protestant theologian (1892–1971) and professor at New York's Union Theological Seminary.

The assertion that King references here is the subject of Niebuhr's 1932 book *Moral Man and Immoral Society*.
7. **Thalidomide:** a sedative drug that was discovered to cause birth defects.

kill your black brothers and sisters with impunity; when you see the vast majority of your twenty million Negro brothers smothering in an airtight cage of poverty in the midst of an affluent society; when you suddenly find your tongue twisted and your speech stammering as you seek to explain to your six-year-old daughter why she can't go to the public amusement park that has just been advertised on television, and see tears welling up in her little eyes when she is told that Funtown is closed to colored children, and see the depressing clouds of inferiority begin to form in her little mental sky, and see her begin to distort her little personality by unconsciously developing a bitterness toward white people; when you have to concoct an answer for a five-year-old son asking in agonizing pathos: "Daddy, why do white people treat colored people so mean?"; when you take a cross-country drive and find it necessary to sleep night after night in the uncomfortable corners of your automobile because no motel will accept you; when you are humiliated day in and day out by nagging signs reading "white" and "colored"; when your first name becomes "nigger" and your middle name becomes "boy" (however old you are) and your last name becomes "John," and when your wife and mother are never given the respected title "Mrs."; when you are harried by day and haunted by night by the fact that you are a Negro, living constantly at tiptoe stance never quite knowing what to expect next, and plagued with inner fears and outer resentments; when you are forever fighting a degenerating sense of "nobodiness"; then you will understand why we find it difficult to wait. There comes a time when the cup of endurance runs over, and men are no longer willing to be plunged into an abyss of injustice where they experience the blackness of corroding despair. I hope, sirs, you can understand our legitimate and unavoidable impatience.

You express a great deal of anxiety over our willingness to break laws. This is certainly a legitimate concern. Since we so diligently urge people to obey the Supreme Court's decision of 1954 outlawing segregation in the public schools, it is rather strange and paradoxical to find us consciously breaking laws. One may well ask, "How can you advocate breaking some laws and obeying others?" The answer is found in the fact that there are two types of laws: there are *just* and there are *unjust* laws. I would agree with Saint Augustine[8] that "An unjust law is no law at all."

Now what is the difference between the two? How does one determine when a law is just or unjust? A just law is a man-made code that squares with the moral law or the law of God. An unjust law is a code that is out of harmony with the moral law. To put it in the terms of Saint Thomas Aquinas,[9] an unjust law is a human law that is not rooted in eternal and natural law. Any law that uplifts human personality is just. Any law that degrades human personality is unjust. All segregation statutes are unjust because segregation distorts the soul and damages the

---

8. **Saint Augustine:** early Christian writer (354–430 CE) and bishop of the North African town of Hippo (in present-day Algeria). (See p. 184).

9. **Saint Thomas Aquinas:** Italian theologian (1224 or 1225–1274) whose *Summa Theologica* (1265–74) is a classic of Christian thought. (See p. 483).

personality. It gives the segregator a false sense of superiority, and the segregated a false sense of inferiority. To use the words of Martin Buber,[10] the great Jewish philosopher, segregation substitutes an "I-it" relationship for the "I-thou" relationship, and ends up relegating persons to the status of things. So segregation is not only politically, economically and sociologically unsound, but it is morally wrong and sinful. Paul Tillich[11] has said that sin is separation. Isn't segregation an existential expression of man's tragic separation, an expression of his awful estrangement, his terrible sinfulness? So I can urge men to disobey segregation ordinances because they are morally wrong.

Let us turn to a more concrete example of just and unjust laws. An unjust law is a code that a majority inflicts on a minority that is not binding on itself. This is difference made legal. On the other hand a just law is a code that a majority compels a minority to follow that it is willing to follow itself. This is sameness made legal.   15

Let me give another explanation. An unjust law is a code inflicted upon a minority which that minority had no part in enacting or creating because they did not have the unhampered right to vote. Who can say that the legislature of Alabama which set up the segregation laws was democratically elected? Throughout the state of Alabama all types of conniving methods are used to prevent Negroes from becoming registered voters and there are some counties without a single Negro registered to vote despite the fact that the Negro constitutes a majority of the population. Can any law set up in such a state be considered democratically structured?

These are just a few examples of unjust and just laws. There are some instances when a law is just on its face and unjust in its application. For instance, I was arrested Friday on a charge of parading without a permit. Now there is nothing wrong with an ordinance which requires a permit for a parade, but when the ordinance is used to preserve segregation and to deny citizens the First Amendment privilege of peaceful assembly and peaceful protest, then it becomes unjust.

I hope you can see the distinction I am trying to point out. In no sense do I advocate evading or defying the law as the rabid segregationist would do. This would lead to anarchy. One who breaks an unjust law must do it *openly, lovingly* (not hatefully as the white mothers did in New Orleans when they were seen on television screaming, "nigger, nigger, nigger"), and with a willingness to accept the penalty. I submit that an individual who breaks a law that conscience tells him is unjust, and willingly accepts the penalty by staying in jail to arouse the conscience of the community over its injustice, is in reality expressing the very highest respect for law.

Of course, there is nothing new about this kind of civil disobedience. It was seen sublimely in the refusal of Shadrach, Meshach and Abednego to obey the laws of

10. **Martin Buber:** Israeli (Austrian-born) Jewish philosopher (1878–1965) and theologian who wrote the well-known ethical treatise *I and Thou* in 1923.

11. **Paul Tillich:** American (German-born) Protestant theologian (1886–1965).

Nebuchadnezzar because a higher moral law was involved.[12] It was practiced superbly by the early Christians who were willing to face hungry lions and the excruciating pain of chopping blocks, before submitting to certain unjust laws of the Roman Empire. To a degree academic freedom is a reality today because Socrates practiced civil disobedience.

We can never forget that everything Hitler did in Germany was "legal" and everything the Hungarian freedom fighters did in Hungary was "illegal." It was "illegal" to aid and comfort a Jew in Hitler's Germany. But I am sure that if I had lived in Germany during that time I would have aided and comforted my Jewish brothers even though it was illegal. If I lived in a Communist country today where certain principles dear to the Christian faith are suppressed, I believe I would openly advocate disobeying these anti-religious laws. I must make two honest confessions to you, my Christian and Jewish brothers. First, I must confess that over the last few years I have been gravely disappointed with the white moderate. I have almost reached the regrettable conclusion that the Negro's great stumbling block in the stride toward freedom is not the White Citizen's Counciler[13] or the Ku Klux Klanner, but the white moderate who is more devoted to "order" than to justice; who prefers a negative peace which is the absence of tension to a positive peace which is the presence of justice; who constantly says, "I agree with you in the goal you seek, but I can't agree with your methods of direct action"; who paternalistically feels that he can set the timetable for another man's freedom; who lives by the myth of time and who constantly advised the Negro to wait until a "more convenient season." Shallow understanding from people of good will is more frustrating than absolute misunderstanding from people of ill will. Lukewarm acceptance is much more bewildering than outright rejection.

I had hoped that the white moderate would understand that law and order exist for the purpose of establishing justice, and that when they fail to do this they become dangerously structured dams that block the flow of social progress. I had hoped that the white moderate would understand that the present tension of the South is merely a necessary phase of the transition from an obnoxious negative peace, where the Negro passively accepted his unjust plight, to a substance-filled positive peace, where all men will respect the dignity and worth of human personality. Actually, we who engage in nonviolent direct action are not the creators of tension. We merely bring to the surface the hidden tension that is already alive. We bring it out in the open where it can be seen and dealt with. Like a boil that can never be cured as long as it is covered up but must be opened with all its pus-flowing ugliness to the

12. **Shadrach, Meshach and Abednego:** In the third chapter of the Book of Daniel, these three young Hebrew men are condemned to die by fire because they refuse to worship a golden image. God saves them from harm, and they end up being promoted to high positions in the Babylonian empire. King invokes them to provide a biblical example of civil disobedience.

13. **White Citizen's Counciler:** After the Supreme Court ordered the desegregation of public schools in 1954, groups known as White Citizen's Councils rose in the South to support continued segregation. Unlike the Ku Klux Klan, the Councils were not secretive or openly violent; however, many committed segregationists were members of both organizations.

natural medicines of air and light, injustice must likewise be exposed, with all of the tension its exposing creates, to the light of human conscience and the air of national opinion before it can be cured.

In your statement you asserted that our actions, even though peaceful, must be condemned because they precipitate violence. But can this assertion be logically made? Isn't this like condemning the robbed man because his possession of money precipitated the evil act of robbery? Isn't this like condemning Socrates because his unswerving commitment to truth and his philosophical delvings precipitated the misguided popular mind to make him drink the hemlock? Isn't this like condemning Jesus because His unique God-consciousness and never-ceasing devotion to his will precipitated the evil act of crucifixion? We must come to see, as federal courts have consistently affirmed, that it is immoral to urge an individual to withdraw his efforts to gain his basic constitutional rights because the quest precipitates violence. Society must protect the robbed and punish the robber.

I had also hoped that the white moderate would reject the myth of time. I received a letter this morning from a white brother in Texas which said: "All Christians know that the colored people will receive equal rights eventually, but it is possible that you are in too great of a religious hurry. It has taken Christianity almost two thousand years to accomplish what it has. The teachings of Christ take time to come to earth." All that is said here grows out of a tragic misconception of time. It is the strangely irrational notion that there is something in the very flow of time that will inevitably cure all ills. Actually time is neutral. It can be used either destructively or construc- tively. I am coming to feel that the people of ill will have used time much more effectively than the people of good will. We will have to repent in this generation not merely for the vitriolic words and actions of the bad people, but for the appalling silence of the good people. We must come to see that human progress never rolls in on wheels of inevitability. It comes through the tireless efforts and persistent work of men willing to be co-workers with God, and without this hard work time itself becomes an ally of the forces of social stagnation. We must use time creatively, and forever realize that the time is always ripe to do right. Now is the time to make real the promise of democracy, and transform our pending national elegy into a creative psalm of brotherhood. Now is the time to lift our national policy from the quicksand of racial injustice to the solid rock of human dignity.

You spoke of our activity in Birmingham as extreme. At first I was rather disap- pointed that fellow clergymen would see my nonviolent efforts as those of the extrem- ist. I started thinking about the fact that I stand in the middle of two opposing forces in the Negro community. One is a force of complacency made up of Negroes who, as a result of long years of oppression, have been so completely drained of self-respect and a sense of "somebodiness" that they have adjusted to segregation, and, of a few Negroes in the middle class who, because of a degree of academic and economic security, and because at points they profit by segregation, have unconsciously become insensitive to the problems of the masses. The other force is one of bitterness and hatred, and comes perilously close to advocating violence. It is expressed in the various black nationalist groups that are springing up over the nation, the largest and best known being Elijah Muhammad's Muslim movement.[14] This movement is nourished by the contemporary frustration over the continued existence of racial discrimination. It is made up of people who have lost faith in America, who have absolutely repudiated Christianity, and who have concluded that the white man is an incurable "devil." I have tried to stand between these two forces, saying that we need not follow the "do-nothingism" of the complacent or the hatred and despair of the black nationalist. There is the more excellent way of love and nonviolent protest. I'm grateful to God that, through the Negro church, the dimension of nonviolence entered our struggle. If this philosophy had not emerged, I am convinced that by now many streets of the South would be flowing with floods of blood. And I am further convinced that if our white brothers dismiss us as "rabble-rousers" and "outside agitators" those of us who are working through the channels of nonviolent direct action and refuse to support our nonviolent efforts, millions of Negroes, out of frustration and despair, will seek solace and security in black nationalist ideologies, a development that will lead inevitably to a frightening racial nightmare.

Oppressed people cannot remain oppressed forever. The urge for freedom will eventually come. This is what happened to the American Negro. Something within has reminded him of his birthright of freedom; something without has reminded him that he can gain it. Consciously and unconsciously, he has been swept in by what the Germans call the *Zeitgeist*,[15] and with his black brothers of Africa, and his brown and yellow brothers of Asia, South America and the Caribbean, he is moving with a sense of cosmic urgency toward the promised land of racial justice. Recognizing this vital urge that has engulfed the Negro community, one should readily understand public demonstrations. The Negro has many pent-up resentments and latent frustrations. He has to get them out. So let him march sometime; let him have his prayer pilgrimages to the city hall; understand why he must have sit-ins and freedom rides. If his repressed emotions do not come out in these nonviolent ways, they will come out in ominous expressions of violence. This is not a threat; it is a fact of history. So I have not said to my people "get rid of your discontent." But I have tried to say that this normal and healthy discontent can be channelized through the creative outlet of nonviolent direct action. Now this approach is being dismissed as extremist. I must admit that I was initially disappointed in being so categorized.

25

14. **Elijah Muhammad's Muslim movement:** Elijah Muhammad (1897–1975) led the Nation of Islam, a group that preached black supremacy and advocated the creation of a separate African-American nation within the United States. Muhammad's most famous disciple was Malcolm X (1925–1965), who broke with the movement after making a pilgrimage to Mecca and fully converting to Islam; the latter process required him to renounce the belief that any one race was superior to any other.

15. *Zeitgeist:* German word meaning "spirit of the time."

But as I continued to think about the matter I gradually gained a bit of satisfaction from being considered an extremist. Was not Jesus an extremist in love—"Love your enemies, bless them that curse you, pray for them that despitefully use you." Was not Amos an extremist for justice—"Let justice roll down like waters and righteousness like a mighty stream." Was not Paul an extremist for the gospel of Jesus Christ—"I bear in my body the marks of the Lord Jesus." Was not Martin Luther an extremist—"Here I stand; I can do none other so help me God." Was not John Bunyan[16] an extremist—"I will stay in jail to the end of my days before I make a butchery of my conscience." Was not Abraham Lincoln an extremist—"This nation cannot survive half slave and half free." Was not Thomas Jefferson an extremist—"We hold these truths to be self-evident, that all men are created equal." So the question is not whether we will be extremist but what kind of extremist will we be. Will we be extremists for hate or will we be extremists for love? Will we be extremists for the preservation of injustice—or will we be extremists for the cause of justice? In that dramatic scene on Calvary's hill, three men were crucified. We must not forget that all three were crucified for the same crime—the crime of extremism. Two were extremists for immorality, and thusly fell below their environment. The other, Jesus Christ, was an extremist for love, truth and goodness, and thereby rose above his environment. So, after all, maybe the South, the nation and the world are in dire need of creative extremists.

I had hoped that the white moderate would see this. Maybe I was too optimistic. Maybe I expected too much. I guess I should have realized that few members of a race that has oppressed another race can understand or appreciate the deep groans and passionate yearnings of those that have been oppressed and still fewer have the vision to see that injustice must be rooted out by strong, persistent and determined action. I am thankful, however, that some of our white brothers have grasped the meaning of this social revolution and committed themselves to it. They are still all too small in quantity, but they are big in quality. Some like Ralph McGill, Lillian Smith, Harry Golden and James Dabbs have written about our struggle in eloquent, prophetic and understanding terms. Others have marched with us down nameless streets of the South. They have languished in filthy roach-infested jails, suffering the abuse and brutality of angry policemen who see them as "dirty nigger-lovers." They, unlike so many of their moderate brothers and sisters, have recognized the urgency of the moment and sensed the need for powerful "action" antidotes to combat the disease of segregation.

Let me rush on to mention my other disappointment. I have been so greatly disappointed with the white church and its leadership. Of course, there are some notable exceptions. I am not unmindful of the fact that each of you has taken some

16. **Bunyan:** English preacher (1628–1688), author of *Pilgrim's Progress*. **Luther:** German reformer (1483–1546) who launched the Protestant Reformation by protesting policies of the Catholic Church.

significant stands on this issue. I commend you, Rev. Stallings,[17] for your Christian stance on this past Sunday, in welcoming Negroes to your worship service on a non-segregated basis. I commend the Catholic leaders of this state for integrating Springhill College several years ago.

But despite these notable exceptions I must honestly reiterate that I have been disappointed with the church. I do not say that as one of the negative critics who can always find something wrong with the church. I say it as a minister of the gospel, who loves the church; who was nurtured in its bosom; who has been sustained by its spiritual blessings and who will remain true to it as long as the cord of life shall lengthen.

I had the strange feeling when I was suddenly catapulted into the leadership of   30 the bus protest in Montgomery several years ago that we would have the support of the white church. I felt that the white ministers, priests and rabbis of the South would be some of our strongest allies. Instead, some have been outright opponents, refusing to understand the freedom movement and misrepresenting its leaders; all too many others have been more cautious than courageous and have remained silent behind the anesthetizing security of the stained-glass windows.

In spite of my shattered dreams of the past, I came to Birmingham with the hope that the white religious leadership of this community would see the justice of our cause, and with deep moral concern, serve as the channel through which our just grievances would get to the power structure. I had hoped that each of you would understand. But again I have been disappointed. I have heard numerous religious leaders of the South call upon their worshippers to comply with a desegregation decision because it is the *law*, but I have longed to hear white ministers say, "Follow this decree because integration is morally *right* and the Negro is your brother." In the midst of blatant injustices inflicted upon the Negro, I have watched white churches stand on the sideline and merely mouth pious irrelevancies and sanctimonious trivialities. In the midst of a mighty struggle to rid our nation of racial and economic injustice, I have heard so many ministers say, "Those are social issues with which the gospel has no real concern," and I have watched so many churches commit themselves to a completely otherworldly religion which made a strange distinction between body and soul, the sacred and the secular.

So here we are moving toward the exit of the twentieth century with a religious community largely adjusted to the status quo, standing as a taillight behind other community agencies rather than a headlight leading men to higher levels of justice.

I have traveled the length and breadth of Alabama, Mississippi and all the other southern states. On sweltering summer days and crisp autumn mornings I have looked at her beautiful churches with their lofty spires pointing heavenward. I have beheld the impressive outlay of her massive religious education buildings. Over and over again I have found myself asking: "What kind of people

---

17. **Rev. Stallings:** The Reverend Earl Stallings (1916–2006), pastor of the First Baptist Church in Birmingham, was one of the eight clergymen who had signed the letter that King was responding to.

worship here? Who is their God? Where were their voices when the lips of Governor Barnett dripped with words of interposition and nullification?[18] Where were they when Governor Wallace gave the clarion call for defiance and hatred?[19] Where were their voices of support when tired, bruised and weary Negro men and women decided to rise from the dark dungeons of complacency to the bright hills of creative protest?"

Yes, these questions are still in my mind. In deep disappointment, I have wept over the laxity of the church. But be assured that my tears have been tears of love. There can be no deep disappointment where there is not deep love. Yes, I love the church; I love her sacred walls. How could I do otherwise? I am in the rather unique position of being the son, the grandson and the great-grandson of preachers. Yes, I see the church as the body of Christ. But, oh! How we have blemished and scarred that body through social neglect and fear of being nonconformists.

There was a time when the church was very powerful. It was during that period   35 when the early Christians rejoiced when they were deemed worthy to suffer for what they believed. In those days the church was not merely a thermometer that recorded the ideas and principles of popular opinion; it was a thermostat that transformed the mores of society. Wherever the early Christians entered a town the power structure got disturbed and immediately sought to convict them for being "disturbers of the peace" and "outside agitators." But they went on with the conviction that they were "a colony of heaven," and had to obey God rather than man. They were small in number but big in commitment. They were too God-intoxicated to be "astronomically intimidated." They brought an end to such ancient evils as infanticide and gladiatorial contest.

Things are different now. The contemporary church is often a weak, ineffectual voice with an uncertain sound.[20] It is so often the arch-supporter of the status quo. Far from being disturbed by the presence of the church, the power structure of the average community is consoled by the church's silent and often vocal sanction of things as they are.

But the judgment of God is upon the church as never before. If the church of today does not recapture the sacrificial spirit of the early church, it will lose its authentic ring, forfeit the loyalty of millions, and be dismissed as an irrelevant social

18. **Governor Barnett:** Ross Barnett (1898–1987) was the governor of Mississippi in 1962, when the Supreme Court ordered that James Meredith (b. 1933), an African American, be admitted to the University of Mississippi. Barnett attempted to nullify the order, swearing that he would go to jail before he would allow a Mississippi school to be integrated.
19. **Governor Wallace:** George Wallace (1919–1998) was elected governor of Alabama in 1962. In his inaugural address, Wallace declared

"segregation now, segregation tomorrow, and segregation forever." In 1963, he stood outside the University of Alabama and tried to prevent two black students from enrolling.
20. **Uncertain sound:** King alludes here to Paul's criticisms of the Corinthian church in 1 Corinthians 14:8: "For if the trumpet give an uncertain sound, who shall prepare himself to the battle?"

club with no meaning for the twentieth century. I am meeting young people every day whose disappointment with the church has risen to outright disgust.

Maybe again, I have been too optimistic. Is organized religion too inextricably bound to the status quo to save our nation and the world? Maybe I must turn my faith to the inner spiritual church, the church within the church, as the true *ecclesia*[21] and the hope of the world. But again I am thankful to God that some noble souls from the ranks of organized religion have broken loose from the paralyzing chains of conformity and joined us as active partners in the struggle for freedom. They have left their secure congregations and walked the streets of Albany, Georgia, with us. They have gone through the highways of the South on tortuous rides for freedom.[22] Yes, they have gone to jail with us. Some have been kicked out of their churches, and lost support of their bishops and fellow ministers. But they have gone with the faith that right defeated is stronger than evil triumphant. These men have been the leaven in the lump of the race. Their witness has been the spiritual salt that has preserved the true meaning of the gospel in these troubled times. They have carved a tunnel of hope through the dark mountain of disappointment.

I hope the church as a whole will meet the challenge of this decisive hour. But even if the church does not come to the aid of justice, I have no despair about the future. I have no fear about the outcome of our struggle in Birmingham, even if our motives are presently misunderstood. We will reach the goal of freedom in Birmingham and all over the nation, because the goal of America is freedom. Abused and scorned though we may be, our destiny is tied up with the destiny of America. Before the Pilgrims landed at Plymouth we were here. Before the pen of Jefferson etched across the pages of history the majestic words of the Declaration of Independence, we were here. For more than two centuries our foreparents labored in this country without wages; they made cotton king; and they built the homes of their masters in the midst of brutal injustice and shameful humiliation—and yet out of a bottomless vitality they continued to thrive and develop. If the inexpressible cruelties of slavery could not stop us, the opposition we now face will surely fail. We will win our freedom because the sacred heritage of our nation and the eternal will of God are embodied in our echoing demands.

I must close now. But before closing I am impelled to mention one other point in your statement that troubled me profoundly. You warmly commended the Birmingham police force for keeping "order" and "preventing violence." I don't believe you would have so warmly commended the police force if you had seen its angry violent dogs

40

21. **Ecclesia:** Latin form of *ekklesia*, the Greek root of English words such as "ecclesiastical." In the early days of the Church, *ekklesia* was used to refer to a Christian community. Later, it came to mean the collective body of the Church or of all Christian believers.

22. **Rides for freedom:** In 1961, a year after the Supreme Court outlawed racial segregation in interstate public facilities, integrated groups of student volunteers rode together on buses throughout the South. The "Freedom Rides" were organized by the Congress on Racial Equality (CORE) and the Student Nonviolent Coordinating Committee (SNCC).

literally biting six unarmed, nonviolent Negroes. I don't believe you would so quickly commend the policemen if you would observe their ugly and inhuman treatment of Negroes here in the city jail; if you would watch them push and curse old Negro women and young Negro girls; if you would see them slap and kick old Negro men and young boys; if you will observe them, as they did on two occasions, refuse to give us food because we wanted to sing our grace together. I'm sorry that I can't join you in your praise for the police department.

It is true that they have been rather disciplined in their public handling of the demonstrators. In this sense they have been rather publicly "nonviolent." But for what purpose? To preserve the evil system of segregation. Over the last few years I have consistently preached that nonviolence demands that the means we use must be as pure as the ends we seek. So I have tried to make it clear that it is wrong to use immoral means to attain moral ends. But now I must affirm that it is just as wrong, or even more so, to use moral means to preserve immoral ends. Maybe Mr. Connor and his policemen have been rather publicly nonviolent, as Chief Pritchett was in Albany, Georgia, but they have used the moral means of nonviolence to maintain the immoral end of flagrant racial injustice. T. S. Eliot has said that there is no greater treason than to do the right deed for the wrong reason.[23]

I wish you had commended the Negro sit-inners and demonstrators of Birmingham for their sublime courage, their willingness to suffer and their amazing discipline in the midst of the most inhuman provocation. One day the South will recognize its real heroes. They will be the James Merediths,[24] courageously and with a majestic sense of purpose facing jeering and hostile mobs and the agonizing loneliness that characterizes the life of the pioneer. They will be old, oppressed, battered Negro women, symbolized in a seventy-two-year-old woman of Montgomery, Alabama, who rose up with a sense of dignity and with her people decided not to ride the segregated buses, and responded to one who inquired about her tiredness with ungrammatical profundity: "My feet is tired, but my soul is rested." They will be the young high school and college students, young ministers of the gospel and a host of their elders courageously and nonviolently sitting-in at lunch counters and willingly going to jail for conscience's sake. One day the South will know that when these disinherited children of God sat down at lunch counters they were in reality standing up for the best in the American dream and the most sacred values in our Judeo-Christian heritage, and thusly, carrying our whole nation back to those great wells of democracy which were dug deep by the Founding Fathers in the formulation of the Constitution and the Declaration of Independence.

Never before have I written a letter this long (or should I say a book?). I'm afraid that it is much too long to take your precious time. I can assure you that it would have been much shorter if I had been writing from a comfortable desk, but what

23. **T. S. Eliot:** British (American-born) poet (1888–1965); the text is from his play *Murder in the Cathedral.*   24. **The James Merediths:** See note 18.

else is there to do when you are alone for days in the dull monotony of a narrow jail cell other than write long letters, think strange thoughts, and pray long prayers?

If I have said anything in this letter that is an overstatement of the truth and is indicative of an unreasonable impatience, I beg you to forgive me. If I have said anything in this letter that is an understatement of the truth and is indicative of my having a patience that makes me patient with anything less than brotherhood, I beg God to forgive me.

I hope this letter finds you strong in the faith. I also hope that circumstances   45 will soon make it possible for me to meet each of you, not as an integrationist or a civil rights leader, but as a fellow clergyman and a Christian brother. Let us all hope that the dark clouds of racial prejudice will soon pass away and the deep fog of misunderstanding will be lifted from our fear-drenched communities and in some not too distant tomorrow the radiant stars of love and brotherhood will shine over our great nation with all of their scintillating beauty.

Yours for the cause of Peace and Brotherhood,
Martin Luther King, Jr.

UNDERSTANDING THE TEXT

1. How does King answer the major criticisms raised in the letter: that the Birmingham demonstrations are being directed by outsiders, that they are making tensions worse, and that they are encouraging disrespect for the law?

2. What portions of the letter speak to people other than (or in addition to) the clergymen to whom it is addressed? Through what elements does King appeal to the letter's potential nonclerical audience?

3. What does King mean by "we would present our very bodies as a means of laying our case before the conscience of the local and national community"?

4. What criteria does King give for determining whether or not a law is unjust? What different definitions of "unjust law" does he propose?

5. Why does King consider white moderates to be more of an obstacle than overt racists to the progress of civil rights? Why does he seem more concerned about the lack of support from those who agree with his ends than about those who want to defeat everything that he stands for?

6. How does King contrast Elijah Muhammad's Black Muslim movement with his own activism? What is the rhetorical effect of this comparison?

7. How does King respond to the charge that he is an "extremist"? In what way does he redefine the traditional definition of "extremism"?

MAKING CONNECTIONS

1. Does King's implicit assertion that the ends of segregation justify the means of breaking the law constitute a Machiavellian argument (p. 405)? How so? Does King say

that any means are acceptable to this end? Or does he argue that certain means (such as violence) are inherently unacceptable?

2. Compare King's views of democracy, civil disobedience, and nonviolence with those of Aung San Suu Kyi (p. 442). How might the two figures be seen as parts of the same philosophical tradition, despite their differences in religion and culture?

3. Thomas Aquinas (p. 483), whom King quotes in this essay for his opposition to unjust laws, is an important thinker in the "just war" tradition. What basic conception of natural law underlies the ideas of "just law" and "just war"?

4. How do King's experiences with segregation compare with the experience of apartheid described in Desmond Tutu's "Nuremberg or National Amnesia: A Third Way" (p. 450)?

WRITING ABOUT THE TEXT

1. Use King's definitions of "just" and "unjust" laws to make the argument that a certain current law (national or local) or policy of your school is "unjust."

2. Think of conditions that would cause you to disobey a law. Write a "Letter from _____" to explain your disobedience.

3. Evaluate the potential effectiveness of nonviolent direct action in different kinds of political systems. Would the kinds of demonstrations that Martin Luther King Jr. staged in Birmingham work in other, more repressive political situations? (Consider, for example, Nazi Germany, where "civil disobedients" were routinely rounded up and shot.) At what point, if any, should a belief in nonviolence give way to advocacy of a "just war"?

4. Examine the rhetorical effectiveness of the "Letter from Birmingham Jail." What aspects of the work made it such an effective argument in its own day?

5. Choose a biblical theme or pattern of biblical allusions that King uses in the "Letter from Birmingham Jail" (such as the writings of Paul, the wanderings of the prophets, the laws of Babylon, etc.). Trace this concept through the letter and show how it supports King's overall argument.

AUNG SAN SUU KYI
from *In Quest of Democracy*
[1990]

IN 1886, the British invaded the Kingdom of Burma and made it part of the massive colonial enterprise known as British India (encompassing present-day India, Pakistan, Burma, Bangladesh, and Sri Lanka). During World War II, Aung San Suu Kyi's father and partial namesake, the nationalist leader Aung San (1915–1947), enlisted the aid of the Japanese to expel the British and proclaim independence. However, Aung San soon became disillusioned by Japanese militarism and fascism, and he turned his forces against the Japanese. As the war ended, Aung San negotiated with the British for Burma's permanent independence, and he would almost certainly have been its first prime minister had he not been assassinated by a rival politician six months before the official transfer of power occurred.

Though she was the daughter of Burma's most revered hero, Aung San Suu Kyi (b. 1945) spent most of her life outside her native country. She attended high school in New Delhi, where her mother was the Burmese ambassador to India. Upon graduating, she studied at England's Oxford University, where she met and married Michael Aris, a leading scholar of Tibetan culture. During this time, events in Burma were quickly deteriorating. The country's democratically elected government was overthrown in 1962 by the Marxist dictator Ne Win (1910 or 1911–2002), whose authoritarian regime plunged Burma deeper and deeper into poverty and international isolation. In 1988, Aung San Suu Kyi was doing advanced graduate work at London's prestigious School of Oriental and African Studies when her mother suffered a severe stroke. She returned to Burma in April 1988, five months before massive popular uprisings ended Ne Win's twenty-six-year rule.

In the chaos that followed the revolts, Aung San Suu Kyi emerged as a strong political leader and democracy advocate, but a military junta seized power (and officially, though controversially, changed the English version of the country's name from Burma to Myanmar). Despite promising free elections, the junta had no intention of handing control to an elected government; they scheduled immediate elections in 1990 under the assumption that no opposition to their rule could organize in such a short amount of time. To ensure their victory, they declared Aung San Suu Kyi ineligible to run for office and placed her under house arrest, and the political party that she had formed, the National League for Democracy (NLD), was barred from taking part in the elections in any way. Nonetheless, the NLD won 82 percent of the popular vote, forcing the junta to void the election and rule as an unelected dictatorship. Instead of taking her rightful place as the elected prime minister, Aung San Suu Kyi remained under house arrest. When she was awarded the Nobel Peace Prize in 1991, her oldest son accepted the award in her stead. She was released in 1995 but was placed under house arrest again from 2000 to 2002 and yet again in 2003. In 2010, she was finally released from house arrest and, in 2012, won a seat in Burma's parliament, where she continues to serve.

In the essay "In Quest of Democracy," a selection from which appears here, Aung San Suu Kyi attempts to answer one of the standard charges made by nondemocratic governments throughout the world: that democracy is a Western form of government and a remnant of imperialism that represents values alien to the non-Western world. To answer this charge, Aung San Suu Kyi argues deductively. First she examines the role of government in Buddhist scripture (nearly 90 percent of the population of Burma/Myanmar is Buddhist). She narrates the story of the original social contract in Buddhist scripture and briefly explains the ten duties of kingship in the Buddhist tradition. She then applies these principles to the present definition of "democracy." The essential elements of democracy, fairness, and respect for human rights, she asserts, have always been present in the Buddhist traditions of her people.

1

Opponents of the movement for democracy in Burma[1] have sought to undermine it by on the one hand casting aspersions on the competence of the people to judge what was best for the nation and on the other condemning the basic tenets of democracy as un-Burmese. There is nothing new in Third World governments seeking to justify and perpetuate authoritarian rule by denouncing liberal democratic principles as alien. By implication they claim for themselves the official and sole right to decide what does or does not conform to indigenous cultural norms. Such conventional propaganda aimed at consolidating the powers of the establishment has been studied, analysed and disproved by political scientists, jurists and sociologists. But in Burma, distanced by several decades of isolationism from political and intellectual developments in the outside world, the people have had to draw on their own resources to explode the twin myths of their unfitness for political responsibility and the unsuitability of democracy for their society. As soon as the movement for democracy spread out across Burma there was a surge of intense interest in the meaning of the word "democracy", in its history and its practical implications. More than a quarter-century of narrow authoritarianism under which they had

1. **Burma:** The Union of Burma was established in 1948, having previously been part of British India. In 1989, the ruling military junta declared that the country would be known as the Union of Myanmar, with the designated short form Myanmar. This change has been adopted by the United Nations and by some other international organizations, but is rejected by prodemocracy forces within Burma because it was not ratified by any elected body. The governments of the United States, Great Britain, and Canada continue to call the country Burma, as does Aung San Suu Kyi.

been fed a pabulum[2] of shallow, negative dogma had not blunted the perceptiveness or political alertness of the Burmese. On the contrary, perhaps not all that surprisingly, their appetite for discussion and debate, for uncensored information and objective analysis, seemed to have been sharpened. Not only was there an eagerness to study and to absorb standard theories on modern politics and political institutions, there was also widespread and intelligent speculation on the nature of democracy as a social system of which they had had little experience but which appealed to their common-sense notions of what was due to a civilized society. There was a spontaneous interpretative response to such basic ideas as representative government, human rights and the rule of law. The privileges and freedoms which would be guaranteed by democratic institutions were contemplated with understandable enthusiasm. But the duties of those who would bear responsibility for the maintenance of a stable democracy also provoked much thoughtful consideration. It was natural that a people who have suffered much from the consequences of bad government should be preoccupied with theories of good government.

Members of the Buddhist *sangha*[3] in their customary role as mentors have led the way in articulating popular expectations by drawing on classical learning to illuminate timeless values. But the conscious effort to make traditional knowledge relevant to contemporary needs was not confined to any particular circle—it went right through Burmese society from urban intellectuals and small shopkeepers to doughty village grandmothers.

Why has Burma with its abundant natural and human resources failed to live up to its early promise as one of the most energetic and fastest-developing nations in Southeast Asia? International scholars have provided detailed answers supported by careful analyses of historical, cultural, political and economic factors. The Burmese people, who have had no access to sophisticated academic material, got to the heart of the matter by turning to the words of the Buddha on the four causes of decline and decay: failure to recover that which had been lost, omission to repair that which had been damaged, disregard of the need for reasonable economy, and the elevation to leadership of men without morality or learning. Translated into contemporary terms, when democratic rights had been lost to military dictatorship sufficient efforts had not been made to regain them, moral and political values had been allowed to deteriorate without concerted attempts to save the situation, the economy had been badly managed, and the country had been ruled by men without integrity or wisdom. A thorough study by the cleverest scholar using the best and latest methods of research could hardly have identified more correctly or succinctly the chief causes of Burma's decline since 1962.

Under totalitarian socialism, official policies with little relevance to actual needs had placed Burma in an economic and administrative limbo where government

2. **Pabulum:** food, or a diet. Because of historical confusion with the word "pablum," or food for infants, the word has come to connote shallow or trite thought.

3. *Sangha:* a collective word for the ordained monks and nuns in the Buddhist religion, similar, in some respects, to the English word "clergy."

bribery and evasion of regulations were the indispensable lubricant to keep the wheels of everyday life turning. But through the years of moral decay and material decline there has survived a vision of a society in which the people and the leadership could unite in principled efforts to achieve prosperity and security. In 1988 the movement for democracy gave rise to the hope that the vision might become reality. At its most basic and immediate level, liberal democracy would mean in institutional terms a representative government appointed for a constitutionally limited term through free and fair elections. By exercising responsibly their right to choose their own leaders the Burmese hope to make an effective start at reversing the process of decline. They have countered the propagandist doctrine that democracy is unsuited to their cultural norms by examining traditional theories of government.

The Buddhist view of world history tells that when society fell from its original   5
state of purity into moral and social chaos a king was elected to restore peace and justice. The ruler was known by three titles: *Mahasammata*, "because he is named ruler by the unanimous consent of the people"; *Khattiya*, "because he has dominion over agricultural land"; and *Raja*, "because he wins the people to affection through observance of the *dhamma* (virtue, justice, the law)". The agreement by which their first monarch undertakes to rule righteously in return for a portion of the rice crop represents the Buddhist version of government by social contract. The *Mahasammata* follows the general pattern of Indic kingship in South-east Asia. This has been criticized as antithetical to the idea of the modern state because it promotes a personalized form of monarchy lacking the continuity inherent in the western abstraction of the king as possessed of both a body politic and a body natural. However, because the *Mahasammata* was chosen by popular consent and required to govern in accordance with just laws, the concept of government elective and *sub lege*[4] is not alien to traditional Burmese thought.

The Buddhist view of kingship does not invest the ruler with the divine right to govern the realm as he pleases. He is expected to observe the Ten Duties of Kings, the Seven Safeguards against Decline, the Four Assistances to the People, and to be guided by numerous other codes of conduct such as the Twelve Practices of Rulers, the Six Attributes of Leaders, the Eight Virtues of Kings and the Four Ways to Overcome Peril. There is logic to a tradition which includes the king among the five enemies or perils and which subscribes to many sets of moral instructions for the edification of those in positions of authority. The people of Burma have had much experience of despotic rule and possess a great awareness of the unhappy gap that can exist between the theory and practice of government.

The Ten Duties of Kings are widely known and generally accepted as a yardstick which could be applied just as well to modern government as to the first monarch of the world. The duties are: liberality, morality, self-sacrifice, integrity, kindness,

---

4. **Sub lege:** "Under the law"; the phrase here refers to a government that is bound by, and accountable to, legal authorities.

austerity, non-anger, non-violence, forbearance and non-opposition (to the will of the people).

The first duty of liberality (*dana*) which demands that a ruler should contribute generously towards the welfare of the people makes the tacit assumption that a government should have the competence to provide adequately for its citizens. In the context of modern politics, one of the prime duties of a responsible administration would be to ensure the economic security of the state.

Morality (*sila*) in traditional Buddhist terms is based on the observance of the five precepts, which entails refraining from destruction of life, theft, adultery, falsehood and indulgence in intoxicants. The ruler must bear a high moral character to win the respect and trust of the people, to ensure their happiness and prosperity and to provide a proper example. When the king does not observe the *dhamma*, state functionaries become corrupt, and when state functionaries are corrupt the people are caused much suffering. It is further believed that an unrighteous king brings down calamity on the land. The root of a nation's misfortunes has to be sought in the moral failings of the government.

The third duty, *paricagga*, is sometimes translated as generosity and sometimes as self-sacrifice. The former would constitute a duplication of the first duty, *dana*, so self-sacrifice as the ultimate generosity which gives up all for the sake of the people would appear the more satisfactory interpretation. The concept of selfless public service is sometimes illustrated by the story of the hermit Sumedha who took the vow of Buddhahood.[5] In so doing he who could have realized the supreme liberation of *nirvana* in a single lifetime committed himself to countless incarnations that he might help other beings free themselves from suffering. Equally popular is the story of the monkey king who sacrificed his life to save his subjects, including one who had always wished him harm and who was the eventual cause of his death. The good ruler sublimates his needs as an individual to the service of the nation.

Integrity (*ajjava*) implies incorruptibility in the discharge of public duties as well as honesty and sincerity in personal relations. There is a Burmese saying: "With rulers, truth, with (ordinary) men, vows". While a private individual may be bound only by the formal vows that he makes, those who govern should be wholly bound by the truth in thought, word and deed. Truth is the very essence of the teachings of the Buddha, who referred to himself as the *Tathagata* or "one who has come to the truth." The Buddhist king must therefore live and rule by truth, which is the perfect uniformity between nomenclature and nature.[6] To deceive or to mislead the people in any way would be an occupational failing as well as a moral offence. "As an arrow, intrinsically straight, without warp or distortion, when one word is spoken, it does not err into two."

10

5. **Sumedha:** In Buddhist tradition, Sumedha was a man who inherited great wealth from his parents but, instead of accepting it, opened his treasury to the people of the village and declared that anyone could take whatever they wanted. Upon renouncing his wealth, Sumedha became a hermit and attained the status of a Buddha.

6. **Nomenclature:** a system of naming. **Uniformity between nomenclature and nature** means that what is said to be true corresponds to what is true.

Kindness (*maddava*) in a ruler is in a sense the courage to feel concern for the people. It is undeniably easier to ignore the hardships of those who are too weak to demand their rights than to respond sensitively to their needs. To care is to accept responsibility, to dare to act in accordance with the dictum that the ruler is the strength of the helpless. In *Wizaya*, a well-known nineteenth-century drama based on the *Mahavamsa* story of Prince Vijaya, a king sends away into exile his own son whose wild ways have caused the people much distress: "In the matter of love, to make no distinction between citizen and son, to give equally of loving kindness, that is the righteousness of kings."

The duty of austerity (*tapa*) enjoins the king to adopt simple habits, to develop self-control and to practise spiritual discipline. The self-indulgent ruler who enjoys an extravagant lifestyle and ignores the spiritual need for austerity was no more acceptable at the time of the *Mahasammata* then he would be in Burma today.

The seventh, eighth and ninth duties—non-anger (*akkodha*), non-violence (*avihamsa*) and forbearance (*khanti*)—could be said to be related. Because the displeasure of the powerful could have unhappy and far-reaching consequences, kings must not allow personal feelings of enmity and ill will to erupt into destructive anger and violence. It is incumbent on a ruler to develop the true forbearance which moves him to deal wisely and generously with the shortcomings and provocations of even those whom he could crush with impunity. Violence is totally contrary to the teachings of Buddhism. The good ruler vanquishes ill will with loving kindness, wickedness with virtue, parsimony with liberality, and falsehood with truth. The Emperor Ashoka[7] who ruled his realm in accordance with the principles of non-violence and compassion is always held up as an ideal Buddhist king. A government should not attempt to enjoin submission through harshness and immoral force but should aim at *dhamma-vijaya*, a conquest by righteousness.

The tenth duty of kings, non-opposition to the will of the people (*avirodha*), tends to be singled out as a Buddhist endorsement of democracy, supported by well-known stories from the *Jakatas*.[8] Pawridasa, a monarch who acquired an unfortunate taste for human flesh, was forced to leave his kingdom because he would not heed the people's demand that he should abandon his cannibalistic habits. A very different kind of ruler was the Buddha's penultimate incarnation on earth, the pious King Vessantara.[9] But he too was sent into exile when in the course of his strivings for

15

---

7. **Emperor Ashoka:** ruler (d. 232 BCE) of the Mauryan Empire, the first political entity that united nearly all of the Indian subcontinent. In the early part of his reign, Ashoka was violent and ruthless, but after converting to Buddhism, he became renowned for his compassionate government and commitment to peace.

8. **Jakatas:** a collection of stories about the Buddha's lives in previous incarnations. Traditionally, the 550 *Jakatas* represent the Buddha's 550 previous lives.

9. **Vessantara:** one of the most recent incarnations of the Buddha, in the best-known *Jakata* tale. As a prince, Vessantara was known for his generosity. As a young king, he gave away a great white elephant that had become a symbol of his country. The people were so disheartened by the loss of the elephant that they lost their confidence in his leadership, leading him to relinquish the throne to his father and become an ascetic.

the perfection of liberality he gave away the white elephant of the state without the consent of the people. The real duty of non-opposition is a reminder that the legitimacy of government is founded on the consent of the people, who may withdraw their mandate at any time if they lose confidence in the ability of the ruler to serve their best interests.

By invoking the Ten Duties of Kings the Burmese are not so much indulging in wishful thinking as drawing on time-honoured values to reinforce the validity of the political reforms they consider necessary. It is a strong argument for democracy that governments regulated by principles of accountability, respect for public opinion and the supremacy of just laws are more likely than an all-powerful ruler or ruling class, uninhibited by the need to honour the will of the people, to observe the traditional duties of Buddhist kingship. Traditional values serve both to justify and to decipher popular expectations of democratic government.

UNDERSTANDING THE TEXT

1. What two kinds of arguments have opponents of democracy in Burma used to discredit their opponents? How does Aung San Suu Kyi refute these charges?

2. Why is democracy a relatively new concept to the Burmese people? In the words of the Buddha, what four causes of decline and decay have prevented Burma from fully prospering? How are these causes relatable to other troubled countries and governments in today's world?

3. By what three names is the legitimate ruler known in Buddhist tradition? What does each name signify? How does Aung San Suu Kyi translate these concepts into a more contemporary setting?

4. How does Aung San Suu Kyi combine the idea of a democratic government with Buddhist principles? How does one support the other? How are the Ten Duties of Kings similar to tenets of a democratic government? How do these duties protect the citizens from the government?

5. To what purpose does Aung San Suu Kyi use the traditional Buddhist stories of Sumedha, Pawridasa, and Vessantara? How does each story support the point that political power ultimately rests in the people's hands?

MAKING CONNECTIONS

1. Compare Martin Luther King Jr. (p. 425), Mohandas K. Gandhi (p. 560), and Aung San Suu Kyi as religious social reformers. In what way does each of them bring religious belief directly to bear on social problems?

2. Compare the ways that the religious views of Aung San Suu Kyi and Desmond Tutu (p. 450) influence their understanding of government's role.

WRITING ABOUT THE TEXT

1. Explore democratic governments' ability to incorporate traditional belief systems into policy. What gives democracy this flexibility? What are the pros and cons of, for instance, religious influences on contemporary American lawmaking?

2. Compare Martin Luther King Jr.'s use of Christianity in the "Letter from Birmingham Jail" (p. 425) with Aung San Suu Kyi's use of Buddhism in "In Quest of Democracy."

3. Compare different notions of the "social contract" across various cultures. How does Aung San Suu Kyi's understanding of this contract differ from Hobbes's (p. 94)?

DESMOND TUTU

Nuremberg or National Amnesia: A Third Way

[1997]

IN 1984, the year that Desmond Tutu (b. 1931) won the Nobel Peace Prize, his country of South Africa was at the center of an international firestorm over its practice of apartheid. Apartheid, or "apartness," was a system of racial segregation that disenfranchised the black South African majority and subjected them to officially mandated inequalities in education, employment, legal status, and police protection. When it began in 1948, apartheid was comparable to the official segregation that existed in the American South and other regions of the world—except that, in South Africa, whites accounted for less than 10 percent of the total population.

By the 1980s, however, the civil rights movement in America and the decolonization of Asia and Africa had eliminated official segregation in nearly every other industrialized nation. South Africa became a pariah nation, subject to boycotts and diplomatic pressures from other countries and increasing protests at home. During this time, Tutu, an Anglican bishop and democracy advocate, became an international symbol of the struggle against apartheid. After winning the Nobel Prize in 1984, he became the Bishop of Johannesburg in 1985 and the Archbishop of Cape Town—as well as the first black cleric to lead the Anglican Church in South Africa—in 1986. All the while, he continued his resistance to apartheid and his advocacy of nonviolent resistance in the tradition of Mahatma Gandhi and Martin Luther King Jr.

Racial tensions nearly plunged South Africa into a civil war. Chaos was averted, however, when F. W. de Klerk (b. 1936) became prime minister in 1989 and, less than a year later, began dismantling the apartheid system. He rescinded the longstanding ban on the African National Congress and released its leader, Nelson Mandela (1918–2013), from jail after twenty-seven years of incarceration. In 1994, Mandela became the president of the newly democratic Republic of South Africa, with F. W. de Klerk as deputy president.

With the transition to democracy, South Africa's new government had to find a way to address the atrocities that had occurred during the apartheid regime without destroying the fragile truce that existed between the old and the new governments. It was Desmond Tutu who provided the solution to this problem. In 1996, Tutu retired as the Archbishop of Cape Town to become the chair of the Truth and Reconciliation Commission, which was set up in an attempt to provide healing, rather than retributive, justice. The commission was empowered to grant amnesty for criminal acts committed by both white officials and black protesters, on the condition that they fully disclosed the crimes for which they were seeking amnesty. Under Tutu's leadership, the Truth and Reconciliation Commission, whose purpose he explains here, became an important element in the creation of a stable democracy in South Africa. "Nuremberg or National Amnesia: A Third Way" is the second chapter of Tutu's 1999 book *No Future without Forgiveness*.

This selection from Tutu's book presents a clear example of an argument based on a Hegelian synthesis (see Chapter 13, p. 668). Tutu considers two antithetical solutions to the problem of dealing with South Africa's past. By placing these propositions in opposition to each other, he succeeds in rejecting them both and constructing a third alternative to take their place.

The debilitating legacy of apartheid is going to be with us for many a long day yet. No one possesses a magic wand which the architects of the new dispensation could wave and, "Hey presto!" things will be transformed overnight into a promised land flowing with milk and honey. Apartheid, firmly entrenched for a long half century and carried out with a ruthless efficiency, was too strong for that. It is going to take a long time for the pernicious effects of apartheid's egregiousness to be eradicated.

Apart from the systematic and devastating violation of all sorts of human rights by the nature of apartheid itself—described by five senior judges in a deposition to the commission as "in itself and in the way it was implemented . . . a gross abuse of human rights"—many South Africans remembered that awful deeds had been perpetrated in the past. They remembered the Sharpeville massacre when, on March 21, 1960, a peaceful crowd demonstrated against the pass laws and sixty-nine people were mown down when the police panicked and opened fire on the demonstrators, most of whom were shot in the back while fleeing.

People recalled the Soweto uprising of June 16, 1976, when unarmed school-children were shot and killed as they demonstrated against the use of the Afrikaans language as a medium of instruction. Afrikaans was regarded as the language of the enforcers of the apartheid policy that an overwhelmingly Afrikaans-speaking political party, the Nationalist Party, had inflicted on the nation from 1948.

South Africa remembered that several people had died mysteriously while they were in police detention. It was alleged by the authorities who might perhaps have been believed by most of the white community—they were certainly not believed by most of the black community—that they had committed suicide by hanging themselves with their belts, or they had slipped on soap while showering, or they tended to have a penchant for jumping out of the windows of the buildings where they were being detained and questioned. Others died, so we were told, from self-inflicted injuries. One such was Steve Biko, the young student founder of the Black Consciousness Movement. It was said he had banged his head against the wall in an inexplicable and quite unreasonable altercation with his interrogators in September 1977. People recalled that when the then Minister of Police was told of Steve's death he had callously and memorably declared that his death "leaves me cold." People recalled that Steve had been driven naked on the back of a police truck over 1500 kilometers to Pretoria, where it was reported he would have received medical treatment, except that he died soon after he arrived there. No one ever explained why he could not have got the emergency treatment in Port Elizabeth where he had been detained, nor why if he had had to be taken to Pretoria he had had to be humiliated, comatose as he was, by being transported without any clothes on.

People remembered the bombing in Amanzimtoti, KwaZulu/Natal, in 1985 when   5
a limpet mine placed in a refuse bin outside a shopping center exploded among holidaymakers doing last-minute Christmas shopping, killing five persons and injuring over sixty.

South Africa recalled the Magoo's Bar bombing of June 1986, when three people were killed and about sixty-nine injured by a car bomb planted by Robert McBride and his two accomplices, allegedly on the orders of a commander of the ANC's armed wing, Umkhonto weSizwe,[1] based in neighboring Botswana.

People had been filled with revulsion when they saw how people were killed so gruesomely through the so-called "necklace," a tire placed around the victim's neck and filled with petrol and then set alight. This horrible way of execution was used by township ANC-supporting "comrades" especially against "sellouts," those who were suspected of being collaborators with the state. It was also used in the internecine strife between warring liberation movements, such as the United Democratic Front (UDF), which largely comprised ANC sympathizers while that party was banned, and the Azanian People's Organization (Azapo), the party espousing the principles of black consciousness developed by Steve Biko and his colleagues. You were appalled that human beings, children even, could actually dance around the body of someone dying in such an excruciating fashion. Apartheid had succeeded only too well in dehumanizing its victims and those who implemented it. People remembered that all this was very much a part of our past, a part of our history.

People were appalled at the carnage in Church Street, Pretoria, in May 1983 when a massive bomb exploded outside the administrative headquarters of the South African Air Force. Twenty-one people died and over two hundred were injured. The ANC claimed responsibility for this outrage.

More recently people recalled the St. James' Church massacre in Cape Town in July 1993. In that attack, two members of the armed wing of the Pan Africanist Congress (PAC)—the liberation movement which had broken away from the ANC in 1959—burst into a Sunday church service and fired machine guns, killing eleven worshipers and injuring fifty-six. Nothing, it seemed, was sacrosanct anymore in this urban guerrilla warfare.

These and similar atrocities pockmarked our history and on all sides it was agreed   10
that we had to take this past seriously into account. We could not pretend that it had not happened. Much of it was too fresh in the memories of many communities.

There was in fact hardly any controversy about whether we should deal effectively with our past if we were going to be making the transition to a new dispensation. No, the debate was not on *whether* but on *how* we might deal with this only too real past.

---

1. **Umkhonto weSizwe:** translates as "Spear of the Nation." [Author's note]

There were those who wanted to follow the Nuremberg[2] trial paradigm, by bringing to trial all perpetrators of gross violations of human rights and letting them run the gauntlet of the normal judicial process. This, it turned out, was really not a viable option at all, perhaps mercifully for us in South Africa. In World War II the Allies defeated the Nazis and their allies comprehensively and were thus able to impose what has been described as "victor's justice." The accused had no say whatsoever in the matter, and because some of those who sat in judgment on the accused, such as the Russians, were themselves guilty of similar gross violations in the excesses perpetrated under Stalin, the whole process left a simmering resentment in many Germans as I found out when I participated in a BBC-TV panel discussion in the very room in Nuremberg where the trial had taken place fifty years previously. The Germans had accepted it because they were down and out and the victors, as it were, could kick the vanquished even as they lay on the ground. Thus the Nuremberg option was rejected by those who were negotiating the delicate process of transition to democracy, the rule of law, and respect for human rights. Neither side could impose victor's justice because neither side won the decisive victory that would have enabled it to do so, since we had a military stalemate.

It is as certain as anything that the security forces of the apartheid regime would not have supported the negotiated settlement which made possible the "miracle" of our relatively peaceful transition from repression to democracy—when most people had been making dire predictions of a blood bath, of a comprehensive disaster that would overwhelm us—had they known that at the end of the negotiations they would be for the high jump, when they would face the full wrath of the law as alleged perpetrators. They still controlled the guns and had the capacity to sabotage the whole process.

As the beneficiaries of a peaceful transition, citizens in a remarkable democratic dispensation, some South Africans—and others in the international community—enjoy the luxury of being able to complain that all the perpetrators ought to have been brought to justice. The fact of the matter is that we do unfortunately have remarkably short memories. We have in our amnesia forgotten that we were on tenterhooks until 1994, within a trice of the most comprehensive disaster, but that, in God's mercy, we were spared all of this. Those who now enjoy the new dispensation have forgotten too soon just how vulnerable and indeed how unlikely it was and why it is that the world can still look on in amazement that this miracle did in fact unfold. The miracle was the result of the negotiated settlement. There would have been no negotiated settlement and so no new democratic South Africa had the negotiators on one side insisted that all perpetrators be brought to trial. While the Allies could pack up and go home after Nuremberg, we in South Africa had to live with one another. . . .

There were other very cogent and important reasons that the Nuremberg trial option found little favor with the negotiators. Even if we had been able to choose it, it would have placed an intolerable burden on an already strained judicial system. We had some experience of cases of this nature because the state had in two major

2. **Nuremberg:** German city where Nazi officials were tried for war crimes after World War II.

trials prosecuted Colonel Eugene de Kock, former head of a police death squad, in 1995 and 1996, and General Magnus Malan, former Minister of Defense, and a number of generals and other military officers in 1996. It had taken a whole bevy of Department of Justice and Safety and Security (police) personnel eighteen months to make a case successfully against de Kock, and since he had been a former state employee, the state was obliged to foot his legal bill, which came to R5 million (nearly U.S. $1 million)—an amount that did not include the cost of the prosecution and its bureaucracy, or an expensive witness protection program. In the case of General Malan and his co-accused, the prosecution failed to nail their men and the costs were astronomical, running into nearly R12 million (U.S. $2 million) just for the defense, which again had to be borne by the state. In a country strapped for cash and with a whole range of pressing priorities in education, health, housing, and other fields, tough decisions had to be made about what the country could be expected to afford.

We also could not have afforded to canvass day in and day out for an unconscionably long time details which from the nature of the case would be distressing to many and also too disruptive of a fragile peace and stability. We certainly would not have been able to have the tenacity of Nazi hunters who more than fifty years later are still at it. We have had to balance the requirements of justice, accountability, stability, peace, and reconciliation. We could very well have had justice, retributive justice, and had a South Africa lying in ashes—a truly Pyrrhic victory[3] if ever there was one. Our country had to decide very carefully where it would spend its limited resources to the best possible advantage.

Other important reasons why the trial option was not a viable one could still be adduced. A criminal court requires the evidence produced in a case to pass the most rigorous scrutiny and satisfy the criterion of proving the case beyond reasonable doubt. In many of the cases which came before the commission, the only witnesses to events who were still alive were the perpetrators and they had used the considerable resources of the state to destroy evidence and cover up their heinous deeds. The commission proved to be a better way of getting at the truth than court cases: amnesty applicants had to demonstrate that they had made a full disclosure to qualify for amnesty, so the normal legal process was reversed as applicants sought to discharge the onus on them to reveal all.

Most distressingly, we discovered in the course of the TRC investigations and work that the supporters of apartheid were ready to lie at the drop of a hat. This applied to cabinet ministers, commissioners of police, and of course those in the lower echelons as well. They lied as if it were going out of fashion, brazenly and with very considerable apparent conviction. In the courts it was the word of one bewildered victim against that of several perpetrators, other officers in the police or armed forces who perjured themselves as they have now admitted in their applications for

3. **Pyrrhic victory:** a victory that inflicts great damage on the victor, named after the Greek king Pyrrhus, whose army defeated the Romans in 280 BCE but, in doing so, took devastating casualties that limited his ability to fight future wars.

amnesty. It would have had to be a very brave judge or magistrate who would find in favor of the solitary witness who would in addition have the further disadvantage of being black facing a phalanx of white police officers who really could never do such a dastardly thing as to lie in court.

No wonder the judicial system gained such a notorious reputation in the black community. It was taken for granted that the judges and magistrates colluded with the police to produce miscarriages of justice. Until fairly recently the magistrates and judges were all white, sharing the apprehensions and prejudices of their white compatriots, secure in enjoying the privileges that the injustices of apartheid provided them so lavishly and therefore inclined to believe that all opposition to that status quo was Communist-inspired and generally supporting the executive and the legislative branches of government against the black person who was excluded by the law from a share in the governance of his motherland. Many judges in the old dispensation were blatantly political appointees and they did nothing to redeem the reputation of the judiciary as a willing collaborator with an unjust dispensation. Of course there were some exceptions, but by and large the dice were heavily loaded against the black litigant or accused or complainant. It will take some time for our black people to have confidence in the police and the judicial system, which was so badly discredited in the bad old days. . . .

When it came to hearing evidence from victims, because we were not a criminal court, we established facts on the basis of a balance of probability. Since we were exhorted by our enabling legislation to rehabilitate the human and civil dignity of victims, we allowed those who came to testify mainly to tell *their* stories in their own words. We did do all we could to corroborate these stories and we soon discovered that, as Judge Albie Sachs, a member of our Constitutional Court, has pointed out, there were in fact different orders of truth which did not necessarily mutually exclude one another. There was what could be termed forensic factual truth—verifiable and documentable—and there was "social truth, the truth of experience that is established through interaction, discussion and debate."[4] The personal truth—Judge Mahomed's "truth of wounded memories"—was a healing truth and a court of law would have left many of those who came to testify, who were frequently uneducated and unsophisticated, bewildered and even more traumatized than before, whereas many bore witness to the fact that coming to talk to the commission had had a marked therapeutic effect on them. We learned this from unsolicited comment by the brother of one of the Cradock Four, ANC-supporting activists who left their homes in Cradock to attend a political rally in Port Elizabeth and never made it back home, having been gruesomely murdered by the police. The brother said to me after one of his relatives had testified at the TRC's first hearing, and before the policemen responsible had confessed and applied for amnesty: "Archbishop, we have told our story to many on several occasions, to newspapers and to the TV.

20

---

4. **"Social truth . . . debate.":** *In The Healing of a Nation?* Alex Boraine, Janet Levy, eds., Justice in Transition, 1995. [Author's note]

This is the first time though that after telling it we feel as if a heavy load has been removed from our shoulders."

Thus the option of trials, which represented one extreme of the possible ways of dealing with our past, was rejected.

Then there were those others who opposed the trial option and suggested rather glibly that we let bygones be bygones. This was much sought after by the members of the previous government and those who had carried out their behest in their security forces. They clamored for a blanket or general amnesty as had happened in, for instance, Chile, where General Augusto Pinochet[5] and his cohorts gave themselves amnesty as a precondition to handing over from their military junta to a civilian government. Even though they agreed to the appointment of a Truth Commission, such a commission would deliberate only behind closed doors and the record of General Pinochet and his government and the security forces would not be scrutinized by the commission, certainly not for the purpose of apportioning blame. It has been important in the whole debate over impunity to point out that General Pinochet and his officers and government forgave themselves, they alone knew what precisely they had done; they were the accused, the prosecution, and the judges in their own case. In the absence of amnesty designed, as it was in South Africa, to establish accountability, I am a strong supporter of the recent extradition proceedings against General Pinochet. It would be quite intolerable that the perpetrator should decide not only whether he should get amnesty but that no one else should have the right to question the grounds on which he had so granted himself amnesty and for what offense.

In the South African case there was to be no general amnesty. This amnesty was not automatic and the applicant had to make an individual application, then appear before an independent panel which decided whether the applicant satisfied the stringent conditions for granting amnesty. So the other extreme, of blanket amnesty, was also rejected. Apart from the reasons given above, it was felt very strongly that general amnesty was really amnesia. It was pointed out that we none of us possess a kind of fiat by which we can say, "Let bygones be bygones" and, hey presto, they then become bygones. Our common experience in fact is the opposite—that the past, far from disappearing or lying down and being quiet, has an embarrassing and persistent way of returning and haunting us unless it has in fact been dealt with adequately. Unless we look the beast in the eye we find it has an uncanny habit of returning to hold us hostage.

The English and Afrikaners in South Africa are a perfect case study in point. During the Anglo-Boer War[6] at the turn of the century, the British incarcerated more than 200,000 people, including Boer women and children and black workers

---

5. **Augusto Pinochet:** a Chilean military dictator (1915–2006) who was ousted in 1988 and, ten years later, arrested in Britain under a Spanish warrant for crimes committed against Spanish citizens during his dictatorship. In 2000, a British court allowed Pinochet to return to Chile rather than extraditing him to Spain to face trial for crimes against humanity.

6. **Anglo-Boer War:** one of two conflicts fought in the late nineteenth century between Great Britain and Dutch settlers, known as Boers, for control of South Africa.

on Boer farms, in what was a new British invention at the time—concentration camps, which were to gain, appropriately, a foul reputation as a special feature of the Jewish Holocaust in Hitler's mad obsession with Aryan purity. Nearly 50,000 of the inmates are estimated to have died in unacceptable conditions. At the end of the war neither side ever sat down with the other to talk about this aspect of their war. It seemed that in time the wounds inflicted then had healed and English and Afrikaner seemed to live happily together. Alas, however, the amicable relationship was only superficial and really quite unstable and uneasy. In 1998 I traveled by road from Zurich to attend the World Economic Forum in Davos. I was accompanied by a young Afrikaner who said he remembered so clearly his grandmother telling him of the awful things that had happened to his people in the concentration camps and he said with some feeling that he was ready to fight the Anglo-Boer War over again whenever he remembered his grandmother's stories.

At Dachau, the former concentration camp near Nuremberg, there is a museum to commemorate what happened there—you can see the gas chambers and the ovens where the bodies of the Jews were incinerated. The gas chambers look so innocuous, like normal shower rooms, until you see the vents through which the lethal gas could be pumped into the chamber. In the museum are pictures of prisoners marching behind brass bands while they are carrying some inmate to his execution—macabre humor indeed. The Germans were so methodical and systematic. They recorded everything, including the experiments they carried out to see what depths and altitudes human beings could tolerate, and of course the guinea pigs were the subhuman, non-Aryan, Jewish inmates and it is all there to see in those photographs, showing faces grimacing like hideous gargoyles.

Over the entrance to this museum are philosopher George Santayana's[7] haunting words, "Those who forget the past are doomed to repeat it." Those who were negotiating our future were aware that, unless the past was acknowledged and dealt with adequately, it could put paid to that future as a baneful blight on it.

To accept national amnesia would be bad for another telling reason. It would in effect be to victimize the victims of apartheid a second time around. We would have denied something that contributed to the identity of who they were. Ariel Dorfman, the Chilean playwright, wrote a play entitled *Death and the Maiden*. The maiden's husband has just been appointed to his country's Truth Commission. While she is busy in the kitchen someone whose car has broken down and who has been helped by her husband enters the house. The woman does not see him but hears him speak and she recognizes his voice as that of the man who tortured and raped her when she was in detention. She is then shown with the man completely at her mercy, tied up and helpless. She holds a gun to him and is ready to kill him because he denies strenuously that he could have done this and tries to produce an elaborate alibi. Much later, he eventually admits that he was the culprit and, very strangely,

25

7. **George Santayana:** Spanish philosopher, novelist, and poet (1863–1952).

she lets him go. His denial hit at the core of her being, at her integrity, at her identity, and these were all tied up intimately with her experiences, with her memory.
Denial subverted her personhood. She was in a real sense her memory, as someone
who has Alzheimer's disease is no longer quite the same person we knew when she
or he possessed all her or his faculties.

Our nation sought to rehabilitate and affirm the dignity and personhood of those
who for so long had been silenced, had been turned into anonymous, marginalized
ones. Now they would be able to tell their stories, they would remember, and in
remembering would be acknowledged to be persons with an inalienable personhood.

Our country's negotiators rejected the two extremes and opted for a "third
way," a compromise between the extreme of Nuremberg trials and blanket amnesty
or national amnesia. And that third way was granting amnesty to individuals in
exchange for a full disclosure relating to the crime for which amnesty was being
sought. It was the carrot of possible freedom in exchange for truth and the stick was,
for those already in jail, the prospect of lengthy prison sentences and, for those still
free, the probability of arrest and prosecution and imprisonment. . . .

Let us conclude . . . by pointing out that ultimately this third way of amnesty was   30
consistent with a central feature of the African *Weltanschauung*[8]—what we know in
our languages as *ubuntu*, in the Nguni group of languages, or *botho*, in the Sotho languages. What is it that constrained so many to choose to forgive rather than to demand
retribution, to be so magnanimous and ready to forgive rather than wreak revenge?

Ubuntu is very difficult to render into a Western language. It speaks of the very
essence of being human. When we want to give high praise to someone we say, "*Yu,
u nobuntu*"; "Hey, so-and-so has *ubuntu*." Then you are generous, you are hospitable,
you are friendly and caring and compassionate. You share what you have. It is to
say, "My humanity is caught up, is inextricably bound up, in yours." We belong in a
bundle of life. We say, "A person is a person through other persons." It is not, "I think
therefore I am." It says rather: "I am human because I belong. I participate, I share."
A person with *ubuntu* is open and available to others, affirming to others, does not
feel threatened that others are able and good, for he or she has a proper self-assurance
that comes from knowing that he or she belongs in a greater whole and is diminished
when others are humiliated or diminished, when others are tortured or oppressed, or
treated as if they were less than who they are.

Harmony, friendliness, community are great goods. Social harmony is for us
the *summum bonum*—the greatest good. Anything that subverts, that undermines
this sought-after good, is to be avoided like the plague. Anger, resentment, lust for
revenge, even success through aggressive competitiveness, are corrosive of this good.
To forgive is not just to be altruistic. It is the best form of self-interest. What dehumanizes you inexorably dehumanizes me. It gives people resilience, enabling them
to survive and emerge still human despite all efforts to dehumanize them.

8. **Weltanschauung:** a German word meaning "worldview."

UNDERSTANDING THE TEXT

1. Why does Tutu believe that the legacy of apartheid will extend far beyond its practice?

2. What kinds of events does Tutu describe to illustrate the crimes of the apartheid regime? Who does he say is responsible for the violence that he cites?

3. What does Tutu see as the flaw in the Nuremberg trials that the Allies conducted after World War II? Why does he say the Nuremberg model would not have worked in South Africa?

4. Why did Tutu feel that it was important to reject the "let bygones be bygones" approach that would have extended blanket amnesty to anybody, on either side, involved in atrocities during the prior regime?

5. What is the point of the play *Death and the Maiden*, by Ariel Dorfman, as Tutu sees it? Why do you think that the woman in the play lets her former torturer go free?

6. How does Tutu translate the African term *ubuntu*? Why is this concept important to his argument?

MAKING CONNECTIONS

1. How does Tutu's understanding of democracy compare to that of Aung San Suu Kyi (p. 442)? How are their views shaped by their religious beliefs?

2. Compare the system of apartheid described by Desmond Tutu with the American system of segregation described by Martin Luther King Jr. in "Letter from Birmingham Jail" (p. 425). How does each writer respond to the political aspect of oppression?

3. Compare the way that Tutu uses the native African concept of *ubuntu* with the way Toni Morrison discusses African views of rhetoric and storytelling in her Nobel lecture (p. 217).

WRITING ABOUT THE TEXT

1. Write an essay that applies the concept of synthesis, as described by Hegel (p. 668), to Tutu's rejection of both the Nuremberg model of justice and "national amnesia." How might Tutu's solution be considered a synthesis of the other two ways that society has used to address horrible crimes committed by the state?

2. Write an essay in which you argue that the amnesty offered by the Truth and Reconciliation Committee in South Africa is incompatible with a belief in justice. Conduct additional research into the process that Tutu describes.

3. Read or watch the play *Death and the Maiden* by Ariel Dorfman (a film version starring Sigourney Weaver and Ben Kingsley is widely available). Use this play as the basis for an argument about either the value of a tribunal such as the Truth and Reconcilition Commission or the problems that prevent such a tribunal from operating effectively.

BARACK OBAMA
A More Perfect Union
[2008]

BARACK OBAMA WAS born in Hawaii in 1961. His parents—whom he would later describe as "a black man from Kenya and a white woman from Kansas"—were both students at the University of Hawaii in Manoa. As a child, Obama lived in Hawaii, Washington State, and Jakarta, Indonesia, the home country of his stepfather. After graduating from high school in Hawaii, Obama studied at Occidental College, Columbia University, and Harvard University before moving to Chicago, Illinois, where he became a professor of constitutional law at the University of Chicago and later a state legislator. In 2004, Obama was elected to the U.S. Senate, and in 2008, he was elected president of the United States, the first African American ever to hold that office. In 2012, he was elected to a second term.

Obama's campaign for the presidency began in February of 2007, just three years after his election to the U.S. Senate. His closest rival for the nomination of the Democratic Party was Senator Hillary Clinton; in the end, Obama won the nomination in one of the closest primary races in recent history and went on to defeat Senator John McCain, the Republican nominee, in November 2008. The most serious threat to Obama's campaign for the Democratic nomination came in March of 2008, when videos surfaced of Reverend Jeremiah Wright (b. 1941), Obama's long-time pastor at the Trinity United Church of Christ in Chicago, making inflammatory statements about the U.S. government and race relations in America. The videos, which showed Wright saying, among other things, that the government had invented HIV "as a means of genocide against people of color," received heavy news coverage and associated Obama with divisive racial politics at a crucial point in a hotly contested Democratic primary.

On March 18, 2008, after several weeks of headlines about the Wright issue, Obama delivered the speech "A More Perfect Union" at the National Constitution Center in Philadelphia, Pennsylvania. In this speech, he responded to those who criticized his relationship with Wright, explaining why he disagreed with Wright and why he refused to denounce him altogether. In addition to addressing his relationship with Wright, Obama used "A More Perfect Union," whose title is taken from the Preamble to the Constitution, to address the broader issue of race in the United States.

Obama uses several rhetorical strategies in his speech. He supports his argument with anecdotes, historical facts, and logical reasoning. Underlying all of these strategies, however, is the creation of an ethos that is sympathetic to the diverse perspectives on race held by different members of his audience. At a number of points in his remarks, Obama refers to personal experiences as a multiracial American in order to establish his authority to speak knowledgeably from several perspectives.

"We the people, in order to form a more perfect union."

Two hundred and twenty-one years ago, in a hall that still stands across the street, a group of men gathered and, with these simple words, launched America's improbable experiment in democracy. Farmers and scholars, statesmen and patriots who had traveled across an ocean to escape tyranny and persecution finally made real their declaration of independence at a Philadelphia convention that lasted through the spring of 1787.

The document they produced was eventually signed but ultimately unfinished. It was stained by this nation's original sin of slavery, a question that divided the colonies and brought the convention to a stalemate until the founders chose to allow the slave trade to continue for at least twenty more years, and to leave any final resolution to future generations.

Of course, the answer to the slavery question was already embedded within our Constitution—a Constitution that had at its very core the ideal of equal citizenship under the law; a Constitution that promised its people liberty, and justice, and a union that could be and should be perfected over time.

And yet words on a parchment would not be enough to deliver slaves from   5
bondage, or provide men and women of every color and creed their full rights and obligations as citizens of the United States. What would be needed were Americans in successive generations who were willing to do their part—through protests and struggle, on the streets and in the courts, through a civil war and civil disobedience, and always at great risk—to narrow the gap between the promise of our ideals and the reality of their time.

This was one of the tasks we set forth at the beginning of this campaign—to continue the long march of those who came before us, a march for a more just, more equal, more free, more caring, and more prosperous America. I chose to run for the presidency at this moment in history because I believe deeply that we cannot solve the challenges of our time unless we solve them together—unless we perfect our union by understanding that we may have different stories, but we hold common hopes; that we may not look the same and we may not have come from the same place, but we all want to move in the same direction—towards a better future for our children and our grandchildren.

This belief comes from my unyielding faith in the decency and generosity of the American people. But it also comes from my own American story.

I am the son of a black man from Kenya and a white woman from Kansas. I was raised with the help of a white grandfather who survived a Depression to serve in Patton's army during World War II and a white grandmother who worked on a bomber assembly line at Fort Leavenworth while he was overseas. I've gone to some of the best schools in America and lived in one of the world's poorest nations.[1]

---

1. **One of the world's poorest nations:** From 1967 through 1971, Obama lived in Indonesia with his mother and his stepfather, Lolo Soetoro, an Indonesian citizen.

I am married to a black American who carries within her the blood of slaves and slaveowners—an inheritance we pass on to our two precious daughters. I have brothers, sisters, nieces, nephews, uncles, and cousins, of every race and every hue, scattered across three continents, and for as long as I live, I will never forget that in no other country on Earth is my story even possible.

It's a story that hasn't made me the most conventional candidate. But it is a story that has seared into my genetic makeup the idea that this nation is more than the sum of its parts—that out of many, we are truly one.

Throughout the first year of this campaign, against all predictions to the contrary,   10
we saw how hungry the American people were for this message of unity. Despite the temptation to view my candidacy through a purely racial lens, we won commanding victories in states with some of the whitest populations in the country. In South Carolina, where the Confederate flag still flies, we built a powerful coalition of African Americans and white Americans.

This is not to say that race has not been an issue in the campaign. At various stages in the campaign, some commentators have deemed me either "too black" or "not black enough." We saw racial tensions bubble to the surface during the week before the South Carolina primary. The press has scoured every exit poll for the latest evidence of racial polarization, not just in terms of white and black, but black and brown as well.

And yet, it has only been in the last couple of weeks that the discussion of race in this campaign has taken a particularly divisive turn.

On one end of the spectrum, we've heard the implication that my candidacy is somehow an exercise in affirmative action; that it's based solely on the desire of wide-eyed liberals to purchase racial reconciliation on the cheap. On the other end, we've heard my former pastor, Reverend Jeremiah Wright, use incendiary language to express views that have the potential not only to widen the racial divide, but views that denigrate both the greatness and the goodness of our nation; that rightly offend white and black alike.

I have already condemned, in unequivocal terms, the statements of Reverend Wright that have caused such controversy. For some, nagging questions remain. Did I know him to be an occasionally fierce critic of American domestic and foreign policy? Of course. Did I ever hear him make remarks that could be considered controversial while I sat in church? Yes. Did I strongly disagree with many of his political views? Absolutely—just as I'm sure many of you have heard remarks from your pastors, priests, or rabbis with which you strongly disagreed.

But the remarks that have caused this recent firestorm weren't simply   15
controversial. They weren't simply a religious leader's effort to speak out against perceived injustice. Instead, they expressed a profoundly distorted view of this country—a view that sees white racism as endemic and that elevates what is wrong with America above all that we know is right with America; a view that sees the conflicts in the Middle East as rooted primarily in the actions of stalwart

allies like Israel, instead of emanating from the perverse and hateful ideologies of radical Islam.

As such, Reverend Wright's comments were not only wrong but divisive, divisive at a time when we need unity; racially charged at a time when we need to come together to solve a set of monumental problems—two wars, a terrorist threat, a falling economy, a chronic health care crisis and potentially devastating climate change; problems that are neither black or white or Latino or Asian, but rather problems that confront us all.

Given my background, my politics, and my professed values and ideals, there will no doubt be those for whom my statements of condemnation are not enough. Why associate myself with Reverend Wright in the first place, they may ask? Why not join another church? And I confess that if all that I knew of Reverend Wright were the snippets of those sermons that have run in an endless loop on the television and You-Tube, or if Trinity United Church of Christ conformed to the caricatures being peddled by some commentators, there is no doubt that I would react in much the same way.

But the truth is, that isn't all that I know of the man. The man I met more than twenty years ago is a man who helped introduce me to my Christian faith, a man who spoke to me about our obligations to love one another, to care for the sick and lift up the poor. He is a man who served his country as a U.S. Marine; who has studied and lectured at some of the finest universities and seminaries in the country, and who for over thirty years led a church that serves the community by doing God's work here on Earth—by housing the homeless, ministering to the needy, providing daycare services and scholarships and prison ministries, and reaching out to those suffering from HIV/AIDS.

In my first book, *Dreams From My Father*, I described the experience of my first service at Trinity:

> People began to shout, to rise from their seats and clap and cry out, a forceful wind carrying the reverend's voice up into the rafters. . . . And in that single note—hope!—I heard something else; at the foot of that cross, inside the thousands of churches across the city, I imagined the stories of ordinary black people merging with the stories of David and Goliath, Moses and Pharaoh, the Christians in the lion's den, Ezekiel's field of dry bones.[2] Those stories—of survival, and freedom, and hope—became our story, my story; the blood that had spilled was our blood, the tears our tears, until this black church, on this bright day, seemed once more a vessel carrying the story

2. **David and Goliath, Moses and Pharaoh, the Christians in the lion's den, Ezekiel's field of dry bones:** All of these references are to biblical stories that speak to persecution and to the eventual triumph of the persecuted. David was a shepherd who killed the giant Goliath. Moses led the Children of Israel out of Egypt in defiance of the pharaoh, who had forced them into slavery. The reference to "Christians in the lion's den" combines the biblical story of Daniel with the story of early Christians being fed to lions in Rome; Daniel was thrown into a den of lions when he refused to stop praying to his god but was ultimately saved by the Lord. The prophet Ezekiel saw a great vision of a field of bones that he brought to life through the power of God.

of a people into future generations and into a larger world. Our trials and triumphs became at once unique and universal, black and more than black; in chronicling our journey, the stories and songs gave us a means to reclaim memories that we didn't need to feel shame about . . . memories that all people might study and cherish—and with which we could start to rebuild.

That has been my experience at Trinity. Like other predominantly black churches across the country, Trinity embodies the black community in its entirety—the doctor and the welfare mom, the model student and the former gang-banger. Like other black churches, Trinity's services are full of raucous laughter and sometimes bawdy humor. They are full of dancing, clapping, screaming, and shouting that may seem jarring to the untrained ear. The church contains in full the kindness and cruelty, the fierce intelligence and the shocking ignorance, the struggles and successes, the love and, yes, the bitterness and bias that make up the black experience in America. 20

And this helps explain, perhaps, my relationship with Reverend Wright. As imperfect as he may be, he has been like family to me. He strengthened my faith, officiated my wedding, and baptized my children. Not once in my conversations with him have I heard him talk about any ethnic group in derogatory terms, or treat whites with whom he interacted with anything but courtesy and respect. He contains within him the contradictions—the good and the bad—of the community that he has served diligently for so many years.

I can no more disown him than I can disown the black community. I can no more disown him than I can my white grandmother—a woman who helped raise me, a woman who sacrificed again and again for me, a woman who loves me as much as she loves anything in this world, but a woman who once confessed her fear of black men who passed by her on the street, and who on more than one occasion has uttered racial or ethnic stereotypes that made me cringe.

These people are a part of me. And they are a part of America, this country that I love.

Some will see this as an attempt to justify or excuse comments that are simply inexcusable. I can assure you it is not. I suppose the politically safe thing would be to move on from this episode and just hope that it fades into the woodwork. We can dismiss Reverend Wright as a crank or a demagogue, just as some have dismissed Geraldine Ferraro,[3] in the aftermath of her recent statements, as harboring some deep-seated racial bias.

But race is an issue that I believe this nation cannot afford to ignore right now. We would be making the same mistake that Reverend Wright made in his offending 25

3. **Geraldine Ferraro:** former member of Congress and 1984 Democratic vice-presidential candidate (1935–2011). Ferraro, who supported Hillary Clinton during the 2008 primary, caused a minor controversy when she told a California newspaper that "if Obama was a white man, he would not be in this position."

sermons about America—to simplify and stereotype and amplify the negative to the point that it distorts reality.

The fact is that the comments that have been made and the issues that have surfaced over the last few weeks reflect the complexities of race in this country that we've never really worked through—a part of our union that we have yet to perfect. And if we walk away now, if we simply retreat into our respective corners, we will never be able to come together and solve challenges like health care, or education, or the need to find good jobs for every American.

Understanding this reality requires a reminder of how we arrived at this point. As William Faulkner once wrote, "The past isn't dead and buried. In fact, it isn't even past."[4] We do not need to recite here the history of racial injustice in this country. But we do need to remind ourselves that so many of the disparities that exist in the African American community today can be directly traced to inequalities passed on from an earlier generation that suffered under the brutal legacy of slavery and Jim Crow.

Segregated schools were, and are, inferior schools; we still haven't fixed them, fifty years after *Brown v. Board of Education*,[5] and the inferior education they provided, then and now, helps explain the pervasive achievement gap between today's black and white students.

Legalized discrimination—where blacks were prevented, often through violence, from owning property, or loans were not granted to African American business owners, or black homeowners could not access FHA mortgages,[6] or blacks were excluded from unions, or the police force, or fire departments—meant that black families could not amass any meaningful wealth to bequeath to future generations. That history helps explain the wealth and income gap between black and white, and the concentrated pockets of poverty that persists in so many of today's urban and rural communities.

A lack of economic opportunity among black men, and the shame and frustration   30
that came from not being able to provide for one's family, contributed to the erosion of black families—a problem that welfare policies for many years may have worsened. And the lack of basic services in so many urban black neighborhoods—parks for kids to play in, police walking the beat, regular garbage pick-up and building code enforcement—all helped create a cycle of violence, blight, and neglect that continue to haunt us.

This is the reality in which Reverend Wright and other African Americans of his generation grew up. They came of age in the late fifties and early sixties, a time

4. **William Faulkner:** American novelist (1897–1962) and winner of the 1949 Nobel Prize for Literature. Here, Obama paraphrases a passage from Faulkner's 1951 novel *Requiem for a Nun*.
5. ***Brown v. Board of Education:*** the 1954 Supreme Court decision that outlawed segregation in public schools.

6. **FHA mortgages:** loans insured by the Federal Housing Administration that help people secure mortgages for which they might otherwise not qualify.

when segregation was still the law of the land and opportunity was systematically constricted. What's remarkable is not how many failed in the face of discrimination, but rather how many men and women overcame the odds; how many were able to make a way out of no way for those like me who would come after them.

But for all those who scratched and clawed their way to get a piece of the American Dream, there were many who didn't make it—those who were ultimately defeated, in one way or another, by discrimination. That legacy of defeat was passed on to future generations—those young men and increasingly young women who we see standing on street corners or languishing in our prisons, without hope or prospects for the future. Even for those blacks who did make it, questions of race, and racism, continue to define their worldview in fundamental ways. For the men and women of Reverend Wright's generation, the memories of humiliation and doubt and fear have not gone away; nor has the anger and the bitterness of those years. That anger may not get expressed in public, in front of white co-workers or white friends. But it does find voice in the barbershop or around the kitchen table. At times, that anger is exploited by politicians, to gin up votes along racial lines, or to make up for a politician's own failings.

And occasionally it finds voice in the church on Sunday morning, in the pulpit and in the pews. The fact that so many people are surprised to hear that anger in some of Reverend Wright's sermons simply reminds us of the old truism that the most segregated hour in American life occurs on Sunday morning. That anger is not always productive; indeed, all too often it distracts attention from solving real problems; it keeps us from squarely facing our own complicity in our condition, and prevents the African American community from forging the alliances it needs to bring about real change. But the anger is real; it is powerful; and to simply wish it away, to condemn it without understanding its roots, only serves to widen the chasm of misunderstanding that exists between the races.

In fact, a similar anger exists within segments of the white community. Most working- and middle-class white Americans don't feel that they have been particularly privileged by their race. Their experience is the immigrant experience—as far as they're concerned, no one's handed them anything, they've built it from scratch. They've worked hard all their lives, many times only to see their jobs shipped overseas or their pension dumped after a lifetime of labor. They are anxious about their futures, and feel their dreams slipping away; in an era of stagnant wages and global competition, opportunity comes to be seen as a zero sum game, in which your dreams come at my expense. So when they are told to bus their children to a school across town; when they hear that an African American is getting an advantage in landing a good job or a spot in a good college because of an injustice that they themselves never committed; when they're told that their fears about crime in urban neighborhoods are somehow prejudiced, resentment builds over time.

Like the anger within the black community, these resentments aren't always expressed in polite company. But they have helped shape the political landscape for at least a generation. Anger over welfare and affirmative action helped forge

35

the Reagan Coalition.[7] Politicians routinely exploited fears of crime for their own electoral ends. Talk show hosts and conservative commentators built entire careers unmasking bogus claims of racism while dismissing legitimate discussions of racial injustice and inequality as mere political correctness or reverse racism.

Just as black anger often proved counterproductive, so have these white resentments distracted attention from the real culprits of the middle-class squeeze—a corporate culture rife with inside dealing,[8] questionable accounting practices, and short-term greed; a Washington dominated by lobbyists and special interests; economic policies that favor the few over the many. And yet, to wish away the resentments of white Americans, to label them as misguided or even racist, without recognizing they are grounded in legitimate concerns—this too widens the racial divide, and blocks the path to understanding.

This is where we are right now. It's a racial stalemate we've been stuck in for years. Contrary to the claims of some of my critics, black and white, I have never been so naïve as to believe that we can get beyond our racial divisions in a single election cycle, or with a single candidacy—particularly a candidacy as imperfect as my own.

But I have asserted a firm conviction—a conviction rooted in my faith in God and my faith in the American people—that working together we can move beyond some of our old racial wounds, and that in fact we have no choice if we are to continue on the path of a more perfect union.

For the African American community, that path means embracing the burdens of our past without becoming victims of our past. It means continuing to insist on a full measure of justice in every aspect of American life. But it also means binding our particular grievances—for better health care, and better schools, and better jobs—to the larger aspirations of all Americans—the white woman struggling to break the glass ceiling, the white man who's been laid off, the immigrant trying to feed his family. And it means taking full responsibility for our own lives—by demanding more from our fathers, and spending more time with our children, and reading to them, and teaching them that while they may face challenges and discrimination in their own lives, they must never succumb to despair or cynicism; they must always believe that they can write their own destiny.

Ironically, this quintessentially American—and yes, conservative—notion of self-help found frequent expression in Reverend Wright's sermons. But what my former pastor too often failed to understand is that embarking on a program of self-help also requires a belief that society can change.

The profound mistake of Reverend Wright's sermons is not that he spoke about racism in our society. It's that he spoke as if our society was static; as if no progress has been made; as if this country—a country that has made it possible for one of

40

---

7. **Reagan Coalition:** Republicans and white, socially conservative Democrats who gave victories to Ronald Reagan in the 1980 and 1984 presidential elections.

8. **Inside dealing:** profiting, usually on the stock market, from information not available to the general public.

his own members to run for the highest office in the land and build a coalition of white and black, Latino and Asian, rich and poor, young and old—is still irrevocably bound to a tragic past. But what we know—what we have seen—is that America can change. That is the true genius of this nation. What we have already achieved gives us hope—the audacity to hope—for what we can and must achieve tomorrow.

In the white community, the path to a more perfect union means acknowledging that what ails the African American community does not just exist in the minds of black people; that the legacy of discrimination—and current incidents of discrimination, while less overt than in the past—are real and must be addressed. Not just with words, but with deeds—by investing in our schools and our communities; by enforcing our civil rights laws and ensuring fairness in our criminal justice system; by providing this generation with ladders of opportunity that were unavailable for previous generations. It requires all Americans to realize that your dreams do not have to come at the expense of my dreams; that investing in the health, welfare, and education of black and brown and white children will ultimately help all of America prosper.

In the end, then, what is called for is nothing more, and nothing less, than what all the world's great religions demand—that we do unto others as we would have them do unto us. Let us be our brother's keeper, Scripture tells us. Let us be our sister's keeper. Let us find that common stake we all have in one another, and let our politics reflect that spirit as well.

For we have a choice in this country. We can accept a politics that breeds division, and conflict, and cynicism. We can tackle race only as spectacle, as we did in the OJ trial, or in the wake of tragedy, as we did in the aftermath of Katrina,[9] or as fodder for the nightly news. We can play Reverend Wright's sermons on every channel, every day and talk about them from now until the election, and make the only question in this campaign whether or not the American people think that I somehow believe or sympathize with his most offensive words. We can pounce on some gaffe by a Hillary supporter as evidence that she's playing the race card, or we can speculate on whether white men will all flock to John McCain in the general election regardless of his policies.

We can do that.

45

But if we do, I can tell you that in the next election, we'll be talking about some other distraction. And then another one. And then another one. And nothing will change.

That is one option. Or, at this moment, in this election, we can come together and say, "Not this time." This time we want to talk about the crumbling schools

---

9. **Katrina:** In 2005, Hurricane Katrina devastated the city of New Orleans, especially its minority communities; many criticized the government for its slow response. **OJ trial:** In 1994, African American actor and former football player OJ Simpson was tried and acquitted for killing his ex-wife, Nicole Brown Simpson, and her friend Ronald Goldman, both of whom were white. Both incidents caused widespread discussion of the role of race in American society.

that are stealing the future of black children and white children and Asian children and Hispanic children and Native American children. This time we want to reject the cynicism that tells us that these kids can't learn; that those kids who don't look like us are somebody else's problem. The children of America are not those kids, they are our kids, and we will not let them fall behind in a twenty-first-century economy. Not this time.

This time we want to talk about how the lines in the Emergency Room are filled with whites and blacks and Hispanics who do not have health care; who don't have the power on their own to overcome the special interests in Washington, but who can take them on if we do it together.

This time we want to talk about the shuttered mills that once provided a decent life for men and women of every race, and the homes for sale that once belonged to Americans from every religion, every region, every walk of life. This time we want to talk about the fact that the real problem is not that someone who doesn't look like you might take your job; it's that the corporation you work for will ship it overseas for nothing more than a profit.

This time we want to talk about the men and women of every color and creed   50
who serve together, and fight together, and bleed together under the same proud flag. We want to talk about how to bring them home from a war that never should've been authorized and never should've been waged, and we want to talk about how we'll show our patriotism by caring for them, and their families, and giving them the benefits they have earned.

I would not be running for president if I didn't believe with all my heart that this is what the vast majority of Americans want for this country. This union may never be perfect, but generation after generation has shown that it can always be perfected. And today, whenever I find myself feeling doubtful or cynical about this possibility, what gives me the most hope is the next generation—the young people whose attitudes and beliefs and openness to change have already made history in this election.

There is one story in particular that I'd like to leave you with today—a story I told when I had the great honor of speaking on Dr. King's birthday at his home church, Ebenezer Baptist, in Atlanta.

There is a young, twenty-three-year-old white woman named Ashley Baia who organized for our campaign in Florence, South Carolina. She had been working to organize a mostly African American community since the beginning of this campaign, and one day she was at a roundtable discussion where everyone went around telling their story and why they were there.

And Ashley said that when she was nine years old, her mother got cancer. And because she had to miss days of work, she was let go and lost her health care. They had to file for bankruptcy, and that's when Ashley decided that she had to do something to help her mom.

She knew that food was one of their most expensive costs, and so Ashley con-   55
vinced her mother that what she really liked and really wanted to eat more than

anything else was mustard and relish sandwiches. Because that was the cheapest way to eat.

She did this for a year until her mom got better, and she told everyone at the roundtable that the reason she joined our campaign was so that she could help the millions of other children in the country who want and need to help their parents too.

Now Ashley might have made a different choice. Perhaps somebody told her along the way that the source of her mother's problems were blacks who were on welfare and too lazy to work, or Hispanics who were coming into the country illegally. But she didn't. She sought out allies in her fight against injustice.

Anyway, Ashley finished her story and then goes around the room and asks everyone else why they're supporting the campaign. They all have different stories and reasons. Many bring up a specific issue. And finally they come to this elderly black man who's been sitting there quietly the entire time. And Ashley asks him why he's there. And he does not bring up a specific issue. He does not say health care or the economy. He does not say education or the war. He does not say that he was there because of Barack Obama. He simply says to everyone in the room, "I am here because of Ashley."

"I'm here because of Ashley." By itself, that single moment of recognition between that young white girl and that old black man is not enough. It is not enough to give health care to the sick, or jobs to the jobless, or education to our children.

But it is where we start. It is where our union grows stronger. And as so many generations have come to realize over the course of the two hundred and twenty-one years since a band of patriots signed that document in Philadelphia, that is where the perfection begins.

60

UNDERSTANDING THE TEXT

1. How does Obama use the phrase "a more perfect union" in the first part of his speech? How does his use of this phrase contrast with its use in the Preamble to the Constitution? (The Preamble is widely available online.) What about the early American republic does Obama present as imperfect?

2. How does Obama's invocation of "my own American story" help shape his ethos? In what way does he suggest his experiences are representative of the larger American experience?

3. What reason does Obama give for his refusal to disown Reverend Wright? What similarities does he find between Wright and his own grandmother? Is the comparison effective? Why or why not?

4. What issues does Obama feel can unite people of all races? Why does he use "This time we want to talk about . . ." to introduce each of these issues?

5. What is the point of the story about Ashley that Obama ends with? How does he invoke Martin Luther King Jr. in this story? Do you believe that this story provides a good conclusion to his remarks? Explain.

MAKING CONNECTIONS

1. Compare Obama's discussion of the role of churches in addressing racial issues with that of Martin Luther King Jr. in "Letter from Birmingham Jail" (p. 425). Consider how the changes in American culture between 1963 and 2008 may affect their views.

2. Compare Obama's experience growing up on the edge of several cultures with those of Gloria Anzaldúa (p. 205). What common threads do you see in these two readings about the spaces between cultures?

3. How do Obama's views of the origins of poverty and inequality compare to Gandhi's (p. 560)? How do both men deal with historical causes for contemporary inequality?

4. Compare Obama's views of reconciliation with those of Desmond Tutu in "Nuremberg or National Amnesia: A Third Way" (p. 450). Though the historical contexts of the two works are very different, they both address the need for different cultures to learn to trust and forgive each other. Do the two selections appear to be motivated by the same overall philosophy of human nature? Explain.

WRITING ABOUT THE TEXT

1. Write an essay in which you compare "A More Perfect Union" to another major speech on race from a different time, such as Martin Luther King Jr.'s "I Have a Dream." (It is widely reprinted and available online.) Explore the ways that the speeches reflect changes in race relations in America.

2. Write an essay in which you analyze how "A More Perfect Union" is designed to appeal to different audiences at the same time. Consider how and how effectively Obama appeals to black and white Americans, to supporters and detractors, to religious voters, and to observers outside of the United States.

3. Watch the video of "A More Perfect Union" (it is available online) and write an essay in which you compare the effects of reading and viewing the speech. How is the experience of watching Obama deliver the speech different from the experience of reading it?

4. Write an essay in which you analyze the role of religious rhetoric in "A More Perfect Union." How does Obama connect religion and race in the United States? How does this affect his view on race relations? How might the speech's religious language and references affect the reactions and perceptions of his audience?

7

WAR AND PEACE

Is War Ever Justified?

War is . . . inevitable unless we change our social system
and outlaw classes, the struggle for power, and possessions;
and in the event of our success warfare would disappear,
as a symptom vanishes when the disease is cured.
—*Margaret Mead, "Warfare:
An Invention—Not a Biological Necessity"*

THE DEDICATION PAGE of Kenneth Burke's highly influential 1945 treatise on rhetoric, *A Grammar of Motives*, reads simply "*Ad bellum purificandum*," a Latin phrase meaning "toward the purification of war." Argument, Burke believed, could be a socially beneficial outlet for the inherent human tendency toward conflict, a tendency that, if not carefully redirected, leads to violence. Rather than trying to eliminate the tendency, Burke held, we should encourage conflict while taking steps to ensure that it involves words and ideas, not guns and bombs. In this way, war can be "purified" into something useful.

History offers a great deal of evidence to support the premise of Burke's argument, that human beings are, by nature, quarrelsome and disposed to war. Early epic poems such as the *Iliad* and the *Mahābhārata* celebrate the prowess of great warriors in glorious combat; the world's major religious texts—such as the Hebrew Bible, the Quran, the *Tao Te Ching*, and the *Bhagavad Gītā*— are replete with references to, and instructions for, warfare; and abundant historical evidence suggests that warfare has been carried out among the peoples of every continent in every historical period.

The reality of war, however, has always been accompanied by the ideal of peace. Few societies—not even militaristic and violent ones—have considered warfare desirable. Indeed, some of the most compelling art, literature, and philosophy has been produced in cultures so saturated by armed conflict that their greatest minds were enlisted to find ways to bring about peace. China's Period of Warring States, for example, lasted 250 years (475–221 BCE), during which seven separate states fought to unify China under one imperial banner. So many philosophers emerged that this time also became known as the Period of the Hundred Schools. Thinkers as diverse as Confucius, Lao Tzu, Mo Tzu, Mencius, Hsün Tzu, and Sun Tzu offered solutions to ending the wars and bringing about peace and stability. A similar burst of creative output is associated with the Peloponnesian Wars, between Athens and Sparta in ancient Greece; with the political instability and civil warfare of the Italian states during the Renaissance; with the Napoleonic Wars, in nineteenth-century Western Europe; and with the almost continuous state of war (either overt or, as in the Cold War, indirect) between various superpowers, for most of the twentieth century.

This chapter begins with two readings from a period that saw some of the most sustained, continuous warfare in the history of the world: China's Period of Warring States. The first of these readings, Mo Tzu's "Against Offensive Warfare," criticizes all parties in war for ignoring the basic rules of human behavior. A very different view is offered by Mo Tzu's contemporary, Sun Tzu, a general who makes no attempt to evaluate the morality of war but simply insists that once the decision is made to engage in an armed conflict, the only rational aim is to win as quickly as possible. Sun Tzu's essay is followed by a logical proof from the medieval Christian writer Thomas Aquinas, who lays out the theological requirements for considering a war "just," and the Renaissance humanist Erasmus of Rotterdam, who argues that war always diminishes the humanity of those who fight.

In the first reading from the twentieth century, anthropologist Margaret Mead refutes the claim that war is inevitable. In her essay "Warfare: An Invention—Not a Biological Necessity," Mead marshals evidence from cultures throughout the world to argue that warfare is not an inherent part of the human condition but rather an invention that emerged to fulfill a certain function. Writing soon after Mead, at the height of World War II, George Orwell moves the discussion of warfare from the abstract to the specific. His essay "Pacifism and the War," confronts head-on the question of what people who love peace should do about a dictator intent on perpetuating violence. Lofty ideals about peace and nonviolence, Orwell insists, have little value when one confronts a ruler who insists on making war.

The final written selections in the chapter present revolutions—one horribly violent and one relatively peaceful—from the perspectives of women who experienced them firsthand. The first of these comes from the transcript of an interview with Marevasei Kachere, a woman who participated in Zimbabwe's War of Independence as a teenager. The second comes from the Nobel lecture delivered by Yemeni journalist Tawakkol Karman, who won the 2011 Nobel Peace Prize for her role in advancing democracy throughout the Middle East in the movement that has become known as the Arab Spring.

This chapter also contains three images designed to capture the human experience of war and peace. Eugene Delacroix's painting *Liberty Leading the People* depicts a battle scene from the French Revolution in which Liberty, an allegory of freedom and the willingness to fight for it when necessary, leads the people of France to victory. Pablo Picasso's *Guernica*, painted soon after German planes bombed thousands of innocent civilians in the Basque village of Guernica, portrays the human cost of war, considered apart from the abstract ideals of its justness or effectiveness. And the final image, a photograph of the British Women of World War II Memorial, speaks to the deep human need to remember those who have made great sacrifices on and off the fields of battle.

In very different and sometimes surprising ways, the texts in this chapter attempt to answer a series of fundamental questions: Is war inevitable? Is peace always desirable? Are ideals worth fighting for, killing for, dying for? Can deep conflict and division be managed without resorting to war? Perhaps no questions have been as important to the shaping of societies in the past, and perhaps no answers are more important to the shaping of humanity in the future.

MO TZU
Against Offensive Warfare
[CIRCA 425 BCE]

CONTEMPORARY READERS OFTEN find the writings of the ancient Chinese phi-losopher Mo Tzu (circa 470–circa 391 BCE) surprisingly accessible. Unlike many of his contemporaries, Mo Tzu did not write in riddles, paradoxes, and short aphorisms. Rather, he wrote in a format very similar to the modern philosophical essay, with a clear thesis statement at the beginning followed by evidence to support it. The content of Mo Tzu's writings also resonates with modern readers, who appreciate many of the arguments that he levied against the Confucians and the Taoists, the principal philosophical opponents of the philosophy, Mohism, that he founded.

Like Mencius and Hsün Tzu, Mo Tzu wrote during the Period of Warring States (475–221 BCE)—two and a half centuries of civil war among seven Chinese king-doms who were struggling for control of the empire. During this time of war, Mo Tzu spoke chiefly of love—universal love, or the love of all human beings, which formed the cornerstone of Mohism. As innocent as this precept seems now, it caused tremendous controversy at the time. Confucians felt that the idea that people should love and respect each other equally undermined the traditional social structure, which called for people to love and respect some (ancestors, parents, elder brothers) more than others. Taoists objected to the Mohist belief that human beings are more deserving of love and respect than any other part of the cosmos, such as insects or rocks.

Along with universal love, Mo Tzu preached the pragmatic philosophy that people should only do that which produces tangible benefit for themselves and others. On these grounds, he opposed much of what was revered in Chinese culture, such as the observance of religious rituals, the staging of elaborate funerals, and the playing of music. These views further alienated him from devout Confucians, whose lives were structured around the rituals that, for Confucius, were essential to a moral life.

The idea of war was a frequent target for Mo Tzu and his followers. The slaughter of other human beings—so common during the Period of Warring States—clearly violated the principle of universal love. But Mo Tzu also believed that war was a foolish waste of resources. The selection presented here is the first, and shortest, of three treatises that Mo Tzu wrote in opposition to war.

Mo Tzu's rhetoric in this passage consists primarily of a series of analogies between war and individual acts of violence or theft. These analogies increase in persuasive power as Mo Tzu presents them and then asks how people can con-demn all of the small atrocities and yet support the same actions when they are conducted on a large scale by states and armies.

If a man enters an orchard and steals the peaches and plums, everyone who hears about it will condemn him, and if those above who administer the government catch him they will punish him. Why? Because he injures others to benefit himself. When it comes to carrying off dogs, swine, chickens, and piglings, the deed is even more unrighteous than entering an orchard to steal peaches and plums. Why? Because the loss to others is greater. It shows a greater lack of benevolence and is a more serious crime. When it comes to breaking into another man's stable and seizing his horses and cows, the deed is even more unrighteous than carrying off dogs, swine, chickens, and piglings. Why? Because the loss to others is greater, and if the loss is greater, it shows a greater lack of benevolence and is a more serious crime. And when it comes to murdering an innocent man, stripping him of his clothing, and appropriating his spear and sword, the deed is even more unrighteous than breaking into a stable and seizing someone's horses and cows. Why? Because the injury to others is even greater, and if the injury is greater, it shows a greater lack of benevolence and is a more serious crime.

Now all the gentlemen in the world know enough to condemn such acts and brand them as unrighteous. And yet when it comes to the even greater unrighteousness of offensive warfare against other states, they do not know enough to condemn it. On the contrary, they praise it and call it righteous. Is this what it means to know the difference between righteousness and unrighteousness?

If someone kills one man, he is condemned as unrighteous and must pay for his crime with his own life. According to this reasoning, if someone kills ten men, then he is ten times as unrighteous and should pay for his crime with ten lives, or if he kills a hundred men he is a hundred times as unrighteous and should pay for his crime with a hundred lives.

Now all the gentlemen in the world know enough to condemn such crimes and brand them as unrighteous. And yet when it comes to the even greater unrighteousness of offensive warfare against other states, they do not know enough to condemn it. On the contrary, they praise it and call it righteous. Truly they do not know what unrighteousness is. So they make a record of their wars to be handed down to posterity. If they knew that such wars were unrighteous, then what reason would they have for making a record of their unrighteous deeds to be handed down to posterity?

Now if there were a man who, on seeing a little bit of black, called it black but, on seeing a lot of black, called it white, we would conclude that he could not tell the difference between black and white. Or if there were a man who, on tasting a little bit of bitterness, called it bitter but, on tasting a lot, called it sweet, we would conclude that he could not distinguish between bitter and sweet. Now when a great wrong is committed and a state is attacked, men do not know enough to condemn it, but on the contrary praise it and call it righteous. Is this what it means to be able to distinguish between righteousness and unrighteousness? So we know that the gentlemen of the world are confused about the distinction between righteousness and unrighteousness.

5

UNDERSTANDING THE TEXT

1. What comparisons does Mo Tzu use to illustrate the immorality of war? Are these comparisons valid? Are they effective in presenting his argument?

2. What is the moral imperative at the heart of all of the actions, including war, that Mo Tzu considers evil? Can his position be reduced to a "golden rule" of appropriate behavior?

3. What is the point of Mo Tzu's discussion of black and white? What is he saying about human perceptions of scale?

4. What does Mo Tzu mean by "offensive warfare"? What do you think he would say about defensive warfare? What conditions does he suggest have to be present to make war immoral?

MAKING CONNECTIONS

1. Compare Mo Tzu's argument in "Against Offensive Warfare" with the argument that he makes in "Against Music" (p. 236). What features do offensive warfare and music have in common?

2. Which of Thomas Aquinas's principles of a just war would Mo Tzu agree with? Which might he disagree with? Why? What might he say about an offensive war conducted to try to achieve a moral or utilitarian purpose?

3. Why is Mo Tzu's utilitarian position so different from Garrett Hardin's argument in "Lifeboat Ethics: The Case against Helping the Poor" (p. 582), which is also based on utilitarian principles?

WRITING ABOUT THE TEXT

1. Analyze the movement that Mo Tzu makes from small-scale to large-scale moral arguments. Evaluate the effectiveness of this movement in terms of inductive reasoning (pp. 655).

2. Write a rebuttal to Mo Tzu's argument by invoking Thomas Aquinas or George Orwell to argue that there are some situations that justify even offensive warfare.

SUN TZU
from *The Art of War*
[400–320 BCE]

VERY LITTLE IS KNOWN about Sun Tzu, the Chinese general reputed to be the author of *The Art of War*, one of the most influential military treatises of all time. Scholars generally date the composition of the text to between 400 and 320 BCE, in the turbulent epoch of Chinese history known as the Period of Warring States (475–221 BCE), which occurred after the Chou Dynasty collapsed and before the Chinese mainland was unified under the Ch'in Dynasty. During this period of turmoil and constant warfare, the philosophies of Confucianism, Taoism, Moism, and Legalism emerged and competed for followers among the warring factions, and organized warfare became the subject of sustained and serious examination.

Though the existence of a historical figure named Sun Tzu cannot be conclusively demonstrated, the influence of *The Art of War* on Chinese military and political thought cannot be underestimated. Chinese texts from the classical period (about 500–200 BCE) refer to it continuously, and it shaped the military strategies of China, Japan, Korea, and Vietnam for nearly 2,500 years. One of Sun Tzu's most recent devotees, the communist leader Mao Tse Tung (1893–1976), used many of the work's principles to seize power in China in 1949.

Like many philosophical texts of ancient China, *The Art of War* is a series of epigrams rather than a consistent or systematic explanation of the author's point of view. Each sentence of Sun Tzu's work is designed to be read and pondered as an individual unit of thought; however, these maxims all work together to produce a pragmatic and surprisingly modern view of the process of warfare. Sun Tzu persuades his readers not through argument, but through a powerfully constructed ethos and through the startling resonance that these maxims have with many people's experiences.

The maxims of *The Art of War* go well beyond giving prescriptions for armed warfare. They touch, often in very deep ways, on the essential structure of human conflict. Perhaps this is why *The Art of War* was reborn in the late twentieth century as a handbook for corporate managers looking for ways to defeat their competition and advance their own product lines. The following maxims from *The Art of War* constitute the whole of Chapter 3, "Attack by Stratagem."

1. Generally in war the best policy is to take a state intact; to ruin it is inferior to this.
2. To capture the enemy's army is better than to destroy it; to take intact a battalion, a company or a five-man squad is better than to destroy them.

3. For to win one hundred victories in one hundred battles is not the acme of skill. To subdue the enemy without fighting is the acme of skill.

4. Thus, what is of extreme importance in war is to attack the enemy's strategy.

5. Next best is to disrupt his alliances.

6. The next best is to attack his army.

7. The worst policy is to attack cities. Attack cities only when there is no alternative.

8. To prepare the shielded wagons and make ready the necessary arms and equipment requires at least three months; to pile up earthen ramps against the walls an additional three months will be needed.

9. If the general is unable to control his impatience and orders his troops to swarm up the wall like ants, one-third of them will be killed without taking the city. Such is the calamity of these attacks.

10. Thus, those skilled in war subdue the enemy's army without battle. They capture his cities without assaulting them and overthrow his state without protracted operations.

11. Your aim must be to take All-under-Heaven intact. Thus your troops are not worn out and your gains will be complete. This is the art of offensive strategy.

12. Consequently, the art of using troops is this: When ten to the enemy's one, surround him.

13. When five times his strength, attack him.

14. If double his strength, divide him.

15. If equally matched you may engage him.

16. If weaker numerically, be capable of withdrawing.

17. And if in all respects unequal, be capable of eluding him, for a small force is but booty for one more powerful.

18. Now the general is the protector of the state. If this protection is all-embracing, the state will surely be strong; if defective, the state will certainly be weak.

19. Now there are three ways in which a ruler can bring misfortune upon his army:

20. When ignorant that the army should not advance, to order an advance or ignorant that it should not retire, to order a retirement. This is described as "hobbling the army."

21. When ignorant of military affairs, to participate in their administration. This causes the officers to be perplexed.

22. When ignorant of command problems to share in the exercise of responsibilities. This engenders doubts in the minds of the officers.

23. If the army is confused and suspicious, neighbouring rulers will cause trouble. This is what is meant by the saying: "A confused army leads to victory."

24. Now there are five circumstances in which victory may be predicted:

25. He who knows when he can fight and when he cannot will be victorious.

26. He who understands how to use both large and small forces will be victorious.

27. He whose ranks are united in purpose will be victorious.

28. He who is prudent and lies in wait for an enemy who is not will be victorious.

29. He whose generals are able and not interfered with by the sovereign will be victorious.
30. It is in these five matters that the way to victory is known.
31. Therefore I say: "Know the enemy and know yourself; in a hundred battles you will never be in peril.
32. When you are ignorant of the enemy but know yourself, your chances of winning or losing are equal.
33. If ignorant of both your enemy and of yourself, you are certain in every battle to be in peril."

UNDERSTANDING THE TEXT

1. Why does Sun Tzu structure his advice on war as a series of short epigrams with no expansion or development? What is the rhetorical effect of this structure? Is it more or less effective than a traditional essay format?

2. What does "subdue the enemy without fighting" mean? How is it possible to achieve victory without conflict? Why would a peaceful victory be considered superior to winning an armed conflict?

3. Why did Sun Tzu hold that "the worst policy is to attack cities"?

4. Why does Sun Tzu place such great importance on a commander's self-knowledge? How is self-knowledge important beyond the scope of military conflict? What kinds of mistakes can be made by people who do not really understand themselves?

5. Can Sun Tzu's philosophy of war be applied beyond the scope of military affairs? Do any of his aphorisms seem relevant to other kinds of human conflict? Why might *The Art of War* be a bestseller among American business professionals?

MAKING CONNECTIONS

1. Can Sun Tzu's view of war be reconciled with Erasmus's view that war and violence destroy our humanity? How might Sun Tzu respond to such an assertion?

2. How might Sun Tzu's advice on warfare be interpreted by George Orwell (p. 508), a former pacifist who believed that the Nazi threat made defensive warfare a moral requirement?

3. Sun Tzu was likely familiar with the teachings of Confucius and Lao Tzu. How does this chapter of *The Art of War* appear to have been influenced by Taoism as found in the *Tao Te Ching* (p. 384) and Confucianism as found in the works of Mencius (p. 78) and Hsün Tzu (p. 84)?

4. What view of human nature do you detect in Sun Tzu's writings? What does he assert as the underlying motivations of most people? How do his views compare with other Chinese writers of the same period, such as Mencius (p. 78) and Hsün Tzu (p. 84)?

WRITING ABOUT THE TEXT

1. Write a chapter of *The Art of War for College Students*, *The Art of War for Corporate America*, or some other version of this classic text for a contemporary audience you know well. What simple, direct aphorisms could be relevant to contemporary situations involving conflict?

2. Analyze one or two underlying assumptions of *The Art of War*. What principle or principles are the aphorisms based on? Are these overall principles stated anywhere in the text, or are they left unstated, and why is this so?

3. Compare *The Art of War* with *The Prince* (p. 405). How do Sun Tzu and Machiavelli agree about the nature of effective leadership? How do they disagree?

LAURENTIUS DE VOLTOLINA
Liber Ethicorum des Henricus de Alemania, circa 1350 (book illustration on parchment).
Wikimedia Commons

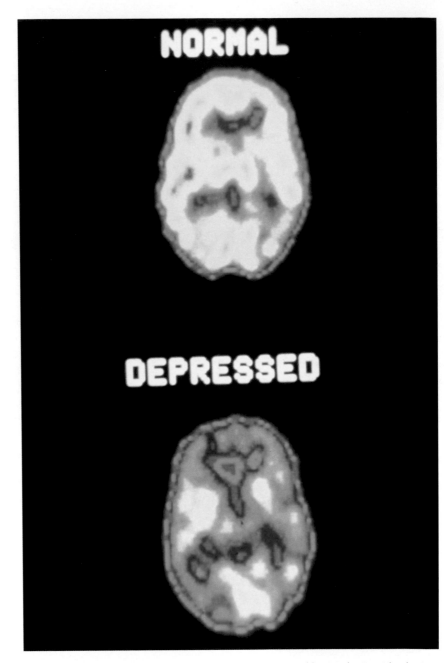

PET scan of a deoxyglucose study that compares a normal human brain with a brain of someone suffering from depression.
Science Source

154

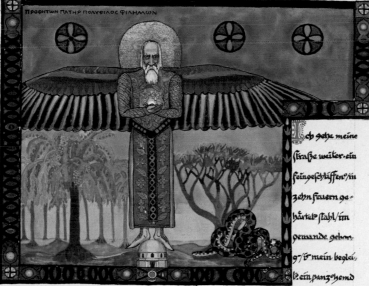

CARL JUNG

Selection from *The Red Book*, date unknown (tempera on paper).

JOHANNES VERMEER
Study of a Young Woman, circa 1665–67 (oil on canvas).
Metropolitan Museum of Art, New York / Wikimedia Commons and Art Resource

WILLIAM BLAKE

The Tyger, 1794 (relief etchings printed in orange-brown).

Metropolitan Museum of Art, New York / Wikimedia Commons

LISA YUSKAVAGE
Babie I, 2003 (oil on linen).
David Zwirner Art Gallery, New York and London / Courtesy of the artist and David Zwirner.

JOSEPH WRIGHT OF DERBY
An Experiment on a Bird in the Air Pump, 1768 (oil on canvas).
National Gallery, London, UK / Bridgeman Art Library

EUGÈNE DELACROIX
Liberty Leading the People, 28 July 1830, 1830 (oil on canvas).
Louvre, Paris, France / Bridgeman Art Library

ST. THOMAS AQUINAS
from *Summa Theologica*
[1265–1274]

THOMAS AQUINAS (1224 or 1225–1274) was born Tommaso d'Aquino to an aristocratic family in Italy and received a classical education, first at the Benedictine monastery of Montecassino, and later at the University of Naples. In 1243, against the strong objections of his family, he joined the recently founded Dominican Order and began to study theology at the University of Paris, where he was eventually awarded a doctorate in theology. He spent his life teaching in universities and writing several massive theological works, which have since become cornerstones of Catholic doctrine.

When Aquinas began his studies, Aristotle's works were becoming increasingly important in Christian Europe, and conflicts between faith and reason were occurring with increasing frequency among European intellectuals. As a devoted student of classical philosophy, Aquinas set out to reconcile Aristotle's rigorous methods of logical analysis with what he believed to be the revealed truths of the Bible and Christianity. He wanted not merely to synthesize Aristotle and the Bible but to reconcile faith and reason as they were understood in his society. By far, his most ambitious work is the *Summa Theologica* ("a summary of theology"), a three-volume work that covers nearly every imaginable topic of Christian ethical and metaphysical belief.

The *Summa Theologica* is a series of thousands of deductive proofs on more than six hundred major subjects. In a typical proof, Aquinas introduces a proposition and lists possible objections to it; he then restates his position clearly and succinctly, citing both the Bible and the writings of the Church fathers, such as St. Augustine, and proceeds to answer the objections in order. Once the proposition is thus "proved"—all possible objections to it answered—it can serve as evidence in a later proof.

The following selection, from the second book of the *Summa Theologica*, is the first of four proofs that Aquinas offers on the subject of war. In this proof, Aquinas lays down the conditions that must be met for an armed conflict to be considered a "just war." As the Middle Ages progressed and Christian nations struggled to reconcile warfare with a religion that emphasizes peace, Aquinas's conditions became the foundation for the "just war theory" in Christian doctrine, a theory that the Catholic Church still applies to wars.

"Whether It Is Always Sinful to Wage War?"

Objection 1: It would seem that it is always sinful to wage war. Because punishment is not inflicted except for sin. Now those who wage war are threatened by Our Lord with punishment, according to Mt. 26:52: "All that take the sword shall perish with the sword." Therefore all wars are unlawful.

Objection 2: Further, whatever is contrary to a Divine precept is a sin. But war is contrary to a Divine precept, for it is written (Mt. 5:39): "But I say to you not to resist evil"; and (Rm. 12:19): "Not revenging yourselves, my dearly beloved, but give place unto wrath." Therefore war is always sinful.

Objection 3: Further, nothing, except sin, is contrary to an act of virtue. But war is contrary to peace. Therefore war is always a sin.

Objection 4: Further, the exercise of a lawful thing is itself lawful, as is evident in scientific exercises. But warlike exercises which take place in tournaments are forbidden by the Church, since those who are slain in these trials are deprived of ecclesiastical burial. Therefore it seems that war is a sin in itself.

On the contrary, Augustine[1] says in a sermon on the son of the centurion: "If the Christian Religion forbade war altogether, those who sought salutary advice in the Gospel would rather have been counselled to cast aside their arms, and to give up soldiering altogether. On the contrary, they were told: "Do violence to no man . . . and be content with your pay". If he commanded them to be content with their pay, he did not forbid soldiering."

I answer that, In order for a war to be just, three things are necessary. First, the authority of the sovereign by whose command the war is to be waged. For it is not the business of a private individual to declare war, because he can seek for redress of his rights from the tribunal of his superior. Moreover it is not the business of a private individual to summon together the people, which has to be done in wartime. And as the care of the common weal[2] is committed to those who are in authority, it is their business to watch over the common weal of the city, kingdom or province subject to them. And just as it is lawful for them to have recourse to the sword in defending that common weal against internal disturbances, when they punish evil-doers, according to the words of the Apostle (Rm. 13:4): "He beareth not the sword in vain: for he is God's minister, an avenger to execute wrath upon him that doth evil"; so too, it is their business to have recourse to the sword of war in defending the common weal against external enemies. Hence it is said to those who are in authority (Ps. 81:4): "Rescue the poor: and deliver the needy out of the hand of the sinner"; and for this reason Augustine says (Contra Faust. xxii, 75): "The natural order conducive to peace

5

1. **Augustine:** early Christian writer (354–430 CE) and bishop of the North African town of Hippo, in present-day Algeria. Augustine's writings in *The City of God* and elsewhere are generally considered the starting point of the Christian "just war" theory.

2. **The common weal:** "commonweal" also; refers to the common interest of the general public.

among mortals demands that the power to declare and counsel war should be in the hands of those who hold the supreme authority."

Secondly, a just cause is required, namely that those who are attacked, should be attacked because they deserve it on account of some fault. Wherefore Augustine says (Questions. in Hept., qu. x, super Jos.): "A just war is wont to be described as one that avenges wrongs, when a nation or state has to be punished, for refusing to make amends for the wrongs inflicted by its subjects, or to restore what it has seized unjustly."

Thirdly, it is necessary that the belligerents should have a rightful intention, so that they intend the advancement of good, or the avoidance of evil. Hence Augustine says (De Verb. Dom.): "True religion looks upon as peaceful those wars that are waged not for motives of aggrandizement, or cruelty, but with the object of securing peace, of punishing evil-doers, and of uplifting the good." For it may happen that the war is declared by the legitimate authority, and for a just cause, and yet be rendered unlawful through a wicked intention. Hence Augustine says (Contra Faust. xxii, 74): "The passion for inflicting harm, the cruel thirst for vengeance, an unpacific and relentless spirit, the fever of revolt, the lust of power, and such like things, all these are rightly condemned in war."

Reply to Objection 1: As Augustine says (Contra Faust, xxii, 70): "To take the sword is to arm oneself in order to take the life of anyone, without the command or permission of superior or lawful authority." On the other hand, to have recourse to the sword (as a private person) by the authority of the sovereign or judge, or (as a public person) through zeal for justice, and by the authority, so to speak, of God, is not to "take the sword," but to use it as commissioned by another, wherefore it does not deserve punishment. And yet even those who make sinful use of the sword are not always slain with the sword, yet they always perish with their own sword, because, unless they repent, they are punished eternally for their sinful use of the sword.

Reply to Objection 2: Such like precepts, as Augustine observes (De Serm. Dom. in   10
Monte i, 19), should always be borne in readiness of mind, so that we be ready to obey them, and, if necessary, to refrain from resistance or self-defense. Nevertheless it is necessary sometimes for a man to act otherwise for the common good, or for the good of those with whom he is fighting. Hence Augustine says (Ep. ad Marcellin. cxxxviii): "Those whom we have to punish with a kindly severity, it is necessary to handle in many ways against their will. For when we are stripping a man of the lawlessness of sin, it is good for him to be vanquished, since nothing is more hopeless than the happiness of sinners, whence arises a guilty impunity, and an evil will, like an internal enemy."

Reply to Objection 3: Those who wage war justly aim at peace, and so they are not opposed to peace, except to the evil peace, which Our Lord "came not to send upon earth" (Mt. 10:34). Hence Augustine says (Ep. ad Bonif. clxxxix): "We do not seek peace in order to be at war, but we go to war that we may have peace. Be peaceful, therefore, in warring, so that you may vanquish those whom you war against, and bring them to the prosperity of peace."

Reply to Objection 4: Manly exercises in warlike feats of arms are not all forbidden, but those which are inordinate and perilous, and end in slaying or plundering. In olden times warlike exercises presented no such danger, and hence they were called "exercises of arms" or "bloodless wars," as Jerome[3] states in an epistle.

UNDERSTANDING THE TEXT

1. What four moral objections to war does Aquinas raise at the beginning of this proof? How does he respond to each one? Are his replies effective? What is the rhetorical effect of Aquinas's raising the objections and then responding to them? What other objections might Aquinas have raised?

2. Choose one of the objections that Aquinas answers and write it as a deductive syllogism (p. 652) with a major premise, a minor premise, and a conclusion.

3. Why does Aquinas consider it necessary for an appropriate "sovereign" to command the waging of war? What would constitute such an authority?

4. What kinds of causes does Aquinas consider sufficient rationale for the waging of war? What kinds of causes does he consider insufficient?

5. Aquinas's third necessary condition for waging war is a pure motive for doing so. Would it be possible, under the terms of Aquinas's argument, for a conflict to meet the first two conditions but be unjust because at least one nation has an impure motive?

6. Does Aquinas sufficiently prove the proposition that participating in a war is not always sinful? How would you argue against him? Try to formulate a logical proof to rebut his arguments.

MAKING CONNECTIONS

1. Compare Aquinas's requirements for a just war with Orwell's view of a necessary war. Does the conflict with fascism, as Orwell describes it, meet Aquinas's standards for a just war? Explain.

2. One of Aquinas's major purposes in the *Summa Theologica* was to harmonize Christian theology with Aristotle's logical methodology. Is the proof he offers here consistent with the philosophy of logic that Aristotle outlines in the *Rhetoric* (p. 177)? Explain.

3. How would Aquinas advise a soldier who was asked to fight in an unjust war? Would he say that it is more important to follow the will of the sovereign or to disobey that

3. **Jerome:** early Christian writer and scholar (circa 347–419 or 420 CE) best known as the translator of the Latin, or "Vulgate," version of the Bible, the standard version in Christian nations throughout the Middle Ages.

will in the way advocated by Martin Luther King Jr. in "Letter from Birmingham Jail" (p. 425)?

WRITING ABOUT THE TEXT

1. Analyze any modern armed conflict using Aquinas's three criteria for a "just war." Consider whether or not these seven-hundred-year-old principles still provide a useful lens through which to view events.

2. Evaluate Aquinas's use of deductive reasoning in this passage. (See p. 652 for an introduction to deductive reasoning.) Does he construct valid syllogisms, in which the conclusions flow automatically from the premises?

3. Contrast Aquinas's "just war" argument with Erasmus's pacifist argument in "Against War."

4. Choose an important contemporary issue and construct a "proof" of your position on it, using this selection from *Summa Theologica* as a model. Follow Aquinas's organization: state a proposition, outline the potential objections to your case, summarize your basic argument, and respond to each objection.

DESIDERIUS ERASMUS
from *Against War*
[1515]

DESIDERIUS ERASMUS (1446–1536), one of the most important thinkers of the European Renaissance, was born in the Dutch city of Rotterdam. He was the out-of-wedlock child of a Catholic priest and grew up with very few luxuries; still, he received a first-class education in the religious schools of the Netherlands, where he learned to speak and write fluently in Latin. At the age of twenty-five, he became a priest, but he received a special dispensation to continue his studies and to serve as the secretary to Henry of Bergen, the Bishop of Cambrai.

Erasmus soon developed a reputation as a first-rate scholar. He studied in both France and England and wrote important works of theology and philosophy in Latin. His critical editions of the New Testament in both Greek and Latin played an important role in the Protestant Reformation, much of which occurred during his lifetime. Like Martin Luther and John Calvin, Erasmus was a frequent critic of the Catholic Church, but he never rejected its authority, believing that it could be reformed most effectively from the inside.

Erasmus was closely associated with the movement of Renaissance scholars and philosophers known as humanism. Humanists believed that people were capable of profound thought and great beauty, and that the works of human culture should therefore be studied. Whereas most of the scholars of previous centuries were cloistered monks studying more abstract logic and obscure theology, humanists lived among regular people and studied those disciplines that we now call "humanities," such as literature, art, and history.

Erasmus brings his profoundly humanistic assumptions to the question of human conflict in this selection from his essay "Against War." Here, Erasmus argues that engaging in any kind of violence requires us to reject what is most human about ourselves and embrace what we have in common with beasts. This essay also demonstrates the rhetorical style that Erasmus made famous in his rhetorical treatise, *De Copia*. He begins with a simple assertion, such as "human beings were made for friendship, not for war," and then deepens this assertion with increasingly elaborate examples.

Dulce Bellum Inexpertis

It is both an elegant proverb, and among all others, by the writings of many excellent authors, full often and solemnly used, Dulce bellum inexpertis, that is to say, War is sweet to them that know it not. There be some things among mortal men's businesses, in the which how great danger and hurt there is, a man cannot perceive till he make a proof. The love and friendship of a great man is sweet to them that be not expert: he that hath had thereof experience, is afraid. It seemeth to be a gay and a glorious thing, to strut up and down among the nobles of the court, and to be occupied in the king's business; but old men, to whom that thing by long experience is well known, do gladly abstain themselves from such felicity. It seemeth a pleasant thing to be in love with a young damsel; but that is unto them that have not yet perceived how much grief and bitterness is in such love. So after this manner of fashion, this proverb may be applied to every business that is adjoined with great peril and with many evils: the which no man will take on hand, but he that is young and wanteth experience of things. . . .

Then first of all if one would consider well but the behaviour and shape of man's body shall he not forthwith perceive that Nature, or rather God, hath shaped this creature, not to war, but to friendship, not to destruction, but to health, not to wrong, but to kindness and benevolence? For whereas Nature hath armed all other beasts with their own armour, as the violence of the bulls she hath armed with horns, the ramping lion with claws; to the boar she hath given the gnashing tusks; she hath armed the elephant with a long trump snout, besides his great huge body and hardness of the skin; she hath fenced the crocodile with a skin as hard as a plate; to the dolphin fish she hath given fins instead of a dart; the porcupine she defendeth with thorns; the ray and thornback with sharp prickles; to the cock she hath given strong spurs; some she fenceth with a shell, some with a hard hide, as it were thick leather, or bark of a tree; some she provideth to save by swiftness of flight, as doves; and to some she hath given venom instead of a weapon; to some she hath given a much horrible and ugly look, she hath given terrible eyes and grunting voice; and she hath also set among some of them continual dissension and debate—man alone she hath brought forth all naked, weak, tender, and without any armour, with most soft flesh and smooth skin.

There is nothing at all in all his members that may seem to be ordained to war, or to any violence. I will not say at this time, that where all other beasts, anon as they are brought forth, they are able of themselves to get their food. Man alone cometh so forth, that a long season after he is born, he dependeth altogether on the help of others. He can neither speak nor go, nor yet take meat; he desireth help only by his infant crying: so that a man may, at the least way, by this conject, that this creature alone was born all to love and amity, which specially increaseth and is fast knit together by good turns done eftsoons[1] of one to another. And for this cause Nature would, that a man should not so much thank her, for the gift of life, which she hath given unto him, as he should thank kindness and benevolence, whereby he might evidently understand himself, that he was altogether dedicate and bounden to the gods of graces, that is to say, to kindness, benevolence, and amity.

---

1. **Eftsoons:** immediately afterward.

And besides this Nature hath given unto man a countenance not terrible and loathly, as unto other brute beasts; but meek and demure, representing the very tokens of love and benevolence. She hath given him amiable eyes, and in them assured marks of the inward mind. She hath ordained him arms to clip and embrace. She hath given him the wit and understanding to kiss: whereby the very minds and hearts of men should be coupled together, even as though they touched each other. Unto man alone she hath given laughing, a token of good cheer and gladness. To man alone she hath given weeping tears, as it were a pledge or token of meekness and mercy. Yea, and she hath given him a voice not threatening and horrible, as unto other brute beasts, but amiable and pleasant. Nature not yet content with all this, she hath given unto man alone the commodity of speech and reasoning: the which things verily may specially both get and nourish benevolence, so that nothing at all should be done among men by violence.

She hath endued man with hatred of solitariness, and with love of company. She hath utterly sown in man the very seeds of benevolence. She hath so done, that the selfsame thing, that is most wholesome, should be most sweet and delectable. For what is more delectable than a friend? And again, what thing is more necessary? Moreover, if a man might lead all his life most profitably without any meddling with other men, yet nothing would seem pleasant without a fellow: except a man would cast off all humanity, and forsaking his own kind would become a beast. 5

Besides all this, Nature hath endued man with knowledge of liberal sciences and a fervent desire of knowledge: which thing as it doth most specially withdraw man's wit from all beastly wildness, so hath it a special grace to get and knit together love and friendship. For I dare boldly say, that neither affinity nor yet kindred doth bind the minds of men together with straiter and surer bands of amity, than doth the fellowship of them that be learned in good letters and honest studies.

And above all this, Nature hath divided among men by a marvellous variety the gifts, as well of the soul as of the body, to the intent truly that every man might find in every singular person one thing or other, which they should either love or praise for the excellency thereof; or else greatly desire and make much of it, for the need and profit that cometh thereof. Finally she hath endowed man with a spark of a godly mind: so that though he see no reward, yet of his own courage he delighteth to do every man good: for unto God it is most proper and natural, by his benefit, to do everybody good. Else what meaneth it, that we rejoice and conceive in our minds no little pleasure when we perceive that any creature is by our means preserved.

Moreover God hath ordained man in this world, as it were the very image of himself, to the intent, that he, as it were a god on earth, should provide for the wealth of all creatures. And this thing the very brute beasts do also perceive, for we may see, that not only the tame beasts, but also the leopards, lions, and other more fierce and wild, when they be in any great jeopardy, they flee to man for succour. So man is, when all things fail, the last refuge to all manner of creatures. He is unto them all the very assured altar and sanctuary.

I have here painted out to you the image of man as well as I can. On the other side (if it like you) against the figure of Man, let us portray the fashion and shape of War.

Now, then, imagine in thy mind, that thou dost behold two hosts of barbarous people, of whom the look is fierce and cruel, and the voice horrible; the terrible and fearful rustling and glistering of their harness and weapons; the unlovely murmur of so huge a multitude; the eyes sternly menacing; the bloody blasts and terrible sounds of trumpets and clarions; the thundering of the guns, no less fearful than thunder indeed, but much more hurtful; the frenzied cry and clamour, the furious and mad running together, the outrageous slaughter, the cruel chances of them that flee and of those that are stricken down and slain, the heaps of slaughters, the fields overflowed with blood, the rivers dyed red with man's blood. And it chanceth oftentimes, that the brother fighteth with the brother, one kinsman with another, friend against friend; and in that common furious desire ofttimes one thrusteth his weapon quite through the body of another that never gave him so much as a foul word.

Verily, this tragedy containeth so many mischiefs, that it would abhor any man's heart to speak thereof. I will let pass to speak of the hurts which are in comparison of the other but light and common, as the treading down and destroying of the corn all[2] about, the burning of towns, the villages fired, the driving away of cattle, the ravishing of maidens, the old men led forth in captivity, the robbing of churches, and all things confounded and full of thefts, pillages, and violence. Neither I will not speak now of those things which are wont to follow the most happy and most just war of all.

The poor commons pillaged, the nobles overcharged; so many old men of their children bereaved, yea, and slain also in the slaughter of their children; so many old women destitute, whom sorrow more cruelly slayeth than the weapon itself; so many honest wives become widows, so many children fatherless, so many lamentable houses, so many rich men brought to extreme poverty. And what needeth it here to speak of the destruction of good manners, since there is no man but knoweth right well that the universal pestilence of all mischievous living proceedeth at once from war. Thereof cometh despising of virtue and godly living; thereof cometh, that the laws are neglected and not regarded; thereof cometh a prompt and a ready stomach, boldly to do every mischievous deed.

Out of this fountain spring so huge great companies of thieves, robbers, sacrilegers, and murderers. And what is most grievous of all, this mischievous pestilence cannot keep herself within her bounds; but after it is begun in some one corner, it doth not only (as a contagious disease) spread abroad and infect the countries near adjoining to it, but also it draweth into that common tumult and troublous business the countries that be very far off, either for need, or by reason of affinity, or else by occasion of some league made. Yea and moreover, one war springeth of another: of a dissembled war there cometh war indeed, and of a very small, a right great war

---

2. **Corn:** before the discovery of the New World, a generic term for grain.

hath risen. Nor it chanceth oftentimes none otherwise in these things than it is feigned of the monster, which lay in the lake or pond called Lerna[3]. . . .

War, what other thing else is it than a common manslaughter of many men together, and a robbery, the which, the farther it sprawleth abroad, the more mischievous it is? But many gross gentlemen nowadays laugh merrily at these things, as though they were the dreams and dotings of schoolmen, the which, saving the shape, have no point of manhood, yet seem they in their own conceit to be gods. And yet of those beginnings, we see we be run so far in madness, that we do naught else all our life-days.

UNDERSTANDING THE TEXT

1. What is the meaning of the proverb that Erasmus begins with, "dulce bellum inexpertis"? How does this set the tone for the essay?

2. What evidence does Erasmus give to support the assertion that human bodies were created for friendship and not for war? Do you find all of his evidence convincing?

3. How does Erasmus move from the physical to mental attributes of human beings? What mental characteristics does he suggest demonstrate that people are not meant to resolve conflicts with violence?

4. What connection does Erasmus see between education and peace? Why does the human desire for knowledge suggest the inhumanity of war?

5. Why does Erasmus move from describing human beings and their characteristics to describing war and its characteristics? What is the rhetorical effect of the balance between these two sets of descriptions?

6. What impact does war, according to Erasmus, have on human populations? How does it frustrate the goals of human beings as he describes in the first section?

MAKING CONNECTIONS

1. Compare Erasmus's views of war to those of the Ancient Chinese philosopher Mo Tzu (p. 476). Could Mo Tzu be called a "humanist"?

2. How do Erasmus's imagined descriptions of war compare to the real descriptions of war in Kachere's "War Memoir" (p. 514)? Does Erasmus's narration give the impression that he had ever witnessed war firsthand?

3. How might George Orwell respond to Erasmus's blanket opposition to war? Do you think that Erasmus would agree with Orwell that there are times when war is the only rational response to evil?

---

3. **Lerna:** a lake in Ancient Greece that was the fabled home of the Hydra—the many-headed water serpent that Heracles fought in Greek mythology.

4. How does Erasmus's view of seeking knowledge compare to that of John Henry Newman in "Knowledge Its Own End" (p. 31)? Does Erasmus believe that the desire to learn can be a good thing in and of itself?

WRITING ABOUT THE TEXT

1. Write an essay about modern war in the style of "Against War," which consists of one or two simple assertions and multiple extensions or examples proving those assertions.

2. Explain how Erasmus's understanding of both the physical and the intellectual characteristics of human beings inform his thinking about war. Evaluate the way that underlying assumptions affect the nature of his argument.

3. Compare the underlying views of human nature in Erasmus's "Against War" and Hobbes's *Leviathan*. Explain how their different starting positions lead to different conclusions.

EUGÈNE DELACROIX
Liberty Leading the People
[1830]

THE FRENCH ARTIST Eugène Delacroix (1798–1863) was the most famous and influential of the Romantic painters, who rejected the balanced, moderate images of the preceding Neoclassical period and emphasized passion and imagination in the creation of beauty. The Romantic movement swept across Europe during the first part of the nineteenth century and included, along with artists such as Delacroix, great writers, composers, architects, and philosophers. Important figures such as William Wordsworth, Samuel Taylor Coleridge, Lord Byron, Johann Wolfgang von Goethe, Ludwig van Beethoven, Richard Wagner, Jean-Jacques Rousseau, and Georg Wilhelm Friedrich Hegel are all associated with European Romanticism.

While Delacroix's paintings depicted contemporary or historical events, they also drew on literature and myth. Stylistically, Delacroix was a transitional figure in European art. He was heavily influenced by Renaissance art, which he studied passionately, but he also drew on impressionism, the painting style of, for example, Monet and Renoir, which dominated the last part of the nineteenth century. The French poet Charles Baudelaire famously referred to Delacroix as "the last of the great artists of the Renaissance and the first of the moderns."

Delacroix's best-known painting, *Liberty Leading the People, 28 July 1830*, was created to celebrate the July 1830 Revolution, which forced France's King Charles X to abdicate in favor of the much more popular and democratic King Louis-Phillippe. However, the painting has become indelibly associated with the French Revolution of 1789, which overthrew the old aristocracy of France and became one of the chief inspirations of European Romanticism. Liberty is allegorically portrayed in Delacroix's painting as a partially nude woman who is striding through a battlefield wearing a Phrygian cap (a hat traditionally associated with liberty in both classical times and during the French Revolution), carrying a musket in one hand and a French flag in the other.

Initial reactions to the painting were mixed. Some people, like Alexandre Dumas, author of such novels as *The Count of Monte Cristo* and *The Three Musketeers*, thought that Delacroix had portrayed the crowd accompanying liberty as too rough and unruly. Others thought that his personification of liberty as a fighting woman was commonplace and vulgar. Having gained in popularity throughout the nineteenth century, the painting is now a recognizable symbol of the idealism behind the French Revolution and of the proposition that freedom must sometimes be won through armed conflict. From 1979 through 1994, the image was featured on the back of France's hundred-franc note.

EUGÈNE DELACROIX
Liberty Leading the People, 28 July 1830, 1830 (oil on canvas)
Louvre, Paris, France / Bridgeman Art Library
See p. C-8 in the color insert for a full-color reproduction of this image.

UNDERSTANDING THE TEXT

1. How would you describe the relationship between the actual scene that the painting depicts and the allegory that it represents?

2. What is the significance of Delacroix's representing liberty as a woman with her breasts exposed? Why might Delacroix have chosen to portray Liberty in this way?

3. What argument about war does the juxtaposition of the items in Liberty's hands make?

4. What kind of social argument might be contained in the depictions of the people accompanying Liberty? (What does their dress indicate about their class status? Do

all the people in the picture appear to be from the same social class?) How would you make this argument in words rather than a picture?

5. What do the lifeless bodies in the foreground of the painting symbolize? Why are they given such a prominent position in the painting?

MAKING CONNECTIONS

1. Compare the figure of Liberty with the sculptures of women's clothing in the Women of World War II Monument. How does each work of art represent the role of women during war time?

2. How do the dead bodies in the foreground of *Liberty Leading the People* compare with the tortured human figures in *Guernica* (p. 497)? How do Delacroix and Picasso view the human costs of war?

3. How does *Liberty Leading the People* make the same point as Orwell's "Pacifism and the War" (p. 508)—that freedom sometimes must be won through violence? Does the painting or the essay argue more effectively? How so? What does this effectiveness suggest about rhetoric?

4. Which writers in this chapter might disagree with Delacroix's and Orwell's point (see #3)? Why?

WRITING ABOUT THE TEXT

1. Interpret *Liberty Leading the People*, focusing on Delacroix's attitude toward war.

2. Write an essay examining the representation of liberty as a woman. What qualities of liberty could plausibly be described as feminine?

3. Research the overall characteristics of European Romanticism and discuss *Liberty Leading the People* as a Romantic painting.

PABLO PICASSO
Guernica
[1937]

IN A CAREER SPANNING more than seventy-five years, the Spanish painter and sculptor Pablo Picasso (1881–1973) produced thousands of paintings and was affiliated with dozens of artistic movements and media. His reputation, already highly esteemed during his life, continued to grow after his death, and he is now seen as one of the most influential artists who ever lived. In May of 2004, one of Picasso's early works, *Boy with a Pipe*, sold at auction for $104.1 million, then the highest price ever paid for a single painting.

In 1907, after more than ten years of painting realistic works, Picasso began working with the French artist Georges Braque (1882–1963) to develop a new artistic style that would eventually be called "cubism." The artistic theory behind cubism holds that an object must be seen from multiple perspectives to be truly understood. Thus, a cubist painting presents its subject from multiple perspectives—front view, side view, back view—all shown at once as part of the same image. Though cubism is only one of the many styles that Picasso used in his paintings, it is the one with which he is most often associated. And it is a style clearly evident in his 1937 masterpiece *Guernica*, which many critics consider his finest painting.

Though Picasso generally did not approve of overtly political art, *Guernica* is perhaps the most famous political statement by any artist in any age. An 11½ × 25½ foot mural commissioned by the Spanish Republican government for the 1937 Paris World's Fair, the painting depicts the bombing of Guernica, a Basque town in northern Spain, by German and Italian forces allied with General Francisco Franco during the Spanish Civil War. The German leader, Adolf Hitler, saw the unprovoked bombing raid against an unarmed civilian population as a way to test the destructive capability of his air force. As a result, an entire town was destroyed, and more than sixteen hundred people were killed. Devastated by the senseless destruction, Picasso created *Guernica* as a response to the brutality of the bombing and the senselessness of war.

PABLO PICASSO
Guernica, 1937 (oil on canvas).
Museo Nacional Centro de Arte Reina Sofia, Madrid, Spain / Bridgeman Art Library.

UNDERSTANDING THE TEXT

1. What is the immediate visual effect of *Guernica*? What is the overall emotional effect? What elements of the painting elicit these reactions?

2. Notice the similarity between the woman holding the baby on the left side of the picture and the woman screaming on the right side. What is the significance of their likeness? Why are both of their heads facing upward at ninety-degree angles from their bodies?

3. Why do animals appear together with the people? What is the significance of the injured horse at the center of the painting and the tortured bull in the top left? Do these figures symbolize human elements of the conflict, or do they simply represent suffering caused by war?

4. What elements of cubism do you see in the painting? How do those elements contribute to Picasso's message?

5. What is the symbolic import of the broken dagger/sword in the bottom-center of the painting?

6. What do you think Picasso wanted to communicate through this painting? Why are glory and dignity absent from the work?

7. What symbolic roles do light sources, such as candles and lightbulbs, play in the painting? Is the painting itself a sort of "light source" designed to illuminate something? If so, what?

MAKING CONNECTIONS

1. Compare the portrayals of war in *Guernica* and *Liberty Leading the People* (p. 494). How are the political messages of both paintings connected to their artistic forms?

2. Compare the depictions of war in *Guernica* and Marevasei Kachere's "War Memoir" (p. 514). Does Kachere's memoir touch on any of the tragic elements of war depicted by Picasso?

3. Compare Picasso's response to fascist brutality to those of Aung San Suu Kyi (p. 442) and George Orwell (p. 508). What similarities and differences do you find?

4. What conception of human nature underlies *Guernica*? How are the animals portrayed in the painting related to that conception? How does Picasso's view of human nature compare with Hobbes's (p. 94) or Wilson's (p. 356)?

WRITING ABOUT THE TEXT

1. Think of a tragedy—personal, national, or global. Write an essay proposing an artwork that would communicate a strong emotional reaction and perhaps create one in the viewer. Would you render the scene visually realistic? What kinds of lines or colors would you use? What would the figures or components of the painting be doing? How would they interact to achieve your vision?

2. Try to translate Picasso's visual rhetoric (p. 614) into words. Does the painting have an overall argument? How does it support that argument? What is lost when visual images are translated into written arguments?

3. Choose a single component of *Guernica*, such as the bull or the mother and child—and interpret its significance within the larger context of the painting. Pay special attention to the possible symbolism of the component.

4. Read two or three interpretations of *Guernica* (hundreds are readily available in any library or on the Internet) and write a paper identifying some of the problems of interpretation, or key areas of disagreement among scholars, that you uncover.

MARGARET MEAD
Warfare: An Invention—Not a Biological Necessity
[1940]

IN 1969, *TIME* MAGAZINE named anthropologist Margaret Mead (1901–1978) the "Mother of the World." This title stemmed in part from Mead's work with young girls in various cultures around the world, but it also recognized the moral and intellectual status that she had earned during her fifty-year career as the world's most famous and respected anthropologist.

Mead was born in Philadelphia in 1901. She earned a doctoral degree in anthropology from Columbia University, where she studied under the legendary anthropologist Ruth Benedict. In 1925, Mead traveled to American Samoa for an extensive fieldwork project studying adolescent girls. She used this research as the basis for her first book, *Coming of Age in Samoa* (1928), which became a bestseller and introduced a generation of nonspecialists to the field of anthropology. In 1929, Mead traveled to New Guinea for a similar study, which resulted in her second major book, *Growing Up in New Guinea* (1930). She continued doing fieldwork throughout the world, but maintained strong ties to New York, where for most of her career she worked at the American Museum of Natural History.

In the course of her career, Mead became known as an expert on both a diverse group of cultures and on human culture generally—on the ways that human beings form, maintain, and modify social relations. She refused to accept the common division of the world into "civilized" and "primitive" cultures, insisting instead that all cultures had things to learn from each other. The accessibility of her scholarly work, combined with her willingness to write articles for the popular press (she wrote a monthly column for *Redbook* magazine for seventeen years), put a human face on the often-obscure discipline of anthropology and gave Mead enormous influence with the American public.

The following essay, "Warfare: An Invention—Not a Biological Necessity," was originally published in *Asia* magazine in 1940. It is based on one of Mead's most cherished beliefs: that people can change by learning from other cultures. In this essay, Mead draws on her vast experience with other cultures to refute the popular argument that the inherent aggressiveness of human beings makes warfare inevitable.

Mead illustrates every major point that she makes with examples drawn from the cultures that she has studied. Each example argues, in effect, that a trait cannot be considered "universal" if there are people anywhere who do not possess it.

Is war a biological necessity, a sociological inevitability, or just a bad invention? Those who argue for the first view endow man with such pugnacious instincts that some outlet in aggressive behavior is necessary if man is to reach full human stature.

It was this point of view which lay back of William James's famous essay, "The Moral Equivalent of War," in which he tried to retain the warlike virtues and channel them in new directions.[1] A similar point of view has lain back of the Soviet Union's attempt to make competition between groups rather than between individuals. A basic, competitive, aggressive, warring human nature is assumed, and those who wish to outlaw war or outlaw competitiveness merely try to find new and less socially destructive ways in which these biologically given aspects of man's nature can find expression. Then there are those who take the second view: warfare is the inevitable concomitant of the development of the state, the struggle for land and natural resources of class societies springing, not from the nature of man, but from the nature of history. War is nevertheless inevitable unless we change our social system and outlaw classes, the struggle for power, and possessions; and in the event of our success warfare would disappear, as a symptom vanishes when the disease is cured.

One may hold a compromise position between these two extremes; one may claim that all aggression springs from the frustration of man's biologically determined drives and that, since all forms of culture are frustrating, it is certain each new generation will be aggressive and the aggression will find its natural and inevitable expression in race war, class war, nationalistic war, and so on.

All three positions are very popular today among those who think seriously about the problems of war and its possible prevention, but I wish to urge another point of view, less defeatist perhaps than the first and third, and more accurate than the second: that is, that warfare, by which I mean organized conflict between two groups as *groups*, in which each group puts an army (even if the army is only fifteen Pygmies) into the field to fight and kill, if possible, some of the members of the army of the other group—that warfare of this sort is an invention like any other of the inventions in terms of which we order our lives, such as writing, marriage, cooking our food instead of eating it raw, trial by jury, or burial of the dead, and so on. Some of this list any one will grant are inventions: trial by jury is confined to very limited portions of the globe; we know that there are tribes that do not bury their dead but instead expose or cremate them; and we know that only part of the human race has had a knowledge of writing as its cultural inheritance. But, whenever a way of doing things is found universally, such as the use of fire or the practice of some form of marriage, we tend to think at once that it is not an invention at all but an attribute of humanity itself. And yet even such universals as marriage and the use of fire are inventions like the rest, very basic ones, inventions which were perhaps necessary if human history was to take the turn it has taken, but nevertheless inventions. At some point in his social development man was undoubtedly without the institution of marriage or the knowledge of the use of fire.

1. **William James's famous essay:** In the 1906 essay mentioned here, the American philosopher and psychologist William James (1842–1910) argues that the natural instincts of human beings toward competition, patriotism, and militarism can be channeled positively into public works projects and the fights against poverty and disease.

The case for warfare is much clearer because there are peoples even today who have no warfare. Of these the Eskimo are perhaps the most conspicuous example, but the Lepchas of Sikkim[2] are an equally good one. Neither of these peoples understands war, not even the defensive warfare. The idea of warfare is lacking, and this lack is as essential to carrying on war as an alphabet or a syllabary[3] is to writing. But whereas the Lepchas are a gentle, unquarrelsome people, and the advocates of other points of view might argue that they are not full human beings or that they had never been frustrated and so had no aggression to expend in warfare, the Eskimo case gives no such possibility of interpretation. The Eskimo are not a mild and meek people; many of them are turbulent and troublesome. Fights, theft of wives, murder, cannibalism occur among them—all outbursts of passionate men goaded by desire or intolerable circumstance. Here are men faced with hunger, men faced with loss of their wives, men faced with the threat of extermination by other men, and here are orphan children, growing up miserably with no one to care for them, mocked and neglected by those about them. The personality necessary for war, the circumstances necessary to goad men to desperation are present, but there is no war. When a traveling Eskimo entered a settlement he might have to fight the strongest man in the settlement to establish his position among them, but this was a test of strength and bravery, not war. The idea of warfare, of one *group* organizing against another *group* to maim and wound and kill them, was absent. And without that idea passions might rage but there was no war.

But, it may be argued, isn't this because the Eskimo have such a low and undeveloped form of social organization? They own no land, they move from place to place, camping, it is true, season after season on the same site, but this is not something to fight for as the modern nations of the world fight for land and raw materials. They have no permanent possessions that can be looted, no towns that can be burned. They have no social classes to produce stress and strains within the society which might force it to go to war outside. Doesn't the absence of war among the Eskimo, while disproving the biological necessity of war, just go to confirm the point that it is the state of development of the society which accounts for war, and nothing else?

We find the answer among the Pygmy peoples of the Andaman Islands in the Bay of Bengal.[4] The Andamans also represent an exceedingly low level of society: they are a hunting and food-gathering people; they live in tiny hordes without any

5

2. **Lepchas of Sikkim:** Sikkim is a small state in the Himalayan mountains of northeastern India. Its original inhabitants, the Lepchas, are noted for their peaceful traditions. About fifty thousand Lepchas still live in India and eastern Nepal.
3. **Syllabary:** a writing system in which a character represents a syllable rather than a single sound (as a character in an alphabet does).

4. **Pygmy peoples of the Andaman Islands in the Bay of Bengal:** Until the twentieth century, the inhabitants of the Andaman Islands, which lie off the eastern coast of India, were hunter-gatherers who had virtually no contact with modern civilization. In 1901, the estimated two thousand Andamanese had twelve distinct, constantly warring tribes.

class stratification; their houses are simpler than the snow houses of the Eskimo. But they knew about warfare. The army might contain only fifteen determined Pygmies marching in a straight line, but it was the real thing none the less. Tiny army met tiny army in open battle, blows were exchanged, casualties suffered, and the state of warfare could only be concluded by a peacemaking ceremony.

Similarly, among the Australian aborigines, who built no permanent dwellings but wandered from water hole to water hole over their almost desert country, warfare—and rules of "international law"—were highly developed. The student of social evolution will seek in vain for his obvious causes of war, struggle for lands, struggle for power of one group over another, expansion of population, need to divert the minds of a populace restive under tyranny, or even the ambition of a successful leader to enhance his own prestige. All are absent, but warfare as a practice remained, and men engaged in it and killed one another in the course of a war because killing is what is done in wars.

From instances like these it becomes apparent that an inquiry into the causes of war misses the fundamental point as completely as does an insistence upon the biological necessity of war. If a people have an idea of going to war and the idea that war is the way in which certain situations, defined within their society, are to be handled, they will sometimes go to war. If they are a mild and unaggressive people, like the Pueblo Indians, they may limit themselves to defensive warfare; but they will be forced to think in terms of war because there are peoples near them who have warfare as a pattern, and offensive, raiding, pillaging warfare at that. When the pattern of warfare is known, people like the Pueblo Indians will defend themselves, taking advantage of their natural defenses, the *mesa* village site, and people like the Lepchas, having no natural defenses and no idea of warfare, will merely submit to the invader. But the essential point remains the same. There is a way of behaving which is known to a given people and labeled as an appropriate form of behavior. A bold and warlike people like the Sioux or the Maori[5] may label warfare as desirable as well as possible; a mild people like the Pueblo Indians may label warfare as undesirable; but to the minds of both peoples the possibility of warfare is present. Their thoughts, their hopes, their plans are oriented about this idea, that warfare may be selected as the way to meet some situation.

So simple peoples and civilized peoples, mild peoples and violent, assertive peoples, will all go to war if they have the invention, just as those peoples who have the custom of dueling will have duels and peoples who have the pattern of vendetta will indulge in vendetta. And, conversely, peoples who do not know of dueling will not fight duels, even though their wives are seduced and their daughters ravished; they may on occasion commit murder but they will not fight duels. Cultures which lack the idea of the vendetta will not meet every quarrel in this way. A people can

5. **The Sioux or the Maori:** The Sioux, or Lakota, are a Native American tribe that originally inhabited the northern Great Plains; the Maori are the indigenous people of New Zealand. The **Pueblo Indians** inhabited the American Southwest.

use only the forms it has. So the Balinese[6] have their special way of dealing with a quarrel between two individuals; if the two feel that the causes of quarrel are heavy, they may go and register their quarrel in the temple before the gods, and, making offerings, they may swear never to have anything to do with each other again. Under the Dutch government they registered such mutual "not-speaking" with the Dutch government officials. But in other societies, although individuals might feel as full of animosity and as unwilling to have any further contact as do the Balinese, they cannot register their quarrel with the gods and go on quietly about their business because registering quarrels with the gods is not an invention of which they know.

Yet, if it be granted that warfare is after all an invention, it may nevertheless be   10 an invention that lends itself to certain types of personality, to the exigent needs of autocrats, to the expansionist desires of crowded peoples, to the desire for plunder and rape and loot which is engendered by a dull and frustrating life. What, then, can we say of this congruence between warfare and its uses? If it is a form which fits so well, is not this congruence the essential point? But even here the primitive material causes us to wonder, because there are tribes who go to war merely for glory, having no quarrel with the enemy, suffering from no tyrant within their boundaries, anxious neither for land nor loot nor women, but merely anxious to win prestige which within that tribe has been declared obtainable only by war and without which no young man can hope to win his sweetheart's smile of approval. But if, as was the case with the Bush Negroes of Dutch Guiana,[7] it is artistic ability which is necessary to win a girl's approval, the same young man would have to be carving rather than going out on a war party.

In many parts of the world, war is a game in which the individual can win counters—counters which bring him prestige in the eyes of his own sex or of the opposite sex; he plays for these counters as he might, in our society, strive for a tennis championship. Warfare is a frame for such prestige-seeking merely because it calls for the display of certain skills and certain virtues; all of these skills—riding straight, shooting straight, dodging the missiles of the enemy, and sending one's own straight to the mark—can be equally well exercised in some other framework and, equally, the virtues—endurance, bravery, loyalty, steadfastness—can be displayed in other contexts. The tie-up between proving oneself a man and proving this by a success in organized killing is due to a definition which many societies have made of manliness. And often, even in those societies which counted success in warfare a proof of human worth, strange turns were given to the idea, as when the Plains Indians gave their highest awards to the man who touched a live enemy rather than to the man who brought in a scalp—from a dead enemy—because killing a man was less risky. Warfare is just an invention known to the majority of human societies by which they permit their young men either to accumulate prestige or

6. **Balinese:** the people of the island of Bali, in present-day Indonesia.
7. **Dutch Guiana:** the country presently known as Suriname, located on the northeast coast of South America between Guyana and French Guiana.

avenge their honor or acquire loot or wives or slaves or sago lands or cattle or appease the blood lust of their gods or the restless souls of the recently dead. It is just an invention, older and more widespread than the jury system, but none the less an invention.

But, once we have said this, have we said anything at all? Despite a few instances, dear to the hearts of controversialists, of the loss of the useful arts, once an invention is made which proves congruent with human needs or social forms, it tends to persist. Grant that war is an invention, that it is not a biological necessity nor the outcome of certain special types of social forms, still, once the invention is made, what are we to do about it? The Indian who had been subsisting on the buffalo for generations because with his primitive weapons he could slaughter only a limited number of buffalo did not return to his primitive weapons when he saw that the white man's more efficient weapons were exterminating the buffalo. A desire for the white man's cloth may mortgage the South Sea Islander to the white man's plantation, but he does not return to making bark cloth, which would have left him free. Once an invention is known and accepted, men do not easily relinquish it. The skilled workers may smash the first steam looms which they feel are to be their undoing, but they accept them in the end, and no movement which has insisted upon the mere abandonment of usable inventions has ever had much success. Warfare is here, as part of our thought; the deeds of warriors are immortalized in the words of our poets; the toys of our children are modeled upon the weapons of the soldier; the frame of reference within which our statesmen and our diplomats work always contains war. If we know that it is not inevitable, that it is due to historical accident that warfare is one of the ways in which we think of behaving, are we given any hope by that? What hope is there of persuading nations to abandon war, nations so thoroughly imbued with the idea that resort to war is, if not actually desirable and noble, at least inevitable whenever certain defined circumstances arise?

In answer to this question I think we might turn to the history of other social inventions, inventions which must once have seemed as firmly entrenched as warfare. Take the methods of trial which preceded the jury system: ordeal and trial by combat.[8] Unfair, capricious, alien as they are to our feeling today, they were once the only methods open to individuals accused of some offense. The invention of trial by jury gradually replaced these methods until only witches, and finally not even witches, had to resort to the ordeal. And for a long time the jury system seemed the one best and finest method of settling legal disputes, but today new inventions, trial before judges only or before commissions, are replacing the jury system. In each case the old method was replaced by a new social invention; the ordeal did not go

8. **Ordeal and trial by combat:** medieval methods of "trying cases." Trial by ordeal subjected the accused to burning or drowning as a way of allowing God to signal guilt or innocence. Trial by combat allowed the accuser to challenge the accused to a duel, which would "prove" the alleged offender's guilt or innocence.

out because people thought it unjust or wrong, it went out because a method more congruent with the institutions and feelings of the period was invented. And, if we despair over the way in which war seems such an ingrained habit of most of the human race, we can take comfort from the fact that a poor invention will usually give place to a better invention.

For this, two conditions at least are necessary. The people must recognize the defects of the old invention, and some one must make a new one. Propaganda against warfare, documentation of its terrible cost in human suffering and social waste, these prepare the ground by teaching people to feel that warfare is a defective social institution. There is further needed a belief that social invention is possible and the invention of new methods which will render warfare as out-of-date as the tractor is making the plow, or the motor car the horse and buggy. A form of behavior becomes out-of-date only when something else takes its place, and in order to invent forms of behavior which will make war obsolete, it is a first requirement to believe that an invention is possible.

UNDERSTANDING THE TEXT

1. What underlying assumption about human nature does Mead reject in this essay? What evidence does she supply for rejecting this assumption?

2. What arguments does Mead support through the examples of the Eskimos and the Lepchas? How do these two tribes differ? In what way are they similar? Which are most important for her argument, their differences or their similarities? How do the examples of the warlike Andaman Pygmies and Australian aborigines complement her arguments?

3. What factors does Mead see as determining whether a civilization will wage war? What kinds of changes would be required to eliminate this tendency?

4. What exactly does Mead mean by categorizing warfare as an "invention"? How does this idea change the traditional view of war? How does it give humanity hope of eliminating war?

MAKING CONNECTIONS

1. Compare Mead's view of human nature with that of Edward O. Wilson in "The Fitness of Human Nature" (p. 356). Would Wilson agree that war is not a biological imperative? Explain.

2. How does Mead's view of human nature compare with those of Mencius (p. 78), Hsün Tzu (p. 84), Hobbes (p. 94), or Machiavelli (p. 405)?

3. Mead studied with Ruth Benedict (p. 112). How might Benedict's theories about the cultural formation of human nature have influenced Mead's assertions about the nature of warfare?

WRITING ABOUT THE TEXT

1. Evaluate the effectiveness of Mead's argument. Does the evidence that Mead presents justify her article's claims? Could other factors account for that same evidence?

2. Define the terms "war," "violence," and "aggression" from Mead's perspective. How does her use of these terms account for some of her differences with one or two other thinkers in this chapter?

3. Consider Mead's contention that social inventions are often replaced with better inventions that solve the same problems. Write an essay speculating about the kind of invention that could achieve the same ends as armed conflict.

4. Examine the fundamental assumptions that Mead makes about human nature. Choose one reading in the chapter "Human Nature and the Mind" as the basis for a comparison.

GEORGE ORWELL
Pacifism and the War
[1942]

"GEORGE ORWELL" is the pen name of Eric Blair (1903–1950), one of the most important and controversial English writers of the twentieth century. Though he published nine novels and several collections of essays and occasional pieces, his reputation as a major author rests almost entirely on two of his last works: *Animal Farm* (1945), a satirical allegory that presents the events of the Russian Revolution as an uprising of the animals on a farm, and *Nineteen Eighty-Four* (1949), a dystopian novel about a futuristic totalitarian society based on surveillance, punishment, and disinformation.

Though Orwell considered himself a socialist and a political liberal, he greatly disdained rigid ideologies—even liberal ones—which, he believed, caused people to be intolerant, irrational, and susceptible to manipulation by cynical, power-hungry politicians. Orwell constantly angered other liberals by attacking their sacred cows and their cherished notions about the world. He especially scorned Soviet Communism, the totalitarianism of which he recognized and attacked at a time when many left-leaning intellectuals in Europe and America were still defending that system, and Spanish, Italian, and German fascism, which he saw as the greatest threat to freedom in history.

Orwell's passionate antifascism during the early stages of World War II led him into a conflict with the liberal pacifist movement in England and America. Though he had once considered himself a pacifist, the aggression of Spain's Francisco Franco, Italy's Benito Mussolini, and, most of all, Germany's Adolf Hitler had convinced him that failure to fight enemies of this kind would eventually cause more suffering and misery than even the bloodiest war. In 1942, he began attacking pacifists in his monthly "London Letter" column in the American magazine *Partisan Review*. His attacks generated numerous responses from pacifists, including letters from the prominent British intellectuals D. S. Savage, George Woodcock, and Alex Comfort. Orwell wrote the following commentary for *Partisan Review* as a collective response to these three letters.

In this response, Orwell identifies one of the most difficult philosophical questions for any pacifist philosophy to answer: how can one respond nonviolently to genuinely evil people, such as Hitler, who will use violence to further their own agendas and who will never respond to nonviolent persuasion? For Orwell, pacifism in the face of unwarranted aggression was morally untenable.

Orwell begins his argument with a single, declarative thesis that he supports through a series of deductive arguments. In the process, he refers to and refutes arguments made earlier by the writers that he is responding to.

Pacifism. Pacifism is objectively pro-Fascist. This is elementary common sense. If you hamper the war effort of one side you automatically help that of the other. Nor is there any real way of remaining outside such a war as the present one. In practice, "he that is not with me is against me." The idea that you can somehow remain aloof from and superior to the struggle, while living on food which British sailors have to risk their lives to bring you, is a bourgeois illusion bred of money and security. Mr Savage remarks that "according to this type of reasoning, a German or Japanese pacifist would be 'objectively pro-British'." But of course he would be! That is why pacifist activities are not permitted in those countries (in both of them the penalty is, or can be, beheading) while both the Germans and the Japanese do all they can to encourage the spread of pacifism in British and American territories. The Germans even run a spurious "freedom" station which serves out pacifist propaganda indistinguishable from that of the PPU.[1] They would stimulate pacifism in Russia as well if they could, but in that case they have tougher babies to deal with. In so far as it takes effect at all, pacifist propaganda can only be effective *against* those countries where a certain amount of freedom of speech is still permitted; in other words it is helpful to totalitarianism.

I am not interested in pacifism as a "moral phenomenon." If Mr Savage and others imagine that one can somehow "overcome" the German army by lying on one's back, let them go on imagining it, but let them also wonder occasionally whether this is not an illusion due to security, too much money and a simple ignorance of the way in which things actually happen. As an ex-Indian civil servant, it always makes me shout with laughter to hear, for instance, Gandhi[2] named as an example of the success of non-violence. As long as twenty years ago it was cynically admitted in Anglo-Indian circles that Gandhi was very useful to the British Government. So he will be to the Japanese if they get there. Despotic governments can stand "moral force" till the cows come home; what they fear is physical force. But though not much interested in the "theory" of pacifism, I *am* interested in the psychological processes by which pacifists who have started out with an alleged horror of violence end up with a marked tendency to be fascinated by the success and power of Nazism. Even pacifists who wouldn't own to any such fascination are beginning to claim that a Nazi victory is desirable in itself. In the letter you sent on to me, Mr Comfort considers that an artist in occupied territory ought to "protest against such evils as he sees," but considers that this is best done by "temporarily accepting the *status quo*" (like Déat or Bergery,[3] for instance?). A few weeks back he was hoping for a Nazi victory because of the stimulating effect it would have upon the arts:

1. **PPU:** the Peace Pledge Union, a pacifist organization founded in 1934 by Richard Sheppard, an Anglican clergyman and radio broadcaster with a large following in England before World War II. Members of the PPU advocated conscientious objection during World War II and often faced persecution and even arrest for their beliefs.

2. **Gandhi:** Mohandas K. Gandhi (1869–1948), Indian political and spiritual leader who led non-violent protests against the British rule of India.
3. **Déat or Bergery:** Marcel Déat and Gaston Bergery were French politicians who collaborated with the Nazi forces occupying France during World War II. Bergery appealed to pacifism in arguing to cooperate with Adolf Hitler.

As far as I can see, no therapy short of complete military defeat has any chance of re-establishing the common stability of literature and of the man in the street. One can imagine the greater the adversity the greater the sudden realisation of a stream of imaginative work, and the greater the sudden katharsis of poetry, from the isolated interpretation of war as calamity to the realisation of the imaginative and actual tragedy of Man. When we have access again to the literature of the war years in France, Poland and Czechoslovakia, I am confident that that is what we shall find. . . .

I pass over the money-sheltered ignorance capable of believing that literary life is still going on in, for instance, Poland, and remark merely that statements like this justify me in saying that our English pacifists are tending towards active pro-Fascism. But I don't particularly object to that. What I object to is the intellectual cowardice of people who are objectively and to some extent emotionally pro-Fascist, but who don't care to say so and take refuge behind the formula "I am just as anti-Fascist as anyone, but——." The result of this is that so-called peace propaganda is just as dishonest and intellectually disgusting as war propaganda. Like war propaganda, it concentrates on putting forward a "case," obscuring the opponent's point of view and avoiding awkward questions. The line normally followed is "Those who fight against Fascism go Fascist themselves." In order to evade the quite obvious objections that can be raised to this, the following propaganda-tricks are used:

1. The Fascising processes occurring in Britain as a result of war are systematically exaggerated.
2. The actual record of Fascism, especially its pre-war history, is ignored or pooh-poohed as "propaganda." Discussion of what the world would actually be like if the Axis[4] dominated it is evaded.
3. Those who want to struggle against Fascism are accused of being whole-hearted defenders of capitalist "democracy." The fact that the rich everywhere tend to be pro-Fascist and the working class are nearly always anti-Fascist is hushed up.
4. It is tacitly pretended that the war is only between Britain and Germany. Mention of Russia and China,[5] and their fate if Fascism is permitted to win, is avoided. (You won't find one word about Russia or China in the three letters you sent to me.)

Now as to one or two points of fact which I must deal with if your correspondents' letters are to be printed in full.

4. **The Axis:** Germany, Italy, Japan, and their allies during World War II.
5. **Russia and China:** A war between Britain and Germany could be viewed by Marxists as simply a clash between two corrupt bastions of industrial capitalism. This could not be said if Russia, the stronghold of world communism, and China, whose communist forces were on the verge of a successful revolution, were counted among Britain's allies in the fight against fascism.

My past and present. Mr Woodcock tries to discredit me by saying that (a) I once served in the Indian Imperial Police, (b) I have written articles for the *Adelphi* and was mixed up with the Trotskyists[6] in Spain, and (c) that I am at the BBC "conducting British propaganda to fox the Indian masses." With regard to (a), it is quite true that I served five years in the Indian Police. It is also true that I gave up that job, partly because it didn't suit me but mainly because I would not any longer be a servant of imperialism. I am against imperialism because I know something about it from the inside. The whole history of this is to be found in my writings, including a novel[7] which I think I can claim was a kind of prophecy of what happened this year in Burma. (b) Of course I have written for the *Adelphi*. Why not? I once wrote an article for a vegetarian paper. Does that make me a vegetarian? I was associated with the Trotskyists in Spain. It was chance that I was serving in the POUM[8] militia and not another, and I largely disagreed with the POUM "line" and told its leaders so freely, but when they were afterwards accused of pro-Fascist activities I defended them as best I could. How does this contradict my present anti-Hitler attitude? It is news to me that Trotskyists are either pacifists or pro-Fascists. (c) Does Mr Woodcock really know what kind of stuff I put out in the Indian broadcasts? He does not—though I would be quite glad to tell him about it. He is careful not to mention what other people are associated with these Indian broadcasts. . . . Most of our broadcasters are Indian left-wing intellectuals, from Liberals to Trotskyists, some of them bitterly anti-British. They don't do it to "fox the Indian masses" but because they know what a Fascist victory would mean to the chances of India's independence. Why not try to find out what I am doing before accusing my good faith?

"*Mr Orwell is intellectual-hunting again*" (Mr Comfort). I have never attacked "the   10
intellectuals" or "the intelligentsia" *en bloc*.[9] I have used a lot of ink and done myself a lot of harm by attacking the successive literary cliques which have infested this country, not because they were intellectuals but precisely because they were *not* what I mean by true intellectuals. The life of a clique is about five years and I have been writing long enough to see three of them come and two go—the Catholic gang, the Stalinist gang, and the present pacifist or, as they are sometimes nicknamed, Fascifist gang. My case against all of them is that they write mentally dishonest propaganda and degrade literary criticism to mutual arse-licking. But even with these various schools I would differentiate between individuals. I would never think of coupling

6. **Trotskyists:** followers of Leon Trotsky (see note 8).
7. **Novel:** *Burmese Days* (1934).
8. **POUM:** *Partido Obrero de Unificación Marxista* (Workers Party of Marxist Unification). In the Spanish Civil War, the POUM was a small, radical faction that opposed both the fascists and the Stalinists, or followers of the Soviet leader,

Joseph Stalin. The POUM followed Leon Trotsky, whom Stalin had exiled after a bitter power struggle. Orwell describes his association with the POUM in his memoir *Homage to Catalonia.* The power struggle between Stalin and Trotsky is the basis for his allegorical novel, *Animal Farm.*
9. **En bloc:** as a group.

Christopher Dawson with Arnold Lunn, or Malraux with Palme Dutt, or Max Plowman with the Duke of Bedford.[10] And even the work of one individual can exist at very different levels. For instance Mr Comfort himself wrote one poem I value greatly ("The Atoll in the Mind"), and I wish he would write more of them instead of lifeless propaganda tracts dressed up as novels. But this letter he has chosen to send you is a different matter. Instead of answering what I have said he tries to prejudice an audience to whom I am little known by a misrepresentation of my general line and sneers about my "status" in England. (A writer isn't judged by his "status," he is judged by his work.) That is on a par with "peace" propaganda which has to avoid mention of Hitler's invasion of Russia, and it is not what I mean by intellectual honesty. It is just because I do take the function of the intelligentsia seriously that I don't like the sneers, libels, parrot phrases and financially profitable back-scratching which flourish in our English literary world, and perhaps in yours also.

12 July 1942
London, England

UNDERSTANDING THE TEXT

1. What kind of case is Orwell making? Does he perceive his audience as supportive, hostile, lacking in information, partially supportive, or unconvinced about the importance of the issue? Support your answer by drawing from the text.

2. What does Orwell mean when he says that during World War II pacifism was "objectively pro-Fascist"? From what you know about this conflict, judge whether it would have been possible to oppose the use of force by one side (the Allies) without supporting the ideology of the other side (the Axis).

3. Why, according to Orwell, was pacifism not permitted in Germany and Japan during World War II?

4. What is the basis of Orwell's distinction between "'moral force'" and "physical force"? Which does he see as more desirable in World War II?

5. What arguments does Orwell characterize as "peace propaganda"? How is this related to "war propaganda"? What kinds of arguments might he see as the cornerstone of all kinds of propaganda?

10. Taken together, these six men represent **the Catholic gang, the Stalinist gang, and the present pacifist . . . gang. Christopher Dawson** was an esteemed Catholic historian whose 1937 essay "The Catholic Attitude to War" argues that true peace is impossible in a flawed world. **Arnold Lunn** was a Catholic aristocrat and adventurer whose attacks on the Trotskyists in the Spanish Civil War earned a rebuttal from Orwell in his 1944 essay "As I Please." **André Malraux** was a major French novelist with communist ties who eventually broke with Stalin and served in the French Resistance. **Rajani Palme Dutt** was the head of the British Communist Party and opposed Britain's entry into World War II. **Max Plowman** was a minor poet and a member of the Peace Pledge Union (PPU). The **Duke of Bedford** refers to Bertrand Russell, the great philosopher and mathematician, who was also a member of the PPU.

6. What mistaken notions about fascism does Orwell attribute to the peace movement?

7. Against what personal attacks does Orwell defend himself? Are his defenses necessary? Are they effective?

MAKING CONNECTIONS

1. Compare Orwell's insistence that pacifism is pro-facist with Erasmus's assertion that war destroys our humanity (p. 488). Would Orwell's argument support the idea that war sometimes prevents greater destruction from occurring? Does Orwell's argument support only defensive warfare? Or would it justify an offensive first strike? Why or why not?

2. How does Orwell's argument about pacifism compare with the just war theory advocated by Thomas Aquinas (p. 483)? Does his argument have religious overtones, or is it completely secular? Explain.

3. What beliefs about human nature are embedded in Orwell's argument? Would he agree with Hobbes (p. 94)? Do you believe that Orwell sees fascism as an extension of or as an aberration from human nature? Why?

4. How might Orwell's dismissal of "moral force" in this essay be reconciled with Martin Luther King Jr.'s very successful use of moral persuasion during the civil rights movement (p. 425)? What differences between the two situations allowed moral force to work in one and not the other?

WRITING ABOUT THE TEXT

1. Write a pacifist response to Orwell. Construct an argument for pacifism's morality, even in the face of unwarranted aggression.

2. Examine how Orwell's arguments about pacifism during World War II would apply to other military conflicts. Discuss whether Orwell's arguments are specific to the kind of ultimate evil represented by Hitler or whether they can be generalized to other armed conflicts.

3. Situate Orwell's argument in the just war tradition. Discuss what Orwell added to that tradition that is not found in the other readings in this chapter.

4. Evaluate the morality of pacifism in "the war on terror," "the war on drugs," or some other contemporary "conflict." Do Orwell's arguments apply?

MAREVASEI KACHERE
War Memoir
[1998]

IN THE 1970s, the African nation of Rhodesia was torn apart by a civil war. For nearly a century, this area of Southeastern Africa had been ruled by European colonizers, first as an outpost of the British Empire and later as a self-governing colony ruled by the white minority descended from the original British settlers. In 1965, as Great Britain was preparing to transfer power to a majority government that would have allowed the native population of Rhodesia to govern itself, the white minority government declared independence from Britain in an effort to maintain power. This Unilateral Declaration of Independence (UDI) sparked a low-level war with Britain and an international response that, through economic sanctions, weakened the existing government considerably and provided the opening for a rebellion by the black majority.

Throughout the 1970s, black Rhodesians slipped across the border to be trained as guerilla fighters in Mozambique and Zambia, whose governments supported the rebellion. After a decade of brutal fighting, the Rhodesian government relented and held popular elections in 1980, which resulted in the end of the minority white government's rule over the native black population. As a result of that election, the colony formerly known as Rhodesia was renamed the Republic of Zimbabwe.

Marevasei Kachere (b. 1961) was born into an agricultural family in a village in the northeastern part of what is now Zimbabwe. In order to prevent people from feeding and sheltering guerilla fighters, the government forced the entire village into a "keep," or a fortified area that could be guarded and locked down. Like many of the young people forced into keeps, Kachere and her friends escaped and joined the resistance forces, which welcomed both male and female fighters into their ranks. In 1976 fifteen-year-old Kachere became a soldier in the liberation army.

"War Memoir" comes from a series of oral interviews conducted with Kachere in 1998. These interviews give a rare glimpse into the mind of a young girl who made the decision to become a soldier, not out of patriotism or a desire for political justice, but simply because the war had made her life as a civilian so dangerous and costly that it seemed safer to join the fighters than to live under government rule in a fortified village.

After the War of Independence, the new government of Zimbabwe offered payouts and monthly pensions to those citizens who fought in the war. The money was in Zimbabwean dollars, which went through several periods of hyperinflation, drastically reducing its value. Two thousand Zimbabwean dollars a month would be worth about $5.50 in U.S. dollars. Kachere's story is an example of how oppressive governments often create the very results that they attempt to suppress.

Marevasei Kachere's "War Memoir" is a rare thing in the history of war writing. It is an account of a war by a combatant who was a teenage girl from a peasant family with very little money or education. Her assessment of the war and of the government that resulted from it is honest, forthright, and uncolored by the propaganda that came from both sides of Zimbabwe's long struggle for independence. It is a story of how war affects the most vulnerable members of a society.

My name is Marevasei Kachere and I was born at Uzumba in Murewa District in 1961, the last in a family of eight children. I went to school at Chidodo when I was eight years old and stayed there up to grade seven. All the children in our family went to school but none of us progressed beyond grade seven, the top class of the primary school. My parents were unusual, as, unlike most parents in our village, they chose to send their daughters to school. This may have been due to the fact that my father had been an only child and so had not experienced discrimination against girls in his family. My education was brought to an end by the Liberation War. I didn't even see the results of my grade seven examinations since we had to leave our home before the results were available. When I eventually came back after the war, I was told that all the school records had been burnt.

Each day, after school, I had to look after the cattle and work in the fields, sometimes helping my father and one of my brothers to plough. I would lead the plough oxen so that they kept on the right course. As with schooling, there was no discrimination in our family between boys and girls as far as work was concerned. Any of us could do anything that had to be done. For instance, my brothers often used to fetch water from the well, something that is considered to be a girl's job. We lived very simply. It was only on special occasions that I was able to eat the food that I loved best—bread and eggs—and that, of course, disappeared along with our hens when we were forced by the Rhodesian soldiers to move into the keep or protected village.

In the early 1970s I used to hear the old people talking about a war and about terrorists, but at first I didn't understand what this meant. Then, round about 1972, when the war was getting hot in the Mount Darwin area, we heard stories that told of terrorists who were invisible. If the Rhodesian soldiers came anywhere near them, they would see only their hats but not the actual people.

We just heard these stories without, as I say, understanding them. Understanding what war was came to us when the soldiers arrived in our district. When they first came they questioned people about the presence of terrorists, and I think that at that period only a few people had been in contact with them, bringing them food and other necessities. But then we were told that on such and such a date we were going to be moved into a keep, although we had no idea what a keep was. So on the appointed day in 1975 the soldiers came and, going from house to house in our village, forced the people at gunpoint to leave with everything they could carry. Anyone who refused to move was shot. And then the soldiers burnt all our houses.

There were no houses in the keep and, at first, people made simple grass shelters   5
to stay in—with no roofs—until they managed to build huts. A whole family was
crowded into each of these shelters, but in my case, I was lucky since my brothers
and sister had married and I was the only one staying with my parents.

The keep was a large area surrounded by a very high barbed-wire fence. It
was so high that one couldn't possibly climb over it and the wires were placed
so close together that no one was able to squeeze through it. There were no two
ways about it—when the soldiers said that we had to stay inside we had no choice.
They were afraid that if we were allowed to go freely in and out we would carry
food to the "terrorists" as they called them. Of course people had to be allowed
to go out at set times to fetch water and to tend the vegetable gardens, and on
these occasions everyone who went out was searched to see if the container he
or she carried held food. And on coming back, if you were carrying a bucket of
water the guards would stir it with a stick to see if there were any explosives in
it. You had to make quite sure that you had brought in enough food and water
for the family for if the gate was kept closed, as it sometimes was, then there
was nothing you could do but go hungry. And if you came back late, after being
outside, you would be shot.

Our school was also inside the fence, and every morning we had to go to school.
The soldiers used to come to check the register to make sure that every child was
present. If anyone was absent the rest of us were beaten with a length of hosepipe—
every one of us—by the soldiers who were trying to get us to say where such and such
a child had gone. We never did say for we believed that if they found out where the
child had gone that child would be killed.

I was not invited by anyone to join the Liberation Struggle, but I was forced into
going by the intolerable circumstances in which we lived. The soldiers used to come
and take us to a place called Mashambanhaka where they put us in drums full of
water and beat us almost to death. This painful routine went on for some time. Even
old people suffered in the same way. Indeed, anybody who was suspected of having
fed the guerrillas was taken out and beaten and then locked in the keep again. I was
tired of being beaten and so I decided I would go out to join the Liberation Struggle.
Doing that, I thought, might lead to my death, but as far as that was concerned I
was under a constant threat of death in the keep, so it was all one whether I stayed
or went. On balance I thought it better to go.

While I was still in the keep some guerrillas arrived at a base called Birimhiri and
a message came that we should prepare sadza and take it the comrades. We cooked
the sadza[1] and on that day we were lucky for the soldiers had gone off to read their
newspapers, and the DA's[2] were holed up in a strong point fortified with sandbags
which was called zvimudburi, so we slipped out carrying the food, and I never came
back. I was with a friend called Kiretti and we just walked saying nothing to each

---

1. **Sadza:** porridge made out of cooked cornmeal.   2. **D.A.:** District Administrator.

other for there was nothing to say; I mean we had no idea what to expect when we arrived at where we were going. This was all done in a moment, completely unplanned. I had not even told my mother that I was going.

That was my first day to meet the comrades. They were just ordinary people, quite visible, wearing uniforms some of which were plain khaki and some camouflage, and carrying their guns which, I noticed, they never let go of since they might have to fight at any moment. We were a bit afraid at first but soon got used to them. There were ten of them altogether. When they had eaten and were about to leave we told them we were going with them; that we wanted to go to Mozambique because we were tired of being beaten. At first they refused to take us and said they were taking boys only, and that though they had taken girls before, they did not encourage those who were very young to go. But we insisted that we were not going back to the keep to be beaten to death or to be injured, as my hearing had been impaired through the punishment I had received. And eventually they agreed.

When we left there were four girls and quite a number of boys from our keep in the group. We did not know what to expect but I did not regret what I had done. We started our journey at night, around eight o'clock, and travelled to Karimimbika which is still in the Uzumba District. Another group of comrades joined us there and we went on, travelling always by night, going via Mudzi and Area 6, and then straight to the border between Rhodesia and Mozambique. My tennis shoes were soon worn out, and I had to make do with the one dress I had been wearing when I left the keep.

After we had crossed into Mozambique we camped at a base called Mubhanana where we stayed for some time, carrying supplies of arms for the comrades who came from Chambere. Then we moved to Zhangara Camp where there were about seven hundred people, including two hundred who were my age. At one stage there were more women than men in this camp, but in my age group there were more boys than girls, and there were no old people. At Zhangara, as in other camps, we were taught politics. Our instructors told us about the war and its origins and said that we should not think of returning home since we had chosen to come and fight for our country's independence.

For my part I never wanted to go back while things were as they were. Yes, I missed my parents, but I was in a large group of young people, all of whom were in the same boat, and that made it easier to forget about your own problems. Most of the time I was happy because I had friends— Ebamore, Tarisai, Mabhunu and Shingirai. We sang together in the choir; in times of hardship we comforted each other; we plaited our hair and mended our clothes. If we were lucky enough to have needles we made small bags in which to keep personal things out of our old dresses. Discipline was fairly strict in the camp. Girls were separated from boys and we never had boyfriends. If a girl did leave camp to meet a boy and was caught she was punished. It wasn't easy to get out of the camp because the exits were guarded. Pregnancies were rare, but girls fell pregnant when they left camp to perform military duties like carrying arms and ammunition. The most common offence for which one was beaten or made to carry ammunition was escaping from the camp to barter clothes for food in the surrounding villages. Beatings were not carried out in the open and we only saw people being called to report for a beating. In all the time I stayed at this camp I never broke the rules, except on one occasion: my friends and I missed a meal because we had stayed too long at the river where we were getting rid of the lice in our hair. Luckily we were not punished for that. [. . .]

We also did some training with "arms," wooden guns that we ourselves had made. Being educated was a big advantage in the camp, and it was the educated ones who were usually the first to be selected to become trainers. I wasn't considered to be educated but I was good at physical activities so I was asked to help with military training. After we had finished the initial training we were allowed to handle real guns, and were given lessons on the different parts of a gun and on how to dismantle and load them. All this time boys and girls were taught together, and we had both male and female instructors. These lessons gave us confidence and a sense of power, so different from how we felt when we were untrained and unarmed.

The most distressing episode in this part of my life was when Tembwe was bombed   15
on November 25, 1977. On that day people were carrying out their duties as usual but another girl and I hadn't gone to work because we were sick. I had an extensive burn on my leg as a result of an accident in the kitchen. Shingi and I had been to the clinic and on our way back we spotted a plane. We were heading for the kitchen, an area of shelters and large drums on fires in which to cook sadza, but before we got there this plane dropped a bomb right in the middle of it. All those on duty in the kitchen were killed—some by the explosion and others by the porridge from the drums. We ran to the river and hid among the reeds but then soldiers appeared and began shooting towards us and I thought I was going to die. I was hit, and the bullet wounds on my leg were deep, but I survived, though it was three months before my injuries healed.

I had never thought of the possibility of dying in a battle before. During my training I had imagined an exchange of gunfire, but nothing more. I had never seen a dead person, but now I saw so many. As we ran to the river I had stepped on the bodies of those who had died, and the thought of that experience horrified me. People die in war and I knew it then all too fearfully.

Soon after the attack on Tembwe I was sent with other survivors to Maroro where I completed my military training. I was then chosen, together with five girls and nine boys, to carry arms—what we called caches—to the comrades who were in the field. These arms—grenades for instance—were packed into sealed bags, and with these we crossed the border into Rhodesia, protected by an armed guard who knew the way. We entered the Mutoko area in July 1978 and went straight to the traditional healer in that area who gave us the go-ahead to operate there. We had been instructed not to seek confrontation with the Rhodesian security forces, and to hide if we came across any. My one experience of action in the field was in Area G. We were having a meal of sadza when we were attacked. We ran away. But four of our comrades were killed by the enemy in this engagement.

In December 1979 a cease-fire was declared. [. . .] We celebrated Zimbabwean Independence on April 18, 1980. We talked about the fact that we had liberated our country and that now no one would be a beggar in his or her own land. We believed that every person in the country would get enough food and a place to stay, and yes, I expected to get a job that matched my education and training. We had great expectations. At that time our leaders told us that what we expected would come true.

As it worked out, some of us were sent to schools, but then the schools were closed. The leaders came and asked for those who wanted jobs, but only the highly educated were taken and given jobs in, for instance, the police force. I stayed behind in that camp while others went off to work, and on top of that they said I was too short to join the police.

Meanwhile, a cousin of mine had come looking for me, as relatives did in those   20
days when family members who had long been lost were returning to these assembly points. As a result I went to see my parents and we wept on one another's necks when we met. They were poor. They had lost everything in the war, and they couldn't help me, nor I them at that time. After staying with them for a short time I went back to Manyene. My hope lay in the promise of jobs that had been made, and I was anxious to get back because I did not want to miss out. [. . .]

Eighteen years after Independence most of the promises made to us remain unfulfilled. We were all promised houses and jobs and a good life, regardless of one's standard of education, but this has not happened.

The hard conditions in the camps in Mozambique have affected my health badly. I think I picked up diseases there from which I have never fully recovered. I would never recommend my daughter to follow my example if such a situation arose again.

The major change of the last couple of years has been the $50,000 payout and the $2, 000 monthly pension. I managed to buy a plough, a cart and two oxen, and I was given land to use. I don't have to dig my field with a hoe anymore. But I think the money is too little. I suffered for too long and the money came too late.

Transcribed by Grace Dube
Translated by Chiedza Musengezi

UNDERSTANDING THE TEXT

1. How were Kachere's parents unusual in their understanding of gender roles? How might this have affected her ultimate decision to join the army?

2. Why does she bring up the rumors of the "invisible" soldiers? How does she understand this term? What does it really mean?

3. Why were the members of her village forced to move into a keep? What did the government hope to accomplish by guarding them at all times?

4. What made Kachere decide to join the army when she was fifteen?

5. How did Kachere's experiences in the military camp compare to those in the keep? Did she experience more or less freedom as a soldier than she did as a civilian?

6. How does she describe her first experience in a battle? How did that experience compare to her expectations?

7. Did the Liberation War accomplish what it set out to do? How does Kachere evaluate the post-revolutionary government? Did it keep its promises to the people?

MAKING CONNECTIONS

1. Compare the way that Marevasei Kachere experienced the War of Liberation with the way that such a war is portrayed by Eugene Delacroix in "Liberty Leading the People" (p. 494). What factors might have prevented Kachere from experiencing liberation the way that Delacroix portrays it?

2. How do Kachere's recollections looking back on an African revolution contrast with Tawakkol Karman's remarks looking forward to the Arab revolutions (p. 524)? Do you think that Karman will eventually experience the disillusion that Kachere displays at the end of her memoir?

3. How do Kachere's experiences as a poorly educated woman compare with those of a well-educated woman like Wangari Maathai (p. 363)? What role do you think education plays in a person's ability to influence a culture?

WRITING ABOUT THE TEXT

1. Discuss how Kachere's experiences of the war were colored by her gender, age, social class, and level of education.

2. Compare Marevasei Kachere's experiences as a peasant farmer with those of the native farmers in Wangari Maathai's "Foresters without Diplomas" (p. 363). What similarities are there in the way that this vulnerable population is treated around the world?

WOMEN OF WORLD WAR II MONUMENT

[2005]

ON JULY 9, 2005, Queen Elizabeth II unveiled a new national monument in the center of London. The Women of World War II Monument was the result of eight years of planning and fundraising by World War II veterans and notable British politicians, including Princess Anne and Baroness Betty Boothroyd. Baroness Boothroyd, the only woman ever to serve as the Speaker of the British House of Commons, made national news in 2002 when she became a contestant on the British version of the game show *Who Wants to Be a Millionaire* in order to raise money for the monument.

Driving the creation of the monument was the recognition that women were crucial to the British war effort in ways that had not been previously recognized. Not only had hundreds of thousands of British women served in the armed forces and as nurses during the war, but millions of women on the home front had stepped into vital community and industrial roles that had been vacated by men. The organizers understood that the monument must commemorate the sacrifices of all these women.

The Women of World War II Monument was created by the well-known British sculptor John Mills. The sculpture itself is a 22-foot-high bronze cenotaph, or grave marker, mirroring the nearby cenotaph monument honoring the fallen soldiers of World War II. Sculpted into the cenotaph are seventeen sets of clothing representing the uniforms worn by women during the war. Some of these are military uniforms, while others represent clothing worn by farmers, factory workers, and police officers—occupations women assumed as part of the war effort. A plaque near the bottom of the monument reads, "This memorial was raised to commemorate the vital work done by over seven million women during World War II."

One of four sides of the Women of World War II Monument, 2005 (bronze).
John Meek / The Art Archive at Art Resource.

UNDERSTANDING THE TEXT

1. Why do you think that a cenotaph, or grave marker, was chosen as the basis of the memorial? How might it have been structured differently to emphasize a different message?

2. Why do you think that the monument features only the uniforms of women who served in World War II and not any images of the women themselves? How would it have been different if actual women had been depicted in the roles represented by the uniforms?

3. Why is it important that both military and civilian uniforms are represented in the monument?

4. What individual uniforms can you make out on the memorial? Are there uniforms or types of dress that should be represented but are not?

MAKING CONNECTIONS

1. Compare the implicit understanding of the Women of World War II Monument with the portrayal of women as soldiers in Marevasei Kachere's "War Memoir" (p. 514).

2. How does the portrayal of women's sacrifice during World War II compare with the portrayal of women's sacrifices in Pablo Picasso's *Guernica* (p. 497)? What do you think accounts for the differences?

3. Do the kinds of women's roles during warfare correspond to the roles for women presented in Christine de Pizan's *Treasure of the City of the Ladies* (p. 397)? Why or why not?

WRITING ABOUT THE TEXT

1. Write a paper about the function of monuments using the Women of World War II monument as a primary example. Explain the role that memorials such as this one play in a society.

2. Pick one of the uniforms in the monument and conduct research into the role that women played in that field or occupation during World War II. Write a research paper presenting your findings.

TAWAKKOL KARMAN
Nobel Lecture
[2011]

IN 2011, Yemeni journalist and human rights activist Tawakkol Karman (b. 1979) became the first Arab woman and the youngest person ever to win the Nobel Peace Prize. Karman has been a visible figure in the movement known as the "Arab Spring"—a wave of pro-democracy protests throughout the Arab world that have resulted in dictators being forced from office in Tunisia, Egypt, Libya, and her native Yemen. Karman shared the 2011 prize with two Liberian women—Ellen Johnson Sirleaf and Leymah Gbowee—"for their non-violent struggle for the safety of women and for women's rights to full participation in peace-building work," as the Nobel Committee stated.

Tawakkol Karman was born into a prominent Yemeni family. Her father is an attorney who once served as the country's minister of legal affairs. She earned an undergraduate degree in business from the University of Science and Technology in Sana'a, Yemen, and a graduate degree in political science at the University of Sana'a. When she completed her schooling, she went to work as a reporter for the Yemeni newspaper *Al-Thawra* (The Revolution).

Karman first came to prominence in 2005 as one of the founders of Women Journalists without Chains, an organization that promotes human rights and advocates for the free expression of ideas in the Arab world. Soon after, she became active in protesting the government of Yemeni dictator Ali Abdullah Saleh, in whose cabinet her father had once served. Her protests and writings against the government led to death threats and an assassination attempt in 2010.

When she won the Nobel Prize in 2011 at the age of 32, Karman immediately became one of the Saleh regime's most prominent opponents. She used this prestige to lobby world leaders to oppose the regime and support the pro-democracy demonstrations that had taken root across the country. Her efforts were successful—in February of 2012, Saleh's 34-year rule came to an end when he stepped down peacefully and left the country. Karman donated her $500,000 in prize money to help the families of those killed in the Yemeni uprisings. Though violence and unrest have continued in Yemen and other countries touched by the Arab Spring, Tawakkol Karman's lecture and example point to a way forward for lasting reform.

In the name of God the Compassionate the Merciful!

Your Majesties, Highnesses, Excellencies, Distinguished Committee of the Nobel Peace Prize, Arab spring and revolution youth in the arena of freedom and change, and all free people of the world: Peace upon you from the Nobel Peace rostrum!

With joy and pleasure I would like to express my gratitude for the honor I was given together with my peace fighter colleagues, Her Excellency the President Ellen Johnson Sirleaf and Mrs. Leymah Gbowee, for this international award, which carries great moral and human meaning. Thank you for the award, which I consider as an honor to me personally, to my country Yemen, to Arab women, to all women of the world and to all people aspiring to freedom and dignity. I accept the award on my behalf and on behalf of the Yemeni and Arab revolutionary youth, who are leading today's peaceful struggle against tyranny and corruption with moral courage and political wisdom.

Alfred Nobel's dream of a world, where peace prevails and wars disappear, has not been achieved yet, but the hope of making it come true has grown large, and the effort to achieve it has doubled. The Nobel Peace Prize still offers this hope spiritual and conscientious momentum. For more than a hundred years, this award has stood as proof of the values of peaceful struggle for rights, justice and freedom, and also as proof of how wrong violence and wars are with all their backfiring and devastating results.

I have always believed that resistance against repression and violence is possible without relying on similar repression and violence. I have always believed that human civilization is the fruit of the effort of both women and men. So, when women are treated unjustly and are deprived of their natural right in this process, all social deficiencies and cultural illnesses will be unfolded, and in the end the whole community, men and women, will suffer. The solution to women's issues can only be achieved in a free and democratic society in which human energy is liberated, the energy of both women and men together. Our civilization is called human civilization and is not attributed only to men or women.

Ladies and gentlemen,

Since the first Nobel Peace Prize in 1901, millions of people have died in wars which could have been avoided with a little wisdom and courage. The Arab countries had their share in these tragic wars, though their land is the land of prophecies and divine messages calling for peace. From this land came the Torah carrying the message: "Thou shalt not kill" and the Bible promising: "Blessed are the peacemakers," and the final message of the Koran urging "O ye who believe, enter ye into the peace, one and all." And the warning that "whosoever killeth a human being for other than manslaughter or corruption in the earth, it shall be as if he had killed all mankind."

However, in spite of its great scientific achievements, the history of humanity is stained with blood. Millions have fallen victims in the rise and fall of kingdoms. That is what ancient history tells us and what recent history confirms! Today's recent evidence tells us that the essence of messages calling for peace has repeatedly been trampled, and the human conscience has often been overrun by the voice of warplanes, rocket and missile launchers, bombs and all means of killing!

5

Ladies and gentlemen,

Mankind's feeling of responsibility to create a decent life and make it worth living with dignity has always been stronger than the will to kill life. Despite great battles, the survival of the human race is the clearest expression of mankind's yearning for reconstruction, not for destruction, for progress, not for regression and death. This tendency is strengthened day after day with all available means of communications, thanks to the rapid and astonishing development of information technology and the communications revolution. Walls between human societies have fallen down and the lives and destinies of societies have converged, marking the emergence of a new phase, a phase where peoples and nations of the world are not only residents of a small village, as they say, but members of one family, despite differences in nationality and race or in culture and language. All the members of this one family interact in all corners of our planet and share the same aspirations and fears. Despite all its missteps, humanity will go on in its march towards what is "beneficial to the people" and will make different cultures, identities and specific characteristics of civilizations come closer to each other on the road towards positive convergence and interaction, both in taking and in giving. Thus, understanding will gradually replace dispute, cooperation will replace conflict, peace will replace war, and integration will replace division.

One can say that our contemporary world, which has been refined and developed by expertise and long experience, good and bad, is marching with confident steps towards the creation of a new world and shining globalization. It will be a new and positive world with human prospects and globalization which will guarantee the values of freedom, truth, justice and cooperation to all human beings. It will be a world where all relationships, dealings and laws will be based on the prohibition of all forms and practices of exclusion and enslavement of man by man. This will mean a globalization with no policies of injustice, oppression, discrimination or tyranny, and a world full of partnership and cooperation, dialogue and coexistence, and acceptance of others. This will mean a globalization where resorting to the law of power and its might, against groups, peoples and nations, in order to deprive them of their liberty and human dignity, will disappear, once and forever. Am I dreaming too much . . . ?

I see on the horizon a glimpse of a new world, of a shining and flourishing globalization. I certainly see the end of a vicious and black history in which so many peoples and nations had experienced horror, tragedies, destruction and disaster. I certainly see the beginning of a humane, prosperous and generous history full of love and fraternity.

Ladies and gentlemen,

Peace within one country is no less important than peace between countries. War is not just a conflict between states. There is another type of war, which is far more bitter, that is the war of despotic leaders who oppress their own people. It is a war of those to whom people have entrusted their lives and destinies, but who have betrayed that trust. It is a war of those to whom people have entrusted their security, but who directed their weapons against their own people. It is the war which today people face in the Arab States. At this moment, as I speak to you here, young Arab people, both women and men, march in peaceful demonstrations demanding freedom and dignity from their rulers. They go forward on this noble path armed not with weapons, but with faith in their right to freedom and dignity. They march in a dramatic scene which embodies the most beautiful of the human spirit of sacrifice and the aspiration to freedom and life, against the ugliest forms of selfishness, injustice and the desire to hold on to power and wealth.

Ladies and gentlemen,

Peace does not mean just to stop wars, but also to stop oppression and injustice. In   10
our Arab region, there are brutal wars between governments and peoples. Human conscience cannot be at peace while it sees these young Arab people, who are in the age of blossoming, being harvested by the machine of death which is unleashed against them by the tyrants. The spirit of the Nobel Peace Prize is the spirit of peace, in which today we look forward in support of the aspiration of the Arab peoples for democracy, justice and freedom. If we support this spirit, the spirit of the Nobel Peace Prize, then we will prove to the despots that the ethics of peaceful struggle are stronger than their powerful weapons of repression and war.

Ladies and gentlemen,

The revolutions of the Arab spring in Tunisia, Egypt, Libya, Yemen and Syria, and the movement towards revolutions in other Arab countries such as Algeria, Morocco, Bahrain, Sudan and others, in terms of motivation, driving power and objectives, didn't take place on isolated islands cut off from all the rapid and astonishing developments and changes which our world is witnessing. The Arab people have woken up just to see how poor a share of freedom, democracy and dignity they have. And they revolted. This experience is somewhat similar to the spring that swept throughout Eastern Europe after the downfall of the Soviet Union. The birth of democracies in Eastern Europe has been difficult and victory emerged only after bitter struggle against the then existing systems. Similarly, the Arab world is today witnessing the birth of a new world which tyrants and unjust rulers strive to oppose, but in the end, this new world will inevitably emerge.

   The Arab people who are revolting in a peaceful and civilized manner have, for so many decades, been oppressed and suppressed by the regimes of authoritarian tyrants who have indulged themselves deeply in corruption and in looting the wealth of their people. They have gone too far in depriving their people of freedom and of the natural right to a dignified life. They have gone too far in depriving them of the right to participate in the management of their personal affairs and the affairs of their communities. These regimes have totally disregarded the Arab people as a people with a legitimate human existence, and have let poverty and unemployment flourish among them in order to secure that the rulers and their family members after them will have full control over the people. Allow me to say that our oppressed people have revolted, declaring the emergence of a new dawn, in which the sovereignty of the people, and their invincible will, will prevail. The people have decided to break free and walk in the footsteps of civilized free people of the world.

All ideologies, beliefs, laws and charters produced by the march of humanity through all stages of its development and growth, as well as all divine messages and religions, without exception, oblige us to support oppressed people, be they groups or individuals. Supporting an oppressed person is not only required because of his need for support, but also because injustice against one person is injustice against all mankind.

Ladies and gentlemen,

What Martin Luther King called "the art of living in harmony" is the most important art we need to master today. In order to contribute to that human art, the Arab states should make reconciliation with their own people an essential requirement. This is not merely an internal interest, but also an international one required for the whole human community. The dictator who kills his own people doesn't only represent a violation of his people's values and their national security, but is also a case of violation of human values, its conventions and its international commitments. Such a case represents a real threat to world peace.

Many nations, including the Arab peoples, have suffered, although they were not   15
at war, but were not at peace either. The peace in which they lived is a false "peace of graves," the peace of submission to tyranny and corruption that impoverishes people and kills their hope for a better future. Today, all of the human community should stand with our people in their peaceful struggle for freedom, dignity and democracy, now that our people have decided to break out of silence and strive to live and realize the meaning of the immortal phrase of Caliph Omar ibn al-Khattab, "Since when have you enslaved people, when their mothers had given birth to them as free ones."

Ladies and gentlemen,

When I heard the news that I had got the Nobel Peace Prize, I was in my tent in the Taghyeer square in Sana'a. I was one of millions of revolutionary youth. There, we were not even able to secure our safety from the repression and oppression of the regime of Ali Abdullah Saleh. At that moment, I contemplated the distinction between the meanings of peace celebrated by the Nobel Prize, and the tragedy of the aggression waged by Ali Abdullah Saleh against the forces of peaceful change.

However, our joy of being on the right side of history made it easier for us to bear the devastating irony.

Millions of Yemeni women and men, children, young and old took to the streets in eighteen provinces demanding their right to freedom, justice and dignity, using non-violent but effective means to achieve their demands. We were able to efficiently and effectively maintain a peaceful revolution in spite of the fact that this great nation has more than seventy million firearms of various types. Here lies the philosophy of the revolution, which persuaded millions of people to leave their weapons at home and join the peaceful march against the state's machine of murder and violence, just with flowers and bare breasts, and filled with dreams, love and peace. We were very happy because we realized, at that time, that the Nobel Prize did not come only as a personal prize for Tawakkol Abdel-Salam Karman, but as a declaration and recognition of the whole world for the triumph of the peaceful revolution of Yemen and as an appreciation of the sacrifices of its great peaceful people.

And here I am now, standing before you in this solemn international ceremony. Here I am, in this unique moment, one of the most important moments of human history, coming from the land of the Arab Orient, coming from the land of Yemen, the Yemen of wisdom and ancient civilizations, the Yemen of more than five thousand years of long history, the great Kingdom of Sheba, the Yemen of the two queens Bilqis and Arwa, the Yemen which is currently experiencing the greatest and the most powerful and the largest eruption of Arab spring revolution, the revolution of millions throughout the homeland, which is still raging and escalating today. This revolution will soon complete its first year since the moment it was launched as a peaceful and popular revolution of the youth, with one demand: peaceful change and the pursuit of free and dignified life in a democratic and civil state governed by the rule of law. This state will be built on the ruins of the rule of a repressive, militarized, corrupt and backward family police rule, which has consistently brought Yemen to the edge of failure and collapse during the last thirty-three years.

Our peaceful and popular youth revolution is not isolated or cut off from the revolutions of the Arab spring. However, with all regret and sadness, I should note that it did not get the international understanding, support or attention of the other revolutions in the region. This should haunt the world's conscience because it challenges the very idea of fairness and justice.

Dear ladies and gentlemen,

Through you and your great universal forum, we send to the world a clear and expressive message in which we emphasize that:

* Our youth revolution is peaceful and popular and is rallied around by the people. It dreams of a free and democratic homeland with no room for tyranny, dictatorship,

20

corruption or failure. I, on behalf of the revolutionary youth, pledge to all people in the world that we are committed to peaceful struggle as a strategic option, without deviation or retreat, regardless of the sacrifices and regardless of the extent of state repression, killing and violence.

- Our youth revolution is peaceful and popular and is motivated by a just cause, and has just demands and legitimate objectives, which fully meet all divine laws, secular conventions and charters of international human rights. Our revolution is determined to fully change the corrupt conditions and ensure free and dignified life, regardless of sacrifices and bitter sufferings, until the establishment of a democratic civil state, a state where the rule of law, equality and a peaceful transfer of power prevail.

- Our peaceful popular youth revolution has succeeded in attracting to its ranks and marches hundreds of thousands of women who have fulfilled, and still fulfill, a major, noticeable and effective role in its activities, and in leading its demonstrations even to the smallest details. Not tens, but hundreds of these women have fallen as martyrs or been wounded for the sake of the victory of the revolution.

- Because of the peaceful popular youth revolution, the voice and thundering march of young people have dominated and the voice of terror and explosive belts, which were employed by Ali Saleh as a justification for his rule, has faded away. The culture of peace is expanding and spreading, and it is finding a place in every neighborhood and street where these young people walk demanding peaceful change and democracy.

- Our peaceful popular youth revolution has demonstrated that the values and objectives of freedom, democracy, human rights, freedom of expression and press, peace, human coexistence, fight against corruption and organized crime, war on terrorism, and resistance to violence, extremism and dictatorship, are values, ideals, demands and objectives of common human interest, and are cherished by the whole international community. These are not subject to division, selectivity or cancellation under the pretext of differences in human characteristics or the requirements of sovereignty in any way.

Distinguished ladies and gentlemen,

I would like to emphasize that the Arab spring revolutions have emerged with the purpose of meeting the needs of the people of the region for a state of citizenship and the rule of law. They have emerged as an expression of people's dissatisfaction with the state of corruption, nepotism and bribery. These revolutions were ignited by young men and women who are yearning for freedom and dignity. They know that their revolutions pass through four stages which can't be bypassed:

- Toppling the dictator and his family
- Toppling his security and military services and his nepotism networks
- Establishing the institutions of the transitional state
- Moving towards constitutional legitimacy and establishing the modern civil and democratic state

Thus, the revolutions of the Arab spring will continue through the effort of youth, who are ready and prepared to launch each stage and to fully achieve its objectives. Today, the world should be ready and prepared to support the young Arab spring in all stages of its struggle for freedom and dignity. The civilized world should, immediately after the outbreak of the revolutions of youth, commence the detention and freezing of the assets of the figures of the regime and its security and military officials. In fact this is not enough, since these people should be brought to justice before the International Criminal Court. There should be no immunity for killers who rob the food of the people.

The democratic world, which has told us a lot about the virtues of democracy and good governance, should not be indifferent to what is happening in Yemen and Syria, and happened before that in Tunisia, Egypt and Libya, and happens in every Arab and non-Arab country aspiring for freedom. All of that is just hard labor during the birth of democracy which requires support and assistance, not fear and caution.

Allow me, ladies and gentlemen, to share my belief that peace will remain the hope of mankind forever, and that the best hope for a better future for mankind will always drive us to speak noble words and do noble deeds. Together, we will push the horizons, one after another, towards a world of true human perfection.

Finally, I ponder myself standing here before you, in this moment, which every   25
man and woman aspires to reach because of the recognition and appreciation it contains. As I do so, I see the great number of Arab women, without whose hard struggles and quest to win their rights in a society dominated by the supremacy of men I wouldn't be here. This supremacy has caused a lot of injustice to both men and women. To all those women, whom history and the severity of ruling systems have made unseen, to all women who made sacrifices for the sake of a healthy society with just relationships between women and men, to all those women who are still stumbling on the path of freedom in countries with no social justice or equal opportunities, to all of them I say: thank you . . . this day wouldn't have come true without you.

Peace be upon you.

UNDERSTANDING THE TEXT

1. Why does Karman begin by quoting the Torah, the Bible, and the Koran? What rhetorical effect does she produce by citing the same message from three different religious texts?

2. How would you describe her view of the future of the Arab world? Would you consider her more optimistic or pessimistic?

3. What does Karman see as the primary characteristics of a just society of the future? What conditions have to be met for a society to be considered just?

4. What two kinds of war does Karman identify? Which type does she see as worse?

5. What does Karman mean by a false "peace of graves"? What kind of peace is achieved by submitting to tyranny and oppression?

6. What four stages of a popular revolution does Karman identify? Why is it important for a revolutionary movement to pass through all four stages?

7. Why does Karman believe that the Arab revolutions cannot be successful unless they fully empower women? How has the "supremacy of men" helped to perpetuate the injustices that she describes?

MAKING CONNECTIONS

1. Compare Karman's view of the false "peace of graves" with Martin Luther King Jr.'s view of "negative peace" in "Letter from Birmingham Jail" (p. 425).

2. How might George Orwell (p. 508) respond to Karman's insistence on peaceful revolution? Is it always possible to confront the forces of oppression and tyranny without using violence?

3. How does Karman's understanding of revolutionary political change compare with Vandana Shiva's understanding of "Earth Justice" (p. 374)? Can there be environmental justice without the kind of political revolution that Karman describes?

WRITING ABOUT THE TEXT

1. Examine Karman's statement that "the peace of submission to tyranny and corruption . . . impoverishes people and kills their hope for a better future." Why does she call this a "peace of graves?" Do you agree?

2. Compare the ways that Tawakkol Karman, Wangari Maathai (p. 363), and Vandana Shiva (p. 374) frame the role of women in social action. How do each of these figures believe that positive social change requires the participation of both men and women?

3. Conduct research into the uprisings collectively referred to as the "Arab Spring." Determine whether or not these uprisings have been consistent with the five principles that Karman outlines (p. 531).

8

◨

WEALTH, POVERTY, AND
SOCIAL CLASS

What Are the Ethical Implications
of Socioeconomic Inequality?

> Ye cannot serve God and mammon.
> —*Matthew 6:24, Luke 16:13*

T HE FREQUENT CONDEMNATIONS of wealth in the New Testament (one of which is quoted above) are reinforced in nearly all of the world's great religious texts. The major religious figures—including Confucius, the Buddha, Jesus, and Mohammed, to name only a few—have consistently taught their followers that focusing on "mammon" (i.e., material things) is spiritually destructive and that allowing fellow human beings to live in poverty is evil. For thousands of years, poverty has been officially condemned by the belief systems that most people in the world subscribe to—yet it persists, and, in many areas of the world, seems worse than ever.

It is difficult to see why the problem of poverty has never been solved, even by societies that clearly have the resources to do so. Understanding this phenomenon means considering how the social mechanisms for distributing wealth are built into a society at a very basic level. The uneven distribution of wealth and the social stratification that accompanies it seem "normal" to most people because they flow directly from cultural assumptions that can be very difficult to question. The Hindu notion of karma, for example, functions as part of an elaborate caste system in which social stratification plays a crucial role in religious duty. Until very recent times, the Christian nations of Europe have viewed members of the aristocratic classes as naturally superior human beings whose right to control vast resources was ordained by God. And in China and other Asian nations, the cardinal Confucian virtue of *li*, which roughly translates as "respect," is manifest when one consistently acts in a way that is appropriate to one's economic and social station in life. The same religions and philosophies that discourage materialism and encourage charity, therefore, can also contribute to social forces that support the unequal distribution of wealth.

Moreover, religious and philosophical teachings tend to focus much more on poverty as it affects individuals than on the large-scale implications of economic policy. Political economics, which emerged in Western Europe in the eighteenth century, was one of the first great intellectual movements in the world to attempt to deal with issues of wealth and poverty on a large scale. Using all of the tools of modern philosophy, science, and mathematics, the great political economists—figures such as John Locke, Adam Smith, Thomas Malthus, Karl Marx, Jeremy Bentham, and John Stuart Mill—studied the same set of problems and came to completely different, mutually exclusive conclusions about the causes of, characteristics of, and cures for poverty. In the end, a macro-level, scientific approach has had as little success in eliminating poverty as a micro-level, religious approach has had.

The readings in this chapter, following the historical arc of the approach to wealth and poverty, move from mainly religious and philosophical texts to works of specialized political economics. The readings begin with a brief selection by Epictetus, a member of the ancient Roman school of philosophy known as Stoicism. He argues that it is not poverty that makes people miserable, but the desire for wealth. Epictetus is followed by a selection from the New Testament's Gospel of Luke, in which Jesus tells two parables that deal directly with wealth and poverty and with the Christian duty to take care of the poor.

Three creative works follow these ancient texts. The first is a poem by one of China's greatest Confucian poets, Po-Chü-i. In "The Flower Market," Po extolls the beauty of flowers being sold to the rich while lamenting the societal cost of such luxuries. The second work is an engraving by the eighteenth-century painter William Hogarth. This engraving, entitled *Gin Lane*, shows a dilapidated London neighborhood whose inhabitants have allowed gin and despair to govern every aspect of their lives. The chapter's other image, Dorothea Lange's *Migrant Mother*, tells a very different story of poverty. This iconic photograph, taken during the Great Depression, depicts a migrant farm worker in Nipomo, California, surrounded by three of her seven children.

The first major economist surveyed in this chapter is Thomas Malthus, who introduced the concept of "overpopulation." Malthus theorized that in any society, population will increase faster than the available food supply, unless it is kept in check by natural catastrophes or by civic regulations. Thus, unchecked population growth will always condemn large segments of a population to live at or below the level of bare subsistence. Malthus's ideas form the basis of Garrett Hardin's twentieth-century critique of food assistance to underdeveloped nations. Such assistance, Hardin argues, is ultimately immoral because it allows a population to grow at an artificially high rate, thus increasing human misery in a severely overpopulated region and guaranteeing the population's collapse. For Hardin, as for Malthus, the most moral institutional response to poverty is to allow nature to take its course when populations exceed the resources of the lands that they inhabit.

A direct contrast to Malthus is given in a speech by Mohandas K. ("Mahatma") Gandhi to a group of British-trained economists in India in 1916. Rather than using his invitation to speak on his plans for "economic progress," as expected, Gandhi questions the very concept of economic progress. He argues that economic progress is inimical to "real" progress, which he defines as moral or spiritual progress. Nearly two thousand years after Jesus first uttered them, Gandhi once again invokes the words quoted at the beginning of this chapter: "Ye cannot serve God and mammon."

Three other selections from the twentieth century portray very different responses to poverty. In the first, French philosopher Simone Weil explains the different kinds of equality that can exist in a society and emphasizes the need for social and economic equality. In "The Day of the Dead," Mexican novelist and philosopher Octavio Paz argues that the Mexican custom of the fiesta—with all of the drunkenness, violence, and transgressive excess associated with it—serves as a crucial counterpoint to the solitary, poor lives that most Mexicans live. In "Rent Seeking and the Making of an Unequal Society," Nobel prize–winning economist Joseph Stiglitz explores both the causes and the consequences of a society where most of the wealth is concentrated in the hands of a few of its members.

EPICTETUS
To Those Who Fear Want
[CIRCA 100 CE]

ADHERENTS OF THE ancient philosophy of Stoicism took great pride in the fact that the two most famous stoics in history were an emperor and a slave. The emperor Marcus Aurelius (121–180 CE) ruled the Roman Empire from 161 to 180, during the height of its power. He was born into great wealth and influence and, for much of his life, commanded the richest and strongest empire that the world had ever known. The slave, Epictetus (55–135 CE), lived a life of poverty and simplicity. His name means simply "one who was acquired," and we know very little about his life other than that he gained his freedom and was banished from Rome in 93 CE. He spent the rest of his life teaching students and living modestly in his native Greece.

Both Marcus Aurelius and Epictetus, Stoics point out, found ways to be content in their circumstances. Accordingly, finding contentment in whatever life one leads is the most important principle of Stoicism. Epictetus and his followers believed that people had very little control over the external facts of their lives. Some were born to great wealth, others to great poverty, and nobody could change the circumstances of their birth. Everybody, however, could shape their own response to those circumstances, which in turn could make the difference between a life of happiness and a life of misery.

Like many of the great figures of antiquity—such as Socrates, Aristotle, Jesus, and Confucius—Epictetus is known to us only through the writings of his followers. One follower in particular, Arrian (86–160 CE), recorded many of the teachings of Epictetus in *The Discourses of Epictetus* (108 CE). Scholars believe that these discourses are Arrian's notes taken during his teacher's lectures, rather than words written or spoken by Epictetus himself. Four of Arrian's original books remain intact; only fragments remain of the rest of his work.

Many of the individual chapters in *The Discourses of Epictetus* take the form of open letters, such as "To Those Who Recommend Persons to Philosophers" and "To Those Who Read and Discuss for the Sake of Ostentation." In "To Those Who Fear Want," the final chapter of the third discourse, Epictetus uses the rhetorical strategy of addressing a hypothetical person who fears falling into poverty. After an initial answer, the selection is structured as a question-and-answer session: the narrator anticipates various questions from the addressee and works to assuage his fears.

Are you not ashamed at being more cowardly and more mean than fugitive slaves? How do they when they run away leave their masters? on what estates do they depend, and what domestics do they rely on? Do they not after stealing a little which is enough for the first days, then afterwards move on through land or through sea, contriving one method after another for maintaining their lives? And what fugitive slave ever died of hunger? But you are afraid lest necessary things should fail you, and are sleepless by night. Wretch, are you so blind, and don't you see the road to which the want of necessaries leads?—Well, where does it lead?—To the same place to which a fever leads, or a stone that falls on you, to death. Have you not often said this yourself to your companions? have you not read much of this kind, and written much? and how often have you boasted that you were easy as to death?[1]

Yes: but my wife and children also suffer hunger.—Well then, does their hunger lead to any other place? Is there not the same descent to some place for them also? Is not there the same state below for them? Do you not choose then to look to that place full of boldness against every want and deficiency, to that place to which both the richest and those who have held the highest offices, and kings themselves and tyrants must descend? or to which you will descend hungry, if it should so happen, but they burst by indigestion and drunkenness. What beggar did you hardly ever see who was not an old man, and even of extreme old age? But chilled with cold day and night, and lying on the ground, and eating only what is absolutely necessary they approach near to the impossibility of dying. Cannot you write? Cannot you teach (take care of) children? Cannot you be a watchman at another person's door?—But it is shameful to come to such a necessity.—Learn then first what are the things which are shameful, and then tell us that you are a philosopher: but at present do not, even if any other man call you so, allow it.

Is that shameful to you which is not your own act, that of which you are not the cause, that which has come to you by accident, as a headache, as a fever? If your parents were poor, and left their property to others, and if while they live, they do not help you at all, is this shameful to you? Is this what you learned with the philosophers? Did you never hear that the thing which is shameful ought to be blamed, and that which is blameable is worthy of blame? Whom do you blame for an act which is not his own, which he did not do himself? Did you then make your father such as he is, or is it in your power to improve him? Is this power given to you? Well then, ought you to wish the things which are not given to you, or to be ashamed if you do not obtain them? And have you also been accustomed while you were studying philosophy to look to others and to hope for nothing from yourself? Lament then and groan and eat with fear that you may not have food tomorrow.

Tremble about your poor slaves lest they steal, lest they run away, lest they die. So live, and continue to live, you who in name only have approached philosophy, and have disgraced its theorems as far as you can by showing them to be useless and unprofitable to those who take them up; you who have never sought constancy, freedom from perturbation, and from passions: you who have not sought any person for the sake of this object, but many for the sake of syllogisms; you who have never

---

1 **Easy as to death:** Epictetus assumes that the recipient of the letter follows the teachings of Stoicism and has therefore proclaimed himself unafraid of death.

thoroughly examined any of these appearances by yourself, Am I able to bear, or am I not able to bear? What remains for me to do? But as if all your affairs were well and secure, you have been resting on the third topic, that of things being unchanged, in order that you may possess unchanged—what? cowardice, mean spirit, the admiration of the rich, desire without attaining any end, and avoidance which fails in the attempt? About security in these things you have been anxious. . . .

Therefore you are now paying the penalty for what you neglected, philosophy: you   5
tremble, you lie awake, you advise with all persons; and if your deliberations are not likely to please all, you think that you have deliberated ill. Then you fear hunger, as you suppose: but it is not hunger that you fear, but you are afraid that you will not have a cook, that you will not have another to purchase provisions for the table, a third to take off your shoes, a fourth to dress you, others to rub you, and to follow you, in order that in the bath, when you have taken off your clothes and stretched yourself out like those who are crucified you may be rubbed on this side and on that, and then the aliptes (rubber) may say (to the slave), Change his position, present the side, take hold of his head, shew the shoulder; and then when you have left the bath and gone home, you may call out, Does no one bring something to eat? And then, Take away the tables, sponge them: you are afraid of this, that you may not be able to lead the life of a sick man. But learn the life of those who are in health, how slaves live, how labourers, how those live who are genuine philosophers; how Socrates lived, who had a wife and children; how Diogenes lived, and how Cleanthes[2] who attended to the school and drew water. If you choose to have these things, you will have them every where, and you will live in full confidence. Confiding in what? In that alone in which a man can confide, in that which is secure, in that which is not subject to hindrance, in that which cannot be taken away, that is, in your own will. And why have you made yourself so useless and good for nothing that no man will choose to receive you into his house, no man to take care of you?: but if a utensil entire and useful were cast abroad, every man who found it, would take it up and think it a gain; but no man will take you up, and every man will consider you a loss. So cannot you discharge the office even of a dog, or of a cook? Why then do you choose to live any longer, when you are what you are?

Does any good man fear that he shall fail to have food? To the blind it does not fail, to the lame it does not: shall it fail to a good man? And to a good soldier there does not fail to be one who gives him pay, nor to a labourer, nor to a shoemaker: and to the good man shall there be wanting such a person? Does God thus neglect the things that he has established, his ministers, his witnesses, whom alone he employs as examples to the uninstructed, both that he exists, and administers well the whole, and does not neglect human affairs, and that to a good man there is no evil either when he is living or when he is dead? What then when he does not

2 **Sophocles . . . Diogenes . . . Cleanthes:** philosophers who taught—and practiced themselves—the value of living simply.

supply him with food? What else does he do than like a good general he has given me the signal to retreat? I obey, I follow, assenting to the words of the commander, praising his acts: for I came when it pleased him, and I will also go away when it pleases him; and while I lived, it was my duty to praise God both, by myself, and to each person severally and to many. He does not supply me with many things, nor with abundance, he does not will me to live luxuriously. . . .

What then, if I shall be sick? You will be sick in such a way as you ought to be.—Who will take care of me?—God; your friends—I shall lie down on a hard bed—But you will lie down like a man—I shall not have a convenient chamber—You will be sick in an inconvenient chamber—Who will provide for me the necessary food?—Those who provide for others also. You will be sick like Manes.[3]—And what also will be the end of the sickness? Any other than death?—Do you then consider that this the chief of all evils to man and the chief mark of mean spirit and of cowardice is not death, but rather the fear of death? Against this fear then I advise you to exercise yourself: to this let all your reasoning tend, your exercises, and reading; and you will know that thus only are men made free.

UNDERSTANDING THE TEXT

1. Why does Epictetus believe that it is shameful to be afraid of poverty? What metaphors does he use to communicate shamefulness?

2. Why does he believe that poverty is not, in fact, shameful? What kinds of things should and should not produce shame, according to Epictetus?

3. Why do you think that Epictetus adopts such an angry and condescending tone toward the hypothetical person afraid of poverty? Why does he say that this person has failed to learn anything from philosophy?

4. According to Epictetus, what is the real fear of those who say they are afraid of hunger? How does he conceptualize the difference between a necessity and a luxury?

5. Why does Epictetus believe that it is irrational to fear a lack of enough food?

6. How, according to Epictetus, should a person who has resolved to accept the inevitability of death respond to life events that lead to death?

MAKING CONNECTIONS

1. Unlike the readings in this chapter by Gandhi (p. 560), Hardin (p. 582), and Stiglitz (p. 594), Epictetus addresses his remarks to one who fears poverty, rather than to wealthy or middle-class people trying to address the poverty of others. How might this rhetorical choice account for the distinct tone and content of his message?

2. Both Epictetus and Seneca were considered Stoics, but their approach to Stoicism was very different. What does Seneca praise in "On Liberal and Vocational Studies" (p. 13) that Epictetus would probably reject?

3. **Manes:** the honored spirits of the dead.

3. How does the question-and-answer format of "To Those Who Fear Want" compare with the dialogue form of Plato's *Gorgias* (p. 166)? Why do you think that each philosopher chose to structure his argument this way?

WRITING ABOUT THE TEXT

1. Evaluate Epictetus's use of logical arguments in "To Those Who Fear Want." Identify and critique possible logical fallacies that he commits.

2. Pick a category of person with which you are familiar (i.e., "Those Who Play Music Very Loud at Night" or "Those Who Answer Every Question in Class") and write an open letter to them in the style of Epictetus.

3. Write a research paper on Stoicism in the ancient world using Epictetus as your primary example of the Stoic philosophy. Draw on "To Those Who Fear Want" for examples of the core Stoic beliefs.

NEW TESTAMENT
Luke, Chapter 16
[CIRCA 90 CE]

AFTER THE CITY OF JERUSALEM was destroyed by the Babylonians in 586 BCE, the region known as Judea was ruled, in succession, by the Babylonian, Persian, Greek, and Roman empires. By the year 30 CE, nearly a thousand years after the golden age of King David (the first ruler of a united Israel), Judea had become a province of Rome. Though the Roman authorities allowed local populations a high degree of religious autonomy, the Jews chafed under foreign rule. Spurred on by prophecies of a "Messiah" who would restore Israel's independence and former glory, a number of revolutionary sects arose in Judea during the first century of Roman rule, culminating in a massive, though ultimately unsuccessful, Jewish revolt in 66 CE. Into this environment, Jesus of Nazareth was born.

Very little about Jesus is known beyond the accounts in the New Testament. His followers clearly believed that he was the Messiah of Hebrew prophecy (the name "Christ" is simply a Greek rendering of the Hebrew word "Messiah"). Just as clearly, Jesus often clashed with the Jewish clergy of his day. The scriptural record contains numerous examples of Jesus's criticizing the priestly class in Jerusalem for focusing on the outward trappings of religious observance and ignoring the true nature of religion, which, for Jesus, was centered around personal devotion and charitable action.

Of the four Gospels, or narratives chronicling the life of Jesus Christ, the Gospel of Luke is the most detailed, and its accounts satisfy the requirements of objective history better than any other scriptural source. The Gospel of Luke also contains the fullest account anywhere of Jesus's parables. A parable is a brief, highly metaphorical narrative used to teach a principle or illustrate a point. In all, the New Testament contains accounts of some forty parables Jesus used to convey important theological points. Fully one-third of Jesus's words in the Synoptic (or biographical) Gospels (Matthew, Mark, and Luke; the Gospel of John, significantly different in form and content, was probably the last to be written) occur in the form of parables. Some of these parables—such as those of the Good Samaritan (Luke 10:30–37), the Lost Sheep (Matt. 18:12–14, Luke 15:3–7), and the Prodigal Son (Luke 15:11–32)—are now among the central metaphors of Western culture.

The following selections from Chapter 16 of the Book of Luke present two parables relating to wealth and poverty. In the first, the Parable of the Unjust Steward, Jesus uses the example of a dishonest steward (or estate manager) to make a point about the moral uses of wealth. In the second, the Parable of the Rich Man and Lazarus, Jesus tells of a reversal of fortunes that typifies many of his parables and other teachings, which emphasize that material prosperity does not indicate God's favor; that people should seek heavenly, rather than earthly, rewards; and that wealth often presents a stumbling block on the way to salvation.

As a rhetorical device, the parable is related to arguments that use analogy and examples to support and develop a claim. While most such arguments draw on existing comparisons, however, the parable constructs its own example or analogy in the form of a narrative. The parables of Jesus are among the most famous examples of this rhetorical device in any culture.

1. And he said also unto his disciples, There was a certain rich man, which had a steward; and the same was accused unto him that he had wasted his goods.
2. And he called him, and said unto him, How is it that I hear this of thee? give an account of thy stewardship; for thou mayest be no longer steward.[1]
3. Then the steward said within himself, What shall I do? for my lord taketh away from me the stewardship: I cannot dig; to beg I am ashamed.[2]
4. I am resolved what to do, that, when I am put out of the stewardship, they may receive me into their houses.
5. So he called every one of his lord's debtors unto him, and said unto the first, How much owest thou unto my lord?   5
6. And he said, An hundred measures of oil. And he said unto him, Take thy bill, and sit down quickly, and write fifty.
7. Then said he to another, And how much owest thou? And he said, An hundred measures of wheat. And he said unto him, Take thy bill, and write fourscore.
8. And the lord commended the unjust steward, because he had done wisely: for the children of this world are in their generation wiser than the children of light.[3]
9. And I say unto you, Make to yourselves friends of the mammon[4] of unrighteousness; that, when ye fail, they may receive you into everlasting habitations.
10. He that is faithful in that which is least is faithful also in much: and he that is   10 unjust in the least is unjust also in much.
11. If therefore ye have not been faithful in the unrighteous mammon, who will commit to your trust the true riches?
12. And if ye have not been faithful in that which is another man's, who shall give you that which is your own? . . .
19. There was a certain rich man, which was clothed in purple and fine linen, and fared sumptuously every day:

1. **Thou mayest be no longer steward:** The master is telling the steward (or estate manager) that he is going to be fired and must present an account of his management, thus giving him time to improve his situation.
2. **I cannot dig; to beg I am ashamed:** The steward is physically unfit for manual labor and reluctant to become a beggar.
3. **Children of light:** The meaning of this passage is that dishonest people (such as the steward) are often more shrewd and practical than honest, righteous people. Since the steward has not been honest, the master says, it is good that he was at least shrewd in his dishonesty.
4. **Mammon:** a Hebrew word meaning wealth or material goods. In this chapter, Jesus personifies "mammon" and presents it as a false god who competes with the true God for allegiance; hence, "Ye cannot serve God and mammon."

20. And there was a certain beggar named Lazarus, which was laid at his gate, full of sores,
21. And desiring to be fed with the crumbs which fell from the rich man's table: 15 moreover the dogs came and licked his sores.
22. And it came to pass, that the beggar died, and was carried by the angels into Abraham's bosom:[5] the rich man also died, and was buried;
23. And in hell he lift up his eyes, being in torments, and seeth Abraham afar off, and Lazarus in his bosom.
24. And he cried and said, Father Abraham, have mercy on me, and send Lazarus, that he may dip the tip of his finger in water, and cool my tongue; for I am tormented in this flame.
25. But Abraham said, Son, remember that thou in thy lifetime receivedst thy good things, and likewise Lazarus evil things: but now he is comforted, and thou art tormented.
26. And beside all this, between us and you there is a great gulf fixed: so that they 20 which would pass from hence to you cannot; neither can they pass to us, that would come from thence.
27. Then he said, I pray thee therefore, father, that thou wouldest send him to my father's house:
28. For I have five brethren; that he may testify unto them, lest they also come into this place of torment.
29. Abraham saith unto him, They have Moses and the prophets; let them hear them.
30. And he said, Nay, father Abraham: but if one went unto them from the dead, they will repent.
31. And he said unto him, If they hear not Moses and the prophets, neither will they 25 be persuaded, though one rose from the dead.

UNDERSTANDING THE TEXT

1. Why does Jesus illustrate his point with a servant's dishonest actions? Is the steward acting righteously or simply acting wisely? How do the two kinds of actions differ?

2. Why does the faithless servant partially forgive the debts of his master's debtors? Why does the master commend him for doing so? Are the servant's reasons for forgiving the debts the same ones for which Jesus praises him?

3. What ultimate point about material wealth is made in the Parable of the Unjust Steward? What uses of wealth does the parable condemn? What uses of wealth does it encourage? What "true riches" does Jesus refer to in verse 11?

4. In the Parable of the Rich Man and Lazarus, why does Lazarus end up in heaven? How does earthly lifestyle relate to eternal destination? According to these two parables, which is the more spiritually admirable and rewarding earthly condition: wealth or poverty?

5. **Abraham's bosom:** heaven, paradise. Abraham was the first and greatest of the Hebrew patriarchs, and to be in his bosom meant to be close to him after death.

5. What are the spiritual dangers of being wealthy, judging from Jesus's parables? Do you agree with the message that poverty is spiritually superior? Is it possible to be wealthy and be a good Christian (or even a good person)? How would one accomplish this?

6. How effectively do these parables argue by analogy? Where do Jesus's analogies illustrate his arguments effectively, and where do they become false analogies, employing insufficiently similar comparisons?

MAKING CONNECTIONS

1. Compare Jesus's portrayal of wealth with Gandhi's in "Economic and Moral Progress" (p. 560). What do Jesus and Gandhi say about the relationship between spiritual and moral "prosperity"?

2. How might some of the figures in Hogarth's *Gin Lane* (p. 548) be read as "parables" similar to those of Jesus in the New Testament? Can you imagine key stories in these characters' lives that would illustrate a moral principle?

3. Compare Jesus and Plato as storytellers. Does Plato use similar techniques to Jesus in "The Speech of Aristophanes" (p. 74)? What are the main differences between these two kinds of stories?

4. How might the Christian understanding of the evils of excess be reflected in the fiestas described by Octavio Paz in "The Day of the Dead" (p. 575), almost all of which celebrate specifically Christian themes or events?

WRITING ABOUT THE TEXT

1. Use a contemporary cultural setting to write a parable with the same message as the Parable of the Unjust Steward. Then write a similar parable that makes an opposite point, such as that money is more important than relationships.

2. The Parable of the Unjust Steward includes a very rare instance of Jesus's praising a person for dishonest actions. Discuss the possible reasons for this apparent incongruity.

3. Compare the teachings of the New Testament in Luke 16 and the *Tao Te Ching* (p. 384) as they relate to material wealth.

PO-CHÜ-I
The Flower Market
[CIRCA 800]

MUCH AS THE PERIOD OF WARRING STATES (475–221 BCE) was the high point of political philosophy in China, the Tang Dynasty (618–907 CE) was the golden age of lyric poetry. The Tang Dynasty provided a period of political stability in China that allowed art and literature to flourish. Then capital of China, Chang'an, was the largest and most advanced city in the world, from which a complex bureaucracy governed more than 50 million households throughout the Chinese Empire. Early in the Tang period, the Buddhist religion of India began to spread throughout China, supplementing the native religions of Confucianism and Taoism.

The most prolific and widely read poet of the Tang Dynasty period was Po-Chü-i (Bai Juyi in pinyin: 772–846 CE), who wrote more than 2,800 poems through his career. Like many Chinese intellectuals of the time, Po spent much of his life in the civil service, a highly organized bureaucracy that required adherence to the Confucian standards of rectitude, propriety, and duty. Po achieved distinction as a bureaucrat and was appointed to several important governorships.

Po was also a devout Buddhist, and his poetry often blends private, Buddhist devotion with a strong Confucian sense of public virtue. As a Buddhist, Po believed that he had a responsibility to address the suffering of other sentient beings; as a Confucian, he believed that the best way to do this was to write poetry capable of influencing public opinion and, particularly, public policy. Many of his best poems call attention to issues such as war, poverty, and economic inequality in the hopes of motivating those in power to address them.

"The Flower Market" is one of Po-Chü-i's best known poems. Most of the poem narrates an experience that would have seemed commonplace to most of his readers: walking through the streets of Chang'an and watching people shopping at an outdoor flower market. Po's words capture this experience elegantly while acknowledging its ordinariness for most well-to-do city dwellers. At the end of the poem, however, we are forced to confront the fact that this simple activity represents an almost unimaginable luxury for the many poor laborers outside of the city.

"The Flower Market" works rhetorically by creating extreme contrasts—between wealth and poverty, luxury and necessity. Through these contrasts, Po gently encourages us to consider the social implications of many commonplace activities.

In the Royal City spring is almost over;
Tinkle, tinkle—the coaches and horsemen pass.
We tell each other "This is the peony season";

And follow with the crowd that goes to the Flower Market.
"Cheap and dear—no uniform price;   5
The cost of the plant depends on the number of blossoms.
The flaming reds, a hundred on one stalk;
The humble white with only five flowers.
Above is spread an awning to protect them;
Around is woven a wattle-fence to screen them.   10
If you sprinkle water and cover the roots with mud,
When they are transplanted, they will not lose their beauty."
Each household thoughtlessly follows the custom,
Man by man, no one realizing.
There happened to be an old farm labourer   15
          Who came by chance that way.
He bowed his head and sighed a deep sigh;
But this sigh nobody understood.
He was thinking, "A cluster of deep-red flowers
Would pay the taxes of ten poor houses."   20

UNDERSTANDING THE TEXT

1. Who do you think is the narrator of the poem? Who is included in the group that the narrator describes as "we"?

2. Which portions of the poem are enclosed in quotation marks? Why? Who is implied to be the author of the quoted material?

3. How should we interpret the description of the flowers as "cheap and dear—no uniform price" in light of the last two lines, which tell us that all of the flowers are "dear" from the old man's perspective?

4. What do you think that Po-Chü-i means by the line "each household thoughtlessly follows the custom?" To what custom might he be referring?

5. How does the presence of the old farm laborer affect your understanding of the poem? Is it significant that this is a character in the poem whom nobody else notices or understands?

6. What is the significance of the farm laborer's lament concerning the taxes of ten poor houses? How would the poem's message change if the line read, "A cluster of deep red flowers could buy *food* for ten poor houses"?

MAKING CONNECTIONS

1. Can you see in Po-Chü-i's poem the seeds of the arguments by Vandana Shiva (p. 374) and Wangari Maathai (p. 363)? What elements of "The Flower Market" could be read as a precursor to what Shiva calls "Earth Justice"?

2. Does "The Flower Market" parallel the argument of Mohandas Gandhi (p. 560) in "Economic and Moral Progress"? What kind of moral progress is Po-Chü-i advocating in the poem?

3. Does Po-Chü-i's Confucian understanding of human nature seem more in line with that of Mencius (p. 78) or that of Hsün-Tzu (p. 84)? Can all three of these views legitimately be called "Confucian"?

WRITING ABOUT THE TEXT

1. Write a paper supporting Po-Chü-i's argument that most people fail to understand the impact of their own luxurious habits on the less fortunate members of society. Use modern examples to support your argument.

2. Compare the way that Po-Chü-i treats the luxury of flowers in "The Flower Market" to the way Mo Tzu treats the luxury of music in "Against Music" (p. 236).

3. Write a paper that incorporates Elaine Scarry's "On Beauty and Being Just" (p. 279) to argue for the value of selling flowers and other beautiful objects in a country with many poor people.

WILLIAM HOGARTH
Gin Lane
[1751]

THOUGH A VISUAL ARTIST, the painter and engraver William Hogarth (1697–1764) was as important to the development of satire in England as were his literary contemporaries Jonathan Swift, Alexander Pope, and Henry Fielding. Many of Hogarth's most famous paintings occur in series with narrative contents, such as *The Harlot's Progress* (1731), *The Rake's Progress* (1735), and *Marriage à la Mode* (1743–45). In each series, between six and eight paintings, taken together, tell cohesive stories that issue strong warnings. Many of Hogarth's early series, or "progresses," were originally oil paintings, but he later re-created them as black-and-white engravings that could be mass produced, sold much more cheaply, and distributed much more widely than the paintings. Their wide dissemination dramatically increased Hogarth's audience and influence.

Hogarth created *Gin Lane* to support the Gin Act, which limited the sale of cheap gin. By the middle of the seventeenth century, gin had become one of the most destructive forces in urban England. Produced cheaply and sold for pennies, gin contributed to rampant alcoholism in England's cities, and was both a symptom and a cause of the extreme poverty and high rates of infant mortality that became the staples of urban life during Hogarth's lifetime. Previous attempts to limit the sale of gin had proved unsuccessful, and the Gin Act, which passed in the summer of 1751, sought to control consumption by doubling the tax on gin and forbidding distillers to sell it directly to the public.

In *Gin Lane*, Hogarth dramatizes the horrific poverty and deprivation that occur in places where cheap gin abounds. The scene emphasizes the effect of gin on children. In the center of the action, a baby falls while its drunken mother reaches for a pinch of snuff. Elsewhere, a child cries as its mother is placed into a coffin, a mother pours gin down the throat of her infant, and a drunken man marches down the street waving a baby impaled on a stick.

But Hogarth is doing more than commenting on the dangers of gin. He is also depicting the effects of poverty. Though Hogarth supported the Gin Act, he also understood that the root of the problem was poverty and that gin had become popular among the poor because it offered a false solution to—and, in the process, exacerbated—this very real problem. *Gin Lane*, which Hogarth originally sold for only a shilling per print, gave the middle and upper classes a rare glimpse into the reality of poverty. Generations of viewers have appreciated *Gin Lane* for reasons that transcend the original sociopolitical context that produced it.

william hogarth *Gin Lane*, 1/51 (engraving).
Bibliothèque Nationale, Paris, France / Lauros–Giraudon / Bridgeman Art Library.

UNDERSTANDING THE TEXT

1. What is happening to the two figures in the foreground of William Hogarth's *Gin Lane*? What is the woman doing while her child falls to its death? What accounts for the man who appears to have starved to death?

2. How does the physical structure of the city reflect the moral structure of its inhabitants? Why is it significant that the only building *not* in disrepair is the pawnbroker's shop?

3. How are children generally treated in *Gin Lane*? What might Hogarth be suggesting by these portrayals?

4. Hogarth is famous for including in most of his engravings dogs and cats whose actions comment on the behavior of human beings. Where do you see examples of this device in *Gin Lane*?

5. How many images of death are in the picture? How many people are or appear to be dead? How can each of these deaths be traced directly to the consumption of gin?

MAKING CONNECTIONS

1. How might Octavio Paz (p. 575) interpret *Gin Lane*'s scenes of drunkenness and excess? How do the actions depicted in this engraving compare with the actions that he describes as part of fiestas?

2. Like Picasso's *Guernica* (p. 597), *Gin Lane* portrays intense violence and suffering. What specific similarities can you find between the two works? What differences?

3. How do *Gin Lane* and *Migrant Mother* (p. 568) differ in their portrayals of poverty?

WRITING ABOUT THE TEXT

1. In a few paragraphs, state, in your own words, the argument that Hogarth makes visually in *Gin Lane*.

2. Write an essay that proposes contemporary images to replace *Gin Lane*. What might symbolize poverty and urban decay in society today?

3. Select one of the characters depicted in *Gin Lane* and write a brief story of that person's life. You may use either the first- or the third-person point of view.

4. *Gin Lane* can be read as both a critique of the poor for drinking gin and a critique of the wealthy for ignoring the poor. Argue for one of these interpretations over the other. Support your argument with a close analysis of the image.

5. Choose a contemporary film, painting, photograph, or literary work that depicts poverty and urban decay. Compare this contemporary source with *Gin Lane*. How do the concerns, elements, and treatments differ? How are they similar?

THOMAS MALTHUS
from *An Essay on the Principle of Population*
[1798]

BEFORE THE ENGLISH ECONOMIST Thomas Malthus (1766–1834) published "An Essay on the Principle of Population," most British economists and politicians believed that population increases were desirable, in that they supplied extra workers on farms and in factories and led to elaborate family systems, which acted as security networks for the old and the unemployed. After the publication of this essay, Chapter 2 of which is excerpted here, the concept of "overpopulation" entered the general European consciousness. Within a generation, population increases began to be seen as threats to, rather than harbingers of, prosperity.

Malthus was an unlikely messenger for the bad news that he bore. He belonged to a wealthy, intellectual family and attended Cambridge University, where he studied for the ministry; upon graduation, he became an Anglican pastor. Deeply religious, he vehemently opposed population-control measures such as abortion and contraception, which he viewed as sinful.

For Malthus, the problem of population could be reduced to a simple, abstract mathematical proposition: that human population, when left unchecked, increases geometrically, while the ability of a given society to produce food increases arithmetically. In practical terms, this means that every society in which the population increases will eventually produce more people than it can feed, thereby condemning a certain percentage of the population to live beneath the subsistence level. When this occurs, poverty becomes a check on population, as people are unable to support more children. This natural check disappears when the food supply catches up to the population level, and the cycle of growth and check begins anew. Malthus believed that while population and food production could increase indefinitely, they could not increase indefinitely at the same rate. Population will always win the race; therefore, some percentage of the human race will always live in poverty.

Most people in the early nineteenth century saw Malthus as a pessimist, and many condemned him for the matter-of-fact way that he dealt with these potentially emotional issues; legislators, however, paid attention to his ideas. In the 1830s, Malthusian principles were invoked by the British Parliament when it dramatically decreased government aid to the poor. Politicians argued that government aid allowed those who could not support children to have them anyway and increase the population, and therefore poverty, even further. Charles Dickens created the character Ebenezer Scrooge—who famously tells a solicitor that those who would rather die than go to a workhouse "had better do it, and decrease the surplus population"—as a satire of precisely this view. Malthus's writings also helped prompt the development of the

British Census, which began in 1801, and they proved a major influence on Charles Darwin's theory of natural selection. As population increases in the twentieth (and so far, the twenty-first) century have confirmed many of Malthus's assertions, his writings continue to influence public policy and social theory.

Malthus supports his claim with statistical data and other facts. All of the facts that he gives, though, were well known to his contemporaries. It is his ability to analyze these facts deductively and produce a seemingly inescapable conclusion that made Malthus's essay so compelling.

I said that population, when unchecked, increased in a geometrical ratio, and subsistence for man in an arithmetical ratio.[1]

Let us examine whether this position be just. I think it will be allowed, that no state has hitherto existed (at least that we have any account of) where the manners were so pure and simple, and the means of subsistence so abundant, that no check whatever has existed to early marriages, among the lower classes, from a fear of not providing well for their families, or among the higher classes, from a fear of lowering their condition in life. Consequently in no state that we have yet known has the power of population been left to exert itself with perfect freedom.

Whether the law of marriage be instituted or not, the dictate of nature and virtue seems to be an early attachment to one woman. Supposing a liberty of changing in the case of an unfortunate choice, this liberty would not affect population till it arose to a height greatly vicious;[2] and we are now supposing the existence of a society where vice is scarcely known.

In a state therefore of great equality and virtue, where pure and simple manners prevailed, and where the means of subsistence were so abundant that no part of the society could have any fears about providing amply for a family, the power of population being left to exert itself unchecked, the increase of the human species would evidently be much greater than any increase that has been hitherto known.

In the United States of America, where the means of subsistence have been more ample, the manners of the people more pure, and consequently the checks to early marriages fewer, than in any of the modern states of Europe, the population has been found to double itself in twenty-five years.

This ratio of increase, though short of the utmost power of population, yet as the result of actual experience, we will take as our rule, and say, that population,

5

---

1. **Geometrical ratio . . . arithmetical ratio:** A geometrical ratio increases by doubling (1, 2, 4, 8, 16, 32, . . .) while an arithmetical ratio increases by simple addition (1, 2, 3, 4, 5, 6, . . .). Though both ratios can double from 1 to 2, simultaneously, the geometric ratio—even if it begins the process at a substantially lower number—will always outstrip the arithmetical ratio.

2. **Vicious:** For Malthus, "vicious" means simply "full of vice," rather than "extremely cruel." A conservative Anglican minister, Malthus believed that adultery, premarital sex, abortion, and contraception were sinful and, therefore, "vicious."

when unchecked, goes on doubling itself every twenty-five years or increases in a geometrical ratio.

Let us now take any spot of earth, this Island[3] for instance, and see in what ratio the subsistence it affords can be supposed to increase. We will begin with it under its present state of cultivation.

If I allow that by the best possible policy, by breaking up more land and by great encouragements to agriculture, the produce of this Island may be doubled in the first twenty-five years, I think it will be allowing as much as any person can well demand.

In the next twenty-five years, it is impossible to suppose that the produce could be quadrupled. It would be contrary to all our knowledge of the qualities of land. The very utmost that we can conceive, is, that the increase in the second twenty-five years might equal the present produce. Let us then take this for our rule, though certainly far beyond the truth, and allow that, by great exertion, the whole produce of the Island might be increased every twenty-five years, by a quantity of subsistence equal to what it at present produces. The most enthusiastic speculator cannot suppose a greater increase than this. In a few centuries it would make every acre of land in the Island like a garden.

Yet this ratio of increase is evidently arithmetical.   10

It may be fairly said, therefore, that the means of subsistence increase in an arithmetical ratio. Let us now bring the effects of these two ratios together.

The population of the Island is computed to be about seven millions, and we will suppose the present produce equal to the support of such a number. In the first twenty-five years the population would be fourteen millions, and the food being also doubled, the means of subsistence would be equal to this increase. In the next twenty-five years the population would be twenty-eight millions, and the means of subsistence only equal to the support of twenty-one millions. In the next period, the population would be fifty-six millions, and the means of subsistence just sufficient for half that number. And at the conclusion of the first century the population would be one hundred and twelve millions and the means of subsistence only equal to the support of thirty-five millions, which would leave a population of seventy-seven millions totally unprovided for.

A great emigration necessarily implies unhappiness of some kind or other in the country that is deserted. For few persons will leave their families, connections, friends, and native land, to seek a settlement in untried foreign climes, without some strong subsisting causes of uneasiness where they are, or the hope of some great advantages in the place to which they are going.

But to make the argument more general and less interrupted by the partial views of emigration, let us take the whole earth, instead of one spot, and suppose that the restraints to population were universally removed. If the subsistence for man that

3. **This Island:** England.

the earth affords was to be increased every twenty-five years by a quantity equal to what the whole world at present produces, this would allow the power of production in the earth to be absolutely unlimited, and its ratio of increase much greater than we can conceive that any possible exertions of mankind could make it.

Taking the population of the world at any number, a thousand millions, for instance, the human species would increase in the ratio of—1, 2, 4, 8, 16, 32, 64, 128, 256, 512, etc. and subsistence as—1, 2, 3, 4, 5, 6, 7, 8, 9, 10, etc. In two centuries and a quarter, the population would be to the means of subsistence as 512 to 10: in three centuries as 4096 to 13, and in two thousand years the difference would be almost incalculable, though the produce in that time would have increased to an immense extent.

No limits whatever are placed to the productions of the earth; they may increase for ever and be greater than any assignable quantity, yet still the power of population being a power of a superior order, the increase of the human species can only be kept commensurate to the increase of the means of subsistence by the constant operation of the strong law of necessity acting as a check upon the greater power.

The effects of this check remain now to be considered.

Among plants and animals the view of the subject is simple. They are all impelled by a powerful instinct to the increase of their species, and this instinct is interrupted by no reasoning or doubts about providing for their offspring. Wherever therefore there is liberty, the power of increase is exerted, and the superabundant effects are repressed afterwards by want of room and nourishment, which is common to animals and plants, and among animals by becoming the prey of others.

The effects of this check on man are more complicated. Impelled to the increase of his species by an equally powerful instinct, reason interrupts his career and asks him whether he may not bring beings into the world for whom he cannot provide the means of subsistence. In a state of equality, this would be the simple question. In the present state of society, other considerations occur. Will he not lower his rank in life? Will he not subject himself to greater difficulties than he at present feels? Will he not be obliged to labour harder? and if he has a large family, will his utmost exertions enable him to support them? May he not see his offspring in rags and misery, and clamouring for bread that he cannot give them? And may he not be reduced to the grating necessity of forfeiting his independence, and of being obliged to the sparing hand of charity for support?

These considerations are calculated to prevent, and certainly do prevent, a very great number in all civilized nations from pursuing the dictate of nature in an early attachment to one woman. And this restraint almost necessarily, though not absolutely so, produces vice.[4] Yet in all societies, even those that are most vicious, the

---

4. **This restraint . . . produces vice:** Malthus believed that young men and women were naturally disposed to form monogamous attachments and begin having children. However, the economic forces listed in the previous paragraph often hinder this process and lead to nonmarital sexual activity, which Malthus equated with "vice."

tendency to a virtuous attachment is so strong that there is a constant effort towards an increase of population. This constant effort as constantly tends to subject the lower classes of the society to distress and to prevent any great permanent amelioration of their condition.

The way in which these effects are produced seems to be this. We will suppose the means of subsistence in any country just equal to the easy support of its inhabitants. The constant effort towards population, which is found to act even in the most vicious societies, increases the number of people before the means of subsistence are increased. The food therefore which before supported seven millions must now be divided among seven millions and a half or eight millions. The poor consequently must live much worse, and many of them be reduced to severe distress. The number of labourers also being above the proportion of the work in the market, the price of labour must tend toward a decrease, while the price of provisions would at the same time tend to rise. The labourer therefore must work harder to earn the same as he did before. During this season of distress, the discouragements to marriage, and the difficulty of rearing a family are so great that population is at a stand. In the mean time the cheapness of labour, the plenty of labourers, and the necessity of an increased industry amongst them, encourage cultivators to employ more labour upon their land, to turn up fresh soil, and to manure and improve more completely what is already in tillage, till ultimately the means of subsistence become in the same proportion to the population as at the period from which we set out. The situation of the labourer being then again tolerably comfortable, the restraints to population are in some degree loosened, and the same retrograde and progressive movements with respect to happiness are repeated.

This sort of oscillation will not be remarked by superficial observers, and it may be difficult even for the most penetrating mind to calculate its periods. Yet that in all old states some such vibration does exist, though from various transverse[5] causes, in a much less marked, and in a much more irregular manner than I have described it, no reflecting man who considers the subject deeply can well doubt.

Many reasons occur why this oscillation has been less obvious, and less decidedly confirmed by experience, than might naturally be expected.

One principal reason is that the histories of mankind that we possess are histories only of the higher classes. We have but few accounts that can be depended upon of the manners and customs of that part of mankind where these retrograde and progressive movements chiefly take place.[6] A satisfactory history of this kind, on one people, and of one period, would require the constant and minute attention of an observing mind during a long life. Some of the objects of inquiry would be, in what

---

5. **Transverse:** connected like the beams of a cross.
6. **Retrograde and progressive:** back and forth. Malthus refers here to the fact that most of the periodic increases and decreases in the population of a society take place among its poorest members, who are the most sensitive to fluctuations in the food supply. Since most of recorded history concerns the upper and middle classes, we do not have a record of these population trends.

proportion to the number of adults was the number of marriages, to what extent vicious customs prevailed in consequence of the restraints upon matrimony, what was the comparative mortality among the children of the most distressed part of the community and those who lived rather more at their ease, what were the variations in the real price of labour, and what were the observable differences in the state of the lower classes of society with respect to ease and happiness, at different times during a certain period.

Such a history would tend greatly to elucidate the manner in which the constant   25 check upon population acts and would probably prove the existence of the retrograde and progressive movements that have been mentioned, though the times of their vibrations must necessarily be rendered irregular from the operation of many interrupting causes, such as the introduction or failure of certain manufacturers, a greater or less prevalent spirit of agricultural enterprise, years of plenty, or years of scarcity, wars and pestilence, poor laws, the invention of processes for shortening labour without the proportional extension of the market for the commodity, and, particularly, the difference between the nominal and real price of labour,[7] a circumstance which has perhaps more than any other contributed to conceal this oscillation from common view.

It very rarely happens that the nominal price of labour universally falls, but we well know that it frequently remains the same, while the nominal price of provisions has been gradually increasing. This is, in effect, a real fall in the price of labour, and during this period the condition of the lower orders of the community must gradually grow worse and worse. But the farmers and capitalists are growing rich from the real cheapness of labour. Their increased capitalists enable them to employ a greater number of men. Work therefore may be plentiful, and the price of labour would consequently rise. But the want of freedom in the market of labour, which occurs more or less in all communities, either from parish laws, or the more general cause of the facility of combination among the rich, and its difficulty among the poor, operates to prevent the price of labour from rising at the natural period, and keeps it down some time longer; perhaps till a year of scarcity, when the clamour is too loud and the necessity too apparent to be resisted.

The true cause of the advance in the price of labour is thus concealed, and the rich affect to grant it as an act of compassion and favour to the poor, in consideration of a year of scarcity, and, when plenty returns, indulge themselves in the most unreasonable of all complaints, that the price does not again fall, when a little rejection would shew them that it must have risen long before but from an unjust conspiracy of their own.

7. **Nominal and real price of labour:** The "nominal price," the actual wage paid to workers, differs from the "real price," which measures the buying power of a given wage by factoring in increases in the prices of goods. Comparisons of the nominal prices of goods or labor are almost meaningless over long periods of time, since the prices of almost everything else increase at the same time. Thus, economists usually use "real wages" as an index of prosperity.

But though the rich by unfair combinations contribute frequently to prolong a season of distress among the poor, yet no possible form of society could prevent the almost constant action of misery upon a great part of mankind, if in a state of inequality, and upon all, if all were equal.

The theory on which the truth of this position depends appears to me so extremely clear that I feel at a loss to conjecture what part of it can be denied.

That population cannot increase without the means of subsistence is a proposition   30
so evident that it needs no illustration.

That population does invariably increase where there are the means of subsistence, the history of every people that have ever existed will abundantly prove.

And that the superior power of population cannot be checked without producing misery or vice, the ample portion of these too bitter ingredients in the cup of human life and the continuance of the physical causes that seem to have produced them bear too convincing a testimony.

UNDERSTANDING THE TEXT

1. What does Thomas Malthus mean when he notes that the human population grows in a "geometrical ratio" but resources grow in an "arithmetical ratio"? What problem does this imbalance eventually create?

2. What assertion does Malthus attempt to support by citing the rate of population increase in the United States? Do you find his use of evidence compelling? Why or why not?

3. Would it be possible, according to Malthusian theory, for the human population to continue to grow unchecked? What natural consequences check the animal and plant populations? What capability checks human populations?

4. Why have most population fluctuations throughout history not been recorded? What does Malthus believe that we would see if we could examine a more complete historical record of population trends?

5. What role do phenomena such as war, plague, and famine play in establishing an equilibrium between food and population?

6. According to Malthus's theory, what is the root cause of poverty? Can the problem of poverty ever be "solved," or is it an inherent feature of any imaginable configuration of society?

MAKING CONNECTIONS

1. Malthus lived at almost the same time as William Hogarth (p. 548) and saw many of the same scenes of urban poverty. However, for Malthus, the root of the problem was not gin, not even inequality, but excess population. What different ways of dealing with the problem of poverty come from these two perceptions of its cause?

2. Compare Malthus's essay with the twentieth-century Malthusian philosopher Garrett Hardin's essay "Lifeboat Ethics: The Case against Helping the Poor" (p. 582). How does Hardin's argument against providing food and other aid to underdeveloped countries follow from Malthus's theory?

3. Charles Darwin cited "An Essay on the Principle of Population" as a major influence on *The Origin of Species* (p. 314). What similarities between the two works can you detect? How might "natural selection" affect human overpopulation?

WRITING ABOUT THE TEXT

1. Research world population growth since 1800, then evaluate Malthus's claim that human population grows geometrically. Conduct similar research to evaluate his claim that food supplies grow arithmetically.

2. Hogarth (p. 548) and Malthus both looked at England during the Industrial Revolution and tried to find the underlying cause of the poverty there. Write an essay outlining what you see as the root cause or causes of poverty within your own society.

3. Dispute Malthus's claim that poverty is an unsolvable problem. Use either historical examples or logical analysis to provide solutions to the problem even in a society with a high population.

4. Examine the connection between vice and poverty. Does poverty cause immoral behavior, or does immoral behavior cause poverty? How do economic factors influence definitions of "morality" and "vice"? Should the unequal distribution of wealth be considered "immoral"? Explain.

MOHANDAS GANDHI
Economic and Moral Progress
[1916]

THOUGH MOHANDAS KARAMCHAND GANDHI (1869–1948) never held a political or religious office, he was the most potent political force in modern India and a spiritual leader—known as "Mahatma," meaning "great soul"—to hundreds of millions of people around the world. His charismatic leadership, shrewd political instincts, and commitment to nonviolent civil disobedience created one of the most successful liberation movements in history and influenced subsequent civil rights movements in the United States, South Africa, Tibet, and Burma.

Gandhi was born in the Indian state of Gujarat, where his father was an important Indian official in the British-controlled government. After studying law in England, he joined an Indian company in South Africa, whose population then included many Indian immigrants. In South Africa, Gandhi confronted the legally sanctioned discrimination that would later develop into the doctrine of apartheid (Afrikaans for "separateness"). Between 1894 and 1914, he developed a philosophy of nonviolent resistance—for which he coined the term *satyagraha*, from the Sanskrit for "truth" and "persistence"—and trained his followers to allow themselves to be punished by the unjust government without using violence to retaliate. His methods were extremely successful, largely because they generated support for his cause around the world and forced the South African government to negotiate with him or face international condemnation.

In 1914, Gandhi returned to India with an international reputation as a skilled mediator and a powerful spokesman for justice. He was soon swept up in the Indian struggle for independence from Great Britain, which had occupied India as its colony since 1858. Using the techniques that he had developed in South Africa, Gandhi led boycotts against British goods, demonstrations against colonial authority, and highly public acts of civil disobedience against unjust laws of the British Empire. In one particularly successful campaign, he led his followers in a march to the coastal village of Dandi to make salt by hand, in direct defiance of the British salt monopoly. More than sixty thousand of Gandhi's followers were arrested, but the demonstrations focused so much world attention on India that the British government agreed to negotiate with Gandhi for the release of all political prisoners in the country.

In 1947, the British government granted India its independence. As part of the agreement, India was divided into two countries: Pakistan, which would be Muslim, and India, which would be Hindu. Only a few months later, Gandhi was assassinated by a Hindu extremist who resented Gandhi for forcing the Indian government to make economic concessions to Pakistan.

Gandhi did not often write for publication. However, various collections of his letters, speeches, and newspaper articles have been published since his death, giving readers key insights into his motivations and character. The speech included here was originally given at the December 22, 1916, meeting of the Muir Central College Economics Society, in Allahabad, India, where Gandhi had been invited to address a group of scholars and students on the topic of "economic progress."

Because Gandhi's audience for these remarks included both Hindus and Christians, he argues from the authority of both religions' scriptural traditions. The majority of these references are to the New Testament—the sacred text of India's colonizers—suggesting a strong desire on Gandhi's part to appeal to Christians on their own rhetorical ground.

When I accepted Mr. Kapildeva Malaviya's[1] invitation to speak to you upon the subject of this evening, I was painfully conscious of my limitations. You are an economic society. You have chosen distinguished specialists for the subjects included in your syllabus for this year and the next. I seem to be the only speaker ill-fitted for the task set before him. Frankly and truly, I know very little of economics, as you naturally understand them. Only the other day, sitting at an evening meal, a civilian friend deluged me with a series of questions on my crankisms.[2] As he proceeded in this cross-examination, I being a willing victim, he found no difficulty in discovering my gross ignorance of the matters. I appeared to him to be handling with a cocksureness worthy only of a man who knows not that he knows not. To his horror and even indignation, I suppose, he found that I had not even read books on economics by such well-known authorities as Mill, Marshall, Adam Smith[3] and a host of such other authors. In despair, he ended by advising me to read these works before experimenting in matters economic at the expense of the public. He little knew that I was a sinner past redemption.

My experiments continue at the expense of trusting friends. For, there comes to us moments in life when about some things we need no proof from without. A little voice within us tells us, 'You are on the right track, move neither to your left nor right, but keep to the straight and narrow way.' With such help we march forward slowly indeed, but surely and steadily. That is my position. It may be satisfactory enough for me, but it can in no way answer the requirements of a society such as yours. Still it was no use my struggling against Mr. Kapildeva Malaviya. I knew that he was intent upon having me to engage your attention for one of your evenings. Perhaps you will treat my intrusion as a welcome diversion

1. **Mr. Kapildeva Malaviya:** Pandit Madan Mohan Malaviya (1861–1946) was a well-known Indian scholar, journalist, and independence advocate and the founder of the Banaras Hindu University.

2. **Crankisms:** eccentricities.
3. **Mill, Marshall, Adam Smith:** John Stuart Mill (1806–1873), Alfred Marshall (1842–1924), and Adam Smith (1723–1790) were important British economists and social theorists.

from the trodden path. An occasional fast after a series of sumptuous feasts is often a necessity. And as with the body, so, I imagine, is the case with the reason. . . .

Before I take you to the field of my experiences and experiments, it is perhaps best to have a mutual understanding about the title of this evening's address: *Does economic progress clash with real progress?* By economic progress, I take it, we mean material advancement without limit and by real progress we mean moral progress, which again is the same thing as progress of the permanent element in us. The subject may therefore be stated thus: 'Does not moral progress increase in the same proportion as material progress?' I know that this is a wider proposition than the one before us. But I venture to think that we always mean the larger one even when we lay down the smaller. For we know enough of science to realise that there is no such thing as perfect rest or repose in this visible universe of ours. If therefore material progress does not clash with moral progress, it must necessarily advance the latter. Nor can we be satisfied with the clumsy way in which sometimes those who cannot defend the larger proposition put their case. They seem to be obsessed with the concrete case of thirty millions of India stated by the late Sir William Wilson Hunter[4] to be living on one meal a day. They say that before we can think or talk of their moral welfare, we must satisfy their daily wants. With these, they say, material progress spells moral progress. And then is taken a sudden jump: what is true of thirty millions is true of the universe. They forget that hard cases make bad law. I need hardly say to you how ludicrously absurd this deduction would be. No one has ever suggested that grinding pauperism can lead to anything else than moral degradation. Every human being has a right to live and therefore to find the wherewithal to feed himself and where necessary to clothe and house himself. But, for this very simple performance, we need no assistance from economists or their laws.

'Take no thought for the morrow'[5] is an injunction which finds an echo in almost all the religious scriptures of the world. In well-ordered society, the securing of one's livelihood should be and is found to be the easiest thing in the world. Indeed, the test of orderliness in a country is not the number of millionaires it owns, but the absence of starvation among its masses. The only statement that has to be examined is whether it can be laid down as a law of universal application that material advancement means moral progress.

Now let us take a few illustrations. Rome suffered a moral fall when it attained   5
high material affluence. So did Egypt and so perhaps most countries of which we have

---

4. **Sir William Wilson Hunter:** member (1840–1900) of the British civil service in India and the author of a number of popular books about India for Western audiences.

5. **'Take no thought for the morrow':** from Jesus' Sermon on the Mount: "Therefore take no thought, saying, What shall we eat? or, What shall we drink? or, Wherewithal shall we be clothed? (For after all these things do the Gentiles seek:) for your heavenly Father knoweth that ye have need of all these things. But seek ye first the kingdom of God, and his righteousness; and all these things shall be added unto you. Take therefore no thought for the morrow: for the morrow shall take thought for the things of itself. Sufficient unto the day is the evil thereof" (Matthew 6:31–34).

any historic record. The descendants, kinsmen of the royal and divine Krishna, too, fell when they were rolling in riches. We do not deny to the Rockefellers and the Carnegies[6] possession of an ordinary measure of morality but we gladly judge them indulgently. I mean that we do not even expect them to satisfy the highest standard of morality. With them material gain has not necessarily meant moral gain. In South Africa, where I had the privilege of associating with thousands of our countrymen on most intimate terms, I observed almost invariably that the greater the possession of riches, the greater was their moral turpitude. Our rich men, to say the least, did not advance the moral struggle of passive resistance as did the poor. The rich men's sense of self-respect was not so much injured as that of the poorest. If I were not afraid of treading on dangerous ground, I would even come nearer home and show you that possession of riches has been a hindrance to real growth. I venture to think that the scriptures of the world are far safer and sounder treatises on laws of economics than many of the modern textbooks.

The question we are asking ourselves this evening is not a new one. It was addressed to Jesus two thousand years ago. St. Mark has vividly described the scene.[7] Jesus is in his solemn mood; he is earnest. He talks of eternity. He knows the world about him. He is himself the greatest economist of his time. He succeeded in economising time and space—he transcended them. It is to him at his best that one comes running, kneels down, and asks: 'Good Master, what shall I do that I may inherit eternal life?' And Jesus said unto him: 'Why callest thou me good? There is none good but one, that is God. Thou knowest the commandments. Do not commit adultery, Do not kill, Do not steal, Do not bear false witness, Defraud not, Honour thy father and mother.' And he answered and said unto him: 'Master, all these have I observed from my youth.' Then Jesus beholding him, loved him and said unto him: 'One thing thou lackest. Go thy way, sell whatever thou hast and give to the poor, and thou shalt have treasure in heaven—come take up the cross and follow me.' And he was sad at that saying and went away grieved—for he had great possessions. And Jesus looked round about and said unto his disciples: 'How hardly shall they that have riches enter into the kingdom of God.' And the disciples were astonished at his words. But Jesus answereth again and saith unto them: 'Children, how hard it is for them that trust in riches to enter into the kingdom of God. It is easier for a camel to go through the eye of a needle than for a rich man to enter into the kingdom of God!'

Here you have an eternal rule of life stated in the noblest words the English language is capable of producing. But the disciples nodded unbelief as we do even to this day. To him they said as we say today: 'But look how the law fails in practice.

6. **The Rockefellers and the Carnegies:** John D. Rockefeller (1839–1937) and Andrew Carnegie (1835–1919) were wealthy American industrialists. **Krishna:** According to Hindu scripture, Krishna is an incarnation of the god Vishnu. He is Arjuna's chariot driver in the *Mahābhārata* and speaks almost all of the text of the *Bhagavad Gītā*.

7. **St. Mark has vividly described the scene:** The scriptural passages quoted in this paragraph and the next are from the tenth chapter of the Gospel of Mark.

If we sell all and have nothing, we shall have nothing to eat. We must have money or we cannot even be reasonably moral.' So they state their case thus. 'And they were astonished out of measure saying among themselves: "Who then can be saved?"' And Jesus looking upon them said: 'With men it is impossible but not with God, for with God all things are possible.' Then Peter began to say unto him: 'Lo, we have left all, and have followed thee.' And Jesus answered and said: 'Verily I say unto you there is no man that has left house or brethren or sisters, or father or mother, or wife or children or lands for my sake and the Gospels, but he shall receive one hundred fold, now in this time houses and brethren and sisters and mothers and children and lands with persecutions and in the world to come eternal life. But many that are first shall be last and the last first.' You have here the result or reward, if you prefer the term, of following the law.

I have not taken the trouble of copying similar passages from the other non-Hindu scriptures and I will not insult you by quoting in support of the law stated by Jesus passages from the writings and sayings of our own sages, passages even stronger if possible than the Biblical extracts I have drawn your attention to. Perhaps the strongest of all the testimonies in favour of the affirmative answer to the question before us are the lives of the greatest teachers of the world. Jesus, Mahomed, Buddha, Nanak, Kabir, Chaitanya, Shankara, Dayanand, Ramakrishna[8] were men who exercised an immense influence over and moulded the character of thousands of men. The world is the richer for their having lived in it. And they were all men who deliberately embraced poverty as their lot.

I should not have laboured my point as I have done, if I did not believe that, in so far as we have made the modern materialistic craze our goal, in so far are we going downhill in the path of progress. I hold that economic progress in the sense I have put it is antagonistic to real progress. Hence the ancient ideal has been the limitation of activities promoting wealth. This does not put an end to all material ambition. We should still have, as we have always had, in our midst people who make the pursuit of wealth their aim in life. But we have always recognised that it is a fall from the ideal. It is a beautiful thing to know that the wealthiest among us have often felt that to have remained voluntarily poor would have been a higher state for them. That you cannot serve God and Mammon[9] is an economic truth of the highest value. We have to make our choice. Western nations today are groaning under the

8. **Nanak . . . Ramkrishna:** Guru Nanak (1469–1539) founded the Sikh religion in India. Kabir (1440–1519) was an Indian mystic whose teachings were important to Hindus and Muslims. Chaitanya Mahaprabhu (1486–1534) was a devotee of Krishna and a social reformer in the Indian province of Bengal; his teachings form the basis for the International Society of Krishna Consciousness (Hare Krishna) in the West. Adi Shankara (eighth century CE) was a well-known Hindu teacher and philosopher. Dayananda Saraswati (1824–1883) was a Hindu reformer. Bhagavan Sri Ramakrishna Paramahamsa (1836–1886) was a well-known Hindu teacher.
9. **Mammon:** a Hebrew word meaning wealth or material goods; Jesus's statement "Ye cannot serve God and mammon" occurs twice in the New Testament, in Matthew 6:24 and in Luke 16:13.

heel of the monster-god of materialism. Their moral growth has become stunted. They measure their progress in £.s.d.[10] American wealth has become standard. She is the envy of the other nations. I have heard many of our countrymen say that we will gain American wealth but avoid its methods. I venture to suggest that such an attempt if it were made is foredoomed to failure.

We cannot be 'wise, temperate and furious'[11] in a moment. I would have our leaders   10
teach us to be morally supreme in the world. This land of ours was once, we are told, the abode of the gods. It is not possible to conceive gods inhabiting a land which is made hideous by the smoke and the din of mill chimneys and factories and whose roadways are traversed by rushing engines dragging numerous cars crowded with men mostly who know not what they are after, who are often absent-minded, and whose tempers do not improve by being uncomfortably packed like sardines in boxes and finding themselves in the midst of utter strangers who would oust them if they could and whom they would in their turn oust similarly. I refer to these things because they are held to be symbolical of material progress. But they add not an atom to our happiness. This is what Wallace,[12] the great scientist, has said as his deliberate judgement.

In the earliest records which have come down to us from the past, we find ample indications that general ethical considerations and conceptions, the accepted standard of morality, and the conduct resulting from these were in no degree inferior to those which prevail to-day.

In a series of chapters, he then proceeds to examine the position of the English nation under the advance in wealth it has made. He says:

This rapid growth of wealth and increase of our power over nature put too great a strain upon our crude civilization, on our superficial Christianity, and it was accompanied by various forms of social immorality almost as amazing and unprecedented.

He then shows how factories have risen on the corpses of men, women and children, how as the country has rapidly advanced in riches, it has gone down in morality. He shows this by dealing with insanitation, life-destroying trades, adulteration, bribery and gambling. He shows how, with the advance of wealth, justice has become immoral, deaths from alcoholism and suicide have increased, the average of premature births and congenital defects has increased, and prostitution has become an institution. He concludes his examination by these pregnant remarks:

10. **£.s.d.:** the standard abbreviations for the three major British monetary units: pounds, shillings, pence.
11. **'Wise, temperate, and furious':** a reference to William Shakespeare's *Macbeth*: "Who can be wise, amazed, temp'rate and furious, / Loyal and neutral in a moment? No man" (2.3.105–06).

12. **Wallace:** Alfred Russel Wallace (1823–1913), a British naturalist who, along with Charles Darwin, articulated the principles of the theory of evolution by natural selection. The passages that Gandhi quotes are found in Wallace's 1913 book, *Social Environment and Moral Progress*.

The proceedings of the divorce courts show other aspects of the result of wealth and leisure, while a friend who had been a good deal in London society assured me that both in country houses and in London various kinds of orgies were occasionally to be met with which would hardly have been surpassed in the period of the most dissolute emperors. Of war, too, I need say nothing. It has always been more or less chronic since the rise of the Roman Empire; but there is now undoubtedly a disinclination for war among all civilized peoples. Yet the vast burden of armaments, taken together with the most pious declarations in favour of peace, must be held to show an almost total absence of morality as a guiding principle among the governing classes.

Under the British aegis,[13] we have learnt much, but it is my firm belief that there is little to gain from Britain in intrinsic morality, that if we are not careful, we shall introduce all the vices that she has been a prey to, owing to the disease of materialism. We can profit by that connection only if we keep our civilization, and our morals, straight, i.e., if instead of boasting of the glorious past, we express the ancient moral glory in our own lives and let our lives bear witness to our past. Then we shall benefit her and ourselves. If we copy her because she provides us with rulers, both they and we shall suffer degradation. We need not be afraid of ideals or of reducing them to practice even to the uttermost. Ours will only then be a truly spiritual nation when we shall show more truth than gold, greater fearlessness than pomp of power and wealth, greater charity than love of self. If we will but clean our houses, our palaces and temples of the attributes of wealth and show in them the attributes of morality, we can offer battle to any combinations of hostile forces without having to carry the burden of a heavy militia. Let us seek first the kingdom of God and His righteousness[14] and the irrevocable promise is that everything will be added with us. These are real economics. May you and I treasure them and enforce them in our daily life.

UNDERSTANDING THE TEXT

1. What does Mohandas Gandhi mean by "economic progress"? What does he mean by "moral progress"? How are the two terms interrelated in this speech?

2. Though Gandhi was a Hindu speaking to a largely Hindu audience, his primary religious source for this speech is the New Testament. Why does he emphasize Christian scriptures? What does this choice say about the ethos (p. 663) he was trying to construct?

---

13. **Aegis:** technically, a shield or breastplate; more commonly, mentorship or guidance.
14. **Let us seek first the kingdom of God and His righteousness:** an allusion to Matthew 6:33:

"But seek ye first the kingdom of God, and his righteousness; and all these things shall be added unto you."

3. What is Gandhi's position on poverty? Does he suggest that moral development requires the renunciation of physical needs? Are extremely poor people morally superior to others? Are wealthy people morally inferior? Explain.

4. What does Gandhi see as "real progress"? Whom does he name as having furthered the real progress of humankind? What traits do these individuals share? What are the "real economics" that he refers to at the end of this speech?

MAKING CONNECTIONS

1. Compare Gandhi's position on the connection between wealth and morality with similar discussions in the New Testament (p. 541) and "The Flower Market" (p. 545). How do these texts, taken together, support the idea of a universal (or at least widespread) religious approach to economics?

2. Would Simone Weil (p. 571) support Gandhi's view that economic progress is at odds with moral progress? Do Gandhi and Weil define "moral" in similar ways?

3. Martin Luther King Jr. cited Gandhi as a major influence on his thinking and social activism. How might "Economic and Moral Progress" have informed "Letter from Birmingham Jail" (p. 425)?

WRITING ABOUT THE TEXT

1. Write your own response to the key question that Gandhi raises: What is the relationship between economic progress and moral progress?

2. Compare Gandhi's arguments about wealth and morality with those of Jesus in the sixteenth chapter of Luke (p. 541). How substantially do the views differ?

3. Refute Gandhi's claim by arguing that many people have been able to accomplish good things through their material wealth.

DOROTHEA LANGE
Migrant Mother
[1936]

OF ALL THE IMAGES OF POVERTY and despair that came out of the Great Depression, none had more impact than Dorothea Lange's *Migrant Mother*. Lange (1895–1965) took this photograph while working for the federal government's Resettlement Administration—later called the Farm Security Administration—a Depression-era agency that attempted to combat rural poverty by purchasing land from subsistence farmers and resettling the farmers on larger tracts of land where they could work in large collectives under the supervision of government scientists. Between 1935 and 1944, the agency employed a number of photographers—including Lange—to create support for their mission by documenting the effects of poverty on sharecroppers, homesteaders, migrant farmers, and other rural victims of the Great Depression.

The photograph now commonly known as *Migrant Mother* is in the Library of Congress under the title "Destitute pea pickers in California. Mother of seven children. Age thirty-two. Nipomo, California." In 1960, Lange recounted her experience the day that the iconic photograph was taken:

> I saw and approached the hungry and desperate mother, as if drawn by a magnet. I do not remember how I explained my presence or my camera to her, but I do remember she asked me no questions. I made five exposures, working closer and closer from the same direction. I did not ask her name or her history. She told me her age, that she was thirty-two. She said that they had been living on frozen vegetables from the surrounding fields, and birds that the children killed. She had just sold the tires from her car to buy food. There she sat in that lean-to tent with her children huddled around her, and seemed to know that my pictures might help her, and so she helped me. There was a sort of equality about it.

For years, this was all that was known about the woman in the image. However, in 1978, a reporter named Emmett Corrigan found her living in a mobile home in Modesto, California. He was able to identify her as Florence Owens Thompson (1903–1983), a Cherokee woman who had moved with her husband from Oklahoma to California in 1922 and was later caught up in the economic hardships of the Depression. Thompson expressed frustration and anger that the picture that had made her face famous had never helped her or her family in any way. Five years later, however, when Americans learned that Thompson was dying of cancer and had no way to pay her medical bills, her family received more than $30,000 in contributions from those who had been moved by the photograph over the years.

dorothea lange *Migrant Mother,* 1936.
Library of Congress.

UNDERSTANDING THE TEXT

1. What does the woman in Dorothea Lange's photograph appear to be looking at? What is she looking away from? What might the direction of her gaze communicate about her state of mind?

2. Why do you think the two older children in the picture have their faces turned away from the camera? What effect might the photographer herself have had on the picture?

3. From what is visible in the picture, what can you tell about the baby that the mother is holding?

4. Imagine that you saw this photograph without any knowledge of the title, the photographer, the cultural and historical context of the photo, or its subject. What would the photograph mean to you? What would you think the photographer was trying to say? How does knowing the context and other information about the photo change how you see it?

MAKING CONNECTIONS

1. Compare the mother in this picture with the mothers in *Gin Lane* (p. 548) and *Guernica* (p. 497). How does each mother respond to the misery of her family? What might account for the differences?

2. Compare *Migrant Mother* with the Women of World War II Monument (p. 521). Could Lange's photograph and/or the monument be classified as a type of propaganda? If so, how?

3. What might Mohandas Gandhi (p. 560) or Garrett Hardin (p. 582) say upon seeing this image? How does it affirm or rebut the arguments that they make?

WRITING ABOUT THE TEXT

1. Write an essay in which you interpret *Migrant Mother* by carefully examining its formal elements, such as shading, lighting, balance, composition, and contrast. Explain how the formal elements of the image reinforce its theme.

2. Show *Migrant Mother* to friends, roommates, or family members who may not be familiar with the picture and ask them what they think it is about. Do not share the title or any information about the photo. Then write an essay in which you compare and contrast their responses. Why do you think they respond as they do?

3. Research when and where *Migrant Mother* was originally published and write an essay explaining the impact (or lack of impact) that it had on its original audience.

SIMONE WEIL
Equality
[CIRCA 1940]

SIMONE WEIL (1909–1943) was born to a wealthy family in Paris. Her parents were Jewish but not observant, and Weil grew up without religious instruction. She was, however, encouraged in her love of languages and classical scholarship, and she mastered ancient Greek and several other languages by age twelve. She attended the best schools in Paris and, in 1928, placed first in the rigorous entrance examination to the elite École Normale Supérieure—ahead of her fellow future philosopher Simone de Beauvoir, who placed second.

Weil was initially attracted to Marxism and radical politics, and she remained active in workers' causes throughout her life. She became disillusioned with Marxism, however, and after a series of intense personal religious experiences, declared her conversion to Christianity in 1938. Weil never joined a church, insisting that Christianity's essence was an unmediated personal experience with God. She also believed that a Christian's life must reflect his or her beliefs. Though she had a graduate degree in philosophy from an elite institution, she frequently applied to do manual labor in factories in order to commune with the workers, and donated a large portion of her income as a teacher to the poor.

After Germany invaded France in 1940, Weil went to England, where she worked for the French Resistance. She was soon diagnosed with tuberculosis. Believing that it would be immoral for her to indulge in physical comforts while her fellow French citizens were suffering under Nazi occupation, she disregarded her doctors' orders to maintain a healthy diet. Instead she subjected herself to near starvation, which hastened her death.

When Weil died, her writings were known only to a few close friends. Since her death, however, selections from her unfinished manuscripts, her personal notebooks, and lecture notes taken by her students have secured her reputation as one of the most important philosophers of the twentieth century. In the selection excerpted here, Weil tries to reconcile the human need for equality with the existing condition of inequality in human societies. To explain this discrepancy, Weil divides inequality into two categories: quantitative inequality, which arises from the inevitable difference in human talents, abilities, occupations, and access to resources, and qualitative inequality, which arises only when we assign different values to people as a result of these differences.

Equality is a vital need of the human soul. It consists in a recognition, at once public, general, effective, and genuinely expressed in institutions and customs, that the same amount of respect and consideration is due to every human being because this respect is due to the human being as such and is not a matter of degree.

It follows that the inevitable differences among men ought never to imply any difference in the degree of respect. And so that these differences may not be felt to bear such an implication, a certain balance is necessary between equality and inequality.

A certain combination of equality and inequality is formed by equality of opportunity. If no matter who can attain the social rank corresponding to the function he is capable of filling, and if education is sufficiently generalized so that no one is prevented from developing any capacity simply on account of his birth, the prospects are the same for every child. In this way, the prospects for each man are the same as for any other man, both as regards himself when young, and as regards his children later on.

But when such a combination acts alone, and not as one factor among other factors, it ceases to constitute a balance and contains great dangers.

To begin with, for a man who occupies an inferior position and suffers from it to   5 know that his position is a result of his incapacity and that everybody is aware of the fact is not any consolation, but an additional motive of bitterness; according to the individual character, some men can thereby be thrown into a state of depression, while others can be encouraged to commit crime.

Then, in social life, a sort of aspirator toward the top is inevitably created. If a descending movement does not come to balance this ascending movement, the social body becomes sick. To the extent to which it is really possible for the son of a farm laborer to become one day a minister, to the same extent should it really be possible for the son of a minister to become one day a farm laborer. This second possibility could never assume any noticeable proportions without a very dangerous degree of social constraint.

This sort of equality, if allowed full play by itself, can make social life fluid to the point of decomposing it.

There are less clumsy methods of combining equality with differentiation. The first is by using proportion. Proportion can be defined as the combination of equality with inequality, and everywhere throughout the universe it is the sole factor making for balance.

Applied to the maintenance of social equilibrium, it would impose on each man burdens corresponding to the power and well-being he enjoys, and corresponding risks in cases of incapacity or neglect. For instance, an employer who is incapable or guilty of an offense against his workmen ought to be made to suffer far more, both in the spirit and in the flesh, than a workman who is incapable or guilty of an offense against his employer. Furthermore, all workmen ought to know that this is so. It would imply, on the one hand, certain rearrangement with regard to risks, on the other hand, in criminal law, a conception of punishment in which social rank, as an aggravating circumstance, would necessarily play an important part in deciding what the penalty was to be. All the more reason, therefore, why the exercise of important public functions should carry with it serious personal risks.

Another way of rendering equality compatible with differentiation would be to take away as far as possible all quantitative character from differences. Where there is only a difference in kind, not in degree, there is no inequality at all.   10

But making money the sole, or almost the sole, motive of all actions, the sole, or almost the sole, measure of all things, the poison of inequality has been introduced everywhere. It is true that this inequality is mobile; it is not attached to persons, for money is made and lost; it is none the less real.

There are two sorts of inequality, each with its corresponding stimulant. A more or less stable inequality, like that of ancient France, produces an idolizing of superiors—not without a mixture of repressed hatred—and a submission to their commands. A mobile, fluid inequality produces a desire to better oneself. It is no nearer to equality than is stable inequality, and is every bit as unwholesome. The Revolution of 1789, in putting forward equality, only succeeded in reality in sanctioning the substitution of one form of inequality for another.

The more equality there is in a society, the smaller is the action of the two stimulants connected with the two forms of inequality, and hence other stimulants are necessary.

Equality is all the greater in proportion as different human conditions are regarded as being, not more nor less than one another, but simply as other. Let us look on the professions of miner and minister simply as two different vocations, like those of poet and mathematician. And let the material hardships attaching to the miner's condition be counted in honor of those who undergo them.

In wartime, if an army is filled with the right spirit, a soldier is proud and happy   15
to be under fire instead of at headquarters; a general is proud and happy to think that the successful outcome of the battle depends on his forethought; and at the same time the soldier admires the general and the general the soldier.

Such a balance constitutes an equality. There would be equality in social conditions if this balance could be found therein. It would mean honoring each human condition with those marks of respect which are proper to it, and are not just a hollow pretense.

UNDERSTANDING THE TEXT

1. What kind of equality does Weil perceive as "a vital need of the human soul"? In what particular area does she believe that human nature most values equality with others?

2. Why does Weil believe that equality of opportunity will always lead to inequality of outcome? How should societies try to deal with this kind of inequality? Would it be possible or advisable to try to eliminate it?

3. Why does Weil believe that both upward and downward mobility are necessary for a true equality of opportunity? Why does she conclude that this level of equality could be socially destabilizing?

4. What does Weil mean by balancing equality and inequality through proportion? In the system she advocates, what additional responsibilities are placed on those who occupy higher social and economic positions? Is this fair?

5. Characterize in your own words the difference between "quantitative" and "qualitative" inequality.

MAKING CONNECTIONS

1. How does Weil's view of the spiritual consequences of inequality compare with those of Mohandas Gandhi in "Economic and Moral Progress" (p. 560)? Does Gandhi deal with respect for others in the same way that Weil does?

2. Do Weil and Joseph Stiglitz (p. 594) share a basic concern about the social consequences of certain kinds of inequality? Would Stiglitz agree with Weil that quantitative inequality is "no inequality at all"?

3. What kind of equality does Eugene Delacroix uphold in *Liberty Leading the People* (p. 494)? How would Weil view this kind of equality? Would she consider it qualitative or quantitative?

4. Does Weil's view of equality match the "Earth Justice" that Vandana Shiva discusses in *Soil, Not Oil* (p. 374)?

WRITING ABOUT THE TEXT

1. Define and contrast the concepts of "quantitative" and "qualitative" inequality as they relate to Weil's essay. Which one more closely represents the kind of social and economic inequalities you observe in your everyday life, and why?

2. Evaluate Weil's claim that the nature of human beings, combined with the nature of societies, makes a balance between equality and inequality necessary in human societies. How might you dispute both parts of this assertion?

3. Compare and contrast Weil's understanding of socioeconomic inequality with that of Stiglitz in "Rent Seeking and the Making of an Unequal Society" (p. 594).

OCTAVIO PAZ
from *The Day of the Dead*
[1950]

FOR MUCH OF THE TWENTIETH CENTURY, Octavio Paz (1914–1998) was Mexico's most famous living poet and one of its most visible public figures. In addition to writing more than forty books—of poetry, essays, criticism, and political commentary—he served as Mexico's ambassador to India from 1962 until 1968. In 1990, he became the first Mexican—and only the fourth Latin American—to win the Nobel Prize for literature.

Paz's most famous prose work is *The Labyrinth of Solitude* (1950). In the nine essays that constitute this book, Paz sets for himself the daunting task of defining Mexican identity. To do this, he analyzes many different layers of Mexico's history, including Aztec myths, Catholic spiritual traditions, the Spanish conquest, French imperialism under Napoleon III, and American militarism in the nineteenth century and economic dominance in the twentieth century. Because the country has been subject to so many different conquests, occupations, and fragmentations, Paz argues, its national character is divided, lacking in confidence, and deeply suspicious.

The key to understanding Mexico is, for Paz, understanding the nature of its people's solitude. This solitude is based not in physical separation but in the inability to form emotional connections. The people who emerge from the pages of *The Labyrinth of Solitude* feel their country's history of poverty, betrayal, and vulnerability in the cores of their beings. "They act," he writes, "like persons who are wearing disguises, who are afraid of a stranger's look because it could strip them and leave them stark naked." *The Labyrinth of Solitude* seeks to understand this condition by looking at myths, customs, language, politics, history, and other representatives of what Paz calls "the psychology of a nation."

The following selection comes from the essay "The Day of the Dead," which deals with one of Mexico's most important holidays. In this selection, Paz attempts to explain the nature of great celebrations, or fiestas, in his country's cultural life. Paz begins with the observation that very poor villages often spend the majority of their collective wealth each year on one or two elaborate fiestas. He notes that elaborate celebrations are much more important to the poor than to the rich, but he also insists that their very nature is shrouded in ambiguity. They simultaneously celebrate life and death, order and chaos, love and hate, and joy and sorrow. Because of this ambiguity, Paz argues, these intensely communal celebrations also preserve the Mexican tradition of solitude.

Paz's purpose in this selection is to explain both the practice of the fiesta and the deep psychology behind this practice. In the process he advances a very subtle thesis about the connection between poverty and occasional excess.

The solitary Mexican loves fiestas and public gatherings. Any occasion for getting together will serve, any pretext to stop the flow of time and commemorate men and events with festivals and ceremonies. We are a ritual people, and this characteristic enriches both our imaginations and our sensibilities, which are equally sharp and alert. The art of the fiesta has been debased almost everywhere else, but not in Mexico. There are few places in the world where it is possible to take part in a spectacle like our great religious fiestas with their violent primary colors, their bizarre costumes and dances, their fireworks and ceremonies, and their inexhaustible welter of surprises: the fruit, candy, toys and other objects sold on these days in the plazas and open-air markets.

Our calendar is crowded with fiestas. There are certain days when the whole country, from the most remote villages to the largest cities, prays, shouts, feasts, gets drunk and kills, in honor of the Virgin of Guadalupe or Benito Juárez.[1] Each year on the fifteenth of September, at eleven o'clock at night, we celebrate the fiesta of the Grito[2] in all the plazas of the Republic, and the excited crowds actually shout for a whole hour . . . the better, perhaps, to remain silent for the rest of the year. During the days before and after the twelfth of December,[3] time comes to a full stop, and instead of pushing us toward a deceptive tomorrow that is always beyond our reach, offers us a complete and perfect today of dancing and revelry, of communion with the most ancient and secret Mexico. Time is no longer succession, and becomes what it originally was and is: the present, in which past and future are reconciled.

But the fiestas which the Church and State provide for the country as a whole are not enough. The life of every city and village is ruled by a patron saint whose blessing is celebrated with devout regularity. Neighborhoods and trades also have their annual fiestas, their ceremonies and fairs. And each one of us—atheist, Catholic, or merely indifferent—has his own saint's day, which he observes every year. It is impossible to calculate how many fiestas we have and how much time and money we spend on them. I remember asking the mayor of a village near Mitla, several years ago, "What is the income of the village government?" "About 3,000 pesos a year. We are very poor. But the Governor and the Federal Government always help us to meet our expenses." "And how are the 3,000 pesos spent?" "Mostly on fiestas, señor. We are a small village, but we have two patron saints."

The translator's footnotes have been omitted.

1. **The Virgin of Guadalupe or Benito Juárez:** The Virgin of Guadalupe, the patron saint of Mexico, is the form that the Virgin Mary purportedly took when she appeared to the Indian convert Juan Diego in 1531 and instructed him to build a church. Benito Juárez (1806–1872), the only Indian to serve as the president of Mexico, remains one of that country's greatest heroes. He led Mexico's famous victory over the French under Napoleon III, who attempted to install a puppet government under the "Emperor" Maximilian.

2. **The Grito:** El Grito de Dolores ("The Shout of Pain"), the sermon by Spanish priest Miguel Hidalgo that launched the Mexican Revolution by detailing Mexico's grievances against Spain. The date of this sermon, September 16, is celebrated as Independence Day in Mexico.

3. **The twelfth of December:** the festival of the Virgin of Guadalupe.

This reply is not surprising. Our poverty can be measured by the frequency and luxuriousness of our holidays. Wealthy countries have very few: there is neither the time nor the desire for them, and they are not necessary. The people have other things to do, and when they amuse themselves they do so in small groups. The modern masses are agglomerations of solitary individuals. On great occasions in Paris or New York, when the populace gathers in the squares or stadiums, the absence of people, in the sense of *a* people, is remarkable: there are couples and small groups, but they never form a living community in which the individual is at once dissolved and redeemed. But how could a poor Mexican live without the two or three annual fiestas that make up for his poverty and misery? Fiestas are our only luxury. They replace, and are perhaps better than, the theater and vacations, Anglo-Saxon weekends and cocktail parties, the bourgeois reception, the Mediterranean café.

In all of these ceremonies—national or local, trade or family—the Mexican opens   5
out. They all give him a chance to reveal himself and to converse with God, country, friends or relations. During these days the silent Mexican whistles, shouts, sings, shoots off fireworks, discharges his pistol into the air. He discharges his soul. And his shout, like the rockets we love so much, ascends to the heavens, explodes into green, red, blue, and white lights, and falls dizzily to earth with a trail of golden sparks. This is the night when friends who have not exchanged more than the pre-scribed courtesies for months get drunk together, trade confidences, weep over the same troubles, discover that they are brothers, and sometimes, to prove it, kill each other. The night is full of songs and loud cries. The lover wakes up his sweetheart with an orchestra. There are jokes and conversations from balcony to balcony, side-walk to sidewalk. Nobody talks quietly. Hats fly in the air. Laughter and curses ring like silver pesos. Guitars are brought out. Now and then, it is true, the happiness ends badly, in quarrels, insults, pistol shots, stabbings. But these too are part of the fiesta, for the Mexican does not seek amusement: he seeks to escape from himself, to leap over the wall of solitude that confines him during the rest of the year. All are possessed by violence and frenzy. Their souls explode like the colors and voices and emotions. Do they forget themselves and show their true faces? Nobody knows. The important thing is to go out, open a way, get drunk on noise, people, colors. Mexico is celebrating a fiesta. And this fiesta, shot through with lightning and delirium, is the brilliant reverse to our silence and apathy, our reticence and gloom.

According to the interpretation of French sociologists, the fiesta is an excess, an expense. By means of this squandering the community protects itself against the envy of the gods or of men. Sacrifices and offerings placate or buy off the gods and the patron saints. Wasting money and expending energy affirms the community's wealth in both. This luxury is a proof of health, a show of abundance and power. Or a magic trap. For squandering is an effort to attract abundance by contagion. Money calls to money. When life is thrown away it increases; the orgy, which is sexual expenditure, is also a ceremony of regeneration; waste gives strength. New Year celebrations, in every culture, signify something beyond the mere observance of a date on the calendar.

The day is a pause: time is stopped, is actually annihilated. The rites that celebrate its death are intended to provoke its rebirth, because they mark not only the end of an old year but also the beginning of a new. Everything attracts its opposite. The fiesta's function, then, is more utilitarian than we think: waste attracts or promotes wealth, and is an investment like any other, except that the returns on it cannot be measured or counted. What is sought is potency, life, health. In this sense the fiesta, like the gift and the offering, is one of the most ancient of economic forms.

This interpretation has always seemed to me to be incomplete. The fiesta is by nature sacred, literally or figuratively, and above all it is the advent of the unusual. It is governed by its own special rules, that set it apart from other days, and it has a logic, an ethic and even an economy that are often in conflict with everyday norms. It all occurs in an enchanted world: time is transformed to a mythical past or a total present; space, the scene of the fiesta, is turned into a gaily decorated world of its own; and the persons taking part cast off all human or social rank and become, for the moment, living images. And everything takes place as if it were not so, as if it were a dream. But whatever happens, our actions have a greater lightness, a different gravity. They take on other meanings and with them we contract new obligations. We throw down our burdens of time and reason.

In certain fiestas the very notion of order disappears. Chaos comes back and license rules. Anything is permitted: the customary hierarchies vanish, along with all social, sex, caste, and trade distinctions. Men disguise themselves as women, gentlemen as slaves, the poor as the rich. The army, the clergy, and the law are ridiculed. Obligatory sacrilege, ritual profanation is committed. Love becomes promiscuity. Sometimes the fiesta becomes a Black Mass.[4] Regulations, habits and customs are violated. Respectable people put away the dignified expressions and conservative clothes that isolate them, dress up in gaudy colors, hide behind a mask, and escape from themselves.

Therefore the fiesta is not only an excess, a ritual squandering of the goods painfully accumulated during the rest of the year; it is also a revolt, a sudden immersion in the formless, in pure being. By means of the fiesta society frees itself from the norms it has established. It ridicules its gods, its principles, and its laws: it denies its own self.

The fiesta is a revolution in the most literal sense of the word. In the confu-   10
sion that it generates, society is dissolved, is drowned, insofar as it is an organism ruled according to certain laws and principles. But it drowns in itself, in its own original chaos or liberty. Everything is united: good and evil, day and night, the sacred and the profane. Everything merges, loses shape and individuality and returns to the primordial mass. The fiesta is a cosmic experiment, an experiment in disorder, reuniting contradictory elements and principles in order to bring about a

4. **Black Mass:** a Satanic parody of the Christian Mass; according to legend, it culminates with a sexual orgy.

renascence of life. Ritual death promotes a rebirth; vomiting increases the appetite; the orgy, sterile in itself, renews the fertility of the mother or of the earth. The fiesta is a return to a remote and undifferentiated state, prenatal or presocial. It is a return that is also a beginning, in accordance with the dialectic[5] that is inherent in social processes.

The group emerges purified and strengthened from this plunge into chaos. It has immersed itself in its own origins, in the womb from which it came. To express it in another way, the fiesta denies society as an organic system of differentiated forms and principles, but affirms it as a source of creative energy. It is a true "re-creation," the opposite of the "recreation" characterizing modern vacations, which do not entail any rites or ceremonies whatever and are as individualistic and sterile as the world that invented them.

Society communes with itself during the fiesta. Its members return to original chaos and freedom. Social structures break down and new relationships, unexpected rules, capricious hierarchies are created. In the general disorder everybody forgets himself and enters into otherwise forbidden situations and places. The bounds between audience and actors, officials and servants, are erased. Everybody takes part in the fiesta, everybody is caught up in its whirlwind. Whatever its mood, its character, its meaning, the fiesta is participation, and this trait distinguishes it from all other ceremonies and social phenomena. Lay or religious, orgy or saturnalia,[6] the fiesta is a social act based on the full participation of all its celebrants.

Thanks to the fiesta the Mexican opens out, participates, communes with his fellows and with the values that give meaning to his religious or political existence. And it is significant that a country as sorrowful as ours should have so many and such joyous fiestas. Their frequency, their brilliance and excitement, the enthusiasm with which we take part, all suggest that without them we would explode. They free us, if only momentarily, from the thwarted impulses, the inflammable desires that we carry within us. But the Mexican fiesta is not merely a return to an original state of formless and normless liberty: the Mexican is not seeking to return, but to escape from himself, to exceed himself. Our fiestas are explosions. Life and death, joy and sorrow, music and mere noise are united, not to re-create or recognize themselves, but to swallow each other up. There is nothing so joyous as a Mexican fiesta, but there is also nothing so sorrowful. Fiesta night is also a night of mourning.

If we hide within ourselves in our daily lives, we discharge ourselves in the whirlwind of the fiesta. It is more than an opening out: we rend ourselves open. Everything—music, love, friendship—ends in tumult and violence. The frenzy of our festivals shows the extent to which our solitude closes us off from communication with the world. We are familiar with delirium, with songs and shouts, with the

---

5. **Dialectic:** the combined effect of two contra-dictory phenomena (p. 678).

6. **Saturnalia:** a riotous, unrestrained celebration, named after the ancient Roman festival of Saturn.

monologue . . . but not with the dialogue. Our fiestas, like our confidences, our loves, our attempts to reorder our society, are violent breaks with the old or the established. Each time we try to express ourselves we have to break with ourselves. And the fiesta is only one example, perhaps the most typical, of this violent break. It is not difficult to name others, equally revealing: our games, which are always a going to extremes, often mortal; our profligate spending, the reverse of our timid investments and business enterprises; our confessions. The somber Mexican, closed up in himself, suddenly explodes, tears open his breast and reveals himself, though not without a certain complacency, and not without a stopping place in the shameful or terrible mazes of his intimacy. We are not frank, but our sincerity can reach extremes that horrify a European. The explosive, dramatic, sometimes even suicidal manner in which we strip ourselves, surrender ourselves, is evidence that something inhibits and suffocates us. Something impedes us from being. And since we cannot or dare not confront our own selves, we resort to the fiesta. It fires us into the void; it is a drunken rapture that burns itself out, a pistol shot in the air, a skyrocket.

UNDERSTANDING THE TEXT

1. In what ways is a Mexican fiesta a form of ritual?

2. Why, according to Octavio Paz, do people in poor nations have a greater desire for elaborate celebrations than do people in wealthy nations?

3. Why do celebrations occasionally result in "quarrels, insults, pistol shots, stabbings"? What aspect of the fiesta encourages these extreme elements? Are they a natural outgrowth of the fiesta?

4. Why does Paz cite the opinion of French sociologists that the fiesta represents "an excess" designed to protect a community "against the envy of the gods"? Does he accept this theory? How does he incorporate it into his own ideas (p. 577)?

5. How do fiestas relate to the established social order in Mexico? Why does Paz call the fiesta a "revolution"? How might the fiesta's short duration relate to its revolutionary nature?

MAKING CONNECTIONS

1. How might Paz respond to Po-Chü-i's "The Flower Market" (p. 545)? Are the expenditures that Mexican villages make on fiestas comparable to the money wealthy people spend on flowers? Why or why not?

2. How does Paz's view of the regulated lawlessness of the fiesta compare with other views of law and disobedience, such as Martin Luther King Jr.'s "Letter from Birmingham Jail" (p. 425) or Aung San Suu Kyi's "In Quest of Democracy" (p. 442)? How might a brief period of controlled chaos be a way to preserve order?

3. How do the drunken revelers in Hogarth's *Gin Lane* (p. 548) compare with the celebrants Paz describes in this selection? What are their key similarities and differences?

WRITING ABOUT THE TEXT

1. In light of Paz's view of the fiesta, examine a party or cultural celebration you have attended. How does Paz's model work as a way to interpret your own experiences?

2. Write an essay criticizing or defending the mayor of a small town for spending all of the town's money on an elaborate celebration when many townspeople lack adequate food, clothing, and shelter.

3. Explore the connection between celebration and revolution. Research not only Mexican fiestas but also different kinds of carnivals, festivities, and other parties in which social orders and categories are, at least for a time, reversed or made unstable.

GARRETT HARDIN

Lifeboat Ethics: The Case against Helping the Poor

[1974]

FOR THE LAST THREE DECADES of the twentieth century, Garrett Hardin (1915–2003), professor of human ecology at the University of California at Santa Barbara, was the most famous American representative of the neo-Malthusian school of thought. Using Thomas Malthus's basic formulation that population increases geometrically while resources increase arithmetically, Hardin insisted that it is ethically imperative for human beings to understand and respect the "carrying capacity" of the earth, and that failure to do so will invite human catastrophe on the largest scale.

In his famous 1968 essay, "The Tragedy of the Commons," Hardin uses a common grazing area, "the commons," as a metaphor for all nonproprietary resources. Because nobody owns a common pasture, everyone may use it for grazing cattle. When the population of cattle using the commons exceeds the commons' carrying capacity, it is in everybody's collective interest to decrease the number of cattle. However, since each individual has an interest in grazing as many cattle as possible on the commons, people will inevitably destroy the pasture by overgrazing it. The tragedy of the commons, then, is that what serves the best interests of everybody collectively usually does not serve the best interests of anybody specifically. Thus, individuals making hundreds of *rational* economic decisions about the use of a common resource will lead, inevitably, to the completely *irrational* destruction of that resource. The tragedy of the commons explains such phenomena as air and water pollution, overfishing, public parking problems, and, most of all, the overpopulation of the earth.

Hardin ended "The Tragedy of the Commons" by stating that "the only way we can preserve and nurture other and more precious freedoms is by relinquishing the freedom to breed." He believed that governments throughout the world should enact mandatory barriers and strong incentive programs to prevent population growth. In a follow-up essay, "Lifeboat Ethics: The Case against Helping the Poor," included here, Hardin argues that the wealthy societies of North America and Western Europe should refuse to subsidize population growth in less-developed countries by providing them with food and other necessities, and that comparatively wealthy nations should severely restrict immigration from poorer countries on the grounds that increased immigration makes local efforts at population control irrelevant to the carrying capacity of the land.

Though Hardin's solutions to the problem are harsh, so much so that they have never been enacted by Western governments, they are solidly rooted in the utilitarian ethic of providing the "greatest good for the greatest number of people." Like Malthus, Hardin believed that overpopulation was the primary cause of human misery in his lifetime and the greatest threat to Earth's future in the long term. Food banks, international aid programs, and unrestricted immigration do not solve this problem, he insisted; they merely allow the number of people who suffer from it to increase.

As the title of this essay implies, "Lifeboat Ethics" relies on a sustained analogy between the "developed" world and a lifeboat. Early in the essay, Hardin offers this analogy as a replacement for the more common analogy of "Spaceship Earth." Moral decisions aboard a lifeboat, he says, must be approached differently than moral decisions aboard a spaceship. The remainder of the essay explores the implications of this analogy as they apply to the world's scarce resources.

Environmentalists use the metaphor of the earth as a "spaceship" in trying to persuade countries, industries and people to stop wasting and polluting our natural resources. Since we all share life on this planet, they argue, no single person or institution has the right to destroy, waste, or use more than a fair share of its resources.

But does everyone on earth have an equal right to an equal share of its resources? The spaceship metaphor can be dangerous when used by misguided idealists to justify suicidal policies for sharing our resources through uncontrolled immigration and foreign aid. In their enthusiastic but unrealistic generosity, they confuse the ethics of a spaceship with those of a lifeboat.

A true spaceship would have to be under the control of a captain, since no ship could possibly survive if its course were determined by committee. Spaceship Earth certainly has no captain; the United Nations is merely a toothless tiger, with little power to enforce any policy upon its bickering members.

If we divide the world crudely into rich nations and poor nations, two thirds of them are desperately poor, and only one third comparatively rich, with the United States the wealthiest of all. Metaphorically each rich nation can be seen as a lifeboat full of comparatively rich people. In the ocean outside each lifeboat swim the poor of the world, who would like to get in, or at least to share some of the wealth. What should the lifeboat passengers do?

First, we must recognize the limited capacity of any lifeboat. For example, a   5
nation's land has a limited capacity to support a population and as the current energy crisis has shown us, in some ways we have already exceeded the carrying capacity of our land.

Adrift in a Moral Sea

So here we sit, say 50 people in our lifeboat. To be generous, let us assume it has room for 10 more, making a total capacity of 60. Suppose the 50 of us in the lifeboat see 100 others swimming in the water outside, begging for admission to our boat or for handouts. We have several options: we may be tempted to try to live by the Christian ideal of being "our brother's keeper," or by the Marxist ideal of "to each according to his needs." Since the needs of all in the water are the same, and since they can all be seen as "our brothers," we could take them all into our boat, making a total of 150 in a boat designed for 60. The boat swamps, everyone drowns. Complete justice, complete catastrophe.

Since the boat has an unused excess capacity of 10 more passengers, we could admit just 10 more to it. But which 10 do we let in? How do we choose? Do we pick the best 10, "first come, first served"? And what do we say to the 90 we exclude? If we do let an extra 10 into our lifeboat, we will have lost our "safety factor," an engineering principle of critical importance. For example, if we don't leave room for excess capacity as a safety factor in our country's agriculture, a new plant disease or a bad change in the weather could have disastrous consequences.

Suppose we decide to preserve our small safety factor and admit no more to the lifeboat. Our survival is then possible although we shall have to be constantly on guard against boarding parties.

While this last solution clearly offers the only means of our survival, it is morally abhorrent to many people. Some say they feel guilty about their good luck. My reply is simple: "Get out and yield your place to others." This may solve the problem of the guilt-ridden person's conscience, but it does not change the ethics of the lifeboat. The needy person to whom the guilt-ridden person yields his place will not himself feel guilty about his good luck. If he did, he would not climb aboard. The net result of conscience-stricken people giving up their unjustly held seats is the elimination of that sort of conscience from the lifeboat.

This is the basic metaphor within which we must work out our solutions. Let   10 us now enrich the image, step by step, with substantive additions from the real world, a world that must solve real and pressing problems of overpopulation and hunger.

The harsh ethics of the lifeboat become even harsher when we consider the reproductive differences between the rich nations and the poor nations. The people inside the lifeboats are doubling in numbers every 87 years; those swimming around outside are doubling, on the average, every 35 years, more than twice as fast as the rich. And since the world's resources are dwindling, the difference in prosperity between the rich and the poor can only increase.

As of 1973, the U.S. had a population of 210 million people, who were increasing by 0.8 percent per year. Outside our lifeboat, let us imagine another 210 million people (say the combined populations of Colombia, Ecuador, Venezuela, Morocco, Pakistan, Thailand and the Philippines) who are increasing at a rate of 3.3 percent per year. Put differently, the doubling time for this aggregate population is 21 years, compared to 87 years for the U.S.

The harsh ethics of the lifeboat become harsher when we consider the reproductive differences between rich and poor.

Multiplying the Rich and the Poor

Now suppose the U.S. agreed to pool its resources with those seven countries, with everyone receiving an equal share. Initially the ratio of Americans to non-Americans in this model would be one-to-one. But consider what the ratio would be after 87 years, by which time the Americans would have doubled to a population of 420 million. By then, doubling every 21 years, the other group would have swollen to 354 billion. Each American would have to share the available resources with more than eight people.

But, one could argue, this discussion assumes that current population trends will   15
continue, and they may not. Quite so. Most likely the rate of population increase will decline much faster in the U.S. than it will in the other countries, and there does not seem to be much we can do about it. In sharing with "each according to his needs," we must recognize that needs are determined by population size, which is determined by the rate of reproduction, which at present is regarded as a sovereign right of every nation, poor or not. This being so, the philanthropic load created by the sharing ethic of the spaceship can only increase.

The Tragedy of the Commons

The fundamental error of spaceship ethics, and the sharing it requires, is that it leads to what I call "the tragedy of the commons." Under a system of private property, the men who own property recognize their responsibility to care for it, for if they don't they will eventually suffer. A farmer, for instance, will allow no more cattle in a pasture than its carrying capacity justifies. If he overloads it, erosion sets in, weeds take over, and he loses the use of the pasture.

If a pasture becomes a commons open to all, the right of each to use it may not be matched by a corresponding responsibility to protect it. Asking everyone to use it with discretion will hardly do, for the considerate herdsman who refrains from overloading the commons suffers more than a selfish one who says his needs are greater. If everyone would restrain himself, all would be well; but it takes only one less than everyone to ruin a system of voluntary restraint. In a crowded world of less than perfect human beings, mutual ruin is inevitable if there are no controls. This is the tragedy of the commons.

One of the major tasks of education today should be the creation of such an acute awareness of the dangers of the commons that people will recognize its many varieties. For example, the air and water have become polluted because they are treated as commons. Further growth in the population or per-capita conversion of natural resources into pollutants will only make the problem worse. The same holds true for the fish of the oceans. Fishing fleets have nearly disappeared in many parts of the world, technological improvements in the art of fishing are hastening the day of complete ruin. Only the replacement of the system of the commons with a responsible system of control will save the land, air, water and oceanic fisheries.

The World Food Bank

In recent years there has been a push to create a new commons called a World Food Bank, an international depository of food reserves to which nations would contribute according to their abilities and from which they would draw according to their needs. This humanitarian proposal has received support from many liberal international groups, and from such prominent citizens as Margaret Mead,[1] U.N. Secretary General Kurt Waldheim, and Senators Edward Kennedy and George McGovern.

A world food bank appeals powerfully to our humanitarian impulses. But before   20 we rush ahead with such a plan, let us recognize where the greatest political push comes from, lest we be disillusioned later. Our experience with the "Food for Peace program," or Public Law 480, gives us the answer. This program moved billions of dollars worth of U.S. surplus grain to food-short, population-long countries during the past two decades. But when P.L. 480 first became law, a headline in the business magazine *Forbes* revealed the real power behind it: "Feeding the World's Hungry Millions: How It Will Mean Billions for U.S. Business."

And indeed it did. In the years 1960 to 1970, U.S. taxpayers spent a total of $7.9 billion on the Food for Peace program. Between 1948 and 1970, they also paid an additional $50 billion for other economic-aid programs, some of which went for food and food-producing machinery and technology. Though all U.S. taxpayers were forced to contribute to the cost of P.L. 480 certain special interest groups gained handsomely under the program. Farmers did not have to contribute the grain; the Government or rather the taxpayers, bought it from them at full market prices. The increased demand raised prices of farm products generally. The manufacturers of farm machinery, fertilizers and pesticides benefited by the farmers' extra efforts to grow more food. Grain elevators profited from storing the surplus until it could be shipped. Railroads made money hauling it to ports, and shipping lines profited from carrying it overseas. The implementation of P.L. 480 required the creation of a vast Government bureaucracy, which then acquired its own vested interest in continuing the program regardless of its merits.

Extracting Dollars

Those who proposed and defended the Food for Peace program in public rarely mentioned its importance to any of these special interests. The public emphasis was always on its humanitarian effects. The combination of silent selfish interests and highly vocal humanitarian apologists made a powerful and successful lobby for

1. **Margaret Mead:** see p. 500.

extracting money from taxpayers. We can expect the same lobby to push now for the creation of a World Food Bank.

However great the potential benefit to selfish interests, it should not be a decisive argument against a truly humanitarian program. We must ask if such a program would actually do more good than harm, not only momentarily but also in the long run. Those who propose the food bank usually refer to a current "emergency" or "crisis" in terms of world food supply. But what is an emergency? Although they may be infrequent and sudden, everyone knows that emergencies will occur from time to time. A well-run family, company, organization or country prepares for the likelihood of accidents and emergencies. It expects them, it budgets for them, it saves for them.

Learning the Hard Way

What happens if some organizations or countries budget for accidents and others do not? If each country is solely responsible for its own well-being, poorly managed ones will suffer. But they can learn from experience. They may mend their ways, and learn to budget for infrequent but certain emergencies. For example, the weather varies from year to year, and periodic crop failures are certain. A wise and competent government saves out of the production of the good years in anticipation of bad years to come. Joseph taught this policy to Pharaoh in Egypt more than 2,000 years ago. Yet the great majority of the governments in the world today do not follow such a policy. They lack either the wisdom or the competence, or both. Should those nations that do manage to put something aside be forced to come to the rescue each time an emergency occurs among the poor nations?

"But it isn't their fault!" some kind-hearted liberals argue. "How can we blame   25 the poor people who are caught in an emergency? Why must they suffer for the sins of their governments?" The concept of blame is simply not relevant here. The real question is, what are the operational consequences of establishing a world food bank? If it is open to every country every time a need develops, slovenly rulers will not be motivated to take Joseph's advice. Someone will always come to their aid. Some countries will deposit food in the world food bank, and others will withdraw it. There will be almost no overlap. As a result of such solutions to food shortage emergencies, the poor countries will not learn to mend their ways, and will suffer progressively greater emergencies as their populations grow.

Population Control the Crude Way

On the average poor countries undergo a 2.5 percent increase in population each year; rich countries, about 0.8 percent. Only rich countries have anything in the way of food reserves set aside, and even they do not have as much as they should.

Poor countries have none. If poor countries received no food from the outside, the rate of their population growth would be periodically checked by crop failures and famines. But if they can always draw on a world food bank in time of need, their population can continue to grow unchecked, and so will their "need" for aid. In the short run, a world food bank may diminish that need, but in the long run it actually increases the need without limit.

Without some system of worldwide food sharing, the proportion of people in the rich and poor nations might eventually stabilize. The overpopulated poor countries would decrease in numbers, while the rich countries that had room for more people would increase. But with a well-meaning system of sharing, such as a world food bank, the growth differential between the rich and the poor countries will not only persist, it will increase. Because of the higher rate of population growth in the poor countries of the world, 88 percent of today's children are born poor, and only 12 percent rich. Year by year the ratio becomes worse, as the fast-reproducing poor outnumber the slow-reproducing rich.

A world food bank is thus a commons in disguise. People will have more motivation to draw from it than to add to any common store. The less provident and less able will multiply at the expense of the abler and more provident, bringing eventual ruin upon all who share in the commons. Besides, any system of "sharing" that amounts to foreign aid from the rich nations to the poor nations will carry the taint of charity, which will contribute little to the world peace so devoutly desired by those who support the idea of a world food bank.

As past U.S. foreign-aid programs have amply and depressingly demonstrated, international charity frequently inspires mistrust and antagonism rather than gratitude on the part of the recipient nation. . . .

Chinese Fish and Miracle Rice

The modern approach to foreign aid stresses the export of technology and advice,   30
rather than money and food. As an ancient Chinese proverb goes: "Give a man a fish and he will eat for a day; teach him how to fish and he will eat for the rest of his days." Acting on this advice, the Rockefeller and Ford Foundations have financed a number of programs for improving agriculture in the hungry nations. Known as the "Green Revolution," these programs have led to the development of "miracle rice" and "miracle wheat," new strains that offer bigger harvests and greater resistance to crop damage. Norman Borlaug, the Nobel Prize–winning agronomist who, supported by the Rockefeller Foundation, developed "miracle wheat," is one of the most prominent advocates of a world food bank.

Whether or not the Green Revolution can increase food production as much as its champions claim is a debatable but possibly irrelevant point. Those who support this well-intended humanitarian effort should first consider some of the fundamentals of human ecology. Ironically, one man who did was the late Alan Gregg, a vice president of the Rockefeller Foundation. Two decades ago he expressed strong doubts about the wisdom of such attempts to increase food production. He likened the growth and spread of humanity over the surface of the earth to the spread of cancer in the human body, remarking that "cancerous growths demand food; but, as far as I know, they have never been cured by getting it."

Overloading the Environment

Every human born constitutes a draft on all aspects of the environment: food, air, water, forests, beaches, wildlife, scenery and solitude. Food can, perhaps, be significantly increased to meet a growing demand. But what about clean beaches, unspoiled forests, and solitude? If we satisfy a growing population's need for food, we necessarily decrease its per capita supply of the other resources needed by men.

India, for example, now has a population of 600 million, which increases by 15 million each year. This population already puts a huge load on a relatively impoverished environment. The country's forests are now only a small fraction of what they were three centuries ago and floods and erosion continually destroy the insufficient farmland that remains. Every one of the 15 million new lives added to India's population puts an additional burden on the environment, and increases the economic and social costs of crowding. However humanitarian our intent, every Indian life saved through medical or nutritional assistance from abroad diminishes the quality of life for those who remain, and for subsequent generations. If rich countries make it possible, through foreign aid, for 600 million Indians to swell to 1.2 billion in a mere 28 years, as their current growth rate threatens, will future generations of Indians thank us for hastening the destruction of their environment? Will our good intentions be sufficient excuse for the consequences of our actions?

My final example of a commons in action is one for which the public has the least desire for rational discussion—immigration. Anyone who publicly questions the wisdom of current U.S. immigration policy is promptly charged with bigotry, prejudice, ethnocentrism, chauvinism, isolationism or selfishness. Rather than encounter such accusations, one would rather talk about other matters leaving immigration policy to wallow in the crosscurrents of special interests that take no account of the good of the whole, or the interests of posterity.

Perhaps we still feel guilty about things we said in the past. Two generations ago the popular press frequently referred to Dagos, Wops, Polacks, Chinks and Krauts in articles about how America was being "overrun" by foreigners of supposedly inferior genetic stock. . . . But because the implied inferiority of foreigners was used then as justification for keeping them out, people now assume that restrictive policies could only be based on such misguided notions. There are other grounds.   35

A Nation of Immigrants

Just consider the numbers involved. Our Government acknowledges a net inflow of 400,000 immigrants a year. While we have no hard data on the extent of illegal entries, educated guesses put the figure at about 600,000 a year. Since the natural increase (excess of births over deaths) of the resident population now runs about 1.7 million per year, the yearly gain from immigration amounts to at least 19 percent of the total annual increase, and may be as much as 37 percent if we include the estimate for illegal immigrants. Considering the growing use of birth-control devices, the potential effect of education campaigns by such organizations as Planned Parenthood Federation of America and Zero Population Growth, and the influence of inflation and the housing shortage, the fertility rate of American women may decline so much that immigration could account for all the yearly increase in population. Should we not at least ask if that is what we want?

For the sake of those who worry about whether the "quality" of the average immigrant compares favorably with the quality of the average resident, let us assume that immigrants and native-born citizens are of exactly equal quality, however one defines that term. We will focus here only on quantity; and since our conclusions will depend on nothing else, all charges of bigotry and chauvinism become irrelevant.

Immigration vs. Food Supply

World food banks move food to the people, hastening the exhaustion of the environment of the poor countries. Unrestricted immigration, on the other hand, moves people to the food, thus speeding up the destruction of the environment of the rich countries. We can easily understand why poor people should want to make this latter transfer, but why should rich hosts encourage it?

As in the case of foreign-aid programs, immigration receives support from selfish interests and humanitarian impulses. The primary selfish interest in unimpeded immigration is the desire of employers for cheap labor, particularly in industries and trades that offer degrading work. In the past, one wave of foreigners after another was brought into the U.S. to work at wretched jobs for wretched wages. In recent years the Cubans, Puerto Ricans and Mexicans have had this dubious honor. The interests of the employers of cheap labor mesh well with the guilty silence of the country's liberal intelligentsia. White Anglo-Saxon Protestants are particularly reluctant to call for a closing of the doors to immigration for fear of being called bigots.

But not all countries have such reluctant leadership. Most educated Hawaiians, for example, are keenly aware of the limits of their environment, particularly in terms of population growth. There is only so much room on the islands, and the islanders know it. To Hawaiians, immigrants from the other 49 states present as great a threat as those from other nations. At a recent meeting of Hawaiian government

40

officials in Honolulu, I had the ironic delight of hearing a speaker, who like most of his audience was of Japanese ancestry, ask how the country might practically and constitutionally close its doors to further immigration. One member of the audience countered: "How can we shut the doors now? We have many friends and relatives in Japan that we'd like to bring here some day so that they can enjoy Hawaii too." The Japanese-American speaker smiled sympathetically and answered: "Yes, but we have children now, and someday we'll have grandchildren too. We can bring more people here from Japan only by giving away some of the land that we hope to pass on to our grandchildren some day. What right do we have to do that?"

At this point, I can hear U.S. liberals asking: "How can you justify slamming the door once you're inside? You say that immigrants should be kept out. But aren't we all immigrants, or the descendants of immigrants? If we insist on staying, must we not admit all others?" Our craving for intellectual order leads us to seek and prefer symmetrical rules and morals: a single rule for me and everybody else; the same rule yesterday, today and tomorrow. Justice, we feel, should not change with time and place.

We Americans of non-Indian ancestry can look upon ourselves as the descendants of thieves who are guilty morally, if not legally, of stealing this land from its Indian owners. Should we then give back the land to the now living American descendants of those Indians? However morally or logically sound this proposal may be, I, for one, am unwilling to live by it and I know no one else who is. Besides, the logical consequence would be absurd. Suppose that, intoxicated with a sense of pure justice, we should decide to turn our land over to the Indians. Since all our other wealth has also been derived from the land, wouldn't we be morally obliged to give that back to the Indians too?

Pure Justice vs. Reality

Clearly, the concept of pure justice produces an infinite regression to absurdity. Centuries ago, wise men invented statutes of limitations to justify the rejection of such pure justice, in the interest of preventing continual disorder. The law zealously defends property rights, but only relatively recent property rights. Drawing a line after an arbitrary time has elapsed may be unjust, but the alternatives are worse.

We are all the descendants of thieves, and the world's resources are inequitably distributed. But we must begin the journey to tomorrow from the point where we are today. We cannot remake the past. We cannot safely divide the wealth equitably among all peoples so long as people reproduce at different rates. To do so would guarantee that our grandchildren and everyone else's grandchildren would have only a ruined world to inhabit.

To be generous with one's own possessions is quite different from being generous   45
with those of posterity. We should call this point to the attention of those who,

from a commendable love of justice and equality, would institute a system of the commons, either in the form of a world food bank, or of unrestricted immigration. We must convince them if we wish to save at least some parts of the world from environmental ruin.

Without a true world government to control reproduction and the use of available resources, the sharing ethic of the spaceship is impossible. For the foreseeable future, our survival demands that we govern our actions by the ethics of a lifeboat, harsh though they may be. Posterity will be satisfied with nothing less.

UNDERSTANDING THE TEXT

1. Why does Garrett Hardin use the lifeboat as his principal metaphor for the earth? How do "lifeboat ethics" differ from "spaceship ethics"? Does limited carrying capacity really make the earth comparable to a lifeboat? What might the global equivalent of a capsized lifeboat be?

2. Why does Hardin reject both the Christian and the Marxist formulations for helping the poor? (See the selection from the New Testament, p. 541). Is his argument entirely contrary to Christian principles?

3. How does Hardin's concept of "the tragedy of the commons" inform this essay? What kinds of "common resources" are compromised by population increases? In what way is the proposed World Food Bank a "commons"?

4. Why does Hardin believe that increasing food production by genetically altering plants and animals is not a good idea? What does he believe will be the result of increasing the world's food supply to support the current population at a subsistence level?

5. What resources other than food does Hardin believe people should consider when making decisions about population and immigration? Which of the things he lists are necessities and which are luxuries?

6. Why does Hardin believe that previous injustices—such as the European conquest of the Americas—are of no practical importance today? Do you agree?

7. What does Hardin see as the difference between absolute justice and the practical necessities of the real world? Does he see "pure justice" as desirable? What assumptions about morality and immorality does Hardin use as the basis for his ethical argument?

MAKING CONNECTIONS

1. How accurately does Hardin represent Malthus's arguments about population growth and human poverty (p. 552)?

2. How well does Hardin counter the arguments of Jesus (p. 541) and Gandhi (p. 560) about the need to help the poor? How do his arguments compare with those of Joseph Stiglitz (p. 594)?

3. To what extent is Hardin's argument a form of Social Darwinism (see the excerpt from "Natural Selection," p. 314)? How would an environment governed by natural selection respond to unchecked population growth within a community?

WRITING ABOUT THE TEXT

1. Write an essay entitled "The Case for Helping the Poor" in which you rebut Hardin. As possible starting points for your essay, consider the positions of Jesus (p. 541), Gandhi (p. 560), and Simone Weil (p. 571).

2. Respond positively or negatively to Hardin's view of immigration. Perhaps take the perspective of an immigrant hoping to enter a wealthy country or of a citizen opposed to that immigrant's entrance.

3. Opponents of population control often argue that the overwhelming catastrophe that Malthus predicted in 1798 and that Hardin predicted in 1974 has not occurred, despite populations having grown at about the expected rates. Write an essay in which you consider whether these facts invalidate Malthusian theory.

4. Using as much demographic data as possible, determine whether world overpopulation is a serious problem. If not, give evidence and support that it is not; if so, propose a solution.

JOSEPH STIGLITZ
Rent Seeking and the Making of an Unequal Society
[2012]

NOBEL PRIZE–WINNING ECONOMIST JOSEPH STIGLITZ was born in Gary, Indiana, in 1943. He was educated at Amherst College, the University of Chicago, and the Massachusetts Institute of Technology, where he received his Ph.D. in 1967. In 2001, he shared the Nobel Memorial Prize in Economics with two other economists for their work in "the foundations for the theory of markets with asymmetric information." He is currently a professor of Business and Economics at Columbia University in New York City.

In addition to his notable academic work, Stiglitz has had a number of roles in shaping economic policy. He was a cabinet member in the Clinton administration, serving as the chair of the Council of Economic Advisors from 1995 to 1997. From 1997 to 2000, he was the chief economist at the World Bank, and, in 2000, he founded the Initiative for Policy Dialogue at Columbia University, a nonprofit foundation and think tank that helps leaders in developing countries think through difficult political and economic challenges.

Stiglitz is the author of more than twenty-five scholarly and popular books, including *Globalization and Its Discontents* (2002), *Fair Trade for All* (2006), and his co-authored economic analysis of U.S. engagement in Iraq, *The Three Trillion Dollar War* (2008). The selection in this chapter is taken from his 2012 *New York Times* bestselling book, *The Price of Inequality.* Here, Stiglitz examines the root causes of the inequalities in wealth and income in American society—inequalities that have risen precipitously since the recession of 2008. "American inequality didn't just happen," he argues. "It was created." The main goal of *The Price of Inequality* is to explain the forces that created it.

In the chapter excerpted here, Stiglitz defines an important factor that contributes to our current economic inequality: the phenomenon that economists call "rent seeking." His discussion uses a very old definition of the word "rent." Today, rent refers to the fee paid to the owner of a piece of property or equipment. Historically, though, it referred to any government allowance that permitted somebody to make an income without doing any work. Today, rent seeking is the process by which those at the top—the wealthiest 1 percent—receive income not by creating wealth, but by taking a larger portion of wealth that could be redistributed to others, for themselves.

Stiglitz draws on several examples and theoretical arguments to argue that rent-seeking activities on the part of wealthy individuals and large corporations have transferred wealth from the poorest members of society to the wealthiest, capturing a larger share of existing wealth for the rich rather than creating new wealth to benefit the entire society. Government actions are necessary to solve the problem of economic inequality, he concludes, because government is the source of the problem.

American inequality didn't just happen. It was created. Market forces played a role, but it was not market forces alone. In a sense, that should be obvious: economic laws are universal, but our growing inequality—especially the amounts seized by the upper 1 percent[1]—is a distinctly American "achievement." That outsize inequality is not predestined offers reason for hope, but in reality it is likely to get worse. The forces that have been at play in creating these outcomes are self-reinforcing.

By understanding the origins of inequality, we can better grasp the costs and benefits of reducing it. . . . Even though market forces help shape the degree of inequality, government policies shape those market forces. Much of the inequality that exists today is a result of government policy, both what the government does and what it does not do. Government has the power to move money from the top to the bottom and the middle, or vice versa. . . .

America's current level of inequality is unusual. Compared with other countries and compared with what it was in the past even in the United States, it's unusually large, and it has been increasing unusually fast. It used to be said that watching for changes in inequality was like watching grass grow: it's hard to see the changes in any short span of time. But that's not true now.

Even what's been happening in this recession is unusual. Typically, when the economy weakens, wages and employment adjust slowly, so as sales fall, profits fall more than proportionately. But in this recession the share of wages has actually fallen, and many firms are making good profits.

Addressing inequality is of necessity multifaceted—we have to rein in the excesses   5
at the top, strengthen the middle, and help those at the bottom. Each goal requires a program of its own. But to construct such programs, we have to have a better understanding of what has given rise to each facet of this unusual inequality.

Distinct as the inequality we face today is, inequality itself is not something new. The concentration of economic and political power was in many ways more extreme in the precapitalist societies of the West. At that time, religion both explained and justified the inequality: those at the top of society were there because of divine right. To question that was to question the social order, or even to question God's will.

However, for modern economists and political scientists, as also for the ancient Greeks, this inequality was not a matter of a preordained social order. Power—often military power—was at the origin of these inequities. Militarism was about economics: the conquerors had the right to extract as much as they could from the conquered. In antiquity, natural philosophy in general saw no wrong in treating other humans as means for the ends of others. As the ancient Greek historian Thucydides

---

1. **1 percent:** a common term used to refer to the wealthiest individuals in a given country.

famously said, "right, as the world goes, is only in question between equals in power, while the strong do what they can and the weak suffer what they must."

Those with power used that power to strengthen their economic and political positions, or at the very least to maintain them. They also attempted to shape thinking, to make acceptable differences in income that would otherwise be odious.

As the notion of divine right became rejected in the early nation-states, those with power sought other bases for defending their positions. With the Renaissance and the Enlightenment, which emphasized the dignity of the individual, and with the Industrial Revolution, which led to the emergence of a vast urban underclass, it became imperative to find new justifications for inequality, especially as critics of the system, like Marx, talked about exploitation.

The theory that came to dominate, beginning in the second half of the nine-   10
teenth century—and still does—was called "marginal productivity theory"; those with higher productivities earned higher incomes that reflected their greater contribution to society. Competitive markets, working through the laws of supply and demand, determine the value of each individual's contributions. If someone has a scarce and valuable skill, the market will reward him amply, because of his greater contribution to output. If he has no skills, his income will be low. Technology, of course, determines the productivity of different skills: in a primitive agriculture economy, physical strength and endurance is what mattered; in a modern hi-tech economy, brainpower is of more relevance.

Technology and scarcity, working through the ordinary laws of supply and demand, play a role in shaping today's inequality, but something else is at work, and that something else is government. . . . Inequality is the result of political forces as much as of economic ones. In a modern economy government sets and enforces the rules of the game—what is fair competition, and what actions are deemed anticompetitive and illegal, who gets what in the event of bankruptcy, when a debtor can't pay all that he owes, what are fraudulent practices and forbidden. Government also gives away resources (both openly and less transparently) and, through taxes and social expenditures, modifies the distribution of income that emerges from the market, shaped as it is by technology and politics.

Finally, government alters the dynamics of wealth by, for instance, taxing inheritances and providing free public education. Inequality is determined not just by how much the market pays a skilled worker relative to an unskilled worker, but also by the level of skills that an individual has acquired. In the absence of government support, many children of the poor would not be able to afford basic health care and nutrition, let alone the education required to acquire the skills necessary for enhanced productivity and high wages. Government can affect the extent to which an individual's education and inherited wealth depends on that of his parents. More formally, economists say that inequality depends on the distribution of "endowments," of financial and human capital.

The way the American government performs these functions determines the extent of inequality in our society. In each of these arenas there are subtle decisions that benefit some group at the expense of others. The effect of each decision may be small, but the cumulative effect of large numbers of decisions, made to benefit those at the top, can be very significant.

Competitive forces should limit outsize profits,[2] but if governments do not ensure that markets are competitive, there can be large monopoly profits. Competitive forces should also limit disproportionate executive compensation, but in modern corporations, the CEO has enormous power—including the power to set his own compensation, subject, of course, to his board—but in many corporations, he even has considerable power to appoint the board, and with a stacked board, there is little check. Shareholders have minimal say. Some countries have better "corporate governance laws," the laws that circumscribe the power of the CEO, for instance, by insisting that there be independent members in the board or that shareholders have a say in pay. If the country does not have good corporate governance laws that are effectively enforced, CEOs can pay themselves outsize bonuses.

Progressive tax and expenditure policies (which tax the rich more than the poor   15
and provide systems of good social protection) can limit the extent of inequality. By contrast, programs that give away a country's resources to the rich and well connected can increase inequality.

Our political system has increasingly been working in ways that increase the inequality of outcomes and reduce equality of opportunity. This should not come as a surprise: we have a political system that gives inordinate power to those at the top, and they have used that power not only to limit the extent of redistribution but also to shape the rules of the game in their favor, and to extract from the public what can only be called large "gifts." Economists have a name for these activities: they call them rent seeking, getting income not as a reward to creating wealth but by grabbing a larger share of the wealth that would otherwise have been produced without their effort. . . . Those at the top have learned how to suck out money from the rest in ways that the rest are hardly aware of—that is their true innovation.

Jean-Baptiste Colbert, the adviser to King Louis XIV of France, reportedly said, "The art of taxation consists in so plucking the goose as to obtain the largest amount of feathers with the least possible amount of hissing." So, too, for the art of rent seeking.

To put it baldly, there are two ways to become wealthy: to create wealth or to take wealth away from others. The former adds to society. The latter typically subtracts from it, for in the process of taking it away, wealth gets destroyed. A monopolist who overcharges for his product takes money from those whom he is overcharging and at the same time destroys value. To get his monopoly price, he has to restrict production.

Unfortunately, even genuine wealth creators often are not satisfied with the wealth that their innovation or entrepreneurship has reaped. Some eventually turn

2. **Outsize profits:** a common way of referring to profits that receive scrutiny and criticism for being extremely large.

to abusive practices like monopoly pricing or other forms of rent extraction to garner even more riches. To take just one example, the railroad barons of the nineteenth century provided an important service in constructing the railroads, but much of their wealth was the result of their political influence—getting large government land grants on either side of the railway. Today, over a century after the railroad barons dominated the economy, much of the wealth at the top in the United States—and some of the suffering at the bottom—stems from wealth transfers instead of wealth creation. . . .

Rent Seeking

Rent seeking takes many forms: hidden and open transfers and subsidies from the   20
government, laws that make the marketplace less competitive, lax enforcement of existing competition laws, and statutes that allow corporations to take advantage of others or to pass costs on to the rest of society. The term "rent" was originally used to describe the returns to land, since the owner of land receives these payments by virtue of his ownership and not because of anything he *does*. This stands in contrast to the situation of workers, for example, whose wages are compensation for the *effort* they provide. The term "rent" then was extended to include monopoly profits, or monopoly rents, the income that one receives simply from the control of a monopoly. Eventually the term was expanded still further to include the returns on similar ownership claims. If the government gave a company the exclusive right to import a limited amount (a quota) of a good, such as sugar, then the extra return generated as a result of the ownership of those rights was called a "quota-rent."

Countries rich in natural resource are infamous for rent-seeking activities. It's far easier to get rich in these countries by gaining access to resources at favorable terms than by producing wealth. This is often a negative-sum game, which is one of the reasons why, on average, such countries have grown more slowly than comparable countries without the bounty of such resources.

Even more disturbing, one might have thought that an abundance of resources could be used to help the poor, to ensure access to education and health care for all. Taxing work and savings can weaken incentives; in contrast, taxing the "rents" on land, oil, or other natural resources won't make them disappear. The resources will still be there to be taken out, if not today, then tomorrow. There are no adverse incentive effects. That means that, in principle, there should be ample revenues to finance both social expenditures and public investments—in, say, health and education. Yet, among the countries with the greatest inequality are those with the most natural resources. Evidently, a few within these countries are better at rent seeking than others (usually those with political power), and they ensure that the benefits of the resources accrue largely to themselves. In Venezuela, the richest oil producer in Latin America, half of the country lived in poverty prior to the rise of

Hugo Chavez—and it is precisely this type of poverty in the midst of riches that gives rise to leaders like him.

Rent-seeking behavior is not just endemic in the resource-rich countries of the Middle East, Africa, and Latin America. It has also become endemic in modern economies, including our own. In those economies, it takes many forms, some of which are closely akin to those in the oil-rich countries: getting state assets (such as oil or minerals) at below fair-market prices. It's not hard to become wealthy if the government sells you for $500 million a mine that's worth $1 billion.

Another form of rent seeking is the flip side: selling to government products at *above* market prices (noncompetitive procurement). The drug companies and military contractors excel in this form of rent seeking. Open government subsidies (as in agriculture) or hidden subsidies (trade restrictions that reduce competition or subsidies hidden in the tax system) are other ways of getting rents from the public.

Not all rent seeking uses government to extract money from ordinary citizens. The private sector can excel on its own, extracting rents from the public, for instance, through monopolistic practices and exploiting those who are less informed and educated, exemplified by the banks' predatory lending. CEOs can use their control of the corporation to garner for themselves a larger fraction of the firms' revenues. Here, though, the government too plays a role, by not doing what it should: by not stopping these activities, by not making them illegal, or by not enforcing laws that exist. Effective enforcement of competition laws can circumscribe monopoly profits; effective laws on predatory lending and credit card abuses can limit the extent of bank exploitation; well-designed corporate governance laws can limit the extent to which corporate officials appropriate for themselves firm revenues.

By looking at those at the top of the wealth distribution, we can get a feel for the nature of this aspect of America's inequality. Few are inventors who have reshaped technology, or scientists who have reshaped our understandings of the laws of nature. Think of Alan Turing, whose genius provided the mathematics underlying the modern computer. Or of Einstein. Or of the discoverers of the laser . . . or John Bardeen, Walter Brattain, and William Shockley, the inventors of transistors. Or of Watson and Crick, who unraveled the mysteries of DNA, upon which rests so much of modern medicine. None of them, who made such large contributions to our well-being, are among those most rewarded by our economic system.

Instead, many of the individuals at the top of the wealth distribution are, in one way or another, geniuses at business. Some might claim, for instance, that Steve Jobs or the innovators of search engines or social media were, in their way, geniuses. Jobs was number 110 on the *Forbes* list of the world's wealthiest billionaires before his death, and Mark Zuckerberg was 52. But many of these "geniuses" built their business empires on the shoulders of giants, such as Tim Berners-Lee, the inventor of the World Wide Web, who has never appeared on the *Forbes* list. Berners-Lee could have become a billionaire but chose not to—he made his idea available freely, which greatly speeded up the development of the Internet.

25

A closer look at the successes of those at the top of the wealth distribution shows that more than a small part of their genius resides in devising better ways of exploiting market power and other market imperfections—and, in many cases, finding better ways of ensuring that politics works for them rather than for society more generally.

We've already commented on financiers, who make up a significant portion of the top 1 or 0.1 percent. While some gained their wealth by producing value, others did so in no small part by one of the myriad forms of rent seeking that we described earlier. At the top, in addition to the financiers, whom we have already discussed, are the monopolists and their descendants who, through one mechanism or another, have succeeded in achieving and sustaining market dominance. After the railroad barons of the nineteenth century came John D. Rockefeller and Standard Oil. The end of the twentieth century saw Bill Gates and Microsoft's domination of the PC software industry.

Internationally, there is the case of Carlos Slim, a Mexican businessman who   30
was ranked by *Forbes* as the wealthiest person in the world in 2011. Thanks to his dominance of the telephone industry in Mexico, Slim is able to charge prices that are a multiple of those in more competitive markets. He made his breakthrough when he was able to acquire a large share in Mexico's telecommunications system after the country privatized it, a strategy that lies behind many of the world's great fortunes. As we've seen, it's easy to get rich by getting a state asset at a deep discount. Many of Russia's current oligarchs, for example, obtained their initial wealth by buying state assets at below-market prices and then ensuring continuing profits through monopoly power. (In America most of our government giveaways tend to be more subtle. We design rules for, say, selling government assets that are in effect partial giveaways, but less transparently so than what Russia did.) . . .

A final large group of rent seekers consists of the top-flight lawyers, including those who became wealthy by helping others engage in their rent seeking in ways that skirt the law but do not (usually) land them in prison. They help write the complex tax laws in which loopholes are put, so their clients can avoid taxes, and they then design the complex deals to take advantage of these loopholes. They helped design the complex and nontransparent derivatives market. They help design the contractual arrangements that generate monopoly power, seemingly within the law. And for all this assistance in making our markets work not the way markets should but as instruments for the benefit of those at the top, they get amply rewarded.

UNDERSTANDING THE TEXT

1. What does Stiglitz see as the government's role in creating economic inequality? How can the government address the problems that arise from this inequality?

2. How do differences in power lead to differences in economic opportunity? How, according to Stiglitz, do people who have power use that power to tilt the economic playing field to their advantage?

3. What does Stiglitz mean by "marginal productivity theory"? To what extent does this theory hold true in our society?

4. What is the difference between "wealth transfer" and "wealth creation"? Which one leads to a greater degree of economic inequality?

5. How does Stiglitz define "rent seeking"? What are some examples of ways that government actions allow some people to generate revenue without expending any labor or assuming any costs?

6. What kinds of innovations tend to produce the greatest wealth? What kinds tend to produce the wealthiest people? Are they the same? Why or why not?

MAKING CONNECTIONS

1. How might you use Stiglitz's arguments to rebut the assertions of Garrett Hardin (p. 582)? Does Stiglitz see poverty as an inherent problem in human society or as a preventable one?

2. How would Stiglitz evaluate the governing philosophies of Lao Tzu (p. 384), who believed that leaders should interfere as little as possible in the economy and allow nature to take its course? What might happen in an advanced economy if government refused to interfere at all?

3. How does Stiglitz's view of equality compare with Simone Weil's in "Equality" (p. 571)? Would Weil feel, like Stiglitz, that the government should address inequality in our society?

WRITING ABOUT THE TEXT

1. Examine the way that "rent seeking" functions in economic areas with which you are familiar. Explore at least one example of an economic activity that makes money without producing anything of value or generating wealth.

2. Research the Gini coefficient, which ranks countries by the level of inequality between their richest and poorest citizens. Describe the features that countries with a low Gini coefficient (ones with more equality) share, and how they differ from countries with high levels of inequality.

3. Write a rebuttal to Stiglitz in which you argue that inequality is inherent in the human condition and cannot be profitably addressed by government action. Use readings in the "Human Nature and the Mind" chapter of this textbook as evidence for your assertions.

PART 2

A GUIDE TO READING AND WRITING

9

⬚

READING IDEAS

READING CAN BE either passive or active. You read passively when, for example, you pick up a piece of writing and read it straight through, starting at the beginning, moving quickly through passages that do not interest you, and putting it aside when you have finished. Many people read passively most of the time—and with very good reason. Passive reading works perfectly well for getting the gist of a piece of writing. It allows for fairly simple information to be communicated from the author to the reader. Passive reading works just fine for skimming the status updates of friends, browsing the Web, or curling up in bed with an entertaining novel.

College-level reading, however, usually requires a more active approach. Reading challenging texts like the ones in this book is not the same as reading the back of a cereal box. No one can read difficult texts without some effort. People who read challenging texts successfully are not necessarily smarter than other people; they have simply mastered a set of strategies that allow them to get the most out of what they read.

This chapter will explore some of these active reading strategies, including prereading, annotating, identifying patterns, reading visual texts, summarizing, and reading with a critical eye. Mastering these skills will allow you to make your way through challenging material—and the texts in this book will give you plenty of practice.

PREREADING

Experienced readers rarely approach difficult texts without a pretty good idea of what they will find. This may sound odd, since the whole point of reading something is to find out what it says. But good readers know that reading is a process that begins long before they physically pass their eyes over the words on a page. Prereading encompasses all of the things that you do before you start reading to increase your capacity to understand the material. In many cases, taking just a few minutes to learn more about what you are going to read can dramatically increase reading comprehension and retention.

Most college textbooks include a fair amount of editorial apparatus to aid in the prereading process. In this textbook the apparatus consists of chapter introductions, headnotes for individual readings, footnotes, endnotes, and study questions. Essay assignments also provide valuable clues to the themes and topics that are important. You might even first read the questions at the end of a reading; they will tell you some of the things to look for when you read the text.

Skimming a text is another good way to get a sense of what you are likely to find in it. A quick reading, in which you look at the beginning, some of the middle passages, and the end, can tell you a lot about the shape of the argument. People whose major reading experience is passive often find it unsettling to read the end of a work before reading the beginning. "Spoiling the ending" is the wrong way to read a mystery novel, to be sure, but it can be a very good way to read a complicated text. You might, for example, find a complicated text's major points summarized in neat little packages at the ends of essays or chapters. If you are struggling with what an author is saying, the end is just as good a place to start understanding it as the beginning. No rule says that you have to go in order.

The key to prereading is to use all of the resources available to you to understand a text *before* you start reading it. Your mind can focus on only so much while you read. Most likely, you try to construct a "big picture" while you read something. In the process, you often skip over important details because you lack a conceptual framework into which you can place these details. If you build the big picture before you start, you begin reading the text with a conceptual framework already in place. Then, when you encounter a new detail or a new bit of evidence in your reading, your mind will know what to do with it.

Questions for Prereading

Here are some of the key questions that you should ask as you gather information in the prereading stage of the reading process:

Who is the author of the work?

The more information you have about an author, the better you will be able to anticipate the kinds of points that he or she will make. In reading a work like Aung San Suu Kyi's "In Quest of Democracy," for example, you can infer certain things about the argument before reading the text, once you know that the author is (1) the daughter of a famous Burmese political leader, (2) a Western-trained academic, (3) a devoted admirer of Mohandas Gandhi and Martin Luther King Jr., (4) the winner of a democratic national election that was invalidated by a military dictatorship, and (5) an outspoken advocate of democracy who was kept under house arrest in her own country. Knowing these key biographical facts—which are readily available in the selection introduction, on the back of any of her books, and on dozens of Web pages—allows you to begin reading "In Quest of Democracy" with a better understanding of Aung San Suu Kyi's general argument, allowing you to focus on her specific claims and her support for those claims.

What was the work's original purpose?

None of the texts in this anthology were written for college students in need of things to write essays about. They all come from historical and rhetorical contexts that shaped both their meanings and their methods of presentation. Even very good readers can misread a text when they ignore the characteristics of the original intended audience. Take, for example, Mo Tzu's "Against Music." To modern readers, this essay might seem like a strict, old-fashioned argument against music. When it was written, however, music was a symbol of luxury, available only to the very wealthy, who enjoyed it at the expense of everybody else. In its original context, "Against Music" was therefore a radical attack on privilege and power.

What cultural factors might have influenced the author?

The further removed you are from an author's culture, time, and place, the more difficult it can be to understand that author's work—even when the work's terminology does not seem especially difficult. To make better sense of texts from different cultures, it can be helpful to learn more about the conventions and concerns of these cultures. The basic argument of Mo Tzu's "Against Music"—that society should not support or allow the production of music—will make very little sense to contemporary readers who do not know that in ancient China music was an extremely expensive luxury available only to the most wealthy members of the aristocracy. Those who attempt to apply Mo Tzu's arguments to modern notions of music will miss the point entirely.

What larger conversation is this text part of?

A written text is part of a larger conversation, and reading a single text is often like listening to only one part of that conversation: you miss most of the questions that have been asked and points that are being responded to. Occasionally, this anthology will give you different texts from the same general historical conversation, such as the debate between Mencius and Hsün Tzu on Confucian notions of human nature, or the opinions of Paley and Darwin on the origins of life on earth.

More often, though, you will need to familiarize yourself with the terms of the discussion that surround a text you are preparing to read. In anthologies, this kind of information might appear in the chapter introductions or in the headnotes or footnotes that accompany texts. You might also locate it with a quick search online. The effort required to learn as much as you can about a text before you start reading it will almost always pay off in increased understanding and retention, and might even save you some time.

Prereading Practice

Read the following passage from John Henry Newman's "Knowledge Its Own End." On your initial reading, do not do any prereading—just read it straight through and then summarize its key points.

> I am asked what is the end of University Education, and of the Liberal or Philosophical Knowledge which I conceive it to impart: I answer, that what I have already said has been sufficient to show that it has a very tangible, real, and sufficient end, though the end cannot be divided from that knowledge itself. Knowledge is capable of being its own end. Such is the constitution of the human mind, that any kind of knowledge, if it be really such, is its own reward. And if this is true of all knowledge, it is true also of that special Philosophy, which I have made to consist in a comprehensive view of truth in all its branches, of the relations of science to science, of their mutual bearings, and their respective values. What the worth of such an acquirement is, compared with other objects which we seek,—wealth or power or honour or the conveniences and comforts of life, I do not profess here to discuss; but I would maintain, and mean to show, that it is an object, in its own nature so really and undeniably good, as to be the compensation of a great deal of thought in the compassing, and a great deal of trouble in the attaining.

Once you have read this passage without any prereading and summarized it, turn to the headnote for this reading (p. 31) and use the information in it to answer the following questions:

1. Who was John Henry Newman, and when did he write?

2. What was the original context of "Knowledge Its Own End"? What was Newman's position when he gave the lecture that would eventually become this essay?

3. How did Newman define the word "Catholic"? What did this definition have to do with his view of education?

4. What did Newman see as the difference between "useful knowledge" and "liberal knowledge"?

After you have answered these four questions, read and summarize the passage again; then compare your second summary to your first one. How has learning key information about the author and text changed your ability to make sense of what you read?

ANNOTATING

After prereading to gather information about a text, your next step is to read the text closely. Your two most important tools will be a good dictionary and a pencil or a pen.

Reading with a dictionary at hand is extremely important, as it allows you to look up words that you do not know. This practice may sound obvious, but many people instead try to figure out the meanings of difficult words by their contexts. Sometimes, this strategy works; sometimes, it does not. If you do not understand a key term that an author uses, you are much less likely to understand the arguments in which the term is used. When you come across a word you don't know, you will want to check a good dictionary.

Your other important close reading tool is a pencil or a pen. As an active reader, you should write while you read. Taking notes on a computer or on a separate piece of paper is a good practice when reading a library book or one borrowed from someone else. Within your own book, annotate the text as you read by underlining key passages, writing comments in the margins, and recording insights as they come to you. Studies have shown that even if you never look again at the annotations that you make, the act of making them will increase the amount of information that you will recall in the future.

As you gain experience with active reading, you will discover annotation tricks and strategies that work for you. Different people annotate texts in different ways, depending on their learning styles and methods of recalling information. Here are a few things to keep in mind as you annotate difficult and unfamiliar texts:

Underline key points and any thesis statement

Whenever you encounter a single statement or part of a paragraph that summarizes one of the author's major arguments, underline it and write something in the margin that tells you that this is a key point. Once you determine that a certain statement summarizes a key part of the argument, you can use this statement as a reference point to see how that argument is supported. (For more on thesis statements, see p. 634.)

Note your insights

As you read an explanation of a difficult idea, a certain part of your brain tries to forge connections between what you are reading and what you already know. This process can produce important insights while you are reading. However, if you do not record these insights, you may very well forget them. Just the act of writing them in the margin helps to make them part of your long-term memory.

Respond to the author

Reading is always part of a dialogue with an author, and marginal notations are a good place to carry on that dialogue. If you strongly agree or disagree with something that you read, make a note of it. These notes will serve you well when it is time to develop your opinions in the form of an essay or in-class writing assignment.

Avoid the temptation to underline or comment too much

Like any good thing, annotating can be overdone. This overkill often defeats the purpose of annotating—if everything is underlined, it becomes impossible to distinguish what is important.

Here, using the same passage from "Knowledge Its Own End" that we used in the section on prereading, is an example of a moderate use of underlining that combines some of the strategies listed above.

What is the purpose of education?

I am asked what is ⟨the end of University Education,⟩ and of the ⟨Liberal⟩ or Philosophical Knowledge which I conceive it to impart: I answer, that what I have already said has been sufficient to show that it has a very tangible, real, and sufficient end, though the end cannot be divided from that knowledge itself. <u>Knowledge is capable of being its own end. Such is the constitution of the human mind, that any kind of knowledge, if it be really such, is its own reward.</u> And if this is true of all knowledge, it is true also of that special Philosophy, which I have made to consist in a comprehensive view of truth in all its branches, of the relations of science to science, of their mutual bearings, and their respective values. What the worth of such an acquirement is, compared with other objects which we seek,—wealth or power or honour or the conveniences and comforts of life, I do not profess here to discuss; but <u>I would maintain, and mean to show, that it is an object, in its own nature so really and undeniably good</u>, as to be the compensation of a great deal of thought in the compassing, and a great deal of trouble in the attaining.

Liberal knowledge = interdisciplinary "useless" knowledge

Thesis: Acquiring knowledge is good in and of itself

Knowledge is a good thing worth obtaining, even if it does not lead to other good things such as wealth or status

IDENTIFYING PATTERNS

Whenever you write, you use, consciously or unconsciously, some kind of organizational pattern. If you are writing about something that happened to you, your organizational pattern will likely be chronological (this happened, then this, and then this . . .); if you are describing a place, you will probably use a spatial order; and so on. When you are reading an unfamiliar text, it helps to try to figure out what kind of organizational pattern the author is using. This knowledge will help you anticipate arguments and conclusions and know where to look for them in the body of the text. Most good writing has characteristics of several different patterns, but often one pattern predominates, if not in an entire essay, at least in a particular passage. Here are some of the more common organizational patterns for written prose:

Chronological order

Historical texts, descriptions of events, personal narratives, and travelogues are often organized chronologically. The narrative begins at one point in time, then moves through the period described, with successive points in time forming the major organizational units of the text. Works such as Marevasei Kachere's "War Memoir" (p. 514) generally use a straightforward chronological pattern to present their ideas.

Spatial order

While descriptions of events are often organized chronologically, descriptions of things and places are often organized spatially. Spatial organization can be used to describe everything from the nucleus of an atom to the universe. When prose accompanies pictures, charts, graphs, or other graphic information, the text's content is oriented spatially to the visual information, as is the case in Carl Jung's *Red Book* (p. 108).

Classification

When an author wants to describe a number of different things—be they kinds of tomatoes, types of clouds, Greek philosophies, or (in the case of what you are reading right now) methods of organizing written information—he or she might create a classification system for the information and then present the information as a list. The list might be set off with bullets, headers, or other formatting information, or it might simply occur normally in the text, with nothing to indicate where the description of one item ends and another begins. For an example of the way that a classification system can organize an essay, consider the various stances toward one's subject matter that Wayne Booth presents in "The Rhetorical Stance" (p. 198).

Claim/support

One of the most common organizational strategies of scientific and philosophical writing—including many selections in *Reading the World*—is to begin by stating a proposition (such as Hsün Tzu's argument that "human nature is evil" or Thomas Malthus's claim that "population grows exponentially while food supply grows arithmetically"), to continue by offering support for that proposition, and to conclude by restating the proposition and explaining its ramifications. This organizational pattern is also commonly used in college essays, with the "proposition" usually called the "thesis statement." (For more on thesis statements, see p. 634.) Once you have identified an essay as being organized in this fashion, you will have a pretty good idea of where to look for the main point: it will probably be stated once in the first paragraph and once again near the end.

Problem/solution

Essays that make specific policy arguments—think of Martha Nussbaum's "Education for Profit, Education for Democracy" (p. 61) or Garrett Hardin's "Lifeboat Ethics: The Case against Helping the Poor" (p. 582)—are often organized from the top down: with the problems that need to be solved stated first, followed by the proposed solutions.

Statement/response

Another common organizational pattern of the readings in this book is statement/ response. This strategy involves quoting or paraphrasing an argument (usually one that you oppose) in the beginning of the essay and then responding to that argument in the remainder of the essay. This form is usually used in texts that rebut other texts and in persuasive essays in which the author anticipates and responds to objections, as Vandana Shiva does in "Soil Not Oil" (p. 374).

Cause/effect

One standard assumption of philosophy and science is that every effect proceeds from a cause. This movement from cause to effect is an important organizational strategy. Some writers who organize their arguments along these lines begin with the cause and move on to explain the effects, as Rachel Carson does in "The Obligation to Endure," (p. 328) when she explains the chemical composition of DDT and then describes its effects on the environment. Many authors, however, present the effects first and then trace them back to a cause, as Joseph Stiglitz does in "Rent Seeking and the Making of an Unequal Society" (p. 594).

Narrative

Stories, or narratives, are an important part of many different kinds of writing. The New Testament parables, the Buddhist *suttas*, African folktales, and the writings of great philosophers, ancient and modern, often rely on short narratives to make or illustrate points. In many of these texts, the narrative is followed immediately by an interpretation, in which the story becomes the basis for some conclusions or discussion, as in Richard Feynman's "O Americano Outra Vez" (p. 53).

Comparison/contrast

When an author is comparing two things—ideas, movements, people, and so on— he or she will often organize the text as an explicit comparison or contrast. Such an organizational pattern usually takes one of two forms. In the first of these forms, the author spends the first half of the essay discussing one subject of the comparison and the second half discussing the other. In the second variation, the author establishes several grounds for comparison and then goes back and forth between the things being compared. In *Reading the World*, perhaps the most straightforward example of this kind of organization is Daniel Kahneman's comparison of System 1 and System 2 in *Thinking, Fast and Slow* (p. 134).

READING VISUAL TEXTS

The word "text" does not apply only to written works. An oral narrative is a text, as is a piece of music, a painting, a photograph, or a film. Works of all these types address audiences, advance ideas, make arguments, and require thoughtful strategies of reading and interpretation. *Reading the World* includes a number of visual texts that can be studied as seriously and interpreted as diligently as the written texts in the book.

Artists, like authors, have objectives, cultural contexts, and recurring concerns, and they respond to historical discussions and debates. You can, therefore, ask the same "prereading" questions of a painting as of an essay. Additionally, there are other reading strategies that you can use with visual texts. For an introduction to some of these strategies, look at the detail on p. 615 from William Hogarth's engraving *Gin Lane* (the full text of which appears on p. 548).

This detail shows two of the scenes in the foreground of the engraving. Knowing only that the engraving is titled *Gin Lane*, you can infer that both of the major figures are intoxicated. One of them, a woman, is reaching for a pinch of snuff while her child falls from her breast and over a railing. The other figure, a man, is holding a glass of gin in one hand and a bottle of gin in the other, and appears to be starving to death. Taken together, the two images present a fairly complete argument, which,

WILLIAM HOGARTH *Gin Lane*, 1751 (engraving, detail).
Bibliothèque Nationale, Paris, France / Lauros–Giraudon / Bridgeman Art Library.

if rendered in prose, would read something like: "Drinking gin is bad because it causes you to ignore your own health and the well-being of your family."

But there is much more to the text than this paraphrase suggests. Here are some important things to look for when "reading" a visual text:

Emotional appeals.   Few images are as emotionally charged as Hogarth's portrayal of a drunken mother allowing her infant child to fall from her exposed breasts to a certain death. The mother's complete lack of concern and the look of pure panic on the infant's face produce a powerful emotional appeal in support of the otherwise bland argument that drinking gin is bad. Most people are extremely affected by emotional appeals, especially when those appeals are made visually. Many people can read words about great suffering, misery, deprivation, and abuse without feeling the emotions that a single picture can convey.

Symbolism. The image of a baby at its mother's breast is a powerful symbol of motherhood and self-sacrifice in cultures throughout the world (see, for example, the wings of the old man in the image from Jung's *Red Book*, which represent the ability to escape the confines of earthly thought). By inverting this symbol, Hogarth taps into a very deep pool of cultural—and even cross-cultural—associations involving infants, mothers, and nursing. Many of the visual texts in this book feature similar kinds of symbolic representation: the gun and the French flag carried by Liberty in *Liberty Leading the People* (p. 494) and the light coming from the lamp in *An Experiment on a Bird in the Air Pump* (p. 308) convey ideas through symbols whose physical forms only suggest their ultimate meaning.

Visual irony. Hogarth was a master of visual irony, much of which requires very close reading of his art. For example, there is a more obvious irony in the fact that the man in *Gin Lane* is starving to death while clutching a large quantity of gin, whose price could have purchased food instead. There is a less obvious but equally important irony, however, in the piece of paper in his basket. It reads, "The downfall of Madam Gin," presumably the title of a broadside ballad he wrote to sell in order to get enough money to buy more gin.

Motifs. If you look at the full version of *Gin Lane* (p. 548), you will see that the two images in this detail are part of larger motifs, or patterns of images that mirror and comment on each other. The "neglected child" motif is refigured in children and infants throughout the picture, including one who is being given a glass of gin instead of a milk bottle, one who is fighting with a dog for a bone, and one who is being carried through the street impaled on a skewer.

Composition. Any visual text includes compositional elements—line, perspective, color, use of space, and so on—that contribute to the work's meaning. In *Gin Lane*, for example, the mother and her infant are foregrounded and brightly lit so that the eye is immediately drawn to them, emphasizing their importance in Hogarth's argument. The dominant lines in the complete engraving—the top of the brick wall, the rooftop pole at the top right, the signpost on the building on the left, and the staircase and its railings—are at random angles to each other to illustrate the unpredictable, disordered world of *Gin Lane*.

All of these elements combine to form an overall impression. If the artist has arranged the elements well, the viewer will gain an overall sense of the text that can itself become a powerful persuasive element. Visual images can create impressions of, among other things, reverence, power, wonder, despair, peace, awe, and patriotism.

SUMMARIZING

As part of active reading, summarizing helps you solidify your own understanding of a text and identify what you need to think about or analyze more closely. The objective of a summary is to boil a large text down to its essential points. Often, teachers will assign essays that consist entirely or partially of summary as a way to evaluate your understanding of difficult material. In other kinds of essays, brief summaries of difficult information can give you a starting point for more sophisticated kinds of writing, such as analysis, synthesis, research, or critique. Here are some suggestions to keep in mind as you create a summary:

Identify the main point

Even if the author does not come to the main point until the middle or the end of an essay, you should identify the main point immediately and put it at the beginning of your summary. Doing so will make clear early on what the text is about, and it will help you focus and organize the rest of your summary.

Identify support for the main point(s)

A summary does not always have to explain every specific bit of evidence that an author uses to support an argument (especially in very short summaries of very long works). It is important, however, for the summary to explain the kinds of evidence (analytical, experimental, statistical, deductive, etc.) that a text employs (see p. 650).

Quote from the text when appropriate

Good summaries often quote from the texts that they summarize, but they do so selectively. Similarly, quotations in a summary should include only a few words here or there to get the point across, rather than large blocks of text that give complete arguments. Quote only when the author has stated something so eloquently that you cannot restate it, or when you want to emphasize the author's own words. Be sure to mark the quotation clearly, in quotation marks, and to cite the page number where the quotation is found.

Use your own words

When you summarize someone else's writing, make sure that you use your own structure as well as your own wording. A summary does not need to move chronologically through the text, relating points in the order that the author presents them. You should employ organizational strategies that fit your own needs, which may or may not mirror those of the author whose text you are summarizing.

READING WITH A CRITICAL EYE

To understand a text, beyond what is being said on the surface, you will need to read the text with a critical eye; that is, you will often need to analyze its assumptions, discover its deeper arguments, and respond to those arguments with ones of your own.

Critical reading is difficult to define, as people in different disciplines use the term differently. In a literature class, "critical reading" may mean examining a literary work to find symbols and motifs, while in a history class, it might mean evaluating the reliability of different sources used to reconstruct a historical event.

Perhaps the best way to define "critical reading" is through its opposite: uncritical reading. Those who read uncritically are likely to be persuaded by the loudest voices rather than the soundest arguments. Such readers tend to gravitate toward arguments that confirm their preconceived ideas, accepting such arguments without serious examination, and they usually reject opinions—and even well-documented facts—that challenge their beliefs. Uncritical readers can be very "critical" in the ordinary sense of the word, but they base their criticisms on how closely authors mirror their own points of view rather than on the texts' merits.

Critical readers, by contrast, approach all texts with a certain amount of skepticism, but they do not reject any argument without a fair hearing. They try to set aside their personal biases long enough to understand what they read. They seek to understand both texts and the contexts in which they are written, including, when appropriate, an author's use of symbolism, imagery, metaphor, and other figurative or rhetorical devices. Once they understand an argument on its own terms, critical readers evaluate its claims, its evidence, and its underlying assumptions both fairly and rigorously. They do not change their minds every time they read something new, but neither do they refuse to consider a new idea because it disagrees with an opinion that they already hold. Reading critically allows us to think critically—learning these skills is a lifelong process, but there are concrete steps you can take to start it:

Think about your own perspective

The process of reading and thinking critically begins with the realization that you have your own perspective. Some aspects of your perspective come from your culture and the time in which you live; others may come from your family, your friends, and your experience of the world. You cannot avoid this situation, nor should you try—it is part of being human. You cannot eliminate your own beliefs, but you can be aware of them, understand where they come from, and take them into consideration when you read something with a perspective different from your own. You need not accept everything that you read—but you should realize when your own perspective might be getting in the way of understanding what a text is saying.

Understand the author's perspective

Just as readers have their own perspectives, so do authors. As a reader, approach a text with a balance of respect and skepticism, being open to an unfamiliar perspective while examining it with the same critical analysis that you apply to your own beliefs. You should approach every text that you read as having been shaped by cultural and individual perspectives, and realize that all such perspectives—your own and everybody else's—come with both insights and stumbling blocks of their own.

Determine how the argument works

All texts make arguments in the sense that they assert at least one point and support that point. These questions can be helpful in determining how an argument works: What is the main point? What are the supporting points? How are different kinds of evidence invoked to back up major and supporting points?

Evaluate the support for a claim

Critical reading involves determining whether a text employs appropriate kinds of evidence for the kind of argument it is making. An author can support his or her claim in different ways, many of which will be covered in Chapter 12. Some claims are supported by statistics, some by experimental data, some by logical analysis, and some simply by the force of the writer's or speaker's personality.

Once you have determined the appropriateness of the kind of evidence that a text employs, you must still determine the strength of that evidence. For example, if statistical evidence is the best way to prove a certain point—such as Garrett Hardin's argument in "Lifeboat Ethics: The Case against Helping the Poor" that the earth's population has exceeded its carrying capacity—you must evaluate the relevance and representativeness of the author's statistics. If drawing out general principles from historical examples is a good way to prove a particular point—such as Machiavelli's assertion in *The Prince* that it is better for a ruler to be feared than to be loved or Octavio Paz's assertion in "The Day of the Dead" that Mexican identity is shaped by profound solitude—you must examine the relevance of the author's or authors' historical examples *and* the relevance of historical examples that have occurred since the texts were written.

Think about underlying assumptions

Most claims have stated points and underlying assumptions. The stated points are the ones that the author makes. The underlying assumptions are the premises that, though never stated, must be true for the argument to succeed. These unstated assumptions may be so obvious that the author does not feel the need to restate

them; they may be assumptions that the author wishes to conceal from the audience; or they may be foundational beliefs so deeply engrained that the author
does not recognize them. When you read, think about the assumptions beneath
the author's claim. What needs to be true for the claim to be true? What would
prevent the claim from being true? The chart below presents some assertions and
the unstated assumptions that underlie them.

STATED ASSERTION	UNDERLYING ASSUMPTION(S)
The best way to derive truth about nature is through direct observation because primary evidence is better than secondary evidence.	Human senses give reliable information and do not deceive us.
Human nature is evil because people are inherently selfish and incapable of genuine concern for other people to the exclusion of self.	Focusing on one's self is evil, and focusing on other people, to the exclusion of one's self, is good.
Democracy is the best form of government because it guarantees the maximum amount of freedom for individuals.	Giving individuals a maximum amount of freedom is a good thing. / Individuals will not use their freedom in ways that harm society and each other.
Helping those in need is important because we owe it to fellow human beings to eliminate as much suffering and misery as we can.	Helping those in need will relieve suffering and will not cause a greater amount of misery in the long term.
Higher education is a good thing because it helps people get good jobs and earn more money throughout their lives.	Earning more money is a good thing.

Of course, every assertion in this chart is debatable. The stated claims in the left-
hand column, while very common, are not self-evident. Every one of them could be,
and has been, disputed. However, even if you generally accept the stated claims in
the left-hand column, their arguments absolutely depend on the unstated assumptions in the right-hand column. Each assumption can also be plausibly debated, and
the rejection of any one would lead to the rejection of the corresponding argument
in the left-hand column.

10

□

GENERATING IDEAS

Most college essays succeed or fail at the idea level. Good ideas are likely to produce good essays. A good idea contains within it the seeds of a good argument and an organized essay. Once you have hit upon a good idea, you will find that your essay is easier to organize, easier to write, and easier to revise.

Very few people simply "have" good ideas. The ability to generate good ideas—and good paper topics—is a skill that can be learned. This chapter will introduce some basic strategies—grouped under considering expectations, exploring your topic, and achieving subtlety—that you can use to move beyond your initial thoughts about a topic and generate worthwhile ideas to write about.

CONSIDERING EXPECTATIONS

The writing process cannot be reduced to a precise set of formulas and equations that will produce "correct" essays in every class that requires writing. Different instructors have different preferences and grade written assignments differently. Sometimes, what works well for one instructor will not work at all for another.

Before you start thinking about a writing topic, then, make sure you understand what your instructor expects from you. If you do not meet these expectations, your ideas will not be judged "good"—even if they represent perfectly sound arguments that might be very successful in other contexts. Here are a few strategies that you can use to make sure that your essay ideas will meet your instructor's expectations:

Understand the assignment

The requirements of an assignment can be very general or very specific. In either case, you must gear your response to the terms of the assignment. Most assignments ask you to perform a certain writing task—to analyze, compare, describe, and so on. It is vital that you understand what this task entails. If you have any questions about the assignment, do not hesitate to ask your instructor to clarify it for you.

Agree/disagree.   Assignments that ask you to agree or disagree will usually give you a proposition to consider. Sometimes, this proposition will be an entire reading, as in "Agree or disagree with George Orwell's points in 'Pacifism and the War.'" More often, the proposition will be a single statement or assertion, such as "In 'Pacifism and the War,' George Orwell states that a pacifist position during wartime is necessarily in favor of the enemy. Agree or disagree with this assertion."

A topic of this sort gives you the opportunity to state your opinion. When instructors assign topics such as this one, they are usually not looking for right or wrong answers. Nor do they want you to simply summarize Orwell's essay and state—at the beginning or the end of the essay—whether or not you approve. An assignment to agree or disagree is asking you to state and defend an opinion; it involves both an argument about what you believe *and* valid reasons for that argument. The quality of the reasons that you give, not your opinion, is the most important part of the assignment.

Analyze.   "Analyze" is one of the most common directions in college-level writing assignments, but it can have many meanings. Generally speaking, to analyze something is to examine it by comparing how its parts relate to a whole or how certain causes produce an effect. In most (but not all) situations, a textual analysis should focus not on agreeing or disagreeing with the text but on showing how different parts of the text operate toward a particular end. An analysis of a literary text often looks at imagery, symbolism, and other kinds of figurative language. An analysis of an argumentative text usually requires you to look at the argument—to see what it claims and how persuasively it supports those claims.

Apply.   One of the best ways to measure how well you understand an argument is to ask you to apply it to a new situation. Consider the following assignment: "Apply George Orwell's reasoning in 'Pacifism and the War' to America's actions in the so-called war on terror." This assignment asks you to consider how the arguments advanced in the original essay—which in this case would include the assertion that refusing to fight an enemy is an act of support for that enemy rather than an act of neutrality—apply to U.S. actions in Afghanistan, in Iraq, and at home. There are, of course, several plausible ways to apply Orwell's argument to this situation. For example, you could argue that, according to Orwell's logic, one could not be a pacifist in the war on terror without being "objectively proterrorist." Or you could argue that, because terrorism is a criminal act rather than a military one, Orwell's argument allows for pacifism (objecting to a military solution to the problem) in the war on terror in a way that it did not allow for pacifism in World War II.

Claim/support.   Many writing assignments involve some kind of claim/support structure, but some assignments specifically ask you to construct and support your own argument. In a college class, these assignments usually require you to develop fully your own opinions about things that you read, but they may or may not ask you to cite specific readings. Often, assignments for this kind of writing are phrased as questions: "Is human nature inherently good?" "Is it ever appropriate to disobey the law?" "When is war a justified response to aggression?" "Do people have a moral obligation to help the poor?" These highly debatable questions are all covered in this book, and, at some point, your instructor will probably require you to express and defend your opinions about issues such as these.

An argument about any issue consists of two parts: the claim and the support. You cannot simply make an assertion such as "Everybody has a moral obligation to help the poor" or "War is justified when people are defending their families." You also need to include a statement that gives a reason for your belief: "Everybody has a moral obligation to help the poor because morality is based on our responses to others" or "War is justified when people are defending their families because taking care of one's family is the most important duty that human beings have." The procedure for embedding a claim and a statement of support in a thesis statement is covered in depth in Chapter 11 (p. 633).

Compare/contrast.   Strictly speaking, "compare" means to show how things are alike, and "contrast" means to show how they are different. Sometimes, an assignment will ask you to "compare and contrast" two things, such as to "compare and contrast the views of Paley and Darwin on the origins of life on earth." Such an assignment asks you to explain similarities and differences in the two texts. Often, instructors simply use the term "compare" as a way to ask you to look for similarities and differences in two or more texts.

Describe.   An assignment to describe something—whether that something is an argument, a painting, or your best friend—asks you to give its essential characteristics without evaluating or taking a position on those characteristics. Though perfect neutrality is rarely possible in a writing assignment (the act of choosing which characteristics to describe conveys an evaluation and a perspective), descriptive writing should present its subject objectively. For example, an assignment that asks you to "describe the situations that led to the emergence of Taoism and Confucianism in ancient China" is asking you to explain a set of historical facts, not to give your opinion about a pair of philosophies.

Respond.   Many assignments ask you to respond to another text or to a specific argument in a text. Such assignments may or may not ask you to "agree or disagree" with the argument. They do, however, require something more than mere approval or disapproval. They require you to use the text that you are responding to as the basis for your own arguments or observations.

An assignment asking you to "respond to Machiavelli's assertion that it is better for a ruler to be feared than loved" is asking you to consider this argument and evaluate its appropriateness. Does this argument work better in some political systems than others? Does it rest on defensible assumptions about human nature? Which leaders might have agreed? Which ones might have disagreed? What would a government look like that completely accepted—or completely rejected—Machiavelli's advice? Each of these questions or their answers would be legitimate starting points for an essay asking you to "respond" to Machiavelli's argument.

Summarize/paraphrase. Some writing assignments ask you to summarize or paraphrase other texts. The two words do not mean exactly the same thing. A *summary* is a short encapsulation of a longer argument, cutting out all but the most important details; a *paraphrase* is a restatement of an argument in your own words, containing most of the original text's detail. A paraphrase of a three-page text should take about three pages, while a summary of such a text could consist of a few carefully worded sentences. When writing about other texts, do not summarize extensively or paraphrase unless you are asked to do so. If you merely summarize or paraphrase an argument that you have been asked to analyze or respond to, you will almost certainly fail to meet your instructor's expectations. (See also "Quoting, Paraphrasing, and Summarizing," p. 685.)

Get responses

To make sure that you have met your instructor's expectations for an assignment, get responses, both to your topic and to your early drafts. You might meet with your instructor to talk about your topic, or you might ask your instructor to comment on drafts. You might also seek out the tutoring resources at your school. Most colleges and universities have a writing center or other tutoring service that can serve as a tremendous resource for improving your writing.

Peer tutors can help writers with every stage of the writing process, not just with the finished product. A good peer tutor will be able to help you think critically about an assignment and brainstorm ideas and essay topics. Occasionally, a tutor will have the expertise to help in areas where you are weak. But sometimes, it just helps to have somebody to bounce ideas off of when you are trying to decide on an essay topic. A peer tutor can also read your essay and point out things that you might miss simply because you are too close to the writing process to view your essay objectively.

Consider your audience and purpose

Before you start writing, ask yourself who you are writing for and what you want to accomplish. The answers to these questions will help you present your ideas appropriately—in a class, this will help you meet your instructor's expectations; outside of school, it will help you effectively reach your intended readers. In both cases, considering your audience and purpose is essential.

Any time that you write for other people, you will be constrained by your audience's expectations. Novelists, journalists, corporate executives, screenwriters, Web designers, and even professors all know that the form, style, and content of their writing must meet certain expectations. "Good writing" in the absolute sense is virtually impossible to define, since writing always occurs in a context of stated or unstated expectations. An effective argument in one context might be totally ineffective in another. Take the following argument as an example: "providing beer in a college dining hall would make the dorms more attractive." This would probably be extremely successful with the student body, much less successful with faculty and administrators, and not successful at all with parents. Part of learning how to be a good writer is learning how to assess these expectations accurately and respond to them effectively.

Just as important as understanding your audience is understanding what you want to accomplish when you write. Different kinds of writing have different purposes. Writing can, among other things, inform, persuade, motivate, express, and entertain. An essay written to persuade your instructor of an argument will be very different from one designed to give an initial impression of a reading. If you begin with a solid understanding of what you want to accomplish when you write, you will be able to incorporate this purpose into every stage of the writing process.

EXPLORING YOUR TOPIC

The strategies listed below are all ways to help you generate ideas. Try them out and see which works best for you. Do not worry about coming up with the perfect topic right away; the process of generating ideas can help you think about different aspects and implications of the topic you finally choose, and you may end up using facets of other ideas in your writing.

Freewriting

The quickest, easiest, and most direct way to fill up an empty piece of paper or blank computer screen is just to start writing. Freewriting is an unconstrained writing exercise in which you simply write down whatever comes to your mind for a set period. The only rule is that you cannot stop writing. A freewriting exercise is designed to tap into the subconscious mind and pull out ideas that may be lurking beneath the surface. To complete such an exercise successfully, you need to override your mind's "editing function" and just write.

Here is a brief example of a freewriting session in response to an assignment to compare the view of liberal education in John Henry Newman's "Knowledge Its Own End" with that in Seneca's "On Liberal and Vocational Studies."

> OK, so I'm supposed to compare what John Henry Newman and Seneca said about education. Both of them talk a lot about liberal education and how it is not supposed to be useful for anything other than itself. When you read them, they sound a lot alike in this way, which is kind of weird since one of them lived in ancient Rome and the other one lived in England like a hundred years ago. Come to think of it, this is probably the biggest difference between them. Seneca lived in a very different kind of society than Newman lived in. Rome was an empire where people owned slaves and were divided into very distinct classes. Newman lived in an industrial country that was pretty much a democracy, at least at the end of his life. Maybe this is why Seneca thought that useful education was a bad thing, and only liberal education was worthwhile, while Newman just thought that they were different things. Most people in Newman's day couldn't afford not to think about how they would earn a living. I guess that's still true today.

This freewriting demonstration follows the usual pattern for such an exercise: it begins with a self-reflective discussion (here I am, doing what I am supposed to be doing), moves to some fairly surface observations about the texts (that both Seneca and Newman talk about liberal education) and then to a statement that, with a lot more refining, could be the basis of a very strong comparison paper: that Newman is more tolerant of practical education than Seneca because Newman lived in a democratic society.

Clustering

Clustering is a good strategy for processing information visually. It consists of drawing some kind of picture that represents the ideas that you are discussing and using that picture to show the relationship between a central, general idea and several more-focused, subordinate ideas. The easiest way to do this is with circles and lines, as in the following diagram, which responds to an assignment to "write a paper that uses Martin Luther King Jr.'s three categories of 'unjust law' to argue that a current law or type of law is unjust."

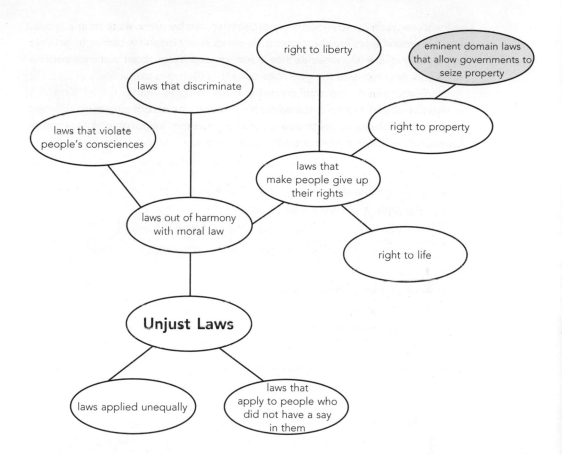

The goal of clustering here is to think of a current law that meets Martin Luther King Jr.'s classification of an unjust law, one that can then be the focus of the essay. Starting simply with "unjust laws," the writer branches out to come up with more-specific kinds of unjust laws. One kind of law, "laws that make people give up their rights," leads the writer to think about different rights, which then leads to the final essay topic: "eminent domain laws," which require people to give up their right to property. In clustering, every idea allows you to jot down several more ideas that are connected to it, so you can continue to refine and develop ideas with increasing layers of specificity. Once you reach an idea that seems workable, you can take it from your cluster and refine it further into an argumentative thesis statement.

Brainstorming

Like freewriting and clustering, brainstorming exercises are meant to get a lot of ideas down on paper without worrying—at least during the exercise—whether they will work for your essay. A brainstorming session can be done alone or in a group, but the ground rules are the same: write down every idea that comes to you, do not try to evaluate the ideas as they come, do not worry about writing complete sentences, and move to the next idea quickly.

Now, imagine staying with the assignment to apply Martin Luther King Jr.'s criteria for unjust laws to a contemporary law and, instead of clustering different kinds of unjust laws, simply throwing out as many ideas as possible. A ten-minute brainstorming session might produce a list like this:

- Slavery
- Segregation laws
- Laws against same-sex marriage
- Laws that give police officers the right to collect information
- Affirmative action laws that treat minorities differently than others
- Prohibition
- Laws that keep women from voting
- Laws that allow countries to attack other countries
- Laws that make it illegal to practice your religion
- Laws against drugs
- Laws that won't let you drink when you are eighteen while others let you be drafted into the army
- Laws that make you wear a helmet or a seat belt
- Laws that don't let you go to the college you want to go to
- Eminent domain laws that allow governments to seize your property
- Laws that don't allow you to defend your house if someone breaks in
- Laws that treat rich people differently than poor people
- Laws that make people homeless
- Laws against people marrying people of other races

Not all the laws on this brainstormed list are suitable for the assignment; some are not current or are not current in the United States, and some are too broad or ill-defined. But a third of these would work very well for the assignment with little or no modification. None of these ideas are thesis statements yet, but they are reasonably good examples of laws that fit the assignment and lend themselves well to good thesis statements and credible essays.

ACHIEVING SUBTLETY

Good writing goes beyond surface issues to explore the deeper meanings and implications of a topic. An argument or idea that digs beneath the surface, that goes beyond the obvious, might be usefully described as "subtle." In a college class, subtle ideas demonstrate to a teacher that you have really thought about an issue, struggled with its complexities, and learned something from an assignment. Once you have come up with a writing topic that meets all the specifications of an assignment, you need to develop and refine your topic to make sure it meets those standards of subtlety—to go beyond the obvious arguments, to do more than just say what you believe about a topic, to *learn* about the topic. This approach turns an acceptable or a good essay topic into a great one.

As you strive for this kind of subtle analysis, keep the following suggestions in mind:

Go beyond your first ideas

The first ideas that will occur to you about a topic will often be the first ideas that occur to everybody else, making the resulting essay "average" by definition. Moreover, the first ideas that occur to you (and everybody else) are rarely very good. Consider an assignment, for example, in which you have been asked to compare the political philosophies of Christine de Pizan and Niccolò Machiavelli. The first thing that someone looking at these two philosophers will notice is that de Pizan is a woman and Machiavelli is a man. From there, many people will conclude that de Pizan's philosophy must be more "feminine" and Machiavelli's more "masculine." The gendered differences between these two authors, however, are by no means the most interesting or significant differences, and they would not lead to the most interesting essay.

Go beyond the standard positions

Issues that are regularly discussed in public forums tend to have easily recognizable "pro" and "con" positions. Sometimes, these standard positions are obvious, knee-jerk reactions to a topic; sometimes, they are well-constructed arguments that have simply been used too often. In most cases, you should steer your own arguments away from these standard arguments, since they are so well known that they will occur to everybody. Even if they are good arguments, they are not *your* arguments, and they do not give you the opportunity to show what kinds of ideas you can come up with on your own.

If the assignment allows it, you might consider staying away entirely from issues that have been discussed so often that few new things are left to say about them. If you do write about such issues, however, approach them with subtlety and avoid the temptation to restate the usual lines of reasoning. Few readers will be persuaded by arguments that simply regurgitate standard lines of thinking.

Consider the following two arguments against legalized abortion, one of the most controversial and often-discussed issues in the modern political landscape:

Argument #1: "Abortion is murder. People who permit or perform abortions are taking innocent human lives, which is the definition of murder, and it doesn't matter how young each life is, since it is a life just the same. A child who has yet to be born is just as valuable as a child who has been born or an adult, so there is no reason why it should be acceptable to kill one if it is not acceptable to kill the other."

Argument #2: "The primary wrong-making feature of a killing is the loss to the victim of the value of its future. . . . The future of a standard fetus includes a set of experiences, projects, activities, and such which are identical with the futures of human beings and are identical with the futures of young children. Since the reason that it is sufficient to explain why it is wrong to kill human beings after the time of birth is a reason that also applies to fetuses, it follows that abortion is . . . seriously morally wrong." (Marquis, Don. "Why Abortion Is Immoral." *The Journal of Philosophy*, vol. 86, no. 4, Apr. 1989, pp. 183–202)

These passages are similar in many ways. Both assert that abortion is immoral because of its impact on a human life, and neither uses religious terms or clichés (see below). The first argument, however, simply strings together the standard, predictable arguments that one usually hears in discussions of abortion.

The second argument—which comes from a famous article by a philosophy professor—goes well beyond the standard arguments. It frames the issue in a way that most people have not considered and adds something new to a very familiar debate. This response is more intellectually challenging than the first and is much more likely to persuade someone who does not already hold an anti-abortion position. It is, in other words, a more subtle approach to the same basic argument.

Avoid clichés

A cliché is an argument, a phrase, a slogan, or a catchphrase that has been used so often that it no longer conveys its original meaning. Sometimes a cliché is simply an overused comparison, such as "dead as a doornail" or "light as a feather," but arguments can also be clichéd. Consider statements such as "When guns are outlawed, only outlaws will have guns," "If you don't like abortion, don't have one," "Make love not war," or "America—love it or leave it." Whatever the original merits of these sentiments may have been, the arguments have become clichés that can be invoked by people who have never seriously considered the complicated issues that they raise.

In college writing, clichés often take the place of serious contemplation about an issue. Clichés discourage the development of new ideas. They tend to be short arguments with little support and inflexible conclusions, and they seem (and only seem) to make further thought unnecessary.

Construct a debatable position

For a claim to result in an interesting essay, it must be arguable. Consider, for example, the following claim and think of the essay that it would produce: "War kills innocent people." Most people would immediately agree that a lot of innocent people die in wars. Many people, however, would argue that the loss of innocent lives is sometimes necessary, even if it is bad. Others would disagree and say that war is always a bad thing, no matter how necessary it may seem. However, the claim that war kills innocent people would not result in an effective essay because it does not take a position that could be reasonably disputed. A better claim might be: "A commitment to pacifism on the part of world leaders is the only way to resolve difficult disputes without bloodshed," or "War is ineffective because it deals with the surface political problems that lead to disputes and not the ultimate problems that cause conflict in the first place."

Consider the implications of an argument

Most arguments have consequences and implications that are not directly stated but that can be clearly understood when read with a subtle, critical eye. When you develop your ideas, keep in mind what unstated assumptions (discussed in Chapter 9, p. 605) they rest on and what their consequences might be. For example, if you are writing an essay about responses to poverty and you want to argue that the government should increase welfare to help lift people out of poverty, then you need to consider the implications of such an argument. One unstated assumption would be that people are poor because of their circumstances and not because of their behaviors—such as drug use or irresponsible spending—which cannot be controlled by welfare payments. Consider also the possible consequences of increasing welfare payments. Would more people go on welfare? Where would the additional money come from—higher taxes? Or would it be taken from the budgets for other social services, such as Medicare or Head Start (an early-childhood-development program)? Would it mean decreasing spending on other programs the government funds, like the National Institutes of Health or the National Endowment for the Arts? You need to consider as many aspects like these as possible in your writing. A subtle, persuasive argument addresses both the implications and the consequences of the claim.

This requirement also applies when you analyze or respond to another person's ideas; an analysis or response that addresses unstated implications of an argument is far more effective than one that does not. Take, for example, Mo Tzu's essay "Against Music" (p. 236). Mo Tzu's stated argument is that music and the pageantry that accompanies it are harmful to society. Rather than focusing on this argument, a deeper reading would analyze the *reason* that Mo Tzu opposed music: music was a luxury that took resources away from society without adding anything to most people's lives. This reasoning has implications for many other things that required or require resources without benefiting the majority of people: past examples include the pyramids of Egypt, the Olympics of ancient Greece, the plays of Shakespeare's Globe Theatre, while present ones include art exhibits, country clubs, and celebrity weddings. A truly subtle analysis of Mo Tzu's argument would account for and examine the implications of his argument that go far beyond what is stated in the text.

Keep going until you have learned something

The reason that most instructors give writing assignments is that they believe, with good reason, that the act of writing can teach you something. If you take an assignment seriously, the experience of creating, developing, and structuring a set of ideas can teach you things that just going to class and reading a textbook cannot.

One way to judge whether you have generated a good idea is to consider seriously whether the idea has changed your outlook. Have you learned something that you did not know, considered something that you never have considered before, changed your opinion about a controversial issue, or learned to look at something in a different way? If you have accomplished any of these things, you most likely have produced a solid, fruitful writing topic.

11

STRUCTURING IDEAS

GOOD IDEAS, EVEN WELL STATED, do not guarantee a good essay. Ideas, no matter how brilliant, must be organized effectively and presented intelligently so they can be understood by a reader. The previous two chapters focused on ways that you interact with both the ideas that you read and the ideas that you generate in response to your reading; both chapters dealt only with you and a text. This chapter will show you how to structure your ideas so that they can be read and appreciated by someone else.

Important structural elements of academic essays include thesis statements, introductions, transitions, and conclusions. This chapter will define these elements and offer techniques to help you use them effectively. Understanding these structural conventions will not only help you produce the kinds of essays that many of your instructors want to receive, it will also help you improve both your thinking and your writing.

In many ways, academic essays that adhere strictly to these guidelines are artificial creations rarely found outside the college classroom—and even in college classes, many teachers will expect you to move beyond these traditional academic writing techniques. But much can be said for the traditional thesis statement and the structural apparatus that supports it. Learning to use them properly can help you stay focused on a single idea and marshal evidence to support a claim, which are essential abilities for every kind of writing: academic, creative, or professional.

However, important as they are, mastering these techniques should not be your goal. They are designed simply to help you reach the ultimate goal of communicating your ideas to someone else. As the ancient Zen masters understood, the methods designed to lead people to enlightenment are not the same thing as enlightenment itself. As you progress as a student and a writer, keep your goal of communication separate from the techniques that you use to achieve it. Intelligent, thoughtful communication is more important than slavish devotion to technique, and these guidelines should be followed only to the extent that they help you reach that goal.

THESIS STATEMENTS

What Is a Thesis?

People can mean two different things when they talk about a "thesis." On the one hand, a thesis is the basic argument that a particular piece of writing makes—the point that an author wants to get across. Most writers, in most circumstances, want to communicate something to an audience; therefore, most writing has a thesis. On the other hand, when writing instructors use the word "thesis," they are usually referring to a thesis statement, a single sentence that summarizes or encapsulates an essay's main argument. Thesis statements of this sort are not required of every kind of writing, nor are they always found in the works of the best professional writers. These writers have learned how to advance a thesis (in the first sense of the word) without creating a single sentence to sum up the argument.

However, composing a thesis statement can be a very useful exercise for developing an argument. It accomplishes several important tasks: (1) it helps you clarify exactly what you are trying to say, which makes the writing process smoother and easier; (2) it serves as a reference point that you can use to eliminate ideas that do not support the main point of the essay; and (3) it tells the reader what kinds of arguments to expect and forecasts what follows.

One common misconception is that a thesis statement should summarize an *essay* rather than an *argument*. The difference is crucial. A thesis statement designed to summarize an essay will usually try to provide a miniature outline and can very quickly become unwieldy. Consider the following example:

There are many differences between Seneca and John Henry Newman: Newman was religious and Seneca was not; Seneca lived in the ancient Roman Empire while Newman lived in Victorian England at a time when it was becoming a modern democracy; and Seneca believed that liberal education was the only good kind of education while Newman believed that both liberal and useful education had their place.

While this sentence may be a good one-sentence summary of a three-to-five-page essay, it does not make a good thesis statement because it does not make an argument. In attempting to summarize everything that the essay says, this sentence does not actually have a point. A better thesis statement would try to summarize less about the essay and more clearly state a major claim:

> Newman's view of liberal education is much less restrictive than Seneca's because the society in which Newman lived required most people to acquire enough useful knowledge to earn a living.

This sentence boils down all of the various ideas in the first example into a single, coherent, focused argument that can serve as the main point that the essay will make.

The Thesis Statement as an Argument

Any argument must have two elements: a claim and support for that claim. Because a thesis statement is always, at some level, an argument, it should also include these two elements. The following sentences would not make good thesis statements because they contain only a claim and do not support that claim:

> Gandhi had a better understanding of poverty than Malthus.

> True objectivity in science can never be achieved.

> Liberal general education is a good idea.

To turn these claims into arguments, and therefore thesis statements, you would have to add a "because clause" (which may or may not contain the word "because"), or a brief statement of support that gives the rationale for the claim:

> Gandhi's understanding of poverty, which takes into account the spiritual side of human nature, is better than that of Malthus, whose analysis is solely economic.

> True objectivity in science requires something that never can be achieved: the presence of a purely unbiased observer.

> Liberal general education is a good idea because it prepares people for a variety of different careers rather than for a single job.

Refining Your Thesis Statement

When you view the thesis statement as an argument, with both a claim and support for that claim, you can use it to test whether your essay's argument works. If the thesis statement is a weak argument, then the chances are very good that the essay is also weak. Keep refining your thesis statement until you are reasonably sure that it is a good argument, and then make sure your essay properly addresses the point of your thesis statement.

Revising a thesis statement is really the same thing as revising the *ideas* in your essay. Here are a few things to keep in mind as you revise a thesis statement:

Present an arguable claim

While this requirement is covered at greater length in the previous chapter (see "Construct a debatable position," p. 630), it is worth repeating that an essay topic—and therefore a thesis statement, which presents the essay topic—needs to be debatable. A thesis statement should present a claim that a reasonable person could disagree with.

Present a single, focused argument

An essay should have a single argument and a focused thesis statement. Unfortunately, the formula for a "five-paragraph essay," the first kind of essay most people learn to write, can often lead to three (or more) separate ideas that are linked together under a common heading. Consider this example:

> Christianity and Islam are similar to each other in their worship of a single God, their belief in a single holy book, and their strong belief in caring for the poor.

While this might appear at first glance to be a workable thesis statement, it actually offers three arguments instead of one—each similarity between Christianity and Islam could be the focus of an entire essay. Consider how this thesis statement could be broken into three more-specific thesis statements:

> Christianity and Islam are similar to each other because both assert the existence of a single, all-powerful deity who stands outside the natural world.

> The most important similarity between Christianity and Islam is that both religions' followers believe that God has spoken to them through a single book rather than through a long tradition of oral narratives.

> The moral codes of Christianity and Islam are nearly identical in that each religion preaches the spiritually destructive nature of material wealth and the importance of taking care of the poor.

Each of these thesis statements could produce an interesting, focused essay, and each would be more effective and interesting than the essay produced by the first example. This kind of streamlining does not mean that an argument cannot have subpoints, or that different paragraphs should not treat different parts of a general assertion. But you have a responsibility as a writer to make very clear how each assertion supports the main thesis.

Make sure your thesis is open enough to allow for further discussion

Consider the following thesis statement:

> Machiavelli's philosophy could never work because he advocates lying and liars always get caught.

A statement such as this would support only a single paragraph or two of argument after the introduction. The problem, of course, is not with the thesis statement but with the ideas in the essay—the author has not thought of enough to say. Consider the following revision:

> While Machiavelli gave valuable advice to the princes and rulers of his own day, the modern notion of the separation of powers makes it unlikely that any leader of a modern democracy could practice these ideas today.

This statement opens up many more possibilities for analysis, discussion, expansion, and examples of the phenomenon that the writer wants to discuss. This thesis, in fact, will serve as the basis for the full sample essay toward the end of this chapter.

Make sure your thesis can be reasonably supported in the assigned essay

While some theses are too focused to allow for further discussion, others are too expansive to be covered in a short essay. For example:

> Lao Tzu's philosophy in the *Tao Te Ching* is so comprehensive that it encompasses every important aspect of what it means to be human.

This thesis might be defensible in a five-hundred-page book, but no writer could adequately defend such a sweeping statement in a three-to-five-page essay. Narrowing the thesis to a manageable assertion will vastly improve the essay. In the example above, choosing one aspect of human nature and exploring how it is treated in the *Tao Te Ching* creates a much more focused thesis statement, which will lead to a much more manageable and interesting essay:

> In the *Tao Te Ching*, Lao Tzu captures an important paradox of human nature: that inaction is often more productive than action.

The most important thing to remember when you are writing your thesis statement is that the claim that you make in it, and the support that you provide for that claim, set the parameters for the rest of your essay. You must be able to tie every assertion that you make in your essay back to the argument that you articulate in your thesis statement.

INTRODUCTIONS

The Introductory Paragraph

The introductory paragraph is where you make your first impression as a writer, and, just as in relationships, first impressions in reading are very difficult to overcome. This is why many experienced writers spend as much time on the first paragraph of an essay as they do on the rest of the essay. (The way that introductory paragraphs affect a writer's "ethos," or credibility, is covered in detail in Chapter 12, p. 649.)

A good introductory paragraph should do three things:

Introduce the purpose of the essay and any important concepts

If your paper is about Newman's and Nussbaum's views on education, your introduction should briefly introduce Newman and Nussbaum and explain, in very basic terms, their views on education. Your goal in the introduction should not be to begin your argument outright, but to clarify all the concepts that you will use in your argument, so that when you use them in the body of your essay, the reader will be familiar with them.

Capture the reader's interest

The introduction should interest the reader in the rest of the essay. It needs to entice the reader to continue reading and convince him or her that something interesting is going to happen in the rest of the essay, that he or she will be educated or entertained or both. (Strategies for doing this are discussed below.)

Provide a platform for any thesis statement

Many writing instructors advise students to place the thesis statement somewhere in the first paragraph, often at or near the end. A thesis statement does not have to go in the introduction, but, if you do choose (or have been instructed) to place it there, it should flow naturally from the introduction. Even if you do not place your thesis statement there, the introduction needs to lay the groundwork for your essential argument, which is summarized in the thesis statement.

Strategies for Beginning

The strategies below can help make your introductory paragraph more effective. All the examples are based on the thesis statement on Machiavelli in the previous section (p. 637); the thesis statement is in bold in each example.

Give historical context

An introduction that offers a meaningful discussion of any key concepts can help to orient readers to your argument:

> In the early sixteenth century, a prince had absolute power over his state. When Machiavelli wrote *The Prince* in 1513, therefore, he set out to teach potential leaders how to best utilize the tyrannical power at their disposal. His advice was clear, concise, and very effective for its time; however, much has changed in the past five hundred years. Since the late eighteenth century—when in their new Constitution America's Founding Fathers experimented with a radical idea called the "separation of powers doctrine"—most of the industrialized democracies in the world have adopted some form of power sharing between their executive, legislative, and judicial branches of government. **While Machiavelli gave valuable advice to the princes and rulers of his day, the modern notion of the separation of powers makes it unlikely that any leader of a modern democracy could practice these ideas today.**

Build your introduction around a key definition

Many times, your essay will introduce, or even revolve around, a key definition that actually defines the argument that you are making. In such cases, it is often a good idea to organize your introduction around this definition:

> One of the most innovative features of the American Constitution is the doctrine known as the "separation of powers." According to this doctrine, the various forms of government authority—legislative, executive, and judicial—should never be concentrated in the same hands, and there should be a system of checks and balances to make sure that no single individual or group obtains enough power to exercise control as a dictator. Without the power of a dictatorship, American rulers have had a very difficult time heeding the advice of the Italian philosopher Niccolò Machiavelli, whose political theories are based on the notion of absolute power that he saw as necessary to the effective running of a state. **While Machiavelli gave valuable advice to the princes and rulers of his day, the modern notion of the separation of powers makes it unlikely that any leader of a modern democracy could practice these ideas today.**

Lead directly into the thesis statement

One of the main purposes of the introduction is to set up the thesis statement. If you keep this in mind as you construct your introductory paragraph, you can often write it in such a way that nearly every sentence in it leads directly into the thesis, thus creating the kind of smooth transition that makes readers feel comfortable moving from your introduction to the body of your paper:

> The absolute power that princes had in Niccolò Machiavelli's time was not entirely a bad thing. In a feudal system of government, a strong ruler with great power can be a good thing for a country, while a weak ruler can cause devastating problems. However, in a society that is no longer feudal, a leader with dictatorial power is no longer so desirable. When America's Founding Fathers wrote the Constitution, they realized this and included a requirement that federal powers be separated into different branches of government; since the late eighteenth century, many other nations have adopted similar measures. **While Machiavelli gave valuable advice to the princes and rulers of his day, the modern notion of the separation of powers makes it unlikely that any leader of a modern democracy could practice these ideas today.**

Start with a question or a quotation

A good quotation can hook readers into your essay by presenting them with something interesting to read right off the bat. Interesting questions addressed directly to the reader have much the same effect. If used skillfully, such an opening hook can be used as the basis for a very effective introductory paragraph. However, keep in mind that this approach can easily become a cliché; use quotations sparingly in your introduction, and only when they apply directly to your topic.

> "Power tends to corrupt," wrote Lord Acton in 1887, "and absolute power corrupts absolutely." Acton's famous maxim is perhaps nowhere better demonstrated than in sixteenth-century Italy, where political power was the ultimate prize in a deadly game that often involved rebellion, assassination, treason, insurrection, and military conquest. When Niccolò Machiavelli wrote *The Prince* in 1513, he set out to tell political rulers exactly how to get the kind of absolute power that Acton warned of. In the America of today, however, people have learned well the lesson that Acton spent much of his life trying to teach. Since the founding of the American democracy, political power has been separated into three different areas—executive, legislative, and judicial—that are never allowed to fall into the same hands. **Thus, while Machiavelli gave valuable advice to the princes and rulers of his day, the modern notion of the separation of powers makes it unlikely that any leader of a modern democracy could practice these ideas today.**

Give a contextualizing example

If you are writing about something that may seem distant or be unfamiliar to your readers, consider starting with an example that might be more familiar. The example can then become a point of reference you can use throughout the paper to help explain more difficult concepts.

In 1974, Richard Nixon became the first president of the United States to resign from office. While it would be difficult to untangle the complicated web of conspiracy and deceit that brought Nixon to this position, most of the scandals known collectively as Watergate share a single motivation: Nixon wanted more power than the Constitution gave him. Being the chief executive officer of the nation was not enough; he also wanted to control legislation and judicial review and to have the power to gather his own intelligence about political enemies. For much of his career, Nixon was a perfect example of a political Machiavellian. However, in 1974 he became a perfect example of the reason that Machiavelli's approach is no longer valid. **While Machiavelli gave valuable advice to the princes and rulers of his day, the modern notion of the separation of powers makes it unlikely that any leader of a modern democracy could practice these ideas today.**

Avoid clichés

Such formulaic introductory phrases as "Throughout history . . . ," "Since the beginning of time . . . ," and "Webster's Dictionary defines . . . " have been used by so many students, in so many contexts, that they have lost whatever effectiveness they might ever have had as ways to introduce an argument.

TRANSITIONS

One of the most important things you can do to communicate your ideas to a reader is to provide transitions between all of the ideas and support that you use to prove your thesis. An effective transition shows how ideas connect and relate to each other; it also smooths the shift between one idea and another. There are three main kinds of transitions in academic writing:

Transitions within a paragraph. An effective paragraph is organized logically, so that the information at the beginning of the paragraph leads logically to the information at the end of the paragraph. Each sentence in a paragraph should flow from the previous sentence and lead directly into the following one. Otherwise, readers can become confused and alienated from your argument. Consider the following two paragraphs:

The ideas of Confucius have been responsible for one of the most important religions in the world: Confucianism. It would be more accurate to characterize Confucius as an "ethical philosopher" rather than as a "prophet" or a "religious figure." Confucius said nothing about the kinds of issues that religions usually deal with: divine beings, miracles, revelation, and the afterlife. He was concerned with constructing an ethical system that people could use to determine correct behavior in any situation.

The ideas of Confucius have been responsible for one of the most important religions in the world: Confucianism. **However**, Confucius himself said nothing about the kinds of issues that religions usually deal with: divine beings, miracles, revelation, and the afterlife. **Instead**, he was concerned with constructing an ethical system that people could use to determine correct behavior in any situation. It would, **therefore**, be more accurate to characterize Confucius as an "ethical philosopher" rather than as a "prophet" or a "religious figure."

Even though the ideas presented in the two paragraphs are identical, the second paragraph is much easier to read. There are two reasons for this. The first reason is structural: in the first example, the second sentence presents an unfamiliar claim (that Confucius should be considered a philosopher rather than a religious figure) that seems to contradict the claim in the first sentence (that the ideas of Confucius have been responsible for an important world religion). Such abrupt changes of thought tend to take readers by surprise. The second paragraph, by contrast, gives the evidence first and proceeds, step by step, to the conclusion, which, by the end of the paragraph, seems natural, logical, and even inevitable. Arranging ideas in a logical order helps you move smoothly from idea to idea.

The second reason that most readers would prefer the second paragraph is that it uses **transition words** such as "however," "instead," and "therefore" to show how ideas are related to each other within the paragraph. These transition words serve as cues that the reader can use to follow the writer's chain of reasoning and see logical relationships between different assertions. Good transition words should reflect the logical relationship between ideas that you are conveying. Some common transition words and phrases include:

ADDITION	**COMPARISON**
In addition to	Similarly
Also	In comparison
Furthermore	In the same way
Moreover	Compared to

CAUSATION	**CONTRAST**
Consequently	In contrast
Because of	By contrast
Thus	However
Therefore	Nevertheless
As a result of	Conversely
Hence	On the one hand
Then	On the other hand
In effect	Instead

Transitions between paragraphs. A well-written paragraph generally centers on a single idea or claim. It is therefore extremely important to demonstrate how the information in one paragraph relates to the information in the next—otherwise, you end up with interchangeable paragraphs that make good points individually but do not add up to a coherent argument.

Transitions to the overall argument. It is not enough simply to show how the ideas in a paragraph relate to ideas in other paragraphs; you must also show how they relate to your overall argument—the argument encapsulated in your thesis statement. Each time you make a new claim, you should demonstrate how this new information relates to the overall thesis of the essay. A transition can link one claim to the thesis statement, and to the next claim.

For an example of the importance of these last two kinds of transitions, read the following sample essay carefully and try to determine how the ideas in it are connected to each other and to the overall thesis statement (which is the same thesis statement that we used when discussing introductions earlier in this chapter).

Machiavelli: Ideas Whose Time Has Come . . . and Gone

In the early sixteenth century, a prince had absolute power over his state. When Machiavelli wrote *The Prince* in 1513, therefore, he set out to teach potential leaders how to best utilize the tyrannical power at their disposal. His advice was clear, concise, and very effective for its time; however, much has changed in the past five hundred years. Since the late eighteenth century—when in their new Constitution America's Founding Fathers experimented with a radical idea called the "separation of powers doctrine"—most of the industrialized democracies in the world have adopted some form of power sharing between their executive, legislative, and judicial branches of government. **While Machiavelli gave valuable advice to the princes and rulers of his own day, the modern notion of the separation of powers makes it unlikely that any leader of a modern democracy could practice these ideas today.**

Machiavelli argues that a leader must constantly prepare for war. While it is certainly true that a modern head of state must be concerned with the defense of the nation, it is no longer the case that he or she alone can make any final decisions about either war or preparation for war. Thus, when George W. Bush decided to send American troops to Iraq, he had to spend weeks lobbying Congress for permission to commit American troops to a foreign engagement and months attempting to raise the money to support them once they were there.

At the heart of Machiavelli's advice is the assumption that a prince is free to tax the people and spend their money as he or she sees fit. While this was true of all princes in Machiavelli's day, it is very rarely the case for leaders today. Executive officers, such as presidents, do not normally have the power to tax people or to spend their money—both of these powers now rest with legislative bodies, such as the House of Representatives and the Senate. During his first term, for example, President Bill Clinton attempted to violate one of Machiavelli's cardinal rules by taxing people heavily in order to finance a generous health care initiative.

Machiavelli's ideas would not work in most countries today. There are, of course, plenty of exceptions to this rule. Many twentieth-century political leaders managed to seize absolute power over their countries—from Hitler, Stalin, and Mussolini in the early part of the century to Pinochet, Mobutu, and Hussein in our time. These leaders have repeatedly shown that absolute power concentrated in a single person is not in the best interests of the state.

If you had trouble seeing the relationships between the main ideas in this paragraph, do not be alarmed. They are very difficult to see, because the essay does not have any transitions in it. It relies on the reader to be able to recognize the connections. The last three paragraphs in this essay are also completely interchangeable. If you were so inclined, you could take a pair of scissors and cut these paragraphs out, replace them in the essay in any order, and neither the flow nor the logic of the essay would suffer.

Now, read the same essay with all the transitions in place. You will notice that the transitions (in bold) account for about a third of the paper's total word count. Also notice that these transitions are not afterthoughts tacked on to each major idea, but integral parts of the structure of each paragraph.

Machiavelli: Ideas Whose Time Has Come . . . and Gone

In the early sixteenth century, a prince had absolute power over his state. When Machiavelli wrote *The Prince* in 1513, therefore, he set out to teach potential leaders how to best utilize the tyrannical power at their disposal. His advice was clear, concise, and very effective for its time; however, much has changed in the past five hundred years. Since the late eighteenth century—when in their new Constitution America's Founding Fathers experimented with a radical idea called the "separation of powers doctrine"—most of the industrialized democracies in the world have adopted some form of power sharing between their executive, legislative, and judicial branches of government. **While Machiavelli gave valuable advice to the princes and rulers of his day, the modern notion of the separation of powers makes it unlikely that any leader of a modern democracy could practice these ideas today.**

One of the most important aspects of the separation of powers doctrine is that it eliminates the ability of any president or prime minister to declare or prepare for war without the consent of a legislative body. Machiavelli argues that a leader must constantly prepare for war and study the art of armed conflict. While it is certainly true that a modern head of state must be concerned with the defense of the nation, it is no longer the case that he or she alone can make any final decisions about either war or preparation for war. In nations that observe the separation of powers principle, both war and peacetime military expenditures have much more to do with budgetary committees than with presidential decrees. Thus, when George W. Bush decided to send American troops to Iraq, he had to spend weeks lobbying Congress for permission to commit American troops to a foreign engagement and months attempting to raise the money to support them once they were there. Machiavelli could not have imagined such a division of power in his own day and could hardly have been expected to anticipate it in his advice to princes.

In addition to preventing leaders from going to war whenever they choose, the separation of powers principle also prevents leaders from taking Machiavelli's advice to avoid lavish expenses and to be content to be considered misers rather than spendthrifts (32–33). At the heart of this advice is the assumption that a prince is free to tax the people and spend their money as he or she sees fit. While this was true of all princes in Machiavelli's day, it is very rarely the case for leaders today. Executive officers, such as presidents, do not normally have the power to tax people or to spend their money—both of these powers now rest with legislative bodies, such as the House of Representatives and the Senate. During his first term, for example, President Bill Clinton attempted to violate one of Machiavelli's cardinal rules by taxing people heavily in order to finance a generous health care initiative. He was prevented from doing this by a power that Machiavelli could not have understood: a legislative body that had to approve all new expenditures by the government.

Our experiences with both war and taxation demonstrate that, even though some modern American presidents and European prime ministers have wanted to put Machiavelli's programs into effect, they have rarely had the concentration of power necessary to be completely Machiavellian. There are, of course, plenty of exceptions to this rule. Many twentieth-century political leaders managed to seize absolute power over their countries—from Hitler, Stalin, and Mussolini in the early part of the century to Pinochet, Mobutu, and Hussein in our time. These leaders have repeatedly shown that absolute power concentrated in a single person is not in the best interests of the state, and their examples have caused countries all over the world to incorporate the separation of powers doctrine into their constitutions. This fact makes Machiavelli's advice increasingly less relevant to our day. Almost all of Machiavelli's advice assumed a leader with absolute power; wherever nations follow the doctrine of the separation of powers, such advice will be of little use to modern politicians.

These transitions relate the various ideas in the paper both to each other and to the overall thesis of the essay: that Machiavelli's ideas would not work in a modern democracy because the separation of powers doctrine would prevent anyone from having the power that he ascribes to princes. Each paragraph extends this argument into some realm of contemporary politics and then explicitly explains how it relates back to the overall thesis. As a result, the entire essay comes across as a single, coherent argument about the contemporary relevance of Machiavelli's political theory.

CONCLUSIONS

Conclusions are important. They give readers a sense of closure and writers the opportunity to tie together various threads of argument into focused assertions or to demonstrate the significance of the cases that they have made in their essays. Consider the conclusion to the sample essay about Machiavelli (p. 644):

> Our experiences with both war and taxation demonstrate that, even though some modern American presidents and European prime ministers have wanted to put Machiavelli's programs into effect, they have rarely had the concentration of power necessary to be completely Machiavellian. There are, of course, plenty of exceptions to this rule. Many twentieth-century political leaders managed to seize absolute power over their countries—from Hitler, Stalin, and Mussolini in the early part of the century to Pinochet, Mobutu, and Hussein in our time. These leaders have repeatedly shown that absolute power concentrated in a single person is not in the best interests of the state, and their examples have caused countries all over the world to incorporate the separation of powers doctrine into their constitutions. This fact makes Machiavelli's advice increasingly less relevant to our day. Almost all of Machiavelli's advice assumed a leader with absolute power; wherever nations follow the doctrine of the separation of powers, such advice will be of little use to modern politicians.

This conclusion is designed to take the two major topics (war and taxation) and link them together as different manifestations of the same thing: the limitations imposed on national leaders by the separation of powers doctrine, an idea that goes hand in hand with the overall thesis. But it also has a secondary function, which is to anticipate and correct a potential weakness: the fact that not every government in the world today believes in the separation of powers, and that there are still dictators today who have the kind of absolute power that Machiavelli envisioned in *The Prince*. By bringing up some of these dictators, the writer demonstrates that he or she has considered this issue and that it does not disprove his or her thesis.

Though there are many ways to bring your essay to a close, below are a few strategies you can employ, along with examples of alternate conclusions to the sample paper that we have been working with:

Refer back to the introduction

If you started your essay with an introductory quotation, question, or historical situation, you can often return to your introduction as the basis for forming a conclusion. Consider the sample introduction on page 641 that begins with a discussion of Watergate as a way to explain the separation of powers. Returning to the story of Nixon's resignation would be an excellent way to conclude an essay that began with such an introduction:

> In Machiavelli's society, leaders were often rebelled against, occasionally exiled, and, not infrequently, assassinated. But no Italian prince in the sixteenth century would ever have done what Richard Nixon was forced to do in 1974: resign and leave office because of a Supreme Court decision forcing him to turn over incriminating evidence to a congressional committee. Supreme Courts and congressional committees simply were not part of the world that Machiavelli inhabited. The fact that they have become such an important part of the world today, and that leaders in democratic countries are prevented from achieving the kind of power that Machiavelli assumed that a prince would have, makes it difficult to see his advice as relevant to American society in the twenty-first century.

Demonstrate the implications of your argument

Sometimes, you can reach the end of an essay only to discover that your argument has some major implications that you have not addressed. The conclusion can be a good place to show how the fairly focused argument that you have been making has broader and more general applications to other kinds of questions and arguments:

> Though America was founded with a separation of powers doctrine designed to prevent any individual from achieving the kind of power that Machiavelli attributed to princes, we have recently been in danger of forgetting what our Founding Fathers did. Recent presidents, from Lyndon Johnson to George W. Bush, have committed troops to long foreign engagements without ever receiving a declaration of war from Congress; congressional committees are famous for attaching spending bills to completely unrelated pieces of legislation; and, in 2000, the Supreme Court divided along partisan political lines to give the presidency of the United States to someone who had not been elected by a majority of the people. The writings of Niccolò Machiavelli do more than show

us what life was like during a particularly violent period of the Italian Renaissance. They warn us what our lives will be like should we ever allow our leaders the power to act unilaterally and with impunity.

Close with a quotation

Just as a quotation can make a good hook for the beginning of an essay, so a quotation can provide an effective way to tie everything together at the end. Furthermore, a well-chosen quotation from someone that the reader recognizes can provide the sense of closure and completeness that should always characterize a concluding paragraph. Beware, however, of using a lengthy quotation—another person's words should not make your argument for you but rather sum up what you have already effectively demonstrated:

> Americans often become annoyed at the inefficiency of our political system. Elections are long and drawn out, debates over important issues are held up by political maneuvering, and the courts, Congress, and the president are forever frustrating each other's plans. The media calls this "gridlock," but scholars of the Constitution call it "checks and balances"—and it is this very inefficiency that prevents rulers from being able to follow Machiavelli's advice completely. It is perhaps this element of democratic inefficiency that Winston Churchill had in mind when he reportedly said that "democracy is the worst form of government in the world with the single exception of all the others."

12

◉

SUPPORTING IDEAS

Though the two terms are often used interchangeably, a claim is not the same thing as an argument. For a claim to become an argument, you need to provide some kind of support. You cannot offer support by simply magnifying the intensity of a claim. The claim that "pornography is extremely disgusting and horribly immoral" offers no more support (that is, no support at all) for its position than the simpler claim that "pornography is immoral."

This chapter will show you how to support a claim and thus turn it into an argument. To begin, you must understand how to provide appropriate evidence to support your claim. You must also understand the different ways that people can be persuaded by arguments. According to Aristotle, the three standard elements of persuasion are logos (appeals to logic and reasoning), pathos (appeals to emotion), and ethos (appeals based on the speaker's character). Understanding these building blocks will make you a stronger reader, as you will be able to identify the methods writers use to make their arguments. And it will make you a better writer, as you will be able to employ them intentionally as you craft your own arguments.

SUPPORTING CLAIMS WITH EVIDENCE

Any time you make a claim, you have a responsibility to support it. Support can come in the form of facts, statistics, authorities, examples, or textual citation. The kind of support that you use depends on the claim that you make: for example, the claim that "affirmative action is not a useful educational policy because it has not increased minority graduation rates" would be best supported by statistical evidence, while the claim that "Mencius and Hsün Tzu held opposing views of human nature" would be best supported by quoting their writings (textual citation). When you think about ways to advance your claim, think about all the possible evidence that you can marshal in support of it.

Facts

Most claims benefit from the support of relevant, well-documented facts. Consider, for example, Charles Darwin's argument in *The Origin of Species*. To support his claim that evolution occurs by means of natural selection, Darwin combines several facts, including Charles Lyell's research showing that the earth is extremely old, Thomas Malthus's calculations about the growth rates of populations, and a summary of existing techniques to breed certain characteristics in livestock and domestic animals. Though these facts do not "prove" Darwin's principles, they create a context in which evolution by natural selection is possible and logical.

Sometimes the facts you need to support your claim are straightforward. A claim that "the benefits of organ donation outweigh any potential risks to the recipient" can be supported by facts about organ donation that are readily available in reference books or on the Web. (For more on finding and evaluating sources, see Chapter 13, p. 668.) At times, however, other factors can complicate the level of support facts can offer. For example, different definitions of a key term can produce different perceptions of what is factual. The number of people living in poverty in the United States is much lower for those who define "poverty" as "living on the street" than for those who define it as "not owning a house and two cars." When using facts to support your claim, make sure they relate directly to your claim and are clearly defined.

Statistics

Statistics are facts that consist of numerical data. Statistical data can be harnessed in support of most claims about society, culture, or the collective facts of a given country or region. For these claims in particular, statistical evidence about birthrates, marriages, deaths, inheritances, lawsuits, and other matters of public record—the data of everyday life—can be extremely useful in making a historical argument that goes deeper than one based on political, military, and cultural leaders' documents, which usually do not reflect most people's lives. In arguments about contemporary societies, statistics can be found to support and refute arguments about race, gender, crime rates, education, employment, industry, income, political affiliation, public opinion, and dozens of other areas where collective behavior can be tracked and measured. An excellent source for many of these statistics in the United States is the *Statistical Abstract of the United States*, which is published each year by the Census Bureau and made available, free of charge, at www.census.gov.

Authorities

In areas where facts and statistics are unavailable or inconclusive, evidence can be gathered from those with an acknowledged expertise in the field. Though appealing to authority cannot prove a fact definitively—even experts make mistakes!—it can explain what is possible, what is likely, and what is impossible, all of which are extremely important in supporting claims. In many cultures, certain texts or authorities have such high status that their support will virtually guarantee many people's acceptance of a claim. The Bible, the Quran, the Buddha's teachings, and Confucius's words have all had this kind of authority in the cultures that have been built around them. However, these texts are not generally acceptable as authorities in modern academic arguments.

Examples

Examples drawn from history, fiction, personal experience, or even one's imagination can often be used to support a claim. Examples drawn from historical or current events are especially persuasive, as they add factual support. Consider how Margaret Mead uses examples in "Warfare: An Invention—Not a Biological Necessity" (p. 500). She begins by giving examples of "primitive" people who do not have a concept of organized warfare—the Lepchas and the Eskimos. Then, to illustrate the point that warfare does not come with increased social development, she gives examples of what she sees as two equally undeveloped groups of people—the Andamans and the Australian aborigines—who fight wars. Each time that she makes a claim about the development of warfare, she provides an example of a culture somewhere in the world that illustrates her point.

Textual Citation

Writing in response to other texts—such as the ones found in this book—often requires you to write interpretively, or to make claims about what texts mean. Interpretive writing requires you to find support for your claim within the source text. For example, if you claim that Christine de Pizan's *The Treasure of the City of Ladies* gives a more accurate view of human nature than Machiavelli's *The Prince* because it accounts for the human potential to do good, you will need to cite portions of de Pizan's text that refer to this potential. Conventions for documenting textual sources are discussed in depth in Chapter 14 (p. 668).

LOGOS: APPEALS TO LOGIC AND REASON

What Aristotle called *logos*, or appealing to logic and reasoning, is an essential part of supporting an argument. While evidence provides the basis of an argument's support, how we apply logic to that evidence—that is, our reasoning—is part of what makes an argument persuasive.

According to classical theories of argument, our minds move in two different directions to reach conclusions. Sometimes, we reach a conclusion by applying a general fact that we know—or belief that we hold—to a specific situation. This is called deductive reasoning. Most people know, for example, that milk is more expensive at convenience stores than at grocery stores. When someone decides to save money by buying milk at a grocery store rather than at a convenience store, that person is reasoning deductively.

Inductive reasoning works in the opposite direction. We reason inductively when we use firsthand observations to form general conclusions. Sometimes, the process of induction is simply referred to as "generalizing." If, after buying milk at a certain grocery store three times and finding it spoiled each time, someone decided never to buy milk at that store again, that person would be reasoning inductively.

Most of us do not consciously decide to reason deductively or inductively to solve problems. Rather, we constantly employ both forms of reasoning at the same time. We gather facts and observations until we can use them to form general conclusions (inductive reasoning), and we use those general conclusions to make judgments about specific situations (deductive reasoning). When we do not have a good understanding of how deductive and inductive reasoning work, however, we can be more easily persuaded by arguments that are weak or misleading. This section will explain how both kinds of reasoning can support claims.

Deductive Reasoning

The basic unit of deductive reasoning is called a syllogism, which can be thought of as a kind of mathematical formula that works with words rather than numbers. In its most basic form, a syllogism contains two premises and a conclusion drawn from those premises:

Major premise (dealing with a category): All dogs have four legs.

Minor premise (dealing with an individual): Rover is a dog.

Conclusion: Rover has four legs.

The major premise asserts that all members of a category share a certain characteristic. In the example above, everyone who belongs to the category of "dogs" shares the characteristic of "four legs." However, the characteristic can apply to other categories, too—for example, cats also have four legs. If we were to represent the major premise above graphically, it would look like this:

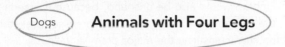

The three simple statements in the syllogism above do not include evidence that Rover is actually a dog; thus, we cannot be sure that the syllogism is true. We can say, though, that *if* all dogs have four legs *and* Rover is a dog, *then* Rover must have four legs. This is because the syllogism is sound, meaning that the premises lead infallibly to the conclusion. A syllogism can be completely true yet unsound. It can also be sound yet demonstrably untrue. Consider the following two arguments:

Major premise: Dogs have purple teeth and green fangs.

Minor premise: Rover is a dog.

Conclusion: Rover has purple teeth and green fangs. (Sound but untrue: the major premise is false.)

Major premise: Basketball players are tall.

Minor premise: Shaquille O'Neal is tall.

Conclusion: Shaquille O'Neal is a basketball player. (True but unsound: simply being tall does not make Shaquille O'Neal a basketball player; plenty of tall people are not basketball players.)

To see why the example above that uses basketball players and Shaquille O'Neal is unsound, consider how the major premise would look if represented graphically:

Because the category of "Basketball Players" is contained entirely within the characteristic of "Tall People," it is logical to assert that all basketball players are tall. It is also logical to assert that someone who is not tall cannot be a basketball player. However, since a large part of the circle representing "Tall People" lies outside the category "Basketball Players," it is not logical to assert that someone who is tall is also a basketball player. If we substitute a different name for "Shaquille O'Neal," it becomes clear why the syllogism is unsound:

Major premise: Basketball players are tall.

Minor premise: Barack Obama is tall.

Conclusion: Barack Obama is a basketball player. (Unsound and untrue)

The following syllogism would also be unsound, because it asserts that if an individual is not in the category named in the major premise (basketball players), he must not have the characteristic in the major premise (tallness):

Major premise: Basketball players are tall.

Minor premise: Barack Obama is not a basketball player.

Conclusion: Barack Obama is not tall. (Unsound and untrue)

To turn the original syllogism into a sound one that asserts that an individual fits the category of the major premise and therefore shares its characteristics, we would need to rewrite it like this:

Major premise: Basketball players are tall.

Minor premise: Shaquille O'Neal is a basketball player.

Conclusion: Shaquille O'Neal is tall. (Sound and true)

A sound syllogism can also assert that an individual who does not share the characteristic in the major premise (in this example, tallness) cannot be part of the category named in the major premise (in this example, basketball players):

Major premise: Basketball players are tall.

Minor premise: George Stephanopoulos is not tall.

Conclusion: George Stephanopoulos is not a basketball player. (Sound and true)

Understanding the structure of syllogisms can be helpful in understanding real-world claims. Consider the following hypothetical statement:

When America was attacked, those who sympathized with these attacks and wished our attackers well opposed going to war in Iraq. At the very moment that terrorists were hoping that we would not go to war, Senator Jones gave a speech on the Senate floor opposing the war. It is important that Americans understand that, in these crucial moments, Senator Jones's sympathies lay with the enemy.

Once we eliminate the political hyperbole in this statement, we are left with a fairly straightforward syllogism:

Major premise: People who support terrorism opposed going to war in Iraq.

Minor premise: Senator Jones opposed going to war in Iraq.

Conclusion: Senator Jones supports terrorism.

Whether or not one considers the premises of this argument to be true, the conclusion is unsound: it states that because the minor premise asserts that an individual shares the characteristic in the major premise (opposing going to war), he must therefore belong to the category in the major premise (people who support terrorism).

When you examine an argument, such as the example above or the ones in this book, think critically about its logic and reasoning. If you were to state the argument in a syllogism, would the syllogism be sound? For example, consider this thesis statement offered earlier in the chapter: "Affirmative action is not a useful educational policy because it has not increased minority graduation rates." Arranged in a syllogism, it would look like this:

Major premise: Useful educational policies increase graduation rates.

Minor premise: Affirmative action has not increased minority graduation rates.

Conclusion: Affirmative action is not a useful educational policy.

Since the minor premise claims that an individual (in this case, a specific instance of educational policy, affirmative action) does not share the characteristic in the major premise, the conclusion that it does not belong to the category in the major premise is sound—and, therefore, the argument is sound (which does not necessarily make it true). Applying this logic to your own arguments can help you ensure that your arguments are sound.

Inductive Reasoning

Inductive reasoning does not produce the kind of mathematical certainty that deductive reasoning does, but it can produce conclusions with a very high likelihood of being true. We engage in induction when we gather together bits of specific information and use our own knowledge and experience to make an observation about what must be true. Inductive reasoning uses observations and prior experiences, rather than syllogisms, to reach conclusions. Consider the following chains of observations:

Observation: John came to class late this morning.

Observation: John's hair was uncombed.

Prior experience: John is very fussy about his hair.

Conclusion: John overslept.

The reasoning process here is directly opposite to that used in deductive syllogisms. Rather than beginning with a general principle (people who comb their hair wake up on time), the chain of evidence begins with an observation and then combines it with other observations and past experience to arrive at a conclusion.

There are three basic kinds of inductive reasoning: generalization, analogy, and statistical inference.

Generalization

This is the most basic kind of inductive reasoning. You generalize whenever you make a general statement (all salesmen are pushy) based on observations (the last three salesmen who came to my door were pushy). When you use specific observations as the basis of a general conclusion, you are said to be making an inductive leap.

Generally speaking, the amount of support needed to justify an inductive leap is based on two things: the plausibility of the generalization and the risk factor involved in rejecting a generalization.

Implausible inductive leaps require more evidence than plausible ones do. More evidence is required, for example, to support the notion that a strange light in the sky is an invasion force from the planet Xacron than to support the notion that it is a low-flying plane. Since induction requires us to combine what we observe with prior experience, and most of us have more prior experience with low-flying planes than with extraterrestrial invaders, it will take more evidence of an alien invasion force to overcome our prior experience of low-flying planes.

An inductive leap is more easily justified—that is, you can supply less support for it—when rejecting it carries a great risk. Consider the following two arguments:

1. I drank milk last night and got a minor stomachache. I can probably conclude that the milk was a little bit sour, and I should probably not drink that milk again.

2. I ate a mushroom out of my backyard last night, and I became violently ill. I had to be rushed to the hospital to have my stomach pumped. I can probably conclude that the mushroom was poisonous, and I should probably not eat mushrooms from my backyard again.

Technically, the evidence for these two arguments is the same. They both generalize from a single instance, and they both reach conclusions that could be accounted for by other factors. However, most people would take the second argument much more seriously, simply because the consequences for not doing so are much more serious.

There are two common errors in generalization: hasty generalization and exclusion.

Hasty generalization.   Inductive fallacies tend to be judgment calls—different people have different opinions about the line between correct and incorrect induction. You commit a hasty generalization, the fallacy most often associated with generalization, when you make an inductive leap that is not based on sufficient information. Another term for this is "jumping to conclusions." Look at the following three statements and try to determine which generalizations are valid and which are hasty.

1. General Widgets is a sexist company. It has over five thousand employees, and not a single one of them is female.

2. General Widgets is a sexist company. My friend Jane, who has a degree in computer science, applied for a job there, and it went to a man who majored in history.

3. General Widgets is a sexist company. My friend Jane applied there, and she didn't get the job.

Because different people can be convinced by different levels of evidence, it can be surprisingly difficult to identify a hasty generalization.

Exclusion.   A second fallacy that is often associated with generalization, exclusion occurs when you omit an important piece of evidence from the chain of reasoning that is used as the basis for the conclusion. If I generalize that my milk is bad based on a minor stomachache and fail to take into account the seven hamburgers I ate after drinking the milk, I have excluded the hamburgers from the chain of reasoning and am guilty of exclusion, which can lead to an invalid conclusion.

Analogy

To make an argument using an analogy is to draw a conclusion about one thing based on its similarities to another thing. Consider, for example, the following argument against a hypothetical military action in the Philippines.

In the 1960s, America was drawn into a war in an Asian country, with a terrain largely comprising jungles, against enemies that we could not recognize and accompanied by friends that we could not count on. That war began slowly, by sending a few "advisors" to help survey the situation and offer military advice, and it became the greatest military disgrace that our country has ever known. We all know what happened in Vietnam. Do we really want a repeat performance in the Philippines?

In other words, this argument is saying the following: A war in the Philippines would be disastrous. Our soldiers had a terrible time fighting in the jungles in Vietnam, and the terrain around Manila is even worse. An argument like this is an example of a valid analogy. It takes an observation (we had a hard time fighting in the jungles of Vietnam), makes a generalization (it is hard to fight modern warfare in a jungle terrain), and then applies it to another instance (we would have a hard time fighting in the jungles of the Philippines).

Analogies can be useful in illustrating key points (such as the inability of modern militaries to contain rebellions based in jungle terrains), but they do not prove their points simply by being analogies. The most common error found in arguments that use analogies is the false analogy. In a false analogy the characteristics considered are irrelevant, inaccurate, or insufficient.

If we decide to attack the Philippines, we should probably do it in January. In 1991, we attacked Iraq in January, and look how well that turned out.

Though it goes through the same process, this analogy is based on irrelevant information (the time of year we attacked Iraq).

Statistical inference

We employ this third variety of inductive reasoning whenever we assume that something is true of a population as a whole because it is true of a certain portion of the population. Politicians and corporations spend millions of dollars a year gathering opinions from relatively small groups of people to form bases for statistical inferences, upon which they base most of their major decisions. Inductions based on statistics have proven to be extremely accurate as long as the sample sizes are large enough to avoid large margins of error. Political exit polls, for example, often predict results extremely accurately based on small voter samples, and the Nielsen ratings report the television viewing habits of over a hundred million households based on sample sizes of about a thousand American families. However, using statistical inference carries the risk of using an unrepresentative sample.

Unrepresentative sample.   This is a statistical group that does not adequately represent the larger group that it is considered a part of. Any sample of opinions in the United States must take into account the differences in race, age, gender, religion, and geographic location that exist in this country. Thus, a sample of one thousand people chosen to represent all of these factors would tell us a great deal about the opinions of the electorate. A sample of one thousand white, thirty-year-old, Lutheran women from Nebraska would tell us nothing at all about the opinions of the electorate as a whole. Because samples must be representative to be accurate, it is a fallacy to rely on straw polls, informal surveys, and self-selecting questionnaires to gather statistical evidence.

Logical Fallacies

Rhetoricians have identified hundreds of different ways that reasoning can be used incorrectly. Understanding the most common of these fallacies can help you recognize where reasoning—your own and that of other people—goes astray. In this way, you can make your own writing more persuasive, and you can avoid being deceived by someone whose arguments are not logically sound.

Post hoc ergo propter hoc

The fallacy of *post hoc ergo propter hoc* (Latin for "after this, therefore because of this") is committed whenever someone asserts or implies that because an event occurred before another event, the first event caused the second. This fallacy is often called simply the *post hoc* fallacy, and it is the abuse of reasoning that allows politicians to take credit for everything good that happened while they were in office—and for their opponents to blame them for everything bad that happened.

> Inflation tripled after Jimmy Carter was elected president. His policies must have been inflationary.

And it occurs in other contexts as well:

> Studies have conclusively proven that 83 percent of people who have died in automobile accidents last year ate ice cream within a month of their accidents. This figure strongly suggests that eating ice cream causes automobile accidents.

> I took Vitamin C and my cold quickly got better. It must be true then that Vitamin C helps to fight colds.

Ad hominem

The fallacy of *ad hominem* (Latin for "against the man") is the assertion that someone's argument or viewpoint should be discounted because of character flaws that have nothing to do with the issues at hand. This fallacy should not be confused with simple name-calling, which is normally not an *ad hominem* fallacy as much as it is simply "being a jerk." Nor should the *ad hominem* fallacy be confused with a legitimate challenge to authority—if someone asserts a point based on his or her own authority, then it is very logical to call that authority into question.

> How can people believe the theory of evolution when it is a well-known fact that Darwin was a deadbeat?

> Rachel Carson's *Silent Spring* is the argument of a bitter woman who had an environmentalist ax to grind. There is no reason to limit DDT use on her account.

Straw man

The straw-man argument is named for a metaphor. The name invokes the image of a fight between a human opponent and a straw dummy dressed to look like a real opponent. When the straw man is knocked down, the human opponent claims victory. A straw-man argument is a summary of an opponent's position that is intentionally weak or easy to refute. By defeating an artificial, constructed version of someone else's argument, a speaker can claim victory, even though he or she has not dealt with the issues at hand.

> Those who want to adopt campus-wide codes against sexist, racist and homo-phobic speech believe that they can prevent such kinds of speech. As noble an idea as this is, realizing the idea is practically impossible. Prejudice, a basic component of human nature, will not be eliminated with the passage of new rules and laws. Those who would try to limit free speech on campus would curtail a vital part of the American Constitution in the name of a pipe dream.

> The problem with antipornography feminists is that they think sex is bad because men are evil. They tell us that any sexual relationship between a man and a woman will demean the woman and enforce the patriarchal hegemony of the man. This idea ignores the fact that a lot of men really do respect and care for women.

Dicto simpliciter

Dicto simpliciter (Latin for "I speak simply") is the illogical assumption that some-thing that is good in general must therefore be good in a particular instance. Those who commit this fallacy are guilty of uncritically applying a general truism to a particular situation. Another word for *dicto simpliciter* is "oversimplification."

> Milk is good for you, so everyone should drink milk.

> Exercise is good, so the college should require a physical education class every semester.

> It is good to date, so you should date me.

Bandwagoning

The fallacy of bandwagoning is the assertion that you should believe something or do something because everybody else does. Bandwagoning works because most people have an innate desire to agree with others—we tend to see a kind of emotional security in doing and thinking as other people do and think. This fallacy is sometimes called *ad populum* (Latin for "appeal to the people").

> Don't be the last person on your street to buy a Clippermeister lawnmower—the only lawnmower that tells the neighbors that you care about the neighborhood as much as they do.

> The "pro-life" position is becoming increasingly difficult to maintain. A recent poll suggested that 85 percent of Americans favor some form of abortion.

False dilemma

The false dilemma, or false dichotomy, is a fallacy that presents two issues as if they are the only possible choices in a given situation. The rejection of one choice in such a situation requires the adoption of the second alternative. False dichotomies should be distinguished from true dichotomies. Sometimes, only two choices exist: everything in the world is either a dog or a nondog, but everything is not either a dog or a cat. In most situations, middle grounds or other options make it irresponsible to force a choice between two alternatives.

> If you are not for the war, you are against the troops. I support the war because I support our troops.

> I am pro-choice because to be otherwise would be antiwoman.

PATHOS: APPEALS TO EMOTION

Aristotle called his second element of persuasion *pathos*, or appeals to emotion. Most people are at least as governed by their emotions as they are by reason, and they are even more likely to be motivated to adopt an opinion or course of action when logical appeals are combined with appeals that work on an emotional level. Advertisers and political campaigns have become extremely good at making these kinds of appeals—often to the point that they exclude logical arguments altogether and appeal only to emotions. They know that emotional appeals work. However, emotional appeals do not have to be manipulative; when used effectively and judiciously, they can help you connect with your reader or illustrate the emotional aspects of an issue.

Below are some of the most common kinds of emotional appeals. All of them can be used in manipulative ways, but they can also all be used in conjunction with other kinds of support to produce extremely compelling and effective arguments.

Sympathy

Most people are moved by the misfortunes of others. When we see victims of injustice, economic hardship, crime, war, or disaster, we sympathize and want to help. Appeals to sympathy or pity tend to be most persuasive when they describe the plights of individuals, and are paired with facts, statistics, and an analysis of large-scale phenomena. For example, in a piece of writing about poverty in less-developed countries, the story of a single child dying of starvation would provide a more effective emotional appeal than would a well-reasoned statistical analysis of childhood death rates in twenty-six nations, but the combination of the two would make for the best argument—it would appeal to both emotion and reason.

Fear

When people do not feel safe, or when they feel that their security (physical or economic) is in jeopardy, they become susceptible to appeals to fear. This is why automakers list safety as a major component of new cars and why politicians fore-ground their commitment to creating jobs and a healthy economy. An appeal to fear creates a sense of fear in the audience and connects its argument to resolving the fear. In the above example of automakers, emphasizing the safety of their cars both puts forth the possibility of being in an auto accident and offers the reassur-ance that if you buy one of their cars, you will be safe. Politicians who emphasize their commitment to creating new jobs and a healthy economy tap into fears of financial struggles and simultaneously offer the reassurance that if they are elected, they will put those fears to rest.

Anger

When writers appeal to anger, they frame an issue in a way that angers an audience and then use that anger to reinforce their claim. Usually, this means telling the audi-ence something that they did not previously know and that, once known, elicits anger.

Most people are moved to a sense of anger by injustice, unfairness, and cru-elty. Exposing unfairness can be an effective way to appeal to this sense of anger. Consider, for example, the following argument:

Shopping at Cheap Stuff is immoral. In order to keep their prices low, they pay subminimum wages with no benefits, and they subject their employees to dangerous working conditions. They have been cited more times than any other corporation for unfair labor practices, and twelve employees during the past year have been killed on the job in unnecessary accidents. The money I save just isn't worth supporting this corporation.

Belonging

Many successful arguments appeal to people's desire to be part of something larger than themselves. An obvious example of this kind of appeal is the appeal to patriotism, or the sense of belonging to a nation. People are often willing to risk their lives for what they believe to be their duty to their country. Appeals to belonging also connect claims to other groups: religious organizations, states, cities, schools, labor unions, fraternities, and so on.

Successful appeals to belonging create a sense in the reader of being part of a larger group. This approach can be very similar to the fallacy of bandwagoning (p. 661). The difference is that an effective appeal does not offer itself as proof of a claim; it simply frames the argument in a way that creates a sense of belonging in the reader. Consider the following argument against censorship:

> The current efforts to censor language and content in popular music and television programs are fundamentally un-American. This nation was founded on ideas of freedom of speech and expression that were considered heretical in Europe but which became the fabric of the Constitution of the United States of America. This principle was enshrined in the First Amendment and is the reason that America has remained a strong country for two hundred years. Those who censor our entertainers destroy part of what makes America a great nation.

The writer here is making an argument by appealing to the larger concept of "America" to which (we assume) the audience belongs. The appeal is grounded in the audience's desire to be part of this larger entity and the values that it espouses.

Pride/Vanity

Appeals to pride and vanity sometimes take the form of simple flattery, but they also include appeals to people's desire to be attractive, professional, and well-thought-of by their peers. As you might expect, this kind of appeal is common in advertising for clothing and cosmetics, as well as for alcohol and cars.

ETHOS: THE WRITER'S APPEAL

According to Aristotle, the most powerful element of persuasion is neither logos (logic) nor pathos (emotion), but ethos, which is also the most difficult of the three terms to define. Although the Greek word *ethos* is the root of our word "ethical," "ethos" does not quite mean "persuasion by appeals to ethics." Rather, it refers to the persuasion through the audience's perception of the speaker. At the heart of Aristotle's notion of ethos is the somewhat circular fact that most people are persuaded by arguments that are made by people that they find persuasive.

A writer's or speaker's ethos, then, is composed of everything that makes an audience consider him or her persuasive. You project a persuasive ethos when you communicate to your audience that you are the sort of person who should be believed: intelligent, well-qualified, and assertive, but also kind, moderate, and sympathetic to their points of view. The ethos of a speaker may include things like tone of voice, level of comfort in speaking, and physical attractiveness. The ethos of a writer may be harder to see, but it is no less important.

Reading someone's writing for the first time is like meeting someone new. We come to the text with certain expectations, which can be met, exceeded, or disappointed. In just a few minutes, we form an impression of the writer that, fair or not, colors the rest of our experience with the work and affects how persuaded we are by its argument. Here are a few things to consider as you work to create a good ethos in your writing:

Establish your credibility

In many kinds of writing, you can appropriately introduce yourself to an audience and explain why you are qualified to give the opinions you are about to give. For example, a very persuasive editorial on the problems faced by single mothers might begin with a paragraph such as this:

> Every time I hear some politician talk about the "single mother" problem, I cringe. To them, single motherhood is a problem to be solved; to me, it is a life to be lived. Five years ago, my husband died, leaving me with three daughters—twelve, nine, and four—to raise by myself. We were not rich, and my husband did not have life insurance. Since then, I have always had a job, sometimes two, and have at times paid more than half of my take-home pay in child care. And yes, I have also been on welfare—not because I am lazy or because I want the government to subsidize my "promiscuous lifestyle," but because I had no other way to feed and house my children.

The writer of this piece not only lays the groundwork for an argument about single mothers but also establishes that her own experience has qualified her to give an informed, thoughtful opinion.

Be generous to other points of view

People want to know that you respect them. When you are writing to a general audience—one in which every reader may have a different opinion on a given issue—be careful to avoid dismissing or disrespecting the people you are trying to persuade. Not only are people much more likely to be persuaded by someone who respects them, but writing that exhibits contempt for others often offends even those who share the opinion being expressed. Look at the following two examples and determine which one projects a more persuasive ethos:

1. There is something rotten in this country: fur. Can you imagine anything more inhumane and immoral than killing an animal just to wear its fur as an expensive coat? The rich women and middle-class posers who participate in the fur trade are probably too dumb to realize that they are wearing the remains of a living creature that was killed just to make their coats fit with this year's fashion trends. If they do know they're contributing to the deaths of innocent animals, then they're just cruel, violent, trend-followers.

2. Society has come a long way since the days when people had to wear the skins of mammoths and saber-toothed tigers to keep warm during the cold winters. Now, synthetic materials can keep us much warmer than the skin of any animal. However, each year, forty million animals are killed to produce commercial fur. Many of these animals are still caught in the wild using painful traps. Millions of decent people who would never treat an animal with wanton cruelty unknowingly participate in just such cruelty when they buy coats, gloves, and other items of clothing made with animal fur.

In the first example, the writer displays contempt and anger for those who wear fur. In the second example, however, the writer maintains a calm, respectful tone and offers those who do wear fur the benefit of the doubt.

Do not show off

Whatever your topic, it is important to show the reader that you know what you are talking about. Carefully research key concepts and make sure to point out relevant facts. But at the same time, avoid being overbearing. Beating people over the head with big words and unnecessary facts is rarely persuasive. The line between competence and arrogance is a fine one, but no distinction is more important to the construction of a persuasive ethos.

Make only claims that you can support

The best way to ruin a good case is to try to make it sound like a great case. If you have evidence to support the claim that affirmative action has had a minimal impact on minority graduate rates, then say so. Do not say "affirmative action has not helped a single person get through school" or "affirmative action has been completely useless over the last twenty years with regard to minority graduation rates." Sometimes, it can even be effective to understate your case a little bit in your introduction and let the evidence speak for itself, as in the following statement:

> In the twenty years that affirmative action programs have been in effect at institutions of higher learning, their actual impact has been difficult to ascertain, but they do not appear to have been a decisive factor in minority graduation rates.

Proofread your writing carefully

When a piece of writing includes shifts in verb tense, sentence fragments, and careless errors in spelling, grammar, and punctuation, readers make certain assumptions about the writer. They might assume that he or she is ignorant, careless, and uneducated. These assumptions may not be true, but they are nonetheless part of the ethos that the writer projects. Careful proofreading can eliminate basic grammatical errors that could seriously injure your ability to be persuasive.

ANTICIPATING COUNTERARGUMENTS

As you build support for your claims, try to anticipate the arguments that might be made against them. This will help you eliminate weaknesses in your argument that might prevent people from being persuaded by your claims. It will also demonstrate to your readers that you are aware of and have considered other positions.

To identify a counterargument, imagine that you were given an assignment to rebut your own argument. What weaknesses do you see that could become the basis for a rebuttal essay? If you know somebody else who can read what you have written with an objective eye and rebut it, ask that person to do so. Conducting research can also help you identify the kinds of arguments that have been made or are currently being made against the position that you are taking.

Once you have identified a counterargument, acknowledge it in your essay and respond to it directly. For example, if you are writing an essay about the importance of liberal education, one counterargument might be that colleges should teach useful job skills instead of a broad range of subjects. You could incorporate this into your essay by saying something like this:

> Some people may object to the argument that colleges and universities should focus on liberal education on the grounds that they would better serve students by providing them with the job skills they will need after college. However, there are plenty of ways that someone can learn how to weld or enter data

into a spreadsheet—internships, part-time jobs, seminars, classes at a trade or vocational school. There is no other way to get the kind of liberal education that a university provides.

The best way to thwart a counterargument is to qualify your own claims—that is, to eliminate absolute claims from your essay, such as "every student can benefit from courses in philosophy" or "nobody learns everything that they need to know for a job in their undergraduate education." When you make claims such as these, they can be refuted with a single counterexample—for example, "the philosophy course I took never benefited me at all" or "as an undergraduate my sister learned everything she needed to know for her job." It is better to avoid such absolutes and say instead that "most students can benefit from courses in philosophy" or "as undergraduates the overwhelming majority of people do not learn everything they need to know for their jobs."

Finally, do not be afraid to cut out any claim that you cannot support. If you have several strong claims and one or two that are weaker or more difficult to support, cut the weakest claims so that they do not give people reasons to reject your entire argument.

13

⊡

SYNTHESIZING IDEAS

WHILE AN ISOLATED IDEA can occur to someone, more-interesting ideas—and, usually, changes in society, science, and scholastic thought—come from connecting several ideas. One name for this kind of connection is "synthesis." As the word *thesis* means a proposition, an argument, or a point of view, synthesis means a combination of different propositions, arguments, or points of view. One hallmark of a strong writer is the ability to synthesize ideas from multiple sources to form his or her own opinions.

Synthesizing ideas requires you to use all of the skills discussed in other chapters of this guide. You must read and understand multiple sources and be able to summarize them quickly and efficiently; discover how to discuss different texts in ways that are meaningful without being clichéd; construct a claim—and in many cases a thesis statement—that asserts an interesting, arguable relationship between different ideas; and locate the evidence necessary to support that claim. This chapter will discuss some of the most common ways to synthesize ideas: summarizing multiple sources, comparing and contrasting, finding themes and patterns, and synthesizing ideas to form your own argument.

SUMMARIZING MULTIPLE SOURCES

Writers often need to summarize, as quickly as possible, what others have said before they can present their own thoughts on an issue. Most often, this kind of writing forms part of a response essay or a research essay.

Writing a literature review, or any other summary of multiple texts, is somewhat different from writing a summary of a single text. It simultaneously requires you to tighten your focus and to make connections between different texts. As you summarize multiple texts in your own writing, keep these suggestions in mind:

Be succinct and selective

The more you have to summarize, the less space you can devote to any one source. While a three-page summary of a single text will include quite a bit of detail about the main and supporting arguments, a three-page summary of ten texts can devote only a few sentences to each text. Choose the points that you want to include carefully, and make sure your wording is as concise as possible. Include only those elements of the text that relate to your overall purpose.

Construct a framework that leads to your ideas

Rather than simply stating the main idea of each text, construct a framework in which you can relate the ideas from multiple texts to each other, so that they all lead directly into your main idea. For example, imagine that you have been given an assignment to write your own definition of "human nature" based on the selections in this book by Thomas Hobbes, Ruth Benedict, and Edward O. Wilson. While simply summarizing each of these texts would adequately convey their major points, framing them so that they relate to each other makes the summary much more focused and concise, and allows you to synthesize them to form your own argument.

> Those who study human nature frequently focus on the interaction between human nature and culture, questioning how much our inherent nature forms our culture—and how much our culture can affect our basic nature. For Thomas Hobbes, human beings are inherently selfish and aggressive, but our own self-interest can compel us to form cooperative societies and develop cultures. Edward Wilson, working from a modern Darwinian framework unavailable to Hobbes, makes a very similar argument. According to Wilson, evolution-shaped attributes very similar to those that Hobbes perceived in human nature—such as the desire to mate and the urge to defend territory—determine the way that we interact with others in society, which forms the basis of culture.
>
> Ruth Benedict places a much stronger emphasis on the way that culture shapes human nature, but she also starts out with inherent (and presumably inherited)

human characteristics. Like Hobbes and Wilson, Benedict believes that human beings across cultures have the same set of inherent traits. Unlike the other two, however, Benedict focuses on the differences among human beings. According to Benedict, human beings in all cultures are born with the same spectrum of characteristics, but those characteristics are encouraged or discouraged to different extents by the cultures in which people live. This view is perfectly compatible with the views of both Hobbes and Wilson; it simply emphasizes the other half of the nature/culture equation.

The framework for this discussion revolves around a single question: how does each author view the interaction between human nature and culture? Once this question has been answered by the three authors whose works are summarized, the writer is free to propose his or her own answer to the question, thus synthesizing the ideas in the summary portion.

COMPARING AND CONTRASTING

One of the most common assignments in college courses is to compare or contrast different texts, concepts, or phenomena. (The format of this assignment is discussed in Chapter 9, p. 605.) To *compare* things means to discuss how they are similar, while to *contrast* things means to show how they are different. However, in general usage, the term "compare" can be used for either operation.

A comparison/contrast assignment involving texts (including visual texts such as paintings or photographs) requires you to make connections between two or more opinions, arguments, theories, or sets of facts. A good comparison/contrast essay, however, does more than just list similarities and differences—when done well, it can become a vehicle for generating a unique and creative synthesis of different ideas.

As with any writing assignment, the key to good comparison and contrast essays is to generate an interesting, subtle topic to write about. Look beyond surface similarities or differences and try to invent, rather than simply discover, a compelling basis for viewing two (or more) texts in relation to each other. Here are a few suggestions to keep in mind:

Choose a single point for comparison

Consider the following thesis statement:

Plato and Machiavelli are very different in their nationalities and their cultures; however, they are similar in the way that they present their ideas. They both emphasize the importance of knowledge, and believe that certain people are superior to others.

This kind of listing is appropriate for prewriting, but it lacks the focus and organization necessary for a good essay. Instead of simply listing similarities and differences, you need to create a framework in which the comparison makes sense. Doing so will often mean choosing a single area of similarity or difference and focusing entirely on that area, as in the following revision of the above statement:

> The crucial difference between Plato and Machiavelli is that Plato sees ultimate truth as existing beyond the material world while Machiavelli believes that material reality is the only truth that matters.

This framework, of course, cannot account for all the differences between Plato and Machiavelli, but it does not have to. A comparison/contrast paper does not need to be exhaustive nearly as much as it needs to be focused. By looking only at Plato's and Machiavelli's views of material reality, you will be able to develop a significant, interesting approach to reading the two texts together.

Do not try to compare everything

Any two things can be compared or contrasted in hundreds of different ways, most of which will not be relevant to your main point. Stick closely to the focus of that essay and be ruthless in cutting out details that do not support your primary claim.

Avoid stating the obvious

Many comparison/contrast assignments deal with pairs of things whose surface similarities or differences are easy to see. When this is the case, consider working against the obvious. Look for ways that clearly similar things are different or that clearly different things are the same. An apple is different from a monster truck, for example, in many ways—so many, in fact, that there is little value in pointing them out. If you can come up with a compelling argument, though, about how an apple is *like* a monster truck (perhaps that they have both become much bigger than they need to be to fulfill their natural functions), you will have a very interesting essay indeed.

The same principle applies when you are comparing ideas. Imagine that you have been asked to compare or contrast a pair of essays whose main points obviously contradict—such as Mencius's chapter on the inherent goodness of human nature and Hsün Tzu's rebuttal essay, "Man's Nature Is Evil." The essays clearly oppose each other, but they also share a number of assumptions about what kinds of behavior constitute "good" and "evil." Finding those assumptions and making them the basis of a comparison paper will be much more interesting than simply repeating the obvious fact that Mencius thought that people were good, while Hsün Tzu thought that they were bad.

Compare underlying assumptions

Beneath every claim is an assumption, a presumption that makes it possible for a claim to be true. The claim that "higher education is a good thing because it helps people get good jobs and earn more money throughout their lives" only holds fast if earning more money is considered to be a good thing. (See Chapter 9, p. 605, for more on this.) The most obvious—and therefore the least subtle—connections between two works will usually be found in what the authors explicitly state. More sophisticated connections can be found in the underlying principles and premises that are necessary for an argument to make sense.

For example, consider this comparison, based on an underlying assumption shared by Plato's "Speech of Aristophanes" and Vandana Shiva's *Soil, Not Oil*:

> On the surface, Plato's philosophical "Speech of Aristophanes" and Vandana Shiva's environmentalist essay *Soil, Not Oil* seem to have nothing in common. One is a whimsical parable about the creation of the human species, and the other is an impassioned plea for a just distribution of resources among the people of the earth. Underneath the surface, however, both selections make the argument that human nature is incomplete and fractured. Plato believes that human beings are partial beings until they find a romantic partner who can complete them. Shiva sees human nature as something that cannot survive long without a connection to nature and the environment. In sum, Plato and Shiva believe that human beings cannot ever be self-sufficient enough to meet all of their own needs.

Neither Plato nor Shiva attempts to prove that people are incomplete; this assumption lies behind the arguments that both make. Keep in mind that an underlying assumption may not be referred to in a text. It is not a major point of an argument, but it is the underlying value or idea that makes the argument possible.

FINDING THEMES AND PATTERNS

Some ideas—particularly those featured in this book, such as the role of law and government or the essence of human nature and the mind—have been explored throughout history in societies that otherwise have little in common. Showing how these ideas influence one another and how they appear in different societies and contexts throughout history can help you synthesize multiple arguments.

Show how ideas interact

One very important way to synthesize arguments is to demonstrate how ideas interact with each other. Ideas can influence other ideas in a number of different ways:

- One idea can be based directly on another idea. For example, William Blake's poem "The Tyger" is based directly on the idea of the sublime articulated by Edmund Burke in *The Sublime and Beautiful*.

- An idea can be based indirectly on another idea. Garrett Hardin's "Lifeboat Ethics," for instance, draws much of its inspiration from Thomas Malthus's *Essay on the Principle of Population*.

- An idea can be influenced by a combination of other ideas. For example, Charles Darwin's *The Origin of Species* was influenced by Charles Lyell's *Principles of Geology*, which established that the earth was much older than people had previously thought, and Thomas Malthus's *Essay on the Principle of Population*, which showed how the competition for resources changed certain aspects of human society.

- An idea can be based on a general perception created by another influential text. For example, Edward Wilson's argument in "The Fitness of Human Nature" draws largely on the framework for understanding nature created by Charles Darwin.

- An idea can synthesize a number of other ideas. For example, Martin Luther King Jr.'s "Letter from Birmingham Jail" cites the work of, among others, Jesus, Gandhi, Henry David Thoreau, and Thomas Aquinas.

- An idea can be formulated as a rebuttal to another idea. For example, Hsün Tzu's "Man's Nature Is Evil" was written in direct rebuttal to Mencius's views in "Man's Nature Is Good."

- An idea can be formulated in general opposition to another system of thought. For example, George Orwell's "Pacifism and the War" opposes the entire ethical position of pacifism.

To demonstrate a pattern of influence among two or more texts, you must first establish that such influence is theoretically possible. You do not have to prove that one author knew another author's work directly. People can be very influenced by ideas whose sources they do not know. However, no idea has been universally influential at every moment in history. It would be difficult to assert, for example, that Plato was influenced by the Buddha's teachings, which were written down thousands of miles away in a culture that had no known contact with Plato's Athens. And it would be impossible to argue persuasively that Plato was influenced by the ideas of Richard Feynman, who lived and wrote more than two thousand years after Plato died.

Once the possibility of influence has been established, the case for influence must be made through very close readings of the relevant texts. Consider an assignment to explore the possible influences of Taoism on Sun Tzu's military theories in *The Art of War*. For the most part, Sun Tzu's ideas could not be further removed from Lao Tzu's. Lao Tzu was a pacifist who abhorred war and believed that it is wrong to try to force people to do anything. Sun Tzu was a military commander who believed that, with the right tools, it is always possible to impose one's will on another. However, both texts came out of China's Period of Warring States, and Lao Tzu's *Tao Te Ching* is unquestionably the older of the two works. Under these circumstances, it is entirely possible that Sun Tzu's work was influenced by the *Tao Te Ching*.

But the fact that Sun Tzu does not directly quote or refer to Lao Tzu means that the case for influence must be made through close reading. To create a persuasive case for influence, begin by listing each text's main points:

TAO TE CHING

- Exertion is unnecessary.

- Leaders should allow things to happen naturally.
- Distinctions between people are counterproductive.
- Genuine power is achieved by allowing others to come to you.
- **The best way to govern people is not to govern them.**
- It is impossible to influence the course of events.
- War is senseless.
- Leaders should always follow "the Way."

THE ART OF WAR

- **The best way to win a battle is not to fight it.**
- An enemy should be taken intact, without destroying cities.
- Understanding military strategy is important.
- Politicians should not interfere with generals.
- Harmonious human relations are important to victory.
- Commanders should know themselves.
- Commanders should know their enemies.

Lurking amid all of the different assertions in these two texts is one undeniable similarity: Sun Tzu, like Lao Tzu, believes that winning through inaction (that is, never having to fight) is superior to winning through action (that is, superior numbers or strategies). Given the prevalence of Taoist ideas during the time in which Sun Tzu wrote, this similarity is not likely coincidental; rather, it is strong evidence of a pattern of influence.

Locate a larger theme

Another way to synthesize ideas is to show how a text fits into a larger theme, or big idea. Many of the selections in this book attest to the fact that human beings struggling with similar questions often come up with similar—or at least partially similar—answers. Cultures and individuals with no connections to each other have arrived at strikingly similar responses to questions such as "Is human nature good or evil?", "Is war ever justified?", and "Do we have a responsibility to those less fortunate than ourselves?"

To see how individual ideas fit into larger themes or patterns, consider the following five images, all of which appear in this book:

- Dorothea Lange: *Migrant Mother* (p. 568)
- Pablo Picasso: *Guernica* (p. 497)
- William Hogarth: *Gin Lane* (p. 548)
- Joseph Wright of Derby: *An Experiment on a Bird in the Air Pump* (p. 308)
- Lisa Yuskavage: *Babie I* (p. 286)

The following chart attempts to describe the mother-and-child theme of each work as it relates to the work's larger theme.

WORK	DESCRIPTION OF MOTHER-AND-CHILD SCENE	OVERALL THEME
Dorothea Lange: *Migrant Mother*	The mother holds a baby to her breast, shelters it from the camera and the squalor of the lean-to.	The determination of a mother to protect her children
Pablo Picasso: *Guernica*	An anguished mother holds the twisted body of a dead child.	The anguish of war
William Hogarth: *Gin Lane*	A drunken mother reaches for a dip of snuff while her infant child falls to its death.	The negative consequences of alcoholism
Joseph Wright of Derby: *An Experiment on a Bird in the Air Pump*	A terrified mother turns away from the experiment while holding her daughter, who looks on with a mix of terror and curiosity.	The mixed reaction to scientific progress during the Enlightenment
Lisa Yuskavage: *Babie I*	A woman who does not appear to be a wife or a mother holds a wilting bouquet of flowers.	The ambiguous position of a woman who does not have a child in a society that values women primarily as wives and mothers

As this chart shows, the connection between the works goes beyond simply the existence of a mother-and-child pair: in each case the relationship between the mother and the child reflects the argument of the overall work. In the painting about anguish, the mother is in anguish over the child; in the painting about alcoholism, the mother's alcoholism causes the child's death. A connection of this kind could lead to a very strong synthesis essay that could go beyond the five works here and draw conclusions about the overall theme of mothers and children in art. The introduction to such an essay might look like this:

Mothers and Children in Art

The bond between a mother and her children goes deeper than the patterns of any particular culture; the mother-child bond has a sound basis in evolution and forms one of the few truly universal elements of the human experience. For this reason, strong connections between mothers and children can be found in almost every human society, and depictions of mothers and children can be found in almost every kind of art. This does not mean, however, that the depictions are all the same. Different cultures value different things at different times, and artistic production usually follows along. However, because the connection between mothers and children is universally strong in human societies, artists from a variety of cultures have been able to use this connection as the basis for a variety of different arguments about the human condition.

SYNTHESIZING IDEAS TO FORM YOUR OWN ARGUMENT

One mark of a strong writer is his or her ability to form ideas that draw upon other sources but are neither slavish imitations of, nor uncritical reactions to, other people's opinions. This synthesis process lies at the very heart of critical analysis.

Synthesizing Ideas: A Model from Classical Rhetoric

When you encounter a new idea, you need not accept it as absolute truth or reject it out of hand. In their discussions of invention, ancient rhetoricians identified five different ways that an idea could affect a reader or a listener. One reaction from a reader or a listener is absolute and uncritical agreement, while another is complete disagreement. Ancient rhetoricians recognized that most reactions fall somewhere in between. The other three cases, explored below, illustrate how your reaction to an idea can lead you to synthesize ideas to form your own.

You can simply become informed about an issue

Often, the process of coming up with your own idea requires nothing more than the knowledge that an issue exists and an understanding of the arguments that compose it. Once you understand how an issue has been defined, you can apply your own experience to make informed judgments about it. It is often valuable to read other people's ideas simply to become informed about the issues that they discuss.

If, for example, you are unaware of the debate among scientists trying to describe human nature as either a biological or a sociological phenomenon ("nature vs. nature"), Edward Wilson's "The Fitness of Human Nature" is probably not going to convince you one way or the other. However, it is enough to give non-specialists a vocabulary for discussing the issues, thereby paving the way for future discussions and arguments.

You can become convinced that an issue is important

Very often people recognize an issue without really understanding its importance or its consequences. This was the case in 1798 when Thomas Malthus wrote *An Essay on the Principle of Population*. People at the time understood that populations were increasing, but they saw this as a good thing because it increased available labor and kept the price of goods down. Malthus, however, demonstrated with compelling arguments that increases in population would eventually outstrip increases in food supply and cause serious catastrophes for societies that did not control their growth rates.

Malthus's arguments awakened people to the dangers of unchecked population growth and opened a door for people to generate their own ideas about how best to deal with the problem. As it turns out, most modern thinkers who label themselves "Malthusian" advocate solutions to the problem of overpopulation that Malthus rejected—they have taken his ideas and synthesized them with other facts, policies, and values to create their own ideas. Malthus was a devout Anglican minister who believed that contraception was a sin and abortion an unspeakable evil. These beliefs, however, have not stopped Malthus's ideas from becoming the cornerstone of modern arguments favoring wide distribution of birth control and universal access to abortion. Those who hold such views are not being inconsistent; they are simply synthesizing Malthus's ideas about the importance of a problem with their own opinions of how best to solve it.

You can agree with only some points of an argument

Though writers often present their ideas as all-or-nothing propositions, you do not have to accept them as such. Most arguments are composed of different elements that often can be separated from each other and accepted on their own. It is perfectly valid to reject some elements of an argument and accept others.

For example, Garrett Hardin's "Lifeboat Ethics: The Case against Helping the Poor" includes the following assertions:

1. Overpopulation is a threat to human civilization.

2. Third-world countries are increasing in population at a rate much faster than first-world countries.

3. Giving food and other kinds of aid to overpopulated countries simply allows them to continue to increase their populations without paying a price.

4. Allowing immigration from overpopulated countries into other countries has the same effect as giving food aid to those countries.

5. Developed nations should therefore close their borders to immigration and stop the policy of giving food or other kinds of aid to overpopulated, underdeveloped countries.

It is possible to accept some of these assertions while rejecting others, and even to agree with Hardin's premises and disagree with his conclusions. One might argue, for example, that food aid is a way to persuade other countries to adopt population control strategies. Or one could present evidence that population decreases when standards of living increase, and that it is in our best interest to raise the standards of living of people in "developing countries" so that they will decrease their own populations naturally. You can combine some of his arguments with your own observations to construct a synthesis that is uniquely your own.

Synthesizing Ideas: A Model from Philosophy

In the early part of the nineteenth century, the German philosopher Georg Wilhelm Friedrich Hegel (1770–1831) developed a system for synthesizing ideas that has become known as "Hegelian dialectic." Hegelian dialectic involves three steps, known to Hegel's students as the thesis, the antithesis, and the synthesis. In Hegel's sense of the word, a thesis is a proposition, an antithesis is an opposite proposition, and a synthesis is a third proposition that resolves the apparent contradiction between the two. Here is an example using the works of Mencius and Hsün Tzu that were discussed earlier in this chapter:

Thesis: Human nature is inherently good (Mencius).

Antithesis: Human nature is inherently evil (Hsün Tzu).

Synthesis: *Neither inherently good nor inherently evil, human nature is inherently self-interested, which can be "good" in some circumstances and "evil" in others.*

In the Hegelian model, the interplay between opposites, which is referred to as a "dialectic," occurs constantly, with each synthesis becoming a new thesis that provokes an antithesis and requires a new synthesis. For example, the "synthesis" statement above can become a new thesis:

Thesis: Human nature is self-interested.

Antithesis: Human nature is altruistic.

Synthesis: *There is no real opposition between selfishness and altruism, since human beings often perceive their own self-interest in helping others in their family and their society.*

And, of course, this synthesis can produce yet another trio of arguments:

Thesis: People help others because they perceive it to be in their own best interest.

Antithesis: People often act altruistically when there is no hope of self-interest, as when soldiers sacrifice their lives to save others.

Synthesis: *Even the utmost altruistic acts can be based on a form of self-interest, as when people who sacrifice their lives to help others derive pleasure from the knowledge that they are doing so.*

At this point, the exercise of resolving antitheses has led us to formulate an idea that is solidly based on the ideas of Mencius and Hsün Tzu without duplicating either of their opinions exactly. Any of the three "synthesis" propositions in this exercise could be refined to make an original and creative thesis. Taken together, they form the basis for the following sample paper, which also draws on ideas from Ruth Benedict and Thomas Hobbes to achieve a synthesis that does not completely accept or reject any of its source materials.

Human Nature, Morality, and Altruism: Are People Good, or What?

As Confucianism became more and more influential in ancient China, even the major Confucians could not agree on one key issue: is human nature essentially good or essentially evil? Mencius, the most influential Confucian besides Confucius himself, weighed in strongly on the side of inherent human virtue. His fellow Confucian, Hsün Tzu, believed the opposite—he felt that people are inherently evil. Though this same debate has been replicated in most of the great religions and philosophies of the world, the terms that it incorporates are problematic. *Human nature can be neither inherently good nor inherently evil, since "good" and "evil" are constructed differently by different cultures.*

In "The Individual and the Pattern of Culture," Ruth Benedict explains how different behaviors can be seen in different moral lights by different cultures. Eating a relative's dead body would be seen as a horribly evil act by someone in New York. Not eating a relative's dead body, on the other hand, would be seen as an unforgivable moral lapse in some parts of New Guinea. With these variations in what constitutes good and evil, it is impossible to ascribe either character trait to humanity in the abstract. The most that can be said is that human beings are inherently disposed or inherently not disposed to act according to the dictates of their home cultures.

One could argue with much more conviction, however, that human beings are inherently self-interested. In certain states, such as the Hobbesian "state of nature," this self-interest leads to a state of "war of all against all." However, Hobbes also argues that human beings, recognizing their self-interest, come together and form societies and act—often altruistically—to preserve those societies. When this is the case, self-interest is at the heart of behavior that both Mencius and Hsün Tzu would undoubtedly have seen as "good." *There is, therefore, no real opposition between selfishness and altruism, since human beings often perceive their own self-interest in helping others in their family and their society.*

Yet there are some occasions—especially in times of war, plague, famine, or great oppression—in which people act altruistically when there is no possibility of this act working in their own favor. A young marine throwing himself on a hand grenade to save his companions, a mother giving the last bit of food to her family and starving to death, a political dissident taking on a totalitarian regime knowing that it will mean death—actions of these sorts can be documented in cultures throughout the world, and yet they do not seem to be accounted for by a theory of human nature as inherently selfish.

However, *even the utmost altruistic acts can be based on a form of self-interest, as when people who sacrifice their lives to help others derive pleasure from the knowledge that they are doing so.* Nothing is wrong with such a feeling. It would be foolish to suggest that people who derived pleasure in helping others were acting "selfishly" in the normal, pejorative sense of the word. It is reasonable, however, to assume that they would not act in this way unless they derived satisfaction from doing so—and satisfaction, even when earned through acts of great self-sacrifice, is "selfish" in the broadest sense of the word.

To return to the debate between Mencius and Hsün Tzu, it is fair to say that the two great Chinese thinkers used the terms "good" and "evil" when they really meant "selfish" and "unselfish." A close examination of human societies, however, supports the argument that no ironclad distinction exists between selfish and unselfish action, since both are, in some way or another, in the perceived self-interest of the people who act. The most that can be said about the "inherent" properties of human nature is that human nature is inherently self-interested—and that this is not necessarily a bad thing.

14

◻

INCORPORATING IDEAS

Since ideas build on other ideas, writing *about* ideas often requires you to refer to another writer's work. And it will often be the case that you will consult not one source but many, and need to document them appropriately.

Almost anybody with a computer or mobile device can access billions of pages of information almost instantly. Materials that once took weeks or months to gather—documents, census records, books, journals, historical records, and rare books—can now be accessed in seconds. We live in an age of information.

As finding sources of information becomes easier, understanding how to evaluate those sources and incorporate them into arguments becomes more and more important. It can be daunting to sift through the many sources at our fingertips—none of us has the time to read a hundred million webpages to find what we are looking for, and, more often than not, people faced with an abundance of information simply end up listening to and believing whoever yells the loudest.

This chapter offers guidance on citing others' ideas, from finding and evaluating sources to incorporating and documenting them. We can thereby avoid, as the great biologist Edward O. Wilson put it, "drowning in information while starving for wisdom." Such interconnection reflects thinking's collaborative nature, which has always been at the heart of ideas that matter.

FINDING SOURCES

The web is a tremendous resource for excellent research material, but it is not the only source, nor does it contain valuable material on every topic. Academic libraries still spend millions of dollars on print-based materials, such as books and journals that contain valuable information not available anywhere else. At the same time, some information is available only online, and the sheer number of documents available makes the internet an essential resource. A good research strategy for most topics will include information in books, journals, electronic databases, archives, and websites.

Library-Based Sources

Books

It is easy to fall into the trap of thinking that any source worth finding can be found online, but this isn't true. For some topics—including many of those discussed in *Reading the World*—printed books remain an important source of reliable information. Most universities spend considerable resources maintaining a print collection, and many important scholarly works are not available online. College students should be very familiar with their schools' libraries and library catalogs.

The library catalog is your main resource for finding books and can be accessed through your library's website. When using the catalog you can search by author, title, subject, or keyword. Many of the books in the catalog may be available in print or online or may be downloadable to your computer or mobile device.

Interlibrary loan

College and university libraries frequently loan materials to each other. Interlibrary loan is especially useful for books, recordings, and videos, but can also be used for journal articles. You can access thousands of library databases at once at *WorldCat* (www.worldcat.org) and use your library's interlibrary loan service to request any materials that you find.

Databases

A lot of important information today is available online on a paid subscription basis. Most college and university libraries subscribe to large database aggregators such as *Academic Search Complete*, *EBSCOhost*, and *LexisNexis*. These databases, in turn, often host smaller and more disciplinary specific databases that you can use.

At most schools, students can log in from remote sites to use the databases to which the school's library has subscribed. These electronic databases are usually the best place to find contemporary journal, newspaper, and magazine articles.

Reference works

Nearly all libraries have a section devoted to reference materials that do not circulate. Reference materials can be either in printed books or in online databases. They are good for giving an overview of a topic and pointing you to other, more specialized resources. Reference materials such as dictionaries, encyclopedias, atlases, almanacs, and bibliographies are often general—*The New Encyclopedia Britannica* is one example. Others are specialized works, such as the *Dictionary of Literary Biography* or the *Encyclopedia of Atmospheric Sciences*, that provide in-depth information on a single field or topic.

Researching Online

General search engines

Most people conduct research online using search engines such as *Google, Yahoo,* or *Bing*. Different search engines use different criteria to scan the entire internet and provide search results based on what other people searching for the same things have found to be most useful.

Search engines work best when you narrow the search by including several keywords in a single search; by using Boolian operators such as "and," "or," and "not" to show relationships between different keywords, or by placing multi-word phrases inside of quotation marks.

Specialized search engines

Some searches are best conducted by specialized search engines, such as *Google Scholar*, which searches only through scholarly sources; *Google News*, which searches only through contemporary news sources; and *CiteSeerX*, which searches scientific documents. You can also search the content of social media sites through specialized search engines such as *Google Blogs* and *Twitter Search*.

Government sites

Many governmental agencies and departments have websites where you can research government reports and statistics. *USA.gov* is where the U.S. government makes its data available.

Portals

Internet portals allow you to browse and search through information connected to a specific topic. The *USA.gov* portal, for example, connects to all of the documents produced by the different offices and departments of the U.S. government. The *DPLA* (Digital Public Library of America) portal connects to high-quality reference information across the internet.

Newspapers and magazines

Most major newspapers and magazines maintain online archives that can be searched for individual stories. Often, some portion of these archives are free, while other portions require a subscription or charge a per-item fee. These archives can be an excellent way to research things that happened in a specific area or to understand how important historical events were understood at the time that they happened.

Digital archives

Many libraries, museums, and research centers have digitized their special collections, making rare books, works of art, concert recordings, old films, and other hard-to-find sources easily available. The Library of Congress, for example, now contains millions of pages of material from its special collection. Other sources include the National Archives, the New York Public Library, and the Internet Archive.

EVALUATING SOURCES

Now that you've located potential sources, your next step is to decide which ones to use. This section will explain ways for you to choose reliable and useful sources.

Never rely on just one kind of source

A good research strategy for most topics will include information in books, journals, electronic databases, web archives, and publicly accessible websites. Good research means going wherever there is good information to be found.

Start with material that has already been evaluated

For each source you work with, begin with information that has already been evaluated by a professional academic librarian. All of the books in a college or university library have gone through such an evaluation, as have the electronic databases to which college libraries subscribe. These databases usually contain academic journals, reference materials, and even the full texts of books that have been reviewed by editors and librarians and found to be appropriate for academic research.

Research the source

Consider a source's author, date of publication, and publisher. Is the author affiliated with any organizations? Was the article published or written recently? If not, is the information it offers out of date? Who is the publisher—a government organization, a private business, a special interest group? Does the publisher have a vested interest in the information being presented? All these factors can affect the reliability of your source.

Read carefully

Another good way to check a source is simply to examine it very carefully. The other articles the source cites may give you important clues to its overall purposes and biases.

Cross-check facts

As a general rule, you should be able to verify whether a piece of information is factual by finding it in more than one source. If the piece of information is disputed, you may have to consult multiple sources and decide on the most accurate way to incorporate the information into your essay.

QUOTING, PARAPHRASING, AND SUMMARIZING

Once you have located and evaluated the sources you would like to use, the next step is incorporating them into your essay—to do so, you may quote, paraphrase, or summarize. Here are a few suggestions for working with quotations, paraphrases, and summaries. More specific suggestions on each kind of citation follow. As a general rule, these three methods help you to illustrate, establish, or support your own argument, but you should not allow quotations, paraphrases, and summaries to speak for you. Whenever you cite—that is, refer to—other people's ideas, your reader must be able to differentiate between those ideas and your own.

Quoting

When you quote a source, you reproduce the language of that source exactly. Quoting is the best choice when the original wording is so eloquent or focused that something would be lost in changing it.

Select quotations carefully

Select a few quotations that express important points within your argument. Make sure that every word of quoted material is relevant to your argument—quotations that are unnecessarily long distract the reader from your ideas.

Introduce the context for a quotation

Let your readers know where your citation originated—who said or wrote it, why he or she is an authority, and where the citation can be found. Establishing that context clarifies the importance of the citation for the reader and, more often than not, will make the cited material more interesting and persuasive.

> **Awkward:** Princes cannot always be moral. "And you have to understand this, that a prince, especially a new one, cannot observe all those things for which men are esteemed, being often forced, in order to maintain the state, to act contrary to faith, friendship, humanity, and religion" (Machiavelli 405).

> **Revised:** Machiavelli writes that, while leaders should try to be moral when possible, they are often required by circumstances to act in ways that are contrary to "faith, friendship, humanity, and religion" (Machiavelli 405).

Maintain control of the verb tense and sentence structure

If you quote someone else's words within your writing, you need to control the verb tense and sentence structure of your writing while still using the exact words of your source. Pay close attention to the verb tenses, subject-verb agreement, and noun-pronoun agreement when you incorporate a quotation into your writing. If you need to, rewrite your sentence or use ellipses or brackets to alter the quotation.

> **Awkward:** Machiavelli believed about princes, "and you have to understand this, that a prince, especially a new one, cannot observe all those things for which men are esteemed" (405).

> **Revised:** Machiavelli did not believe that rulers should be immoral simply for the sake of immorality, but he did believe that practically minded political leaders did not have the luxury of observing "all those things for which men are esteemed" (405).

Use block style for long quotations

Block quotations are a good strategy for analyzing long passages from a text or for citing passages that are difficult to summarize and extremely important for your argument. However, you should use this strategy sparingly—only when the material is extremely important and there is no better way to incorporate it into your essay.

If you use a block quotation, introduce it clearly and then present the quotation indented five spaces from the left margin. Here is an example of how a block quotation looks within an essay:

> One of Machiavelli's most controversial points is that leaders must be willing to act in immoral ways when doing so will preserve the stability of their government:
>
>> A prince, especially a new one, cannot observe all those things for which men are esteemed, being often forced, in order to maintain the state, to act contrary to faith, friendship, humanity, and religion. Therefore it is necessary for him to have a mind ready to turn itself accordingly as the winds and variations of fortune force it, yet, as I have said above, not to diverge from the good if he can avoid doing so, but, if compelled, then to know how to set about it. (405)

See pp. 692–97 for more guidelines on how to use block quotations in MLA and APA styles.

Use ellipses (. . .) and brackets ([ ]) to indicate changes in a quotation

Occasionally, you will be able to create a very poignant short quotation by using just the beginning phrases and ending phrases from a long paragraph. Or you might find that a word or two in the middle of a sentence would confuse your reader by referencing material in a section of the text that you are not quoting. In instances such as these, you may use ellipsis marks (. . .) to indicate the omission of words in quoted material.

If you need to change the text of a quotation, use brackets ([ ]) to indicate the altered text. You most commonly will use brackets to change the verb tense to make the quoted material compatible with your own syntax, so that you can use the quotation in the middle of your sentence. Adding a phrase in brackets can also allow you to clarify a confusing term or substitute a noun for a pronoun.

For example, the extended block quotation above from Machiavelli's *The Prince* could be effectively altered within an essay like this:

> Machiavelli argued that it was "necessary for [a prince] to have a mind ready to turn itself accordingly as the winds and variations of fortune force it . . . not to diverge from the good if he can avoid doing so, but, if compelled, then to know how to set about it" (405).

Ellipses and brackets are acceptable when used to focus an argument or to clarify meaning, but they should never be used to change the meaning of the quotation or misrepresent the author's intent.

Paraphrasing

Paraphrase if you do not need to reproduce the exact wording of a source, but wish to restate its information. A paraphrase uses your own words and sentence structure, includes the source's main points and details, and is usually the same length as the original.

Indicate source

Whenever you use someone else's ideas, you need to credit them—even if the wording is entirely your own (as it must be in a paraphrase). For guidelines on documenting your sources in MLA and APA styles, see p. 692.

Use your own words and your own sentence structure

By definition, a paraphrase must be in your own words and your own structure. One common way of trying to get around this rule is the "half-baked paraphrase," which attempts to use slightly different words to reproduce the ideas in a source. The first paragraph below comes from Margaret Mead's essay "Warfare: An Invention—Not a Biological Necessity"; the second is an example of a half-baked paraphrase of the same passage:

> **Source:** Warfare is just an invention known to the majority of human societies by which they permit their young men either to accumulate prestige or avenge their honor or acquire loot or wives or slaves or sago lands or cattle or appease the blood lust of their gods or the restless souls of the recently dead. It is just an invention, older and more widespread than the jury system, but none the less an invention. (500)

> **Improper paraphrase:** According to Margaret Mead, war is only a discovery that most human cultures have in common, one that enables them to allow their youth to acquire honor or revenge or to get money, women, servants, property, or livestock or to placate their deities' desire for blood or the souls of those who have died recently. War is simply a discovery, one that has been around longer than trial by jury, but still a discovery. (500)

The second paragraph is far too close in sentence structure and wording to be a true paraphrase; the writer has not really used his own words. Here is an example of a proper paraphrase of the same passage:

> **Proper paraphrase:** Margaret Mead argues persuasively that warfare is not an inevitable product of human nature. Rather, it was invented in most (not all) societies as an economic or religious tool, to permit young men in that society to become wealthy or worship appropriately. Although it is older and more common than many other inventions, like the jury system, it too was created for a purpose. (500)

Enclose in quotation marks any wording that is not your own

If you find in writing a paraphrase that you want to use wording from the original source, make sure that you enclose it in quotation marks. It should be clearly distinguished from your own wording and be properly documented. (See p. 692 for information on how to document sources.)

Summarizing

If you want to highlight only the most important details of a passage, summarize. Unlike quotations or paraphrases, summaries should not include details. Instead, summaries highlight the aspects of a source that are most important or most relevant to your argument. Keep your summaries short and focused, trim away any extraneous detail, and concentrate on what's most important. See, for example, how the following passage uses summaries to highlight and compare the main ideas from two texts:

> Even liberal modern philosophers cannot agree with each other about our moral responsibility to the poor. On the one hand, in "Two Principles of Justice," John Rawls insists that a basic understanding of fairness requires us to distribute our resources in a way that everybody would see as fair if they viewed it from a neutral perspective (354). Garrett Hardin, on the other hand, believed that giving food, money, or other resources to poor people, especially those in less developed countries, is actually an immoral action. In "Lifeboat Ethics: The Case against Helping the Poor," Hardin argues that the earth's carrying capacity is limited and that it is unfair to allow people to exceed this capacity by having more children than the planet can support—thus placing everyone in danger (360).

Use your own words

Like a paraphrase, a summary by definition must be in your own words. Avoid using words and phrases similar to those in the source.

Indicate the source

Whenever you use or cite someone else's ideas, you need to credit them—even if the wording is entirely your own. For guidelines on documenting your sources in MLA and APA styles, see p. 692.

DOCUMENTING SOURCES

Whenever you use another's ideas or refer to a source in your writing, you need to provide documentation—identifying information—for your source. Plagiarism is any use of another person's idea without proper documentation. Whether it's intentional or not, plagiarism is an act of academic dishonesty that can have serious repercussions. Plagiarism includes (1) using the exact words of a writer without quotation marks, (2) using a writer's words, ideas, or both without an in-text citation or other form of documentation, and (3) paraphrasing or summarizing another writer's ideas by using the language or sentence structure of the original source. All of the following elements must be documented:

Ideas you have summarized or paraphrased from a source

It is plagiarism to summarize, paraphrase, or just use someone's ideas without attributing those ideas to their source. For examples of paraphrases and summaries, see pp. 688–89.

In the example from "Warfare: An Invention—Not a Biological Necessity" on p. 500, it would have been dishonest for the writer of the paraphrase to take credit in any way for the basic idea of Mead's essay: that warfare is an invention that spread from culture to culture rather than an inherent element of the human condition. Any idea that you borrow from another source must be attributed to that source, even if all the writing is your own.

Visuals that you did not create—photographs, tables, charts, graphs, and so on—must also be cited. If the visuals are ones you created, make sure that you acknowledge the work as your own.

Facts that are not considered common knowledge

In the middle of "Warfare: An Invention—Not a Biological Necessity," Margaret Mead writes that the Andaman pygmies living in the Bay of Bengal had a knowledge of organized warfare long before they ever encountered Europeans or other more technologically sophisticated societies. Even if you use this fact in another context (say in an essay about the organization of pygmy tribes), you must still cite Mead as the basis for this information, because it is not what scholars call "common knowledge."

In this context, "common knowledge" refers to the kind of information that is generally known or that is easily available in reference works. For example, the facts that the Andaman Islands are in the Bay of Bengal and that the native inhabitants of these islands are pygmies can be readily found in reference books and online, making them part of the pool of general knowledge. You would not need to cite Mead (or anyone else) as your source for these facts.

Approaches or organizational strategies borrowed from a source

Creating interesting, subtle frameworks for discussing ideas is one of a writer's most important skills. If, in searching for such a framework, you borrow from someone else's work, you must acknowledge it. Imagine, for example, that, in searching for a way to compare Machiavelli's *The Prince* and de Pizan's *Treasure of the City of Ladies*, you came across a website comparing them as "political theories," "cultural theories," and "theories of history." If you used these three categories in your own essay, you would need to acknowledge the website as your source—even if your actual comparisons did not borrow at all from the original source.

Anyone who has helped you develop your ideas

Whenever you collaborate with other people on your writing, make sure you give them proper credit. (Keep in mind that your instructor might not allow collaboration of any kind, in which case the ideas that you come up with must be entirely your own.) Contributions from other students, professors, colleagues, friends, and family should be acknowledged either in the body of the text or in a footnote or an endnote that explicitly gives credit where it is due. A note such as "Thanks to Dr. Mary Johnson of the Department of Psychology for her contribution to my understanding of Freud's concept of the ego" can be placed either at the end of an essay or at the point in your argument where the relevant discussion occurs.

DOCUMENTATION STYLES

Different academic disciplines use several different styles to document sources. Two common styles for undergraduate writing are the Modern Language Association (MLA) style and the American Psychological Association (APA) style. Before writing an essay, determine which style your instructor prefers and refer to an official style guide for detailed instructions on using that style. The guidelines that follow are not a replacement for a style manual, which provides much more detail on different kinds of documentation.

MLA Style

This style originated for the discussion of literature and is currently used in many humanities disciplines. MLA format places a minimal amount of information in an in-text citation and puts full bibliographical citations at the end on a Works Cited page.

In-Text Documentation

When you cite another source in your own writing, place enough information in parentheses for the reader to locate the source on your Works Cited page. If you have already identified your source, put the page number in parentheses immediately after the citation. Place the parentheses after the closing quotation marks but before the period:

> According to civil rights leader Martin Luther King, a law is unjust if it "is a code that a majority inflicts on a minority that is not binding on itself" (435).

If you're citing a source that doesn't have page numbers, such as a website, include the paragraph or section number in parentheses:

> According to the Nobel Prize organization, King "led a massive protest in Birmingham, Alabama, that caught the attention of the entire world, providing what he called a coalition of conscience, and inspiring his 'Letter from a Birmingham Jail'" (par. 3).

Quotations that run for more than four lines should be set off in blocks, without quotation marks. In the block-quotation format, the parenthetical citation comes after the period:

> King criticized the view that laws should always be obeyed by citing the example of Nazi Germany's laws against helping Jews:
>
> > We should never forget that everything Adolf Hitler did in Germany was "legal" and everything the Hungarian freedom fighters did in Hungary

was "illegal." It was "illegal" to aid and comfort a Jew in Hitler's Germany. Even so, I am sure that, had I lived in Germany at the time, I would have aided and comforted my Jewish brothers. (436)

If a paragraph does not give enough information to identify a citation, then include the author's name parenthetically:

Many people believe that disobeying laws that are unjust is actually an expression of "the very highest respect for the law" (King 435).

If you have two works by the same author, add a word or phrase from the title to identify the work:

King draws three different distinctions between "just laws" and "unjust laws" ("Letter" 434-35).

Bibliographical Citations

Full bibliographical citations are given at the end of an essay on a separate page titled "Works Cited." The Works Cited page lists sources alphabetically by author, or, if an author is unavailable, by title. When an author is listed multiple times, the listings are arranged alphabetically by title. For sources found online, the examples below include date of access; MLA notes, however, that this element is optional. Additionally, when providing source information for online databases, MLA permits either a URL or DOI. Below are the formats for some of the most common kinds of citations that you will need on your Works Cited page. For further details, consult the *MLA Handbook* (8th ed., 2016) and *The MLA Style Center* (style.mla.org).

One-Author Book
Elshtain, Jean Bethke. *Just War against Terror: The Burden of American Power in a Violent World.* Basic Books, 2003.

Multiple-Author Book (Two Authors)
Malless, Stanley, and Jeffrey McQuain. *Coined by God: Words and Phrases That First Appear in the English Translations of the Bible.* W. W. Norton, 2003.

Work in an Anthology
Weil, Simone. "Equality." *Reading the World: Ideas That Matter,* edited by Michael Austin, 3rd ed., W. W. Norton, 2015, pp. 571-73.

Single-Author Print Journal Article
Weinberger, Jerry. "Pious Princes and Red-Hot Lovers: The Politics of Shakespeare's *Romeo and Juliet.*" *The Journal of Politics,* vol. 65, no. 2, May 2003, pp. 350-75.

Multiple-Author Print Journal Article (Three or More Authors)
Weaver, Constance, et al. "To Grammar or Not to Grammar: That Is *Not* the
     Question!" *Voices from the Middle*, vol. 8, no. 3, Mar. 2001, pp. 17-33.

Scholarly Edition
Austen, Jane. *Sense and Sensibility*. Edited by Claudia Johnson, W. W. Norton, 2001.

Print Magazine Article
Hawass, Zahi. "Egypt's Forgotten Treasures." *National Geographic*, Jan. 2003,
     pp. 74-87.

Online Magazine Article
Samuelson, Robert J. "The Changing Face of Poverty." *Newsweek*, 17 Oct. 2004,
     www.newsweek.com/changing-face-poverty-130129. Accessed 9 Oct. 2005.

Print Newspaper Article
Farenthold, David. "Town Shaken by Lobster Theft." *The Washington Post*,
     9 Oct. 2005, p. A3.

Online Newspaper Article
Dowd, Maureen. "Sacred Cruelties." *The New York Times*, 7 Apr. 2002,
     www.nytimes.com/2002/04/07/opinion/07DOWD.html. Accessed 9 Oct. 2005.

Journal Article from an Electronic Database
Moore, Kathleen D. "The Truth of the Barnacles: Rachel Carson and the
     Moral Significance of Wonder." *Environmental Ethics*, vol. 27, no. 3,
     Fall 2005, pp. 265-77. *Philosophy Documentation Center*, doi: 10.5840/
     enviroethics200527316. Accessed 9 Oct. 2005.

Work on a Website
Nasr, Seyyed Hossein. "The Meaning and Concept of Philosophy in Islam." *Islamic
     Philosophy Online*, edited by Muhammed Hozien, Islamic Philosophy Online,
     Inc., 5 May 2007, www.muslimphilosophy.com/ip/nasr=ip1.htm. Accessed
     23 Apr. 2009.
Gross, Daniel. "The Quitter Economy." *Slate*. Slate, 24 Jan. 2009, www.slate
     .com/articles/business/moneybox/2009/01/the_quitter_economy.html.
     Accessed 26 Apr. 2009.

APA Style

APA style is used in most social sciences, including education, nursing, and social
work. In-text citations in the APA style give a publication date as well as a name,
with full bibliographic information provided on a References page.

Before writing an essay, determine which style your instructor prefers and refer to an official style guide for detailed instructions on using that style. The following table gives brief guidelines in MLA and APA styles for some of the most common documentation tasks. This table is not a replacement for a style manual, which provides much more detail on different kinds of documentation.

In-Text Documentation

When you summarize the contents of an article, document the source by placing the date immediately after the author's name:

> King (1963) discusses the role of civil disobedience in trying to change unjust laws.

APA guidelines require page numbers at the end of quotations. This is also true if you paraphrase a passage or cite a fact that can be found on a specific page:

> King (1963) defined an unjust law as one "not rooted in eternal and natural law" (p. 434).

> King (1963) argued that moral laws take precedence over human laws (p. 434).

In APA articles, it is not unusual to have two sources by the same author (since someone working on a given topic in the social sciences will often contribute to several papers as part of an overall study). If the texts are from the same year, use lowercase letters to distinguish between different articles:

> King (1963b) asserted that people have a moral obligation to disobey unjust laws.

If your text does not contain enough information to identify a source that you are citing, give the name, date, and, if necessary, page number of that source in the parenthetical citation:

> Many in the civil rights movement argued that civil disobedience was a moral duty (King, 1963, p. 434).

If you need to quote more than forty words, set the quotation off in a block. For block quotations, indent five spaces from the left margin and type the quoted text without quotation marks. The parenthetical citation comes after the period:

> King (1963) also believed that laws that were not unjust in their nature could be applied in unjust ways:

> Sometimes a law is just on its face and unjust in its application. For instance, I have been arrested on a charge of parading without a permit. Now, there is nothing wrong in having an ordinance which requires a permit for a parade. But such an ordinance becomes unjust when it is used to maintain segregation and to deny citizens the First Amendment privilege of peaceful assembly and protest. (p. 435)

If you are citing a source that does not have a page number—such as a webpage—include instead the number of the paragraph where the information can be found, using either the ¶ symbol or the abbreviation "para."

> According to the Nobel Prize organization, King "led a massive protest in Birmingham, Alabama, that caught the attention of the entire world, providing what he called a coalition of conscience, and inspiring his 'Letter from a Birmingham Jail'" (para. 3).

Bibliographical Citations

Full bibliographical citations are given at the end of an essay on a separate page titled "References." The References page lists works alphabetically by author, or, if an author is unavailable, by title. When an author is listed multiple times, the listings are arranged by date. Below are the formats for some of the most common kinds of citations that you will need on your References page.

Single-Author Book
Elshtain, J. B. (2003). *Just war against terror: The burden of American power in a violent world*. New York, NY: Basic Books.

Multiple-Author Book (Fewer than Four Authors)
Malless, S., & McQuain, J. (2003). *Coined by God: Words and phrases that first appear in the English translations of the Bible*. New York, NY: Norton.

Works in an Anthology
Weil, S. (2015). Equality. In M. Austin (Ed.), *Reading the world: Ideas that matter* (pp. 575–78). New York, NY: Norton. (Original work published 1940)

Single-Author Journal Article (Paginated by Volume)
Weinberger, J, (2003). Pious princes and red-hot lovers: The politics of Shakespeare's *Romeo and Juliet*. *Journal of Politics, 65*, 370–375.

Multiple-Author Journal Article (Paginated by Issue)

Weaver, C., McNally, C., & Moerman, S. (2001). To grammar or not to grammar: That is *not* the question! *Voices from the Middle.* 8(3), 17–33.

Scholarly Edition

Austen, J. (2001). *Sense and sensibility* (C. Johnson, Ed.). New York, NY: Norton.

Magazine Article—Monthly

Hawass, Z. (2003, January). Egypt's forgotten treasures. *National Geographic, 203.* 74–87.

Magazine Article—Weekly

Samuelson, R. J. (2004, October 18). The changing face of poverty, *Newsweek, 144,* 50.

Newspaper Article

Farenthold, D. (2005, October 9). Town shaken by lobster theft. *The Washington Post,* p. A3.

Article from an Electronic Database

Moore, K. D. (2005). The truth of the barnacles: Rachel Carson and the moral significance of wonder. *Environmental Ethics,* 27(3), 265–277. Retrieved from Academic Search Premier database.

Work that Appears Only Online

Nasr, S. H. (2007, May 5). The meaning and concept of philosophy in Islam. Retrieved April 23, 2009, from http://www.muslimphilosophy.com/ip/nasr-ipi.htm

Gross, D. (2009, 24 January). The quitter economy. *Slate.* Retrieved from http://www.slate.com/id/2209617

Online Work also in Print

Dowd, M. (2002, April 7). Sacred cruelties (Electronic version). *New York Times* Retrieved from http://www.nytimes.com/2002/04/07/opinion/07DOWD.html

SAMPLE DOCUMENTED ESSAY (MLA FORMAT)

Clarissa Porter
Professor Croft
English 101, Section 10
February 13, 2015

Human Nature in Mencius and Hsün Tzu

     Mencius and Hsün Tzu were both Chinese scholars living during the Period of Warring States. They were both self-professed Confucians, and they both believed that rites and rituals were necessary in order to perfect human beings. Both Mencius and Hsün Tzu gave a lot of thought to questions of human nature, but, as many writers and scholars have pointed out, they came to very different conclusions. Mencius believed that human beings were inherently good, and that they only act in evil ways when their natural goodness is perverted. Hsün Tzu, on the other hand, believed that human nature is inherently evil and must be corrected by strict religious observances. These differences, however, have often been exaggerated. Mencius and Hsün Tzu have certain theoretical differences about the abstract concept of human nature, but their view of what humans should do is nearly identical.

     The differences between Mencius and Hsün Tzu have been the subject of substantial commentary. In *China's Imperial Past*, for example, Charles O. Hucker asserts that

> Whereas Mencius's conception of the essential goodness of human nature has led some specialists to characterize him as a tenderhearted idealist, it is universally agreed that the last great Confucian thinker of the formative age, Hsün Tzu, was an unsentimental, ruthlessly tough-minded rationalist. His characteristic intellectual approach was "Humbug! Let's consider the facts." (82)

Porter 2

Hucker's characterization here is backed up by the authors themselves. Mencius argues that "human nature is inherently good, just like water inherently flows downhill. There is no such thing as a person who isn't good, just as there's no water that doesn't flow downhill" (79). Hsün Tzu directly contradicts this. "Mencius," Hsün Tzu says, "states that man's nature is good, and that all evil arises because he loses his original nature. Such a view, I believe, is erroneous" (86). Even the title of Hsün Tzu's essay, "Man's Nature Is Evil," betrays his fundamental difference with Mencius.

The difference between the two Confucian scholars is fundamental, but is it important? Some scholars believe that the differences between them stem from different views of morality but that, in the words of David E. Soles, "they are in substantial agreement as to the empirical facts of human nature" (123). Soles believes that the differences between Mencius and Hsün Tzu are real, but that these differences are not the result of the two considering sets of facts about human behavior. Both philosophers acknowledge that human beings sometimes act morally and sometimes immorally. They differ drastically in what they see as the root cause for this behavior—Mencius believes that people are immoral when they deny their natures and Hsün Tzu believes that they are immoral when they do not. Amazingly, though, these differences do not result in any practical differences in the behavior that they recommend.

Like Confucius, Hsün Tzu believes that we must all shape our characters through an elaborate series of purifying rituals. These rituals, he believes, turn inherently evil people into moral beings:

> Mencius states that man is capable of learning because his nature is good, but I say that this is wrong. It indicates that he has not really understood man's nature nor distinguished properly between the basic nature and conscious activity. The nature is that which is given by Heaven; you cannot learn it, you cannot acquire it by effort. Ritual principles, on the other hand, are created by sages; you can learn to apply them, you can

work to bring them to completion. That part of man which cannot be learned or acquired by effort is called the nature; that part of him which can be acquired by learning and brought to completion by effort is called conscious activity. This is the difference between nature and conscious activity. (85)

Conscious activity is just as important to Mencius, who, according to the online *Stanford Encyclopedia of Philosophy*, "regarded the transformative power of a cultivated person as the ideal basis for government. In addition, he spelled out more explicitly the idea that order in society depends on proper attitudes within the family, which in turn depends on cultivating oneself." Mencius believed that people should engage in ritual self-cultivation through the very same Confucian rituals advocated by Hsün Tzu.

For Hsün Tzu, Confucian rituals are necessary to change human nature into something good. For Mencius, they are necessary to cultivate raw human nature, which is already good, into the polished attributes of a gentleman. Their philosophical views could not be farther apart, but in the end, the behavioral norms that they expound are very similar, and their dedication to Confucian rituals is identical. Their enmity is limited to the realm of the abstract. In practice, they would have us do the same things, albeit for very different reasons.

Porter 4

Works Cited

Hsün Tzu. "Man's Nature Is Evil." *Reading the World: Ideas That Matter*, edited by Michael Austin, 3rd ed., W. W. Norton, 2017, pp. 84-92.

Hucker, Charles O. *China's Imperial Past: An Introduction to Chinese History and Culture.* Stanford UP, 1975.

Mencius. "Man's Nature Is Good." *Reading the World: Ideas That Matter,* edited by Michael Austin, 3rd ed., W. W. Norton, 2017, pp. 78-82.

Shun, Kwong Loi. "Mencius." *The Stanford Encyclopedia of Philosophy*, Winter 2004 ed., edited by Edward N. Zalta, plato.stanford.edu/archives/win2004/entries/mencius. Accessed 11 Feb. 2009.

Soles, David E. "The Nature and Grounds of Xunzi's Disagreement with Mencius." *Asian Philosophy*, vol. 9, no. 2, 1999, pp. 132-33.

15

REVISING AND EDITING

WRITING IS NOT A PRODUCT but a process—a draft can always be revised, reshaped, reformed, and improved. Once you've finished a draft of an essay, it's best to put it aside for a day or two and then approach it with a fresh eye—a "re-vision."

Revising a draft often means reimagining it from the ground up. During revision you'll want to rethink the basic ideas of your essay and rewrite the text as needed. You may revisit several stages of the writing process, perhaps doing more research, revising your thesis, and reorganizing your draft. Just as a renovated building often looks nothing like it did before renovations, it is not uncommon for writers to find that, after two or three revisions, almost nothing remains of the drafts that they started with.

Once you've completed rethinking and rewriting—a process you may go through several times—it's time to edit. This is the time to correct errors in spelling, punctuation, and grammar, and check for other mechanical issues.

In the following pages are guidelines and suggestions for the revision process—for rethinking, rewriting, and editing your essays.

RETHINKING

Give yourself plenty of time

Good writing takes time. You cannot create and revise multiple drafts the night before an essay is due. Your best essays will be the ones that you start well in advance of their due date and keep thinking about until they are done. This does not necessarily mean that you must spend more time on a paper than do those who procrastinate until the very end. Six hours spread over a week will almost always produce a better paper than six hours spent the night before it is due.

Ask other people to read your draft and provide feedback

The very act of writing suggests an audience, and, to be sure, your instructor will generally be the final audience for your efforts. But it is usually a good idea to get feedback on a draft during the revision process. A friend, a classmate, or a writing tutor can let you know if you have effectively translated your ideas into written words—and even if the ideas were worth translating in the first place.

Reread the assignment and make sure that you have followed it correctly

Good writing, as discussed in Chapter 10, meets the expectations of its audience. When the audience is a teacher who has given you an assignment, you must make absolutely certain that you have followed the instructions as closely as possible. Refer to the assignment guidelines when you have finished a draft and again when you're revising—just to make sure that, in the process of crafting your essay, you have not strayed away from the assignment or failed to answer a critical question asked by the instructor.

Identify your thesis and consider how each part of the essay supports it

It's not unusual to discover what you are trying to say while you are writing your first draft. If you find that, by the end of your draft, you're focusing on a different thesis from the one you started with, you'll want to revise your original thesis statement or revise other parts of your essay. In either case, make sure that your entire essay, all your evidence, develops and supports the same thesis—and make sure that that thesis is clearly indicated.

Don't be afraid to throw out ideas that don't work

One of the hardest things for any writer to do is to cut out words, sentences, or whole paragraphs that he or she has spent a substantial amount of time creating.

After we labor over a piece of writing, we feel an ownership of, and even a responsibility to, the words that we have brought into being. But nobody has good ideas all of the time, and even good ideas can be extraneous if they don't support the thesis. If you decide that an idea is not worth pursuing, or that it doesn't support or develop your thesis, you must be willing to cut it—even if it means scrapping the entire paper and starting over from scratch.

REWRITING

Make sure that your introduction and conclusion are consistent with each other

In the same way that ideas can drift away from the thesis during the course of writing a paper, conclusions can drift away from introductions. Use the revision process as an opportunity to revisit these two crucial paragraphs and make sure that they are working together. You might revise your introduction so that it anticipates your conclusion or revise your conclusion so that it refers to or extends your introduction—just make sure that the two paragraphs tie your essay together. This will encourage readers to view your essay as a self-contained, coherent argument.

Make sure that you have clear transitions between all major ideas

Transitions between ideas are an important part of orienting a reader to your paper (see p. 641). They can also be difficult to include in a first draft, since you are so often discovering ideas through the process of writing. You should therefore check the beginning and end of each paragraph and revise as needed to include transitions that move readers gracefully and seamlessly from one idea to the next.

Look for ways to eliminate useless words and phrases

It's easy to fall into the trap of using more words than are needed to convey an idea. But fewer words often mean clearer, more elegant prose. If you look carefully at your first draft, you will probably find it full of "deadwood": "there is" or "there are" at the beginnings of sentences; wordy constructions such as "because of the fact that"; and unnecessary additions and qualifications of all kinds. As you rewrite, look for ways to eliminate extra words that do not add meaning.

Pay attention to your ethos

As we discussed in Chapter 12, readers usually judge writers by the ethos (p. 663)—the overall persona—projected in a piece of writing. During the revision process, pay special attention to the ethos that you are projecting. This is the time to build rapport and establish credibility with your readers by striking the right tone and making sound arguments.

EDITING

Make sure that you have documented every source

As we saw in Chapter 14, the line between accidentally omitting documentation of a quotation and plagiarizing a paper is very thin. As you prepare your final draft for submission, make sure that you have properly documented every outside source that you used in any way.

Refer to a handbook or other source for grammar and usage questions

Many instructors require or recommend a handbook for composition courses. Handbooks contain a wealth of information about grammar rules, punctuation conventions, documentation styles, and other nuts-and-bolts elements of writing. If your instructor has chosen a specific handbook, use it faithfully. If not, select one in your library or bookstore and refer to it when revising your papers.

Read your entire essay out loud to catch any errors you might have missed

Just as reading sentences out loud can help you catch awkward passages, reading an entire essay out loud, carefully and slowly, can help you see missing words, extra characters, spelling errors not caught by spellcheckers, and other problems with your paper that can result from carelessness.

REVISING AND EDITING CHECKLIST

During the revision process, keep the following questions in mind.

Ideas

- Have you met the guidelines for the assignment? (See "Considering Expectations," p. 621.)
- Have you generated an idea that is original enough to make an impact on the reader? (See "Achieving Subtlety," p. 628.)
- Is the idea sufficiently focused? (See "Refining Your Thesis Statement, p. 635.)

Structure

- Is there an arguable, well-written thesis? (See "Thesis Statements," p. 634.)
- Does the introductory paragraph set up the thesis and define key terms in the essay? (See "Introductions," p. 638.)
- Are there solid, well-constructed transitions between all major ideas? (See "Transitions," p. 641.)
- Does the concluding paragraph tie together major arguments in the essay and bring the whole to a definite conclusion? (See "Conclusions," p. 646.)

Argument

- Have you considered how your audience will respond to your arguments? How have you appealed to your audience? (See "Considering Expectations," p. 621, and "Supporting Ideas," p. 649.)
- Have you constructed a persuasive ethos? Is it reasonable and knowledgeable? (See "Ethos: The Writer's Appeal," p. 663.)
- Are all of your major claims supported with appropriate evidence? (See "Supporting Claims with Evidence," p. 650.)
- Do all of the supporting arguments in the essay support the main thesis? That is, are they relevant and focused? (See "Supporting Ideas," p. 649.)

Correctness

- Have you integrated all quotations, paraphrases, and summaries smoothly into your own writing? (See "Quoting, Paraphrasing, and Summarizing," p. 685.)
- Have you properly documented all outside sources according to the style guide required by the assignment? (See "Documenting Sources," p. 690.)
- Have you read your essay out loud to check for awkward phrasing and to catch errors that you might miss reading silently? (See "Editing," p. 705.)
- Have you proofread carefully and corrected any errors in grammar, spelling, or punctuation? (See "Editing," p. 705.)

Credits

Gloria Anzaldúa: "How to Tame a Wild Tongue" from *Borderlands/La Frontera: The New Mestiza*. Copyright © 1987, 1999, 2007, 2012 by Gloria Anzaldúa. Reprinted by permission of Aunt Lute Books. www.auntlute.com.

Matsuo Bashō: From *Narrow Road to the Interior and Other Writings* by Matsuo Bashō, translated by Sam Hamill. Copyright © 1998 by Sam Hamill. Reprinted by arrangement with The Permissions Company, Inc., on behalf of Shambhala Publications Inc., Boston, MA. www.shambhala.com.

Ruth Benedict: Excerpt from *Patterns of Culture* by Ruth Benedict. Copyright 1934 by Ruth Benedict; copyright renewed © 1961 by Ruth Valentine. Reprinted by permission of Houghton Mifflin Harcourt Publishing Company. All rights reserved.

Wayne C. Booth: "The Rhetorical Stance," *College Composition and Communication*, Vol. 14, No. 3, Oct. 1963. Published by National Council of Teachers of English.

Calvin Martin Bower: "Boethius' 'The Principles of Music', an Introduction, Translation, and Commentary," Ph.D. dissertation, Peabody College for Teachers of Vanderbilt University, 1967, University Microfilms no. 67-15,005. Reprinted by permission of the author.

Nicholas Carr: From *The Shallows: What the Internet is Doing to Our Brains* by Nicholas Carr. Copyright © 2010 by Nicholas Carr. Used by permission of Atlantic Books Ltd and W. W. Norton & Company, Inc.

Rachel Carson: "The Obligation to Endure" from *Silent Spring*. Copyright © 1962 by Rachel L. Carson, renewed 1990 by Roger Christie. Reprinted by permission of Frances Collin, Trustee and Houghton Mifflin Harcourt Publishing Company. All rights reserved. All copying, including electronic, or re-distribution of this text, is expressly forbidden.

Po Chü-I: "The Flower Market" from *Chinese Poems*, translated by Arthur Waley (George Allen & Unwin, 1946). Reprinted by permission of The Arthur Waley Estate.

Barry Commoner: Excerpt(s) from *The Closing Circle: Nature, Man, and Technology* by Barry Commoner, copyright © 1971 by Barry Commoner. Used by permission of Frances Collin,

Index